Property Management

Kathryn Haupt
Inger Faraz
Dawn Henry
David Jarman
Joe Reiner

Rockwell Publishing Company

Copyright© 2012
By Rockwell Publishing Company
13218 N.E. 20th
Bellevue, WA 98005
(425)747-7272 / 1-800-221-9347

First Edition

ISBN: 978-1-887051-90-3

PRINTED IN THE UNITED STATES OF AMERICA

Table of Contents

Chapter 13: Managing Industrial Property 367

Chapter 14: Complying with Federal, State, and Local Laws 393

Chapter 1

Property Management: An Overview

Outline

Professional Property Management

In the most general sense of the term, **property management** refers to the administration, operation, and maintenance of a piece of real estate. But the term is often used more narrowly, to refer to the management of real estate by a professional property manager who is working on behalf of the property owner.

Many different kinds of properties lend themselves to professional management, from single-family residences to large industrial complexes. These properties may be owned by individuals, investment groups, developers, corporations, financial institutions, or even governments.

Depending on the type and size of a managed property, the manager's duties will range from advertising vacant space and negotiating leases, to rent collection and recordkeeping, to physical maintenance and tenant relations. In addition to these day-to-day duties, a property manager might also arrange financing for the property or handle risk management issues. Some property managers are responsible for creating and executing long-term strategies designed to maintain or increase the managed property's value. Of course, whatever the manager's specific tasks, his primary function is to achieve the owner's short- and long-term goals.

Given the variety of property management services, it's not surprising that there are many different types of property managers. Some property managers specialize in a certain property type or size, while others limit their work to a specific management function, such as leasing or asset management. Some managers handle many properties, while others manage just one large property. In some cases, managers work and even live on-site at the properties they manage.

Property managers may be employed by management firms or real estate brokerages, or work within property management divisions of large corporations or financial institutions. Other property managers are hired directly by individual owners.

As you can see, the property management profession encompasses a variety of employment opportunities.

Who Uses Property Managers?

There are three general categories of property management clients:

- investor-owners,
- incidental or interim owners, and
- institutional owners.

Investor-Owners. Investment property is property that is not occupied by the owner. In most cases, an investment property is an **income-producing property** (also called **income property**). In other words, the property isn't held just for appreciation; it also generates rental income.

Investor-owners may be individuals or investment syndicates, such as a partnership or a limited liability company. (Investment syndicates are discussed in greater detail in Chapter 3.) Although some investor-owners do manage their own properties, others discover that management takes too much of their time or requires very specialized knowledge and skills. This is especially true in regard to larger properties with multiple tenants. Investors usually decide it makes more sense to rely on professional property managers to operate and maintain these properties.

The vast majority of property under professional management in the United States is income-producing property, held by investor-owners. For that reason, this book will focus primarily on the management of income-producing property. However, much of the information presented also applies to property owned by incidental/interim and institutional owners.

Incidental or Interim Owners. Some owners never planned on owning investment property, but are nevertheless forced to deal with its management. These owners may be responsible for investment property only temporarily, or they may acquire it incidentally. For instance, an estate administrator may find himself briefly responsible for a home after the owner's death, or someone might receive an out-of-state property as an inheritance. Other examples of incidental or interim owners include banks and other lenders that acquire property through foreclosures, and government agencies that obtain property through seizure (such as a drug seizure).

Incidental and interim owners often intend to sell the property as soon as possible, but need someone to manage it in the meantime.

Institutional Owners. The final category of property owner includes institutional owners: corporations, institutions, and agencies that occupy and use their properties. Institutional owners include private companies, nonprofit organizations, colleges and schools, government entities, and the military.

Property managers employed by institutional owners are often called **facilities managers**, and the managed property may be referred to as **institutional property**.

Development of the Property Management Profession

Throughout history, owners of extensive real estate holdings have hired others to assist with various property management tasks. In ancient times, landowners employed land stewards to maintain their estates; during the Middle Ages, feudal lords used managers to handle rent collection. It wasn't until the 20th century, however, that property management developed into a recognized profession. During this period, a number of technological innovations as well as economic and social changes led to a dramatic increase in the need for professional property management.

Around the turn of the nineteenth century, thanks to the development of steel framing and high-speed elevators, high-rise office buildings and apartment complexes sprang up in cities across the country. These buildings accommodated more tenants, contained more common space, and offered more varied facilities than their low-rise predecessors; as a result, these buildings required more management services. Also, because these large buildings were much more expensive to develop, they were often owned by groups of investors rather than individuals. All of these factors translated into a greater demand for professional property management.

A significant event that increased the demand for property managers was the Great Depression. After the stock market crash of 1929, hundreds of thousands of borrowers defaulted on their mortgages, resulting in mass foreclosures. Banks and other lenders desperately needed management services to handle the residential and commercial properties they had suddenly acquired. It was during these years that many financial institutions formed their own property management departments.

Following World War II, the United States experienced a construction boom. Increased prosperity, high rates of employment, and widespread automobile ownership all contributed to a sharp increase in both commercial and residential construction. Indeed, it was during

4 Chapter 1

 New York City Skyscrapers

One of the first buildings to utilize both steel-frame construction and high-speed elevators was the Woolworth Building, which opened to great fanfare on April 24, 1913 in New York City. The tallest building in the world at the time, the Woolworth Building stood 792 feet and 58 stories high. Designed by architect Cass Gilbert in the neo-Gothic style, the Woolworth Building cost $13.5 million to build (which was paid for in cash by retail magnate Frank Woolworth). The building held the title of world's tallest building until 1930, when first 40 Wall Street and then the Chrysler Building towers were completed. The 77-floor Art Deco Chrysler Building held the title of world's tallest building for 11 months, until the Empire State Building was completed in 1931.

The 1,453-foot, 102-story Empire State Building was the first building to have more than 100 floors. It remained the tallest building in the world until 1972; today it is the third tallest building in the United States and the 15th tallest in the world. It has 73 elevators, houses over 1,000 businesses, and has its own zip code. It is considered the second-largest office complex in the United States, after the Pentagon.

this period that the "suburb" was born. Shopping centers appeared, and office and industrial parks were built, all creating even more need for property management.

In the 1960s and 1970s, condominiums became popular. Also, real estate investment trusts (REITs), pension funds, and insurance companies began investing heavily in large-scale income-producing properties. As the country's population increased in the following decades, so did the number of multi-family residences, common interest developments, and other increased-density developments, all of which required some level of property management. Future decades will no doubt bring more technological, economic, and cultural developments that will also affect how real estate is owned and managed.

Regulation of Professional Property Managers

Many occupations are regulated by the government to protect the public from unscrupulous or incompetent practitioners, and property management is no exception. As property management developed into an established profession, most states introduced licensing requirements and began regulating property management business practices. Property managers are also subject to a number of federal, state, and local fair housing and other antidiscrimination laws. And, because the property manager is the agent of the property owner, property managers must also comply with state laws regulating agency relationships.

Licensing. To ensure property managers have a minimum level of education and skill, most states require professional property managers to hold either a real estate license or a property manager's license. Typically, license requirements apply when someone engages in any of the following activities on behalf of another, in exchange for compensation:

- leasing,
- offering to lease,
- negotiating lease terms,
- collecting rent, or
- soliciting rental listings.

Exemptions. Even in states where a license is required, some property management activities may be exempt from the licensing requirement. For example, a person generally doesn't need a license to manage his own property, and a license may not be required if the property manager is acting without compensation. Typically, a resident manager (a building manager who lives on the premises) does not need to be licensed. And an unlicensed family member of the property owner may be allowed to help with certain tasks that would otherwise require a license.

In some states, property managers may employ unlicensed assistants to perform a limited number of activities that would normally require a license, such as showing property or collecting rent.

A few states offer a separate community association manager's license for those engaged solely in community association management. (Community association managers are hired by condominium and subdivision owners associations to manage common areas and respond to residents' needs.) See Chapter 10 for more information on community association management.

Licensing requirements. License candidates are generally required to complete real estate coursework and pass an examination. Age and experience requirements may apply as well. The licensee may need to maintain professional liability insurance or a surety bond, and continuing education courses may be required to renew the license.

Regulation of Business Practices. Most state licensing agencies also regulate property management business practices. For example, state regulations usually dictate how property managers must handle security deposits and other trust funds. Other regulations might require a manager to keep certain documents (such as lease agreements) for a certain number of years. Many states regulate the format and content of advertising.

Property managers must also be familiar with federal, state, and local laws and regulations regarding fair housing, landlord-tenant relations, antidiscrimination, and antitrust issues. (Compliance with these laws is discussed in greater detail in Chapter 14.)

Agency Law. The relationship between a property manager and her client (the owner) is an agency relationship: the manager is the owner's agent, and the owner is the agent's principal. As such, the relationship will be governed by general agency law. The manager/agent is authorized to represent the owner/principal in dealings with third parties, such as tenants, suppliers, and contractors. Furthermore, the manager owes the owner fiduciary duties, meaning that she has a legal obligation to protect and promote the owner's interests. The manager can be held liable for failing to meet this obligation.

Some states have passed real estate agency statutes that expand or replace the general agency laws that would normally apply to the relationship between a property manager and an owner. (For more information on agency relationships, see Chapter 3.)

Types of Managed Properties

Many different types of property lend themselves to property management services. In fact, the only types of property that are rarely managed professionally are raw land (unimproved property) and agricultural property.

Managed properties may be divided into four broad categories:

- residential,
- office,
- retail, and
- industrial.

Residential property includes single-family homes, duplexes, apartment buildings, and manufactured/mobile home parks. This category also includes common interest developments in which units are individually owned, such as condominiums, cooperatives, and planned unit developments. Most property managers work with residential real estate.

The **office property** category includes everything from small office buildings to business parks and high-rise complexes. **Retail property** includes stand-alone buildings, strip malls, local shopping centers, and regional malls. **Industrial property** includes warehouses and manufacturing facilities. Industrial property can be either stand-alone or part of an industrial park.

Some real estate may take the form of a **mixed-use property**: multi-level buildings with ground-floor retail space and upper-level office or residential units, which may be set up as condominiums. Not all condominiums are residential; some retail or office properties are developed as condominiums (the units are owned by the businesses that occupy them).

Properties that don't fit into any of these categories are termed **special-purpose properties**. Examples of special-purpose properties include hospitals and nursing homes, schools and colleges, places of worship, military housing, theaters, hotels and motels, resorts, clubs, and other recreational facilities. Often, these are institutional properties, meaning that they are occupied by the corporation or institution that owns them.

The Property Manager's Role

A property manager's main task is to manage the property in a manner that helps the property owner achieve his investment goals. Naturally, most owners of income-producing property are concerned primarily with maximizing the property's income. A second (and often equally important) goal is protecting and perhaps even increasing the property's value.

The manager's role is slightly different with institutional property, because the owner/client occupies and uses the property. Maintaining the property's value is still important, but instead of focusing on generating income, the manager works to ensure that the property meets the owner's current needs.

Whatever the client's goals, the property manager will work with the client to develop a **management plan** based on those goals. The management plan serves as a blueprint for the property's management. (For more on management plans, see Chapter 4.)

In addition to developing the management plan, the manager may also be responsible for many other management tasks. These may be day-to-day or long-term tasks, and include things like:

- analyzing the market to determine appropriate rental rates;
- creating budgets and paying operating expenses;
- hiring and supervising staff (on-site managers, maintenance, security, etc.) and contractors;
- overseeing maintenance of the property;
- marketing the property;
- screening potential tenants;
- negotiating lease terms;
- addressing tenants' needs and requests;
- collecting rents and any assessments or fees;
- minimizing risk and insuring against loss;
- accounting, recordkeeping, and handling of trust funds; and
- reporting to the owner.

The type and size of the property will determine the tasks required. Managing a suburban four-unit apartment building is very different from managing a downtown high-rise office building.

Career Possibilities for Property Managers

With so many different types of managed properties and such a wide range of property management tasks, it's no surprise that aspiring property managers can choose from a variety of jobs. In this section, we'll look at the various employers a property manager might work for, the types of positions available, and the specializations he might pursue.

Employment Arrangements

Employment arrangements can range from working as a sole proprietor (providing property management services to many different property owners) to working as an employee of a large corporation and managing the many properties owned by that corporation. Let's take a brief look at possible employment arrangements.

- **Property management companies.** Property management companies vary greatly both in size and the services they offer. A sole proprietorship or small firm might specialize in just one type of managed property; a larger firm might handle all types of properties.

- **Real estate brokerages.** Some licensed real estate agents specialize in property management services; others handle sales transactions as well.
- **Financial institutions.** Some banks need property managers for the real estate they hold in trust; lenders may employ managers to handle properties they own temporarily as a result of foreclosure.
- **Large corporations.** Companies with significant real estate assets often have their own real estate divisions. Property managers are hired by these divisions to manage the corporate real estate holdings.
- **Institutional owners.** Some institutional owners (such as schools, hospitals, and hotels) outsource their property management needs to private companies, but most employ facilities managers directly.

Property Management Positions

As the property management profession has evolved, so has the range of employment opportunities available. Specific job titles and descriptions vary from one organization to another, but the following are some of the positions commonly available in the industry.

Site Manager. A site manager (also called an on-site manager) is a resident manager in an apartment or other residential building, or a building manager in an office building. A site manager is responsible for the hands-on, day-to-day tasks required to manage a single property, including leasing, rent collection, physical maintenance, handling tenant complaints, and basic recordkeeping and accounting. On the other hand, site managers typically aren't involved in long-term management planning and decision-making.

A site manager often works under the supervision of a property manager, rather than reporting directly to the property owner. Some site managers are licensed as real estate agents; others are not. Depending on state law, however, an unlicensed site manager may be limited to certain tasks.

Property Manager. The title of property manager (or property supervisor) generally describes someone who manages a portfolio of properties for several clients, but can also refer to someone managing a single large property. A property manager usually works directly with the property owners, preparing management plans for client approval, consulting with clients about major decisions, and providing clients with regular operating and financial reports. A property manager may perform the same day-to-day management functions as an on-site manager, or she may be responsible for supervising on-site managers.

Regional and Executive Managers. When a property manager supervises on-site managers rather than performing hands-on management functions, she may be called a regional manager or executive manager. A regional manager may also be responsible for handling the management business itself. An executive manager is often the owner or an executive officer of a property management firm, overseeing its general operations and marketing efforts.

Asset Manager. Asset managers handle the long-term planning for a client's property or portfolio of properties. For example, an asset manager evaluates whether the property is serving its highest and best use (the use that produces the greatest return on the investment). Similarly, an asset manager is responsible for helping an owner decide when or even whether a certain property should be purchased or sold. An asset manager may also consult with the client regarding alternative uses for the property, and will help implement any desired change in its use.

Specializations

Many managers specialize in a particular category of property and also in a particular size of property within that category. For example, two property managers specialize in residential property, but one handles only single-family rental homes, while the other manages only large condominium complexes.

There are other types of specializations as well. For example, some property managers are primarily engaged in community association management. Other specializations include managing hotels and resorts, vacation homes, housing for the elderly, public housing for low-income tenants, military housing, and shopping centers.

Professional Development for Property Managers

As the property management industry developed and expanded, the number of professional property management associations also grew. Some of these associations serve the general property management industry; others cater to specific segments, such as apartment managers or facilities managers.

Property managers can benefit greatly from associating with one or more of these organizations. Professional associations provide invaluable networking opportunities, as well as other resources such as written publications and training. Most associations have adopted codes of ethics that serve as guidelines for their members' conduct. And many offer various designations and credentials for those who meet certain education, experience, and examination requirements.

Professional Associations

Among the most prominent property management associations are the Institute of Real Estate Management (IREM®), the Building Owners and Managers Association International (BOMA®), the National Apartment Association (NAA®), and the National Association of Residential Property Managers (NARPM®).

IREM. The Institute of Real Estate Management was founded in 1933 by a group of real estate firms; it is an affiliate of the National Association of REALTORS®. Its members include both residential and commercial real estate managers. IREM offers management courses and conferences, and publishes a journal on property management.

IREM first offered a Certified Property Manager (CPM®) designation in 1938. Later, it added the Accredited Management Organization (AMO®), Accredited Residential Manager (ARM®), and Accredited Commercial Manager (ACoM) credentials. IREM also offers several forms of non-credentialed membership, including student and academic memberships.

BOMA International. BOMA International, the oldest property management group in the U.S., began in 1907 as a national organization of local and regional property management groups and associations. Since then, it has expanded to include members in Canada and a number of other countries. Its members own, manage, develop, and supply commercial properties. BOMA lobbies on behalf of the commercial real estate industry, and produces a number of industry publications.

Another association, the Building Owners and Managers Institute (BOMI), is affiliated with BOMA; it is a nonprofit organization that provides education and training programs. BOMI offers a number of professional designations, including Real Property Administrator (RPA®), Facilities Management Administrator (FMA®), Systems Maintenance Administrator (SMA®), and Systems Maintenance Technician (SMT®).

National Apartment Association. The National Apartment Association, created in 1939, is an organization of state and local apartment housing associations. Its members include apartment managers, developers, builders, and suppliers. NAA provides education

 Codes of Ethics

Most property management associations, including IREM, have adopted codes of ethics that set standards for the professional conduct of their members. Members generally must pledge to uphold these codes of ethics as a condition of membership.

Here is an excerpt from IREM's Member Pledge:

I pledge myself to maintain the highest moral and ethical standards consistent with the objectives and higher purpose of the Institute.

I pledge myself to seek and maintain an equitable, honorable, and cooperative association with fellow Members of the Institute and with all others who may become a part of my business and professional life. I recognize and support the need to preserve and encourage fair and equitable practices and competition among all who are engaged in the profession of real estate management.

I pledge myself to place honesty, integrity, and industriousness above all else and to pursue my gainful efforts with diligent study and ongoing education so that my services shall be beneficial to the general public and my obligations to my clients shall always be maintained at the highest possible level.

IREM actively enforces its code of ethics and has established a disciplinary process that includes an investigation and review by its Board of Ethical Inquiry and a hearing by its Ethics Hearing and Discipline Board. If a member is found to have violated the code, he may be subject to a letter of censure, membership suspension for up to three years, or termination of his membership altogether.

and training, and offers several different professional designations, including Certified Apartment Manager (CAM), Certified Apartment Maintenance Technician (CAMT), and National Apartment Leasing Professional (NALP).

National Association of Residential Property Managers. The National Association of Residential Property Managers, founded in 1988, is an organization of property managers who specialize in managing single-family homes and other small residential properties. Its members include real estate licensees engaged primarily in residential property management, as well as their employees. NARPM® offers the Residential Management Professional (RMP®) and Master Property Manager (MPM®) designations for individuals, as well as the Certified Residential Management Company (CRMC®) designation for property management firms.

Designations and Certifications

We've already mentioned that many professional property management organizations offer a range of certifications and designations for members that meet education and experience requirements, and/or pass an examination. These credentials can be useful to managers seeking employment, as evidence of a baseline level of knowledge and skill.

Although we list brief descriptions of the requirements for the most common designations/certifications below, you should contact the conferring organization directly for the most current information.

> ▶ **Advocacy**
>
> In addition to offering networking opportunities, training, and education, most property management associations also engage in lobbying and other advocacy on behalf of the industry sectors they each represent. For example, BOMA, which represents commercial owners and managers, lobbied hard against rent control measures in the 1950s and then again in the 1970s. More recently, after 9/11, BOMA's lobbying efforts contributed to the passage of federal laws intended to help businesses purchase terrorism risk insurance at reasonable rates. Similarly, IREM and NAA have advocated against changes in lead-based paint rules and the Americans with Disabilities Act that would increase requirements for rental property owners and managers.

Certified Property Manager (CPM®). IREM's Certified Property Manager designation is probably the most widely recognized property management credential. Candidates for the CPM designation must:

- have a real estate license, if required by state law;
- affiliate with the National Association of REALTORS® and receive approval by the local IREM chapter;
- acquire at least three years of real estate management experience;
- submit three letters of recommendation;

- complete IREM coursework;
- prepare an actual management plan or pass a management plan skills assessment; and
- pass a certification exam.

Accredited Residential Manager (ARM®). IREM's Accredited Residential Manager certification is for managers specializing in residential management. ARM candidates must:

- be approved by the local IREM chapter;
- complete IREM coursework;
- submit three letters of recommendation;
- have at least one year of real estate management experience; and
- pass a certification exam.

Certified Apartment Manager (CAM®). Those seeking NAA's Certified Apartment Manager designation must:

- complete required coursework;
- have at least one year of experience in the apartment industry; and
- pass a certification exam.

Residential Management Professional (RMP®) and Master Property Manager (MPM®). The Residential Management Professional and Master Property Manager designations are conferred by NARPM®. Although they don't require a certification exam, these designations do require residential property management experience. To receive the RMP designation, the candidate must:

- hold a real estate license, if required by state law;
- complete at least 100 unit years of experience (one unit year equals management of one residential unit for one year);
- manage at least 25 residential units during the candidacy period;
- complete NARPM coursework, including an ethics course; and
- submit letters of recommendation.

The MPM designation requires a candidate to:

- have an RMP designation;
- hold a real estate license, if required by state law;
- complete at least 500 unit years of experience;
- manage at least 50 residential units during the candidacy period;
- complete NARPM® coursework, including an ethics course; and
- submit letters of recommendation.

Real Property Administrator (RPA®). BOMI's Real Property Administrator designation doesn't require a certain number of experience hours, but candidates do have to complete courses in building design, operation, and maintenance; real estate investment and finance; environmental health and safety; and ethics. In addition, two elective courses must be

"Green" Certifications

In recent years, the real estate industry has seen a trend favoring environmentally sustainable, energy-efficient building principles and operating practices. Several organizations offer "green" certifications to property managers who complete certain training. For example, the National Association of REALTORS® offers a Green Designation for members who complete coursework and pass an examination. Similarly, the National Affordable Housing Management Association and the National Apartment Association Education Institute offer a Credential for Green Property Management™ (CGPM™) for candidates who complete 16 hours of coursework.

Holding one of these certifications allows a manager to market himself as educated in the latest advances in cost-cutting green technology and practices. This background can be attractive not only to investors and owners who prioritize environmentally friendly practices, but also to those interested in saving money through energy- and water-efficiencies.

chosen from asset management, real property administration, leasing and marketing, and managing the organization.

Certified Shopping Center Manager (CSM). The Certified Shopping Center Manager designation, conferred by the International Council of Shopping Centers, requires at least four years of experience in shopping center management (coursework may be substituted for the fourth year of experience) in addition to passing an exam.

Chapter Summary

1. Most of the property under professional management in the United States is income-producing property, held by investor-owners. However, owners who acquire property incidentally or are holding it temporarily also hire property managers, as do companies and entities that occupy and use the property they own.

2. The demand for professional property management grew dramatically throughout the 20th century, in large part due to the advent of large residential and commercial structures with generous amounts of common space and numerous tenants. These buildings include the high-rise office and residential buildings that began to appear at the turn of the century, as well as the shopping centers, industrial parks, condominiums, and other increased-density developments that became common later on.

3. In most states, professional property managers must hold either a real estate license or a property manager's license. Exemptions usually apply to those managing their own property, living on-site, or assisting a family member with certain management tasks.

4. Managed property may be categorized as residential (single- and multi-family buildings, manufactured/mobile home parks, and common interest developments), office, retail, industrial, and special-purpose (hospitals, nursing homes, schools, churches, military housing, hotels, and recreational facilities).

5. Property managers may work directly for property owners, or may be employed by property management companies or real estate brokerages. Some property managers work for banks, corporations that invest in real estate, and institutional owners.

6. Common positions in property management include site manager, property manager, regional/executive manager, and asset manager. Many managers specialize in a particular type and/or size of property.

7. Property management professional associations offer networking opportunities, education, and training. Two of the most prominent associations are the Institute of Real Estate Management (IREM) and the Building Owners and Managers Association International (BOMA®).

8. Many professional associations offer credentials to those who fulfill certain education, experience, and exam requirements. A widely recognized credential is the Certified Property Manager (CPM®) designation conferred by IREM.

Key Terms

Income-producing property – Investment property that is held not just for appreciation, but also because it generates rental income.

Incidental/interim owners – Property owners who are responsible for an investment property only temporarily or incidentally (for instance, because of a foreclosure or an inheritance). These owners often plan to sell the property as soon as possible, but need managers in the meantime.

Institutional owners – Property owners who occupy and use their own properties, such as corporations, private schools and colleges, and government agencies.

Institutional property – Property that is used by the company or organization that owns it. Examples include college campuses and hospital complexes.

Facilities manager – A property manager employed by an institutional owner to manage the property it is occupying.

Residential property – Property where people reside; it includes single-family homes, duplexes, apartment buildings, and manufactured/mobile home parks. Residential property also includes condominiums, cooperatives, and planned unit developments. Residential real estate is the largest source of demand for professional property management.

Special-purpose property – Property that does not fit into the categories of residential, office, retail, or industrial property. Examples of special-purpose properties include hospitals and nursing homes, schools and colleges, places of worship, military housing, theaters, hotels and motels, resorts, clubs, and other recreational facilities.

Management plan – A plan that serves as a blueprint for the property's management; it addresses the financial and operational strategy for managing a property.

Site manager – A resident manager in an apartment or other residential building, or a building manager in an office building. A site manager is responsible for the day-to-day tasks required to manage a single property, including leasing, rent collection, physical maintenance, and handling tenant complaints. (Also called an on-site manager.)

Asset manager – A manager who handles the long-term planning for a client's property, including evaluating whether the property is serving its highest and best use and implementing any desired change in the property's use.

Institute of Real Estate Management (IREM®) – A professional association that offers property management courses and conferences, and publishes a journal of property management. It is an affiliate of the National Association of REALTORS®, and its members include both residential and commercial property managers.

Building Owners and Managers Association International (BOMA®) – The oldest property management group in the U.S. (founded in 1907); it is an organization of local and regional property management groups and associations. BOMA lobbies on behalf of the commercial real estate industry, and produces a number of industry publications.

National Apartment Association (NAA®) – This organization, created in 1939, is composed of state and local apartment housing associations. Its members include apartment managers, developers, builders, and suppliers.

National Association of Residential Property Managers (NARPM®) – An organization founded in 1988 for those who specialize in managing single-family homes and other small residential properties.

Certified Property Manager (CPM®) – The most widely recognized property management credential; offered by IREM. Candidates must fulfill a variety of requirements, including training, experience, and passing an exam.

Accredited Residential Manager (ARM®) – An IREM certification for managers who specialize in residential management. Candidates must fulfill a variety of requirements, including training, experience, and passing an exam.

Green certifications – Certifications that allow managers to market themselves as educated in the latest advances in green technology and practice. The National Association of REALTORS®, the National Affordable Housing Management Association, and the National Apartment Association Education Institute all offer green designations.

Chapter Quiz

1. Which of the following is an example of a special-purpose property?

   a) Industrial park
   b) Hotel
   c) Planned unit development
   d) Strip mall

2. An asset manager's services would likely include:

   a) recommending properties to purchase
   b) selecting tenants
   c) routine property maintenance
   d) All of the above

3. Which of the following is not a type of industrial property?

   a) Warehouse
   b) Light manufacturing plant
   c) Distribution facility
   d) Nursing home

4. The primary function of the manager of an income-producing property is:

   a) generating income for the owners
   b) preserving and/or increasing the value of the property
   c) achieving the objectives of the owners
   d) All of the above

5. A residential site manager typically isn't responsible for:

   a) paying utility bills
   b) supervising maintenance and support staff
   c) screening tenants and collecting rents
   d) investment decisions

6. Which of these organizations is an affiliate of the National Association of REALTORS®?

   a) Institute of Real Estate Management (IREM®)
   b) National Apartment Association (NAA®)
   c) Building Owners and Managers Association (BOMA®)
   d) National Association of Residential Property Managers (NARPM®)

7. Which of the following is not one of the main types of managed properties?

   a) Retail
   b) Industrial
   c) Agricultural
   d) Residential

8. A bank takes ownership of a home after foreclosing on a mortgage loan. In this situation, the bank is known as an:

   a) investor-owner
   b) incidental or interim owner
   c) institutional owner
   d) None of the above

9. A private university that owns the campus on which it is located would be categorized as an:

   a) investor-owner
   b) incidental or interim owner
   c) institutional owner
   d) None of the above

10. The increased demand for professional property management can be traced to the development of:

    a) structural steel framing and high-speed elevators
    b) condominiums
    c) suburbs and shopping centers
    d) All of the above

Answer Key

1. b)   A hotel is a special-purpose property; the other options are all examples of residential, retail, or industrial property.

2. a)   Instead of directly managing an individual property, an asset manager is involved in long-term planning. This role includes helping the owner determine whether and when a property should be bought or sold.

3. d)   A nursing home would be considered a type of special-purpose property.

4. d)   The manager will be tasked with generating income for the property owner, preserving (or increasing) the value of the property, and achieving the owner's goals and objectives.

5. d)   Site managers handle day-to-day management tasks, but aren't necessarily involved in long-term planning and decision-making.

6. a)   IREM® represents both residential and commercial property managers, and offers a Certified Property Manager® designation.

7. c)   Property managers don't routinely work with agricultural property.

8. b)   In this situation, the bank is an interim owner.

9. c)   An institutional owner occupies and uses the property it owns.

10. d)   All of these things contributed to the dramatic increase in the demand for professional property management in the 20th century.

Chapter 2

The Economics of Real Estate Investment

Outline

Introduction

The real estate market is simply one part of the national, and even global, economy. The same forces and principles that shape the economy as a whole also shape the real estate market. For example, supply and demand determines the price of real estate, just as it does any other commodity, and the real estate market moves through cycles, as does the economy as a whole.

Real estate (especially income-producing property) is an investment for its owner, so property managers should understand the basic economic principles that affect investments—both the economic considerations that affect investments generally and the factors that affect real estate investments in particular.

This chapter begins by reviewing basic investment terminology and concepts. After that, we discuss how real estate investments work and how they compare to other types of investments. We then examine how business cycles and supply and demand affect prices. Finally, we consider various private and governmental factors that impact the real estate market.

Investment Basics

An **investment** is any allocation of funds that is expected to generate a profit for the owner. There are many different types of investments, including:

- real estate,
- stocks,
- bonds,
- commodities (oil, gold, wheat, etc.), and
- certificates of deposit (CDs) and savings accounts.

The money earned on an investment is called a **return**. Different types of investments generate different types of returns. For instance, the return on a savings account comes in the form of interest. Bonds pay dividends, and the return on most stocks takes the form of both dividends and appreciation. (A **dividend** is a pro rata share of the corporation's earnings that is distributed to each shareholder. **Appreciation** is an increase in an investment's value over time.) The return on real estate investments usually takes the form of both rents and appreciation.

Debt Investments and Ownership Investments

Investments come in two forms: debt investments and ownership investments. With a **debt investment**, an investor lends money to an individual or a business entity. The investor allows the borrower to use his funds in exchange for interest. For instance, if a bank makes a mortgage loan, it's a debt investment that generates interest income for the bank.

A savings account is also a debt investment. The depositor essentially lends money to a bank or other depository institution, which the bank then uses to make loans to other customers. The bank will pay the depositor interest for use of his funds. Bonds work in a similar way. A bond is a certificate of indebtedness issued by a government or a business entity. An investor who buys a bond loans money (the cost of the bond) to the bond issuer. On the bond's maturity date, the issuer must repay the "loan" amount, plus interest.

With an **ownership investment**, the investor uses her money to acquire title to an asset (or a portion of the asset), rather than merely lending her money to someone else. Real estate is an ownership investment, and so are shares of corporate stock. (A stockholder buys a fractional ownership interest in the company that has sold the stock.)

Ownership investments can provide the investor with two types of returns. First, these investments usually generate income during the period of ownership. Stocks may pay dividends, while real estate can generate rent. Second, if demand for the investment increases, its value will also increase, and the investor will get a return on the investment in the form of appreciation.

Certain types of investments are known as securities. A **security** is any instrument representing either a debt or ownership investment that does not carry with it a right to direct managerial control over the business. Stocks and bonds are both securities, for example. Although a stockholder is an owner, and usually has a right to vote on the company's direction at a shareholder's meeting, the shares themselves do not confer a right to manage the enterprise in any hands-on sense. The sale of securities is strictly regulated by federal and state law.

Key Investment Characteristics

Most investors have only a certain amount of capital to invest, and they decide where to put their dollars after carefully weighing the potential risks and benefits of various investment choices. Typically, investors analyze investment opportunities by examining three key characteristics:

- safety,
- liquidity, and
- yield.

These characteristics are interrelated. For example, the safer and more liquid an investment is, the less likely the investment is to pay a high return (yield). On the other hand, an investor who's willing to take on more risk may come out ahead with higher profits.

Let's take a look at each of these three investment characteristics.

Safety. Safety refers to the investment's riskiness; a safe investment is one in which the investor has a low risk of losing her money. The rate of return may be modest, but the investor is unlikely to lose her original investment.

The U.S. government backs Treasury securities such as T-bills, making these among the safest investments. Savings accounts are also very safe. Even though the money is deposited into privately owned banks, checking and savings deposits are insured by the federal government. As long as a depositor's funds at a particular bank don't exceed the $250,000 maximum that is covered by federal deposit insurance, he will not lose his money, even if the bank fails and goes out of business. Of course, the returns on government securities and bank deposits are relatively low.

Speculative investments, such as stocks, generally offer higher rates of return, but are correspondingly riskier. When someone invests in stocks, he runs the risk of losing his entire investment.

Assessing the safety of all but the most straightforward investments is something of a guessing game.

> **Example:** Bernie invests $14,000 (half of his savings) in the stock of a startup company called U-Turn. The company is developing a medical device that will—if successful—cause the value of the stock to skyrocket. However, the device turns out to have dangerous side effects and the FDA refuses to approve it. The company's stock tumbles to 25% of the price Bernie paid. Worried, Bernie sells his stock; as a result, he loses about three-quarters of his original $14,000 investment.

Mortgage investing. Stocks aren't the only risky investments. Investors can purchase mortgages and mortgage-backed securities, which were traditionally thought of as fairly safe investments. The rigorous loan underwriting process that lenders used when making loans (plus government backing in some instances) created a sense of security. However, in the years leading up to the 2007 recession, lenders became so eager to make mortgage loans that they loosened traditional underwriting standards. The financial crisis that began in 2007 came about in part because of home loans based on faulty or even fraudulent underwriting standards. Many loans that were considered safe investments ended up in default.

Liquidity. Liquidity refers to whether an asset can be converted into cash quickly and easily. Liquid investments can be cashed out right away when funds are needed for emergency expenses or a better investment opportunity crops up elsewhere. In contrast, an illiquid investment is "locked up" and the funds are not immediately available for other purposes.

A savings account is perhaps the most liquid type of investment; it can be converted into cash at any time, simply by going to the bank. Certificates of deposit (CDs), stocks, bonds, and mutual funds are somewhat less liquid; they may take a little time to convert into cash, and service or penalty fees may apply. Tangible items, such as a piece of art or an automobile, are much less liquid. It may take a long time to find an interested buyer and then negotiate the sale.

Real estate is one of the least liquid assets. It may take months or even years to sell a property, particularly during a slow market or if the property is an unusual one. If the need to sell the property is urgent, the seller may have to accept a price that's well below market value.

The usual trade-off for liquidity is a lower yield. A savings account, for instance, is very liquid but pays little in the way of a return, often only a fraction of a percent in annual interest. Investments with a similar degree of safety but which lock up funds for a longer period of time, such as bonds or CDs, usually pay a somewhat higher rate of return.

Yield. An investment's **yield** is the rate of return on the investment. Yield is usually expressed as a percentage.

> **Example:** An investor puts $1,000 into a one-year certificate of deposit. At the end of the year, he gets $1,030 back. Thirty dollars of this amount is interest. The investor has received a 3% yield on his investment.

For some investments, like a bond or a CD, the yield is fixed at the outset. The investor knows with near certainty what she will receive at the end of the investment's term. Other investments, however, are highly uncertain, including real estate. The actual yield may turn out to be much more or much less than hoped for, depending on the characteristics of the individual project or enterprise, as well as the overall state of the economy.

As a general rule, the riskier the investment, the higher the yield must be to attract investors. An investor faced with two investments of comparable risk will choose the one that promises a higher yield. A risky investment that offers a low yield will attract few investors.

Investors also expect a higher yield for longer-term investments (as a trade-off for having their capital tied up for an extended period). Investors will avoid long-term investments that do not offer a better return than short-term investments.

Diversification

Investors have competing needs; they want safe investments that protect their original investment, but they also want a high yield. That is why experts recommend that investors **diversify**: invest in a mix of stocks, bonds, real estate, and commodities (such as gold). A diversified portfolio helps protect the investor from financial disaster should one type of investment suffer severe losses. (A **portfolio** is the mix of investments that a person owns, plus any cash reserves.)

The ideal portfolio will contain a variety of investments, including ones that are extremely safe (such as savings accounts), those that are fairly safe and generate reliable dividends or income (such as bonds offered by established companies), and those that are somewhat risky but offer a potentially high return (such as stocks and real estate). Some portfolios may also include investments that provide tax benefits; for example, the interest earned from municipal bonds is usually tax-free.

Investing in Real Estate

Investing in real estate is not for everyone. However, many investors like the tangible aspect of real property and they know that, historically, real estate has generated a considerable amount of wealth. In this section, we'll examine some of the advantages and disadvantages of investing in real estate.

Advantages of Real Estate Investment

The three biggest advantages of real estate investment involve cash flow, appreciation, and leverage. Real estate ownership may also offer tax advantages and we'll look at that topic briefly, but most of our discussion of taxation takes place in Chapter 5.

Cash Flow. Most real estate investors expect their income-producing properties to generate at least some positive cash flow. In other words, after the operating expenses and mortgage payments have been deducted from the property's income, there is some cash left over for the investor/owner.

Many other kinds of investments offer no cash flow. This is true of commodities (such as oil or wheat), collectibles (such as coins or artwork), and even certain stocks, as some companies don't pay dividends. The owner gets no income from these investments until she actually sells the asset. A successful real estate investment can provide more immediate financial rewards.

Appreciation and Equity. Historically, most real estate has increased in value over time. This appreciation may occur because of the efforts of the owner, or because of external factors such as a growing demand for that type of property. Of course, while real estate usually appreciates over time, it may also experience periods of depreciation during economic downturns.

An increase in the property's value causes a corresponding increase in the investor's equity. (**Equity** is the difference between a property's value and the liens against it.) Equity also increases as the loans against the property are paid off.

An investor can borrow against her equity and then use the loan funds to expand her business or make other investments. Although equity in real estate isn't a liquid asset per se, equity loans can be an important source of cash for an investor.

Leverage. One advantage associated with real estate investment is leverage: using borrowed money to invest in an asset. When an asset is purchased with borrowed funds and then appreciates, the investor earns a profit not only on the money she invested (the downpayment), but also on the money she borrowed to purchase the property. Thus, the return is much greater than it would've been had the investor paid the full purchase price in cash.

> **Example:** Waltham, Inc. purchased an apartment building for $645,000. The company made a $64,500 downpayment and borrowed the rest of the purchase price. The rent generated by the property covered all of the property's operating expenses, plus the mortgage payment and income taxes. The property appreciated at an average rate of 3% per year for ten years.

> ### ▶ *Sale-Leasebacks*
>
> Even if an investment property isn't rented out—for instance, because the owner uses the building for its headquarters—the owner can still take advantage of the equity in the property. The owner can borrow against the equity, as mentioned, or alternatively use a sale-leaseback arrangement.
>
> In a sale-leaseback, the owner sells the property to another investor, but then leases the property back from that investor. The seller continues to use the property for her business, and typically uses the lump sum from the sale to strengthen or expand the business. (Sale-leasebacks aren't limited to privately owned property. The Arizona state government, in the midst of the financial crisis in 2010, arranged a sale-leaseback of several of its office buildings, receiving $735 million in the transaction.) After a sale-leaseback, the seller-turned-renter can deduct the lease payments on the property as a business expense.
>
> Many sale-leaseback arrangements include a buyback clause, which states that the seller will (or may) buy the property back at fair market value after a specified number of years. This protects the seller from being forced to move operations at the end of the lease.

At the end of the ten years, Waltham sold the property for $866,826. After selling costs and paying off the loan balance, the company netted about $150,000 profit on its original $64,500 downpayment investment. That's over double the amount invested, a fairly healthy rate of return, even when spread over ten years.

Tax Deductions. Although a property manager rarely (if ever) prepares the owner's tax return, the manager will certainly want to understand the general nature of the deductions available to real estate investors.

Real estate investors may take deductions for expenses that might not be deductible with other kinds of investments. These include deductions for depreciation, mortgage interest, and operating expenses (such as repairs and insurance premiums). We'll explain these deductions in more detail in Chapter 5.

Property managers should also be aware that investors who want to sell a property can defer payment of taxes on the gain by using an installment sale or, alternatively, a 1031 exchange (exchanging one real property for another). If an investor chooses a 1031 exchange, her property manager can play an important role in identifying another property for the exchange.

Disadvantages of Real Estate Investment

Along with the advantages of investing in real estate, there are a few disadvantages as well, including illiquidity, high risk, high cost, complexity, and immobility.

Tax-Deferred Exchanges

Investors who want to sell a property that has appreciated may face stiff taxes on their profit. A 1031 exchange (named after section 1031 of the tax code) can delay the tax bill, however. The seller of an income property or a property used in a trade or business may defer taxation on any gain realized from the sale by exchanging the property for a **like-kind property** instead. (You may hear these transactions referred to as a "tax-free" exchange, though "tax-deferred" is more correct since it's presumed that eventually the property will be sold and the taxes paid.)

The like-kind rule allows exchanging real estate for any other piece of real estate, regardless of its particular use; for instance, an apartment complex may be exchanged for a commercial building. However, real property can't be exchanged for other kinds of property, such as stocks or an art collection.

Generally, when simply exchanging one property for another, no gain or loss is recognized on the deal, and neither party owes income tax on the transaction. However, if the exchange includes something other than like-kind property—such as money paid to compensate for the difference in values between the properties—that amount (referred to as **boot**) is taxable. Boot may also include a difference in mortgage balances owing on the properties exchanged; if Party A to the transaction assumes a larger mortgage on his new property, this represents a payment of money to Party B, since Party B now owes less money to the bank (this is called **debt relief**).

Illiquidity. As we've mentioned, real estate is not a liquid investment; it can take months to sell a property even in a favorable market, and much longer during an economic downturn. An investor who needs money quickly or who wants to escape a poor investment may find there is no easy way out. By contrast, stocks or mutual funds can be sold fairly quickly; the investor can receive the cash from the sale within days or even hours.

Risk of Loss. The recent real estate downturn reminded everyone that investing in real estate can be risky. Even if an investor makes what looks like a wise buy, the investment property could still lose value because of a downturn in the local or national economy. Unexpected problems with the property itself could crop up, such as previously undetected structural problems or toxic mold. Even investors who carefully research a property's condition may find operating expenses running higher than expected. A negative cash flow could force the investor to sell the property quickly, increasing her losses.

Cash Outlay. Most investors finance a significant portion of a property's purchase price; however, the required downpayment is still a very large sum of money. Some investors simply don't have the necessary capital. Even those who have the capital may not want to put all their available cash into one investment; this lack of diversification increases the risk of a devastating loss.

Note that an investor who doesn't have enough money to buy property outright can still participate in the real estate market by buying an interest in a real estate trust or syndicate. These trusts and syndicates hold and manage property on behalf of a number of investors.

Expert Knowledge. Purchasing and managing real estate requires expert knowledge. Is the property likely to appreciate in value over the coming years? Will its income exceed its operating expenses? What will be the demand for this type of space next year? In five years? In ten years? How will regional growth (or decline) affect the property? This type of information about a particular property is hard to come by. Picking the right investment property requires a level of knowledge about the local real estate market and its quirks that only an insider would know. The need for expert knowledge doesn't end with the purchase. Managing a property is time-consuming and the learning curve is steep.

On the other hand, some investors enjoy being actively involved in the purchase and management of real estate investments, either on their own or with the help of a property manager. Some investors prefer this type of hands-on investment to investing in securities such as stocks, where they have no control over operational decisions.

Immobility and Permanence. Real estate, by definition, is immobile; it is permanently fixed in one place. This means that a property's surroundings have a very large impact on its value, and yet they're entirely out of an investor's control. For instance, if the property's neighborhood starts to decline because of a nuisance or an economic downturn, the property can't be packed up and moved to a better area.

Because each property is unique and at the mercy of its environment, a real estate investor must engage in careful long-term planning and research, even more so than with other types of investments.

Determining How Much to Pay for a Property

Let's assume that an investor has weighed the pros and cons of investing in real estate and has decided to take the plunge. How does the investor decide what price to pay for a property?

Other aspects being equal, investors will pay more for a property that generates a larger income. This is why appraisers valuing income-producing property use the amount of income generated by the property to estimate the property's market value, employing what is called the **income approach to value**.

In the income approach, an appraiser takes the property's annual net operating income and divides it by the rate of return that the investor expects (the "cap rate"). Net operating income is the amount of income left over after paying for the property's operational (day-to-day) expenses.

Net operating income (NOI) ÷ Capitalization rate = Value

Example: An investor is interested in a small office building that generates an annual net operating income of $100,000. The investor wants at least a 7% rate of return on her investment. Applying the income approach formula for this investor would produce a value for the building of $1,428,571 ($100,000 ÷ 0.07 = $1,428,571).

Principle of Substitution

The principle that a buyer won't pay more for a similar, equally desirable item that he could get from another seller, unless there is an unreasonable delay in acquiring the substitute item, is known as the principle of substitution. This principle is the basis for all of the methods that an appraiser may use to estimate a property's value.

For example, the income approach to value presumes that an investor will not pay more for a property that does not generate a greater net income than substitute properties. The principle also comes into play with approaches that are more suited to buyers of residential properties, as well; for instance, a buyer will not pay more for a property than he will for a substitute property with similar features and amenities.

The cap rate that is used to determine a property's value will vary, depending on both the rate of return for similar investments in the current market and the investor's tolerance for risk. Different investors expect different returns on their investments, and thus the same property will have a different value for each investor.

If an investor is unsure about which cap rate to use, she can use market data to determine what rate of return other investors find acceptable. For instance, if she knows that a comparable property has an annual NOI of $100,000 and recently sold for $1,000,000, that would suggest that a 10% capitalization rate is appropriate for this type of property. (Appraisers have other methods of selecting capitalization rates as well, but these are beyond the scope of our discussion here.)

Economic Forces and Business Cycles

Returns from a real estate investment are often unpredictable because they depend on factors that are external to the property itself, such as economic forces and social trends. In this section, we'll explain basic economic concepts (such as markets and the law of supply and demand) that have an impact on real estate investments. We'll also look at the related concepts of business and real estate cycles.

Markets

A property's income—and thus its value—depends a great deal on the local market. For instance, the local market dictates the rental rates that can be charged for a particular type of space. A tenant will not pay $1,200 a month for a one-bedroom apartment if he can rent a similar apartment in the same market for $800 a month. The local market will also impose a limit on the miscellaneous income that can be collected, and determine the general cost of management expenses.

A **market** is defined as any arena in which buyers and sellers exchange a product. The "product" can be vegetables, stocks and bonds, or real estate. Depending on the product, the market will be local, regional, national, or international.

In the real estate rental market, the product is rental space and the geographical area is usually local (a residential tenant wants to live in a particular city, near her job and family, and would not be interested in housing hundreds of miles away). The real estate market can often be broken down into many smaller markets, such as higher-priced homes near a lake, commercial space in the downtown corridor, etc.

Although real estate values are local, investors and property managers alike should stay on top of trends in the regional and national economy. Factors such as state and federal spending and tax rates often have an effect on the local market.

The Principle of Supply and Demand

So what factor in the local market has the most impact on the price of an item? The answer is the supply of and demand for that item. Prices in a market depend on the quantity of goods available in the market—the supply—and the desire among potential purchasers for those particular goods—the demand.

Economists illustrate the effects of supply and demand on each other as an "X" on a graph. (See Figure 2.1.) As demand increases, supply decreases, and vice versa: as supply increases, demand decreases. The point where the two lines of the X intersect on the graph represents a market where supply and demand are in balance.

When demand for a product exceeds the supply, prices tend to go up as buyers compete with each other for the product. Economists call this a **seller's market**, because the higher prices benefit sellers. These higher prices encourage an increase in production, and sellers then have more goods to sell. In the case of real estate, more sellers put their property on the market. When the supply increases, the market price will begin to fall as sellers compete with each other to find buyers. This is called a **buyer's market**. Next, the presence of bargains attracts more buyers to the market, and once again the demand will begin to outstrip supply. The cycle begins anew and continues to repeat itself.

> **Example:** A college town lacks enough rental units within walking distance of the university to house all the current students. Without enough units to go around, rents there are high compared to other parts of town. Students without a lot of money live in the cheaper outlying parts of the city.
>
> The high rents in the university area attract the attention of several developers. They buy land in the area and build some large apartment complexes, flooding the market with new units. Suddenly university area landlords must lower rents and make other concessions in order to keep their buildings reasonably full. However, the discounted rents attract the attention of students who live farther out and gradually most of the available units fill up. At this point, any further influx of renters will cause the market to favor the landlords again and rents will rise to relatively high levels once more.

Of course, market price isn't the only thing that drives demand; any number of other factors may come into play. For instance, returning to our college town example, if the university decided to admit several thousand additional students, that would increase the

Figure 2.1 Relationship between supply and demand

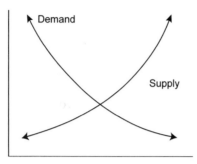

demand for apartments in the neighborhood considerably, regardless of what prices are doing.

Increased demand for one commodity may spur demand for a related commodity. Demand for new furniture tends to go hand-in-hand with demand for houses, for instance. A serious housing downturn can spill over into many other sectors of the economy, not only reducing demand for the items that go into new empty houses (furniture and appliances) but also for the raw materials used to build houses (lumber and drywall).

Measuring Supply and Demand. One way owners and property managers can gauge supply and demand for their product is by studying the absorption rate. The **absorption rate** is the length of time—usually expressed as a certain number of months—that it would take for the existing amount of vacant space to be rented at the rate people are currently signing leases (under the assumption that no additional space comes onto the market or that no other changes upset the balance).

The absorption rate is determined by dividing the total amount of space available for lease in a market by the current rate of demand for that kind of space.

> **Example:** A market has 240,000 square feet of leasable office space available. The current rate of office leasing is about 80,000 square feet a year. Thus, it would take about 36 months to absorb the current supply.

Developers and lenders usually consult the absorption rate before deciding whether to proceed with a new project. For instance, if it's taking 24 months for current office space to be absorbed into the market, developers are much less likely to proceed with the construction of a new office building than if the absorption rate is only five months.

Business Cycles

As we discussed earlier, supply and demand move in a constant cycle, with increased demand pushing up prices and increased supply pushing down prices. These cycles happen not just in the markets for particular commodities, but in the regional, national, and global economies. These economies go through repeating cycles of expansion followed by contraction. When demand is high, businesses are able to make easy profits and expand their business. When demand is low, businesses slash prices, lay off workers, and cut costs. These cycles, generally speaking, are known as **business cycles**.

A business cycle has three different stages:

- prosperity,
- recession, and
- recovery.

Prosperity. Prosperity is a period of sustained, stable growth and overall economic health. Employment levels are high and people earn enough income to pay for basic necessities with cash left over for at least some discretionary spending. As consumer spending increases, businesses expand—creating more jobs at higher salaries—and the expansion continues.

Unfortunately, periods of prosperity inevitably burn themselves out. Demand for goods or services grows until prices increase, forcing consumers to cut back on spending. As consumption declines, production falls off, employment declines, and the economy enters a recession.

Recession. In a recession, the economy slows down. Technically, a **recession** occurs when the gross domestic product (the market value of all goods and services produced in the United States) declines for at least six months. However, people tend to use the term for any significant period of time when growth is slow and unemployment is high. A severe, long-term recession is called a **depression**.

Recessions are inevitable in the normal cycles of supply and demand. Sometimes, though, a failure in a particular economic sector can trigger a national recession. For example, the bursting of first the dot-com bubble in 2000 and then the housing bubble in 2008 precipitated and intensified the recessions that followed. Business failures and job losses in those particular sectors led to less demand for goods and services throughout the general economy.

Recovery. A period of recovery eventually follows every recession. The length of recessions varies widely, ranging from several months to a number of years; but at some point, prices will have declined enough that consumers once again start purchasing. This early growth, like a recession, may start in one sector of the economy and spread throughout the larger economy. For instance, a new technology might grow a particular part of the economy, and job growth and increased incomes in that sector will lead to more consumption everywhere. Eventually, once the benefits have filtered into the entire economy, another period of prosperity will begin.

Business cycles can be short, especially when they're confined to a particular, volatile sector of the economy; but generally they tend to play out over a number of years. Almost every decade has suffered one or two periods of recession among longer periods of growth and prosperity.

Even though a property manager's day-to-day concerns are mostly shaped by conditions in the local real estate market, he should keep an eye on the national economic news: nationwide business cycles can have a significant impact on decisions the property manager will have to make. Anticipating changes in demand and setting rents at an appropriate level to maintain full occupancy are hallmarks of a successful property manager, and

Economic Indicators

Economic forecasters tend to focus on several widely accepted economic indicators that can help predict future economic growth or contraction. Economists call these leading indicators. The Conference Board, a nonprofit organization, publishes a report that weighs ten of the most important leading indicators, including new orders, jobless claims, the money supply, and so on.

One particularly important leading indicator, especially in the real estate context, is the number of new building permits. An increase in building permits indicates that developers are optimistic about the future demand for residential or commercial space, and that soon they will be putting more money into the economy as they pay for labor and materials. Other real estate-related indicators, such as new and existing home sales, are also helpful in gauging the health of the broader economy.

While leading indicators help forecast economic activity, other indicators trail behind. Employment, for instance, is a well-known trailing indicator. Employers tend to lay people off in response to economic contraction, rather than ahead of it, and unemployment rates tend to remain elevated even after the economy resumes growing: businesses need to work through backlogged inventory before they can start increasing production and thus resume hiring.

since those are shaped by national as well as local factors, some familiarity with business cycles is necessary.

Real Estate Cycles

Business cycles shape the economy as a whole, but various sectors of the economy also have cycles of their own. Real estate—commercial real estate in particular—is notorious for boom and bust cycles that are more pronounced than those in the broader economy.

During the prosperity phase of a real estate cycle, developers jump onboard with an abundance of projects, trying to take advantage of the big profits that are currently available. But as more and more projects are finished, a period of **overbuilding** begins. The number of new units eventually exceeds the demand for them, and prices drop. Instead of reaping the profits they anticipated, developers end up having to cut rents on newly finished buildings and abandon any further development plans. This phase, known as **adjustment** in real estate cycles, corresponds with the recession phase in general business cycles.

Once the cycle bottoms out, after a period of **stabilization**, a new phase of development will begin, corresponding with the recovery phase of the business cycle.

The real estate market's cycles may or may not coincide with the more general business cycles. They also tend to be local or regional; a big increase in local unemployment because a large employer left town would put downward pressure on real estate values even if the overall national economy is healthy. On the other hand, a severe national recession could affect the real estate values across the country.

The same real estate cycle can have different effects on different segments of the real estate market. For example, suppose high unemployment rates have decreased home values and increased foreclosure rates. In this environment, the property manager for a homeowners association might find it difficult to collect homeowner dues and pay for necessary repairs to the building. But suppose that same manager is also managing a large apartment complex. Since many people can no longer afford to buy new homes (or even afford the payments on the homes they already own), the occupancy rate at that apartment complex may increase and the cost of tenant concessions decrease, as more tenants move in and existing tenants renew their leases.

Factors Affecting Real Estate Supply and Demand

Many other factors besides business cycles play a role in supply and demand. We'll end this chapter by looking at some of these other factors, which include both social and business trends, and government actions.

Social and Business Trends

Changes in how we live and work can affect the supply of and demand for real estate in a particular market.

Population Changes. The number of people living in a region can change because of fluctuations in the local birthrate or because people are either moving in or out of the area. A population that's increasing will tend to extend the prosperity phase of a real estate cycle, keeping demand for living space high. The opposite is also true: a declining population generally has a negative impact on the value of real estate.

A rental market can be affected greatly by seasonal population changes. For instance, a college town might have low demand for rentals during the summer months but high demand during the rest of the year, while a beachside resort might have a high demand for rentals during the summer months but low demand for the rest of the year.

Business Cycles. Business expansion or contraction can have a big impact on a local real estate market. Expansion can lead to new construction of commercial properties, while contraction can lead to high vacancy rates in existing commercial buildings. These business cycles can also affect residential markets, because employment opportunities (or lack of them) directly affect the demand for housing.

An increase in local wages may increase demand for upper-end rental units that have more amenities, or it could diminish the demand for rental units by converting more renters into homeowners. Conversely, a decrease in earning power may create more demand for rentals because fewer people are able to afford houses, or it may decrease demand for rental units as more people take in roommates or move in with family members.

Demographic Changes. Shifts in the demographic makeup of the population can have a significant impact on supply and demand. A change in the size of households or in the average age of residents may lead to changes in the types of units that people desire. An increase in families with young children would lead to an increase in the demand for units with two or three bedrooms. On the other hand, an increase in young professionals or in senior citizens would lead to less demand for large units, and greater demand for smaller, low-maintenance properties.

Technological Changes. Technological changes also create new patterns of demand. For instance, increasing numbers of people opt to shop online. This trend will have a significant impact on the demand for retail space in coming years. Online retailers can store their products in warehouses in cheaper rural areas and sell directly from these locations, rather than depending entirely on storefronts in more expensive, densely populated areas. Similarly, an increase in telecommuting may reduce the future demand for office space.

Social Trends. Social trends that affect supply and demand include forces that cause migrations from urban to suburban areas, and vice versa. Environmental concerns may cause people to choose to live closer to work to cut down on energy consumption. Or the popularity of growing your own food may encourage people to leave densely populated urban areas in favor of a detached home with space for a small garden.

Changes in consumer preference can have a huge impact on retail development. For instance, upscale stores clustered around outdoor plazas have become more popular in recent years. Many traditional enclosed shopping malls, the mainstays of retail during the late 20th century, look increasingly dated, leaving owners to wonder whether to refurbish or convert them to entirely new uses.

Government Factors

The list of possible influences on supply and demand for real estate is nearly endless, but some of the most important ones are controlled (at least partially) by the government. The government affects the real estate market in many ways, but it does so chiefly through:

- monetary policy (setting interest rates and controlling the money supply),
- regulation of lending institutions,
- mortgage industry involvement,
- tax policy, and
- land use laws.

Let's begin with a look at how the government's monetary policy affects the real estate market.

Interest Rates and Money Supply. In theory, banks can charge whatever rate of interest they want. However, in practice, they are limited by both the interest rates that other banks are charging and by the actions of the federal government.

The Federal Reserve helps implement U.S. **monetary policy** by controlling key interest rates, such as the rate charged to banks that borrow money from the Fed. The Fed works to lower rates when it sees economic weakness and believes it must stimulate more borrowing and consumption. Conversely, it raises rates when inflation threatens, in order to keep the economy from overheating.

The Federal Reserve also has other tools for implementing the government's monetary policy. It can change the **reserve requirements** imposed on banks. For instance, it can require banks to keep a greater portion of their deposited funds out of circulation, which in turn would decrease the money available for mortgage loans. The decrease in the supply of money would cause interest rates to rise.

The Fed can also buy or sell Treasury securities. These transactions are known as **open market operations**. Like reserve requirements, open market operations can increase or decrease the money supply. Selling securities to investors takes money out of circulation and ties up funds that might be invested elsewhere. When the government buys securities, on the other hand, it puts money back into circulation, providing investors with cash to buy property.

These actions by the Fed affect interest rates both directly (through control of key interest rates) and indirectly (by affecting the nation's money supply). Interest rates affect the real estate market in many ways: high interest rates make it difficult to get financing for new development projects. Higher rates also make it harder for individual home buyers to purchase homes. Under these conditions, current rental space can become more valuable as the demand for it increases. On the other hand, higher interest rates mean that investors may want a higher return on their real estate investments (since competing investments may be offering a higher interest rate). This could put downward pressure on the value of real estate. (Remember, the higher the cap rate desired by investors, the lower the market value of investment property.)

Lower interest rates tend to make potential renters more likely to purchase homes instead of renting, but also make real estate development more attractive because of the lower cost of borrowing the necessary funds.

Lending Institution Regulation. The federal government oversees the lending and investment practices of the nation's largest financial institutions. The strictness of government regulations on lending institutions can affect the overall availability of credit.

For example, during the loose regulatory regime of the early 2000s, credit was freely available. However, this lack of strict oversight probably ended up harming the economy; the large number of risky loans made during this period helped precipitate the financial crisis that began in 2007. On the other hand, if regulators over-tighten lending rules, the flow of funds can dry up, causing problems throughout the economy.

Mortgage Industry Involvement. The availability of mortgage financing influences investor demand for real estate. Most people, including investors, can't afford to buy property without borrowing most of the money.

The federal government is heavily involved in the mortgage industry in order to promote homeownership. For instance, the government manages two agencies, Fannie Mae and Freddie Mac, which were created to help strengthen the housing market. These agencies buy mortgage loans from lenders, package them as mortgage-backed securities, and sell the loans in the secondary market. This helps provide a smooth flow of mortgage funds throughout the country, assuring that local lenders will have money on hand to lend.

Two other agencies, the Federal Housing Administration and the Department of Veterans Affairs, also play important roles. These agencies insure or guarantee home loans in order to encourage lenders to lend to borrowers whose income might not be adequate for conventional loans.

Borrowers must meet the underwriting standards set by these agencies before they can obtain loans. In recent years, higher credit score requirements and other heightened qualifying standards have contributed to slowing home sales. As stricter standards shrink the pool of buyers, more people end up renting simply because they can't obtain purchase loans. This trend favors investment in rental housing.

In the wake of the most recent recession, the federal government's role in residential real estate came under fire. A reduction in the level of support given by the federal government to the housing market would probably reduce the amount of mortgage funds available to buyers.

Tax Policy. State and local governments impose taxes on real property to fund their operations. Tax rates can vary significantly from one area to another, and this may affect the desirability of a particular state or county as a place to invest. High tax rates tend to discourage new development. At the same time, if the high property taxes are used to pay for high-quality public services, infrastructure, and public schools, the area will be attractive to buyers, tenants, and developers.

The federal government's main source of funds is the income tax. The income tax code includes exemptions and deductions that are designed to encourage particular endeavors deemed socially beneficial, from the development of sources of alternative energy to the construction of low-income housing. The current income tax code encourages real estate investment by allowing deductions for depreciation, mortgage interest, and operating expenses. (These deductions are discussed in Chapter 5.)

Environmental and Land Use Regulation. Environmental and land use regulations affect the amount of land that is available for development. Environmental laws generally limit the usability of certain parcels of land. For instance, shoreline restrictions may limit the use of ocean or lakefront property.

Land use and zoning laws may either restrict development or open it up. For example, if an area of raw land is zoned for single-family homes, the development potential is much more limited than if it were zoned for multi-family or a mixed residential/commercial use.

When the zoning for an area is changed to allow a wider range of development, it is referred to as "downzoning."

> **Example:** A neighborhood zoned for multifamily use has entered a decline. Hoping to rejuvenate the neighborhood and bolster property tax revenues, the city rezones the area to allow commercial development. As a result, the owners of two apartment buildings in the neighborhood tear down their buildings and replace them with small strip malls.

The effect of any zoning change is apt to help some investors and hurt others. In our example, the owners of nearby apartment buildings now face decreased competition and may be able to raise rental rates. On the other hand, any owners of nearby shopping center properties will face fresh competition for tenants as a result of the zoning change. They may have to lower store rents or spend money remodeling in order to compete with the freshly built strip malls.

Governmental actions related to real estate will always produce winners and losers. Owners and property managers who stay informed of proposed changes will have the best opportunity to make them work to their own advantage.

Chapter Summary

1. Investors buy real estate hoping to make a profit. Returns on a real estate investment may take the form of appreciation and rent payments.

2. With an ownership investment, such as real estate, the investor takes title to an asset. Debt investments, by contrast, involve an investor lending money to an individual or business entity in return for interest.

3. Investors assess the safety, liquidity, and yield of an investment. Safety refers to the riskiness of the investment. Liquidity refers to how easily the asset can be converted to cash. Yield is the rate of return on the investment. Investments that are safe and liquid tend to have the lowest yields.

4. Advantages of real estate investment include cash flow and appreciation (which increases the owner's equity, and can be used as collateral for additional borrowing). Real estate investors can benefit from applying the principle of leverage. Real estate investment also offers certain tax deductions.

5. Disadvantages of real estate investment include illiquidity (difficulty of converting the asset into cash), the risk of loss, the large cash outlay required to get started, the need for expert knowledge, and the immobility and permanence of land.

6. Net operating income is the rental income that a property generates, minus operating expenses. An appraiser can use net operating income to estimate the property's market value.

7. Prices in a market are shaped by the supply of, and demand for, an item. As supply rises, prices tend to drop. As supply shrinks, prices generally rise.

8. The economy tends to move through cycles called business cycles. A business cycle has three distinct phases: prosperity, recession, and recovery. The real estate market also tends to move through its own cycles, which often closely follow broader business cycles.

9. Factors affecting demand include changes in population and in people's buying power, demographic changes, and changes in taste or fashion.

10. The government engages in many activities that help shape the real estate market. These include setting monetary policy (including influencing interest rates), regulating lending institutions, involvement in mortgage markets, and tax policy. The government also influences the real estate market through environmental and land use regulation.

Key Terms

Investment – An allocation of funds expected to generate a profit for the investor.

Appreciation – An increase in an investment's value over time.

Debt investment – An investment in which an investor lends money to an individual or business entity.

Ownership investment – An investment in which the investor acquires an asset or an ownership interest in an asset.

Securities – Investments where the investor does not have a managerial interest, only the right to receive payments (such as with shares of stock).

Safety – The degree of risk associated with an investment; in particular, the likelihood of losing money on the investment.

Liquidity – The ability to convert an asset to cash quickly.

Yield – The rate of return on an investment for the investor; a high-yield investment is one that is highly profitable.

Portfolio – The various investments that an investor owns.

Cash flow – The remainder of the rental income received by an investor after paying the property's operating expenses and mortgage payment.

Equity – The difference between a property's market value and the liens against the property.

Leverage – Using borrowed money to invest in an asset.

Net operating income (NOI) – The rental income that a property generates, minus its operating expenses.

Supply – The quantity of a particular product available in a market.

Demand – The desire among potential purchasers for a particular product in a market.

Absorption rate – The length of time, usually expressed in months, for the existing amount of vacant space to be rented under current conditions.

Business cycle – The pattern of repeated waves of growth and decline that characterizes the movement of the economy.

Prosperity – The phase in a business cycle where growth is sustained and stable.

Recession – The phase in a business cycle when the economy is contracting, characterized by increased unemployment and falling prices.

Recovery – The phase in a business cycle where growth starts to resume after a recession has bottomed out.

Real estate cycles – Cycles of growth and contraction that occur specifically within the real estate sector; these often closely track broader business cycles.

Monetary policy – The federal government's control over the size of the money supply; implemented primarily through the Federal Reserve.

Chapter Quiz

1. An investor buys a certificate of deposit (CD) that pays 3.4% interest. This interest is the CD's:
   a) rate of appreciation
   b) dividend
   c) rate of return
   d) liquidity factor

2. An investor purchases an apartment complex, with the investor managing it himself and renting it out to tenants. This is an example of a/an:
   a) debt investment
   b) ownership investment
   c) sale-leaseback
   d) security

3. You can cash out an investment in a savings account or in a mutual fund quickly and easily. However, it may take months or even years to sell real property. This is why investors say real estate has poor:
   a) leverage
   b) liquidity
   c) appreciation
   d) yield

4. The amount of money left after paying a rental property's operating expenses and mortgage each month is known as:
   a) appreciation
   b) cash flow
   c) equity
   d) leverage

5. The term "leverage" refers to:
   a) a tax-deferred exchange of two like-kind properties
   b) real estate's ability to appreciate faster than inflation
   c) the property's market value, minus the value of liens against it
   d) using borrowed money to purchase an asset

6. Which of the following is an advantage of investing in real estate?
   a) Possibility of appreciation
   b) Immobility
   c) Cash outlay needed to obtain a property
   d) Degree of knowledge needed to choose and manage properties

7. An investor decides that she would like a 10% rate of return on her real estate investment. An appraiser uses that knowledge, plus a property's $200,000 annual net operating income, to determine that the property would be worth $2,000,000 to that investor. The appraiser has used what percentage as the cap rate?
   a) 1%
   b) 5%
   c) 10%
   d) None of the above; the cap rate isn't expressed as a percentage

8. A developer builds a large new apartment building in a town where there is a shortage of rental units and where rents are high. This will:
   a) increase demand, which will lower rents
   b) increase demand, which will raise rents
   c) increase supply, which will lower rents
   d) increase supply, which will raise rents

9. Demand for a commodity may be increased by a change in:
   a) fashion or tastes
   b) population
   c) purchasing power
   d) All of the above

10. Periods of broader prosperity tend to spur _____ in real estate markets, which tends to further exacerbate the subsequent downturn by adding excess supply to the real estate market.

    a) adjustment
    b) inflation
    c) overbuilding
    d) stabilization

11. Which of the following government entities does not participate in the federal government's active involvement in the mortgage market?

    a) Fannie Mae
    b) Federal Housing Administration
    c) Federal Reserve
    d) Department of Veterans Affairs

12. The federal government has a large role in setting:

    a) absorption rates
    b) interest rates
    c) cap rates
    d) supply of rental units

13. In a particular real estate market, there are 50 leasable units currently on the market, and the number of units that are typically leased in that market in a typical year is 100. How long would it take the market to absorb that backlog of supply?

    a) Three months
    b) Six months
    c) One year
    d) Two years

14. Faced with an overheated, inflationary economy, the federal government would attempt to do what with interest rates?

    a) Raise them
    b) Lower them
    c) Keep them the same
    d) None of the above; the federal government can't influence interest rates

15. The Federal Reserve requires member banks to hold an additional 1% of their deposits in their vaults, in order to be available on demand to depositors. This is an example of the Fed manipulating the money supply through:

    a) deficit spending
    b) key interest rates
    c) open market operations
    d) reserve requirements

Answer Key

1. c)   A loan is a form of investment and the interest paid on the loan is the investment's rate of return.

2. b)   Any investment where an investor owns an asset, or an interest in an asset, is an ownership investment. Ownership of an apartment building isn't a security; that term is used to describe investments where the investor has no managerial control, as with stocks or bonds.

3. b)   Liquidity describes whether an asset can be converted into cash quickly. Real estate, which may take a long time to sell, is not a liquid asset.

4. b)   Subtracting operating expenses and the mortgage payment from monthly rental income leaves the property's cash flow.

5. d)   Leverage is the use of borrowed funds to invest in an asset. When the asset appreciates, investors profit not only on the funds they invested but also on the funds they borrowed.

6. a)   Real property, unlike other investments (such as CDs or bonds), may gain value over time; this is appreciation.

7. c)   A capitalization rate represents the rate of return that an investor expects to receive on the money invested in an investment. An appraiser may use net operating income, divided by the capitalization rate, to find a property's value.

8. c)   By adding more apartment units to the rental market, the developer is adding supply. If supply increases to the extent that it exceeds demand, rents will drop.

9. d)   Changes in population, in purchasing power, or in people's tastes may all lead to changes in demand for a particular commodity.

10. c)   The "overbuilding" phase of the real estate cycle tends to happen in concert with the prosperity period of the broader business cycle. Building projects launched during this phase tend to enter the market once it is already in decline, adding excess supply to a market where demand is already falling.

11. c)   Fannie Mae is a secondary mortgage agency that buys and resells mortgage loans, while the FHA and VA insure or guarantee mortgage loans. The Federal Reserve is not actively involved in the mortgage industry, although its ability to affect interest rates certainly means it has an impact on mortgage lending.

12. b)   The federal government, through the actions of the Federal Reserve, greatly influences market interest rates. This is one the most significant ways in which the government shapes the real estate market.

13. b)   This question asks you to calculate the absorption rate for this type of property. If there are 50 units available and 100 units are absorbed per year, it would take half a year (or six months) to work through this supply of units.

14. a) The Federal Reserve controls key interest rates; raising these rates tends to discourage borrowing and encourage savings and will slow the economy down.

15. d) Reserve requirements are one of the Fed's tools for controlling the money supply. Requiring banks to keep more deposits in reserve takes more funds out of circulation in the economy, which may have the effect of raising interest rates.

Chapter 3

Working with Management Clients

Outline

Introduction

A property manager's job is to handle the financial and physical aspects of the owner's property in a manner that will achieve the owner's goals. Since those goals are determined by the owner and her expectations for her investment property, the property manager and the property owner must be able to work together.

This chapter examines the relationship between the manager and the property owner (the client). We'll begin by describing the different types of entities that own investment property. Next, we'll explain the legal relationship between the owner and the manager, and the duties and liabilities created by that relationship. We'll then explore aspects of working with a new owner: the owner's goals, the contents of a typical management agreement, handover procedures, and recordkeeping and reporting. We'll end the chapter by discussing what happens when the manager and owner decide to terminate their relationship.

Types of Property Owners

A property manager might work with an individual property owner, a small business, or a large investment company. The differences between these types of owners can have a significant impact on the manager-client relationship, so an understanding of the different forms of business entities is crucial to the property manager's success.

Sole Proprietorships

A business that is made up of one individual is called a **sole proprietorship**. A sole proprietor may own just one investment property or he may own several. He will often have another source of income besides the investment property, such as a job or another business.

Sole proprietorships are the most common form of business entity, mainly because sole proprietorships are easy and inexpensive to form. But this business type also offers other advantages to the owner. First, the simplicity of the arrangement allows for lower administrative and legal costs. Second, the business owner doesn't need to answer to anyone else: he has complete control over the business's management decisions and day-to-day operations. Finally, the owner has more privacy; he isn't required to disclose as much financial information as he would if he were a member of a partnership or other shared business arrangement.

But these advantages come at a price. A sole proprietor with limited resources usually can't afford to purchase large, expensive properties such as those owned by groups of investors. (Of course, this is not a disadvantage to those owners who prefer smaller properties that are easier to manage.) And because a sole proprietor acts alone, he has no one to share the risks and responsibilities.

The biggest disadvantage to sole proprietorship, though, is **unlimited liability**. Unlimited liability means that the sole proprietor is personally liable for the business's debts. In other words, if the business is unable to pay its obligations, the creditors can collect the debt from the individual owner.

Example: Mary is a sole proprietor. In addition to her personal residence, Mary also owns a ten-unit apartment building. A tenant sues Mary because Mary didn't clear the icy walkway one winter morning and the tenant slipped and fell. A judgment is entered against Mary for $20,000. If there aren't enough funds in Mary's business account to pay this debt, the tenant can go after Mary's personal residence and personal bank account to satisfy the judgment.

In contrast, as we'll discuss in the next section, some business arrangements provide investors with **limited liability**, meaning that members' personal assets are protected from business liabilities. In some states, an individual can choose to operate her business as a corporation or a limited liability company instead of as a sole proprietorship, in order to gain limited liability protection. But this could mean giving up the simplicity, privacy, and control that comes with a sole proprietorship.

> ### ▶ *Married Couples Only*
>
> California allows married couples to classify their business as a sole proprietorship. Despite California's Domestic Partner Rights and Responsibilities Act, however, domestic partners must classify their business as a partnership. The city of San Francisco provides a notable exception: the form to register a sole proprietorship in the city specifically allows domestic partners to operate as a sole proprietorship.

Married Couples. Typically, a sole proprietor is an individual person. If two or more people wish to start a business or buy an investment property, they will often form some type of business syndicate to do so. (We'll discuss syndicates shortly.) However, there's a limited federal exception for married couples who own a business together. Until 2007, only married taxpayers in community property states could treat a shared business as a sole proprietorship. But the IRS now gives this special treatment to all married couples. To qualify, the married couple must be the only owners of the business, and both spouses must materially participate in running the business. Other reporting and tax rules apply, so married couples should consult a tax attorney or accountant before treating their business as a sole proprietorship for tax purposes.

Some states (such as California) allow married couples to treat their business as a sole proprietorship for state income tax purposes; other states require married couples to treat the business as a partnership. In some limited cases, registered domestic partners may also treat their business as a sole proprietorship.

Working with Sole Proprietors. In many ways, a sole proprietor is much easier to work with than any other type of business entity. A property manager with a sole proprietor for a client doesn't have to worry about conflicts between partners, and he doesn't need to obtain consent from several owners before addressing non-routine problems. On the other hand, a sole proprietor may want to be very involved in managing the property, and may take up a fair amount of the property manager's time.

Business Syndicates

Things get a little more complicated when two or more people want to purchase an investment property together. These people may be business associates, but they might also be siblings, roommates, or casual friends. The more formal these owners make their business relationship, the easier it is for the property manager. Without a formal business arrangement, multiple owners could easily misunderstand their rights and obligations. Will all the owners expect to vote on management decisions, or will they appoint a single owner to speak for the group? Are all of them equally liable for management expenses, property repairs, etc.? A business agreement should address these issues ahead of time, to save time and help avoid misunderstandings.

Co-owners may choose to formalize their business relationship by creating an investment group, or syndicate. The term **syndicate** does not have a precise legal definition, but in most cases, it is a formally organized business entity such as a corporation, a partnership, or a limited liability company. (Each of these will be discussed in more detail in the following sections.)

With a syndicate, title to the investment property is usually held in the business entity's name, rather than in the names of the individual investors.

> **Example:** Peter and Ahmed are real estate investors who have formed a corporation called "Sunset Properties." When they purchase an investment property, title to the property will be held in the name of "Sunset Properties," rather than in Peter's and Ahmed's names individually.

Syndicate investors often have limited liability. If the syndicate becomes insolvent, the investors will lose their investment, but their personal assets may be protected from the syndicate's creditors.

> **Example:** After several bad investment decisions, "Sunset Properties" goes out of business, leaving behind over $400,000 in outstanding debts. In most cases, neither Peter nor Ahmed (nor any of the other corporation's investors) will be personally responsible for those unpaid bills.

Someone who organizes an investment syndicate may be referred to as the **syndicator** or the **sponsor**. A syndicator may manage the syndicate and the investment property herself, or the syndicate may hire a professional property manager.

In some cases, interests in a real estate syndicate are considered securities, like stocks and bonds. If so, a syndicator offering them to potential investors must comply with federal and state securities laws. Of course, anyone who is considering forming a syndicate should seek expert legal and financial advice before proceeding.

One advantage of forming a syndicate is that investors can usually purchase much larger, more expensive properties than they could on their own. Other advantages and disadvantages vary depending on the type of business entity created. Some common types of investment groups include:

- corporations,
- general partnerships,
- limited partnerships,

- limited liability companies (LLCs),
- trusts, and
- joint ventures.

Corporations. A corporation is owned by its shareholders: individuals who purchase shares of stock in the company as an investment. A corporation may be an extremely large company with thousands of shareholders and publicly traded stock (that is, stock that is bought and sold on a public stock exchange). But it may also be a small or medium-sized company with only a few shareholders (sometimes called a **closely held corporation**). A real estate investment syndicate organized as a corporation is likely to be on the smaller side.

The money invested by the shareholders provides the corporation with operating capital. The corporation's income may be distributed to the shareholders in the form of **dividends**.

A corporation must be organized in compliance with formal requirements prescribed by state law. The particular requirements vary by state, but all states require **articles of incorporation** to be filed with the secretary of state's office. The articles of incorporation establish the corporation's name, list the name and address of each incorporator, explain the share structure, and include a general statement of purpose.

A corporation is legally a separate entity from its shareholders. The law treats it as an artificial individual: it can enter into contracts, own property, incur debts, and sue and be sued.

Management. The shareholders of a large corporation often have very little direct involvement in its management. They may only receive annual reports and vote on an occasional major issue. How much management input an individual shareholder has depends on the corporation's bylaws and how many shares of stock she owns.

The real power behind a corporation is the board of directors. The directors govern the corporation's affairs in accordance with its bylaws. They appoint **corporate officers**—the president or chief executive officer (CEO), vice president, treasurer, and corporate secretary—who run the business on a day-to-day basis. The officers are not automatically authorized to convey or encumber the corporation's real property, however; these actions must be expressly authorized by a resolution of the board.

Liability. The primary advantage of the corporate form of organization is that individual shareholders are protected from liability for the corporation's debts.

> **Example:** A few years ago, Nguyen paid $3,000 for shares of stock in the ABC Corporation. His shares are now worth $3,600.
>
> The ABC Corporation is found liable for a serious injury that occurred on one of its industrial properties, and a $250,000 judgment is entered against the corporation. The judgment creditor can file a lien against the corporation's assets if the judgment is not paid.
>
> However, the creditor cannot proceed against Nguyen to collect the judgment. Nguyen's home, bank accounts, and other property are protected because the corporation is a separate legal entity. Nguyen may lose his original $3,000 investment if the corporation goes out of business because of the judgment, but that is the extent of his liability.

Because of this special legal status, corporations are closely regulated by state and federal laws.

> ▶ *Double Taxation*
>
> Double taxation is a potential problem only for corporations. The other entities described in the text—partnerships, limited partnerships, limited liability companies, and joint ventures—do not have to pay taxes on their profits before distributing them to investors. The profits are taxed only as investors' personal income.
>
> A small or medium-sized corporation can avoid double taxation if it qualifies as an S corporation (as opposed to a C corporation, which is the designation for a regular corporation). To qualify as an S corporation, a company must have no more than 100 shareholders, and none of the shareholders can be foreign investors. An S corporation is allowed to pass its income on to shareholders without first paying corporate income taxes, just like a partnership or an LLC.

Taxation. For all of its advantages, the corporate form of ownership generally has one major disadvantage: **double taxation**. First the company must pay corporate income taxes on its profits; then, when the profits are distributed to the shareholders as dividends, the shareholders must pay personal income taxes on those dividends.

General Partnerships. A general partnership is an association of two or more individuals who operate a business as co-owners for profit. A general partnership is created by express agreement (either oral or written). If there is a written contract, the terms of the contract will usually govern the partnership. If the partnership agreement isn't in writing, state law governs the partnership.

A general partnership is appealing to many investors. It doesn't require the formal structure of a corporation and it is relatively easy to set up. The partners in a general partnership all share in the profits and management of the business. Unless otherwise agreed, each one has an equal share of the profits and losses, and each has an equal voice in the management and control of the business.

Unlike corporations, income from a general partnership is not taxed prior to its distribution to the partners. Instead, each partner is responsible for paying taxes on his share of the income.

Liability. The chief disadvantage of a general partnership is that each partner has unlimited liability for the acts of the partnership. In other words, if the business is unable to pay its debts, its creditors can collect the money owed from an individual partner's personal assets.

> **Example:** Phillips, Quen, and Reichman own the PQR Company, a general partnership. PQR is sued for breach of a construction contract, and a judgment is entered against the company for $105,000. When PQR fails to pay the debt, the judgment creditor claims a lien against Phillips's home. Phillips ends up paying the entire $105,000 judgment to protect his home from foreclosure.

Of course, Phillips could demand reimbursement from Quen and Reichman for their share of the judgment, but this personal liability contrasts sharply with the protection enjoyed by a corporate shareholder.

Partnership property. In general, property acquired for the partnership's business, plus anything purchased with partnership funds, is partnership property. Title to partnership property may be held in the partnership's name. Alternatively, it may be held in the name of one or more of the partners, as long as the deed makes reference to the partnership.

Unless otherwise agreed, each partner has a right to use and possess all partnership property for partnership purposes. Partnership property is not subject to claims by creditors of individual partners; it can be reached only by creditors of the partnership.

If property is acquired in the partnership's name, it can be conveyed only in the partnership's name. Any authorized partner can sign the deed. A partner is not a co-owner of the partnership property and can't transfer her interest in the partnership property to someone outside the partnership, except when all of the partners transfer the entire property. Nevertheless, unless otherwise agreed, one partner may assign her interest in the partnership itself to an outsider. That gives the assignee a right to share in the partnership's profits. It does not make the assignee a partner, however, or give her the right to intervene in the management of the business.

When a partner dies, his interest in partnership property vests in the surviving partners. The deceased partner's estate has a right to an accounting and a share of the partnership profits, but it does not have an interest in the partnership property.

Limited Partnerships. A limited partnership, like a general partnership, is an association of two or more persons as co-owners of a business. A limited partnership has one or more general partners, plus one or more **limited partners**. The rights and duties of general partners in a limited partnership are the same as in a general partnership. The limited partners, however, have limited liability and may play a limited role in management.

Like corporate shareholders, limited partners are protected from the business's debts. As a result, limited partnerships are more strictly regulated than general partnerships. Limited partnerships generally require a written agreement. Laws vary from state to state, but in general, a limited partnership must register with the secretary of state. The registration form will ask for the name and address of all general partners and the location where the names and addresses of all limited partners are kept. If a certificate of limited partnership is not filed, or the names and addresses are not available as required, all of the partners may be considered general partners.

Limited Liability Companies (LLCs). Real estate investors often choose the limited liability company (LLC) form of business entity because it combines the advantages of a corporation with the advantages of a partnership.

An LLC is created by drawing up an LLC agreement and filing **articles of organization** with the state. There is great flexibility in structuring the management of a limited liability company. LLC owners (called **members**) can choose virtually any manner of allocating income, losses, or appreciation among themselves. Once the LLC is created, initial and annual reports usually must be filed with the state.

Management. LLCs have the flexibility of a general partnership when it comes to managing the business. Management of the LLC may be placed in the hands of its members, or assigned to one or more managers (who may or may not be LLC members).

In a **member-managed** limited liability company, every member has agency authority; that is, all managing members can bind the LLC with their actions. Normally, all decisions are made by the majority of LLC members. Alternatively, the LLC agreement may create a structure in which certain persons or classes of members have different management powers, duties, and voting rights.

In a **manager-managed** limited liability company, ordinary members do not act as agents of the LLC, only the managers do. Usually, designated managers may be appointed or removed by a majority of the members.

Liability. An attractive aspect of the LLC business form is that all of its members enjoy limited liability like that of corporate shareholders or limited partners. (But members and managers are usually liable for any acts or omissions on behalf of the LLC that constitute gross negligence, intentional misconduct, or a knowing violation of the law.)

Taxation. As noted earlier, a major disadvantage to the corporate form of ownership is the double taxation imposed on many corporations and their stockholders. LLC income, on the other hand, is taxed as the personal income of each member, in the same manner as partnership income.

Trusts. In a trust, one or more **trustees** manage property for the benefit of one or more **beneficiaries**. Title to the property is held by the trustees, who have only the powers expressly granted in the trust instrument (the document that created the trust).

A **real estate investment trust** (REIT) is a trust that is used as a form of business ownership. REITs qualify for tax advantages if they meet certain requirements set by the Internal Revenue Service (IRS). For example, to qualify for these tax advantages, trusts must have at least 100 investors, and at least 75% of their investment assets must be in real estate.

A qualifying REIT avoids double taxation. As long as at least 90% of its income is distributed to the investors annually, the trust pays taxes only on the earnings it retains. Yet the investors, like corporate stockholders, are shielded from liability for the REIT's debts. Shares in REITs are securities, subject to federal regulation.

Joint Ventures. A joint venture is similar to a partnership, except that it is created for a single project or a limited series of business transactions, rather than as an ongoing business of indefinite duration. There are no formal requirements for the creation of a joint venture. For the most part, they are governed by the same rules that apply to general partnerships, so the participants in a joint venture typically have unlimited liability.

The Legal Relationship Between Manager and Client

In the last section we examined the different types of owners/clients who use a property manager's services. Now, let's take a closer look at the manager-client relationship itself and the legal rules that govern it.

Agency Relationship

An agency relationship arises when one person authorizes another to represent him in dealings with third parties. The parties in an agency relationship are the **agent**, the person who's authorized to represent another, and the **principal**, the party who authorizes and controls the actions of the agent. Persons outside the agency relationship who deal with the principal through the agent are called **third parties**. A **subagent** is an agent (or representative) of the agent.

> **Example:** Carol owns an apartment building. She hires ABC Property Management to manage her building. ABC, in turn, hires Sue as a leasing consultant to show apartments to prospective tenants.
>
> ABC Property Management is the agent and the property owner (Carol) is the principal. Sue, the leasing consultant, is ABC's subagent, while prospective tenants are third parties.

Agency Law. An agency relationship has significant legal implications. For a third party, dealing with the agent can be the legal equivalent of dealing with the principal. For instance, when an agent who is authorized to do so signs a lease or makes a promise, it's as if the principal signed the lease or made the promise. And in some states, if the agent does something wrong, the principal may be held liable to third parties for harm resulting from the agent's wrongdoing.

These general rules are part of agency law, a body of law that applies to agency relationships in nearly any context, including the relationship between a lawyer and his client, or between a real estate agent and a property seller. In most cases, it also applies to property managers and their clients. Agency law varies from state to state, and some states have passed laws that specifically control the agency relationship between a property manager and her client. In those states, the real estate agency statute will supersede general agency law.

In states where property managers are regulated by the real estate license law, they may have the duty to disclose their agency status. For example, a manager may be required to disclose to a prospective tenant that he represents the property owner during negotiations, and not the prospective tenant.

Agency Authority. A property manager's authority is usually described in the management agreement, which is the contract between the manager and the property owner (discussed later in this chapter). The principal grants the manager authority to act on his behalf and defines the extent (or scope) of that authority. The property manager may be treated as the property owner's **general agent** in regard to the property; this means he is given relatively broad authority to handle all matters connected with the property, such as marketing, maintenance, and hiring and firing personnel. Or, the management agreement may make the manager a **special agent**, an agent who has only limited authority to act on behalf of the owner, often for only a single function or transaction.

Authorized actions of agent binding on principal. A principal is generally bound by the actions of her agent, as long as those actions fall within the scope of the agent's authority. For example, if a property manager is authorized to enter into maintenance and supply contracts on behalf of the property owner, then a contract signed by the manager has the same effect as a contract signed by the owner.

Liability for unauthorized acts. Under some circumstances, the principal may be held **vicariously liable** for harm to third parties caused by the agent while the agent was acting within the scope of his authority. The agent's actions may have been negligent, or they may have involved deliberate wrongdoing, such as intentional misrepresentation. The rules concerning vicarious liability vary from state to state. Vicarious liability generally applies to employer-employee relationships as well as to agency relationships.

Fiduciary Duties. An agency relationship is a fiduciary relationship. A **fiduciary** is a person who stands in a special position of trust and confidence in relation to someone else. The other party has a legal right to rely on the fiduciary, and the law holds the fiduciary to high standards of conduct.

An agent owes fiduciary duties to the principal from the first moment the agency relationship begins, and the agent must continue to fulfill those duties until the relationship ends. The fiduciary duties required by law vary from state to state, but they generally include all of the following:

- **Care and skill.** The agent must use reasonable care and skill when acting on behalf of the principal.
- **Obedience.** The agent must carry out the principal's instructions.
- **Utmost good faith.** The agent must act with honesty and integrity in regard to the principal.
- **Loyalty.** The agent must put the principal's interests ahead of the interests of third parties, and also ahead of the agent's own interests; the agent must avoid conflicts of interest.
- **Confidentiality.** The agent cannot reveal the principal's confidential information to third parties. (This duty continues even after the end of the agency relationship.)
- **Disclosure of material facts.** The agent must disclose to the principal any information that could influence the principal's judgment in a transaction.
- **Accounting.** The agent must account to the principal for all funds handled on the principal's behalf.

 Secret Profits

The issue of **secret profits** illustrates fiduciary duties in a manager-client relationship. Under agency law, it's a violation of fiduciary duty for a manager to profit from his relationship with the client in any way without disclosing it to the client and obtaining her consent.

For example, suppose a manager accepts a kickback (a fee, a gift, a discount, or any other form of benefit) for purchasing supplies from a particular vendor for use on the client's property. If the manager fails to inform the client of this kickback, it creates a conflict of interest, violating the duty of loyalty. It may also violate the manager's duty to disclose material facts.

A property manager can be held liable to a client for damages that result from failure to fulfill fiduciary duties.

Employment Status

Another legal distinction that affects the manager-client relationship is whether the manager is considered an independent contractor or an employee. An **independent contractor** is hired to perform a particular task and generally uses his own judgment to decide how the task should be completed. An employee, on the other hand, is hired to perform whatever tasks the employer requires and is usually told how to accomplish each task. An **employee** is supervised and controlled much more closely than an independent contractor. In addition, various employment and tax laws apply only to employees and not to independent contractors.

A property manager is almost always an independent contractor in relation to the property owner. In fact, property managers often act as independent contractors for several different owners at the same time. The owner/client contracts with the property manager to perform a specific task: managing the owner's property. Beyond that, however, the property manager usually sets his own hours, decides how and when to perform his duties, and uses his own discretion when deciding how best to complete the contract. Property managers who work as independent contractors are sometimes called "fee managers."

However, sometimes a property manager works for a property owner as a salaried employee. The employer may be an institutional property owner (such as a large company, a college, a hotel, or a hospital), a financial institution, or possibly a large investment syndicate that owns many properties.

Trustees

Another role that a property manager may be called upon to fill is that of a **trustee**. In a trust, the trustee is given legal title to a property, along with the responsibility for holding and managing the property on behalf of the beneficiaries, who receive and retain equitable title to the property.

This arrangement is most common when a property manager works for a financial institution. The financial institution serves as a trustee under a testamentary trust or a living trust, managing property that is held in trust for one or more beneficiaries. The trustee is a fiduciary in relation to the beneficiaries, and must manage the trust property in accordance with the terms of the trust instrument.

Trusts are strictly regulated, and trust agreements are complex financial and legal instruments. A property manager who works in the capacity of trustee must be sure she understands the special nature of her obligations and liabilities.

Working with a New Client

Now that we've examined the legal relationship between the client and the manager, let's turn to the actual working relationship. When a property manager begins working with a new client, she must discover the client's goals for the property and prepare a management plan to fulfill those goals. The manager and her client will enter into a management agreement, which is the contract that will govern their working relationship. The manager will then follow certain procedures to take over the reins from the owner or from a previous manager. Let's take a look at each of these steps in more detail.

Determining the Client's Goals

As we said earlier, a property manager's job is to manage the financial and physical aspects of the client's property in the way that will best achieve the owner's goals. The manager should explore these goals with the client early in the working relationship. The client may have specific financial goals, such as generating a certain amount of monthly income. She may also have nonfinancial goals, such as helping the community. These goals, along with the client's personality, will impact the property manager's approach to managing the property.

Financial Goals. Investors usually expect some form of financial return on their investments, but those expectations vary from client to client. Some investment property owners want immediate high returns, while others prefer a modest income with low risk and little effort. These financial goals have a direct bearing on how the manager goes about her job.

If the client's goal is a quick, high return on her investment, she may authorize only those improvements that are necessary to maintain or increase the property's net income. (This attitude is more likely when the owner has acquired the property incidentally, such as by inheritance.) On the other hand, if the client's focus is more on the long term, she may be more interested in maintaining the property's value than generating a large income stream.

Income tax considerations are often a big part of the client's financial goals. For example, some owners use their investment properties as tax shelters, so annual operating losses are acceptable. While the manager should try to understand the owner's tax goals, she should never give tax advice to the owner. (Income tax considerations are discussed in more detail in Chapter 5.)

Keep in mind that an owner's financial goals often change during her period of ownership.

> **Example:** When Sarah was 40, she purchased a small residential apartment building as an investment. Sarah worked full time and was interested in the investment property primarily as a tax shelter to help offset her earnings. Now, 25 years later, Sarah is considering retirement and the investment property will be an important part of her retirement income. With that in mind, Sarah's goal changes: she is less concerned about a tax shelter, and more concerned that the property generates a steady, reliable cash flow that will meet her monthly living expenses.

Nonfinancial Goals. While an investor's financial goals are typically the primary consideration, a property manager shouldn't overlook the client's nonfinancial motivations. These motivations can vary greatly among clients, and may include:

- **Pride of ownership.** The desire to own and be associated with something that's considered desirable, both by the client and by other people.

- **Nonfinancial self-interest.** The client's own use of the property (he may live, work, or do business there himself).
- **Social benefit.** The desire to provide a good place for others to live, work, or do business; wanting to contribute to the surrounding community by offering public amenities like benches or a fountain; or addressing aesthetic issues and environmental considerations.

Values, Attitudes, and Personality. A client's financial and nonfinancial goals usually reflect his values, attitude, and personality. The property manager who can identify some of these factors will find it easier to tailor a management plan to the client's needs and desires. For example, the property manager should try to determine the client's aversion to risk. A conservative or timid investor will be less inclined to try bold new ideas.

Difficult Clients. A client may have a clearly defined goal, but be unwilling to invest the time or money that is necessary to achieve that goal. Or the manager and client may have conflicting personalities that make working together difficult. And sometimes a client may ask the property manager to do something unethical or even illegal. Working with these types of owners can be very difficult.

It's virtually always better for the property manager to end a relationship with a difficult client as quickly as possible. A difficult client can be a serious drain on the manager's time and resources, and could also damage the manager's professional reputation, particularly if the client wants to engage in unlawful activity, such as discriminating against tenants. Terminating a manager-client relationship will be discussed later in this chapter.

Developing a Management Proposal

After determining the client's goals and values, the property manager prepares a management proposal. A **management proposal** is an analysis of the property's current status (physical, financial, and operational) compared to competing properties in the market, and a list of recommended changes that would help the client meet her ownership goals.

The management proposal is similar to a listing presentation made by a real estate agent to a home seller. The proposal demonstrates to the owner that the manager has the knowledge, skill, and expertise to manage the property in a professional manner. (Once the management proposal is approved by the client, it's known as a management plan. Management plans are covered extensively in Chapter 4.)

Management Agreement

The legal relationship between a property manager and a client begins when they sign a management agreement. As mentioned, a **management agreement** is a contract that establishes and defines the working relationship between the property owner and the property manager.

Most states require the management agreement to be in writing and signed by both parties. Additional rules may also apply. For example, some states require property management agreements for more than 90 days to have a definite termination date. Property managers who are subject to a state's real estate license law may have to meet other requirements as well, such as agency disclosure rules.

Regardless of whether it's required or not, it's always a good idea to put a management agreement in writing. Professional associations and multiple listing services often provide preprinted management agreement forms for general use (see the example in Figure 3.1); special agreements or unusual provisions should be drafted by the parties' attorneys.

The management agreement should set forth all of the terms and conditions of the manager-client relationship, including the:

- identity of the parties and the property,
- duration of the agreement,
- grant of authority,
- manager's responsibilities,
- property owner's obligations, and
- manager's compensation.

Identity of Parties and Property. The management agreement must identify the owner and the manager, and it must be signed by both parties. If the property has more than one owner, the agreement must be signed by all of them, unless one of the owners has the legal authority to sign on behalf of the other owners. If the property is owned by an entity, such as a corporation, the agreement must be signed by an authorized representative of that entity (for example, a corporate officer authorized to sign by a resolution of the board of directors). If the property manager is acting on behalf of a management firm, she usually signs the agreement as a representative of the management firm.

> **Example:** Three brothers, Albert, Bryan, and Carl, own two small office buildings. They would like to hire XYZ Property Management to manage the buildings. Mark, a representative of XYZ Property Management, meets with Albert (who lives nearby) to propose a management plan and to negotiate the management agreement. Albert confers with his brothers and all three agree to hire Mark and XYZ Property Management.
>
> However, Albert doesn't have the authority to sign on Bryan and Carl's behalf, so Mark will need to get the signatures of all three co-owners on the management agreement before it will be valid.

The agreement must also adequately identify the property to be managed. If the property is a rental home or small retail building, a street address may be sufficient. That may not be enough for a larger property; the agreement must leave no doubt as to the location and boundaries of the property and buildings that are to be managed. (A legal description is generally not required for a management contract to be valid, although it's always a good idea to include one.)

Duration of Agreement. The duration of the agreement generally depends on the type of property as well as the client's goals. The client who wants a property manager to oversee complex physical and operational renovations to the property should be willing to commit to a longer contract. And of course, a commercial property manager will not want to invest a lot of effort into setting up management systems if the owner has only committed to a six-month agreement.

Figure 3.1 Property management agreement

CALIFORNIA ASSOCIATION OF REALTORS®

PROPERTY MANAGEMENT AGREEMENT
(C.A.R. Form PMA, Revised 4/11)

_____ ("Owner"), and
_____ ("Broker"), agree as follows:

1. **APPOINTMENT OF BROKER:** Owner hereby appoints and grants Broker the exclusive right to rent, lease, operate and manage the property(ies) known as _____,
_____ and any additional property that may later be added to this Agreement ("Property"), upon the terms below, for the period beginning (date) _____ and ending (date) _____, at 11:59 PM.
(If checked:) ☐ Either party may terminate this Property Management Agreement ("Agreement") on at least 30 days written notice _____ months after the original commencement date of this Agreement. After the exclusive term expires, this Agreement shall continue as a non-exclusive agreement that either party may terminate by giving at least 30 days written notice to the other.

2. **BROKER ACCEPTANCE:** Broker accepts the appointment and grant, and agrees to:
   A. Use due diligence in the performance of this Agreement.
   B. Furnish the services of its firm for the rental, leasing, operation and management of the Property.

3. **AUTHORITY AND POWERS:** Owner grants Broker the authority and power, at Owner's expense, to:
   A. **ADVERTISING:** Display FOR RENT/LEASE and similar signs on the Property and advertise the availability of the Property, or any part thereof, for rental or lease.
   B. **RENTAL; LEASING:** Initiate, sign, renew, modify or cancel rental agreements and leases for the Property, or any part thereof; collect and give receipts for rents, other fees, charges and security deposits. Any lease or rental agreement executed by Broker for Owner shall not exceed _____ year(s) or ☐ shall be month-to-month. Unless Owner authorizes a lower amount, rent shall be: ☐ at market rate; OR ☐ a minimum of $ _____ per _____; OR ☐ see attachment.
   C. **TENANCY TERMINATION:** Sign and serve in Owner's name notices that are required or appropriate; commence and prosecute actions to evict tenants; recover possession of the Property in Owner's name; recover rents and other sums due; and, when expedient, settle, compromise and release claims, actions and suits and/or reinstate tenancies.
   D. **REPAIR; MAINTENANCE:** Make, cause to be made, and/or supervise repairs, improvements, alterations and decorations to the Property; purchase, and pay bills for, services and supplies. Broker shall obtain prior approval of Owner for all expenditures over $ _____ for any one item. Prior approval shall not be required for monthly or recurring operating charges or, if in Broker's opinion, emergency expenditures over the maximum are needed to protect the Property or other property(ies) from damage, prevent injury to persons, avoid suspension of necessary services, avoid penalties or fines, or suspension of services to tenants required by a lease or rental agreement or by law, including, but not limited to, maintaining the Property in a condition fit for human habitation as required by Civil Code §§ 1941 and 1941.1 and Health and Safety Code §§ 17920.3 and 17920.10.
   E. **REPORTS, NOTICES AND SIGNS:** Comply with federal, state or local law requiring delivery of reports or notices and/or posting of signs or notices.
   F. **CONTRACTS; SERVICES:** Contract, hire, supervise and/or discharge firms and persons, including utilities, required for the operation and maintenance of the Property. Broker may perform any of Broker's duties through attorneys, agents, employees, or independent contractors and, except for persons working in Broker's firm, shall not be responsible for their acts, omissions, defaults, negligence and/or costs of same.
   G. **EXPENSE PAYMENTS:** Pay expenses and costs for the Property from Owner's funds held by Broker, unless otherwise directed by Owner. Expenses and costs may include, but are not limited to, property management compensation, fees and charges, expenses for goods and services, property taxes and other taxes, Owner's Association dues, assessments, loan payments and insurance premiums.
   H. **SECURITY DEPOSITS:** Receive security deposits from tenants, which deposits shall be ☐ given to Owner, or ☐ placed in Broker's trust account and, if held in Broker's trust account, pay from Owner's funds all interest on tenants' security deposits if required by local law or ordinance. Owner shall be responsible to tenants for return of security deposits and all interest due on security deposits held by Owner.
   I. **TRUST FUNDS:** Deposit all receipts collected for Owner, less any sums properly deducted or disbursed, in a financial institution whose deposits are insured by an agency of the United States government. The funds shall be held in a trust account separate from Broker's personal accounts. Broker shall not be liable in event of bankruptcy or failure of a financial institution.
   J. **RESERVES:** Maintain a reserve in Broker's trust account of $ _____.
   K. **DISBURSEMENTS:** Disburse Owner's funds held in Broker's trust account in the following order:
       (1) Compensation due Broker under paragraph 8.
       (2) All other operating expenses, costs and disbursements payable from Owner's funds held by Broker.
       (3) Reserves and security deposits held by Broker.
       (4) Balance to Owner.
   L. **OWNER DISTRIBUTION:** Remit funds, if any are available, monthly (or ☐ _____), to Owner.
   M. **OWNER STATEMENTS:** Render monthly (or ☐ _____), statements of receipts, expenses and charges for each Property.
   N. **BROKER FUNDS:** Broker shall not advance Broker's own funds in connection with the Property or this Agreement.
   O. **KEYSAFE/LOCKBOX:** ☐ (If checked) Owner authorizes the use of a keysafe/lockbox to allow entry into the Property and agrees to sign a keysafe/ lockbox addendum (C.A.R. Form KLA).

4. **OWNER RESPONSIBILITIES:** Owner shall:
   A. Provide all documentation, records and disclosures as required by law or required by Broker to manage and operate the Property, and immediately notify Broker if Owner becomes aware of any change in such documentation, records or disclosures, or any matter affecting the habitability of the Property.
   B. Indemnify, defend and hold harmless Broker, and all persons in Broker's firm, regardless of responsibility, from all costs, expenses, suits, liabilities, damages, attorney fees and claims of every type, including but not limited to those arising out of injury or death of any person, or damage to any real or personal property of any person, including Owner, for: **(i)** any repairs performed by Owner or by others

Owner's Initials (_____)(_____)   Broker's Initials (_____)(_____)

PMA REVISED 4/11 (PAGE 1 OF 3)

Reviewed by _____ Date _____   EQUAL HOUSING OPPORTUNITY

PROPERTY MANAGEMENT AGREEMENT (PMA PAGE 1 OF 3)

Owner Name: _____ Date: _____

hired directly by Owner; or **(ii)** those relating to the management, leasing, rental, security deposits, or operation of the Property by Broker, or any person in Broker's firm, or the performance or exercise of any of the duties, powers or authorities granted to Broker.

C. Maintain the Property in a condition fit for human habitation as required by Civil Code §§ 1941 and 1941.1 and Health and Safety Code §§ 17920.3 and 17920.10 and other applicable law.

D. Pay all interest on tenants' security deposits if required by local law or ordinance.

E. Carry and pay for: **(i)** public and premises liability insurance in an amount of no less than $1,000,000; and **(ii)** property damage and worker's compensation insurance adequate to protect the interests of Owner and Broker. Broker shall be, and Owner authorizes Broker to be, named as an additional insured party on Owner's policies.

F. Pay any late charges, penalties and/or interest imposed by lenders or other parties for failure to make payment to those parties, if the failure is due to insufficient funds in Broker's trust account available for such payment.

G. Immediately replace any funds required if there are insufficient funds in Broker's trust account to cover Owner's responsibilities.

5. **OWNER REPRESENTATIONS:** Owner represents that, unless otherwise specified in writing, Owner is unaware of: **(i)** any recorded Notice of Default affecting the Property; **(ii)** any delinquent amounts due under any loan secured by, or other obligation affecting, the Property; **(iii)** any bankruptcy, insolvency or similar proceeding affecting the Property; **(iv)** any litigation, arbitration, administrative action, government investigation, or other pending or threatened action that does or may affect the Property or Owners ability to transfer it; and **(v)** any current, pending or proposed special assessments affecting the Property. Owner shall promptly notify Broker in writing if Owner becomes aware of any of these items during the term of this Agreement.

6. **TAX WITHHOLDING:** If owner is not a California Resident or a corporation or LLC qualified to conduct business in California, Owner authorizes Broker to withhold and transmit to California Franchise Tax Board ("FTB") 7% of the GROSS payments to Owner that exceed $1,000 received by Broker, unless Owner completes and transmits to Broker FTB form 589, nonresident reduced withholding request, FTB form 588, nonresident withholding waiver, or FTB form 590, withholding exemption certificate.

7. **DISCLOSURE:**

A. **LEAD-BASED PAINT**
   (1) ☐ The Property was constructed on or after January 1, 1978.
   OR **(2)** ☐ The Property was constructed prior to 1978.
       (i) Owner has no knowledge of lead-based paint or lead-based paint hazards in the housing except:_____
       _____.
       (ii) Owner has no reports or records pertaining to lead-based paint or lead-based paint hazards in the housing, except the following, which Owner shall provide to Broker:_____.

B. **POOL/SPA DRAIN**
   Any pool or spa on the property does (or, ☐ does not) have an approved anti-entrapment drain cover, device or system.

8. **COMPENSATION:**

A. Owner agrees to pay Broker fees in the amounts indicated below for:
   (1) Management: _____.
   (2) Renting or Leasing: _____.
   (3) Evictions: _____.
   (4) Preparing Property for rental or lease: _____.
   (5) Managing Property during extended periods of vacancy: _____.
   (6) An overhead and service fee added to the cost of all work performed by, or at the direction of, Broker: _____.
   (7) Other: _____.

B. This Agreement does not include providing on-site management services, property sales, refinancing, preparing Property for sale or refinancing, modernization, fire or major damage restoration, rehabilitation, obtaining income tax, accounting or legal advice, representation before public agencies, advising on proposed new construction, debt collection, counseling, attending Owner's Association meetings or _____
   _____
   If Owner requests Broker to perform services not included in this Agreement, a fee shall be agreed upon before these services are performed.

C. Broker may divide compensation, fees and charges due under this Agreement in any manner acceptable to Broker.

D. Owner further agrees that:
   (1) Broker may receive and keep fees and charges from tenants for: **(i)** requesting an assignment of lease or sublease of the Property; **(ii)** processing credit applications; **(iii)** any returned checks and/or (☐ if checked) late payments; and **(iv)** any other services that are not in conflict with this Agreement.
   (2) Broker may perform any of Broker's duties, and obtain necessary products and services, through affiliated companies or organizations in which Broker may own an interest. Broker may receive fees, commissions and/or profits from these affiliated companies or organizations. Broker has an ownership interest in the following affiliated companies or organizations:
   _____
   Broker shall disclose to Owner any other such relationships as they occur. Broker shall not receive any fees, commissions or profits from unaffiliated companies or organizations in the performance of this Agreement, without prior disclosure to Owner.
   (3) Other: _____.

9. **AGENCY RELATIONSHIPS:** Broker may act, and Owner hereby consents to Broker acting, as dual agent for Owner and tenant(s) in any resulting transaction. If the Property includes residential property with one-to-four dwelling units and this Agreement permits a tenancy in excess of one year, Owner acknowledges receipt of the "Disclosure Regarding Agency Relationships" (C.A.R. Form AD). Owner understands that Broker may have or obtain property management agreements on other property, and that potential tenants may consider, make offers on, or lease through Broker, property the same as or similar to Owner's Property. Owner consents to Broker's representation of other owners' properties before, during and after the expiration of this Agreement.

Owner's Initials (_____)(_____)   Broker's Initials (_____)(_____)

PMA REVISED 4/11 (PAGE 2 OF 3)

Reviewed by _____ Date _____

EQUAL HOUSING OPPORTUNITY

PROPERTY MANAGEMENT AGREEMENT (PMA PAGE 2 OF 3)

Owner Name: _____   Date: _____

10. NOTICES: Any written notice to Owner or Broker required under this Agreement shall be served by sending such notice by first class mail or other agreed-to delivery method to that party at the address below, or at any different address the parties may later designate for this purpose. Notice shall be deemed received three (3) calendar days after deposit into the United States mail OR ☐ _____.

11. DISPUTE RESOLUTION

A. MEDIATION: Owner and Broker agree to mediate any dispute or claim arising between them out of this Agreement, or any resulting transaction before resorting to arbitration or court action, subject to paragraph 11B(2) below. Paragraph 11B(2) below applies whether or not the arbitration provision is initialed. Mediation fees, if any, shall be divided equally among the parties involved. If, for any dispute or claim to which this paragraph applies, any party commences an action based on a dispute or claim to which this paragraph applies, without first attempting to resolve the matter through mediation, or refuses to mediate after a request has been made, then that party shall not be entitled to recover attorney fees, even if they would otherwise be available to that party in any such action. THIS MEDIATION PROVISION APPLIES WHETHER OR NOT THE ARBITRATION PROVISION IS INITIALED.

B. ARBITRATION OF DISPUTES: (1) Owner and Broker agree that any dispute or claim in law or equity arising between them regarding the obligation to pay compensation under this agreement, which is not settled through mediation, shall be decided by neutral, binding arbitration, including and subject to paragraph 11B(2) below. The arbitrator shall be a retired judge or justice, or an attorney with at least 5 years of residential real estate law experience, unless the parties mutually agree to a different arbitrator, who shall render an award in accordance with substantive California Law. The parties shall have the right to discovery in accordance with Code of Civil Procedure § 1283.05. In all other respects, the arbitration shall be conducted in accordance with Title 9 of Part III of the California Code of Civil Procedure. Judgment upon the award of the arbitrator(s) may be entered in any court having jurisdiction. Interpretation of this agreement to arbitrate shall be governed by the Federal Arbitration Act.

(2) EXCLUSIONS FROM MEDIATION AND ARBITRATION: The following matters are excluded from mediation and arbitration hereunder: **(i)** a judicial or non-judicial foreclosure or other action or proceeding to enforce a deed of trust, mortgage, or installment land sale contract as defined in Civil Code § 2985; **(ii)** an unlawful detainer action; **(iii)** the filing or enforcement of a mechanic's lien; and **(iv)** any matter that is within the jurisdiction of a probate, small claims, or bankruptcy court. The filing of a court action to enable the recording of a notice of pending action, for order of attachment, receivership, injunction, or other provisional remedies, shall not constitute a waiver of the mediation and arbitration provisions.

"**NOTICE: BY INITIALING IN THE SPACE BELOW YOU ARE AGREEING TO HAVE ANY DISPUTE ARISING OUT OF THE MATTERS INCLUDED IN THE 'ARBITRATION OF DISPUTES' PROVISION DECIDED BY NEUTRAL ARBITRATION AS PROVIDED BY CALIFORNIA LAW AND YOU ARE GIVING UP ANY RIGHTS YOU MIGHT POSSESS TO HAVE THE DISPUTE LITIGATED IN A COURT OR JURY TRIAL. BY INITIALING IN THE SPACE BELOW YOU ARE GIVING UP YOUR JUDICIAL RIGHTS TO DISCOVERY AND APPEAL, UNLESS THOSE RIGHTS ARE SPECIFICALLY INCLUDED IN THE 'ARBITRATION OF DISPUTES' PROVISION. IF YOU REFUSE TO SUBMIT TO ARBITRATION AFTER AGREEING TO THIS PROVISION, YOU MAY BE COMPELLED TO ARBITRATE UNDER THE AUTHORITY OF THE CALIFORNIA CODE OF CIVIL PROCEDURE. YOUR AGREEMENT TO THIS ARBITRATION PROVISION IS VOLUNTARY.**"

"**WE HAVE READ AND UNDERSTAND THE FOREGOING AND AGREE TO SUBMIT DISPUTES ARISING OUT OF THE MATTERS INCLUDED IN THE 'ARBITRATION OF DISPUTES' PROVISION TO NEUTRAL ARBITRATION.**"

Owner's Initials _____ / _____	Broker's Initials _____ / _____

12. EQUAL HOUSING OPPORTUNITY: The Property is offered in compliance with federal, state and local anti-discrimination laws.

13. ATTORNEY FEES: In any action, proceeding or arbitration between Owner and Broker regarding the obligation to pay compensation under this Agreement, the prevailing Owner or Broker shall be entitled to reasonable attorney fees and costs from the non-prevailing Owner or Broker, except as provided in paragraph 11A.

14. ADDITIONAL TERMS: ☐ Keysafe/Lockbox Addendum (C.A.R. Form KLA); ☐ Lead-Based Paint and Lead-Based Paint Hazards Disclosure (C.A.R. Form FLD) _____

15. TIME OF ESSENCE; ENTIRE CONTRACT; CHANGES: Time is of the essence. All understandings between the parties are incorporated in this Agreement. Its terms are intended by the parties as a final, complete and exclusive expression of their Agreement with respect to its subject matter, and may not be contradicted by evidence of any prior agreement or contemporaneous oral agreement. If any provision of this Agreement is held to be ineffective or invalid, the remaining provisions will nevertheless be given full force and effect. Neither this Agreement nor any provision in it may be extended, amended, modified, altered or changed except in writing. This Agreement and any supplement, addendum or modification, including any copy, may be signed in two or more counterparts, all of which shall constitute one and the same writing.

Owner warrants that Owner is the owner of the Property or has the authority to execute this contract. Owner acknowledges Owner has read, understands, accepts and has received a copy of the Agreement.

Owner _____   Date _____
Owner _____
        Print Name   Social Security/Tax ID # (for tax reporting purposes)
Address _____ City _____ State _____ Zip _____
Telephone _____ Fax _____ E-mail _____

Owner _____   Date _____
Owner _____
        Print Name   Social Security/Tax ID # (for tax reporting purposes)
Address _____ City _____ State _____ Zip _____
Telephone _____ Fax _____ E-mail _____

Real Estate Broker (Firm) _____   Date _____
By (Agent) _____   DRE Lic. #: _____
Address _____ City _____ State _____ Zip _____
Telephone _____ Fax _____ E-mail _____

THIS FORM HAS BEEN APPROVED BY THE CALIFORNIA ASSOCIATION OF REALTORS® (C.A.R.). NO REPRESENTATION IS MADE AS TO THE LEGAL VALIDITY OR ADEQUACY OF ANY PROVISION IN ANY SPECIFIC TRANSACTION. A REAL ESTATE BROKER IS THE PERSON QUALIFIED TO ADVISE ON REAL ESTATE TRANSACTIONS. IF YOU DESIRE LEGAL OR TAX ADVICE, CONSULT AN APPROPRIATE PROFESSIONAL.

This form is available for use by the entire real estate industry. It is not intended to identify the user as a REALTOR®. REALTOR® is a registered collective membership mark which may be used only by members of the NATIONAL ASSOCIATION OF REALTORS® who subscribe to its Code of Ethics.

Published and Distributed by:
REAL ESTATE BUSINESS SERVICES, INC.
a subsidiary of the California Association of REALTORS®
525 South Virgil Avenue, Los Angeles, California 90020

Reviewed by _____ Date _____

PMA REVISED 4/11 (PAGE 3 OF 3)

PROPERTY MANAGEMENT AGREEMENT (PMA PAGE 3 OF 3)

Many agreements set a minimum term (such as one year) and provide for the contract to continue indefinitely until either party gives the other notice of termination (usually 30 days' notice). Another common arrangement is an initial one-year term with automatic renewals for each subsequent year unless notice of termination is given by one of the parties at least 30 days before the expiration of the current term.

Some states require management contracts to have a definite termination date. If no date is required and the contract is silent on the issue, the contract will terminate after a reasonable amount of time (such as 180 days).

Most agreements have provisions that set out consequences for terminating the contract before expiration of the term or without proper notice. Terminating the management contract is discussed at the end of this chapter.

Grant of Authority. The property manager needs an express grant of authority from the owner to act on her behalf. As we mentioned earlier, the manager may be authorized as a general agent (empowered to make decisions regarding the property without consulting the owner) or as a special agent (empowered only to show apartments, provide maintenance services, and supervise leasing activities).

Designated decision-makers. However broad the manager's day-to-day authority may be, there will always be decisions that must be made by the owner. For instance, expensive repairs usually must be approved by the property owner.

If the property has more than one owner, the management agreement should state which co-owner the manager must consult. In the absence of such a provision, the manager may be required to obtain the consent of all co-owners.

Manager's Responsibilities. Along with the manager's authority, the manager's responsibilities should be clearly stated in the management agreement. Of course, many of these responsibilities are determined by the type of property being managed, as well as the client's goals. As we discuss some of the more common duties, keep in mind that a particular management agreement may include different or additional provisions.

Financial responsibilities. A property manager's financial responsibilities typically include collecting income, paying expenses, managing the property's bank accounts, and submitting net income to the property owner. (We'll briefly outline financial responsibility here; the topic is covered more thoroughly in Chapter 5.)

- **Collecting income.** The manager is in charge of collecting the property's income. Income sources include rent, late payment fees, and miscellaneous income from other sources, such as vending and laundry machines.
- **Managing accounts.** The property manager will usually be in charge of the property's operating account, trust accounts for security deposits and similar funds, and the reserve fund for unexpected repairs or planned future improvements. Managing the accounts includes not only supervising deposits and withdrawals, but also includes reconciling the accounts on a regular basis.
- **Paying expenses.** The manager pays the property's regular operating expenses, such as maintenance and utilities, and he may also be responsible for paying other types of expenses, such as property taxes and debt service.

- **Sending net income to owners.** The management agreement should set a regular schedule for sending the property's cash flow to the owner. If there's more than one owner, the agreement should stipulate the percentage of income each owner will receive.

The management agreement should address other financial issues as well, including:

- **Operating deficits.** Sometimes a property's expenses will exceed its income. The agreement should specify how such a deficit should be handled. One common practice is for the owner to keep a certain amount on deposit in the operating account to cover periodic deficits.
- **Audits.** The agreement usually gives the property owner the right to audit the property's accounts at any time. Alternatively, the agreement may set a schedule of periodic audits, for example, on a quarterly or yearly basis.

General management duties. The agreement will also describe the property manager's general management duties. These day-to-day activities often include:

- **Managing staff and payroll.** The property manager will usually have the task of hiring, supervising, and firing staff. He may also manage employee benefits and handle payroll, which includes paying premiums for workers compensation insurance and managing payroll taxes. (Staffing is discussed in Chapter 9.)
- **Advertising.** Advertising plans and objectives are usually detailed in the management plan. The management agreement should state the property manager's responsibility for implementing these plans, such as placing newspaper advertisements, maintaining the property website, and ordering signs. (Marketing is discussed in Chapter 6.)
- **Selecting tenants.** The property manager is usually responsible for leasing the space, including setting rental rates, accepting applications, screening tenants, and signing leases. For commercial properties and larger residential properties, however, these tasks may be delegated to a leasing agent. (Leasing is discussed in more detail in Chapter 7.)
- **Entering into contracts.** Many property managers contract with outside companies to handle certain daily activities, such as maintenance and landscaping. The manager may also need to contract with suppliers for office products, cleaning products, and so on. (See Chapter 9.) The management agreement should detail the manager's responsibilities in these areas.
- **Arranging property repairs and alterations.** Most income property will eventually need some kind of repair, equipment replacement, or alteration. These may be required in order to address safety hazards or insurance or legal requirements, or to fulfill lease agreements. A well-drafted management agreement will specify the maximum amount the manager can spend for certain types of expenses without prior approval.
- **Enforcing lease terms.** The property manager is usually responsible for enforcing lease terms and evicting tenants when necessary. (Handling problem tenants is discussed in Chapter 8.)

Reporting requirements. The management agreement should also specify how often and in what form the manager must provide reports of the property's financial performance. (The different types of financial reports are discussed in Chapter 5.)

Property Owner's Obligations. To help avoid misunderstandings between the parties, the management agreement should spell out the property owner's obligations during the management period. At minimum, the owner must agree to provide the manager with any information, records, and documents the manager needs to effectively manage the property. In addition, the owner's obligations may include:

- **Insuring the property.** Traditionally, the property owner has been responsible for insuring the property. Now, some property managers negotiate and obtain loss prevention insurance for the properties they manage. In either case, the management agreement should specify the types of insurance and coverage required. It should require that the manager be named as an additional insured party on all policies; otherwise, the insurance company may refuse to deal directly with the manager in the event of a claim. (Insurance is discussed in Chapter 15.)
- **Ensuring compliance.** The owner must keep the property in compliance with landlord-tenant laws and other legal requirements, such as state and federal disability laws, or health and safety codes. The management agreement should indemnify the manager against liability for noncompliance. However, the manager is usually responsible for notifying the owner of potential noncompliance, and the agreement should state this as well. (Complying with federal, state, and local laws is discussed in Chapter 14.)
- **Providing funds for shortfalls.** As we mentioned earlier, the agreement should address potential operating deficits. Whether or not a fund is established for this purpose, the agreement is likely to require the owner to provide adequate funds to cover any shortfalls.
- **Providing funds for capital expenditures.** As with regular operating expenses, an owner must make funds available to cover capital expenditures when needed. If the manager is not authorized to set aside a portion of the net operating income for reserves, then the agreement should include a provision obligating the owner to either maintain a reserve fund or provide funds when needed. (Reserves are discussed in Chapter 5.)

Manager's Compensation. The management agreement should specify the manager's compensation, including how that compensation will be calculated and when and how it will be paid. Compensation may be a flat fee, a percentage of the property's gross income, a commission on new rentals, fees for special services, or a combination of these types. Compensation is completely negotiable between the owner and manager, and will depend to some degree on the type of property to be managed and the type of services the property manager offers.

A flat (or fixed) fee may be based on square footage or on the number of units or tenants. A flat fee compensation arrangement is more common for the managers of some kinds of institutional property, homeowners associations, and condominium associations.

Alternatively, the manager's compensation may be a percentage of the property's gross income. This method provides an incentive for the manager to increase the property's income. The specific percentage is negotiable between the parties, and will depend in part on the type of property, the extent of services provided, the number of units, and the property's income. Often, the agreement provides for a minimum monthly guaranteed fee regardless of the property's income.

Some agreements allow the manager to collect a bonus for each new lease or lease renewal, or when specified leasing goals are met. However, this could create an incentive for the manager to encourage tenant turnover. The owner and manager should exercise special care when negotiating a leasing bonus provision to ensure that it is fair and that it promotes a healthy, stable income with minimal turnover.

Finally, the management agreement should address any separate fees the manager may charge for special services that aren't part of the manager's regular responsibilities, such as overseeing remodeling projects or tenant alterations. While these fees may be individually negotiated, managers often simply use a schedule of fees for extra services. Some managers use special service fees to discourage clients from unnecessarily demanding too much of their time.

Handover Procedures

After the management agreement has been signed, the property manager begins the task of taking over management of the property from the owner or a previous property manager. This process is sometimes called the **handover** or takeover.

When taking over management of a property, the manager should obtain the following:

- **Owner information.** Name, home address, business address, telephone umber(s), and email address; social security number or tax ID number; and how the owner holds title.
- **Contact information.** Names, phone numbers, and email addresses for the owner's accountant, lawyer, on-site managers, service contractors, suppliers, vendors, mortgage company, insurance agent, architect and/or construction firm (for newly built property), and any other relevant service providers.
- **Property information.** Building plans and specifications; unit floor plans; systems maintenance logs and contracts; an inventory list for any personal property on the premises; copies of building keys; contracts for work in progress, if any; contracts and/or records for on-site vending machines; and the previous year's operating statement.
- **Accounts payable ledger.** Ledger, along with bills and account numbers, for mortgage loan(s), utilities, property taxes, insurance policies, janitorial and maintenance services, and any other routine recurring charges to the property.
- **Leasing information and documents.** Copies of all current leases; listing of all rental units; rent schedules; rent rolls and a list of delinquent accounts; names and payment histories of current tenants; records for any new leasing or evictions currently in progress; and any other available tenant information.

- **Employment records.** Records on any property employees; employment taxes; and payroll records.
- **Banking account statements and funds.** Bank statements for all operating accounts, trust accounts, and reserve accounts associated with the property.

With this information in hand, the new manager is ready to set up her own recordkeeping and management system. This can be a complicated process, and communication with the owner during this time is key to a smooth transition. As we look at some of the steps involved in a typical handover, keep in mind that different types of property may require a different amount of time to be spent on each step. Basic handover procedures include:

- **Setting up client records.** An accurate, reliable recordkeeping system is the first and most important tool for a property manager. Without good records, a manager cannot fulfill his fiduciary duties to the client. Client records are discussed in more detail in the next section.
- **Setting up accounts.** The property should have its own bank account for daily operations, such as collecting rent and paying expenses. Depending on state law, it may also be practical (and legally required) to establish additional accounts, such as trust accounts. (Trust accounts are covered in more detail in Chapter 5.)
- **Establishing a working capital fund.** At the time of the handover, the manager should have working capital equal to one month's expenses, including employee wages and debt service (assuming the manager is responsible for paying those expenses). These funds may be provided by the owner or transferred from the previous property manager.
- **Transferring security deposits.** All security deposits being held by the owner or previous manager must be accounted for and transferred to the new manager. In some states, the law requires the landlord to keep residential security deposits in a separate trust account and notify tenants of the name and address of the bank in which their deposits are held.
- **Notifying parties.** All tenants, account holders, service contractors, and vendors should be notified that a new property manager has taken over management of the property. The notice should state that all related correspondence, bills, payments, and statements are to be sent to the new property manager, and should also provide relevant contact information.
- **Inspecting the property.** As soon as possible after the handover, the new manager should inspect the property thoroughly and prepare an inspection report for the owner. The manager should document all necessary repairs (to both vacant and occupied units), which should be taken care of promptly.

Client Records

After the handover, it's imperative that the manager establish and maintain a secure system for recording and storing all relevant information about the property. As you will recall, one of the fiduciary duties that an agent owes to his principal is that of accounting. A good system of recordkeeping ensures that the manager is able to fulfill this duty.

The client's records may be kept electronically or in paper format. The decision between the two is typically based on the style, frequency, and detail of the reports requested by the client, as well as the manager's existing business model. Electronic records must be backed up on a regular basis to a safe, off-site location. Key documents should be kept in a fireproof safe or safe deposit box.

Organization. For each property under the manager's control, he should keep folders (electronic or hard copy) that contain the following information:

- a general folder for the management contract, deed or title information, and mortgage documents;
- a folder for the management plan and underlying research;
- one or more folders for copies of correspondence with the owner and with tenants or customers;
- a folder for leases and tenant information;
- one or more financial folders for checks, receipts, disbursement records, bank statements, budgets, and monthly and annual financial reports;
- an insurance folder for policies, claims, and related correspondence;
- an employment folder for employee records, and payroll and withholding information;
- a maintenance folder for work orders, work logs, and purchase orders; and
- a service contract folder for contracts and bids submitted by contractors.

Tickler System. A tickler system should be a part of every manager's recordkeeping system. This is a system of electronic reminders that alerts the manager when bills are coming due, such as property tax or insurance payments. She should also receive alerts when leases, insurance policies, and service contracts are about to expire.

Communicating with the Client

A good property manager will keep her client informed of the property's performance on a regular basis. The management agreement should specify exactly which reports are required, and when and how they will be submitted to the owner. Although state licensing laws may impose minimum reporting requirements on the property manager, the frequency and detail of the reports is generally decided by the manager and the client.

The type and frequency of reports often depends on how involved the client wants to be in the management of the property. An owner with extensive property holdings may not want to be bothered with detailed, time-consuming reports. On the other hand, a retired person with only one income-producing property may wish to receive much more information about his investment.

It is the property manager's job to organize and summarize the information from his records so that the client can understand it. Straightforward, jargon-free language is usually best.

Reports

A management agreement usually requires the manager to submit a written financial report on a monthly basis. The monthly report provides information about the property's finances for the previous month, such as the rent roll (rent collections), receipts and disbursements, net operating income, and cash flow. The monthly report may also summarize the manager's leasing and marketing efforts, as well as any maintenance or tenant problems.

The management agreement may require financial reports on a quarterly and yearly basis. The manager is also usually expected to provide the client with an annual profit and loss statement and an annual operating budget. (Financial reports are discussed in more detail in Chapter 5.)

Methods of Reporting. The management agreement should stipulate how the client prefers to receive the monthly, quarterly, and annual reports. Written reports are sometimes required by state law, and almost always required by the management agreement. Formal reports may be sent by mail, by fax, or delivered in person. Alternatively, the client may prefer to receive reports in electronic format (by email, for example).

Regardless of the method used, property managers should keep copies of all reports on file. State law may require the reports to be kept for a certain period of time (such as three years), but managers may want to keep them for longer periods.

Some managers of larger properties use property management software that gives the owners around-the-clock access to financial data and other reports. (This data should be encrypted for the owner's safety.) The property owner simply logs on to a website (using a user ID and password), and is able to see up-to-date financial and leasing information on his property. Of course, these type of client "portals" should not take the place of the more formal monthly written reports. They simply provide another way for the property manager to communicate with her client.

Keeping in Touch

Managers should do more than simply send financial reports to their clients. A telephone call, an email, or a personal visit to explain a particular proposal or problem or just to touch base is often advisable. Again, the level of contact will be determined largely by the type of client and property being managed.

Some property managers use newsletters (printed or electronic) to keep their clients informed of certain issues, such as recent changes to the building code or the landlord-tenant law. Others use websites and blogs to relay such information. But none of these should replace one-on-one communication with the client.

> **Example:** Ed manages several apartment complexes. He sends each of his clients a monthly email newsletter discussing any upcoming legal changes or other issues that may affect the community. In January, Ed's newsletter describes a new law, effective in June, that will require smoke detectors in certain types of rental units. After inspecting each property, Ed follows up this announcement with a report to each individual client. Each report lists the number of units affected by the law, the number of smoke detectors that need to be installed, and the cost to bring each unit into compliance.

It's a good idea to arrange a formal, in-person meeting if a monthly report is especially unusual or complicated. This may be the case when a property's income was markedly less than expected, or if operating expenses exceeded the budgeted amount. An in-person meeting allows the manager to address openly and honestly any questions the client may have—both about that particular financial report and any other issues the client may wish to discuss.

Consultation and Decision-Making

If non-routine decision-making is required, the manager should get the client's input. A good manager is able to gauge how much involvement the client wants, and is careful not to request her input too often. On the other hand, if there is real doubt about what the best course of action is and what the client would choose to do, the manager should definitely seek the client's opinion. When in doubt—ask! When a property has more than one owner, the manager should consult with the person who has decision-making authority.

If an emergency arises that calls for quick action, the manager should use his own best judgment to get the situation under control, and then set up a meeting with the client. At that time, the manager should inform the client of the incident and get input concerning follow up procedures.

Terminating a Manager-Client Relationship

When a property management relationship terminates—because the agreement has expired or because one of the parties wanted to end the relationship—the property's keys, operating funds, records, and security deposits must be turned over to the owner or transferred to a new property manager.

When a property management relationship for a larger property ends, the parties may execute a **termination agreement** (usually on the advice of their attorneys) that spells out the status of all major management duties and expenditures, and designates who is responsible for payment or reimbursement of any expenses.

Early Termination

As we discussed earlier, a management agreement creates an agency relationship between the property owner and the property manager. Because agency requires the consent of both parties, either of them can withdraw consent and terminate the agency at any time. However, if the agreement has a minimum term or an expiration date, early termination may be a breach of contract. If so, the breaching party may be required to pay damages to the other party for any financial losses that result from the termination.

> **Example:** Minh is the property manager for Oceanside Apartments. She signed a one-year management agreement with the owner in March. The agreement states that Minh is to be paid a flat fee of $2,000 per month. In December, the owner informs Minh that he is terminating their management agreement because he's found another company that offers more services. Under the terms of the agreement, the owner must pay Minh two

months' worth of fees for terminating the contract early. Because the owner has breached the contract, he must pay Minh $4,000.

When the parties to a contract agree in advance that a certain sum of money will serve as full compensation for a breach of the contract, the sum is referred to as **liquidated damages**. In the event that liquidated damages are not available, or if the breaching party fails to pay the damages as agreed, the non-breaching party may have to sue to recover any financial losses.

If the manager is entitled to special compensation (such as a leasing bonus), the management agreement should address what happens if the owner terminates the contract while the manager is in the middle of negotiations with a prospective tenant.

> **Example:** Returning to our previous example, let's say that Minh was entitled to a $100 leasing bonus for every apartment she leased. When the agreement was terminated, Minh had been negotiating a lease with a prospective tenant for several weeks. Under the terms of the management agreement, Minh is entitled to her bonus if the prospective tenant signs a lease within 60 days after her contract is terminated.

This type of provision protects the property manager when the owner terminates the contract early. Other provisions may protect the owner. For example, the management agreement may provide that the contract can be terminated early without liability under certain circumstances—such as when the owner sells the property, or the property becomes subject to bankruptcy or foreclosure proceedings.

Chapter Summary

1. Investment property owners may be sole proprietorships or business syndicates. Common forms of business syndicates include corporations, general partnerships, limited partnerships, limited liability companies (LLCs), trusts, and joint ventures.

2. The relationship between a property manager and his client is usually an agency relationship, which gives the manager (agent) the authority to act on the client's (principal's) behalf when dealing with third parties. The manager usually acts in a fiduciary capacity, managing trust funds, contracts, and the facilities on the property owner's behalf. A property manager may be an independent contractor or an employee in relation to the client.

3. A property manager's job is to handle the financial and physical aspects of the client's property in order to achieve the client's goals. The client's goals may be financial, such as a rapid return on her investment, or they may be nonfinancial, such as creating a nice place for others to live. A client's values and attitudes, such as a willingness to take financial risks, help shape the client's goals.

4. The management agreement is a contract that establishes and defines the working relationship between the client and the property manager. The agreement should set out all the terms of the manager-client relationship, such as the duration of the agreement, the manager's responsibilities and duties, the property owner's obligations, and the manager's compensation.

5. After the management agreement has been signed, the manager and client should follow certain procedures to transfer management of the property from the owner or former manager to the new manager. These steps include: setting up client records, establishing bank accounts and a working capital fund, arranging for the transfer of tenant deposits, performing a property inspection, and notifying all interested parties of the new management.

6. The property manager must keep her client informed of the property's performance and operations through monthly, quarterly, and annual reports. The frequency and content of the reports should be specified in the management agreement. Financial reports provide information about the property's rent roll, receipts and disbursements, net operating income, and cash flow. The manager may also provide a periodic report on leasing and marketing efforts, as well as an annual profit and loss statement and an annual operating budget.

7. Either the manager or the client can terminate the manager-client agency relationship at any time, although early termination of the management agreement may be a breach of contract.

Key Terms

Sole proprietorship – A business owned by one individual.

Unlimited liability – When a business owner is personally liable for the business's debts.

Limited liability – When a business owner's personal assets are protected against liabilities connected with the business.

Syndicate – Any group of investors who pool their investment capital to purchase investment property.

Syndicator/sponsor – Someone who organizes an investment syndicate.

Corporation – A form of business ownership in which individuals (shareholders) purchase stock in the company as an investment.

Dividends – Income from a corporation that is periodically distributed to its shareholders.

Closely held corporation – A corporation with comparatively few shareholders.

Articles of incorporation – A document filed with the secretary of state's office that establishes the corporation, lists the name and address of each incorporator, explains the share structure, and includes a general statement of purpose.

Corporate officers – Those appointed by a corporation's board of directors to run the business on a day-to-day basis.

Double taxation – When income from a company is taxed at the corporate level, and then taxed again at the individual shareholder level.

S corporation – A type of corporation that is allowed to pass its income on to shareholders without first paying corporate income taxes.

C corporation – A regular corporation that is subject to double taxation.

General agent – An agent who has authority to handle all matters for the principal in certain specified areas.

Special agent – An agent who has limited authority to do a specific thing or conduct a specific transaction.

Vicarious liability – A principal's liability for harm to third parties that is caused by the agent while acting within the scope of his authority.

Fiduciary – A person who holds a special position of trust and confidence in relation to someone else.

Management agreement – The contract that establishes and defines the working relationship between a property owner and her property manager.

Termination agreement – A document that formalizes the termination of a property management agreement and spells out the status of all major management duties and expenditures.

Chapter Quiz

1. A major disadvantage of a sole proprietorship is that the owner:
   a) has less control over decision making
   b) bears all risk and liability
   c) may have less money to invest
   d) Both b) and c)

2. The type of property most suitable for an all-inclusive flat fee compensation arrangement is:
   a) retail space
   b) a school
   c) light industrial property
   d) an office building

3. Which type of business entity gives the owners the most personal liability?
   a) S corporation
   b) general partnership
   c) LLC
   d) Both a) and c)

4. Someone who is hired to perform a particular task and is left to decide how and when to go about accomplishing it is called a/an:
   a) independent contractor
   b) employee
   c) corporate officer
   d) limited partner

5. Someone who organizes an investment syndicate may be referred to as the:
   a) syndicator
   b) organizer
   c) sponsor
   d) Both a) and c)

6. The term "risk aversion" refers to which of the following questions?
   a) Is the owner vicariously liable for the manager's actions?
   b) Does the form of ownership impose unlimited liability on the owner?
   c) Is the manager an employee or an independent contractor?
   d) How much financial uncertainty is the client comfortable with?

7. In which situation is it least likely that one of the parties will be liable to the other for breach of contract?
   a) The owner and manager have a 3-year agreement, but after a year the owner realizes their working styles are simply incompatible and decides to terminate the relationship
   b) The owner and manager have a 3-year agreement that the owner terminates after 2.5 years because she is selling the property
   c) The agreement between owner and manager has 3 months remaining, and the manager decides to terminate the relationship immediately. The property currently has a zero vacancy factor, and there are no outstanding tasks
   d) Any of the above situations are equally likely to result in liability for breach of contract

8. An owner who is interested in rapid, high returns will be more interested in:
   a) paying for quick property improvements that can immediately increase the property's value or rental income
   b) keeping rents slightly lower than market to minimize turnover
   c) maintaining a conservative approach in planning for long-term capital improvements
   d) None of the above

9. The document most in need of an attorney's thorough review is the:
   a) management plan
   b) management agreement
   c) annual operating budget
   d) annual profit and loss statement

10. Which of the property owners listed below is most likely to have direct involvement with the day-to-day decisions affecting the property?

    a) A shareholder in a real estate investment corporation
    b) A general partner in a limited partnership
    c) A regular member of a manager-managed LLC
    d) A large institutional investor

11. The property owner's obligations to the manager include:

    a) keeping the property insured
    b) providing funds when there is a shortfall
    c) providing funds for necessary capital expenditures
    d) All of the above

12. The scope of a property manager's authority is most reliably defined by:

    a) the property management agreement
    b) whether the manager is an employee or an independent contractor
    c) whether the manager is a universal agent or a special agent
    d) whether the owner is vicariously liable for the agent's actions

13. The most critical step for a property manager when beginning to manage a property is:

    a) setting up client records
    b) performing a comprehensive property inspection
    c) obtaining the property owner's social security number
    d) obtaining all keys to the property

14. An owner and manager agree in advance that a certain sum of money will be full compensation should one of them breach the management agreement. This sum is known as:

    a) limited liability
    b) early termination
    c) liquidated damages
    d) compensatory damages

15. Which of the following roles has the property manager holding legal title to the property?

    a) Universal agent
    b) Special agent
    c) Trustee
    d) General agent

Answer Key

1. d) A sole proprietor bears all risk and liability associated with the investment, and because he doesn't share the investment with anyone else, the owner may have less funds to purchase investment property.

2. b) Usually non-income property is most suitable for a flat fee arrangement. The charge may be per square foot or per unit, depending on the use.

3. b) In a general partnership, the individual partners are personally liable for the partnership's business debts. This means that the partners' personal assets can be sold to satisfy the partnership's business debts. Owners of S corporations and limited liability companies enjoy limited liability.

4. a) The distinction is between whether the person hired is an independent contractor or an employee. Property managers are almost always independent contractors.

5. d) The syndicator or sponsor may manage the syndicate and the investment property herself, or the group may hire a professional property manager.

6. d) A property owner with high risk aversion will be less likely to try new ideas that may increase income, and will be more conservative in her overall approach to property management objectives.

7. b) Management agreements often contain a provision that allows the contract to be terminated if the owner sells the property.

8. a) An owner who's after immediate high returns will want to do whatever increases the returns from the property as quickly as possible. Such a client will be willing to pay for property improvements only if they can be done in a short time frame and will have an immediate impact on net income and value.

9. b) The management agreement is the contract between the property manager and owner, and should be drafted or at least approved by an attorney.

10. b) Corporate shareholders and non-designated members in a manager-managed LLC all have limited roles in management activities. Institutional investors rarely get involved in the day-to-day management of the property. Only a general partner in a limited partnership will have responsibility for management decisions.

11. d) All of these options are the owner's responsibilities. The owner is also ultimately responsible for keeping the property and operations in compliance with lease requirements and legal requirements, though the manager is responsible for notifying the owner of any violations.

12. a) A property manager's authority is granted and defined in the management agreement. The amount and type of authority granted to the manager determines what type of agency/employment relationship is created and what liability is assumed, not the other way around.

13. a) Although all of the listed tasks are important, an accurate, reliable record-keeping system is the first and most important tool in managing property; without good records, a property manager cannot fulfill his fiduciary duty of accounting.

14. c) A liquidated damages clause in a contract specifies a sum of money that will compensate the non-breaching party in the event the other party breaches the contract. This eliminates the need for a lawsuit to ascertain damages.

15. c) All of the roles listed are fiduciary roles. Only that of trustee requires that the property manager hold legal title to the property. The beneficiaries hold equitable title.

Chapter 4

Developing a Management Plan

Outline

Introduction

In the last chapter, we examined the manager-client relationship and explained how to establish a working relationship with a new client. A critical step in that process is developing a management plan, which is the focus of this chapter. We'll begin with a basic overview and discussion of the purposes of a management plan. Then we'll discuss the types of analyses involved in a management plan's preliminary study. Next, we'll cover preparing the management plan and presenting it to the client. We'll end the chapter with a brief look at ongoing management planning.

The Management Plan

A **management plan** represents a property manager's strategy for physically and financially managing a property in the manner that will best achieve the client's goals. A good management plan is the result of careful research and analysis by the property manager, and will address every aspect of management, including:

- the property's competitive position in relevant markets,
- the property's physical condition,
- the property's financial condition, and
- operations (such as staffing and maintenance).

A management plan often begins as a **management proposal**—a document that is used to persuade a prospective client to hire the property manager. The proposal is usually the manager's first chance to make a good impression on a potential client. Once the client decides to use the property manager's services, the proposal becomes the management plan. The management plan serves as the manager's roadmap while she is managing the property. (For the sake of simplicity, we'll use the term "management plan" to refer to both a management proposal and the approved version of the management plan, unless otherwise noted.)

Other important functions of the management plan include clarifying the client's goals and educating the client about the property's condition and status in the market. The plan can also be used to illustrate the manager's strategies and clear up any misunderstandings about the manager's role.

If the client is considering making improvements or other changes to the property, a management plan can indicate whether her ideas are feasible. If appropriate, the plan may be used to suggest alternative changes that would help achieve the client's objectives more efficiently.

In the last chapter we discussed identifying a client's financial and nonfinancial goals. It's important to keep these goals firmly in mind when researching and preparing the management plan; they will determine the type and amount of information the property manager will need to examine.

> **Example:** Michael is preparing a management plan for a prospective client. The property is a two-story apartment building occupied by middle-income tenants, but many of the units need some updating. If the client's goal is to modernize the units but still market to middle-income tenants, Michael will research other middle-income properties to find out what amenities and finishes are considered standard. But if the client's goal is to convert the apartments into luxury units, Michael will need to gather information about other rentals that cater to high-income tenants.

If the client's goal is to generate the most income possible from the property, the property should be put to its **highest and best use**, which is the most profitable use a property can be put to. To be the highest and best use, a use must be reasonable in light of all legal, economic, and physical limitations.

> **Example:** Returning to the previous example, let's say that all of the apartment buildings in the neighborhood are modern high-rise buildings. In that case, the older two-story apartment building may not be the highest and best use of the property. To achieve the highest net return, the owner may have to replace the two-story apartment building with a high-rise apartment building.

Preparing the Management Plan

Preparing a management plan begins with research and analysis to determine the property's current situation and its future prospects. This process of research and analysis is known as the **preliminary study** and is comprised of five different types of analyses: regional analysis, neighborhood analysis, property analysis, market analysis, and an analysis of alternatives.

In the first three analyses, the manager gathers and evaluates data on the region, the neighborhood, and the property itself. This information is then used in the market analysis to evaluate how the subject property compares to its competition, and to set rental rates for the subject property. In the analysis of alternatives, the manager evaluates any physical or operational changes that could help him achieve the owner's goals more quickly or more cost-effectively. The following sections will examine each of these steps in more detail.

Regional Analysis

In a regional analysis, the property manager considers the "big picture": the economic and demographic conditions that affect the supply of and demand for property in the general area where the subject property is located. (**Demographics** refers to characteristics of a human population, such as average family size and median age.)

Metropolitan Statistical Areas

The first step in a regional analysis is identifying the region to be researched. Usually, this means identifying the Metropolitan Statistical Area in which the property is located. A **metropolitan statistical area** (MSA) is defined by the federal Office of Management and Budget as an area with at least one urbanized population center of 50,000 or more and a high degree of social and economic conformity. There are currently 366 MSAs in the United States.

Certain large MSAs, with population cores of over 2.5 million people, are divided into smaller regions called metropolitan divisions. There are currently 29 Metropolitan Divisions in the United States. The Office of Management and Budget has also defined 576 micropolitan statistical areas, which are similar to MSAs but have smaller urban population clusters of between 10,000 and 50,000 people.

Once the property manager has identified the relevant metropolitan statistical area, metropolitan division, or micropolitan statistical area, he can begin gathering and evaluating the economic and demographic information for the region.

Gathering and Evaluating Regional Data

When gathering data for the regional analysis, the property manager is interested in both current conditions and future trends. It's important to know whether the region is

 Metropolitan Statistical Areas (MSAs)

The following is a sampling of a few of southern California's metropolitan and micropolitan statistical areas, including the metropolitan divisions contained within the Los Angeles MSA.

San Diego–Carlsbad–San Marcos	Metropolitan Statistical Area # 41740
Santa Barbara–Santa Maria–Goleta	Metropolitan Statistical Area # 42060
Modesto	Metropolitan Statistical Area # 33700
Bishop	Micropolitan Statistical Area # 13860
Crescent City	Micropolitan Statistical Area # 18860
San Jose–Sunnyvale–Santa Clara	Metropolitan Statistical Area # 41940
Fresno	Metropolitan Statistical Area 23420
Los Angeles–Long Beach–Santa Ana	Metropolitan Statistical Area # 31100
Los Angeles–Long Beach–Glendale	Metropolitan Division # 31084
Santa Ana–Anaheim–Irvine	Metropolitan Division # 42044

Source: U.S. Office of Management and Budget

Population Shifts

A population shift is a change in the relative numbers of different groups of people that make up a population. For instance, after World War II, the population of the United States generally began to move away from cities into suburbs, thanks in part to the automobile. And while the westward expansion of the 1800s now seems merely a part of the history books, modern Census data show that the population of southern and western states continues to grow. In fact, 2010 Census data revealed that over the previous ten years, Nevada's population grew over 35%, more than any other state. In comparison, most of the New England states grew less than 5%.

Source: United States Census

likely to experience growth, is fairly stable, or is entering a period of decline. With these considerations in mind, the manager will look for information about:

- **Population size.** Is the population increasing or decreasing, and at what rate?
- **Demographic profile.** What is the average family size? What is the average age of the population?
- **Economic conditions.** What is the employment rate and average income, and have they been increasing or decreasing? What are the major industries and who are the major employers? Is this a tourist area?
- **Infrastructure.** What are the major sources of transportation and is the area well-served by major utilities?
- **Other government and social issues.** What is the social and political climate like? Are the tax rates high? What kind of schools are available?

Sources of Regional Data

The United States Census Bureau website (www.census.gov) is the primary federal source for regional economic and demographic data. The foundation of that data is the U.S. Census, which is taken once every ten years and collects both population and housing information. Data from the federal census is the basis for nearly all demographic statistics available in the United States.

The Census Bureau also performs several other useful surveys, including:

- **The Economic Survey.** Every five years (in years ending in "2" and "7"), the Census Bureau collects and compiles information about manufacturing, construction, retail, and other business sectors.
- **The American Community Survey.** This survey provides yearly population and housing statistics.

- **The Statistical Abstract of the United States.** This survey provides statistics on the social, political, and economic organization of the United States. Information available includes such statistics as the number and size of shopping centers, and family debt to income ratios.
- **The American Housing Survey.** Performed in odd-numbered years by the Census Bureau on behalf of the Department of Housing and Urban Development (HUD), this survey collects national data on types and sizes of housing units; household characteristics; income; housing and neighborhood quality; housing costs; and equipment and fuels.

In addition to the above surveys, the Census Bureau compiles information about market absorption rates (discussed in Chapter 2), vacancy rates, new home construction, housing patterns, and so on. All of this information is available in printed form, and much of it is also searchable via the Census Bureau website based on state, county, city, zip code, and other demographic or economic factors.

Other Sources of Data. Of course, the federal government isn't the only source of information available to property managers. State and local government agencies, local business groups (such as the Chamber of Commerce), the Board of REALTORS®, and local multiple listing services may offer similar data about regional economic and demographic conditions. Financial institutions, such as banks and mortgage companies, may also provide data.

Another source of information is trade and professional organizations, such as the:

- Institute of Real Estate Management (IREM®),
- Building Owners and Managers Association International (BOMA®),
- National Apartment Association (NAA®), and
- National Association of Residential Property Managers (NARPM®).

Finally, several companies are in the business of compiling statistics from the above federal, state, local, and trade organization sources. Other companies sell mapping software that allows users to view statistics based on defined geographic areas.

A property manager usually works in one general area and will be able to use the same regional data for multiple clients. But to ensure that each regional analysis is accurate, she must update her research at least annually, if not more often.

Neighborhood Analysis

The next step in the preliminary study is the neighborhood analysis. A neighborhood analysis is similar to a regional analysis, but the manager narrows her focus to the area immediately surrounding the subject property. Depending on the area in question, a neighborhood may consist of several square miles or only a few city blocks. Property managers don't have a precise definition for "neighborhood"; they tend to use the term in more or less the same way it's generally used. For the purposes of this discussion, we'll define a **neighborhood** as a geographic area in which the residents share common characteristics or the properties share a similar land use.

Defining Neighborhood Boundaries

Often, a natural or artificial barrier creates one or more of a neighborhood's boundaries. Natural barriers include rivers and lakes, coastlines, steep hills and deep ravines, and so on. Nature preserves and greenbelts are also natural barriers, even though they've been "created" by people. Artificial barriers, on the other hand, include highways, railroads, golf courses, parks, airports, and even large buildings or complexes, such as a college or university.

> **Example:** The city clerk's office of Seattle, Washington keeps an online database of neighborhood boundaries. The University District, for example, is bounded on the southern side by portions of Lake Washington and Lake Union, on the western side by an interstate freeway, and on the northern and eastern sides by a park and several major roads.

The natural and artificial barriers in the above example are visible and easily observed by a property manager. But, as we'll discuss next, other types of artificial barriers aren't so easily recognized. These invisible barriers nevertheless serve to delineate one neighborhood from another.

Zoning. One example of an invisible boundary is **zoning**. Zoning ordinances divide a community into areas (zones) that are set aside for specific types of uses, such as agricultural, residential, commercial, or industrial. The line that divides an area zoned for residential use from an area zoned for agricultural use may serve as a boundary of that residential neighborhood.

But zoning alone won't necessarily define a neighborhood. A single area zoned for residential use may contain several different neighborhoods. For instance, one single residential zone may include an area of older, historic homes that constitute one neighborhood, as well as a new subdivision that constitutes another neighborhood. Likewise, one neighborhood in an industrial area might consist of heavy manufacturing facilities, while an adjacent neighborhood in the same zone is made up primarily of warehouses.

Economic and Social Barriers. Economic and sociological factors may also play a role. If an area filled with upscale homes and expensive shops borders an area of run-down homes and discount stores, the two areas are likely to be considered different neighborhoods. And ethnic or religious differences can also serve as barriers. For example, in some cities, certain ethnic groups historically congregated in particular areas, either by choice or because of prejudices. Even if residents of those ethnic groups have since drifted away, those areas typically remain distinct neighborhoods.

> **Example:** In the Los Angeles of the 1800s, people of Chinese or Japanese descent tended to settle in the "Chinatown" or "Little Tokyo" neighborhoods. Today, although most Los

Angeles residents of Chinese or Japanese descent live outside these neighborhoods, the Chinatown and Little Tokyo neighborhoods have maintained their unique cultural flavor.

While a neighborhood boundary formed by a river or coastline is easy to discern, the subtle difference between neighborhoods that results from ethnic or economic differences may be much harder to recognize. As a result, the property manager will not be able to rely on maps alone; he may have to define the neighborhood based on a physical inspection and careful data analysis.

Gathering and Evaluating Neighborhood Data

Once the property manager has defined the boundaries of the subject property's neighborhood, he'll begin gathering and evaluating neighborhood data, including information on land use and zoning, property types and values, rental and vacancy rates, characteristics of the local population, curb appeal, local amenities and transportation, and whether the neighborhood itself is in a period of growth or decline.

Land Use and Zoning. Property managers look for neighborhood trends—such as changes in population size and increased consumer spending—that indicate an area is growing or has the potential to grow. But growth can be limited by land use planning and zoning ordinances. For example, a mostly residential neighborhood may not be able to sustain more growth if the area isn't zoned for high density housing.

The manager must also consider the amount and type of any **impact fees** that apply. Impact fees are upfront fees municipalities charge developers to help offset the costs of additional public services required by developments. In some cases, these fees may be high enough to discourage further development.

Property Types. Next, the property manager will determine which type of property is dominant in the neighborhood. If a residential area is zoned for both single-family homes and apartment buildings, which is more common? If an area is zoned for commercial use, are more properties office buildings or storefronts?

Property Values. A manager can learn a lot about a neighborhood by studying its property values. Obviously, current property values will be important to the manager's property and market analyses, but historic property values are important to the neighborhood analysis. By studying the changes in neighborhood property values over time, the manager can identify trends. Have property values been increasing or decreasing in recent years, and at what rate? Is this likely to continue? A pattern of increasing values is a sign of growth, while a pattern of decreasing values raises a red flag.

Rental Rates. The property manager will also be interested in both current and historic rental rates. For residential properties, she'll want the average rental rates for one-, two-, and three-bedroom apartments. For commercial properties, she'll gather information about the average cost per square foot of leased space. She'll also be on the lookout for trends: have average rents increased or decreased over the years, and at what rate?

Vacancy Rates. Vacancy rates tend to fluctuate, so managers look for overall trends in the demand for rental properties. Are occupancy rates rising or falling? How fast are these changes occurring?

The property manager will also want to compare vacancy rates between different types of properties. Is there more demand for one-bedroom or two-bedroom apartments, or for single-family homes? Is the vacancy rate lower for retail properties or office properties?

Demographics and Economic/Education Levels. The manager will need to gather information about the neighborhood's residents. Are they mostly students, single working adults, or families? What is the median age? Are they mostly one-income or two-income families, or are they primarily retirees? Commercial and industrial property managers will also be interested in this sort of information; depending on the size of the neighborhood, the residents may be a source of customers and employees.

Similarly, the overall economic status and average educational level of neighborhood residents is important. What is the average income and employment rate? Is the population mostly made up of high school graduates or college graduates? Again, these are potential customers, renters, and employees, so the demand for certain types of stores, rental properties, and businesses will depend in part on the population's economic and educational levels.

Curb Appeal and Distinctive Features. "Curb appeal" refers to a neighborhood's overall condition and appearance. Does it feature nicely manicured lawns and well-landscaped properties, or run-down buildings and streets with potholes?

A neighborhood's distinctive features can also help or hurt property values and rents. In a residential neighborhood, walking trails and a nearby park or lake may increase value; conversely, a nearby prison is likely to decrease value. Other features that may impact value include the presence of schools, religious institutions, restaurants, and shopping centers.

Commercial property managers will be interested in some of the same features. For instance, a nearby beach or tourist attraction will bring potential customers to the area and may help dictate which types of restaurants and retail stores will prosper.

Transportation Issues. Residential tenants want quick access to employment areas, while commercial tenants want customers to have easy access to their stores and offices. Does the neighborhood have easy access to major highways and other commuter routes? What kind of public transportation is available? Are there any plans to expand transportation options in the near future?

Stage in Neighborhood Life Cycle. Finally, the property manager will want to consider the neighborhood's overall condition. So far, she's been looking for trends in property values and vacancy rates; now she'll consider the larger picture. Overall, how is the neighborhood doing? Is it constant or changing? If it's changing, is it in a period of growth, with new construction, a growing population, and increased demand? Or is the neighborhood in a period of decline, with a decreasing population, high vacancy rate, and many closed businesses?

Sources of Neighborhood Data

Some of the same sources of information used for the regional analysis, such as the local multiple listing service or the Chamber of Commerce, can also be used for the neighborhood analysis. Often, data are available for smaller geographic areas such as zip codes or even city blocks.

Zoning and land use planning information should be obtained from the appropriate local agency. A good place to start is the city or town's local building department or planning board.

As with regional data, a property manager may keep neighborhood data on file for future clients. Of course, even when a region's overall status seems fairly stable, individual neighborhoods within that region may be changing at a faster rate. Neighborhood information should be updated at least annually, if not more often, to ensure its accuracy.

Property Analysis

After gathering and evaluating data on the region and neighborhood in which the subject property is located, the property manager turns to the property itself. The goal of the property analysis is to review every aspect of the property relevant to its management.

Most of the information necessary for the property analysis can be obtained from the property owners, but the manager should also perform a careful inspection of the property. The gathered data concern the property's basic physical attributes, attractiveness and condition, management and leasing, and financial status.

Basic Physical Attributes

First, the property manager takes stock of the property's basic physical features. This includes the property's location in the neighborhood, the size of the lot, and the measurements and features of both the building and any individual units and spaces within it.

Location. The manager will evaluate the property's location within the surrounding neighborhood. Is the property prominently located and easy to spot, or is it on a side street and difficult to find? For a commercial property, the manager will be especially concerned with the property's proximity to high-traffic areas. Residential managers, on the other hand, might be more concerned with the property's distance from commuter roads, parks, schools, and so on.

Lot Size. Next, the property manager notes the size of the lot and its building-to-land ratio (how much of the lot is occupied by the building itself). For residential properties, is there outdoor space for recreational use? For industrial properties, is there sufficient space for equipment, storage, and easy access by delivery trucks?

Measurements and Features. Finally, the property manager will note the measurements and features of the buildings, including:

- **Building size.** What is the square footage? How many floors?
- **Number of units or spaces.** How many units or spaces are available? If there are different types of units (one-bedroom, studios, etc.), how many of each type are available?
- **Unit sizes and layouts.** What size are the apartments (in square feet by type—one-bedroom, two-bedroom, etc.) or commercial spaces? How are the units and spaces configured? For residential spaces, are the units accessible from separate, outdoor entrances, or from interior hallways? For commercial properties, is the building meant to be open to the public, with a reception area in front, or is this an office building composed of many smaller spaces?

Attractiveness and Condition

Next, the property manager examines the property's overall attractiveness and condition. She'll be concerned with the property's exterior features and curb appeal, as well as the condition of the common areas, rental space, and the building's operating systems.

Exterior Condition. The property manager will record the age and architectural style of the building. She'll also note the composition and approximate age of the roof, and indicate whether it needs repairs or cleaning.

Next, she'll study the condition of the grounds and landscaping. Is the area well-manicured? Are there gardens and pedestrian paths, landscape lighting, and mature trees and plants? Crumbling walkways and overgrown grassy areas should be noted. And what about the condition of any fences or sheds? Are they solidly constructed and freshly painted, or are they falling apart?

Common Areas. The condition and attractiveness of the common areas is very important, both for residential and commercial properties. Are the lobby and hallways clean, well-lit, and in good repair? Is the parking lot paved or gravel, and is it well-maintained? Are parking spaces clearly marked and is there sufficient lighting? What other public facilities—bathrooms, for example—are available and what shape are they in? For each feature, the property manager should be sure to write down any safety hazards or other problems.

Rental Space. Of course, the property manager will also be concerned with the general attractiveness and condition of the rental spaces. Do residential units have modern appliances, fixtures, and finishes, or do they need updating? (This question isn't necessarily asked about commercial space, which is usually is built out after leasing.) The condition of wall and floor surfaces should be observed: are they new or in need of repairs? As with the common areas, she'll want to note if the rental space appears to be clean and well-maintained, or if there are health or safety problems that need to be addressed.

Unique Features. Unique and unusual features should also be listed. In a residential building, these features might include balconies with great views, or a swimming pool or other recreational facilities. A commercial space might have a nice outdoor courtyard that could be used by employees and customers.

Operating Systems. Finally, the manager will want to gather information about the property's operating systems. How modern is the electrical system? Is the property wired for high-speed Internet? Is the plumbing in good shape? Have the elevators been inspected recently?

The property's HVAC system should be examined. Is there air conditioning? What kind of fuel is used to power the heat and hot water systems? Are residential units served from a common source or do units have individual hot water heaters? Information about the age and overall condition of these systems should also be included.

Management and Leasing

Once the property manager has gathered information about the size and physical condition of the property, his next step is to take a closer look at day-to-day operations. His goal is to determine how well the property is currently being managed in all areas, including leasing and tenant relations, staffing, management policies, and marketing.

Leasing and Tenant Relations. The property's occupancy rate is extremely important. This includes the current occupancy level as well as past occupancy levels.

> **Example:** Carol is conducting a property analysis for a three-story commercial building that contains mostly retail stores on the first floor, with office space on the upper two levels. While examining the property's leases and other records, Carol discovers the following information:
> - The building is currently 80% occupied, but the overall occupancy rate over the past 20 years has averaged over 90%.
> - There are ten units in the building; eight are occupied. Three tenants are located on the first floor: one café and two retail clothing stores. The remaining tenants occupy the upper floors and consist of three doctors, a dentist, and a medical transcription service.
> - Six of the units are subject to long-term leases that won't expire for at least three years. The remaining two leases will expire within the year.
> - Historically, 60% of tenants have renewed their leases at the end of the lease term.
>
> Carol includes all of this information in her notes on the property.

When reviewing the status of current leases, the manager should note any concessions (such as free rent) that may impact renewal negotiations. The property manager should also review any documented tenant problems, including late payments, bounced checks, and complaints about excessive noise.

Staffing. Questions the property manager should ask include: what kind of staff is currently working on-site? Do the staff do most of the work themselves, or do they use outside companies for maintenance and repairs? Who handles the leasing? Is there enough on-site staff to address tenant problems in a timely manner? The manager should list each staff member, all salaries and benefits, and whether there are any unfilled positions. He should also make a list of any jobs that are contracted out to others.

Policies, Procedures, and Legal Compliance. Next, the property manager will want to examine the policies and procedures regarding pets, security deposits, late payment fees, maintenance, tenant complaints, parking, move-in and move-out checklists, and so on. If state or local law regulates any of these items (such as how security deposits are handled), the manager should check to see if the legal requirements are being met and note any problems found.

Compliance with other federal, state, and local laws should also be investigated. For instance, is there any evidence of health or safety code violations? Were past problems taken care of in a timely manner? Are all federal and state disability laws followed? All potential legal problems should be carefully documented.

Marketing. Finally, the property manager examines the current marketing strategy. Depending on the type of property, marketing methods can include radio or television advertisements, billboards or signs, newspaper and magazine ads, and Internet advertising. The property manager will want to examine how much money is spent on advertising in each medium, and the rate of success for each type.

> **Example:** Raul is preparing a management plan for ABC Apartments, a 35-unit apartment building. He learns that ABC has an overall marketing budget of $5,000 per year. Approximately 40% of this budget is spent on print advertising (such as newspapers), 40% on direct marketing (mailings), and 20% on Internet advertising. These figures will help him determine his own marketing budget later on.

Financial Condition

Naturally, a property manager will be very interested in the property's financial condition. An analysis of the property's overall financial health will help the manager determine whether the current strategies are working or need improvement.

Income. The property's primary source of income will almost always be rent, but other types of income (such as from vending machines and parking spaces) should also be listed. Residential managers will want to determine not only the total amount of rent received for all units, but also the amount of rent received for each type of unit. Commercial managers will want to note the income received per square foot of leased space.

> **Example:** When gathering information about an apartment building's income, Lee notes the following monthly totals:
>
> | | | |
> |---|---|---|
> | Income from one-bedroom units: | 10 @ $600 per month | $6,000 |
> | Income from two-bedroom units: | 5 @ $700 per month | $3,500 |
> | Income from vending machines: | | $235 |
> | Income from laundry facilities: | | $475 |
> | Income from leased parking spaces: | 20 @ $25 per month | $500 |
> | **Total income:** | | **$10,710** |

Expenses, Reserves, and Insurance. Expenses must also be documented. Typical expenses include maintenance fees, staff salaries, supplies, utilities, insurance, taxes, administrative costs, and advertising, among other things. The property's debt service is also important; **debt service** is the principal and interest due on any mortgage or other outstanding debts. Any recent unusual expenses, such as the cost of replacing a leaky roof or a broken water heater, should also be listed.

Cash reserves are funds set aside for both planned and unplanned maintenance or repairs. The property manager should note the balance of the cash reserve account, how the reserve amount is determined, and recent expenditures and deposits. She should also note whether the reserves have been sufficient to handle emergencies, unanticipated expenses, and any planned improvements. (Reserves are discussed in greater detail in Chapter 5.)

Finally, the property manager will want to examine the amount and type of insurance coverage maintained on the property. She should note the cost of these policies, the amount of any deductibles, and whether the policies are current.

Market Analysis

Using the information gathered during the regional, neighborhood, and property analyses, the property manager is now ready to complete a market analysis. In a market analysis, the manager evaluates how the subject property compares to competing properties; this information is then used to set rental rates for the subject property.

Defining the Relevant Market

The first step in performing a market analysis is determining the relevant market for comparison. In most cases, the relevant market will be a small segment of a larger market. This smaller segment, known as a **submarket**, is usually made up of buildings that are similar in size and character, with similarly sized rental units or spaces, and with comparable rental rates.

> **Example:** Peter is performing a market analysis for a small commercial building that consists of a half-dozen rental spaces, configured for and used by small retail shops. The spaces lease for an average of $30 per square foot, per year. Nearby, there is a high-rise office complex that rents for approximately $55 per square foot, a shopping mall with 140 stores that rents for approximately $44 per square foot, and three strip malls that rent for $29, $30, and $33 per square foot.
>
> The office complex isn't a comparable property because its size and character are too different from those of a small commercial building. And although the shopping mall caters to retail tenants, its size and character are also not similar enough to those of the subject property. Instead, Peter should focus on the submarket, which would include the three strip malls (small commercial buildings that cater to the same kind of retail tenants as the subject property).

The manager also must choose the geographical limits for the relevant market. Is the property's immediate neighborhood the appropriate market, or should other similar, nearby neighborhoods be included?

Example: Sarah is doing a market analysis for a rental home in the Green Hill neighborhood, a neighborhood of single-family homes bordered on two sides by a university. She knows from her research that 70% of the tenants in Green Hill are graduate students who are married with families. The Sunset neighborhood, on the other side of the university, also consists of single-family homes that appeal to graduate students. Since prospective tenants are likely to choose homes in either neighborhood, Sarah decides that the relevant market includes both Green Hill and Sunset.

Comparing the Subject Property to the Competition

Real estate agents are familiar with the sales comparison approach to value (also called the market data approach to value) that is used when preparing a competitive market analysis (CMA). The comparison process used in a property manager's analysis is essentially the same, except that adjustments are made to rental rates rather than to sales prices. Let's take a closer look at how this process works.

Comparables. The property manager's first step is to gather information about comparable properties in the submarket. To be suitable as comparables, these properties must be similar to the subject property in size, number of rental units or spaces, and amenities. At least three or four comparables should be used to provide an accurate picture of the competition.

Information the property manager should gather about the comparables will vary based on whether the subject property is residential or commercial. For example, a residential property manager will want to note a comparable's amenities, such as a swimming pool and views, while a commercial property manager would look into the availability and cost of parking. Regardless of the type of property, the property manager will want to gather information about a comparable's:

- location, size, age, and condition;
- number, type, and size of rental spaces or units;
- equipment and amenities;
- utilities and other recurring expenses;
- rental rates and other sources of income; and
- vacancy rates.

For market analysis purposes, the manager may use a comparison worksheet (either paper or electronic) similar to the one shown in Figure 4.1, for commercial property, or 4.2, for residential property. The appropriate elements for comparison will depend not only on the type of property, but also on the subject property's location and its particular features and amenities. (The relative importance of various features for each major type of income property will be discussed in Chapters 10 through 13.)

As you can see, the worksheets have spaces to enter specific information about the subject property along with each of the comparable properties. The property manager then evaluates how the subject property—in its current condition—differs from each comparable, for better and for worse. By considering the subject property in its current condition, the manager establishes a baseline for measuring how various improvements and other differences affect rent. Note that if the subject property includes different types of rental

Figure 4.1 Comparison worksheet for market analysis – commercial property

Market Analysis Comparison Grid for Commercial Property

Subject property: _____ Date: _____

Type of property: _____

	Subject	Comparable 1	Comparable 2	Comparable 3
Property Name				
Base rent (sq. ft./year)				
Concessions (–)				
Pass-through expenses (+)				
Tenant improvements (+)				
Total (effective rent)				
Vacancy rate				

Elements	Description	Difference	$ adj.	Difference	$ adj.	Difference	$ adj.
Location							
Prestige							
Transportation access							
Business services							
Employee services							
Crime and safety issues							
Other							
Building & Site							
Age of building							
Overall curb appeal							
Grounds							
Building exterior							
Entry and/or lobby							
Other common areas							
Other							
Special Factors (list)							

Adjustments should be stated in dollars per square foot per year. For example, +0.20 means the comparable's rental rate is increased by twenty cents per square foot, and –1.50 means the rate is decreased by $1.50 per square foot.

	Subject	Comparable 1		Comparable 2		Comparable 3	
Elements	**Description**	**Difference**	**$ adj.**	**Difference**	**$ adj.**	**Difference**	**$ adj.**
Systems & Operations							
Energy efficiency (HVAC)							
Elevators							
Telecommunications							
Staffing							
Security							
Other							
Parking							
Lot, covered, or garage							
Parking ratio or index							
Visitor spaces available							
Tenant parking cost							
Rental Space							
Location within building							
Layout issues; floor plate							
Quality							
Condition							
Storage							
Special features							
Other							
Adjustment Totals							
Net Adjustments							
Adj. rent per rentable sq.ft.							
R/U ratio (×)							
Adj. rent per usable sq.ft.							
Total no. of adjustments							
Comments:							

Figure 4.2 Comparison worksheet for market analysis – residential property

Market Analysis Comparison Grid for Residential Property

Subject property: _____ Date: _____

Type of unit: _____

	Subject	Comparable 1	Comparable 2	Comparable 3
Property Name				
Rental rate (monthly)				
Concessions (–)				
Effective rent				
Vacancy rate				

Elements	Description	Difference	$ adj.	Difference	$ adj.	Difference	$ adj.
Location							
Prestige							
Access to transportation							
Nearby tenant services							
Crime and safety issues							
Buildings & Site							
Number of bldgs/units							
Age of building(s)							
Grounds							
Building exterior(s)							
Entry and/or lobby							
Other common areas							
Systems & Operations							
Energy efficiency (HVAC)							
Elevators							
Staffing							
Security							
Parking							
Lot, covered, or garage							
Visitor spaces available							
Tenant parking cost							

Adjustments should be stated in dollars per month. For example, +10 means the comparable's rental rate is increased by $10.00 per month, and –22 means the rate is decreased by $22.00 per month.

Elements	Subject Description	Comparable 1 Difference	$ adj.	Comparable 2 Difference	$ adj.	Comparable 3 Difference	$ adj.
Amenities							
Pets allowed							
Internet/cable TV							
Clubhouse or party room							
Rec or exercise facilities							
Laundry facilities							
Other							
Rental Unit							
Location in complex							
Square footage (est.)							
Layout							
Overall quality/condition							
Number of bathrooms							
Storage							
Carpets & flooring							
Window treatments							
Stove & refrigerator							
Dishwasher							
Other appliances							
Air conditioning							
Balcony, deck, or patio							
Fireplace							
Other							
Utilities Paid by Owner							
Adjustment Totals							
Adjusted Rent							
Adjusted rent per sq.ft.							
Total no. of adjustments							
Comments:							

spaces (a residential building with studios, one-bedroom units, and two-bedroom units, for example), the manager prepares a separate worksheet for each type of rental space.

Once the manager has filled out the worksheet, he'll need to estimate a dollar value for each feature or amenity. He then adjusts the rent of each comparable upward or downward to reflect differences between the comparable and the subject property. The resulting figure indicates how much the comparable would be renting for if it were essentially the same as the subject property.

The worksheet results are used to evaluate the subject property's current rental schedule. (A **rental schedule** is a list of the rental rates assigned to the different types of units.) Are the subject property's rental rates at, below, or above market rates?

> **Example:** Marcus is doing a market analysis for the Santiago Apartments, where one-bedroom apartments with modern amenities and lake views currently rent for $795 per month. His market research shows that the rental rate for similar apartments in the neighborhood, after adjustments, is $845 per month. This tells him that the one-bedroom units in the Santiago building are priced below market rates.

Armed with this information, the property manager can now set appropriate rental rates for the subject property.

Setting Rental Rates

One of the most important elements of a property manager's market analysis and management plan is her suggested rental rates for the subject property. Rent is an investment property's primary source of income, and the property manager's goal is to set a rental rate that will maximize the owner's return on investment. Choosing the optimum rent for a unit requires striking a balance between maximizing income and maximizing occupancy. For example, while a 0% vacancy rate sounds ideal, it could indicate that the property's rental rates are too low.

> **Example:** An office complex is at 100% occupancy, with an average rent of $37 per square foot. However, a market analysis reveals that similar properties rent for $41 per square foot and have an occupancy rate of 95%.

On the other hand, if rents are too high, the vacancy rate will be higher than necessary.

> **Example:** Returning to our previous example, suppose instead that the office complex struggles to maintain a 60% occupancy rate while renting space at $37 per square foot. A market analysis reveals that similar properties with occupancy rates over 90% are renting at $29 per square foot.

How high a vacancy rate is acceptable will depend on the type of property, general economic conditions, supply and demand in the rental market, and the owner's goals. To establish what's acceptable, the manager will compare the subject property's vacancy rate to the vacancy rates of several comparable properties.

> **Example:** Let's look at our original example once again: the office complex with a 100% occupancy rate and rental rates that are below market value. The owner would like to raise his rental rates but doesn't want to let the occupancy rate drop too far. Comparable

> **Average Rental Rates in the United States**
>
> The number of bedrooms is a major factor in determining average residential rental rates across the United States.
>
> **Average gross rent in the United States**
>
> | | |
> |---|---|
> | Studio: | $891 |
> | One bedroom: | $858 |
> | Two bedrooms: | $1054 |
> | Three bedrooms: | $1345 |
>
> Source: www.myapartmentmap.com/rental_data, August, 2012

properties with an occupancy rate of 90% are renting for $45 per square foot, while properties with a vacancy rate of 95% are renting for $41 per square foot. If the owner wants his property's occupancy rate to remain above 95%, the maximum amount he can charge is $41 per square foot.

Setting rental rates involves one final step: the manager chooses a basic rental rate for each type of unit or space in the subject property, and then adjusts that basic rate for specific units or spaces depending on their features.

> **Example:** After completing her market analysis, Carla decides that the basic rental rate for a one-bedroom apartment in the subject property should be $800 per month. One-bedroom apartments with a balcony, however, will rent for $850 a month, while one-bedroom apartments on the top floor, featuring a view of the ocean, will rent for $975 a month.

Analysis of Alternatives

Now that the property manager has completed the regional, neighborhood, property, and market analyses, the last step before preparing the final management plan is to conduct an analysis of alternatives. In the **analysis of alternatives**, the property manager evaluates possible operational and physical changes to the property.

Until now, the property manager has been considering the subject property in its current ("as is") condition. The analysis of alternatives, on the other hand, considers "what if"—what if the apartments were converted to condominiums? What if the parking lot was reconfigured to accommodate more customers during peak business hours? What if the units' old carpeting was replaced with hardwood floors, and the kitchens were updated with new cabinetry and appliances?

As always, the property manager is working to maximize the owner's profit. So in the analysis of alternatives, the manager must consider whether each change would increase the property's net operating income. As we mentioned in Chapter 2, net operating income (NOI) is rental income, minus operating expenses. The higher the NOI, the higher the property's value, and the greater the owner/investor's return on her investment. (Calculating NOI will be discussed in the next chapter.) To increase the property's NOI, the manager might suggest reducing operating expenses, raising the occupancy rate, or raising rents. Even if a particular change won't increase the property's NOI, it may nevertheless be necessary to preserve the property's value.

> **Example:** An apartment building currently rents one-bedroom apartments for $850 per month, but the kitchens haven't been updated in ten years. A newly built apartment building nearby will be opening soon and is also offering one-bedroom apartments for $850, but with modern appliances and granite countertops in the kitchens. Updating the kitchens in the subject property won't allow the building manager to charge more for one-bedroom apartments, but it may be necessary if he doesn't want the occupancy rate to plummet.

Finally, a change may be necessary in order to comply with insurance or legal requirements, even if the change results in no increase (and perhaps even in a decrease) in NOI.

> **Example:** To comply with the local building code, the property manager of a large apartment building recommends that smoke detectors be installed in every bedroom. The addition of the smoke detectors won't increase the property's NOI, but it will bring the building into compliance with the law.

Proposed Changes

As we just discussed, a property manager may include proposed changes in her analysis of alternatives for any one of a number of reasons: to increase property value or income, to preserve property value and income, or to comply with insurance or legal requirements. Whatever the reason, proposed changes will usually fall into one of three categories: operational changes, physical changes, or changes in use. Let's take a closer look at each category.

Operational Changes. Operational changes don't directly affect a property's physical appearance or use; instead, they impact how a property is managed. Operational changes include changes made to rental rates, marketing activities, maintenance schedules, staffing, and so on.

The operational change the property manager is most likely to suggest is an increase or decrease in rental rates. In some cases, the suggested adjustment will simply bring the subject property's rates in line with comparable properties on the market. But the manager may also suggest a rent increase or decrease in conjunction with other proposed changes.

> **Example:** To attract more retail tenants, a property manager suggests remodeling a property's storefronts and adding larger windows. His market analysis indicates that if the owners agree to this change, rent for the spaces can be raised from $27 per square foot to $29 per square foot.

Regardless of the reason for the proposed increase or decrease, any rental rate change must be supported by the market analysis. Simply raising the rent to cover the cost of other changes, or to increase the net operating income, will likely result in increased vacancies if the new rates aren't in line with market rates.

Other operational changes are designed to increase or preserve the NOI by decreasing expenses while increasing efficiency. For example, the manager might suggest changing certain types of maintenance supplies.

> **Example:** During her inspection, the property manager noticed that the maintenance staff currently uses several specialty cleaning products for various jobs around the building. She suggests switching to a general cleaning solution that can be used for 75% of these jobs, reducing the need for so many specialty products and saving the building's owners over $500 per year.
>
> The manager might also suggest switching to more expensive, higher-quality supplies if they will last longer or work more efficiently, saving money in the long run.

The property manager may also suggest operational changes involving staff, wages, and outside personnel. For example, many office and residential buildings hire cleaning companies and maintenance companies (such as landscaping services) to perform routine tasks around the property. The property manager may suggest changing to cheaper or more efficient vendors. Alternatively, she may suggest renegotiating existing contracts, either to reduce monthly costs or to increase the amount and type of services provided.

> **Example:** A shopping mall currently contracts with a janitorial service to clean the public areas of the mall. The mall's administrative offices, however, are cleaned by a separate cleaning service. To reduce expenses, the property manager suggests renegotiating the janitorial contract so that a single company is responsible for cleaning both areas of the mall. He estimates this change will save $5,000 per year.

Finally, the property manager may make suggestions to improve how a property is marketed or managed, such as increasing Internet advertising or changing the building's pet policy.

Physical Changes. Often, a property manager will propose physical changes to the property that are designed to increase, or at least maintain, the property's value. Almost every property is vulnerable to a loss in value (known as **depreciation**) over a period of time. (Depreciation as it refers to taxes will be discussed in Chapter 5.) Two common causes of depreciation are physical deterioration and functional obsolescence. To correct physical deterioration or functional obsolescence, a property manager may suggest physical changes known as rehabilitation and remodeling.

Rehabilitation. Rehabilitation refers to correcting curable physical deterioration. **Physical deterioration** is depreciation caused by wear and tear on (or damage to) a building's physical components. Broken windows, leaky roofs, peeling paint, termite damage, and worn carpeting are all examples of physical deterioration.

Physical deterioration can be curable or incurable. If the cost of correcting the problem is less than the value that would be added by the correction, then it is curable; otherwise, it is incurable. Curable physical deterioration is sometimes referred to as **deferred maintenance**.

> **Example:** Since a fresh coat of paint often adds more to the value of a rental property than the cost of the painting, the need for repainting is usually considered curable physical deterioration. On the other hand, the cost of repairing a cracked foundation may far

exceed any increase in value that would result from the repairs. So the cracked foundation would be considered incurable physical deterioration.

Remodeling. Remodeling (or modernization) attempts to address depreciation caused by design defects. Whether the design is defective from the start or simply becomes outdated over time, the resulting loss in value is called **functional obsolescence**.

> **Example:** Today's commercial tenants want buildings that are wired for high-speed Internet access. Older buildings without this feature have suffered a loss in value due to functional obsolescence.

Like physical deterioration, functional obsolescence is either curable or incurable. The same test applies: if the defect can be remedied at a cost that is less than the resulting increase in value, then it is curable; otherwise, it is incurable.

> **Example:** Inadequate ceiling insulation in a rental house is likely curable functional obsolescence, because additional insulation can be installed at a reasonable cost. A rental house with substandard ceiling heights, on the other hand, probably suffers from incurable functional obsolescence, since it would be prohibitively expensive to increase the height of the walls.

Changes in Use. The highest net operating income and return on the owner's investment is usually achieved when the property is operating at its highest and best use. So

---

 Examples of Functional Obsolescence

Here are some examples of functional obsolescence in residential and commercial/industrial rental properties.

Residential properties:

- A three-bedroom apartment or house with only one bathroom
- An apartment with no washer and dryer hookups in an area where they are common
- Window air conditioning units in an area where central HVAC is common
- An apartment kitchen that isn't plumbed for a dishwasher
- Apartment units without storm windows
- A bedroom that is only accessible by passing through another bedroom

Commercial and industrial properties:

- Loading docks that are too small
- No elevator
- A public restroom that can only accommodate one person at a time (as opposed to one with multiple separate stalls)
- Multi-story warehouse facilities
- A building that isn't wired for modern computer and Internet usage

an analysis of alternatives may suggest a change in the property's use. For instance, the analysis may indicate that the best return on an owner's investment would be achieved by converting an apartment building to condominiums. Although such a change in use may be complicated and expensive, it may be financially justifiable.

Note that while a change in use may involve adapting or converting an existing building (such as turning apartments into condos), it can also involve the demolition of an existing building and the construction of an entirely new one.

The Cost-Benefit Analysis

The changes suggested in an analysis of alternatives always come with costs, of course. The basic tool for evaluating the economic effect of a proposed change is a cost-benefit analysis. A **cost-benefit analysis** is a technique that is used to determine the costs and the benefits of a particular change over a given period of time. Unless the benefit exceeds the cost of the proposed change, the change won't be considered financially justifiable.

Calculating Cost. The first step in a cost-benefit analysis is to calculate the cost of the proposed change, including both tangible and intangible costs.

Tangible costs include labor, materials, shipping costs, and so on. Intangible costs are harder to quantify, but must be included if the cost-benefit analysis is to be a reliable indicator of the true cost of a proposed change. An intangible cost, for example, might be the business lost during the construction phase of a retail property's remodel.

> **Example:** A commercial building houses several retail stores and a restaurant. The building is getting old and its occupancy rate has dropped over the last several years. The property manager estimates that the property's value and occupancy rate can be increased if the building's exterior is remodeled and modernized. Her proposed changes include new walkways, larger and more energy-efficient windows, and new landscaping near the entrance. Tangible costs include the cost of landscaping materials, new windows, and labor. But the property manager must take into account the intangible costs as well, including difficulties in finding tenants for empty space during the construction period, and possibly lower rents because tenants may lose business during construction (assuming that tenants pay a percentage of their income as part of their rent payments).

Calculating Benefit. The next step in the cost-benefit analysis is to calculate the financial benefit that will be gained from the proposed change.

> **Example:** Returning to the previous example, let's say that the suggested improvements (which will be paid for with funds from the owner's reserve account) will cost $100,000. Once they're completed, however, there's a reduction in operating expenses. For instance, replacing the old lobby windows with new, energy-efficient windows will decrease the property's energy costs by $1,200 a year. Also, rents can be raised because the building is more appealing to the tenants' customers. Between the decrease in operating expenses and the increase in rent, the property's net operating income is increased by $10,000 per year. So the return on investment (ROI) will be 10%. ($10,000 NOI increase ÷ $100,000 cost = 10% ROI.)

In our example, the property's NOI will increase by $10,000 annually once the new changes are in place. But this isn't the only benefit to consider when weighing the pros and cons of making the improvements. The manager must also calculate how this increased NOI will increase the property's value.

> **Example:** Returning to the above example once again, let's assume the property has an 8% capitalization rate. The manager can calculate the increase in the property's value like this:
>
> $10,000 Increase in NOI ÷ .08 Cap rate = $125,000 Increase in value – $100,000 Cost of improvement = $25,000 Net increase in value.

(The concepts of return on investment and capitalization rates were discussed in Chapter 2.)

A tax expert should also evaluate any possible tax benefits of the proposed change, such as depreciation deductions. (Depreciation deductions are discussed in Chapter 5.)

Other Factors to Consider. Several other factors must be considered when determining the overall cost versus benefit of a suggested change or improvement. First, as was the case in the previous example, the increase in income generated by an improvement may eventually offset the cost of making the improvement. This period of time over which the cost is recouped is known as the **payback period**.

Knowing the payback period for each change suggested in the analysis of alternatives is important. If one alternative has a payback period of one year, while the other has a payback period of five years, the first alternative will probably be much more attractive to the client.

The property manager must also consider whether the client has sufficient cash available for each alternative. Financing an expenditure instead of paying cash will not only increase the cost of the change (because of the interest on the borrowed money), but will increase the payback period as well.

Preparing and Presenting a Management Plan

Once the manager has completed the preliminary study—the regional analysis, neighborhood analysis, property analysis, market analysis, and analysis of alternatives—she's ready to prepare the management plan for the client. The manager doesn't need to follow any specific format. The management plan may be relatively brief or very detailed, depending on the type of property, the client's goals, how well the property is doing, and how conditions are changing. In this section, we'll take a look at some of the more common components of a management plan.

Components of a Management Plan

While the management plan need not be presented in any particular format, most plans are likely to contain the following components in one form or another:

- executive summary;
- statement of the client's objectives;
- narrative presentation of the regional, neighborhood, and market analyses;

- report on the property's current ("as is") status;
- list of proposed changes and accompanying cost-benefit analyses;
- marketing plan;
- short- and long-term budgets; and
- conclusion and recommendations.

Let's take a look at each of these components.

Executive Summary. The amount of information included in a management plan can overwhelm some clients. Other clients have neither the time nor the desire to read over an entire management plan, especially a long one. So most management plans include an executive summary, which outlines the information contained in the body of the plan and allows the client to quickly see the recommendations and other main points without having to read the entire document.

The executive summary should consist of brief statements that highlight each of the plan's main points; these statements should be in the same order in which the topics appear in the main report. Technical language (such as "Metropolitan Statistical Data") and jargon (for example, using "NOI" for "net operating income") should be avoided. The executive summary should be easily understood by the average reader.

The executive summary doesn't just benefit the client—a well-prepared and thorough executive summary can be a useful blueprint for the property manager to follow when presenting and discussing the management plan with the client.

Statement of Client's Goals. In this section, the property manager sets forth her understanding of the client's goals for the property. The client's goals not only shaped the manager's preliminary analysis, but they also determined the types and amount of information included in the final management plan. A statement of the client's objectives serves to remind the client of the scope of the manager's analysis, including any limitations that the client has imposed.

> **Example:** The owner of a small apartment building wants to increase the property's value. He's willing to invest additional funds, as long as he can recoup his costs through increased rental income within five years. When writing the statement of the client's objectives, the property manager will be sure to include this five-year limitation.

Narrative Presentation of Regional, Neighborhood, and Market Analyses. The property manager has likely compiled a significant amount of statistics during his research. While only a fraction of that data may make its way into the management plan, even that reduced amount can still be difficult for a layperson to understand. So the property manager will use this section to present and summarize the results of the regional, neighborhood, and market analyses in descriptive terms. He explains what information he included, why he included it, and how that information led him to make his final recommendations.

The property manager will also point out and explain any trends he noticed while gathering data. Most clients won't recognize or understand trends simply by looking at numbers and percentages, so the manager needs to convey this information to his client in easy-to-understand terms.

Report on Property's Current Status. It's always helpful for the client to have a thorough understanding of her property's current status before reading about the manager's proposed changes. Information on the property's status is usually divided into two categories: physical condition and management operations.

The description of the property's physical condition should contain enough detail to provide an accurate and realistic picture of the property. For example, the manager might include information about the property's:

- grounds (size, landscaping, etc.);
- common or public areas (lobby, swimming pool, etc.);
- units or rental spaces (size, layout, condition, etc.); and
- physical plant (electrical, plumbing, HVAC systems, maintenance areas, etc.).

The property manager will also describe the current status of management operations, such as details about the property's:

- on-site staff (number of employees, wages);
- rental schedule (for one-bedrooms, two-bedrooms, etc.);
- leasing (occupancy rates, lease expiration dates);
- tenants (average family size, median age, mix of businesses);
- maintenance (types of problems, unresolved issues);
- insurance (types of insurance, status of policies, deductibles); and
- legal compliance issues (disability access, habitability, trust accounts).

A client who doesn't visit the subject property often (or who owns multiple properties) may not be familiar with the property's current status and will appreciate this information. Other clients will already be quite familiar with the information presented in this section; regardless, it serves as a reminder of the data the manager used when making his recommendations.

Proposed Changes and Cost-Benefit Analyses. Depending on the client's goals, the manager may simply recommend updated rental rates and conclude the management plan. However, most property managers will have identified changes that can or should be made to increase income, preserve the property's value, or satisfy insurance or legal requirements. If so, these proposed changes should be discussed in more detail.

First, the property manager should list any recommended physical changes, such as painting the lobby, installing new carpeting, or repaving parking lots, and explain why each change is recommended. Each proposed change should be accompanied by a cost-benefit analysis that details the cost, expected benefit, and payback period.

Next, the property manager will list any proposed operational changes, such as a recommendation to hire additional staff or to change landscaping maintenance contractors. Any recommendation to raise or lower rental rates will also be discussed. Again, for each proposed change, a detailed cost-benefit analysis must be provided.

As we discussed earlier, the cost-benefit analysis for each proposed physical or operational change should indicate how it will impact the property's net operating income, the client's return on investment, and the property's value.

Marketing Plan. If the manager has extensive new ideas for marketing the property, he might decide to present them in a separate section of the management plan. Otherwise, notes about the current marketing plan can be included in the report on the property's current operations, and ideas for minor adjustments can be included in the "proposed changes" section. (Marketing is discussed in greater detail in Chapter 6.)

Short- and Long-Term Budgets. A management plan usually includes a one-year projected **operating budget**, estimating the property's income and expenses for the coming year on a month-by-month basis. This budget is generally based on the property in its current condition, but it should reflect any proposed change in rental rates.

Any proposed changes in income or expenses (such as hiring additional staff or installing vending machines) should be discussed in the proposed changes section. If the client approves any of these changes, the property manager will update the operating budget accordingly. (See Chapter 5 for how to prepare an operating budget.)

The management plan may also include a long-range budget, showing predicted changes in income and expenses over a specified number of years. A five-year long-range budget is common, but any period may be used depending on the client's goals and the type of property. A long-range budget is especially appropriate when the client is making a major investment in property or when the property manager has proposed a significant change in operations.

Finally, the management plan may include a **capital budget** for reserve funds used to replace equipment or make improvements. (As we discussed earlier, the amount of reserves will be included in the operating budget as an expense.) The capital budget details how these reserves will be spent. To determine whether current reserves are adequate, the manager must estimate the cost of anticipated future replacements and improvements. She then divides that cost by the number of months before the expenditures will be made to find the monthly amount needed for reserves.

> **Example:** A property manager estimates that the building's HVAC system will need to be replaced in three years and will cost $20,000. The amount that must be set aside each month in the reserve fund is approximately $556.
>
> $$\$20,000 \div 36 \text{ Months} = \$556 \text{ Per month}$$

When calculating this amount, the manager should take into account the interest that will accrue on the funds over time. However, the property manager must also allow for inflation. If the accumulating interest cannot keep up with the rate of inflation, the reserve funds won't be enough to pay for the improvement.

Conclusion and Recommendations. The last section of the management plan is a conclusion summarizing the property manager's recommendations. The manager should state plainly what she thinks should be done to meet the client's goals, making sure to distinguish essential changes from those she believes to be optional. If there's more than one way to achieve the client's goals, the manager should indicate which option she prefers, and why.

Making the Plan Professional

Some management plans will consist of only a few pages; others will be hundreds of pages long. Regardless of its length, the plan should appear organized and thorough. A professional-looking management plan may convince a new client that the property manager is a skilled professional whose judgment can be trusted. On the other hand, typos, trivial discrepancies, and a general lack of attention to detail may cause the client to doubt the property manager's competence.

It's always a good idea to have someone else proofread the plan before it's presented to the client. The manager may also want to ask a trusted layperson to look over the executive summary to make sure that it's free of jargon and understandable to someone outside the property management business.

Simple organization can go a long way toward making the management plan look more professional. For instance, the property manager may want to present the management plan in a binder that includes:

- a title page that identifies the property, the owner, and the manager;
- the **letter of transmittal** (a cover letter from the manager to the client, presenting the report);
- a table of contents;
- photos and/or maps of the neighborhood and property that illustrate points made in the report; and
- appendices, such as charts showing regional, neighborhood, or market data, or a list of sources where such data was found.

Once all this information has been gathered in a neat, organized, professional format, it's time to present the management plan to the client.

Presenting the Management Plan

Ideally, the property manager will review the most important elements of the management plan with the client in person. This is especially true if the plan is long or complicated, or if it includes a number of major proposed changes that require additional explanation. Whether the management plan is long and complicated, or fairly simple and short, the manager should at least be sure to point out the executive summary and the conclusion.

Once presented with the management plan, the client has several options. The client may:

- approve the manager's proposal as presented, authorizing all suggested changes and expenditures;
- authorize only the expenditures that are necessary to preserve the property's value (i.e., to address deferred maintenance);
- decide against making any immediate changes to the property or operations;

- ask the property manager to make changes to his proposal and to resubmit the updated plan for consideration; or
- decide not to hire the property manager.

The property manager may want to revise the management plan if some of the client's goals were clarified during the presentation, or if the client had questions about additional options that weren't included in the original analysis. Of course, the property manager may decide against taking the time or expense to make changes to the management plan, especially if the prospective client seems difficult or unlikely to accept realistic suggestions. And if the client wants to hire the manager but refuses to consider important suggestions, the property manager must decide whether working with the client on those terms will be acceptable.

Ongoing Management Planning

For the most part, this chapter has discussed management planning from the point of view of a property manager working to win the business of a new client. It's important to remember, however, that management planning is a process that continues even after the manager has been hired.

As we noted earlier, the property manager must keep his regional, neighborhood, and market analyses updated with current information. Updating data should take place at least annually, or more frequently in a particularly volatile market. As that information is updated, the manager may want to revisit the management plan to account for those changes. At the very least, the manager should reconsider the management plan annually, and be prepared to make further recommendations to the client as needed.

Over time, it's also likely that the client will make requests that weren't accounted for in the original management plan. For instance, a residential property owner may decide that he'd like to put in a swimming pool, or a commercial property owner may decide that she'd like to reconfigure the space to attract doctors instead of retail stores. When those requests are made, the property manager can (and probably should) use a management plan to analyze the proposed changes in light of the market and the client's new goals.

Chapter Summary

1. A management plan is a property manager's strategy for the physical and financial management of a property. A property manager may prepare a management plan for a prospective client or to educate a current client about the feasibility of proposed physical or operational changes to the property.

2. Before preparing the management plan, the property manager performs a preliminary study consisting of a regional analysis, a neighborhood analysis, a property analysis, a market analysis, and an analysis of alternatives. During the preliminary study, the property manager gathers and analyzes the data, looking for trends.

3. In a regional analysis, the property manager analyzes the economic and demographic conditions that affect the supply of and demand for property in the metropolitan statistical area (MSA) where the subject property is located.

4. A neighborhood analysis is similar to a regional analysis but focuses on the area immediately surrounding the subject property. Neighborhood boundaries are determined by natural barriers (such as rivers) and artificial barriers (such as major roads, or economic or ethnic divisions). The property manager will look at land use and zoning, property types and values, rental and vacancy rates, local demographics, and whether the neighborhood is in a period of decline, stability, or growth.

5. In the property analysis, the manager gathers information about the subject property's current condition. This includes data on physical attributes, general attractiveness and condition, management and leasing, and the financial condition.

6. Information gathered in the regional, neighborhood, and property analyses will be used to perform the market analysis, which compares the subject property to competing properties. By comparing size and type of units or spaces, amenities, and so on, the property manager can set rental rates for the subject property that will strike a balance between maximizing rent and minimizing the vacancy rate.

7. In the analysis of alternatives, the property manager evaluates possible operational and physical changes that would increase the property's net operating income, preserve the property's value, or comply with insurance or legal requirements. Changes may be recommended to address deferred maintenance or to cure functional obsolescence. For each proposed change, the property manager must perform a cost-benefit analysis and calculate a payback period.

8. While there is no set formula for a property management plan, typical components include an executive summary, a statement of the client's objectives, a narrative report of the preliminary study, a list of proposed changes, short- and long-term budgets, and a concise summary of recommendations. The final plan should be well-organized and presented in a professional manner.

Key Terms

Management plan – A property manager's strategy for the physical and financial management of a property.

Highest and best use – The most profitable use a property can be put to, given legal, economic, and physical limitations.

Preliminary study – The process of research and analysis used by a property manager to determine a property's current status and future prospects.

Regional analysis – A preliminary study that focuses on the general economic and demographic conditions that affect the supply of and demand for property in the general area where the subject property is located.

Demographics – Characteristics of a human population, such as average family size, median age, and household income.

Metropolitan statistical area (MSA) – An area, along with adjacent territory, with at least one urbanized population center of 50,000 or more and a high degree of social and economic conformity.

Micropolitan statistical area – An area, along with adjacent territory, with at least one urban population cluster of at least 10,000 but less than 50,000 and a high degree of social and economic conformity.

Neighborhood – A geographic area in which the residents share common characteristics or the properties share a similar land use.

Zoning – Ordinances that divide a community into areas set aside for specific types of land use, such as agricultural, residential, commercial, or industrial.

Impact fees – An upfront fee charged to developers to help offset the cost of additional public services required by a new development.

Curb appeal – The overall condition and appearance of an area or property.

Debt service – The monthly or yearly amount required to pay interest and principal on an outstanding debt.

Market analysis – An evaluation of how the subject property compares to competing properties.

Submarket – In a market analysis, a smaller segment (such as luxury high-rise rental units) of the larger relevant market (such as apartment buildings).

Rental schedule – A list of the rental rates assigned to the different types of units or spaces in a property.

Analysis of alternatives – The process of evaluating possible operational or physical changes that are intended to increase a property's income, preserve the property's value, or comply with legal or insurance requirements.

Deferred maintenance – A curable (fixable) loss of value due to wear and tear or damage to the building.

Functional obsolescence – A loss of value due to design defects or outdated elements.

Cost-benefit analysis – A technique used to analyze the costs and benefits, over a given period of time, of a physical or operational change to a property.

Payback period – The period of time it takes to offset the cost of an improvement.

Operating budget – A budget that estimates a property's income and expenses for the coming year on a month-by-month basis.

Capital budget – A budget showing how reserve funds will be used to replace equipment or make improvements over time.

Letter of transmittal – A cover letter for a management plan, from the property manager to the client.

Chapter Quiz

1. A management plan may be used to:
   a) persuade a prospective client to hire the property manager
   b) educate the client about the property's overall condition
   c) analyze the feasibility of the client's goals for the property
   d) All of the above

2. The characteristics of a human population, such as average family size, are known as:
   a) social profiling
   b) demographics
   c) sociographics
   d) regional analysis

3. The U.S. Census is conducted once every:
   a) year
   b) two years (in odd-numbered years)
   c) two years (in even-numbered years)
   d) ten years

4. A subject property is located in an area of apartment buildings and single-family homes that is known as "Little Saigon." The area consists of six square blocks, bordered on one side by a river, and on the other by a major road. This area would most likely be referred to as the subject property's:
   a) region
   b) neighborhood
   c) submarket
   d) metropolitan statistical area

5. A property manager performing a neighborhood analysis will be concerned with all of the following except:
   a) local property values
   b) local vacancy rates
   c) transportation
   d) outdated appliances in the subject property's rental units

6. Jim is performing a market analysis for a commercial building designed to house a half-dozen small retail stores. The most relevant submarket for comparables will include:
   a) all rental buildings, including apartment buildings
   b) all commercial rental space, including enclosed malls and office buildings
   c) commercial buildings designed for a similar size and number of retail tenants
   d) all commercial buildings within one mile

7. A property manager has a list showing that one-bedroom units in the subject property rent for $650 a month, while two-bedroom units in the subject property rent for $800 a month. This list is known as the:
   a) rental schedule
   b) occupancy rate
   c) rental income ratio
   d) net operating income

8. A rental property needs new paint and new carpeting. These issues are examples of:
   a) functional obsolescence
   b) deferred maintenance
   c) planned obsolescence
   d) capital improvements

9. A commercial rental property is an older building without air conditioning. As a result, retail tenants must use fans and open windows during warm summer months. This is an example of:
   a) functional obsolescence
   b) deferred maintenance
   c) planned obsolescence
   d) capital improvements

10. Sally is preparing a management plan for a prospective client. Comparable properties all have swimming pools, while the subject property does not. When suggesting that the client install a swimming pool to be competitive, Sally should provide a/an:

    a) list of companies that install swimming pools
    b) cost-benefit analysis
    c) impact sheet
    d) amenities survey

11. An apartment building has washers and dryers in the basement that all tenants must share. The property manager estimates that rents can be increased by $50 a month if the client modernizes each unit so that it can accommodate private washers and dryers. It will take five years for the increased rent to offset the cost of this change. That five-year period is known as the:

    a) revitalization period
    b) rehabilitation period
    c) payback period
    d) capital recovery period

12. An estimate of a property's income and expenses for the coming year is known as a/an:

    a) capital budget
    b) long-range budget
    c) operating budget
    d) cost-benefit analysis

13. To determine how much should be set aside each month to create a reserve fund, a property manager should:

    a) multiply the net income by 5%
    b) estimate the cost of the improvements, then divide by the number of months until the improvements will be needed
    c) estimate the cost of the improvements, then divide by the number of tenants
    d) estimate the cost of the improvements, then set aside 5% of that amount each month

14. The management plan will likely include which of the following components?

    a) Executive summary
    b) Marketing plan
    c) Narrative report of regional trends
    d) All of the above

15. The optimum rent for a rental unit results in:

    a) a vacancy rate of 0%
    b) a vacancy rate of less than 5%
    c) the highest rent possible
    d) a balance between maximizing income and minimizing vacancies

Answer Key

1. d)   Although a management plan is most commonly used to convince a prospective client to hire the property manager, it can also be used to educate the client about the property's current condition and to analyze the feasibility of the client's ideas for the property.

2. b)   Demographics refers to the characteristics of a human population, such as average family size, median age, and so on. Demographic information is used when conducting a regional analysis, but a regional analysis includes many other types of data (such as transportation and government issues) as well.

3. d)   The U.S. Census, taken once every ten years, compiles information on population and housing in the United States.

4. b)   A neighborhood is a geographic area in which the people share common characteristics or the properties share a similar land use. Neighborhoods may be bordered by natural boundaries, such as rivers, or by artificial boundaries, such as roads.

5. d)   A property manager performing a neighborhood analysis will be concerned with local property values and vacancy rates, as well as transportation in the area. Information about the subject property's current condition (such as its appliances) will be gathered and analyzed in the property analysis, not the neighborhood analysis.

6. c)   A submarket is made up of buildings and rental units of a similar size and character to the subject property. Other types of properties, even if they are rental properties, are not comparables and will not provide reliable information for the market analysis.

7. a)   A rental schedule is a list of the rental rates assigned to the different types of rental units.

8. b)   Physical deterioration is a loss of value caused by wear and tear or physical damage to the property. When the deterioration can be cured (fixed), it's known as deferred maintenance.

9. a)   Functional obsolescence is a loss of value caused by design defects, such as an apartment building with outdated appliances, or a commercial retail property without central air conditioning.

10. b)   Each change suggested in the analysis of alternatives should always be accompanied by a cost-benefit analysis, which analyzes the costs and benefits of the proposed change. The change cannot be justified unless the short- or long-term benefit exceeds the cost of the change.

11. c)   The payback period is the time it will take for increased income generated from an improvement to offset the cost of that improvement.

12. c)   The operating budget estimates the property's income and expenses for the coming year on a month-by-month basis.

13. b) To budget for capital improvements and repairs, the property manager should first estimate the total cost, then divide that cost by the number of months before the improvement or repair will be necessary. The resulting figure should be set aside each month in the reserve fund.

14. d) Management plans need not follow any particular format, but most plans include an executive summary, a statement of the client's objectives, a narrative presentation of regional or neighborhood trends, proposed changes, short- and long-term budgets, a proposed marketing plan, and a conclusion.

15. d) The ideal rental rate will result in a balance between maximizing income and minimizing vacancy rates. A vacancy rate that's too low may indicate that the rental units are underpriced. On the other hand, if the rental rates are too high and not supported by the market, vacancy rates may be too high.

Chapter 5

Financial Aspects of Property Management

Outline

Introduction

As a property manager, you don't need to have an accounting degree or be a tax expert. However, you will need fundamental accounting and budgeting skills, along with a basic understanding of the income tax ramifications of real estate ownership. We'll begin this chapter with a discussion of accounting, trust fund handling, and property management bank accounts. Next, we'll look at income and expenses, cash flow, and preparing a budget. We'll discuss creating monthly, quarterly, and annual financial reports for the client. Finally, we'll examine how income from investment property is taxed, and common tax deductions that property owners may take.

Accounting

Accounting refers to keeping records of financial transactions (bookkeeping) and preparing reports based on those records. It's crucial for a property manager to keep accurate records of all the financial transactions that take place while managing each property in her portfolio.

There are several reasons why the manager should keep financial records. For starters, accounting is a fiduciary duty that every agent owes to her principal. In addition, the license laws in almost all states impose recordkeeping and accounting requirements on property managers. Not only do most management agreements establish a contractual duty to keep good records, but property owners need accurate records for income tax purposes. Finally, detailed records help the owner and manager evaluate whether the property is generating the net income that it should.

Accounting Methods

There are three basic accounting methods to choose from. Usually, the property manager will select his accounting method based on the advice of an accountant. The three choices are:

- **Cash-basis accounting.** Income is recorded when received; expenses are recorded when paid.
- **Accrual-basis accounting.** Income is recorded when due; expenses are recorded when incurred.
- **Modified cash-basis accounting.** Expenses that are not due monthly (such as annual insurance premiums or property taxes) are accounted for as they accrue (for example, each month would show $1/12$ of an annual insurance premium). However, income is recorded only when received.

The straightforward quality of the cash-basis system appeals to some property managers, especially those who manage small or even medium-sized properties. However, the accrual system is generally preferred. It is almost certainly the better choice for owners who require monthly reports. With the cash system, monthly income or expenses may differ significantly from one month to the next.

Example: Suppose that in February, a large annual bill comes due. If February's statement is prepared using the cash-basis method, the owner may think that something unusually bad has happened, when in fact the business is proceeding normally.

On the other hand, if a number of tenants fail to pay their rent in February, the accrual-basis method may imply that more cash is on hand than there actually is. Since the modified-cash method records income only when it is received, but also balances non-monthly bills over the course of the year, this hybrid method strikes many managers and owners as the best choice.

Whatever system is used—cash, accrual, or modified-cash—the method must be applied consistently over time and throughout the bookkeeping system. An owner who wants to change to a new accounting method must obtain approval from the IRS.

Accounting Software

Most property managers use computer software to handle their accounting needs. Managers of smaller properties may use general business software, such as a spreadsheet program like Excel. However, applications specifically designed to meet property management needs may prove to be more satisfactory.

Property management software can generate:

- monthly, quarterly, and annual reports;
- Schedule E for tax reporting;
- categories and subcategories for expenses;
- running totals of income and expenses;
- bank records;
- payroll and inventory records; and
- purchase orders and maintenance records.

This more sophisticated software may also offer email integration (for handling communications with clients, vendors, and tenants), image attachments (photos from move-in/move-out inspections, scanned driver's licenses, and tenant applications), automatic vacancy

 Software Costs

At one time, the cost of property management-specific programs placed these tools outside the reach of many smaller businesses, but recently costs have come down dramatically. Some good programs are available in the neighborhood of $100 to $200. And a few programs are even free, at least for owners of a small number of units.

Some software developers, generally those who offer online (cloud-based) programs, don't sell their software outright, but instead charge a monthly fee based on the number of units (for example, $20 a month for 30 units or less).

posting to craigslist or other websites, bank account integration (including statement reconciliation), and integration with online rent payments by tenants.

No matter what software is used, both onsite and offsite backup is critical. Property management software is increasingly web-based, which can simplify backups. Web-based products may also be easier in terms of software updating and maintenance.

Trust Funds and Bank Accounts

All of the money that a property manager holds or handles on behalf of a client, such as tenant rent payments, security deposits, or reserve funds, is considered **trust funds** and must be treated as such. Thus, under the laws of most states, client funds may not be **commingled** (mixed together) with the property manager's own funds—either with his business or personal funds.

The property manager is liable for any loss caused by the misappropriation of client funds by an employee. One way the manager can address this danger is by purchasing fidelity bonds on her employees; fidelity bonds are usually purchased from an insurance company. We discuss bonding more fully in Chapter 15.

Typically, state law requires trust funds to be held in a bank account that must be labeled as a trust account. Segregating funds into a special trust account makes it harder for a manager to convert a client's funds to his own use, either deliberately or accidentally. (Conversion is another term for misappropriation.) Also, if a client's funds were not kept in a separate account, they could be frozen or claimed by the manager's or owner's creditors.

Many property management firms keep client funds in a **pooled trust account**, to avoid the expense and awkwardness of numerous separate bank accounts.

> **Example:** Jim manages several small office buildings owned by different owners. His state's real estate license law allows property managers to deposit trust funds (mainly tenant rents and security deposits) from all the management company's clients into a single (pooled) trust account. Individual trust accounts for each property owner aren't required.
>
> Property management accounting software allows Jim to keep track of how much each client, and each tenant, has in the pooled account.

Trust Account Requirements

State license laws typically include detailed requirements for trust accounts. For starters, state law might require a trust account to be opened in the property manager's name as it appears on his license, in a recognized financial institution in the state where the manager is doing business.

If the license law allows interest-bearing trust accounts, there are usually rules as to who receives the interest. In many states, the interest belongs to the owner, not the manager, unless the management agreement says otherwise.

License laws usually include rules concerning the payment of bank service charges for trust accounts. In some states, the manager may keep a limited amount of her own money in a trust account to cover the service charges. In other states, this is prohibited; the manager must arrange for trust account service charges to be withdrawn from his general account.

State laws generally require the property manager to deposit trust funds soon after they come into the manager's possession. For example, some states require trust funds to be deposited into a trust account by the next business day after receipt; other states allow a 48- or 72-hour time frame. A manager must know the trust account rules in her state, and stay apprised of any changes in the law. Trust account infractions are one of the most common reasons for disciplinary action.

Trust Account Categories

Managers who handle income-producing property typically maintain three different trust accounts:

- an operating account,
- a reserve fund account, and
- a security deposit account.

Each month, the manager should reconcile the bank statement for each account with her own records of account deposits and withdrawals. As mentioned, property management software can help with this task. The manager should address any discrepancies immediately. Many managers may be tempted to postpone reconciliations, but that procrastination could result in disciplinary action if the manager is audited.

Operating Account. The operating account is a simple (generally non-interest-bearing) checking account for ordinary receipts and expenditures. The manager deposits the property's rents and other income into the account, and pays the operating expenses out of the account.

Reserve Fund Account. The reserve fund account is used to accumulate funds that will be used to pay for capital expenditures such as a roof replacement. These funds are called **reserves**. The manager may be authorized to make regular deposits into the reserve fund from the operating account, or she may get money directly from the owner. The reserve fund account is usually an interest-bearing checking or money market account. The amount of funds in a reserve account may be substantial, so naturally the owner will want the best interest rate possible.

A property manager may also use the reserve fund account to accumulate funds for operating expenses that are paid annually or semi-annually, such as property taxes and insurance premiums. By allocating money each month for these expenses, the monthly financial report will give a truer picture of the property's bottom line (in cases where modified cash-basis accounting isn't being used). Also, these operating funds can earn a reasonable interest rate in the reserve account.

Note that institutional owners, such as insurance companies, might not make contributions to a reserve account. This is because the typical institutional owner already has sufficient assets on hand to pay for any major expenses that arise. It's also likely that this kind of owner would want to handle its own reserve funds, rather than having a property manager do so.

Security Deposit Accounts. Almost all owners and managers require their tenants—both residential and commercial—to provide a security deposit at the beginning of the tenancy. Generally, state laws require landlords to put tenant security deposits into a trust account.

In some states, the law requires residential landlords to pay their tenants interest on the security deposits. A few states and municipalities even specify the interest rate. On the other hand, some states have no requirements at all concerning interest on deposits. If the owner isn't required by law to pay interest to the tenants, then the accruing interest can be a modest additional source of operating income for the property.

Deposit Insurance

All bank accounts used for client funds should be federally insured. Indeed, the license law as well as the property management agreement may require this.

Currently, the Federal Deposit Insurance Corporation (FDIC) insures all funds in non-interest-bearing checking accounts, with no limitations. Thus, FDIC insurance would apply to all the funds in the typical operating account, which is usually a simple checking account. (This unlimited coverage rule is set to expire at the end of 2012, although there is a good chance the law will be extended.)

On the other hand, trust accounts for reserves and security deposits are often deposited into interest-bearing accounts; coverage limits do apply. The FDIC will insure up to $250,000 in an interest-bearing checking account.

What about insurance coverage on a pooled checking account when the total amount of funds exceeds $250,000? (Remember, a pooled account contains the funds of more than one client.) According to an opinion letter issued by the FDIC:

> When an agent holds funds owned by more than one principal in a single deposit account [such as a pooled trust account], the ownership interest of each principal in the commingled account would be added to any other funds held in an individual capacity by that person at the same bank.

In other words, each principal (each client/owner) is insured for up to $250,000, regardless of the total amount deposited in the account. However, if one property owner happens to have her own account at the same bank as the pooled account, all of the owner's funds in that individual account will be counted along with her funds in the pooled account; the FDIC $250,000 insurance limit will apply to the total of those funds. Thus, the percentage of an owner's deposits that are insured may be less than either she or her manager supposes. Given the number of bank mergers over the last few years, this may be a more common problem than it would appear. To get the full $250,000 coverage on the trust funds, the property owner may need to transfer her personal funds to a different financial institution.

The FDIC imposes one additional requirement before a property owner can claim insurance coverage on funds that were deposited into the manager's account. The name on the manager's account must indicate that the funds are held on behalf of another—that is, in a fiduciary capacity. The name of the account, pooled or not, should include the word "trust" or "escrow" or something similar (for example, "Applebaum Property Management, LLC Trust Account").

Gross Income and Operating Expenses

Before we can address planning and tax issues, we need to lay a foundation by discussing two fundamental financial concepts important to managing income property: gross income and operating expenses. A firm grasp of these concepts is key to making a property profitable.

Gross Income

There are two sources of income for a typical investment property: rental payments and miscellaneous fees. Residential properties may generate significant miscellaneous income. Fees can be collected for:

- cable TV and Internet,
- parking,
- tenant storage units,
- special tenant services (such as carpet or window cleaning),
- coin-operated washers and dryers,
- vending machines and ATMs,
- utility charges paid by tenants, and
- interest on tenant security deposits (in some states).

Office and retail properties may also receive income from at least a few of these sources. Office, retail, and industrial properties sometimes generate additional income by charging tenants for extra services, such as security and grounds maintenance.

All miscellaneous income is added to the rental income to arrive at the property's **gross income**. Gross income is the amount of money earned by the property before the operating expenses have been paid.

Operating Expenses

Operating expenses include all of the costs of maintaining, operating, and managing the property. Operating expenses do not include debt service (principal and interest payments on any mortgages), nor the income tax that the owner must pay on income from the property.

As we'll see later, capital expenditures (expenditures that increase the property's value or prolong its useful life) are not operating expenses. We will discuss capital expenditures in more detail later in the chapter.

Controlling operating expenses is one of a property manager's chief tasks. One way of measuring how well a property is managed is to calculate the percentage of gross income that is represented by the operating expenses. This is called the **operating expense ratio**. The formula for determining the operating expense ratio is:

Operating expenses ÷ Gross income = Operating expense ratio

Example: Last year, a six-unit apartment building earned $64,000 of rental income, plus $1,000 of other income, for a total gross income of $65,000. The year's operating expenses were $26,400. Taking the operating expense of $26,400 and dividing it by the gross income of $65,000 yields the number .406 or approximately 41%. In other words, about 41% of the property's gross income was spent on operations.

Operating Expense Ratios

An owner or a manager can compare the operating expense ratio (OER) of his property to that of similar properties to get a sense of how well his property is managed. It's important to compare only similar properties, however. There's not much point in comparing the OER of a newer building with that of an older building. Older buildings generally require more maintenance and cost more to heat and cool, making operating expenses higher. (Note that the price of older buildings should be lower to reflect the higher operating expenses, all other factors being equal.)

What are some typical OERs? The OER for a residential apartment building commonly ranges from the low- to mid-40s. According to a National Apartment Association survey, a newer building might have an OER of 40%, while 46% is more typical for buildings over 20 years old. Office space isn't vastly different. A 2010 Institute of Real Estate Management survey found a median OER of 46% for downtown office properties and 43% for suburban office properties.

Fixed vs. Variable Expenses. A property manager has little or no control over some operating expenses (such as property taxes) but, for other expenses, careful management can make a big difference.

A distinction is sometimes drawn between fixed and variable operating expenses. **Fixed expenses**, like insurance premiums, occur at regular intervals and do not go up or down throughout the year in response to the occupancy rate. **Variable expenses**, like maintenance expenses, tend to vary with the occupancy rate and/or may not occur every year.

The distinction between fixed and variable expenses is important. Suppose a manager would like to increase occupancy rates by lowering the rental rate. Deciding whether this is a good idea requires more than merely multiplying the lower rent by a higher number of occupied units. Variable costs will rise, while fixed costs generally won't. Dividing expenses into these two categories will make the profitability analysis easier and more accurate.

A property manager shouldn't assume that a particular type of expense is always fixed or always variable. For example, an employee's pay may be fixed if he is on salary, but variable if he is part-time and paid on an hourly basis. Some variable expenses, such as maintenance costs for computers, phones, and photocopiers, can be converted into fixed expenses by purchasing service contracts.

Managers often try to reduce expenses by contracting out certain services. For instance, instead of hiring a security staff, it may be cheaper to use a security firm. This could reduce salaries, decrease management time, and even lower the building's insurance premiums. Of course, each situation is different, but property managers should be aware that a little creativity can help reduce "fixed" expenses.

Operating Expense Categories

Every property manager assigns operating expenses to slightly different categories and subcategories. There is no right or wrong way to do this, as long as the categories are clear to the property owner—the important thing is to use the chosen categories consistently. For example, the same categories and subcategories used to log expenses should also be used when creating budgets.

It's also a good idea to pay attention to how many categories and subcategories are used. Too many categories can make it difficult to focus on the bigger picture, but two few categories can obscure important details.

> **Example:** Jeanette owns 35 rental houses. She purchased washers and dryers for all of her properties instead of leasing them from a laundry servicing company. Recently, the dryers have started requiring repairs at a much higher rate than the washing machines.
>
> Jeanette's property manager puts all the laundry repairs into one expense category called Laundry Machines. This could mask the problem Jeanette is having with her dryers, and it might be useful to break down this repair item into two subcategories, one for Dryers and one for Washing Machines. This amount of detail would probably be useful for the property manager; however, including these two subcategories in the owner's financial reports might create too much clutter.

Now that we've discussed operating expenses generally, let's look at the main categories of expenses.

Property Taxes. Property taxes include both general real estate taxes and special assessments. As the example in Figure 5.1 suggests, property taxes can be a property's largest operating expense. This is especially true if a sizeable special assessment is levied during the year.

Figure 5.1 Pie chart showing expenses for an eight-unit apartment building

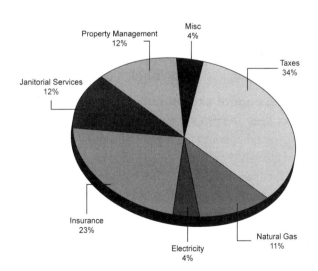

General real estate taxes. State and local taxing authorities levy general real estate taxes each year, based on the value of the property. General real estate taxes are usually the main source of revenue for funding public services.

Typically, general property taxes are paid in two installments, one at the beginning of the year and one in mid-summer or fall. As noted earlier, a manager may "pay" property taxes on a monthly basis by accumulating the prorated amounts in the reserve fund trust account.

Special assessments. Special assessments are taxes levied to pay for a particular public improvement project that will benefit the assessed property but not all the properties in the tax district. For example, special assessments might be used to pay for street and sidewalk improvements or the addition of a neighborhood park. Special assessment taxes can often be paid in installments. As with general real estate taxes, a manager may budget for a special assessment on a monthly basis.

Insurance. Insurance is another significant operating cost. The two main kinds of coverage are hazard insurance (which covers losses resulting from damage to the property itself) and liability insurance (which covers losses resulting from personal injuries that occur on the property).

Premiums are usually charged annually, but may be paid in monthly, quarterly, or semiannual installments. Again, the manager may budget for these on a monthly basis.

Insurance is discussed in more detail in Chapter 15.

Utilities. Utilities include electricity, gas, heating oil, water and sewer, and garbage and recycling removal. Internet and cable may be an expense item in some situations. The cost of these utilities will differ widely by region, and sometimes by season as well.

Commercial tenants and tenants of single-family houses usually pay at least some utilities directly. The same is often true for apartment tenants if there are submeters for each of the units. Even in apartment buildings without submeters, the expense of a given utility is often passed on to tenants via pro rata or flat-rate shares of the building's bill.

Maintenance. Maintenance costs usually include groundskeeping expenses, as well as the cost of maintaining the building—the labor, materials, and supplies needed for cleaning, upkeep, and repairs. We'll look at maintenance in detail in Chapter 9.

Ordinary repairs vs. capital expenditures. The costs of **ordinary repairs** (corrective maintenance) that keep the property in good operating condition are considered **operating expenses**. On the other hand, if a repair adds long-lasting value to the property, it's generally considered a **capital expenditure**. For example, replacing a leaking roof or an old furnace is a capital expenditure.

As we'll discuss at the end of the chapter, ordinary repair expenses and capital expenditures are treated quite differently for income tax purposes. They're also handled differently in the budgeting process, a topic we'll get to shortly. For now, it's enough to understand that unlike ordinary repair expenses, capital expenditures are not considered operating expenses.

Other Expenses. Here are some other common expense items:

- security (equipment and services);
- marketing;
- miscellaneous supplies (such as office supplies);
- miscellaneous services (such as key-making);
- legal costs (such as attorney's fees); and
- management fees and the owner's own administrative costs.

Net Operating Income

Now that we've explained gross income and looked at operating expenses, we have the elements we need to calculate a property's **net operating income** (NOI). The formula for calculating this key figure is shown here.

Gross income – Operating expenses = Net operating income

For most owners and managers, NOI is the basic monetary measure of success. This is because it can be used to measure the owner's return on investment. The **return on investment** (ROI) is essentially the "interest rate" paid on the money that the owner has invested in the income-producing property. The formula for calculating the ROI is:

NOI ÷ Capital invested = ROI

Example: Featherton has invested $50,000 into an investment property that is generating a net operating income of $5,000 per year. This means she is getting a return of 10% per year on her investment.

$5,000 ÷ $50,000 = 10% ROI

The NOI figure has a second use, as well. As we explained in Chapter 2, appraisers can estimate a property's value using net operating income (NOI ÷ Capitalization Rate = Value).

A property's ROI and value are primarily the property owner's concern. Here, we are going to focus on what the NOI means to the property manager. Net operating income is essentially the property's useful income—its bottom line—and a manager is usually working to increase this figure.

How can a manager increase net operating income? The short, obvious answer is by increasing gross income and/or by decreasing expenses. Let's turn our attention to how these financial goals might be accomplished. (Keep in mind that small fiscal changes can add up over the course of a year.)

Increasing Gross Income

There are many ways to go about enhancing revenue. The basic methods of generating more income involve increasing:

- rent,
- occupancy,

- the collections rate,
- leasable space, or
- miscellaneous fees.

Note that we discuss revenue enhancement in more detail in the chapters that deal with specific types of property.

Raising Rents. A manager should exercise caution when considering rent increases. The rents charged by comparable properties will necessarily limit the size of any rent increase. And even raising rents to the highest competitive level could discourage tenants from remaining in the property over the long term. (Long-term tenants are desirable because they keep lease renewal expenses low.)

However, if the premises are improved in some way, the manager may be more successful in raising rents. For instance, shopping center signage, awnings, and other exterior elements could be modernized. The plumbing fixtures, appliances, or window treatments in vacant residential units could be updated. New, inexpensive services could be offered, such as signing for and holding packages for later pickup. These types of improvements help distinguish the property from the competition and make it more attractive to tenants.

Of course, making expensive improvements, such as adding an exercise room or other recreational facility, would also make a property more attractive. However, this kind of improvement must be analyzed carefully, to avoid overstepping the owner's budget or overimproving the property.

Improving Occupancy Rates. The most obvious way to increase occupancy is to lower rental rates. Of course, this could have the effect of decreasing the net operating income. Nonetheless, a modest decrease in rent may pay off overall if it causes a significant increase in occupancy. But be careful: the type of tenants attracted by the lower rates may be less economically viable in the long run. Offering free rent for a month or two may be a better option than lowering the monthly rate.

The manager can also improve occupancy rates by improving tenant satisfaction. Prompt, courteous responses to tenant complaints generally translate into happier tenants. Happier tenants tend to stay longer, and are also likely to provide good referrals.

Increasing Rent Collections. It is often difficult to achieve both increased rent and increased occupancy rates. However, increasing rent collections is nearly always possible, regardless of what other steps are taken to increase income. Reducing instances of overdue or unpaid rent is always worthwhile. Late notices should be sent promptly (the first day rent is overdue), and the manager should personally contact the tenant right away. Notices to tenants don't have to be hostile or cold, but they should strike a firm tone.

Sometimes managers are reluctant to pursue collections or evictions. However, while a nonpaying tenant may give a comforting illusion of occupancy, he also drives up management costs and sometimes even damages the property. Further, he takes up space that a paying tenant could be occupying.

One way to increase rent collections is to screen potential tenants very carefully. Are there any red flags that might indicate potential payment problems? Would using a screening company work better than in-house screening? We will revisit the topic of leasing practices in Chapter 7.

Adding Leasable Space. While it may seem impossible to generate additional leasable space, managers should pause to consider whether they are using leasable space for their own office or storage needs. If so, that space might be converted into storage space that could be rented out, or even converted into another small unit.

In a shopping center, the manager can add leasable space by installing kiosks. She can also sell advertising space in corridors or other public areas. A manager can upgrade vacant warehouse space by adding utilities and some finish work to create inexpensive retail or office space.

Increasing Miscellaneous Revenue Sources. Managers should keep an eye on what fees comparable properties charge for various tenant services such as storage, parking, cable, or security. Perhaps current rates for these services could be raised, or the manager could begin charging for services that were previously offered for free. Adding services, such as a health club or meeting space, can pay off. Significant improvements could increase the property's tax assessment or insurance costs, however, which must be weighed against the increase in income.

Finally, the manager could raise late fees and other similar charges. Increased late fees mean that either tenants pay more promptly or higher fees are collected—a positive result either way.

Decreasing Expenses

Another way to increase NOI is by decreasing expenses. Aside from salaries (if there are any), typically the three biggest categories of operating expenses are property taxes, insurance, and utilities. We'll take a quick look at ways to reduce each of these items.

Property Taxes. It's possible to reduce a tax bill by appealing the assessment. This is generally more successful during a recession, when property values are declining. However, some property owners appeal their tax bill every year as a matter of course.

Insurance. The property manager should discuss insurance coverage with several insurance companies, as rates can vary considerably. He should also ask the insurance agent if there are any property improvements or other actions the manager could take that would reduce rates. For example, adding an alarm system is not very expensive, but could significantly reduce property insurance premiums.

Utilities. While many utility bills are passed on to tenants, some are routinely paid by the owner, and these should be kept as low as possible. Heating and cooling bills can be reduced by creating and following a schedule for cleaning heating, ventilation, and air conditioning (HVAC) equipment and changing filters. Improving insulation and replacing older HVAC equipment with more energy-efficient models can also dramatically reduce utility bills, although the initial expense of the upgrade will take some time to recover.

Other Expenses. Of course, contracts for building upgrades and services provided by outside companies—such as groundskeeping or janitorial service—should be awarded based on a bidding process. Property managers should insist on paying competitive rates for services. A little extra care in making sure that prices are reasonable can go a long way toward keeping expenses under control.

Disposition of the Net Operating Income

Typically, the property manager will give the full amount of the NOI to the property owner each month. However, sometimes the management agreement calls for the manager to make the mortgage payment out of the income, and/or deposit some of the income (usually an agreed percentage) into the property's reserve fund account for later use.

Cash Flow

Net operating income is one measure of the property owner's return on investment; cash flow is another. As explained in Chapter 2, cash flow is spendable income—the amount of money generated by an asset after all of the expenses connected with it have been paid.

Here's how to calculate cash flow:

$$\text{NOI} - \text{Debt service} = \text{Cash flow}$$

Remember, debt service means the payments of principal and interest on the property's mortgage loans.

In addition to increasing the NOI, the owner (or manager) might be able to increase a property's cash flow by refinancing the current mortgage loan. Of course, refinancing is generally worthwhile only if interest rates have fallen significantly since the owner obtained the existing loan.

Cash flow can be used to pay for capital expenditures, reserves, or the owner's personal income taxes. However, these items don't necessarily need to be paid out of the property's cash flow. The funds to pay these expenses could come from the property owner's savings or other source of income. Whether the property manager or the owner is responsible for making these payments will depend on the terms of the property management agreement.

Another important measure of profitability is the property's **after-tax cash flow**. This is the cash flow minus the income taxes paid by the owner on the property's income.

Preparing the Annual Operating Budget

We've explained how net operating income is calculated, and examined some key sources of income and expenses. A manager needs to understand these elements in order to carry out one of her most important tasks: creating the **annual operating budget**.

As mentioned briefly in Chapter 4, each year the manager prepares an operating budget. As you can see from the sample operating budget shown in Figure 5.2, the budget doesn't have to—and probably shouldn't—be very complicated. While it's certainly possible to

Figure 5.2 Operating budget

Annual Operating Budget		
Income		
6 studios @ $670/month	$670 × 6 × 12 =	$48,240
8 studios @ $700/month	$700 × 8 × 12 =	67,200
7 one-bedrooms @ $910/month	$910 × 7 × 12 =	76,440
9 one-bedrooms @ $1,110/month	$1,110 × 9 × 12 =	119,880
3 two-bedrooms @ $1,490/month	$1,490 × 3 × 12 =	+ 53,640
Potential gross rental income		365,400
Vacancy/collection loss factor: 7.5%	$365,400 × .075 =	− 27,405
Other income (storage, vending machines)		+ 1,800
Total Effective Gross Income (EGI)		**$339,795**
Expenses		
Property taxes		$41,410
Insurance		18,960
Utilities (common areas)		42,630
Maintenance and repairs		47,200
Office expenses		970
Management fees		+ 23,785
Total Operating Expenses		**$174,955**
Projected Net Operating Income (NOI)		**$164,840**

create a complex budget (especially with property management software), it's preferable to be able to read and understand the budget at a glance.

The operating budget sets out the property's expected income and operating expense figures for each month in the coming year. These numbers are estimates; variations are to be expected as the year unfolds. Ideally, the budget is based on historical numbers that are updated to reflect any changes in prices and other factors. This is sometimes called **incremental budgeting**.

The operating budget may be created in conjunction with a capital budget if a major expense is anticipated (see Figure 5.3 for an example of a capital budget). The capital budget shows how the reserves will be spent. Often the long-range operating budget (usually covering five years) will be updated at the same time.

When a property has no past income or expense data, **zero-based budgeting** is used. Zero-based budgeting relies on figures that are typical for similar properties in the same market. Zero-based budgeting must be used with brand-new properties. It might also be used by properties that are in fiscal trouble or are undergoing other major transformations.

Figure 5.3 Capital expense budget (for building an apartment complex)

Uses of Funds	Cost
Land	$802,103
Site work	283,330
Construction	3,144,736
Tenant improvement work	106,162
Environmental studies & remediation	84,916
Demolition	127,957
Personal property	59,829
Architecture/engineering	232,732
Testing & inspections	53,333
Construction consultant	50,000
Legal – Construction loan closing	35,380
Legal – Permanent loan	25,000
Legal – Syndication	25,000
Legal – Organization	5,000
Title, escrow, and recording – construction loan	7,718
Title, escrow, and recording – permanent loan	17,500
Appraisal	7,500
Municipal & utility fees	137,913
Conventional construction loan interest (10 mos.)	55,000
Construction interest after completion (16 mos.)	71,000
Soft construction loan interest	27,211
Predevelopment loan interest	2,104
Permanent loan fees	6,000
Permanent loan fees/capital campaign expenses	16,000
Rentup & marketing	31,875
Developer fee	350,000
Development consultant	138,750
Taxes prior to construction	15,000
Insurance	23,925
Construction loan fees/expenses	42,547
Capitalized operating reserve	82,979
Soft cost contingency	50,000
Syndication consultant	35,000
Audit	15,000
Relocation	306,000
Repayment of construction loan	2,309,221
Total Project Costs	**$8,783,721**

For these properties, the previous year's operating data would not be relevant to their current situation.

Potential Gross Rental Income

The first step in preparing an operating budget is to carefully estimate the gross income that the property is likely to generate during the coming year—income from both rents and any miscellaneous sources. To do this, first determine the property's **potential gross rental income**. (This may also be called potential gross income, or PGI; it's also referred to by other names, such as gross scheduled income.)

When determining potential gross rental income, property managers distinguish between market rent and contract rent. The **market rent** for a particular unit or space is the amount that would be charged if the unit or space were offered for lease in the current market. (See Chapter 4 for a discussion of how property managers estimate market rents.) The **contract rent** is the amount that is currently charged for a particular unit or space under the terms of an existing lease.

The manager generally uses contract rent in calculating the property's potential gross rental income. If a unit or space is currently available for lease, the manager will use the market rent instead. If a unit or space is currently leased, but the lease is due to expire during the course of the year, a combination of the contract rent and the market rent may be used.

The manager takes the monthly rental figure for each unit or space, adds them up, and multiplies that number by 12 to get the annual potential gross rental income. Of course, the calculation is more complicated when the rent varies from month to month (for example, as with a percentage lease—see Chapter 7).

Deducting a Vacancy and Collection Loss Factor. For many properties, particularly larger apartment or office properties, full occupancy throughout the year rarely happens. And for any type of property, some of the rent that is owed may not be collected. This is doubly true during times of economic stress.

The manager uses a vacancy and collection loss factor (often called a **bad debt and vacancy factor**) to reduce the property's potential gross income to reflect the reality of vacancies and problems with rent collection. This factor is expressed as a percentage, and might be around 5% for a smaller residential property. However, 10% or more is a typical number for most larger residential properties and office buildings.

When choosing a vacancy and collection loss factor, a manager shouldn't just use an industry average, but should instead choose a percentage based on the amount of rent actually collected from the property in recent years.

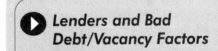

▶ Lenders and Bad Debt/Vacancy Factors

Note that even if a multi-tenant building is 100% occupied, a lender is likely to apply at least a 5% vacancy factor when determining the maximum loan amount for the property. The lender has to consider occupancy over the entire life of the loan, not just for a given year. The property owner should keep this in mind when applying for financing.

Example: Two years ago, a strip mall's potential gross rental income was $948,000; the rental income actually collected was $840,000 (88.6% of $948,000). Last year, the potential gross rental income was $975,000 and the rental income actually collected was $861,000 (88.3% of $975,000). Based on those figures, the manager might choose 11.5% as the vacancy and collection loss factor.

If the local economy has recently experienced an uptick or a downturn, a manager might decide to adjust the loss factor up or down accordingly. It's a good idea to include a note in the budget that explains any assumptions made about the economy (or any other factors) that might affect projected income.

After subtracting the vacancy and collection loss factor from the potential gross rental income, the resulting figure is added to the potential miscellaneous income (such as parking or vending machine fees). The sum of these two sources of income equals the **effective gross income** (EGI) predicted for that year. The EGI is the amount of money that should be available to pay operating expenses.

Estimating Operating Expenses

The second step in preparing an operating budget is to make detailed estimates of the operating expenses for the year, allocating a specific amount for each category of expense. As with income, any special assumptions made about expenses should be explained in the budget. If the property is new or has no reliable figures for past expenses, the zero-based budgeting method discussed earlier should be used.

 ### Budgets for Homeowners Associations

Many states strictly regulate homeowners associations (which govern subdivisions and condominiums) in order to protect individual homeowners and buyers. California, for instance, requires that the association's annual budget contain all of the items listed below. Item 1 is the operating budget, while items 2-7 concern reserves and the capital budget.

1. Estimated revenue and expenses using accrual-basis accounting
2. Total cash reserves
3. Estimated remaining life of major components
4. Estimated current replacement cost of major components
5. Amount of any construction defect-related award or settlement
6. Cash reserves analysis (whether reserves will meet capital costs of funding for future repair, replacement, or additions to major components)
7. Statement of methods used to develop budget and funding plan

Any property manager should consider including these items in his budget.

Subtracting expenses from income will produce the projected net operating income for the coming year. But what if this income amount isn't enough to cover the property's expenses or to meet the client's investment goals?

Discovering this kind of shortfall is a primary reason for preparing a budget. The manager and owner can discuss the problem and arrive at tentative solutions before a cash flow crisis occurs. Possible solutions will involve the two methods of building up the NOI: reducing expenses and increasing income.

> **Example:** Expenses have been cut to the bone at Cozy Apartments. Despite this, the manager's annual operating budget alerts the owner, Lucy, to a potential problem. By the end of the year, the property won't be generating enough revenue to meet the debt service payments, let alone pay for any necessary repairs.
>
> After several discussions, Lucy and her property manager decide to increase parking and storage fees right away (which is allowed under the terms of the lease). Then, in July, they will raise the rent for any new tenants. By the end of the year, they will raise the rent for all renewing tenants.
>
> Thanks to the budget planning process, Lucy and the property manager have ample time to warn tenants of the upcoming fee/rate hikes, and they can avert a potential financial crisis.

Financial Reports

Now let's look at the financial reports that are submitted to the property owner on a monthly, quarterly, and annual basis. These financial reports may be referred to as cash flow reports, profit and loss statements, earnings statements, or statements of operations.

Although the operating budget plays a role in the preparation of these reports, the reports are quite different from the operating budget. Financial reports are a summary of the income and expenses that actually occurred; the operating budget is merely a plan or prediction of what might (and hopefully will) happen.

Property management accounting software makes generating financial reports fairly easy, but there is no standard format that must be used. Whatever form the report takes, keep in mind that most clients appreciate plain English and helpful summaries of key information.

The content and frequency of the reports will be dictated by the terms of the property management agreement. Property managers should also be sure to meet any disclosure requirements that might be imposed by state law.

Some commercial leases may require the manager to give tenants financial reports. This is especially true in the retail setting when the tenant pays a percentage of the property's operating expenses. In this case, the lease often gives the tenant a right to certain information, such as the property's expenses and degree of occupancy.

Contents of Financial Reports

Most financial reports include the following items:

- **Summary of operations.** A brief description of income and expenses, summarizing the information that's presented more fully in the rest of the report.
- **Rent roll.** A report on rent collections (a list of the total amount of rent earned, both collected and uncollected).

- **List of owner contributions.** A list of any sums that were contributed by the property owner.
- **Statement of receipts.** A list of all other income and payments that were received.
- **Statement of disbursements (cash disbursements report).** A list of all expenditures that were made (including both operational and capital expenditures, and debt service).
- **Reserve account report.** A list of all deposits into and withdrawals from the property's reserve fund account.
- **Budget comparison.** A comparison of the actual income and operating expenses for the reporting period to the amounts budgeted.
- **Narrative report of operations.** A letter to the client that explains the information that's presented in numerical form in the rest of the report.

On most financial reports, these components (except for the summary of operations) appear simply as line items. In other words, the report itself can be fairly simple, often just a single page that shows the property's income and expenses using the same categories found in the operating budget. This makes comparing actual income and expenses to projected income and expenses much easier. Accounting software allows the manager to break down categories of expenses and income, so the owner can ask for greater detail if he wants it.

The annual and quarterly reports will usually contain the same items that appear in the monthly statement. Owners often pay more attention to the annual statement than to the quarterly or monthly reports. They feel the annual report gives them a true picture of both the profitability of the property and whether the manager is doing a good job.

Monitoring Expenses and Revising Budgets

An important element of a financial report is the budget comparison statement. The budget comparison statement often shows up next to the actual income or expense figure.

Example:

Grounds maintenance . . . . $7,892 (amount budgeted: $6,500)

It is the property manager's job to analyze and then explain to the owner any significant discrepancies between the budgeted and actual figures. If discrepancies start to show up for a given expense on a regular basis, the budget may need to be adjusted for the rest of the year. Of course, sometimes patience is advised: events may happen later in the year that make adjustments unnecessary.

Example: The budget for an office park lists a monthly sum for groundskeeping, which includes items such as snow removal, lawn mowing, and summer watering. January brings heavy snow, and several months of the groundskeeping budget is used up just keeping the parking lot clear of snow and ice.

The manager and owner get together and consider increasing the budget for groundskeeping, which would reduce the owner's return on his investment. They decide to take a wait-and-see approach. As it happens, the summer months—which are often hot and dry—are unusually rainy, significantly reducing the need for watering. The lower water bills more than make up for the earlier cost of the snow/ice removal, and no change to the budget is required.

Income and Expense Statement for Tax Purposes

Sometimes, it is the manager's responsibility to prepare an annual income and expense statement for tax purposes. This statement is used by the owner or her accountant or other tax expert to prepare a tax return. This statement resembles a normal annual profit and loss statement, but the tax version also accounts for depreciation deductions on capital assets. We'll explain the concept of depreciation in the next section.

Income Tax Ramifications of Real Estate Ownership

We will conclude this chapter with an overview of the income tax issues related to real estate ownership. While property managers must not give tax advice, they should have a good grasp of the general tax issues involved in real property ownership. The perspective gained from this knowledge will prove valuable to both the manager and the owner.

First we'll look at tax deductions available to rental property owners; then we'll consider income tax on the sale of investment property.

Tax Deductions Available to Rental Property Owners

There are four basic types of deductions available to investment property owners:

- depreciation,
- mortgage interest,
- operating expenses, and
- operational losses.

Depreciation Deductions. Buildings and equipment wear out over time. The loss in value caused by wear and tear is referred to as **depreciation**, and the IRS allows investment property owners to deduct depreciation from their income. Since land does not wear out, only the portion of property value attributable to the buildings is eligible for this deduction. (Another term for the depreciation deduction is the **cost recovery deduction**, because the annual deductions eventually allow the owner to "recover" the cost of the building.)

Calculating depreciation deductions. Property depreciates gradually, so a taxpayer is not allowed to depreciate the entire value of the property all at once. Instead, the Internal Revenue Code determines the "life" of the property—which is a certain number of years—and the taxpayer can deduct a percentage of the property's value every year of the property's life.

For residential rental real estate placed into service during or after 1987, the depreciation period (the life of the property) is 27.5 years. ("Placed into service" refers to the date the property is first occupied, which isn't necessarily the date the property was purchased or construction was completed.) The depreciation period for nonresidential rental property is 39 years.

While there are different ways to calculate depreciation, the simplest method is to divide the cost of the depreciable asset (the building) by the life of the property (the total number of years scheduled for the depreciation of that type of property).

> **Example:** A rental home has a value of $250,000. The land is worth $100,000 and the building is worth $150,000. According to the IRS, the life of the building is 27.5 years.
>
> $$\$150,000 \div 27.5 = \$5,454.55$$
>
> Therefore, the investor can deduct about $5,455 every year for 27.5 years. At the end of this time period, the entire $150,000 will have been depreciated (recovered).

As with other income tax issues, a tax expert should be consulted when depreciation questions arise.

Mortgage Interest and Points. Mortgage interest on investment property is completely deductible. Discount points and any origination fee paid at closing are considered prepaid interest and therefore are deductible as mortgage interest.

Operating Expenses. For some types of properties, operating expenses can be the owner's largest tax deduction. We discussed operating expenses earlier in the chapter. Remember, these expenses include property taxes, hazard insurance, utilities, advertising, maintenance, and repairs—anything that isn't a capital expenditure.

Operational Losses from Rental Property. Operational losses are deductible up to a point. An operational loss (also called an operating loss) occurs when the rental property's annual expenses exceed its annual income. (Don't confuse operational losses with income lost due to vacancies—if a rental unit sits vacant for all or part of the year, that lost income is not deductible, it merely reduces the amount of the property's income.)

Let's start with a little background. The IRS considers all rental income to be passive income. **Passive income** is income that a taxpayer earns from an enterprise (such as a limited partnership) in which he doesn't materially participate. But what if a rental property owner materially participates in the management of the property? That doesn't matter, because rental income is always considered to be passive income.

As a general rule, passive losses—losses from passive investment activities—can be deducted only from passive income, not from ordinary income (ordinary income includes wages, dividends, interest, etc.). However, passive losses from the operation of rental real property receive special treatment, as long as the taxpayer actively participates in the property's management (and meets certain income requirements). In these cases, up to $25,000 in operational losses from rental property can be deducted from the owner's ordinary income.

The employment of a property manager doesn't necessarily mean that the owner isn't actively involved in management. However, the taxpayer does have to share decision-making authority with the property manager. Many owners will meet this requirement, but they should document their activities in case the IRS questions the assertion of active involvement in the property's management.

Example: Jenks, a plumber, owns an apartment building. A property manager handles all the day-to-day management tasks, but Jenks reviews and approves all expense/repair requests over $200, approves all new tenants, and personally hires the resident manager. Last year the property's annual operating expenses were $115,000 and the rental income was $100,000. Because Jenks actively participates in the management of the property, this $15,000 passive loss is deductible from Jenks's ordinary income. That means Jenks can take a $15,000 deduction against the $58,000 salary he earns as a plumber.

Not every rental property owner who actively participates in the management of his property can take advantage of passive loss deductions. There are significant restrictions. For example, the taxpayer can't be involved in any other passive activities, and his adjusted gross income can't exceed a certain amount (the deduction begins phasing out at $100,000).

On the other hand, if the taxpayer/owner is a real estate professional who materially participates in rental property activities, there is no $25,000 limit on the amount of operational losses that the real estate professional can deduct from her ordinary income.

Income Tax on the Sale of Property

When a property owner sells an investment property, he will have to pay tax on any gain realized from the sale. The amount of gain from the sale is determined by the following formula:

$$\text{Sales price} - \text{Adjusted basis} = \text{Gain (or loss)}$$

While this is a simple formula, determining the adjusted basis can be tricky. The first step is to figure out the **initial basis**, which is the amount of money the owner spent to acquire the property. This includes the purchase price plus closing costs and any money spent on evaluating the purchase.

 Examples of Capital Improvements

Below is a list of items that generally qualify as capital improvements and would be subtracted from a property's initial basis. However, each property is different; what constitutes a capital improvement for one property might not qualify for another.

- Burglar alarm installation or upgrading
- Roof replacement
- Remodeling
- Electrical upgrade
- Asbestos removal (or remedying any other environmental hazard)
- Insulation costs
- Drainage work
- Certain legal costs that add value to property

To the initial basis, add any capital expenditures (money spent on capital improvements). As we discussed earlier, capital improvements are items that add to the long-term value of the property, such as a new roof or the addition of a parking garage. Selling costs are also added to the initial basis.

Some items must be deducted from the initial basis. Any allowable depreciation deductions must be subtracted from the initial basis, whether or not the owner actually took these deductions.

These various additions and subtractions to the initial basis result in the adjusted basis figure: Initial basis + Capital expenditures − Depreciation = Adjusted basis.

> **Example:** To keep things simple, let's assume that Martinez purchased a rental house on January 1, five years ago, for $200,000 (including closing costs). The value of the structure is $125,000. He rented the property out for exactly five years before he sold it for $220,000 on December 31. During that time, he made no capital expenditures. To calculate his gain on the sale of the property, he must deduct the amount of allowable depreciation deductions (whether he took them or not) from his initial basis, then deduct that adjusted basis from the sales price.
>
> $125,000 ÷ 27.5 × 5 years = $22,727 Depreciation deductions
>
> $200,000 Initial basis − $22,727 Depreciation = $177,273 Adjusted basis
>
> $220,000 Sales price − $177,273 Adjusted basis = $42,727 Gain
>
> Martinez had a taxable gain of $42,727 on the sale of his rental property.

Capital Gains and Losses. The IRS classifies real estate as a capital asset. Thus, any gain on the sale of real estate is a capital gain (and any loss would be a capital loss). There are two kinds of capital gains: short-term and long-term. Short-term capital gains result from the sale of a capital asset held for a year or less. Long-term capital gains result from the sale of a capital asset held for more than one year.

The IRS taxes short-term capital gains at the investor's regular income tax rate (this rule would apply to many "property flippers," for example). However, the IRS gives favorable treatment to those who hold capital assets longer than a year. The tax rate applied to most long-term capital gains is considerably lower than the rate for ordinary income.

As for capital losses, taxpayers can subtract these losses from any gains made on the sale of other capital assets. If a taxpayer ends up with a net capital loss, she can deduct the amount up to $3,000 from her regular income. Any loss over $3,000 may be carried over to subsequent years.

As we've said, most property managers do not give property owners tax advice or perform tax calculations. Completing tax returns on income properties requires specialized knowledge. However, a general understanding of tax basics will help a manager better understand the owner's concerns, and equip him for more accurate planning and budgeting.

Chapter Summary

1. Accounting refers to keeping records of financial transactions and preparing reports based on those records. Property management software is typically used for these tasks. Bookkeeping is done either on a cash basis, where income is recorded when received and expenses recorded when paid, or on an accrual basis, where income is recorded when due and expenses are recorded when incurred. A combination of the two methods may also be used.

2. Trust funds are funds that a property manager holds or handles on behalf of a client. A client's funds should not be commingled with the property manager's own funds, whether business or personal. In most cases, state law requires that trust funds be held in a bank account called a trust account. Managers who handle income-producing property typically maintain three different trust accounts: an operating account, a reserve fund account, and a security deposits account.

3. Income consists of rent and also money from miscellaneous sources (parking, storage fees, vending, etc.). Net operating income can be increased by increasing rents, the occupancy rate, collections, or leasable space, or by finding ways to decrease expenses (such as insurance, utilities, or maintenance fees).

4. Each year, the manager prepares an operating budget, estimating income and expenses for the coming year. The manager uses a vacancy and collection loss factor to estimate how much to reduce the property's potential gross income to account for unleased space and uncollected rents. The operating budget is often created in conjunction with a capital budget if a major expense is anticipated. Often a long-range budget will also be updated at this time.

5. Typically, the manager must provide monthly, quarterly, and annual financial reports to the owner. These financial reports generally contain a statement of receipts and disbursements, reserve fund accounting, and a budget comparison to show how the expenses and income are tracking the figures projected in the operating budget. Revisions should be made to the budget if significant shortfalls develop.

6. Real property investors may take deductions for depreciation, mortgage interest, and operating expenses. Operational losses may also be deductible, in most cases up to $25,000. The gain on a sale of investment property is taxable. The amount of gain is determined by the formula: Sales price − Adjusted basis = Gain.

Key Terms

Cash-basis accounting – Accounting system where income is recorded when received and expenses are recorded when paid.

Accrual-basis accounting – Accounting system where income is recorded when due and expenses are recorded when incurred.

Modified cash-basis accounting – Accounting system where annual or semi-annual expenses are debited monthly as they accrue, but income is recorded only when received.

Accounting software – Software designed to handle accounting and generate financial reports for the owner.

Trust funds – Money that a property manager holds on behalf of a client. Trust funds should be held in an account separate from the manager's business or personal funds.

Operating account – A checking account used for ordinary receipts and expenditures, into which the manager deposits the property's rents and other income, and out of which he pays the operating expenses.

Reserve fund account – An account, often interest-bearing, that is used to accumulate reserves to pay for capital expenditures (such as a roof replacement or new refrigerators for the tenants of an apartment building).

Deposit insurance – Currently, funds held in a noninterest-bearing checking account are insured by the Federal Deposit Insurance Corporation (FDIC) with no limit on the amount. Deposits in interest-bearing accounts are insured up to $250,000.

Bad debt and vacancy factor – A percentage used to reduce the property's potential gross rental income to account for vacancies and uncollected rents.

Gross income – The amount of money from the property that's available before operating expenses have been paid.

Net operating income (NOI) – The amount of money left over from gross income after paying the property's operating expenses. Gross income – Operating expenses = Net operating income.

Operating expense ratio – The percentage of effective gross income that represents the property's operating expenses. This figure can be compared to industry averages to determine management efficiency.

Ordinary repairs – Routine repairs (corrective maintenance) that keeps the property in good operating condition.

Capital expenditure – An expense that adds long-lasting value to the property (for example, replacing a roof or furnace).

Cash flow – The amount of spendable income generated by an asset after all of the expenses connected with it have been paid.

Operating budget – A budget that sets out the property's expected income and operating expenses for the coming year.

Monthly statement – A financial report given to the owner that shows actual income and expenses for a given month, usually combined with a comparison to the budgeted income and expenses.

Depreciation deductions – A deduction from income of a certain percentage of the property's value each year to account for physical deterioration. Residential real estate is depreciated over 27.5 years, and other investment real estate is depreciated over 39 years.

Adjusted basis – The initial amount spent to acquire a property, plus capital expenditures, minus depreciation deductions, and plus selling costs. Adjusted basis is subtracted from the sales price to determine the amount of taxable gain when an investment property is sold.

Passive income – Income a taxpayer earns from an enterprise (such as a limited partnership) that he doesn't materially participate in. The IRS considers all rental income to be passive income.

Capital gain – Profit realized from the sale of a capital asset. If the asset was held for more than one year, it is a long-term capital gain; if the asset was held for one year or less, it is a short-term capital gain.

Chapter Quiz

1. Which of the following is not an accounting method?
   a) Accrual
   b) Cash-basis
   c) Adjusted basis
   d) Modified cash-basis

2. Tracy manages several small apartment buildings for various owners. She sets up a checking account for her business and deposits all funds relating to the various properties into the account. She also deposits some of her management fees into this account, and pays her office expenses out of it. She keeps scrupulous records of all deposits and withdrawals to make sure that by the end of the month she hasn't used more money for personal purposes than she has actually deposited. This is:
   a) acceptable, provided the accounting is strictly accurate
   b) commingling, but not conversion, making it legal
   c) conversion and commingling, and illegal
   d) legal in some states but not in others

3. Property managers often set up a separate trust account for all of the following items, except:
   a) operations
   b) security deposits
   c) insurance
   d) reserves

4. Which of the following is not a fixed expense?
   a) Heating and cooling
   b) Property taxes
   c) Insurance premiums
   d) Management fee

5. Which of the following is the formula for determining net operating income?
   a) Gross income – Operating expenses
   b) Gross income + Operating expenses
   c) Gross income ÷ Operating expenses
   d) Gross income × Operating expenses

6. Do operating expenses include debt service for the mortgage on the property?
   a) Yes, debt service is an operating expense
   b) Yes, in part; debt service on mortgages other than the purchase loan is an operating expense
   c) No, debt service isn't an operating expense
   d) Yes, unless the management agreement provides otherwise

7. What term refers to the amount of money that remains after payment of debt service?
   a) Equity
   b) Cash flow
   c) NOI
   d) ROI

8. Cash flow might be used to handle the cost of:
   a) capital projects
   b) payments into a reserve fund
   c) owner's personal income taxes
   d) Any of the above

9. The operating budget is prepared:
   a) monthly
   b) twice yearly
   c) annually
   d) every five years

10. Potential rental income minus _____ results in an estimate of effective gross income.
    a) EGI
    b) market rental rates
    c) a bad debt and vacancy factor
    d) an operating expense ratio

11. Two years ago, a property's potential gross rental income was $335,000; the rental income actually collected was $305,855. Last year, the potential gross rental income was $342,500; the rental income actually collected was $315,100. Based on those figures, what figure would the manager choose as the vacancy and collection loss factor?

    a) 11%
    b) 8%
    c) 5%
    d) 3%

12. All of the following income tax deductions are available to rental property owners except:

    a) depreciation
    b) mortgage interest
    c) operating expenses
    d) mortgage principal payments

13. Residential rental property is depreciated over how many years?

    a) 10
    b) 17.5
    c) 27.5
    d) 39

14. Norman manages a small, rundown motel property for his mother. Mother and son decide to completely renovate the property. The cost breakdown is as follows: roof replacement, $11,000; unit remodeling, $28,000; general cleaning, $3,000; hiring security, $400 (monthly); and an electronic billboard out by the highway, $18,000. What are the total capital expenditures and what are the total annual operational expenditures?

    a) $47,000 (capital expense) and $17,800 (operational expense)
    b) $57,000 (capital expense) and $7,800 (operational expense)
    c) $64,800 (capital expense) and $0 (operational expense)
    d) $0 (capital expense) and $64,800 (operational expense)

15. Kerry earns $37,000 a year as a dance instructor. She owns an older four-unit apartment building. One of her tenants leaves mid-year and Kerry is unable to re-rent the unit, meaning she loses $6,000 in rent. Her operating expenses for the year exceed her rental income by $2,500. How much can she deduct for the year under the operational loss deduction?

    a) $2,500
    b) $6,000
    c) $8,500
    d) $25,000

Answer Key

1. c) Adjusted basis is a figure used in calculating the gain, if any, on a sale of property; it isn't an accounting method.

2. c) This situation involves both commingling and conversion. This is illegal in all states.

3. c) A separate trust account isn't set up for insurance payments. Sometimes insurance payments are paid into the reserve account, however, so the full amount is ready when the annual bill comes due.

4. a) Heating and cooling expenses vary month-to-month and therefore aren't fixed expenses.

5. a) The correct formula is: Gross income – Operating expenses = Net operating income.

6. c) Debt service isn't an operating expense; it is paid out of the net operating income. This is standard accounting practice, and a management agreement wouldn't specify otherwise. However, the agreement might state that the manager is to pay the debt service out of the net operating income.

7. b) Cash flow is the money left to the owner after operating expenses and debt service have been taken care of. ROI (return on investment) is calculated by dividing the NOI by the amount of capital invested.

8. d) The cash left over after operating expenses and debt service is available for capital expenses, reserves, and paying income tax.

9. c) An operating budget is prepared each year.

10. c) The bad debt and vacancy factor is more formally called the vacancy and collection loss factor.

11. b) For the past two years, the vacancy factor has been approximately 8%. Barring a sharp change in economic conditions, the manager would probably stick with that figure.

12. d) An owner can deduct interest on a mortgage, but not the repayment of the principal itself.

13. c) Residential rental property is depreciated over 27.5 years and other investment real estate is depreciated over 39 years.

14. b) The roof ($11,000), remodeling ($28,000), and highway sign ($18,000) are all capital expenses because they add long-term value to the property. Security (12 months × $400 = $4,800) and cleaning ($3,000) are operational expenses.

15. a) Generally, operational losses are deductible up to $25,000 a year; Kerry has a $2,500 operational loss.

Chapter 6
Marketing

Introduction

Part of the property manager's job is to make sure that the client's property generates a reliable income. Since the property's income comes primarily from rent, attracting and retaining tenants is crucial. The most common way for the property manager to find tenants is through **marketing**: the process by which a business promotes and sells a product or service to a customer.

In this chapter, we'll begin by discussing some general marketing principles: knowing the product, knowing the customer, and branding. Then we'll take a look at how to market a property for lease: how to identify potential tenants, and how to choose the most cost effective type of advertising. Next, we'll examine how to evaluate the effectiveness of the manager's marketing efforts. We'll also review the use of public relations and, finally, end the chapter with an overview of laws that pertain to advertising.

General Marketing Principles

Let's begin by examining two of the most basic marketing rules: know your product, and know your customer.

Knowing the Product

In general, a **product** is anything, such as a good or service, that can be marketed or sold to the public. A product may have both tangible and intangible qualities.

> **Example:** ABC Company sells metal widgets. XYZ Company also sells metal widgets. Both company's widgets serve the same purpose and are used by the customer in the same way. However, ABC Company's product is known for being a "quality widget" while XYZ Company's product is known for being a "budget widget." Both companies are selling the same item—metal widgets—but they are not necessarily selling the same product.

When marketing rental property, the property manager first needs to identify the product being sold. This may be a one-bedroom apartment, a 5,000-square-foot retail space, or a warehouse.

In addition to the bare-bones facts regarding size, price, and location, the property manager should note any features that accompany the basic product. These might include services or items that tenants expect to come with an apartment rental. Examples include parking, garbage removal, cable television, and Internet access.

Commonly expected features will vary from market to market. In suburban areas, a designated parking space or two may be expected to go with a residential unit; in a city, where parking is at a premium, prospective tenants may consider parking a special feature. Special features are what make a property unique, and property managers should be especially careful to note features that make the property stand out from its competition.

> **Example:** Sarah is the property manager for a retail property. There are several competing properties in the area, all of a similar size and price-per-square-foot, and with similar amenities. However, the property Sarah manages is closest to a busy subway station.

Figure 6.1 Anatomy of a product

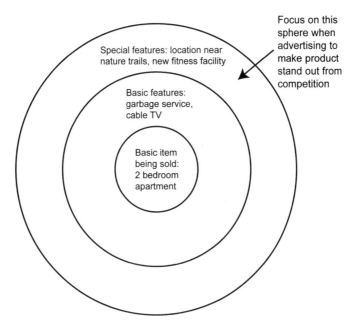

In the previous example, the retail property's location is its special feature—what sets it apart from its competition. Other examples of special features might include a view, a rooftop garden, or proximity to a park or a shopping center.

Knowing the Customer

To market effectively, familiarity with the product isn't enough. In any given market, there may be thousands of people who are interested in leasing property. But not all of those renters will be interested in your particular property. Some will be looking for apartments, for example; others will be searching for retail or industrial space.

Ideally, marketing efforts will attract qualified prospects. A **qualified prospect** is someone who has a need for the product, as well as the financial means to acquire it. It's important to focus marketing efforts on the customers who will be potential tenants. In other words, managers should engage in targeted marketing. **Targeted marketing** refers to dividing a large group of potential customers into smaller groups, and then focusing marketing efforts on one or two key segments.

> **Example:** Sam manages a 50-unit apartment building consisting of two- and three-bedroom units near the local graduate school. The size of the apartments makes them ideal for graduate students with families. Rather than send flyers to every graduate student, Sam focuses his marketing efforts on graduate students who are married and have one or more children.

Of course, when targeting specific groups of people, managers must be careful not to violate federal and state fair housing laws. We'll discuss these types of laws later in this chapter.

Identifying the Target Market. The first step in targeted marketing is to identify the target market. Who will the manager market to, and how will he find them?

The most common method of breaking down (or segmenting) a market is based on demographics. As we discussed in Chapter 4, **demographics** refers to characteristics of a human population or a segment of that population, such as average family size or median age. When determining a target audience for a marketing campaign, the property manager may segment the market based on education, household size, or economics (salary); land use (residential, retail, offices); location; or preferred leisure activities (outdoor enthusiasts or art connoisseurs).

> **Example:** Carlos is developing a marketing plan for a small apartment building near the city's business core. Carlos could market the building to everyone in the county, including rural farmers and college students, but it would be much more efficient (and less costly) to market only to those people who work downtown.

As the example above demonstrates, one of the most important ways to limit the target market is by geographic location. This is done primarily to limit the cost of the marketing campaign. For example, running a television ad across the entire state to find renters for a single-family residential property is not a good use of advertising dollars.

The property manager can use regional and neighborhood data collected while developing a management plan to narrow his target audience (see Chapter 4).

Generational Marketing. Generational marketing is a special way of segmenting a market not just by age, but also by social, economic, and psychological factors. Generational marketing tries to identify the values and shared experiences of certain groups of society. Marketers can then tailor their advertising and marketing efforts to appeal to their target audience.

> **Example:** Sita is developing her marketing plan for an apartment building located near the local university. She wants to market to college and graduate students, but can only afford either newspaper ads or Internet marketing. After learning that the younger generation rarely reads newspapers and expects instant access to information online, Sita decides to focus her energy and her budget on Internet advertising.

A resourceful property manager can market a property in different ways to different target audiences.

> **Example:** An apartment building has a fitness facility and free cable. The manager could appeal to busy professionals by focusing on the advantages of an on-site gym. On the other hand, when marketing to college students she might focus on the benefits of free cable TV.

Branding

Branding is the process of developing and creating a company's or product's image in the minds of the target audience. A brand can be a name, term, symbol, design, or idea that people associate with a product or company.

> **Example:** A retirement community in Anytown uses the slogan "Always Active" on all of its signs and marketing materials. The community is next to several nature trails, has a tennis court, and is within walking distance of many local amenities. The community

Cultural Generations

Understanding the characteristics of each generation will enable you to market more effectively.

- **Matures.** Matures include those born before 1945. They were shaped by the Great Depression and both World Wars. Matures are considered to be loyal, hardworking, and to value stability. They are not very active online, except for perhaps email and Facebook. They prefer traditional forms of marketing, including newspapers, television, and face-to-face sales. They believe hard work is the key to success.

- **Baby boomers** (1945–1964). Baby boomers were born in the years after the World Wars, and were shaped by the Kennedy assassination, the Vietnam War, and the civil rights movement. They believe education and knowledge are the keys to success. Both traditional and Internet advertising will appeal to them. They are considered to be motivated by success, so advertising that appeals to that motivation is more likely to catch their interest.

- **Generation X** (1965–1979). Generation X is composed of the children of the baby boomers. They came of age when things seemed to be falling apart: Watergate, the fall of the Berlin Wall, and various U.S. economic crises (recessions, gas shortages, etc.). Gen X-ers are often the children of divorce, adding to their sense of change and distrust, but also their sense of independence. Gen X-ers are considered to be distrustful of advertising (and authority in general). They are cynical and wonder what the "catch" is. Marketing to Gen X-ers can involve both traditional and Internet advertising, but Gen X-ers value the Internet as a way to find information for themselves. Plain, simple messages based on facts seem to work best.

- **Millennials** (1980–2000). Millennials have almost always had the Internet and computers. They like instant access to information and obtain almost all their information online. Their generation is shaped by rapid leaps in technology, and so what's "new" will always appeal to them. Millennials are optimistic and lack the perceived rebelliousness of the previous generation, seeming to value family and traditions. Marketing based on starting conversations and forming connections (such as Facebook and Twitter) may be especially successful.

- **Generation Z, or the Internet generation** (2001 to the present). It's too soon to define this generation, but it's likely to be shaped in part by the events of 9/11, the recession, and the housing bust. It's predicted that the Internet will continue to play an increasing role in marketing to this and subsequent generations.

also sponsors numerous activities, such as dance classes and yoga. Soon, when active retirees think about choosing a place to retire to in Anytown, they immediately think of that community.

Branding is more important for larger rental properties (and their management companies) than for smaller rental properties. Regardless of the product, though, to deliver a clear branding message, it's important to first know both the product and the customer. The property manager needs a clear vision of the image she wants to convey, and must then deliver the message in a way that reinforces that branding vision.

Branding has many benefits. First, it creates loyalty. Repeat customers return because they associate the company or the product with a certain ideal. Second, branding can help a product or property stand out from the crowd. Finally, branding helps to target potential customers by positioning the property within a certain market segment.

Marketing Property for Lease

Now that we've explained some of the basic principles of marketing, let's take a closer look at how these principles apply to marketing a property for lease. (We'll examine marketing a property management business and related issues later in this chapter.)

Deciding how to market a property for lease is one of the property manager's most important jobs: without tenants, there is no income. The property manager needs to know how to select a target audience, which type of marketing is appropriate, and how to evaluate the results of the marketing plan.

Targeting Potential Tenants

As we just discussed, it's important to "know your customer." When marketing properties for lease, this means knowing the type of person or company who is likely to rent the property. That's who must be reached with marketing efforts.

> **Example:** Marco manages a luxury apartment building. His target audience is someone in a high income bracket who is in the market for residential rental property. He's not likely to pay for television advertising—while that would reach some qualified prospects, he would also spend a lot of money advertising to thousands of people who are completely uninterested in his property. His advertising dollars might be better spent on a tasteful display ad in a local publication that features fine dining and high-end luxury goods.

Sometimes property managers need to be creative when determining who their potential tenants are. For instance, an apartment in a university district may appeal to more than just college students: families and retirees may appreciate the energy in the area, as well as the inexpensive cultural events offered on college campuses.

How Much Advertising?

After the target market has been identified, the property manager needs to consider how much advertising is needed. If there are no current or anticipated vacancies, it may not be necessary to market the property at all. This is especially true of single-family rental units or small apartment buildings, or commercial spaces with long-term leases and very little turnover. On the other hand, large residential buildings are likely to have constant turnover. With leases expiring on a regular basis, continual advertising may be necessary.

Sometimes, marketing is a good idea even when vacancy rates are low. For instance, advertising can be used to improve the property's public image (see the discussion of public relations later in this chapter).

The location of the property may also help determine the amount of advertising that's required. In a high traffic area, for example, a "for lease" sign may be all that's needed; in a remote area, other forms of advertising may also be required.

Advertising Methods

A property manager has a variety of options when it comes to choosing the type of advertising that's best for the property. When determining the best option, she should consider the reach and frequency of each advertising method. **Reach** refers to the size of the audience exposed to the advertising. A statewide television ad has a much larger reach than a classified ad in a local newspaper. **Frequency** refers to the number of times each ad will appear. For example, an ad in a newspaper may run only once a week, while an Internet ad may be viewed 24 hours a day.

In general, advertising falls into two categories: traditional marketing, which involves media like signage and newspaper ads; and Internet marketing, which utilizes websites, social networking, and other forms of Internet advertising. Most property managers will probably want to use some combination of these methods, so let's take a closer look at each.

Traditional Advertising Methods. Traditional advertising methods are those that were used before computers and the Internet became commonplace, including signage, classified advertising, display advertising, "For Rent" magazines, and direct mail.

Many property managers still rely heavily on traditional methods of advertising. In some situations, traditional marketing can be more effective than Internet marketing: it depends on the geographical area, the target customer, and the type of property.

> **Example:** Carol manages a small apartment building in Retirementville, Florida. Her research indicates that 75% of the town's population is 65 or older, and that empty

 Advertising Agencies

Some property managers, especially those managing very large residential or commercial properties, choose to hire advertising agencies to handle the marketing. While this increases the cost of marketing considerably, it may be worth it if a very professional marketing campaign is desired.

Advertising agencies are usually paid in one of three ways:

- flat fee per project;
- contract for a certain period of time (such as one year); or
- by commission (such as 15% of the advertising cost).

apartments in the building have been filled by referrals and walk-ins. Furthermore, a local poll shows that 80% of the town's residents over the age of 65 "seldom" or "almost never" use the computer. Based on this information, Carol decides to focus her marketing efforts on traditional signage and classified ads.

Signage. All properties should display a sign with the property manager's contact information, even if there are no current vacancies and other types of advertising are being used. Prospects who contact the manager after seeing a sign are strong prospects: they've already seen the building and are interested enough to make contact. With other advertising methods, the prospect may make contact, only to visit the property and dislike what he sees.

The manager should use a type of sign that reflects the building's overall image, and the sign should be professional-looking and easy to read. Include only the most important information, so as not to overwhelm the reader who may be driving or passing by quickly. Use color when possible, and be sure the font is easy to read from a distance. Note that local ordinances may restrict the size and type of sign that may be displayed, so check the rules in your area.

Signage may not be as effective as other methods of advertising in low-traffic areas—if the building is on a side street, for example—but it's still a good idea to post a sign on the property.

Classified advertising. Classified advertising is still a popular choice among many property managers. Classified advertising involves simple, brief ads, usually in a newspaper or magazine. Classified ads can be used to advertise a single available unit, multiple vacancies, or the property as a whole.

Classified advertising can be very cost-effective, depending on the newspaper's circulation. However, classified ads reach a large audience, so they need to be well-designed and well-written to attract only qualified prospects.

> **Example:** Earl manages a fourplex in a busy part of town. He places a classified ad that reads, "Two-bedroom, one-bath unit for rent in nice building. Call 555-5555." Earl receives lots of calls about the apartment, but many of the callers just want to know how much the rent is and whether utilities are included. After learning that the rent is $1,000 per month and utilities are extra, the majority of callers say, "That's out of my budget" and hang up. Earl could have saved himself a lot of time and effort if he'd included the rental amount in his ad.

As our example shows, classified ads should be straightforward and include basic information about the building or unit, including:

- the type of space available (such as "two-bedroom unit" or "800-square-foot office space on second floor");
- the rent per unit or per square foot, amount of security deposit, and whether utilities are included;
- the property's location, either a specific address or a general location (such as "near university" or "on Pine Street"); and
- the number to call for more information.

This type of information will help ensure that only qualified prospects respond to the classified ad.

Many newspapers make their classified ads available online. In such cases, the property manager may be able to include a link to photographs or the property's website. (We'll discuss Internet advertising later in this chapter.)

Display advertising. Display advertising is similar to classified advertising, but in addition to text, ads often include logos, pictures, maps, or other visual elements. Because display ads are so visual, their location in the newspaper or magazine is important. In general, the larger the ad, the more it will cost, and premium spots may cost extra.

Because display ads are more expensive than classified ads, they should be well-designed. Many property managers hire professionals to create the ads; however, software is available that can help a creative manager design her own ads using simple templates. Display ads can often be printed and used as flyers.

Display ads are used most often for commercial properties and larger residential properties. They are typically used to advertise the property as a whole, or several categories of available units, rather than a single vacancy. Property managers may also use display advertising during **lease-up**, that time period when a new property enters the market and the manager is seeking the first tenants. It's also useful for advertising remodeled buildings.

"For Rent" magazines. An alternative to newspapers or magazines is the "For Rent" magazines that are often available at supermarkets, the chamber of commerce, real estate offices, and other businesses. The magazines are usually free for consumers; property managers pay to buy ads in them. The ads can be fairly small or as large as a half or full page. Some of these publications are black and white newsprint, while others are glossy, full-color publications.

Because of the cost associated with purchasing ad space in these publications, the ads usually promote entire apartment of office buildings, rather than individual units. These publications may also be used to advertise newly completed buildings or remodeled properties.

Direct mail. Another form of traditional advertising is direct mail. Direct mail can be expensive, and it's not a very effective means of promoting individual properties unless definite prospects can be identified.

> **Example:** Bill wants to advertise a 1,000-square-foot retail space that was previously used as a restaurant. He could send direct mail to the entire town, at a substantial cost. But it would be far less expensive if Bill could identify graduates of the local cooking school. That way, he's targeting just the sort of prospective tenants he needs, and not wasting money advertising to hundreds or thousands of people who wouldn't be interested.

Direct mail can refer to sending stamped envelopes or advertisements via the postal service, or to sending email (or e-flyers) electronically. While email can be considerably less expensive than traditional direct mail, the same problem exists: it's not very effective unless it's targeted at the right individuals. Also, anyone using email to advertise properties must comply with federal and state anti-spam laws. (Advertising laws are discussed at the end of this chapter.)

Internet Advertising. Of course, most property managers no longer rely solely on traditional marketing methods. With the advent of computers and the Internet, it is more and

> **▶ Top Apartment Shopping Tools**
>
> Internet rental listing services: 80.9%
>
> Online classified websites (such as craigslist): 46.2%
>
> Word of mouth: 31.1%
>
> Local newspaper: 27.1%
>
> *Source: Apartments.com 2011*

more common to see property managers with websites, blogs, and social media accounts. In fact, statistics show that 75 – 80% of prospective tenants begin their property search online.

There are certain advantages to Internet marketing. For one thing, the Internet is "always on"—prospective tenants can get information about available properties 24 hours a day, whether the manager is there to answer the phone or not.

Another advantage of Internet marketing is the ability to target specific segments of the market easily. Search engines can bring renters looking for properties directly to the manager's website, while websites like craigslist allow a property manager to target specific geographic areas.

But perhaps the greatest advantage of Internet marketing is the ability to track the results of marketing efforts. Most online advertising websites keep statistics on how many people have viewed the ads, clicked links within the ads, and so on. Other tracking tools (such as "hit counters") allow the property manager to see how many people have visited the property's website. (We'll discuss evaluating marketing efforts in more detail later in this chapter.)

Now let's take a closer look at three of the most common ways to utilize Internet marketing: websites, rental listing services, and social networking tools.

Property websites. A website can consist of a simple page containing information about a property or building and the property manager's contact information. It may also be an elaborate site with links to virtual tours, floor plans, other properties owned by the same business, and information about the surrounding area.

Many potential tenants begin their rental search online, and these prospects will form their first impression of the property based on the website. A luxury high-rise building with state-of-the-art amenities is poorly represented by an amateur website, and potential tenants may be dissuaded from scheduling an appointment. On the other hand, a well-designed website with up-to-date information may convince a prospect that even a modest property is well cared for by a responsive manager.

When designing a website, both the property type and the client's needs should be considered. Here are some tips for designing and maintaining a website:

- **Use a professional.** As we said, a well-designed website is important; unless the manager (or one of the manager's staff) is extremely tech-savvy, it's worthwhile to hire a professional to create and maintain the website.

- **The website should reflect the property.** The style and tone of the website should reflect the feel of the property itself.
- **Details count.** Make sure there are no spelling or grammatical errors, every link on the website works properly, and information is easy to find.
- **Update often.** A website with outdated information will frustrate potential tenants, and give them the impression that the property manager doesn't care about her tenants or her property.

In some cases, a client with multiple properties will want a single website, with the home page including general information pertinent to all the properties, and individual pages for each property (or available unit/space).

> **Example:** Dai is the property manager for Sunshine Rentals, a company that owns three apartment buildings in town. Sunshine Rentals has one website for the company's rental process, late fees, pet policy, and other general information. That website also has links to individual webpages for each of the three properties. Each of these webpages gives specific details about that property, including rental rates, floor plans, local amenities, and virtual tours of individual units.

Alternatively, there may be a separate website for each property. This is especially helpful if the owner has very different types of properties, such as a fourplex in an older part of town, a 20-unit luxury building in a high-rent district, and a small retail space downtown.

Whatever type of website is used, it should include as much useful information as possible. The more information a prospect can find on the website, the less time the manager will waste fielding calls or emails from prospects who can't afford or don't want the type of property offered.

Many property management firms also maintain websites for their own businesses, oriented toward finding new clients. We'll discuss this type of website later in the chapter.

Rental services. A rental listing service is a website that's designed to bring tenants and property managers together. The rental service charges a fee to property managers to advertise individual units and entire buildings. Tenants can then search for certain types of properties by location, cost, features, and amenities. Property managers may find this type of service worth the expense, as it often results in qualified prospects.

Some services cater to both residential and commercial properties, but others specialize in one or the other. Look for a service that provides plenty of feedback and ways to track its effectiveness.

Social networking websites. Social networking may not result in a lot of qualified prospects, but it is an important (and cost-effective) part of branding. Use of websites such as Facebook, Twitter, LinkedIn, and blogs allows a property manager to show current and prospective tenants that he is knowledgeable about the market and cares about his tenants.

Social networking also gives the manager the opportunity to announce changes in procedures, newly-available units, special events, or problems that need to be addressed. It's a good way to stay in contact with and get feedback from current tenants. This helps keep tenants happy, leading to more lease renewals and tenant referrals. In addition, social networking can turn into viral marketing. **Viral marketing** occurs when customers actually market a product by word of mouth or by networking on the Internet.

Example: Mike manages an office complex. As part of his marketing efforts, he maintains a blog and a Facebook account, where he shares articles and information about the local market, business and office resources, and news about local events. People who follow his blog and Facebook account often share Mike's articles with their friends and business associates. Soon Mike is seen as one of the most knowledgeable property managers in the area: when someone has a property that needs to be managed, they are likely to go to Mike. Mike's social media efforts benefit himself as well as his clients.

A property manager should be careful to maintain a professional image at all times. The manager should monitor social networking sites on a regular basis, addressing tenant comments and questions in a timely, courteous manner.

Other Forms of Advertising. Although the forms of traditional and Internet marketing described above are the most common methods used by property managers, there are other forms that may be appropriate depending on the type and size of the property.

Some simple forms of advertising that can be effective include:

- **Bulletin boards.** Bulletin boards are usually better for advertising smaller properties, or when the manager is able to target very specific audiences. Examples include an apartment catering to retirees advertised on a senior center bulletin board; corporate housing advertised on the employer's bulletin board; or an apartment near nature trails advertised at a store that sells sporting equipment. Managers of large or expensive properties may find bulletin boards too casual, however.
- **Flyers/brochures.** Flyers and brochures can be expensive, but at times they're worth the cost. Managers can create flyers for individual units or for the client's property as a whole. (Ideally, a flyer for an individual unit will discuss

 QR Codes

Quick Response (QR) codes have been around for years, but have only been utilized as a marketing tool in the U.S. fairly recently. QR codes can be used on any type of printed material (such as business cards or property flyers), as well as emails, websites, and so on. You can generate a code using any of several free online QR code generators. Consumers with code readers (also available for free download) on their smartphones can then scan the QR code and will be taken directly to the URL that was entered. Want to try it out? Scan this code with your smartphone and see where it goes!

the property as whole, too). Flyers and brochures should look professional, and should fit the property's overall image. Professional flyers and brochures can be handed to visitors, put on display in model units, and mailed to prospects who call for more information.

- **Marketing to current tenants.** Some property managers find that marketing to current tenants is a good way to get referrals. Managers can send information about available units to current tenants by email or newsletter.

  Some property managers offer incentives for referrals ($100 off the next month's rent, for example). However, state laws vary on such incentives. Some states prohibit them altogether; others limit the number of times a current tenant can be compensated for referrals in a certain period of time (such as three times per year).

- **Open house/model unit.** Holding an open house in a staged model unit (in larger or new properties) can be a good way to bring prospects to the property. A skilled property manager or sales team may be able to convert some of those prospects into tenants.

Of course, any unit open to the public must be clean, with no outstanding maintenance issues. Ideally, the property will be staged with neutral furniture and colors so prospective tenants can easily imagine their own possessions in the space. Whoever shows the unit must be ready to answer questions about rental procedures, amenities, local features, and the property management team.

Larger properties, such as office buildings, major retail properties, and high rise residential properties may use more elaborate marketing techniques, such as:

- **Billboards.** One way to target a specific audience is to place a billboard in an advantageous location. For instance, advertising a new commercial building or an in-city apartment building on a billboard along a commuter road could reach hundreds of prospective tenants.

- **Radio and television.** Radio and television advertising is very expensive. While it reaches a very large audience, it doesn't target qualified prospects very effectively. However, radio and television advertisements may be cost-effective for new buildings during the lease-up period.

- **Promotional presentations.** Promotional presentations at local or national events (such as trade shows) may be appropriate for large buildings—commercial or residential—during a lease-up period. Ideally, the presenter will have a scale model and/or floor plans available, as well as videos, brochures, and contact information. Promotional presentations are rarely an effective way to market individual units or smaller properties (very expensive individual units, such as a remodeled penthouse, may be an exception to this rule).

Incentives

Managers may also use incentives to market the property to potential tenants. Incentives may be offered to current tenants for referrals (where allowed by law; see above) or to incoming tenants. The type and amount of the incentive depends on vacancy rates for the building itself and for the area as a whole.

Incentives for existing tenants might be a flat fee (such $100 per referral) or a discount on future rent. Incentives for new tenants might include a free month's rent, free cable TV, free parking, or other amenities. The incentives for commercial tenants may include free rent, free or reduced-rate remodeling, and so on.

Marketing the Property Management Business

Many of the marketing principles and techniques we've discussed can be used to market the property manager's own business. In this case, the manager's product is her management services. As when marketing a retail space or commercial property, the manager should identify the special features that make her property management services unique.

> **Example:** Rosa is just starting her residential property management company. There are several other companies in the area that offer the same basic services. However, Rosa's company is going to disburse client funds on the fifteenth of each month, rather than on the last day of each month (which is what all the other companies do). This is the special feature that Rosa will focus on when marketing her property management business to prospective clients.

When targeting potential customers, the property manager must consider the types of buildings she manages. A manager who specializes in office buildings will focus on a different market segment than one who primarily manages single-family homes and small apartment buildings. Additionally, the manager should consider what type of client she wants to work with, such as corporations, individual owners, or institutions. (See Chapter 3 for more on the different types of rental property owners.)

Management Company's Website

The property manager's website serves several purposes. First, it's a place for the manager to advertise his management services and highlight the type of clients and properties he works with. If the manager prefers to work with corporate clients and office space (as opposed to sole proprietors and single-family homes) the website should communicate this information. Again, it's a matter of finding qualified prospects. The manager should clearly state what services he offers; this will reduce calls from unqualified prospects. Of course, the website should also highlight the manager's experience and credentials. Always include positive testimonials from current and former clients and tenants.

The manager's website is a good place to advertise the properties he's currently managing. Not only does this show potential clients the kind of properties the manager handles, it also helps his existing clients by sending some traffic to the websites of those properties.

The property manager's website can serve as a source of information for tenants, setting forth the rules regarding late fees, pets, parking, and so on. The website may also function as a site for making online rental payments, submitting repair requests, and emailing questions or complaints directly to the manager.

Finally, the manager can use the website to illustrate his knowledge of the neighborhood, the industry, and the local market. This can be done through a blog, or by linking to social networking sites, such as Facebook or Twitter. Not only does this serve to develop his branding, but it can also result in referrals and additional business.

Advertising

A property manager has a variety of options for advertising her property management business. These include on-site signage (at both her business location and currently managed projects) and classified ads. Online directories are usually available, where the manager can list her company and her services. Facebook, Twitter, and websites like craigslist are also good places to advertise the manager's services. Any ad, sign, or online posting for a currently managed property or unit should list the manager's name, phone number, and website. (Depending on state law, additional information may be necessary.)

As always, the manager should choose the type of advertising based on the target audience (corporate or individual clients), type of property (residential, office, or retail), and budget constraints. The manager should be sure to track and evaluate her advertising results, and make changes to her advertising plan when necessary. We'll talk about how to evaluate advertising efforts shortly.

Networking/Referrals

Networking at trade shows and other local events is a good source of future clients, as are referrals from satisfied current and past clients. Real estate professionals who focus on selling property may also be a good source of referrals.

> **Example:** Claudia is a real estate agent. When the market is slow, some of her sellers decide to rent their properties instead of trying to sell them. Claudia's real estate company doesn't do property management, so she refers these clients to A-1 Property Management. She's worked with the company for years, and knows that her clients will be happy with the company's services. In return, A-1 Property Management refers buyers and sellers to Claudia when the opportunity arises.

Legal Limitations. Property managers should be careful to understand federal and state laws governing referrals. For example, as we'll discuss soon, it would be a violation of the federal Fair Housing Act to ask only white tenants for referrals.

In addition, only a minority of states allow payment of referral fees or rent concessions to current tenants (unless they are licensed real estate agents). Even in states where it's allowed, state law usually limits the amount of the fee ($100 is a common figure) and how often per year it can be claimed (for instance, no more than five times in any twelve-month period). Check state law to see if referrals are permitted or regulated before offering them to clients or tenants.

Direct Solicitation

Direct solicitation can be a very effective method of advertising property management services. Of course, identifying potential clients (rather than sending mail to an entire town, for example) will help focus marketing dollars more effectively. Some property managers purchase mailing lists, which are available for both U.S. mail and email. Phone number lists are also available. Of course, property managers who use such lists must comply with federal and state anti-spam and Do Not Call laws (these laws are discussed at the end of this chapter).

The property manager may be able to identify potential prospects by researching rental properties in the area. If a property lacks tenants or suffers from deferred maintenance (like overgrown landscaping or peeling paint), it may need new, more professional management. By sending the property owner information about his services, a manager may be in a position to gain a new client when the current property management contract terminates.

Contacting Potential Clients. A property manager can contact potential clients directly by mail or by phone. This initial contact is the manager's first opportunity to make a good impression. She should be prepared to answer the owner's questions about her services, why her property management company is superior to others in the area, and why the owner/prospect should think about using her services.

The property manager's goal is to get the potential client to request a management proposal. (We discussed property management proposals in Chapter 4.) At that point, the manager can work on converting the prospect into a client.

Evaluating the Effectiveness of Marketing

The goal of marketing is to produce the greatest number of qualified prospects for the least amount of time and money. That's why it's important for the property manager to continually evaluate the cost-effectiveness of both her overall marketing plan and her individual marketing efforts. Methods of evaluating the effectiveness of marketing include traffic reports, prospect cards, and conversion ratios.

Traffic Reports

Traffic reports track the number and type of prospects obtained, and how each prospect heard about the property. The manager should record whether the prospect was a drop-in visitor, a phone contact, a website visitor, or an email user. The manager should also note the source of each prospect: did the person hear about the property (or the manager) from the Internet, a newspaper ad, a sign, or from friends or other real estate professionals?

It's useful to break down each source into subcategories. For instance, the manager may want to know whether the Internet prospect came from his website, craigslist, Facebook, a rental service, or an online advertisement. Many prospective tenants use multiple sources to find rentals (especially when searching online), so the more information, the better.

The manager will typically give the property owner some form of a traffic report. This is often a weekly or monthly report, depending on the owner's needs and the size of the property. See Figure 6.2 for an example of a simple monthly traffic report.

Prospect Cards

Prospect cards list information about individual prospects. These cards (which can be on paper or on the computer) include more detailed information than traffic reports, and are used by the manager to follow up with potential clients or tenants.

The manager can fill out the cards when the prospect visits the property or calls for information. Alternatively, the prospect could fill out the card online, via the property's website or the manager's website.

Information that should be included on the prospect card includes:

- the prospect's contact information (name, address, phone number, email);
- the source of the prospect's referral (Internet, newspaper ad, sign);
- when the prospect is planning to move; and
- the type of property the prospect is interested in.

If the prospect is interested in residential property, the manager should note whether the prospect is interested in a one-, two-, or three-bedroom unit, or any other preferences she might have. Commercial property managers will want to note the prospect's desired square footage, type of property (small retail, large retail, etc.), intended use of the space, remodeling needs, and other items (such as whether the prospect needs janitorial or land-scaping services). See Figure 6.3 for an example of a simple prospect card.

Figure 6.2 Monthly traffic report

Monthly Traffic Report

Month: _____ May _____

Total inquiries: ___ 57 _____

Telephone: ___ 37 _____

Walk-in: ___ 20 _____

Total showings: ___ 24 _____

Total rentals: ___ 4 _____

Source of inquiry	Phone call	Walk-in	Showing	Rental
Sign:	1	1	2	0
Referral:	8	7	10	1
Newspaper:	12	4	5	1
Internet:	16	8	7	2

Figure 6.3 Prospect card

Prospect Card

Thank you for your interest in ABC Apartments!   Date: _____

Name: _____ Phone number: _____

Address: _____ Email address: _____

Which type of unit do you prefer?   1BD   2BD   3BD   *(please circle one)*

How many people will be living in the unit? _____

Pets?   Y   N   *(please circle one)*

Will you need parking?   Y   N   *(please circle one)*

When are you interested in moving? _____

How did you hear about us? _____

Cost Per Prospect and Conversion Ratio

As we said earlier, marketing is effective if it brings qualified prospects to the property. One way to measure a marketing plan is to track the cost per prospect for each type of advertising used. The **cost per prospect** evaluates the money spent on a particular method of advertising based on the number of prospects generated by that method.

> **Example:** If a manager spends $100 in newspaper advertising, and that advertising results in 10 prospects, the cost per prospect is $10.
>
> $100 Ads ÷ 10 Prospects = $10 Per prospect
>
> If that manager spends $100 on flyers, and the flyers bring in only two prospects, the cost per prospect is $50.
>
> $100 Ads ÷ 2 Prospects = $50 Per prospect

The manager in this example would probably conclude that the newspaper ads are a much more cost-effective way to advertise the property. However, the cost per prospect is not the only number the manager needs to consider. She also needs to track and evaluate the conversion ratio. The **conversion ratio** measures how many prospects it takes to get a signed lease, expressed as a percentage. (Note: to convert a ratio into a percentage, divide the first number by the second number, then multiply by 100.)

> **Example:** Let's return to the previous example. Although the newspaper ads bring in 10 prospects, only one of the prospects ends up signing a lease. Therefore, the conversion ratio for the newspaper advertising is 1:10, or 10% (1 ÷ 10 = .1 × 100 = 10%).

The flyers brought in two prospects, one of whom signs a lease. The flyers cost more per prospect, but the conversion ratio is 1:2, or 50% ($1 \div 2 = .5 \times 100 = 50\%$). This may be because the flyer has pictures of the property and a diagram of the floor plan, while the newspaper ad does not; the flyer attracted fewer prospects, but those who called were more interested.

In this case, the property manager might conclude that the flyers are a better use of advertising dollars, because they resulted in better qualified prospects. Or he might conclude that the newspaper ads need to be reworded, in order to attract more people who are actually interested in the property.

Following Up with the Owner

The last step in evaluating the effectiveness of marketing efforts is following up with the property owner. Along with sending the owner the weekly or monthly traffic report, the manager should also be prepared to give more detailed reports on the effectiveness of each type of advertising, the cost per prospect, and the conversion ratio. When necessary, the manager should be prepared to suggest changes to the current advertising methods or to the advertising budget (via a revised management plan or marketing plan). As we discussed in Chapter 4, the manager should include a cost-benefit analysis for any proposed changes.

Public Relations

As noted earlier, an important part of marketing involves effective branding: positioning the product (the property) in the mind of the consumer as representing a certain desirable quality. An apartment building may want to brand itself as family-friendly, or a retail space may want to be known as a destination for high-end shoppers.

Creating and keeping this reputation is known as **public relations**, and should be an ongoing part of a property manager's marketing plan. Public relations involves more than just periodic announcements to the news media; it also includes involvement with community activities and the ability to respond to negative events when they happen.

Community Involvement

Community involvement is a natural extension of networking. Opportunities will arise for the manager to participate in local events, and this participation is a form of advertising. In addition, community involvement helps with branding. For example, if the manager is trying to attract families to his residential properties, he may choose to sponsor a Little League team. If the manager wants to appeal to upscale professionals and luxury clients, he may decide to hold a wine tasting or art event.

Some activities have a specific generational appeal. For example, a manager of a retirement community with lots of veterans may want to sponsor the town's Memorial Day parade or participate in placing flags at the cemetery.

The manager must choose her activities carefully, though. The event should never be negative or controversial. Finally, the manager must always behave professionally and courteously at public events.

Announcements

Of course, getting involved in community events does little good if no one knows about it. Announcements (also known as press releases) are one way to make sure potential clients hear about your involvement in the community. Press releases can also be used to inform the community about property renovations, sales figures, major new tenants, and so on.

> **Example:** Here's a short press release for a residential property:
>
> *Sheridan Property Management is pleased to announce that Riverview Apartments has recently undergone a complete renovation. All units now feature stainless steel appliances and granite countertops. A model unit can be viewed at 123 Riverview Drive, and the public is encouraged to stop by on Saturday for a tour.*

Larger properties often send press releases to local media to announce the lease-up period of a new property. Sometimes, the property will end up as the focal point of a more general newspaper or television story about the local real estate market. Of course, this acts as free advertising and is almost always welcome.

All types of properties can use their website, blog, and social media sites (such as Facebook and Twitter) to draw attention to press releases. This integrated approach to marketing offers a cost-effective way to reach a larger number of people at little additional cost.

For larger properties, the property manager should consider issuing internal press releases to ensure current tenants are aware of upcoming changes to the property, opportunities for community involvement, staff changes, and other types of news. This helps current tenants feel involved, which in turn makes them more likely to provide feedback, renew their leases and make referrals. The manager can send out internal press releases separately (via U.S. mail or email) or include them in regular weekly or monthly newsletters.

Responding to Negative Events

Regardless of how well a property is managed, problems inevitably occur. Responding in a positive manner to such issues is also a part of public relations.

The property manager may need to address negative events such as:

- changes that affect tenants (such as price increases, new rules, upcoming construction noise, and changes in the services offered);
- crime (such as burglaries, car thefts, and personal assaults), not just within the property but in nearby areas and buildings;
- tenant-caused problems (such as noise and trash);
- unique events that may cause disruption (such as weather-related problems, political or social incidents, nearby activities such as planned protests, and parades); and
- for commercial buildings, loss of tenants (especially anchor tenants).

Responding quickly and effectively to problems accomplishes several things. First, it minimizes any disruption to tenants. A quick response also reduces the risk of potential liability for the property owner. It also preserves the reputation of both the property and the manager, and reduces the chance of similar problems occurring in the future. Finally, tenants appreciate knowing they can count on management to act quickly, which increases the likelihood of both lease renewals and referrals.

Advertising Laws

Whether you prefer using traditional marketing methods or the Internet, it's important to be aware of the various laws—both state and federal—that regulate your advertising practices. Some laws are designed to make sure your advertising isn't discriminatory. Other laws—such as real estate laws—require certain disclosures in your marketing materials. And some laws restrict unsolicited marketing.

Antidiscrimination Laws

Both state and federal fair housing laws apply to property management marketing activities. For example, under the federal Fair Housing Act, it is illegal to use advertising that indicates or implies a preference, restriction, or intent to discriminate against potential tenants on the basis of their race, color, national origin, religion, gender, disability, or familial status. (The groups of persons protected under the Fair Housing Act and other antidiscrimination laws are referred to as **protected classes**. Other state and federal laws protect additional classes. We'll discuss this in Chapter 14.)

Other examples of unlawful marketing practices include advertising only in certain neighborhoods for discriminatory reasons, and refusing to show a property to a particular protected class of renter.

An ad can violate antidiscrimination laws even if the manager doesn't intend to discriminate in her advertising.

> **Example:** A flyer that describes an apartment building as "Near local church and synagogue" may seem to indicate that Muslims are unwelcome, even if that was not the intention of the ad. Likewise, using only Caucasian models in a display ad or flyer could send a message that minorities are not welcome, even if that was not the intent.

Many property managers send advertisements to current tenants in search of potential renters. While such solicitations are not necessarily discriminatory, they can have a discriminatory effect when:

1. persons of a particular race or ethnic background are singled out for exclusion (copies of the solicitation are not sent to them); or
2. the solicitation suggests that the recipient can control the type or character of the person who will lease the property. For example, if a solicitation suggests that a tenant can "uphold the standards of the community" by referring potential renters, the tenant might infer that he can control the race or ethnicity of new residents.

Finally, it's always a good idea to include the fair housing logo in all advertising materials. And state or city law may require property managers to display a letter-size fair housing poster in a prominent location, such as the door to the leasing office or in the model unit. (For more on antidiscrimination laws and protected classes, see Chapter 14.)

State License Law

When the property manager is a real estate licensee, advertising that is misleading under state and federal laws may also be a violation of a state's real estate license law, and could be grounds for disciplinary action. Sanctions usually include fines and possibly suspension or revocation of the real estate agent's license, so it's important to know and understand these regulations.

Blind Ads. Many states prohibit blind ads. This means that advertisements must include the real estate company's name as licensed. An ad that does not state the company's name is a **blind ad** and may violate the license law.

Additionally, states may require that a real estate agent advertising her own rental property disclose in the ad that she is a real estate licensee.

Advertising on the Internet. Now that advertising on the Internet is so common, many states have developed guidelines requiring a real estate licensee to disclose his licensed status fully in all Internet communications. For example, Washington has particularly stringent requirements for Internet advertising. To meet the requirement for full disclosure, a Washington licensee must disclose:

- the licensee's name, the name of the firm with which the licensee is affiliated, the city and state in which the licensee's office is located, and the states in which the licensee holds a real estate license; and
- the firm's name as registered, the city and state in which the firm is located, and the states in which the firm is licensed.

State guidelines may also include suggestions on how to meet the disclosure requirements for various types of Internet advertising, such as websites, email, discussion groups, chat sessions, and banner ads. Property managers should check with their state to be sure that they are complying with all state advertising disclosure laws.

Unsolicited Marketing

While some federal and state laws regulate advertising content, others regulate the methods used to deliver that content. These restrictions are commonly called **Do Not Call** or **anti-spam** laws.

For example, it's not permissible to call individuals who have registered with the Do Not Call Registry maintained by the Federal Trade Commission. Violators of the law could be fined up to $16,000 per incident. The manager should understand these rules and obtain a copy of the registry before engaging in any cold calling. (It is not a violation of the law to contact actual clients or to return calls.)

Federal and state laws also apply to unsolicited email. For example, the federal law that restricts unsolicited emails is known as the **CAN-SPAM Act** (short for Controlling the Assault of Non-Solicited Pornography and Marketing Act). More information regarding the specific requirements of the federal Do Not Call laws and the CAN-SPAM Act can be found at the Federal Trade Commission's website at www.ftc.gov.

Phone and email marketing efforts may also violate individual state laws. Violators of these laws can be subject to substantial fines, so a manager must be sure to check the requirements in her particular location.

Chapter Summary

1. A product is any good or service that can be marketed or sold to the public. Marketing should focus on the unique qualities of goods and services that make them stand out from their competition.

2. A manager should know the customer and use targeted marketing to identify potential tenants and clients. Demographics are used to identify the target audience. Focusing marketing efforts on people who actually need the type of property being offered will result in more qualified prospects.

3. Branding is the process of developing and maintaining a certain image in the mind of consumers. A brand can be a name, term, symbol, design, or idea that people associate with the property manager or building.

4. The property manager must determine how much advertising is necessary and what would be most cost-effective. Ideally, advertising will generate a large number of qualified prospects at the lowest possible cost per prospect.

5. Traditional advertising methods include signage, classified and display advertising, "For Rent" magazines, and direct mail. Internet advertising includes websites, rental services, and social networking sites. Additionally, some property managers may also use bulletin boards, flyers and brochures, marketing to current tenants, open houses and model units, billboards, radio and television ads, promotional presentations, or incentives to advertise their business or rental properties.

6. Public relations involves creating and maintaining a positive reputation among tenants, clients, and the public. Community involvement and informational press releases are both good ways to develop and keep a positive reputation. But it's equally important for property managers to respond to negative events in a professional and timely manner.

7. Both federal and state laws regulate advertising by property managers. The manager must be sure to comply with anti-discrimination laws, state laws regarding disclosures in advertisements by real estate licensees, and state and federal anti-spam and Do Not Call laws.

Key Terms

Marketing – The process by which a business promotes and sells a product to customers.

Product – Anything that can be marketed or sold.

Targeted marketing – Dividing a large group of potential customers into smaller groups, then focusing marketing efforts on one or two key segments of those groups.

Demographics – Characteristics of a human population or a segment of that population, such as average family size, median age, education level, etc.

Generational marketing – A special way of segmenting a market, not just by age but also by social, economic, and psychological factors.

Branding – The process of developing an image for a company, product, or person in the marketplace.

Qualified prospect – A person that has the need for a particular product or service as well as the ability to purchase it.

Reach – The size of an audience targeted by an advertisement.

Frequency – The number of times an advertisement will appear in a given medium.

Lease-up – The initial period when a new rental property enters the market and is seeking its first tenants.

Viral marketing – A type of marketing that occurs when customers market a product themselves, often by word of mouth or on the Internet.

Traffic report – A record of the number and type of prospects who call or visit, including how they heard about the property.

Prospect cards – Forms that are used in person or online to gather information about individual prospects, including name, address, the type of property desired, and how the prospect heard about the property.

Cost per prospect – An amount of money spent on a type of advertising, divided by the number of prospects the advertising generates.

Conversion ratio – A measure of how many prospects it takes to get a signed lease, expressed as a percentage.

Public relations – The process of creating and maintaining a positive image in the community.

Protected classes – Groups of persons protected under the federal Fair Housing Act and other federal and state antidiscrimination laws.

Blind ad – An ad that violates state licensing law by failing to disclose the real estate firm's name as licensed.

Do Not Call Law – A federal law that prohibits calling individuals who have registered with the Do Not Call registry.

CAN-SPAM Act – A federal law that restricts unsolicited emails.

Chapter Quiz

1. An example of a product a property manager may market is:

   a) a two-bedroom, one-bath apartment unit

   b) the property manager's services

   c) excellent customer service

   d) All of the above

2. Ben manages an office building whose tenants consist primarily of doctors, dentists, and other medical professionals. When advertising vacant space in the building, which targeted segment should Ben market to in order to generate the greatest number of qualified prospects?

   a) The 4,263 people who stated in a recent survey that they "rent" rather than own their homes

   b) All 275 local businesses in town

   c) The 64 medical professionals who currently lease space in the area

   d) College graduates

3. In general, Internet marketing can be effective when marketing to all of the following, except:

   a) millennials

   b) matures

   c) baby boomers

   d) Gen X-ers

4. The manager of a large residential rental property wants to attract young families. When attempting to brand their image, which phrase might be the most appropriate?

   a) "Grow with us!"

   b) "Retire in style!"

   c) "Where business matters!"

   d) "Luxury is worth it!"

5. Juan wants to advertise his single-family rental property. Which type of advertising is likely to generate the most qualified prospects in a cost-effective manner?

   a) A state-wide radio ad

   b) A billboard on the freeway near the property

   c) An ad in the rental section of several local communities' newspapers

   d) A display ad in a garden magazine with 100,000 subscribers

6. A sign on a rental property should:

   a) include as much detail as possible, such as testimonials and late-payment policies

   b) state the property manager's name and phone number

   c) be in a font that is easy to read from a distance

   d) Both b and c

7. Display advertising may include any of the following except:

   a) pictures and floor plans

   b) text

   c) logos

   d) a virtual tour

8. Sam maintains a blog to advertise his property management business and available units. He also posts information about the local market and upcoming events. Soon, people are sharing Sam's posts with their friends and recommending his services. This is known as:

   a) viral marketing

   b) shared commerce

   c) public utilization

   d) business equity

9. A summary of basic information about the number and type of prospects that visit or call a property is called a:

   a) prospect card
   b) traffic report
   c) conversion ratio
   d) press release

10. When Salim shows a model unit in his building, he gives the visitors a short form to fill out with some basic information, such as their names and phone numbers, the type of property they are looking for, when they plan to move, and how they heard about the property. Salim is asking them to fill out a:

    a) prospect card
    b) traffic report
    c) lease
    d) marketing report

11. When evaluating his marketing efforts for the month of May, Jim notices that it cost $50 to send out 1,000 flyers, which resulted in five calls. He also spent $100 to take an ad out in the local newspaper with 500 subscribers, which resulted in six calls. Which method of marketing is the most cost-effective?

    a) The flyers, because they only cost five cents each
    b) The flyers, because they cost less per qualified prospect than the newspaper ad
    c) The newspaper ad, because it resulted in more calls
    d) The newspaper ad, because the cost per prospect is only about $17

12. A property manager may want to send out a press release about which of the following events?

    a) A new swimming pool
    b) Recent crime at a nearby building
    c) The loss of an anchor tenant in a shopping mall
    d) All of the above

13. All of the following would violate the federal Fair Housing Act, except:

    a) an ad for a property in a Hispanic neighborhood that uses white, African-American, and Hispanic models
    b) an ad that states, "Near local mosque!"
    c) an ad for a property in a Hispanic neighborhood published only in Hispanic newspapers
    d) asking for referrals only from white tenants

14. Brad is a real estate licensee who manages several rental properties for his brokerage firm. Brad's state licensing law requires him to include the name of his firm as licensed in all of his ads. If Brad fails to do so, this results in a:

    a) violation of the CAN-SPAM Act
    b) blind ad
    c) license law violation
    d) Both b and c

15. Violating the federal Do Not Call law can result in a fine, per violation, of up to:

    a) $1,000
    b) $7,500
    c) $10,000
    d) $16,000

Answer Key

1. d) Products include both tangible items and services, such as an apartment unit or property management services, but also intangible qualities, such as good customer service.

2. c) Qualified prospects are those who have a need for the property. Marketing to all renters or local businesses might generate in a lot of interest, but few qualified prospects for an office building that caters to medical professionals. Although there are only 64 medical professionals in town, marketing to them is likely to result in the highest number of qualified prospects for the least amount of money.

3. b) Matures include older generations born before 1945. While they use the Internet, they primarily do so for social reasons, and prefer traditional forms of marketing, such as newspapers and face-to-face sales.

4. a) Of the options, branding that includes the phrase "Grow with us!" is the most likely to create a family-oriented image in consumers' minds.

5. c) A billboard, display ad in a magazine, or radio ad might reach a large number of people, but the cost per qualified prospect would likely be quite high. Of the options given, local newspaper ads would probably generate the most qualified prospects cost-effectively.

6. d) Too much information on a sign can overwhelm the viewer, who may be passing by quickly. However, the sign should state the manager's name and phone number and be easy to read from a distance.

7. d) Display ads may contain text as well as pictures, floor plans, logos, and so on. Virtual tours are more likely to be used in Internet advertising.

8. a) Viral marketing happens when customers market a product or service for the business, usually by word of mouth.

9. b) A traffic report is a summary of basic information about the number and type of prospects that visit or call a property, while a prospect card collects specific information about each prospect.

10. a) A prospect card is used to gather information about individual prospects who call or visit a property, and these cards provide a useful way for property managers to follow up with potential tenants.

11. b) While the flyers only cost five cents each, it's the number of qualified prospects they generate that matters. In this case, the flyers are more cost effective than the newspaper ad, because while the newspaper ad generated 6 prospects, the cost per prospect was about $17 each ($100 ÷ 6 = $17). The flyers generated fewer prospects, but the cost per prospect was only $10 each ($50 ÷ 5 = $10).

12. d) Press releases can be used not only to announce positive changes (such as a new swimming pool) but also to address negative events, such as nearby crime or the loss of an anchor tenant in a retail space.

13. a) Ads may violate the Fair Housing Act if they seem to indicate a preference for a certain type of renter. Using models in display ads that represent many types of people is one way to avoid violating the Fair Housing Act.

14. d) A blind ad is an ad that doesn't state the real estate firm's name as licensed. In most states, it is a license law violation.

15. d) Violating the federal Do Not Call law can result in a fine of up to $16,000 per incident.

Chapter 7

Leasing

Outline

Introduction

As we discussed in the last chapter, finding the right tenants for a property begins with marketing. Once the manager has an adequate pool of applicants, the challenging task of selecting qualified tenants begins.

The first part of this chapter takes a look at the process of selecting tenants. We'll begin with a discussion of the tenant application, followed by a summary of the aspects of an applicant's background the manager should investigate (such as credit, rental, and employment history). Next, we'll discuss how to evaluate this information to determine whether the applicant will make a suitable tenant.

The second part of the chapter examines leases, which govern the relationship between an owner (via her manager) and the tenant. We will focus on key provisions of a lease contract, such as rent, maintenance, and alterations.

Finally, the chapter concludes with a look at the practicalities of signing a lease.

Selecting Tenants

Both the manager and the owner want tenants who will:

- keep the property in good condition,
- pay the rent on time,
- harmonize well with other tenants, and
- stay for a reasonably long time.

A solid application process is the best way to find tenants who meet these requirements. The tenant selection process consists of three steps: application, screening, and acceptance (or denial).

Application Process

The manager begins the application process by gathering information about the prospective tenant(s).

Application Form. The manager of even a simple residential property should have applicants complete an application form. Use of a form serves two purposes. First, it ensures that full data is collected for every applicant in an efficient manner. Second, a standardized form means that each applicant is asked the same questions; this is the best way to avoid discriminatory bias, or the appearance of it, in the tenant selection process.

Of course, the owner or manager must be diligent about requiring applicants to complete all portions of the forms or much of the value will be lost.

Residential tenant applications. Many property management service websites offer application forms that can be downloaded and used for free (many professional associations also have forms). The sample form shown in Figure 7.1 is typical for a residential tenancy. Items covered by the form include personal information, rental and employment history, asset information, and references.

A statement above the signature line on the application form authorizes the landlord to investigate the applicant's background, including credit, employment, and criminal history. Obtaining this permission from the applicant is critical. The **Fair Credit Reporting Act** (FCRA) requires written authorization from an individual before running a background check on him.

Many states require that residential tenants receive a receipt for any fees and deposits they pay. A line at the bottom of the application form serves as the tenant's receipt for the application fee. Even when not required by law, receipts are a good business practice.

Commercial tenant applications. Compared to residential forms, commercial tenant applications are usually much more complicated. Whether the leased space is office, retail, or industrial, the application form may run half a dozen pages or more.

Along with the basic questions found in a residential rental application, most commercial application forms also request a description of:

- business operations,
- the names and roles of employees,
- the owner/lease signer's role in the business,
- any financing, and
- any planned improvements to the leased space.

This list isn't exhaustive. Note that the last item is subject to negotiation and may actually be the landlord's responsibility, as we'll discuss later in the chapter.

The application form, along with its accompanying documentation, is often referred to as the **qualification package**. The contents of the package varies according to the type of the property (retail, office, or industrial), but generally depends more on the size of the tenant business and whether it is new or established.

Figure 7.1 Sample residential rental application form

RENTAL APPLICATION
(Each adult resident must complete a separate form and pay a separate screening fee.)

Applicant name _____ Phone # _____ DOB _____

SS #_____ Driver's license # _____ State _____ Exp. _____

Rental History

Current address _____ City _____ State _____ Zip _____

Landlord's name _____ Phone # _____ How long at address _____

Previous address _____ City _____ State _____ Zip _____

Landlord's name _____ Phone # _____ How long at address _____

Employment History

Present employer _____ How long at job _____

Address _____

Position _____ Monthly income _____ Phone # _____

Assets

Name of bank _____ Account # _____

Automobile: Yr _____ Make _____ Model _____

State/License Plate # _____

Legal History

Have you ever been party to an eviction? [ ] Yes [ ] No

If yes, describe _____

Have you ever filed for bankruptcy? [ ] Yes [ ] No

If yes, describe _____

Personal References

Name_____ Relationship _____ Phone #_____ Yrs. known ____

Name_____ Relationship _____ Phone #_____ Yrs. known ____

Proposed Occupants

Total number of adults _____ Total number of children (under age 18) _____

Names and relationships of all occupants _____

_____

Describe all pets _____

I CERTIFY that the above answers are true and complete. I authorize investigation of all statements in this application for screening to determine my suitability as a tenant (including credit check and criminal background screening).

Signature _____ Date _____

Received from applicant a non-refundable fee of $_____ dollars for tenant screening.

Almost every qualification package includes the application form and the following documents:

- profit and loss statements,
- tax returns,
- personal financial statements,
- operating budget and five-year budget,
- business plan,
- business entity organizational documents (LLC agreement, articles of incorporation, or partnership agreement),
- franchise agreement (if any), and
- resumes of key personnel in the business.

Many of these documents, such as the personal financial statement, should be signed.

Businesses usually have to provide two or three years' worth of financial statements and tax returns. Landlords may require owners of small- and medium-size businesses to personally guarantee the lease (discussed in more detail at the end of the chapter). If so, the owners need to provide personal financial statements and tax returns. Some landlords hire outside experts, such as accountants or other consultants, to evaluate complicated financial documents.

Of course, new businesses won't be able to provide business tax returns and financial statements. But because startups fail at a relatively high rate and pose a significant risk of default, a landlord evaluating a startup applicant should pay extra attention to the business plan, budgets, and resumes of key personnel.

Identification. A property manager must require identification from an applicant before signing a lease. An Executive Order under the Patriot Act requires landlords to check the names of prospective tenants (or the officers, partners, or sole proprietors of a prospective tenant's business) against the Specially Designated Nationals watch list maintained by the Office of Foreign Assets Control. (This order is discussed in greater detail in Chapter 14.)

A manager should ask to see a driver's license or other photo identification when accepting a lease application. Photocopy or scan the ID if possible and attach a copy to the application.

Reservation Fee. Some residential property managers require that an applicant submit a reservation fee to hold the space for two or three days while the manager performs the background check. Reservation fees aren't used with commercial properties.

Reservation fees are used to discourage applicants who are not serious or who are unlikely to qualify for the apartment. However, the fee may also discourage good applicants, so many managers avoid using them. To some degree, whether a reservation fee is charged is a matter of what the market will bear: in a market with few available spaces, renters may not be dissuaded by reservation fees.

Note that technically a "fee" is nonrefundable while a "deposit" is refundable if certain conditions are met. If the money won't be refunded, the receipt given to the applicant must state that the money is nonrefundable (this is true with any money accepted by the manager). Never call a nonrefundable fee a "deposit."

Often, the reservation fee is not a fee at all, but a deposit; if the tenant is approved, the money is either returned, credited to the first month's rent, or applied to the security deposit. (Returning the money may be simpler than making credits or deductions, which can end up confusing both parties.)

Investigating the Applicant

With the application in hand, the manager or owner can begin the process of investigating the applicant's background to determine if she will be suitable as a tenant. The investigation focuses on information contained on the application—legal history (both criminal and civil), rental history, employment, and general financial creditworthiness. A manager often starts with a screening service to check the applicant's background, then personally investigates other information contained on the application form.

Screening Services. For a fee, a screening service collects, analyzes, and summarizes legal and personal information about a potential tenant. The applicant usually pays the screening fee.

It's important to use a reputable service, both to increase the likelihood of receiving accurate information and to make sure that the screening service complies with various statutes (chiefly, the Fair Credit Reporting Act).

Residential applicants are screened early in the process. With commercial applicants, a screening service may be used somewhat later, after there's evidence that a lease agreement can actually be reached. When the applicant is a business, the manager might screen several individuals: the owners, any guarantors, and the business entity itself, unless it is a start-up.

Screening services require a manager to provide basic identifying information about herself, and to state a legitimate reason for making a background check. The services require this to avoid helping identity thieves and also to comply with FCRA requirements. Managers of larger properties may have to open a commercial screening account; this involves an onsite inspection of the rental business by the screening service to verify the landlord's legitimacy.

Some screening services allow the tenant to submit his information directly to the website and pay for the investigation; the manager then receives a simple analysis on viability. This approach protects the applicant's privacy, but removes the manager from the process to such an extent that it has yet to achieve widespread usage.

Legal history. A number of screening databases rely on information voluntarily supplied by banks or other nongovernment parties, such as landlords. That means the quality of the information may vary. Also, inexpensive reports on an applicant's civil and criminal history must be taken with a grain of salt. There is no universal criminal database, for example—at least not one available to non-law-enforcement personnel. A truly thorough report on legal history requires a time-consuming county-by-county search of records, likely to cost more money than a screening warrants. (Many counties now allow online searches that a manager could perform himself, but again, this can be quite time-consuming.)

Even when the manager is using a screening service, the tenant application should still ask about legal problems. If the tenant fails to answer honestly about something later

Screening Service Costs and Coverage

A screening service might charge $16–$20 for a basic search (SSN validation, Patriot Act check, evictions, bankruptcies, criminal convictions, and sex offender registration). This may include a basic credit recommendation. A full credit report might cost another $10, meaning a total of around $25–$30 at most sites.

Here are the types of databases a typical screening service will use:

- **Consumer credit.** Information from the three major national credit reporting agencies: Experian, TransUnion, and Equifax.
- **Business credit.** Information from a national credit reporting agency.
- **County criminal.** Varies by state, as some counties do not report criminal data information. Manual search of county criminal cases can be conducted. Fee varies.
- **Office of Foreign Assets Control/Patriot Act.** National database.
- **Sex offender.** Information from state sex offender registries.
- **Social security.** National database.
- **Bankruptcy.** National database.
- **Liens, judgments.** Varies by state. Manual search of county civil court records available. Fee varies.
- **Evictions.** National database.
- **NSF checks/debits.** National database.

revealed in the screening, that should be a red flag. Also, if the tenant does report a problem, such as a bankruptcy, a simple conversation with the applicant can clarify the situation.

> **Example:** Jakob checks a box on the apartment rental application form to indicate a past bankruptcy. Instead of rejecting the application, the apartment manager gives him a call. "That bankruptcy was about four years ago," Jakob explains. "I was laid off and had a lot of medical bills from a serious accident. But I'm fine now, and I've switched to a much more stable job." The manager thanks him for the information and proceeds with the screening. When the bankruptcy shows up in the screening report, the manager isn't taken by surprise and can give the issue proper consideration.

Personal Investigation. If the screening service indicates a reasonably sound applicant, then and only then will the manager invest time and effort in further investigation, generally by contacting the applicant's current and/or past employers and landlords.

Although the typical application requests personal references, many managers feel that calling an applicant's friends is a waste of time. Indeed, many small scale landlords don't bother contacting anyone, although this lack of diligence can backfire.

With a commercial applicant, the manager will decide who to contact on a case-by-case basis. At a minimum, as with residential applicants, landlords and employers (if relevant) get contacted. Professional references should be checked as well.

When contacting landlords or employers, a manager should use the phone book, a reverse directory, or official telephone numbers supplied in the screening service report. This ensures that the phone number is legitimate and not an applicant's friend posing as someone official.

The manager should be prepared to ask questions about the applicant's:

- rental history,
- employment history, and
- financial status.

Rental history. Both residential and commercial managers should speak to the applicant's current and past landlords. It's important to speak to past landlords, as current ones may withhold information in an effort to get rid of a problem tenant.

When speaking to other landlords, the manager should ask whether the applicant:

- paid rent on time,
- violated the lease or building rules,
- had any bounced (insufficient funds, or NSF) checks, and
- gave proper move-out notice.

Here's an example of why it's important to speak to a past landlord.

> **Example:** Terry is applying for a one-bedroom unit at ABC Apartments. A check of his legal history showed he had a clean record. However, at his previous address (a small apartment building), he verbally abused other tenants while drunk. These tenants never felt threatened enough to call the police, but the manager finally told Terry to move out or she would evict him. Terry promptly moved out and the manager let it go at that. Even though court records showed nothing, a short chat with Terry's former landlord would prove invaluable to ABC's manager.

Landlords of smaller and medium-sized buildings may be quite forthcoming, as they may know their tenants fairly well. Landlords of larger properties, with less personal interaction, often won't say much more than whether the tenant paid rent on time and if they would rent to her again.

Employment history. Most employers, especially larger ones, won't say much about a past or present employee except to confirm the dates of employment and the employee's job title. Other employers will say more. In either case, making the call is worthwhile to confirm basic employment information contained in the application. If a concern develops about employment, the manager can always ask the applicant to show her pay stubs as part of the verification process.

Financial status. Residential property managers don't usually investigate an applicant's assets. Instead, the manager relies on a credit report to get a financial picture of the applicant (including outstanding debt amounts and payment history). With authorization from the applicant, banks may verify some basic information about accounts as well.

Figure 7.2 Sample excerpt from a credit report

Creditor: Lendorama Financial
Account History Information

	Experian	TransUnion	Equifax
Account number	1334****	1334****	0-1334****
Type	Student Loan	Student Loan	Student Loan
Condition	Open	Open	Open
Responsibility	Individual	Individual	Individual
Pay status	60 days late	30 days late	30 days late
Date opened	06/01/2007	06/2007	06/2007
Date reported	07/01/2012	07/2012	07/2012
Balance & limit	Bal. $42,821	Bal. $42,577	Bal. $42,577
Payment & terms	$494.36 for 180 mo.	$494.36 for 180 mo.	Payment $494.36
High balance	$55,000	$55,000	$55,000
Past due	$988.72	$494.36	$494.36
Remarks:			

Seven-year Payment History for Account

	Experian	TransUnion	Equifax
30 days late	1	1	1
60 days late	1	1	0
90 days late	0	1	0

For a commercial applicant, where much more is at stake, the manager runs a credit check on the business owners as well as the entity itself. However, further investigation is usually required to verify financial information not addressed by a simple credit check.

> **Example:** An applicant for office space provides a personal financial statement that lists $230,000 worth of equity in a residence. The house shows up on the credit report with a mortgage of $98,000. To determine if the claim of equity is accurate, the manager must have at least a rough idea of the home's market value. She might content herself with a quick online estimate, or require the applicant to pay for an appraisal.

When examining qualification package documents, make sure that they square up with each other. For example, does the current year's personal and/or business financial statement make sense when compared to the previous years' statements?

Reaching a Decision about the Applicant

Once a manager has investigated the applicant thoroughly, it's time to decide whether to accept or reject the application. Finances aren't the only consideration. While one goal is a tenant who pays the rent on time, it's also desirable to have a tenant who maintains the property, fits in well with the other tenants, and seems to promise a long tenancy.

Written Evaluation Standards. Every property manager should use a set of written standards for evaluating applicants. Written standards help the manager make unbiased decisions. These standards also provide evidence of a fair decision-making process should a disgruntled applicant file a fair housing complaint with the state licensing agency or a civil rights agency.

The standards for residential applicants will differ from those used with commercial applicants.

Evaluating Residential Applicants. Here are some typical standards for a residential tenant (with sample minimum requirements in parentheses):

- gross income (two or three times the monthly rental amount);
- evictions (none, five years ago, or ten years ago);
- criminal convictions (none, five years ago, or misdemeanor only);
- positive landlord reference; and
- bankruptcy (none, discharged, at least five years ago).

The manager shouldn't set minimums that he can't or won't follow. Exceptions destroy the whole point of the list; therefore, the minimums should be set realistically low. Once an applicant meets those minimum standards, the manager can then use a checklist to rate the qualified applicants on a number of other factors.

> **Example:** The manager for Evergreen Apartments requires, at minimum, that applicants be currently employed. Sophie meets this qualification, as does another applicant, Joel. The manager's checklist, however, gives more consideration to applicants who have been employed at the same job for over five years. Sophie has been employed as a nurse for seven years at the same hospital, while Joel has been working for seven months as a janitor for the local school district. Although both meet the minimum employment qualification, it's likely that the manager will consider Sophie's employment history more favorably.

These checklists may contain 20 to 30 items concerning the applicant's financial strength, employment, rental history, and various other matters. The applicant gets points for each item that he satisfies. So, for instance, the applicant might earn points for the presence of a checking account, a credit score over 550, and so on. The applicant must usually score a certain predetermined minimum number of points in order to rent a unit (in addition to meeting the basic minimum standards).

The points assigned to each item on the checklist are often based on the manager's experience with prior tenants.

> **Example:** Meg has managed Sunset Apartments for ten years. In her experience, applicants with a steady job and a favorable rental history make better tenants. So along with scoring various other factors, Meg gives each applicant one point if they've worked at the same job for one year, two points for working at the same job for two to three years, and three points for working at the same job four or more years. She applies a similar point system to the number of years applicants have lived at the same address.

Screening services can weigh many of these same factors and will simply approve or reject an applicant. Managers who want to avoid the effort of a point calculation system may go this route. However, before relying on a screening service's overall evaluation, the manager must satisfy herself that the service's standards are fully adequate and comply with antidiscrimination laws.

Evaluating Commercial Applicants. It's difficult to generalize standards for evaluating commercial applicants—so much depends on the size and nature of the business under consideration. We'll discuss the topic briefly in this section; it will be covered more extensively in Chapters 11–13, which deal with specific types of commercial properties.

The evaluation of commercial tenants often involves weighing many of the same factors used to evaluate residential tenants (and gives rise to the same concerns about discrimination). But the process is more complicated, with more considerations, and a thorough evaluation generally requires more than a simple checklist or point system. Acceptable credit and legal histories for both the owners and the business entity itself are a must, and an in-depth financial analysis is typically necessary as well.

The financial analysis often begins by determining whether the business owner possesses a substantial net worth in the form of real estate, stocks, or other assets. Substantial assets can be a big plus: the presence of reasonably unencumbered assets gives the landlord something to go after should the tenant default on the lease.

Of course, a manager would prefer a tenant who is unlikely to default. The manager should ask himself the following questions:

- Do the financial statements paint a picture of sound financial health?
- Do the operational and five-year budgets seem plausible?
- Does the business plan make sense?
- Do the individuals who will run the business have sufficient experience?

For larger businesses, the manager often can't answer these questions without expert help from professionals, such as accountants, appraisers, and lawyers. The largest property managers may have these professionals on staff; smaller offices employ professional consultants as needed.

Notifying the Applicant

Once the manager has considered the application objectively, she'll decide whether to accept or deny the applicant. Then she will notify the applicant of her decision.

The manager should notify the applicant in writing, whether the application is accepted or denied. In fact, the Fair Credit Reporting Act requires notifying a rejected applicant in writing if the denial was based on credit issues, such as a low credit score. (Any action based on credit and considered "adverse," such as requiring a larger-than-normal security deposit, requires written explanation. For more discussion of the FCRA, see Chapter 14.) The denial notification must include the explanation for the adverse action along with certain other information. See Figure 7.3 for a sample letter that meets the FCRA requirements.

A copy of the written notification should be kept on file, as with all other application materials.

Figure 7.3 Denial of tenancy letter

Dear Mr. Adams,

Unfortunately, we are denying your application for residency at the Carriage House Apartments in the city of Tomlinson.

The reason(s) for denying your application is/are checked below:

[ ] Adverse history at previous rental properties. You have the right to make a written request to us within 60 days of this letter for a disclosure of the nature of this information.
[X] Insufficient employment history.
[X] Insufficient income.
[X] Information in a consumer credit report obtained from: see list below.
[ ] A consumer credit report containing information insufficient to our need was obtained from: see list below.
[ ] The fact that the consumer reporting agency contacted was unable to supply any information about you: see list below.

The consumer reporting bureau that provided your credit report was *AccuCredit, 20122 Airport Way, Bay City, Anystate.*

The above-named company may also have obtained information on you from one or more of the consumer reporting agencies whose names, addresses, and phone numbers are listed below. The following (checked) consumer reporting agencies supplied your credit information:

[X] Experian (TRW) Consumer Assistance, P.O. Box 949 Allen, TX 888-397-3742
[X] TransUnion Consumer Relations, P.O. Box 2000 Chester, PA 800-888-4213
[X] CBI/Equifax Credit Information Services, P.O. Box 740241 Atlanta, GA 800-685-1111

You have the right to receive a free copy of your credit report(s) from the reporting company, if you so request within 60 days of receiving this letter. However, the reporting company did not make the decision to take the adverse action and cannot give the specific reasons for it. You can dispute the accuracy or completeness of the report with the reporting company; generally, this can be done online.

Thank you for your application.

Sincerely,

Gerry Karl, Manager
Carriage House Apartments

Retention of Records

Management should save all completed applications and background check documentation for both accepted and rejected applicants. There's always a chance, however slim, that a rejected applicant will file a discrimination claim with a state or federal civil rights agency. The application documentation will give the owner and property manager written evidence of the basis for denying occupancy. In addition, application documentation can show that the selection criteria have been applied consistently over the years, creating a strong defense against any discrimination claim.

A few owners of small rental properties don't bother with application forms or even background checks, preferring to talk to the applicant and "go with their gut." However, for the reasons we've just mentioned, it's always best to base a decision on written data that thoroughly supports the manager's conclusion.

How long should application documentation be kept? Five years is a minimum; ten is safer. Note that the law requires the safeguarding of personal information found in tenant application and screening reports. Printed material should be kept in locked file cabinets and shredded when no longer needed. Electronic material should be protected with passwords.

Lease Provisions

In some cases, once a potential tenant's application has been approved and the applicant notified, lease negotiations begin. The extent of the negotiations will depend in part on whether the property is residential or commercial.

Most residential leases don't involve much negotiation. The rent amount is usually nonnegotiable and the property manager and tenant simply have to agree on a start date. The manager fills out a few blanks in a lease form and both parties sign.

Residential lease agreements are usually only a page or two long. In contrast, a commercial lease document may run dozens of pages and have numerous addenda. During negotiations, some lease provisions may undergo many revisions with various individuals consulting on the details—the property manager, an accountant, a lawyer, and so on.

In this section, we'll discuss important provisions found in virtually every lease. Where appropriate, we'll offer suggestions for negotiating key points. Keep in mind, however, that provisions specific to certain types of rental properties will be discussed in more detail in their appropriate chapters. (See Chapters 10–13.)

Property managers typically earn a commission (a percentage of the rent collected) on the properties they manage. Some managers may be tempted to take less qualified tenants simply because they are willing to pay more, resulting in a bigger commission for the manager. That is a mistake. A manager should always be able to answer "yes" to the following question: Is this tenant the right one for the owner's property? Accepting an unqualified tenant just to earn a quick commission violates the manager's fiduciary duties of loyalty and good faith as an agent. Unethical property managers subject to state licensing law may be violating statutory provisions as well.

Moreover, ethical choices simply make good business sense. An unqualified tenant will eventually result in headaches for both the manager and the owner.

Now let's take a look at some of the more common lease provisions, including the:

- description of the premises,
- rental term,
- date of possession,
- rent amount,
- security deposit,
- maintenance provision,

- use of premises,
- possession and quiet enjoyment,
- provision for alterations and improvements,
- rules of tenancy,
- insurance requirements,
- rules for assignment and subleasing,
- right of first refusal, and
- option to renew.

Description of Premises

Many leases start out by describing the property being rented. With residential tenancies, the premises description doesn't usually need to be complicated. Typically a street address—along with a unit number for apartments—suffices.

Commercial property leases generally require more. The lease provision should contain a formal legal description of the property. A survey may be needed if the building or space is new.

Space Diagram. If the leased premises are just one part of a building (for example, a mall or office building), then the parties should supplement the legal description with a floor plan diagram that indicates the leased space as a shaded portion of the floor plan. The diagram should then be referenced in the Premises clause and attached as an addendum to the lease.

Common areas should also be indicated on the diagram. When appropriate, the diagram may show private areas (such as the property manager's office or the utility room) that are

> ### ▶ *Commercial Lease Negotiation: Questions for the Manager*
>
> 1. Did you thoroughly research the tenant's business before formulating goals for the lease negotiation?
> 2. Have you committed your negotiation goals to writing? (Doing so helps you stick to your guns.)
> 3. Have you allowed enough time to reach your negotiation goals? (You don't want to give in just because you're bumping up against a deadline.)
> 4. Are you sure that the person you're negotiating with has the power to make decisions?
> 5. If you're on a negotiation team, are roles clearly assigned (lead negotiator, secondary negotiator, note taker, and so on)?
> 6. Have you practiced role playing with your team members so that you can easily overcome likely objections to the negotiation goals?
> 7. Will you be producing the first draft of the lease? Make it a goal to produce the first draft—this allows you to frame the discussion of any issues that weren't resolved in the initial negotiation.

separate from public or common areas. Finally, if the tenant has a right of first refusal or an option to expand the leased space (discussed below), the diagram should indicate the possible expansion area.

The space diagram is an easily understood visual aid that can help avoid confusion or arguments down the road.

Square Footage. Residential leases sometimes state the approximate number of square feet rented. But because residential spaces are usually priced by the unit, and not per square foot, the actual square footage is not as essential.

Commercial space. With commercial leases, an accurate square footage figure is almost always critical. Many commercial spaces are advertised and rented based on a certain dollar figure per square foot. In addition, commercial tenants usually pay a proportionate share of the building's operational expenses based on the amount of square footage leased, as we'll discuss shortly. Both of these factors make accurate square footage an important part of the lease. The Building Owners and Managers Association (BOMA) publishes industry standards for measuring floor space.

Property managers use several different terms when discussing floor space:

- usable area,
- rentable area, and
- gross area.

Usable area is the number of square feet that a tenant can physically occupy. It excludes the building's common areas, such as corridors, elevators, stairwells, building lobby, and services areas.

Rentable area includes the space that the tenant occupies exclusively (the usable area) plus most or all of the building's common areas. Unlike the gross area, discussed below, the rentable area is measured from the inside of the building's outer walls. Sometimes certain parts of the building, such as a basement, aren't counted as rentable area.

The ratio of the rentable area to the usable area is referred to as an **R/U ratio**. R/U ratios are often used to determine how much the tenant will pay towards the common areas. The larger the R/U ratio, the more the tenant is spending on common areas. Newer buildings usually devote less space to common areas than older buildings, meaning newer buildings often have lower R/U ratios. However, newer buildings also typically charge higher rent, so their lower R/U ratio may not help the tenant. Nonetheless, all things being equal, a low R/U ratio will strike tenants as desirable.

Rather than use a precise R/U ratio to determine rent, a building manager may simply charge an **add-on factor** to account for the rent that must be paid on common areas. The add-on factor may or may not be the same as the actual R/U ratio; it's a common practice in some communities for the same add-on factor to be used for all buildings. This simplifies negotiations and increases predictability for potential tenants who are shopping around.

Gross area (or construction area) is the building's entire floor area, measured to the outside surface of its outer walls. This includes all enclosed floors, basements, and mechanical equipment floors. In some places, gross area rather than rentable area is used to determine the square footage of a building's common areas. You may hear this referred to as the "New York method."

Lease Term

The next typical provision of a lease agreement concerns the **term**, or amount of time, the property will be leased.

Residential lease terms generally run for one year. However, half-year terms aren't unusual and nine-month terms are sometimes seen in rental housing around college campuses.

Leases for office space often run three to five years, with space in better quality buildings sometimes leasing for seven years. Local shops usually rent for three- to five-year terms, but restaurants and other businesses that invest a good deal in fixtures may seek a ten-year term or longer. Anchor tenants generally try to lock down the space with 20-year terms, with multiple options to renew. And for industrial tenants, where the financial commitment to the space is often tremendous due to the installation of specialized equipment, lease terms may run considerably longer, such as 30 years or more.

Managers may prefer a relatively short term, especially if getting a new tenant (or renewing the current lease) is the only way to increase the rental amount. However, tenant turnover is very costly and many managers prefer longer leases for that reason. If a longer lease is used, the manager should address the need for rent increases with some kind of escalation clause. (Escalation clauses are discussed later in this chapter.)

> ▶ **Letter of Intent**
>
> Negotiating a commercial lease for a medium- or large-sized tenant is often a long process. Naturally, neither the manager nor the tenant wants to invest time and money in detailed negotiations unless it's reasonably certain that a deal can be worked out. To address this concern, the parties may begin the process by drafting a letter of intent. The letter of intent is a signed—though generally non-binding—document. It sets out a barebones agreement on the significant lease issues: square footage, start date, length of term, rent amount, and so on.
>
> A quick agreement on key points vastly reduces the danger of a walkaway late in the game. If the parties can't even agree on the basics, why proceed to detailed lease negotiations?

Types of Leaseholds. Leases may be classified by the nature of their terms. A **term tenancy** (also called an estate for years) is a leasehold having a fixed term. Almost all term tenancies run for whole years, as in the three- or five-year terms we've mentioned. However, the term may be measured in days or months as well—for example, a 65-day summer vacation lease would be a term tenancy.

The term tenancy automatically expires when the end of the term is reached.

> **Example:** Nolan starts college and rents an apartment for a nine-month period, planning to return home for the summer. He has a term tenancy. He doesn't have to give the landlord notice as June approaches and school ends. He simply has to be out of the premises by the term's end date.

In the above example, if Nolan decided to stay on in the apartment rather than going home for the summer, and the landlord accepted rent without having Nolan sign a new lease, Nolan's tenancy would be month-to-month.

A month-to-month tenancy—or any other tenancy that automatically renews for a certain period—is called a **periodic tenancy**. Many periodic tenancies are month-to-month residential tenancies that follow the end of a term tenancy. A periodic tenancy is properly terminated by giving the other party notice before the end of the period. The law typically requires 30 days' notice, though some states allow residential tenants a shorter period, such as 20 days.

With commercial property, simply lapsing into a month-to-month lease after the expiration of the term is much less common. Both the manager and the tenant want more stability than is offered by a lease that can be terminated with only 30 days' notice (or whatever notice period is required). If the parties want to continue their relationship, but the tenant has no options to renew, or has already used them up, they will have to negotiate a new lease.

Date of Possession

A residential lease term usually begins as soon as the tenant is entitled to possession. That is, the lease begins on the date when the premises are available for occupancy (whether or not the tenant moves in on that date). The possession date should be stated in the lease agreement.

Generally, commercial leases also start from the date of possession. However, for retail space the start date may be a month or two after the tenant takes possession, giving the business time to set up and begin generating income.

Premises Not Ready. Sometimes the previous tenant illegally holds over past the termination date, or departs on time but leaves so much damage that the manager can't get the premises ready by the start date. If the manager can't deliver possession when promised, the new tenant is probably entitled to compensation. A residential landlord might have to reimburse the tenant for the cost of renting a motel room and storage fees for the tenant's possessions.

A commercial tenant who can't occupy the premises when promised may have more significant losses. In theory, the landlord could be responsible for income lost in the period the tenant was unable to occupy the property. To reduce the landlord's exposure, and to avoid costly lawsuits, many commercial leases address this problem with a liquidated damages provision in the Possession section. In the case of a small bookstore, for example, the provision might state that for every day the premises remain unavailable, the tenant will receive $200 off his rent. This figure would be many times that for larger businesses.

Start Date Uncertain. Commercial tenants often request remodeling or a build out of the leased space. **Remodeling** involves renovations to already existing space (changing the type of flooring in a lobby, for example). A **build out**, on the other hand, refers to creating the desired space from an empty shell. This would include building individual offices within a large empty space, for example. When there's a remodel or build out situation, it's often impossible to set an exact start date because it's difficult to judge when work will be completed. The lease may simply say something like, "start date to be 45 days after premises are ready."

When the premises are being remodeled or built out, the lease should contain an addendum with a work schedule, construction standards, and an anticipated occupancy date. The parties can amend the lease with an actual possession date once construction is close to completion. This leaves a clear record of when occupancy actually commenced, which is important for determining the rental amount and when the term will end.

If the tenant insists on a definite start date despite extensive construction requirements, and wants to enforce the start date with a liquidated damages provision, the manager will usually pass on the potential cost to the contractor. The contractor may be offered an on-time completion bonus for meeting the deadline, but will also be charged late penalties if construction takes longer than promised.

Rent Amount

Obviously, one of the most important provisions in a lease concerns the amount of rent the tenant will pay. In residential settings, the manager usually states a certain monthly rent; there's little or no negotiation. Commercial rent negotiations, on the other hand, can be quite protracted.

Both residential and commercial leases are often classified by the method used to determine the amount of the tenant's rent. There are three common categories of leases based on the type of rent calculation: gross, net, and percentage. Let's take a quick look at each.

Gross Lease. Most residential leases are gross leases. The tenant pays a fixed amount of rent to the manager and the manager foots the bill for all of the operating expenses incurred in running the property. (The utility company may bill the tenant directly for usage in his unit, however.)

> **Example:** Isako owns a small apartment building. Tenants pay her a set amount of rent each month depending on whether they have a one-bedroom or a studio. Isako bears all the building's operation costs: maintenance, insurance and taxes, garbage and recycling, and energy use (common area heating and interior and exterior lighting). Her tenants have gross leases.

Net Lease. Most commercial leases are net leases. In a net lease, the manager charges (or "passes through") some or all of the property's operating costs to the tenant in addition to rent. Operating costs include the costs associated with the common areas, such as utilities, cleaning, and repairs. These costs are called **common area maintenance** (CAM) **charges**. Operating costs also include the taxes and insurance associated with the tenant's premises and any private (manager-occupied) areas. In other words, operating costs include all of the expenses of running a property.

When the landlord passes through maintenance, tax, and insurance costs to the tenant, the lease is known as a **triple net lease** (or fully net lease). A triple net lease means that the owner's entire monthly rent stream is net income. All of the rent money is available for paying the mortgage or anything else that the property owner desires. With a triple net lease, the net income generated by the property is straightforward and fixed—income won't fluctuate month-to-month because of expenses.

Not all net leases are triple net, however. For instance, the landlord might not charge the tenants for the cost of insurance or property taxes.

Net lease tenants usually require the manager to bid out all significant maintenance contracts, in order to minimize the costs charged back to the tenant. They may also want to receive copies of contractor maintenance bills so that they can make sure the calculation of their pro rata share is correct.

Calculating a tenant's pass-through share. In a net lease, the tenant usually pays a share of the operational expenses based on the percentage of space in the building that the tenant occupies. Let's look at an example that focuses on CAM charges.

> **Example:** Hobby Horse, a gift and crafts shop, leases a 1,000-square-foot shop in a building with 20,000 square feet of rentable space. The manager charges each tenant a share of CAM costs based on the ratio of the rented space to the building's total amount of currently rented space. The building is fully occupied.
> CAM charges for July total $9,000. How much of that will Hobby Horse have to pay?
>
> $$1,000 \text{ sq. ft.} \div 20,000 = 5\%$$
> $$\$9,000 \times .05 = \$450$$
>
> Hobby Horse will pay $450 in CAM charges in addition to January's rent.

In the above example, actual monthly CAM costs are used. However, quite often the expense figures billed back to a net lease tenant each month are based on budgeted (expected) costs rather than the actual bills. This simplifies bookkeeping. At the end of the year, the actual costs are tallied up and then the tenant either gets debited or credited depending on whether actual costs ran higher or lower than expected.

In a triple net lease, the tenant is often required to contribute to the manager's reserve account. A reserve account is money set aside each month to fund major repairs to the building when necessary. However, some tenants can successfully negotiate this requirement out of their leases. Larger tenants, such as major department stores, have enough capital behind them to handle their share of a major repair cost if one arises.

Percentage Lease. Many retail tenants pay a fixed **minimum rent** (often called the **base rent**), plus an additional percentage of their gross sales. For instance, a boutique in a mall might pay a minimum rent of $2,000 per month, plus 5% of monthly sales over $30,000.

In theory, a percentage arrangement can benefit both parties. The tenant starts out with relatively low rental costs and gets a chance to get her business up and running. And because the landlord stands to profit from the tenant's success, the relationship between the two parties may be more cooperative. Further, the landlord may be more inclined to make the entire property more attractive to customers, since the more successful a tenant is, the more the landlord profits.

The tenant's method of reporting gross sales must be spelled out clearly in the lease. "Gross sales" is a generic term and open to interpretation. The tenant will want as many deductions to the gross sales figure as possible, reducing the amount she has to pay. The manager will want just the opposite, both to maximize rent and to make it easier to figure out whether the tenant is paying the agreed-upon share.

Percentage Rents in a Neighborhood Shopping Center

The gold standard for information about percentage rents and other kinds of shopping center lease data is *Dollars & Cents of Shopping Centers*. This book comes out every few years. It's published by the International Council of Shopping Centers and it doesn't come cheap (about $300 for nonmembers).

Below are some sample percentage rent ranges. Note that the range overall is from 1% to over 7%. Lower margin stores, such as groceries, pay smaller percentages. This is also true within a particular industry: some types of restaurants have thinner margins than others. To get the maximum realistic percentage rate, the property manager must have a good grasp of a particular tenant's business.

Typical Percentage Rents for a Neighborhood Shopping Center

Drugstores	2.5–4.0%
Jewelry Stores	6.0% or More
Restaurants	4.0–7.0%
Shoes	5%
Gift Shops	3.0–6.0%
Supermarkets	1.0–2.0%

Escalation Clauses. Whether a commercial lease is gross, net, or percentage, it's likely to contain a rent escalation clause. An **escalation clause** calls for a rent increase at fixed intervals, typically once a year. (Residential leases rarely contain escalation clauses, partly because these leases rarely last longer than a year.)

There are several variations on escalation clauses, differing mainly in the way they are calculated. Some types simply specify a fixed annual increase (using a stated percentage or dollar amount), or base the periodic increase on a designated inflation index (for example, the Consumer Price Index). Other types base the increase on the property's total operating expenses for a certain specified time period. Let's look at two of these types of clauses more closely.

Under an **operating expense escalation clause**, the tenant pays a proportionate share of any increase in operating expenses over and above the expenses generated in the first full year of the lease. The increase may be based on known or merely estimated increases. If the tenant is billed for additional expenses based on estimates, adjustments will be made later, once the actual costs are known. In either case, the manager must provide the tenant with written calculations for the tenant's share of the increase, and the method of calculation must be consistent with the method described in the lease.

An **expense stop escalation clause** sets a limit on how much the property owner is expected to pay toward operating expenses in a given year. For instance, a "stop" might be set at $10 of operating expenses per rented square foot per year. If the actual expenses come in at or below $10 per square foot, the tenant's rent will not increase. If they come in at $11 per square foot, the tenant will be responsible for the additional $1 per square foot. The manager usually adjusts the tenant's rent based on projected operating expenses, with any excess refunded back to the tenant once actual costs are known at the end of the year.

Due Date and Late Fees. Rent customarily falls due on the first of the month. Automatic payment through a checking account or credit card is becoming more common. Some states prohibit residential landlords from requiring the use of auto payment—or any other particular method of payment. However, if a tenant develops payment problems, this rule may not apply.

> **Example:** Thor works part-time and has trouble making rent. He lives in a state that generally prohibits landlords from requiring cash payments. However, the law makes an exception for tenants who have written bad rent checks. Unfortunately, Thor falls into this category. In order to avoid additional bounced check fees, the landlord requires Thor to pay rent by cash or certified check.

In percentage leases, the first of the month may not be a practical due date for the percentage portion of the rent. Ideally, the manager cooperates with the tenant in picking a date that makes sense. For example, in some states businesses must calculate their gross sales by a certain date each month for the payment of state business taxes; requiring the percentage portion of the rent on this date makes better sense than the first of the month. Alternatively, some tenants pay percentage rent quarterly. Quarterly payment reduces the tenant's bookkeeping burden, since gross income must already be calculated quarterly in order to file federal income tax returns.

Sometimes commercial tenants seek a lease provision requiring the manager to send the tenant notice if rent is late. After receiving the notice, the tenant then has a specified amount of time (such as three days) to make the payment. In theory, this prevents the tenant from being charged a late fee just because the manager made a bookkeeping error, though in practice the tenant's goal may be to gain a few extra days in case the business has trouble coming up with rent. As with any provision strongly favoring one party, the likelihood of obtaining this concession depends on market conditions and the particular tenant.

Security Deposit

Most tenants must give the manager a security deposit to cover any expenses associated with a breach of the lease contract, such as a default on the rent or damage to the premises beyond normal wear and tear.

State landlord-tenant laws place restrictions on the deposits that may be required of residential tenants. (Residential security deposits are discussed in greater detail in Chapter 10.) Commercial tenants, however, are generally not protected by these laws and are free to negotiate whatever arrangements they want with the landlord. The law presumes that commercial tenants have the resources to hire an attorney and are as sophisticated about leasing as the landlord.

However, keep in mind that all managers holding security deposits (and other monies in trust) do so as fiduciaries. This means that the fiduciary duties of accounting and fairness apply in both residential and commercial settings.

Deposit Amount. One month's rent is the typical amount, even with commercial tenants. Some states limit how much a residential landlord may require as a security deposit (for example, a maximum of two months' worth of rent).

If a commercial tenant's business success seems questionable, and the risk of default above average, managers will often seek a larger security deposit than usual. Of course, the manager doesn't want to increase the chance of default by requiring the tenant to set aside a crippling amount of money.

Another situation may inspire a manager to require a larger-than-ordinary deposit: when the manager will be spending a lot of money to remodel or build out the premises for the tenant. A manager in this situation wants to make sure that the tenant stays for the whole lease term, and a large security deposit encourages the tenant to do so.

On the other hand, a powerful, well-known commercial tenant may be able to avoid making a deposit altogether. The manager may be satisfied with a letter of credit from a bank indicating that the tenant has plenty of money to compensate for a breach of the lease contract.

Tenants with sufficient leverage may demand interest on their security deposit. (Some states require that residential landlords pay their tenants interest on security and other deposits.)

Refunding the Deposit. When a tenancy ends, the manager should refund the security deposit as promptly as possible; in fact, state law may impose a deadline for returning the deposit. If any funds are being withheld, the manager usually must give the tenant a written explanation and itemized list of deductions. Of course, if it turns out that the deposit isn't large enough to cover repair expenses or unpaid rent amounts, the landlord may sue the tenant for the difference.

Maintenance

In residential buildings, the manager handles maintenance and cleaning of the common areas. Tenants clean their own units and are usually required to perform simple maintenance tasks, such as replacing burnt out light bulbs in the unit. More involved maintenance tasks, such as unplugging a drain or fixing a leaky faucet, usually fall to the manager.

In a commercial building, the manager almost always handles maintenance of the common areas. Managers want to avoid the danger of tenants hiring subpar contractors who may do more harm than good. And a manager who contracts maintenance for the whole building should get cheaper rates than a tenant could obtain for small jobs. In theory, these savings are passed on to the tenants.

Some managers provide maintenance services inside the leased spaces, such as office janitorial services. Other tenants prefer to hire their own janitors.

Use of Premises

Every lease, residential or commercial, should contain a **use clause**. In a residential lease, the use clause states that the tenant may use the unit for residential purposes only, and the unit can be used only by the tenant and the tenant's guests. This provision prohibits commercial or illegal uses.

All commercial leases prohibit illegal uses and the use of hazardous materials (or limit them for certain industries). Generally speaking, the manager wants the most narrow use clause possible, one that permits only the tenant's current use. Conversely, the tenant wants the broadest possible provision, one that authorizes any legal commercial use. A narrow use clause prevents the tenant from expanding into uses that damage the business of other tenants; a broad use clause allows the tenant's business to evolve to meet changing market conditions.

> **Example:** An upscale women's clothing store is negotiating a lease in a mid-size shopping plaza. The manager wants to limit the store to selling upscale women's clothes and nothing else, to prevent the tenant from taking business away from an accessories retailer in the plaza.
>
> In contrast, the tenant wants the lease's use provision to end with the phrase, "and every other legal commercial use." That way, if the store decides it wants to add new types of products, such as leather goods or perfumes, or expand with a discount line, it may do so.

Note that in larger shopping centers, narrow use clauses are less important; a wide variety of choice attracts customers in numbers sufficient to support several competitors.

Competition is less of an issue with office buildings and industrial tenants. Still, even managers of these properties need to exercise care with use provisions. For example, they would want to prevent a new use that would put added strain on the shared facilities—such as a use that translates into more crowded parking lots or increased usage of electricity.

Noncompete Clause. Retail tenants in a new shopping center, especially anchor tenants, may be able to secure a noncompete clause. In a **noncompete clause**, the landlord promises to include use provisions in all other leases (from that point forward) that ban a competing use. For example, a coffee chain might require a noncompete clause that prohibits the sale of espresso by anyone else in the shopping center.

The demand for inclusion of a noncompete clause has eased somewhat, as experience and studies show that competition often improves a store's bottom line. The array of competing choices in a mall or shopping center tends to draw more customers to the location.

Hazardous Substances. As noted, the use provision in most commercial leases limits or prohibits the use of hazardous chemicals or otherwise restricts environmentally hazardous activities on the premises.

The hazardous substances provision in an industrial lease is often quite detailed, enough so that the subject may be handled in a provision separate from the use clause. These provisions may include landlord inspection rights, insurance requirements, and indemnification language stating that if environmental claims are brought against the landlord, the tenant will cover the legal costs and pay any fines, judgments, or settlements.

Possession and Quiet Enjoyment

Every lease contains an implied or express promise from the landlord that the tenant's possession of the property will not be disturbed, either by the landlord or third parties making a lawful claim to the property. This is called the **covenant of quiet enjoyment**. The

Improvement Allowance Amounts

The dollar amount a manager is willing to pay for tenant improvements varies tremendously. With office premises in good shape, more or less usable as-is, the manager may offer only $5–6 per square foot, enough to cover the cost of repainting and new carpet. If, in addition to paint and carpet, the tenant needs a moderate amount of construction, that might bring the total to $20 per square foot. When allowances reach this range, managers may require a five-year or longer lease.

To build out an entirely unimproved space to high quality office space, the allowance can run as high as $60 per square foot or higher.

covenant of quiet enjoyment applies even if it isn't stated explicitly in the lease agreement, and cannot be waived by the parties. The tenant is guaranteed exclusive possession and quiet enjoyment of the leased premises.

Quiet enjoyment also refers to the tenant's right to privacy. The landlord and any service provider hired to work on the property cannot unreasonably intrude on the tenant. Just what is considered unreasonable intrusion will depend on the nature of the need to enter the property and the type of property (residential tenants enjoy the highest level of protection). Protections afforded to residential tenants are discussed in Chapter 10.

Alterations and Initial Improvements

Many alterations clauses in residential leases prohibit the tenant from making so much as a nail hole without first getting written permission from the manager. Other managers are more generous, allowing a few nail holes to hang pictures (so long as they are repaired at the end of the lease), but preventing larger changes—like painting the walls—without the manager's permission. The degree of actual enforcement varies from manager to manager, of course.

Managers in commercial settings know that businesses must customize their premises in order to maximize profits. Indeed, especially with new retail and office buildings, interior space is often left unfinished until a tenant is found. Management then builds out offices or storefronts or whatever other interior structures the tenant needs. The same is often true of industrial space as well.

The manager, rather than the tenant, usually undertakes the actual construction. The manager hires contractors and supervises the remodeling or initial improvements in cooperation with the tenant. This lets the manager maintain quality standards throughout the building.

In other cases, especially with major retail businesses, the tenant handles the build out or remodeling, and the manager retains the right to approve the construction plans and inspect the work.

Figure 7.4 Excerpts from a typical work letter

> Landlord, in cooperation with the tenant, will arrange to have the following work performed:
>
> 2. **Demolition:** Demolition of existing partitions, doors, suspended ceilings, and floor finishes within the tenant's space.
>
> 5. **Steel:** Steel installation for supporting tenant-requested equipment mounted on the floor, ceiling, and roof. Steel modifications must be reviewed and approved by the landlord's structural engineer at tenant's cost...
>
> 6. **Partition Walls, Floors & Ceilings:** Tenant partitions shall consist of 3 5/8" metal 20 gauge studs, 24" OC, full height, floor to deck, with type C ½" gypsum board, and R-11 wall insulation. The landlord will pay all the construction costs of new walls between new tenant spaces and building common areas (lobbies and corridors)...
>
> 12. **Mechanical:**
>
>   . . .
>
>   C. The building HVAC system runs during normal business hours only. The costs of design, purchase, and installation of additional HVAC systems to address tenant requirements for 24/7 heating and cooling systems, and for tenant-requested server rooms where the potential BTU per hour output exceeds normal capacities, is not part of the tenant allowance.

Tenant Improvement Allowance. No matter who is performing the work, the manager often contributes a certain amount of money toward the work via a "tenant improvement allowance." The tenant can choose whatever improvements she wants, at whatever price, but must pay for any costs that exceed the manager-provided allowance.

The allowance is usually expressed as a certain dollar amount per square foot. The amount varies according to the current condition of the premises, the length of the lease, and how profitable the rent is likely to be. The health of the economy also plays a role, affecting both construction costs and how eager managers are to please tenants.

Work Letter. Rather than clutter the lease with build-out or remodeling plans and specifications, completion dates, and so forth, the parties usually attach an addendum called a **work letter** to the lease. As you can see in Figure 7.4, work letters can get quite detailed. Notice that in provision six of this work letter, the landlord contributes money over and above the tenant improvement allowance. This is common when the work to be done will improve the common areas or the space of another tenant in the building.

Rules

Residential property managers typically impose a set of tenant rules, usually in the form of a lease addendum that covers various issues of tenant conduct. (Residential lease rules are also discussed in Chapters 8 and 10.) Most of the rules address relatively minor matters, such as smoking, noise, pets, and the hours of use for an exercise facility or laundry room. The lease will usually allow the manager to adjust the rules as necessary during the tenancy.

Rules for commercial tenants generally govern issues such as employee parking, freight elevator usage, and window signs.

> **Example:** A mall landlord has a rule that tenants cannot use the service corridors for storage due to the danger of fire, blocked access to exits, and the burden on cleaning staff.

The rules for commercial tenants may be contained in the various provisions of the lease, or they may be found in a tenant handbook. This handbook also covers the landlord's administrative procedures and other useful information.

Insurance

Increasingly, residential property managers are requiring tenants to have renter's insurance. **Renter's insurance** protects the tenant's personal property within the rental unit in the event of damage or loss. The manager's insurance, on the other hand, doesn't cover loss to a tenant's property from theft, fire, or other cause unless the management was at fault. Renter's insurance also provides liability protection for any accidents or injuries to the tenant or the tenant's guests. A residential renter's insurance policy costs about $100 a year.

Managers require tenants to carry renter's insurance because it can cut down on the amount or size of claims made against the manager's policy, thus reducing costs. Requiring tenants to carry insurance may also lower the manager's premiums.

Commercial landlords always require tenants to maintain liability insurance. (This covers claims made against the tenant for injuries or property damage caused by the tenant's negligence.) A million dollar coverage policy was once standard, but many landlords now require double that amount. Most tenants must also get various other kinds of insurance, including fire, theft, and (if relevant) boiler and plate glass insurance.

The tenant provides evidence of the necessary insurance coverage by providing a **certificate of insurance** to management each year. The property manager's software should allow the manager to log these certificates and note when they are about to expire. The manager can then send out renewal notices. A lease's insurance requirement is of no use if the manager allows a tenant to let insurance coverage lapse. We will return to the topic of insurance in Chapter 15.

Assignment and Subleasing

Most leases require the landlord's prior written consent to any assignment or sublease. In an **assignment**, the original tenant transfers the right to possess the leased premises for the remainder of the lease term to someone else. In a **sublease** (also called a sublet), the transfer involves only some of the remaining term, or just some of the space; in other words, with a sublease, the original tenant retains part of the leasehold estate.

Example: Albert signs a lease to rent an apartment from January 1 to December 31. On June 1, Albert transfers possession of the property to Sarah for a term beginning June 1 and ending December 31. This is an assignment, because it's for the entire remaining lease term.

Now assume that Albert is just going away for the summer and transfers possession of the property to Sarah for three months, ending August 31. This is a sublease, because Albert will resume possession after Sarah's possession ends.

In an assignment, the new tenant (assignee) becomes liable to the landlord for rent, and the original tenant becomes secondarily liable for the rent. The landlord must attempt to collect rent from the assignee; only if collection efforts fail can he go after the assignor (the original tenant).

With a sublease, the new tenant (the sublessee) pays rent to the original tenant, rather than to the landlord. The original tenant is still liable to the landlord. This arrangement is sometimes referred to as a **sandwich lease**, since the original tenant is in the middle, sandwiched between the landlord and the sublessee.

As we said, most leases require the landlord's prior written consent to any assignment or sublease. However, in many states this consent cannot be unreasonably withheld, especially for commercial leases. Still, a tenant should try to have the "consent cannot be unreasonably withheld" language added to a lease if it's not already there; this will help avoid later debate.

It is usually considered reasonable for the landlord to refuse an assignment or sublease if the new tenant isn't creditworthy. In addition, in the commercial setting, consent might be withheld if the new tenant's business is too different from the original, would violate non-compete provisions, or would result in a less desirable tenant mix.

Right of First Refusal

Sometimes commercial leases contain a provision that gives the tenant a right of first refusal to rent adjacent space if and when the space becomes available. In other words, before the manager can offer the space to a new tenant, it has to offer the space to the neighboring tenant on the same terms that would be granted to the new tenant.

Example: A dentist rents space in a medical building. The lease gives the dentist the right to expand into the office next door if that space becomes available. After a year, the doctor next door moves his practice downtown. A prospective tenant offers the landlord 35 dollars per square foot for the empty space. The landlord can't sign a lease with the prospective tenant unless the dentist waives her right of first refusal.

The right of first refusal specifies how long the tenant has to exercise the right after receiving notice that the space is available. (This period is usually only a few days.)

On rare occasions, the manager of an office building grants an outright option on existing adjacent vacant space. The option is a promise by management to hold the space open for a certain period of time. The option may last for only be a few months, or it may last several years. A long-term option is usually offered only if the tenant is taking most of the space already—for example, a business that rents two-thirds of a floor in an office building. Generally speaking, options are a sign that there are too many spaces for lease in the market.

Managers should be wary of granting rights of first refusal and options. These rights tie up space and make it difficult to enter into deals with new tenants.

Option to Renew

A residential lease may contain an option for the tenant to renew his lease at the end of the term, and may offer favorable terms for doing so. Many managers find this preferable to tenant turnover—advertising for new tenants, going through the application process, and possibly dealing with empty space. This is especially true when the market is steady and the lease is only for a year.

Commercial landlords often give the tenant an option to renew its lease as a way to make a lease more attractive.

> **Example:** A toymaker leases a warehouse for five years with two five-year options to renew. Before the end of the first five years, the manufacturer gives notice that he will be staying on for the next five years. However, after a total of ten years in the premises, he retires. He does not exercise the second option to renew and the landlord rents the warehouse to someone else.

In the above situation, a landlord would probably prefer the tenant to simply sign a 15-year lease with no options. That would provide certainty. However, most businesses, especially new ones, are often hesitant to commit to such long-term leases. This makes renewal options particularly attractive to tenants.

Of course, the manager should seek terms that make the renewal option as favorable as possible to the landlord. We discuss renewals in more detail in the next chapter.

Signing the Lease

Once the tenant and manager have negotiated the lease terms and committed the lease provisions to writing, it's time to sign the agreement. Most state laws require a lease contract to be in writing; even when a written contract isn't required, it's still a good business practice. We'll end this chapter with a brief discussion of general signing practices.

Who Must Sign

In a residential lease, every adult who will live in the unit should sign the lease agreement. Anyone who signs the lease as a tenant becomes liable for any nonpayment or other breach.

A person can't enter into a lease without contractual capacity. This means possessing mental competence and, generally, being over 18 years of age. Minors can void a lease in many states, so managers of residential property should make note of birth dates when running credit checks and/or examining IDs. If the manager wants to rent to a minor, the signature of a parent or other adult guardian may be needed.

As a general rule, a lease signature does not have to be notarized, but the manager must check state law on this point. Sometimes a long-term (usually commercial) lease is recorded, and it typically must be notarized before it can be recorded.

Signing by Business Entities. It may not be obvious who should sign a commercial lease on behalf of a business tenant. Let's take a look at a few general rules.

A corporate officer signs on behalf of a corporation. A resolution from the board of directors authorizing the individual to sign is necessary. With a partnership, any general partner can usually sign a lease and bind the entire entity to the lease terms. However, it's better to obtain a resolution from the partnership authorizing a particular partner to sign. Alternatively, all the partners may sign the document.

A landlord should have her attorney review the documents that authorize signatures. (It's also a good idea for an attorney to determine whether the entity was validly formed.)

Personal Guaranty. For local businesses, startups, or any other business that seems to possess a relatively high risk of failure, most managers require that each owner (as well as the entity) personally sign the lease. Sometimes, instead of having the owner personally sign the lease, a separate document called a **guaranty** is used. A manager cannot judge the value of this guaranty without examining the owner's personal financial statement, which should be part of the tenant qualification package.

In some cases, the manager and the tenant compromise on the guaranty, limiting it to a certain period—say the first two years of a startup. After that, the owner has no personal liability even if the business later defaults on the lease.

Chapter Summary

1. The owner and property manager want tenants who will help keep the property in good condition, pay rent on time, harmonize well with other tenants, and stay a reasonably long time. Evaluating all applicants using the same written standards and the same application form will help the property manager make rational decisions and avoid illegal discrimination.

2. Applicants for commercial space submit a qualification package, which includes the application form, as well as profit and loss statements, tax returns, personal financial statements, operating budget and five-year budget, business plan, entity organizational documents (such as articles of incorporation), and resumes of key personnel.

3. A screening service will give the manager information about the individual's employment, creditworthiness, and civil or criminal history. However, the manager should also personally contact employers and talk to past landlords.

4. Tenants should be notified in writing of acceptance or rejection of their application. The Fair Credit Reporting Act requires notifying a rejected applicant in writing if the denial was based on credit issues, such as a low score. The denial letter must state the reason for the rejection.

5. Residential leases are short and don't usually involve much negotiation. Commercial leases are often long and complicated and may involve many drafts as the parties discuss various terms concerning rent amount, build-out, pass-through shares, etc.

6. Important provisions in a lease include a description of the premises, the rental term, the possession date, the rent amount, the security deposit, maintenance, use of the premises, alterations/initial improvements, rules, insurance, assignment/subleasing, the right of first refusal, and the option to renew.

7. Generally, leases must be in writing. In a residential lease, all adult occupants should sign the lease. With a commercial lease, an authorized representative of the business entity signs the lease. In addition, the manager may require that the owners of the business sign the lease in their personal capacity.

Key Terms

Fair Credit Reporting Act (FCRA) – A federal law that requires a landlord who denies an application for tenancy because of the applicant's poor credit to notify the applicant in writing, explaining the denial and stating how an individual can correct any misinformation in his credit report.

Qualification package – The collection of documents submitted by a commercial tenancy applicant; these documents typically include financial statements, business plans, tax returns, budgets, etc.

Screening services – For a fee, various companies will provide background information about a tenant applicant, including employment history, past addresses and landlords, credit history (credit report), and some limited legal history.

Tenant mix – The mix of tenant types found in a building or development. With shopping centers, the property manager wants a mix of tenant businesses that complement each other, building customer traffic for the facility as a whole.

Acceptance or denial letter – A letter, sent by a property manager to all applicants, notifying them whether their application was accepted or denied. The FCRA requires that denials based on credit factors be explained to the applicant.

Lease term – In a lease contract, the amount of time a property will be leased.

Letter of intent – A preliminary nonbinding agreement used in contract lease negotiations to state basic lease terms, such as the start date and rent amount, while detailed negotiations are worked out.

Term tenancy – A leasehold with a fixed term. Also called an estate for years.

Periodic tenancy – A tenancy (often month-to-month) that automatically renews at the end of the lease term unless one party gives notice.

Remodeling – Renovations to already existing rental space.

Build out – Creating a desired rental space from a larger, unfinished space.

Gross lease – A lease where the landlord absorbs operational costs such as maintenance, taxes, and insurance rather than directly charging the tenant her share of these amounts. This is the opposite of a net lease and is the most common type of lease for residential tenancies.

Net lease – A lease where the landlord passes through to the tenant a pro rata share of operational costs, such as maintenance, taxes, and insurance, so that the rent itself is pure net income. This is the opposite of a gross lease and is the most common type of lease for commercial tenancies.

Percentage lease – A lease where the landlord charges a fixed minimum or base rent plus some percentage of the tenant's gross sales. This lease is limited to retail tenants.

Escalation clause – A clause in the rent provision of a lease providing that the rent will rise on a certain date (usually the anniversary of the lease) by a certain percentage. Alternatively, a cost of living index may be used to adjust rent according to the rate of inflation.

Use clause – A provision in a lease that limits the tenant's use of the property to one purpose, and also prohibits illegal or hazardous uses.

Noncompete clause – A provision prohibiting the landlord from leasing space to competing businesses; sometimes found in shopping center leases.

Covenant of quiet enjoyment – A promise (actual or implied) by the landlord that the tenant's possession of the property will not be disturbed, either by the landlord or by a third party with a lawful claim to the property.

Tenant improvement allowance – A certain amount of money given to a tenant by a landlord that will be used to build out or remodel the premises at the start of a tenancy.

Certificate of insurance – A certificate issued by an insurer to a tenant, to give proof of coverage.

Assignment – When the original tenant transfers the right to possess the property to someone else for the remainder of the lease term.

Sublease – When the original tenant transfers part of the property to someone else for the remainder of the lease term, or part or all of the property to someone else for part of the lease term.

Right of first refusal – A provision in a commercial lease that gives the tenant the right to rent adjacent space if the space becomes vacant.

Option to renew – A provision in a lease contract that gives the tenant the option to renew his lease at the end of the lease term for another similar rental period.

Personal guaranty – When a small business owner signs the lease personally, along with the business entity; this makes the owner personally liable (along with the entity) for a breach of the lease.

Chapter Quiz

1. Which of the following is NOT a recommended procedure for handling tenant applications?
   a) Keeping the applications on file, whether accepted or not
   b) Using a standardized application form
   c) Going with intuition or "gut-feelings" when evaluating applicants
   d) Relying strictly on written standards to evaluate applicants

2. A commercial tenant qualification package usually includes:
   a) personal financial statements
   b) tax returns
   c) budgets
   d) All of the above

3. Which of the following laws makes it necessary for a manager of commercial property to check a tenant applicant's name against a certain list before signing a lease?
   a) FIRPTA
   b) Patriot Act
   c) FCRA
   d) 1099-S Reporting Act

4. Experian, TransUnion, and Equifax are all:
   a) property manager professional organizations
   b) tenant screening services
   c) credit reporting bureaus
   d) None of the above

5. The Fair Credit Reporting Act requires:
   a) notifying applicants of a credit-based denial of tenancy or other adverse action
   b) posting landlord rules in prominent places, such as elevators
   c) not determining creditworthiness based solely on credit scores
   d) mandatory use of credit scores when determining creditworthiness

6. Which of the following is implied in every commercial lease?
   a) Habitability
   b) Quiet enjoyment of the premises
   c) Rent escalation
   d) Both a) and b)

7. A lease for 18 months is a _____ tenancy.
   a) two-year
   b) commercial
   c) month-to-month or periodic
   d) term

8. Alessandro rents premises for his deli in a commercial block. The utility companies bill him directly for his water, garbage, electricity, etc. He doesn't pay property taxes or any of the landlord's other operating expenses. What kind of lease does Alessandro have?
   a) Gross
   b) Net
   c) Triple net
   d) Term

9. Just before Alessandro's three-year lease term expires, the manager says that he is willing enter into a new lease (there is no renewal option). However, in addition to minimum or base rent, the manager wants to start passing through to Alessandro the taxes, insurance, and other operating costs associated with the property. This would be:
   a) illegal
   b) a net lease
   c) a gross lease
   d) an escalation clause

10. A store pays a minimum rent of $1,000 per month plus 2% of gross sales up to $25,000, and 4% of sales above that amount. This a _____ lease.
    a) base-proportional
    b) sales
    c) net
    d) percentage

11. Which of the following lease provisions constitutes an escalation clause?

    a) Escalators will be turned off 30 minutes after the mall closes
    b) The parties agree to arbitrate all disputes; if arbitration proves unsuccessful, the complaining party may file a lawsuit
    c) On September 1st of each year, the rent will increase by 3%
    d) If space adjoining the tenant's location becomes vacant, the tenant will have five days to notify the manager that he wishes to expand into this space

12. The lease for Kendrick's Gifts states that if the retail space on the north side of the store becomes available, Kendrick's may rent it by giving notice to the manager within a certain period of time. This clause is called a/an:

    a) option
    b) right of first refusal
    c) subordination provision
    d) Nothing; a manager would never grant this kind of right

13. A tenant gives her manager a potentially refundable amount of money equal to one month's rent; the tenant does this in order to help guaranty her performance of the obligations under her lease. This money is a/an:

    a) advance payment of rent
    b) security deposit
    c) application fee
    d) CAM charge

14. The manager and the tenant can settle the details of the construction that will take place before the tenant moves into the premises in an addendum to the lease called a:

    a) letter of intent
    b) work letter
    c) guaranty
    d) disclosure statement

15. Who must sign a lease for a corporate tenant?

    a) The owner(s) of the business
    b) An officer of the corporation authorized by resolution of the board of directors
    c) A notary public
    d) All of the above

Answer Key

1. c) A property manager should avoid making decisions based on anything other than written standards. Written standards help cut down on mistakes and provide a defense in case a rejected applicant alleges illegal discrimination.

2. d) A tenant qualification package normally includes all of these documents, as well as a business plan, organizational documents, and key personnel resumes.

3. b) The Patriot Act requires that commercial landlords not rent to applicants before checking the applicants' names against the Specially Designated Nationals watch list maintained by the Office of Foreign Assets Control.

4. c) Experian, TransUnion, and Equifax are the three major credit reporting agencies. They produce credit reports used by individuals and businesses, including tenant screening services.

5. a) If poor credit history played a role in denying an applicant a tenancy, FCRA requires notifying the applicant in writing and providing an explanation along with other information.

6. b) Every commercial landlord has an implied duty to provide tenants with quiet enjoyment of the premises. In a residential tenancy, every landlord has this duty in addition to a duty to provide habitable premises.

7. d) Term tenancies are any tenancy for a fixed period of time, whether a certain number of days, months, or years. If the parties do nothing, term tenancies expire automatically at the end of the term, unlike periodic tenancies which continue on for successive periods unless the parties take action to terminate the tenancy.

8. a) In a gross lease, the tenant pays a flat monthly rent designed to cover the manager's operating costs and provide additional income. In a fully net lease, the manager charges rent, but also bills the tenant a pro rata share of all operating costs.

9. b) In a net lease, some or all of the property's operating costs are passed through (charged) to the tenant.

10. d) A percentage lease usually has a fixed amount of rent, called minimum rent (or base rent), plus an additional amount of rent that is calculated as a percentage of gross sales above a certain dollar level.

11. c) Many commercial leases contain a rent escalation clause. The clause provides that on a certain date (usually the lease's anniversary), the rent will increase by a particular dollar amount or percentage.

12. b) The right to lease space if, and only if, it becomes available is called a right of first refusal. An option gives an absolute right to rent a certain space, meaning the manager must keep the space unrented while the option is in effect.

13. b) A refundable deposit given to the manager to help cover the cost of a breach of the lease by the tenant is called a security deposit. One month's rent is the usual amount of the security deposit.

14. b) A work letter is one name that is used to refer to a lease addendum that spells out the plans, specifications, and dollar amounts for improvements to the leased premises.

15. b) A corporation is bound to a lease by the signature of an agent; the agent is an officer of the corporation authorized to sign the lease by a resolution of the corporation's board of directors.

Chapter 8

Working with Tenants

Outline

Introduction

Working with tenants can be one of the most challenging yet rewarding aspects of property management. And since no rental property can succeed without a solid tenant base, it's also one of the most important aspects of property management. We'll begin with a discussion of various ways to establish and maintain strong tenant relationships. Then we'll focus on how best to handle rent collection. Next, we'll address tenant retention. After that, we'll look at breaches of the lease. Finally, we'll discuss ways in which a tenancy terminates.

Creating a Strong Manager-Tenant Relationship

A tenant relationship that begins on a positive note creates a strong foundation for the rest of the tenancy. In this section, we'll discuss the tenant welcome and walkthrough. Then we'll look at ways to maintain communication after the tenant moves in. Finally, we'll discuss how to respond to requests and complaints, and how the manager can provide various tenant services that will strengthen the manager-tenant relationship.

Welcoming the Tenant

Management can make a tenant feel valued and respected beginning with the very first contact. Answering a prospective tenant's questions about the property courteously and promptly will get the relationship off to a good start. Once a lease has been signed, the manager can welcome the new tenant by providing help with the move-in or perhaps by giving a "welcome to the building" gift.

Moving Assistance. Tenants will appreciate moving-day help whether they're moving into a one-bedroom apartment or a large commercial space. Management can provide hand trucks, rolling carts, or any other equipment available for the task. If appropriate, available staff can lend a hand to move larger items.

Of course, larger commercial tenants are likely to use a professional moving service. If the business is relocating from outside the area, the manager can send the new tenant information about local service providers such as exterior sign companies and Internet service providers.

Tenant Gifts. A welcome gift can set the tone for a friendly tenant relationship. The manager should give the gift to the tenant on moving day or shortly thereafter.

Management should choose a gift based on the lease term and the type of rental property. For residential tenants signing a one-year lease, for example, a small inexpensive gift (a basket of snacks or a gift card to a local business) is appropriate. Some landlords like to give a move-in kit that includes items such as trial-size cleaning supplies, tips on local restaurants, and a map.

A more substantial gift is justified for a large commercial tenant that has just signed a five-year lease. What's considered an appropriate gift will depend on the tenant's business, as well as the amount of concessions given during lease negotiation. Options might include pens imprinted with the company's name and new address, magazine subscriptions for the tenant's lobby, or perhaps tickets to sporting or other local events.

The property owner should preapprove any gift, either on a case-by-case basis or under a blanket authorization in the management agreement. An authorization in the management agreement should detail exactly what types of gifts are allowed as well as a per-gift spending limit.

The Walkthrough

It's important to complete a walkthrough when the tenant moves in. In a **walkthrough**, the manager and the tenant walk through the property together, assessing its current condition. But the walkthrough is more than just a chance to inspect the property's condition and to hand over keys; it's also part of the welcoming process and an opportunity to provide important information and answer questions. For example, the manager can give the tenant instructions on how to operate appliances or other equipment, and go over property rules (such as quiet hours).

Inspection. The manager and tenant should use a walk-through checklist (also called a move-in/move-out inspection form) to note the property's condition. Some tenants want to be alone in the rental space when they complete the form. Provided the management agreement allows her to do so, the manager can leave the checklist with the tenant and instruct him to return the completed form within a certain number of hours. However, allowing the tenant to complete the checklist on his own is not a substitute for a manager/tenant in-person walkthrough. And, of course, when the tenant has completed the form, the manager should verify the reported information.

Tenant Rules. The property manager should give the tenant a copy of the property's rules when the lease is signed or during the walkthrough. (As we discussed in Chapter 7, property rules supplement the lease provisions.) An example is shown in Figure 8.1.

All expectations for tenant conduct should be covered in one well-organized, readable document (sometimes called a **tenant handbook**). To some degree, the handbook's content will depend on the type of property involved, but topics covered generally include:

- use of common areas,
- conduct of tenants and guests,
- cleanliness and safety,
- maintenance and repairs,
- emergency procedures,
- payment and late fee policies, and
- security deposit information.

Maintaining Communication

After the chaos of the initial move-in subsides, the tenancy will settle into its normal routine. But a manager shouldn't let the goodwill created during the welcome process go

Figure 8.1 Sample residential tenant rules

Rules and Regulations

These Rules and Regulations are legally binding and are hereby incorporated into your lease. Any violation of these rules constitutes a default under the lease agreement, and may be grounds for eviction or other legal action.

Rental payments: Rent is due by 5:00 p.m. on the first day of each month. Payments can be made by personal check or automatic wire transfer. A $25 NSF fee will be charged on all returned checks. A late fee of $10 per day (up to a maximum of $70 per month) will be charged for all payments made after the first of the month.

Keys: Two unit keys and one mailbox key are provided. Tenant is prohibited from making additional copies and distributing them to anyone who is not named in the rental application. Installation of additional locks without prior consent of Landlord is prohibited. Upon move-out, a $35 charge will be assessed for re-keying of any lock.

Excessive noise: Audio devices such as stereos, televisions, musical instruments and the like must be kept at a reasonable volume at all times. Between the hours of 10:00 p.m. and 7:00 a.m., Tenant is prohibited from allowing any noise inside her living unit that is audible from outside of the unit. Tenant must not engage in any activity that unreasonably interferes with other tenants' peaceful use of their own leased premises.

Balconies: Balconies and porches are not to be used for storage. Patio furniture, a small barbecue, and up to three small potted plants are allowed; any additional items should be stored out of sight. Balconies and porches must be kept neat and clean at all times.

Parking: Tenants all have assigned parking spaces. Additional overflow guest parking is provided in the areas with unnumbered spaces. Do not park in any numbered space except your own assigned space; if you do, your vehicle may be ticketed and/or towed at your expense.

---

to waste. Managers can continue to foster tenant relationships by maintaining good communication throughout the lease term.

Management should encourage every tenant to give feedback and to communicate any problems as soon as they occur. This approach, combined with prompt action to address problems, helps create loyal tenants.

Good communication is also financially beneficial to the owner. Encouraging prompt reporting of maintenance issues can save thousands of dollars in repair costs, since the manager can address small problems before they become big ones. Also, a good rapport with tenants can translate into more timely rent payments and a higher tenant retention rate. Finally, a good communication system will diminish the impact of tenant conflicts if they arise.

Regular Updates. A manager should take the time to provide her tenants with regular updates. These updates encourage a sense of community among the tenants, and also demonstrate the manager's interest in the property.

In many cases, the manager and owner together will decide on the frequency and format of tenant updates. The manager can use a webpage to provide updates. Tenants find website updates non-invasive; on the other hand, the information could easily get overlooked. Email alerts may work better, but are more intrusive; it's important that they contain only relevant and informative content. Newsletters are a third option that many managers employ.

> **Example:** Jennifer manages a large industrial property that has 15 long-term tenants. The area was rezoned not long ago to allow mixed industrial, retail, and office uses, and construction is taking place on many nearby properties. Streets are crowded with construction vehicles and often close temporarily to allow heavy equipment to be brought in. New information about street closures and other inconveniences surfaces almost daily.
>
> Jennifer should establish a webpage where she can post updates for her tenants. This format would allow her to keep her tenants informed without constantly bombarding them with email alerts or flyers. She could add website links to various government sources for information about construction, road closures, building permits, and so forth.

> **Example:** Kenneth manages a 50-unit apartment complex. The building is about 70 years old and in relatively good shape. Many of the tenants are elderly and don't use the Internet often (if at all). Kenneth prints out a monthly newsletter which he leaves in the lobby of the building. He includes some community news he thinks might be relevant to most of his tenants, news about the building, and seasonal maintenance reminders, such as: "The cold weather is approaching. Please make sure your heat is working properly and send any repair requests to my attention."

Soliciting Tenant Input. Managers can solicit tenant input through a variety of means, from the classic low-tech suggestion box to the use of more sophisticated web-based surveys. The best method will depend on a number of factors. If the property has a large number of tenants, Internet communication may be the way to go. On the other hand, for commercial properties with just a few large tenants, the manager should visit each tenant on a regular basis. In any case, the manager will want to have an accurate and efficient system for tracking tenant requests and management responses.

Responding to Requests and Complaints

A system for soliciting input isn't worth much if the manager doesn't respond properly to the issues raised by tenants. The manager should respond to every request promptly and treat everyone with the same level of patient, friendly interest. If a tenant's request is unreasonable, calmly explain why.

Begin with a simple acknowledgement of the request/complaint and an estimate of when the problem will be fixed or investigated. The manager's procedures manual should set out timelines for handling various types of requests; a manual for residential property should also reflect any deadlines mandated by the state landlord-tenant law.

To avoid charges of discrimination under federal and state fair housing laws, be sure to treat all requests and complaints equally, regardless of the tenant's race, ethnicity, sex,

Life-Threatening Issues

Property managers field all kinds of complaints: noisy neighbors, parking problems, broken fixtures—the list is nearly endless. All issues should be dealt with as soon as reasonably possible. However, the law requires that certain life-threatening issues be remedied immediately. Life-threatening issues include:

- carbon monoxide fumes;
- smoke detectors that aren't working;
- gas leaks;
- blocked fire exits;
- electrical hazards (such as exposed wires);
- a security issue in a unit (such as broken locks or windows); and
- threats of physical violence by another tenant or a visitor.

Issues that may threaten a tenant's health but aren't considered immediately life-threatening include:

- improper garbage storage/removal;
- unsanitary living conditions of other tenants; and
- air quality (such as sewer odor and mold issues).

or membership in any other protected class. Keep careful written records of the initial complaint or request, management's response, and the reason why the request was denied, if applicable.

Requiring Written Requests. It's a good idea to require tenants to submit all but the most minor requests or complaints in writing. Keeping a supply of pre-printed forms handy makes this easier for the tenants. Requiring written requests can prevent a tense situation from escalating into something worse. An angry tenant who comes into the manager's office to vent about his neighbor may calm down when he's given a form and asked to put his complaint in writing. Also, a written request is much easier to follow up on.

Of course, if a tenant calls to report a burst pipe in his unit, the first thing to do is turn off the water main and call the plumbing service. Requiring a written request in an emergency situation would not be appropriate. However, a maintenance report should be completed after dealing with an emergency, just as would be done after a normal request.

Tenant Services

Another way to create and preserve tenant goodwill is to offer more services. Tenant services serve a double purpose; they not only make tenants happier, but they also create extra income for the property. And even when a tenant has no use for the offered service, she may appreciate knowing the option is available.

The kind of services offered depends on the type of property involved. Potential tenant services include:

- **Housekeeping.** Management customarily provides janitorial services to office and certain other commercial tenants. However, managers can also provide cleaning services to residential tenants, either as a complimentary perk for those paying a high rent or as a service paid for by the tenant.
- **Private rental of common areas.** Large residential apartment complexes with extensive clubhouse facilities often rent space for weddings and other events.
- **Doorman, concierge, and related conveniences.** These kinds of services are usually offered in luxury highrise apartments and high-end office buildings. However, any apartment building with a management office can offer to handle packages and deliveries for tenants, either for free or for a slight charge.
- **Painting and interior decoration.** The landlord may provide interior decorating and painting services for commercial spaces.

Rent Collection

Now that we've looked at establishing strong manager-tenant relationships, let's turn our attention to rent collection and related recordkeeping. (Note that this is a general discussion of rent collection; for more information on this topic as it relates to specific types of properties, see Chapters 10–13.)

Rental income pays for the property's expenses (including the property manager's fee), and it's critical for the manager to receive rent payments in a dependable manner. A good rent collection system, along with a reliable method of recordkeeping, will help the manager meet this goal.

Property management software with a rent collection feature is a good idea for properties of any size. There are many computer programs that can collect and report rental payments online, identify delinquent renters, automatically generate late notices and assess late fees, and issue an eviction notice.

Keep in mind that the rental agreement must spell out all rental payment terms (sales amount, due date, and late fees). A manager will find it difficult, if not impossible, to enforce any terms that are not clearly set forth in the agreement. The landlord should also carefully explain the rental payment provision to the tenant at the lease signing. The tenant should understand from the outset that on-time payment is a priority and that delinquencies are taken seriously.

Rent Collection System

A dependable rent collection system generally consists of three parts: billing, late notices, and late fees.

Billing. Because most residential leases specify a fixed monthly rental amount, a rent bill usually isn't necessary; it's sufficient that the tenant knows where and when to deliver or deposit the rent.

In a commercial lease, however, the monthly rental amount often varies. For example, a tenant may pay a portion of the building's operating expenses, such as property taxes, insurance, utilities, and maintenance. Since some of these additional charges vary from month to month, tenants need monthly bills to tell them exactly how much is due.

Late Notices. Late notices are an effective rent collection tool. A manager who issues a one-day late notice sends a message to tenants that late payments are unacceptable, regardless of whether a late fee is charged.

Property management software can produce these notices automatically. However, when a manager is dealing with just a few large commercial tenants, it may be better to make a phone call or visit the tenant.

Late Fees. There are several ways to structure late fees. The four most common arrangements are:

- **Flat percentage.** A flat percentage, such as 5%, of the amount due after a certain date (for example, 3 to 10 days after rent is due). However, this fee structure may inadvertently encourage partial payments, since the percentage is charged only on the amount overdue.
- **Flat fee.** A straight fee, such as $25 or $50, that becomes due after a certain date (usually 3 to 10 days after the rent is due). However, as with a flat percentage, once rent is overdue there's little incentive to pay it quickly.
- **Daily fee.** A daily flat fee charged beginning on a certain date (for example, $5 per day from the 3rd day after rent is due) until rent is fully paid. This method has the advantage of continuing to encourage prompt payment.
- **Flat fee plus daily fee.** A flat fee charged a certain number of days after rent is due (such as $25 or $50), and an additional smaller daily fee charged until rent is paid in full.

The late fee method should be chosen with care, as it will have an effect on how tenants regard their payment obligations. Whatever fee structure the landlord chooses, it's important to enforce it consistently and firmly.

Instead of imposing a late fee, some landlords like to set the rent at a slightly higher rate and then give discounts to those who pay before the due date; they feel this fosters a more positive attitude toward timely rent payments.

Exceptions. Occasionally, a late rent payment should be accepted without imposing a late fee. Sometimes tenants are in the midst of an emergency situation that justifies an exception to the rules. For instance, perhaps a spouse has died or is very ill, and the other spouse is too preoccupied with other matters to make the rent payment on time. If exceptions are going to be made, however, the policy allowing them should be clearly spelled out in the management agreement.

When granting exceptions, the manager must strive for consistency to avoid claims of favoritism or discrimination. Keep in mind that granting exceptions may have the unintended effect of encouraging future instances of late rent. In addition, repeated instances of accepting late rent may constitute a waiver of the lease's due-date provisions and weaken a case for eviction in court.

Recordkeeping

In addition to using property management software to track rental payments and issue late notices, landlords also depend on software to generate two important schedules: a rental ledger and a rent roll. These two schedules help the manager (and the owner) track tenant information and plan for the future.

Rental Ledger. A rental ledger is the primary tenant rent record, containing a separate ledger sheet for each tenant. Each ledger sheet usually has columns for the following information:

- tenant name,
- tenant phone number,
- unit number,
- current rental rate,
- amount of security deposit,
- move-in date,
- lease expiration date (or status of month-to-month),
- any recurring charges,
- pass-through charges (for commercial tenants),
- late charges incurred,
- payments made, and
- balances owed.

This ledger makes it easy for the manager to check a tenant's payment and leasing status at a glance. This information is also useful when it's time to consider lease renewal, which we'll discuss shortly. It's also useful when the manager or owner is determining whether to make an exception to the late payment penalty rule. (Tenants with an excellent payment history might get a one-time break from the late payment penalty.)

Rent Roll. The rent roll contains much of the same information that appears in the rental ledger, but the rent roll is organized by unit or space rather than by tenant, with a separate entry for each unit or space (whether rented or not). An example of a rent roll for a residential building is shown in Figure 8.2.

Management software can take the data in the rent roll and rent ledger and use it to generate rent collection and delinquency reports, vacancy reports, and lease expiration projections.

Breaching Lease Agreements

Inevitably a landlord will have to deal with tenants who breach their leases. And occasionally the landlord himself may breach a lease. We'll discuss both situations in this section.

A **breach** occurs when one party violates a provision of their contract (the lease agreement). If the breach is serious enough to justify terminating the lease, it's known as a **material breach**. There are a number of ways to breach a lease agreement; we'll briefly cover some of the more common ones.

Figure 8.2 Rent roll

Rent Roll								
Property: Magnolia Heights					**Period:** April			
Owner: S.T. Jones					**Prepared by:** M. Smith			
Unit No.	Occupant	Previous Balance	Current Rent	Date Received	Other Amounts	Description	Total Received	Balance Due
101	G. Tsui	0	$1,200	4/1	—	—	$1,200	0
102	F. Brown	$900	$900	4/9	—	—	$1,800	0
103	K. Plane	0	$900	4/2	$100	Parking	$1,000	0
104	C. Flynn	0	$1,050	4/1	—	—	$1,050	0
105	P. Sneed	$1,050	$1,050	4/15	—	—	$1,050	$1,050
106	L. Hurt	0	$1,050	4/1	$100	Parking	$1,150	0
107	E. Winn	0	$900	4/2	—	—	$900	0

Breach by the Landlord

A landlord breaches a lease if she violates one of its implied provisions—the right to quiet enjoyment or (in a residential lease) the right to habitable premises—or any of the lease's express provisions.

Quiet Enjoyment. Every lease, residential and commercial, contains an **implied covenant of quiet enjoyment** (see Chapter 7). This means that a landlord cannot disrupt the tenant's use of the property, nor can he allow others to do so.

> **Example:** Suzanne, a massage therapist, rents a small office to meet with clients. The landlord decides to remodel the surrounding offices and begins performing the work himself. The demolition and construction noise go on for months, interfering with Suzanne's therapeutic massage practice. The landlord has breached the covenant of quiet enjoyment.

Another example of a breach of the covenant of quiet enjoyment would be a landlord's failure to control the late-night noise of certain tenants in an apartment building after other tenants have complained.

The covenant does not prevent the landlord from entering the unit for a reasonable purpose, such as making repairs or showing the space to prospective tenants, provided the manager gives the tenant sufficient notice.

If the landlord's intrusions are sufficiently prolonged and serious, they may amount to a material breach that justifies termination of the lease.

Habitability. Every residential lease agreement carries the landlord's **implied warranty of habitability**. Habitability means that the residence meets all building and housing code regulations that affect health and safety. If the property does not meet code requirements and the tenant notifies the landlord of the defect, the landlord must correct the problem within a certain period of time prescribed by state law. If the landlord fails to repair the problem, he has breached the lease. We'll say a little more about this warranty in Chapter 10.

Other Lease Provisions. In addition to the implied covenants described above, the landlord might also breach any of the express lease provisions that benefit the tenant. Examples include the failure to provide promised improvements to the premises, violation of a noncompete clause in a commercial lease, or a continued failure to perform maintenance duties required by the lease.

Breach by the Tenant

Generally speaking, a lease imposes more duties on a tenant than it does on a landlord, so there are many more ways that tenants can (and do) breach leases. Any of the following violations would justify termination if the landlord decided to pursue the issue. However, the landlord would need to give the tenant notice of the breach and a chance to remedy the violation before he could terminate the lease and evict the tenant. (Evictions are discussed later in this chapter.)

Failure to Pay Rent. The tenant must keep rent payments current. She must also pay when due all utility bills and other pass-through charges the she is responsible for. Failure to meet this obligation is a material beach and justifies terminating the lease.

Failure to Maintain the Premises. A tenant who causes significant damage to the premises has breached the lease. (Note that if the security deposit is more than sufficient to cover the damage, landlords may not bother terminating the lease.)

Engaging in a Prohibited Use. Most leases prohibit the tenant from using the property for any purpose that is contrary to the intended purpose of the lease. With a residential tenant, prohibited uses may include running a business out of the residence or increasing the number of occupants to a greater number than allowed by the lease.

Commercial tenants can violate use provisions in a variety of ways. With an industrial tenant, for example, a prohibited use might include adding a chemical manufacturing process that creates environmental liability for the landlord. With a retail tenant, a prohibited use could include adding a new service or different merchandise—such adding a coffee bar to a clothing boutique—when that use wasn't mentioned in the original lease. (Retail use provisions are often tightly written to avoid tenants competing with each other.)

Violating Property Rules. As we mentioned earlier, the tenant must abide by all of the landlord's property rules. Breaking any of these rules generally constitutes a breach of the lease.

> **Example:** Picasso Workspaces is an old factory that has been divided up into artist studios. One of the property rules prohibits the tenants from sleeping in their spaces at night. One tenant loses her apartment lease and starts sleeping in her studio to save money. She has violated the property rules and breached the lease.

A tenant can also breach the lease if he fails to obey any state or local laws that relate to the use of the premises. Such failures that might violate the lease include creating unsanitary conditions, for instance, or using the premises for illegal drug activity.

Retaining Tenants

Effective property managers know that their property's success depends on retaining good tenants. In this section, we'll discuss the importance of tenant retention, look at how to retain good tenants, and discuss the particulars of lease renewals.

Importance of Retention

There are three basic advantages to retaining tenants: avoiding lost rental income, saving on remodeling and refurbishing costs, and avoiding the marketing and administrative expenses that are associated with leasing out space. An existing tenant is also a known quantity; the tenant can be counted on to provide a steady rental income. A new tenant may look good on paper but until there is a history of regular payments, each new tenant is a gamble.

Lost Income. The most obvious advantage to retaining a tenant is avoiding the loss of rental income while the manager looks for a replacement tenant. The manager must prepare the property for showing, market the property, screen applicants, and finally sign a lease agreement. Meanwhile, the property is sitting empty for days, weeks, or even months.

Commercial landlords may also end up paying carrying costs for expenses that the tenant normally covers, such as utilities, property taxes, insurance, and maintenance. These extra costs add up quickly and can become a significant financial drain if the manager can't find a new tenant right away.

Remodeling/Refurbishing. Empty space must often be refurbished or remodeled before the new tenant moves in. This is true to a varying degree for all types of rental property. For example, most residential apartment units will need a thorough carpet cleaning or a new coat of paint between tenants. Commercial space typically requires significant improvements to meet the needs of the new tenant, and these improvements are usually completed at the landlord's expense.

Marketing and Administrative Expenses. Naturally, a renewing tenant renders marketing efforts unnecessary. This represents a savings not only on advertising fees, but also on the manager's time and effort in responding to inquiries, showing the property, and researching the backgrounds of prospective tenants. Managers who use leasing agents for these tasks will save money by not having to pay an agent's commission.

How to Retain Good Tenants

A strong manager-tenant relationship is the surest path to retaining good tenants. As we made clear at the outset of this chapter, the effort to build a relationship begins before the tenant moves in and continues throughout the lease period. Tenants who feel welcomed, listened to, and who have their needs met reasonably quickly tend to stay put.

Don't take a long-term tenant's renewal for granted. Some modest improvements to the leased space may be worth considering even though the tenant is still under lease and isn't pushing for a concession. For example, a long-term residential tenant may tire of waiting for a new refrigerator or some other improvement and look for a new apartment—especially if she has seen empty units get various upgrades over the years.

Getting Rid of Bad Tenants. Of course, not all tenants are worth retaining. Those who habitually pay their rent late or who are a constant source of problems are often more trouble than they're worth. Getting rid of a poor tenant is usually a simple matter of not renewing the lease. However, in some circumstances the manager will be required to provide notice. (We'll discuss notice requirements shortly.)

As an alternative to not renewing the lease, the manager could insist on new lease terms that fully address the tenant's past problems. For instance, if the tenant is chronically late paying the rent, the manager might raise the rent, increase the size of security deposits, or impose a higher late payment penalty. The new terms should be serious enough to either discourage the tenant from renewing the lease, or protect the owner's financial interests if the tenant chooses to stay.

 Giving Notice

The type of leasehold largely determines what notice, if any, a party must give to terminate a tenancy.

Estate for years (term tenancy). An estate for years is created by an express agreement that specifies a definite term (one with a fixed beginning and end date). For residential leases, the term is usually one year. These types of leases are also used for short vacation leases or multi-year commercial leases.

As a general rule, an estate for years terminates automatically when the term expires; neither party needs to give notice. However, many leases, particularly commercial ones, require the parties to state in advance whether they wish to renew or not.

Periodic tenancy. A periodic tenancy has no fixed termination date; the tenancy renews automatically unless one party gives notice to the other. (The most common periodic tenancy is a residential month-to-month tenancy.)

The notice required to terminate a periodic tenancy generally mirrors the length of the lease period. For example, 30 days' notice is required for a month-to-month periodic tenancy, although some states require residential landlords to give 60 days' notice. The landlord does not have to give the tenant a reason for terminating the tenancy.

Lease Renewals

The lease renewal process will vary depending on the type of lease and the type of tenant. Generally, the steps include sending the tenant a renewal notice, following up with the tenant, negotiating the new lease terms, and then signing the new lease.

Renewal Notice. The manager should have a system that notifies him of upcoming lease expiration dates; the system might involve property management software or simply notations on a desk calendar. Renewal notices (for good tenants) should be sent a reasonable amount of time before the lease will expire. The appropriate amount of advance notice depends on the type of tenant and the lease term. Two months should be plenty for the typical residential tenant with a one-year lease, while six to nine months is advisable for a commercial tenant with a three- to five-year lease.

> **Example:** Davis Properties manages a 330-unit apartment complex. The management software generates form renewal letters 40 days before each lease is due to expire and prints the letter for mailing (provided the tenant hasn't been flagged for non-renewal). The program can also generate email renewal notices if the tenant has indicated a preference for email communications.

Personal Follow-Up. The manager should follow up on the renewal notice with personal contact. A phone call often suffices for a simple residential renewal, but most commercial leases justify a visit. This face-to-face meeting allows the manager to find out whether the tenant wants to renew, and to discuss the rent or any other terms (such as renovations) that either party wants to renegotiate.

With a small commercial tenant, such as a retail store in a strip mall, all the negotiations may be completed in the first meeting. With larger tenants, however, the initial contact is just the beginning of a longer negotiation process.

The manager should schedule the first meeting early enough so that if the tenant fails to renew the lease, there is still time to find a replacement tenant before the lease terminates.

Renewal Negotiations. Renewal negotiations generally focus on the same items that were central to the initial lease negotiations (discussed in Chapter 7). The following three items are critical to virtually all renewal negotiations:

- length of the lease term;
- rental amount; and
- repairs, alterations, and renovations.

Initial and renewal negotiations differ in some important ways, however. First, when the renewal negotiations begin, the tenant now has a track record, so the landlord has a better idea of how valuable the tenant is and how far to go in accommodating requests.

> **Example:** Boss Tweeds is an excellent retail tenant and draws lots of foot traffic to Sandy Shores Mall. The store always pays its rent on time, and the amount of percentage rent it pays is considerable because store sales are high year-round. The store's five-year lease is up for renewal. In this case, the owner and property manager are willing to offer significant concessions to renew the lease for another five years. Concessions might include improvements to the retail space or a discount on CAM charges.

Example: At the other end of Sandy Shores Mall is Scads of Plaids, an average tenant whose merchandise appeals to a very limited market. Sales are lackluster, and the store occasionally has trouble getting rent in on time. If vacancy rates are low, the property manager may not want to renew this lease. On the other hand, if the market is poor and vacancy rates are expected to remain high, the manager may have little choice but to renew—possibly even with some concessions. Finally, in a hybrid situation, where the market is stagnant but expected to improve before long, the manager might want to negotiate a short lease renewal, which will allow the manager to revisit the tenancy later, when the market is better.

Another distinction between initial and renewal lease negotiations is that both parties have a sense of how the practicalities of the lease are working out. For example, say an office tenant has problems paying rent by the first of the month because the business normally doesn't collect the bulk of its income until the fifth of the month. Under the current lease, late penalties begin to accrue on the second day of the month. It's a reasonable concession for the manager to agree to a late fee provision that doesn't impose penalties until later in the month.

On the other hand, suppose a retail tenant is habitually late in submitting her report of gross receipts, which is used to calculate her rent for the month. There is no justifiable reason for the tardiness; the tenant simply doesn't seem to consider it a priority. Assuming the manager wants to renew the lease, he may seek a higher penalty for each day the report is late.

As with any lease negotiation, the manager must keep current and future market conditions in mind. If inflation rates are high, the manager may want to raise the rent considerably, or reevaluate the escalation clause to be sure the formula is keeping up with costs. In times of projected deflation, the manager will want to lock in the current rental rate for as long as possible.

Deciding what terms to offer a renewing tenant can be difficult, especially in commercial situations. The manager must keep current on market conditions, know his client's financial goals, and maintain an accurate performance history for each tenant. All of this information will help the manager negotiate lease renewals.

Termination of Tenancy

Now that we've discussed dealing with tenants old and new, let's look at how the landlord-tenant relationship ends. Generally, tenancies terminate by lease expiration, abandonment, surrender, eviction, or through foreclosure, destruction, or condemnation of the rental property.

Lease Expiration

Many tenancies simply end when the lease expires. Either the tenant wants to move on despite the manager's retention efforts, or the manager is happy to see the tenant go. The lease expiration date approaches, notice is given if the lease requires it, and then the tenant moves out and the tenancy ends.

The tenant and manager should go through the premises and complete a move-out inspection report. The inspection allows the landlord to compare the current condition of the premises to the condition before the tenant moved in (when an inspection was also made). Most state residential landlord-tenant acts require a move-in and move-out inspection, but it's a good idea with many types of commercial spaces as well. Depending on the condition of the unit or space, the landlord will refund some or all of the tenant's security deposit; state law generally dictates a deadline by which a residential tenant must receive the refund.

The tenant may agree to an exit interview, which gives the manager an opportunity to find out more about why the tenant has decided to move. During the interview, the tenant may be more forthcoming than usual with his opinions about the rental rate, management and policies, neighbors, etc.

If the lease term expires and the tenant remains without the landlord's consent, the landlord can begin eviction proceedings (see below).

Notice of Termination. As noted, a lease sometimes requires a party to give notice of intent to terminate. And periodic tenancies, such as month-to-month tenancies, always require a termination notice. The amount of notice required depends on the original lease agreement's terms and on state law, but 20 or 30 days' notice is usually required.

> **Example:** Under the law of Washington State, a party to a commercial lease who wishes to terminate a month-to-month tenancy must give the other party 30 days' notice. In contrast, a residential tenant in that same state only needs to give 20 days' notice.

Abandonment

Abandonment occurs when a tenant leaves the premises before a fixed lease term expires. The term also applies if a tenant departs without giving the advance notice required to properly end a month-to-month tenancy. Commercial tenants usually abandon a space because of financial problems. For a residential tenant, reasons also include family issues or the need to relocate for a job.

In most cases, a tenant who abandons the premises has breached the lease agreement and is liable for the remaining rent payments as they become due. The manager generally has a duty to mitigate (lessen) the damages by re-renting the property as soon as possible. In a reasonably active rental market, re-renting may be easy; in that case, the manager may not even bother to pursue the abandoning tenant for damages.

A landlord may presume abandonment under certain conditions. For example, abandonment might be presumed if the rent becomes overdue by a certain number of days and the manager reasonably suspects that the tenant has vacated the premises.

When a tenant is late paying his rent and appears to have vacated the premises, the manager may deliver a **notice of belief of abandonment**. (Some states require this for residential tenants.) The notice essentially states that the manager will repossess the property if the tenant fails to respond within a certain time. If there is no response, the manager can retake the premises.

Tenant's Personal Property. Frequently, the landlord will find some personal property left behind by an abandoning tenant. State law usually spells out detailed procedures for handling any personal property a residential tenant abandons.

Generally, the tenant cannot recover the property without reimbursing the landlord for any costs incurred in storing the property. If the tenant fails to recover the property within the statutory period, the landlord can dispose of it, and should sell the property if it has some monetary value. Some states allow the landlord to withhold from the proceeds any lease monies owing (such as unpaid rent); other states do not. If there are proceeds owed to the tenant, they must be sent to the tenant. If the tenant's whereabouts are unknown, the manager must hold the proceeds for a certain period, such as one year.

If the tenant left behind only a small amount of property, some states shorten or eliminate this entire process. For example, the law might provide that if the property appears to be worth less than $250 dollars, the landlord can dispose of it within seven days after sending the tenant notice to reclaim the property.

State statutes typically don't address a commercial tenant's abandoned property. However, these states may have case law indicating that a commercial landlord must give the tenant a reasonable opportunity to recover the property.

Surrender

Surrender (also known as mutual agreement) occurs when the parties agree to terminate a lease before the date stated in the lease agreement. This happens when a tenant needs to get out of the lease for financial or other reasons and the landlord agrees (usually because re-renting the premises will be relatively easy or even profitable).

> **Example:** Oscar rents a house from Felix under a one-year lease. Five months into the lease term, Oscar gets a promotion that requires him to move to another state. Demand for housing is very strong, and Felix knows that he can charge a new tenant higher rent. He agrees to let Oscar out of the lease without any liability for the rent remaining under the lease term.

Surrender can also occur when a landlord wants to redevelop or refurbish the property. The tenant is often willing to give up his lease in return for a cash payment that covers the tenant's costs to move and rent property elsewhere, plus a little extra.

Eviction

An eviction occurs when the manager expels the tenant from the property. The manager cannot simply force the tenant to leave the property, however. If the tenant refuses to leave when requested, the manager must go through the legal process of an **unlawful detainer action**, discussed below. Landlords should never take matters into their own hands. A manager who attempts a **self-help eviction** (forcing the tenant out with threats or by cutting off the utilities) instead of filing an unlawful detainer action may end up defending a costly lawsuit. And be aware that the eviction process cannot be used to discriminate against someone unfairly or to retaliate against a tenant who has made legitimate repair requests or exercised other legal rights.

Process of Lawful Eviction. Generally, there are four stages to the eviction process: a notice to quit or cure the tenant's breach of the lease; filing an unlawful detainer action

Figure 8.3 Notice to pay or quit

NOTICE TO PAY RENT OR QUIT

TO _____, TENANT, in unit _____:

You must pay the rent and all other charges owing on your unit, pursuant to a written lease for the premises described below, in the amount of $_____, for the period from _____ to _____, or give up possession of the premises within THREE DAYS after service on you of this notice; otherwise the undersigned will institute legal proceedings against you to declare a forfeiture of the lease and collect all amounts owing plus legal fees and costs.

The premises referred to are commonly known as:

_____ [address, unit number]

_____ [city, state, zip code]

Signed: _____   Dated: _____
        (Landlord)

---

in court; a court hearing; and then—if the landlord wins the hearing—an eviction order followed by physical removal. We'll briefly discuss each of these stages.

Notice to Quit or Cure Breach. As soon as a tenant becomes delinquent in her rent payments or otherwise breaches the lease agreement, the manager should issue a late payment notice or a notice to correct the violation.

Alternatively, if the manager wants to proceed as quickly as possible to the eviction stage, he can deliver an eviction notice to the tenant (skipping a simple late payment notice or notice to correct the violation). In many states, this notice is called a **three-day notice** or a notice to pay/cure or quit premises. This notice informs the tenant that legal action will be taken unless the outstanding amount is paid (or other violation cured) within three days. Note that state law will dictate the actual deadline; some states require up to ten days' notice. The landlord must strictly conform to all state and local rules concerning the format and delivery of the notice. A sample notice to pay rent or quit for a residential property is shown in Figure 8.3.

Many states exempt the landlord (at least a residential landlord) from the notice requirement if the tenant is involved in illegal drug-related activity. In such situations, the landlord can proceed directly to court by filing an unlawful detainer action.

Note that the manager must have the owner's approval to commence eviction proceedings, whether that consent is given on a case-by-case basis or granted broadly in the management agreement.

Filing the Unlawful Detainer Action. If the tenant fails to bring the rent current or to correct the specified lease violation, the manager may file an unlawful detainer action with the appropriate court. The tenant must be served with a summons and a copy of the complaint. Again, state and local rules govern the procedures that must be followed.

A tenant may move out voluntarily after being served with the complaint. If the tenant remains but fails to respond to the complaint, the landlord can request a default judgment. If the tenant responds in a timely manner (by filing an answer in the court proceeding), the judge will hold an eviction hearing.

While an experienced property manager may have a relatively easy time handling the first few steps of the eviction process on her own, it's best to enlist the help of an attorney if the tenant contests the eviction. In some jurisdictions an attorney is required.

Hearing. Tenants may raise various defenses in an unlawful detainer action. For example, a tenant might claim that the eviction action violates the tenant's civil rights or is illegal retaliation for the tenant's complaint about the unit's habitability.

A tenant may also claim that nonpayment of rent was justified because a constructive eviction occurred. **Constructive eviction** means that the landlord has caused or permitted a substantial interference with the tenant's possession of the property; in these circumstances, the tenant may be justified in withholding rent payments or even abandoning the lease altogether.

After hearing evidence concerning a breach of the lease, the judge will rule in favor of the tenant or the landlord. However, a judgment for the landlord won't necessarily result in an eviction order. Instead, the judge may simply order the tenant to bring the rent current (or remedy whatever violation exists). Generally, the losing party must pay the other party's legal costs.

 ### Retaliatory and Discriminatory Evictions

In an eviction hearing, a tenant might raise the defense that the landlord is pursuing eviction because the tenant made legitimate repair requests or reported substandard living conditions to a local government entity. A landlord who does this has engaged in retaliatory eviction, which is illegal.

Another illegal use of the eviction process is discriminatory eviction. No landlord can evict a tenant due to her membership in a class protected by antidiscrimination laws. A discriminatory eviction will open up the landlord to significant statutory penalties (see Chapter 14).

Managers can guard against unsubstantiated claims of unfair eviction by keeping good records of all interactions with tenants (including both formal notices and any conversations or correspondence), in order to establish legitimate grounds for an eviction.

Eviction Order and Removal. If the judge does issue an **eviction order** (also called a writ of ejectment or a writ of possession), the order must be served on the tenant. Usually the county sheriff's department handles this. The order specifies the deadline for the tenant to move out. The landlord should have the sheriff's department conduct the actual physical eviction if the tenant continues to remain on the premises after this date.

Once the eviction is complete and the tenant and her personal property are removed from the premises, the landlord should change the locks and conduct an inspection. Then she can begin the process of preparing the property for a new tenant.

Just Cause Exception. As a general rule, either party can terminate a periodic tenancy for any reason. But in some cases, the law limits a residential landlord's power to terminate the tenancy. This is true for tenancies in government-assisted housing (such as Section 8 housing). It also applies in some cities that have "just cause" eviction ordinances. In these situations, a landlord generally can't terminate a periodic tenancy unless the tenant has committed a material breach of the leasehold agreement. A material breach (the just cause for termination) exists if the tenant does any of the following:

- fails to pay rent,
- materially damages the rented property,
- substantially interferes with another tenant's quiet enjoyment,
- uses the premises illegally, or
- otherwise materially breaches the lease agreement.

Normal eviction procedures must be followed. Even in a community with a just cause eviction ordinance, exemptions apply to certain types of property and in certain situations. For example, the ordinance may not apply to smaller buildings (those with one to four units) where the owner lives in one of the units. Any property manager who may be affected by this type of ordinance should obtain more detailed information from local sources.

Foreclosure, Destruction, or Condemnation

Foreclosure, destruction, or condemnation may also terminate a tenancy under certain circumstances.

Foreclosure. When a lien against a commercial property is foreclosed because the owner has defaulted on a loan or other obligation, this generally terminates the leases of all the tenants. However, foreclosure doesn't usually terminate a residential lease. A recent federal law requires the buyer of foreclosed residential property to honor a tenant's lease until the expiration date. There is an exception if the buyer intends to occupy the property herself, in which case she must give the tenant at least 90 days' notice before terminating the lease and evicting the tenant.

Destruction of the Property. The destruction of the entire leased property will terminate a lease. But if the lease includes both the land itself and the building(s) on it, the destruction of the building doesn't entirely frustrate the purpose of the lease—so the tenant may be required to pay rent to the end of the lease period. Note that while this rule might apply to a land-user such as a farmer, it wouldn't apply to a tenant renting a single-family house with a yard.

Condemnation. The government can take private property for public use through a process called **condemnation**. Condemnation of a property will terminate any existing lease. However, the government must reimburse the property owner for the fair market value of the condemned property and also pay the tenant for the value (if any) of the remaining leasehold.

Chapter Summary

1. A good relationship with tenants is an important aspect of rental property success. It begins from the first contact with a prospective tenant and continues throughout the entire course of the relationship, including the walkthrough, complaint-handling, rent collection, lease renewal, and move-out.

2. Every tenant should receive a copy of the property rules, which covers such topics as use of common areas, noise, safety and cleanliness, and emergency procedures.

3. Every manager should foster good communications with tenants with regular updates about the property, and by encouraging feedback and questions. Updates can take the form of traditional paper newsletters, emails, an interactive website, a personal visit, or some combination of these.

4. The manager should establish a protocol for handling complaints and requests, get everything in writing as soon as possible, and treat all tenant requests and complaints seriously and with courtesy.

5. An efficient rent collection system may include rent bills, late notices, and late fees. Most managers use property management software to handle these tasks. The manager and owner should agree on rules for waiving late fees. Possible late fee structures include the flat percentage, flat fee, daily fee, and on-time discount. Accurate recordkeeping is essential if late notices are going to be sent out promptly and late fees assessed fairly. Basic records include a rental ledger and a rent roll.

6. A landlord may breach the lease by violating the tenant's right of quiet enjoyment and, in a residential tenancy, failing to maintain habitability. A tenant may breach the lease by failing to pay rent or engaging in a prohibited use of the property.

7. Retaining good tenants is a top priority for every property manager, as it eliminates the uncertainty and rental downtime associated with finding new tenants. It also saves on marketing and remodeling or refurbishing costs. The property manager should maintain a notification system for upcoming lease expiration dates and begin negotiating new leases before they expire.

8. A tenancy may terminate through expiration, surrender, or eviction. A lease may also terminate due to foreclosure, destruction of the property, or condemnation.

Key Terms

Walkthrough – An inspection by the landlord and tenant conducted before move-in in which the parties note any damage to the rental property.

Tenant handbook – An organized document or manual given to new tenants, explaining the building's rules and other tenant expectations.

Rent bill – The monthly rent invoice for commercial tenants. The bill takes into account any percentage rent and the tenant's share of operating expenses, such as taxes, insurance, utilities, and maintenance charges.

Rental ledger – A list of each tenant's payment history, organized by tenant; it lists such things as rent rate, security deposit, lease expiration date, recurring and pass-through charges (if any), payments made, late charges incurred, and balances owed.

Rent roll – A list of every rental unit or space. The list includes the current tenant's name and phone number, rental rate, lease terms and payment status, and amounts due, if any.

Breach – Violation of a provision of a contract by one party; when the breach is serious enough to justify terminating the contract (lease agreement), it's known as a material breach.

Implied covenant of quiet enjoyment – An implied right in a lease that assures the tenant of freedom from any unreasonable intrusion by the landlord or anyone else.

Implied warranty of habitability – An implied lease provision that requires a residential landlord to provide living quarters that are safe, clean, and fit for human habitation.

Estate for years – Also known as a term tenancy, an estate for years is created under an express lease that specifies a fixed term (of any length) by establishing a beginning date and an ending date.

Periodic tenancy – Also called a month-to-month tenancy, a periodic tenancy has no fixed termination date, and is characterized by periodic automatic renewal when rent is paid.

Expiration – Most tenancies end when the lease expires; the expiration date approaches, notice is given, if required, and then the tenancy ends.

Abandonment – When a tenant leaves the premises before a lease expires (or without giving proper notice terminating a periodic tenancy).

Notice of belief of abandonment – Notice given by a landlord when it appears the tenant has abandoned the rental property; if the tenant fails to respond by the deadline, the landlord may follow state rules to remove and dispose of the tenant's personal property.

Surrender – When the tenant or the landlord mutually agree to terminate a lease before its expiration date.

Eviction – The legal process for removing a tenant from a rental property before the end of the lease term.

Self-help eviction – Illegally forcing a tenant to move by using threats or harassment, cutting off utilities, or by changing locks.

Constructive eviction – A situation where a landlord causes or permits a substantial interference with the tenant's possession of the property, in which case the tenant may be allowed to withhold rent or even abandon the lease.

Just cause exception – A prohibition in a few jurisdictions against termination of a residential periodic tenancy by a landlord unless the tenant has committed a significant breach of the lease agreement, such as failure to pay rent or illegal use of the property.

Foreclosure – When a creditor (such as a lender) forces a piece of real property to be sold to pay off the creditor's lien against the property.

Condemnation – A court process in which the government takes private property for a public use in exchange for paying fair market value.

Chapter Quiz

1. A property manager can guard against a tenant's unfair allegation of failure to maintain the property by:

   a) requiring tenants to make complaints and maintenance requests in writing

   b) documenting both the repair actions and the follow up with the tenant

   c) insisting that the complaining tenant produce proof of the inadequacy of repair efforts

   d) Both a) and b)

2. An implied lease provision that requires a residential landlord to keep the property in livable condition and in compliance with local building and safety codes is the:

   a) covenant against unreasonable eviction

   b) warranty against constructive eviction

   c) warranty of habitability

   d) duty to disclose

3. An implied right in every lease that requires the landlord to respect the tenant's privacy and to protect the tenant from the intrusions of others is called the:

   a) Fair Credit Reporting Act

   b) covenant of quiet enjoyment

   c) implied warranty of privacy

   d) right to tenant security

4. When handling repair requests, the manager should do all of the following, except:

   a) respond to every request promptly

   b) keep records of why the repair request was denied

   c) require a written request before responding to emergency situations

   d) treat all requests equally, regardless of the tenant's race

5. A lease violation that is serious enough to justify terminating the lease is known as a:

   a) warranty breach

   b) breach of trust

   c) material breach

   d) None of the above

6. A tenant's duties under the lease include:

   a) not interfering with other tenants' quiet enjoyment

   b) maintenance and protection of the premises

   c) timely rent payments

   d) All of the above

7. A rental property is sold in a foreclosure sale. Which of the following statements is true?

   a) The buyer must honor all commercial leases.

   b) The buyer may terminate residential leases immediately.

   c) The buyer must honor all residential leases, without exception.

   d) The buyer must honor all residential leases, unless she intends to occupy the property herself.

8. All of the following are likely examples of a material breach of a lease contract when done without the landlord's permission, except:

   a) a tenant who knocks down a wall in order to open up his kitchen to the living room

   b) an industrial tenant who changes from manufacturing clothing to producing petroleum products

   c) a residential tenant whose lease imposes a late charge on the third of the month, and who pays the rent and the late charge on the fourth of the month

   d) a retail tenant who fails to pay its pass-through charges

9. If a tenant fails substantially to comply with the landlord's building rules, the landlord should issue a notice:

   a) to cure or quit
   b) to depart
   c) of abandonment
   d) of nonrenewal

10. Maria rents an apartment. In the last three months, she's put in several requests for management to repair the heating system in her unit, but nothing has been done and now winter is setting in. This is an example of:

    a) inadvertent eviction
    b) informal eviction
    c) constructive eviction
    d) comprehensive eviction

11. A landlord's records include information organized by rental space (rather than by tenant), detailing the occupant of each unit or whether it's vacant, the amount of rent due, and whether rent has been paid on time. This is an example of a/an:

    a) rent ledger
    b) rent roll
    c) expense and vacancy register
    d) rent expense report

12. Juan is the landlord for ABC apartments. A tenant is arrested for dealing drugs, and Juan would like to evict the tenant. The legal process of evicting a tenant is known as a/an:

    a) unlawful detainer action
    b) notice of legal termination
    c) writ of lawful repossession
    d) motion to readmit

13. The most effective means of minimizing lost income due to a vacancy is:

    a) retaining existing tenants
    b) immediate and aggressive marketing to prospective tenants upon vacancy
    c) quick remodeling to attract more prospective tenants
    d) significantly lowering monthly rent to attract more prospective tenants

14. Bob pays $700 per month in rent to his landlord. Bob's lease expired six months ago. Bob probably has what kind of leasehold?

    a) Estate for years
    b) Tenancy at will
    c) Periodic tenancy
    d) Tenancy at sufferance

15. Even if the tenant and landlord are in full compliance with the lease terms, the lease will terminate if the following happens:

    a) an unlawful detainer action
    b) destruction of the premises
    c) condemnation of the property by a government entity
    d) Both b) and c)

Answer Key

1. d)   It's not absolutely necessary to require a written request before starting work on a repair, but a property manager should require the request be put in writing eventually (noting the date when the request was first made). This practice establishes a timeline and gives the manager the ability to rebut a tenant's accusations of delay or non-responsiveness, if necessary.

2. c)   The implied warranty of habitability is present in every residential lease and requires the landlord to provide living quarters that are fit for human habitation and that comply with safety and health codes.

3. b)   Every tenant has the right to quiet enjoyment (also known as peaceful enjoyment) of the premises. This means that the landlord must respect the tenant's privacy and notify the tenant in advance if he will be entering the property.

4. c)   While it's a good idea to have tenants put all maintenance and repair requests in writing, emergency situations should be dealt with immediately. The problem and how the situation was handled should then be documented after the emergency is over.

5. c)   Some lease violations constitute material breaches of the lease agreement, meaning that they are serious enough to warrant terminating the lease altogether.

6. d)   To remain in compliance with the lease, a tenant is legally required to not interfere with other tenants' quiet enjoyment, to maintain the premises, and to pay rent on time.

7. d)   If the buyer intends to occupy the property herself, she may terminate a residential lease after giving the tenant 90 days' notice.

8. c)   While a failure to pay rent and other charges (such as pass-through charges) is usually a material breach, a residential tenant who is one day late on rent and pays the late fee as required in the lease is unlikely to be committing a material breach of the lease contract.

9. a)   A notice to cure or quit puts the tenant on notice that if she fails to correct the specified lease violation within the given time period, the landlord will begin an unlawful detainer action.

10. c)   Constructive eviction occurs when the landlord causes or permits a substantial interference with the tenant's possession of the property. A violation of the implied warranty of habitability and/or the landlord-tenant law (by failing to make heat, water, or other utilities available) is an example of such interference.

11. b)   A rent roll contains much of the same information as a rental ledger (such as the tenant's name, unit number, and balance owed); however, it is organized by unit rather than by tenant.

12. a)   The legal process to evict a tenant is known as an unlawful detainer action.

13. a)   The most effective way to minimize rental downtime is to retain good tenants. Landlords should make every reasonable effort to keep existing tenants happy so that they will choose to stay when their leases expire.

14. c)   Bob has a periodic tenancy. Each month when he pays the rent, the tenancy renews automatically for one month.

15. d)   A lease will terminate if the property is condemned or destroyed, such that the tenant can no longer use the property for the intended use of the lease.

Chapter 9

Staffing and Maintenance

Introduction

The day-to-day operation of managed property can be a considerable undertaking, often too much for any one person to handle. In fact, a large property, like an office tower or a shopping mall, may need dozens of people to keep it functioning. Even someone who manages a small residential property will occasionally need to contract with outside help for major repairs or tax preparation.

In this chapter, we'll look at the issues of staffing and maintenance. We'll begin with staffing options for different types of property, categories of jobs and functions, and issues associated with hiring and firing staff. Then we'll look at the different types of maintenance and the procedures for setting up maintenance schedules. Finally, we'll briefly discuss environmental issues and also employee safety.

Staffing Managed Property

Managing rental property often means managing people. All properties periodically need maintenance and repair, which means contractors or other workers must be hired and supervised. Managers may also need help to clean or repair units between tenants. The day-to-day management of larger properties (leasing, rent collection, bookkeeping, and maintenance) may call for a whole team of employees.

There are legal requirements associated with hiring, compensating, and firing workers (both independent contractors and employees), and property managers need to be aware of their responsibilities. But before we discuss these requirements, let's first take a look at how a manager determines staffing needs.

Staffing Needs

The number of staff required by a particular property varies considerably, depending on the size and type of the property. A large property may require many different people to handle maintenance, tenant services, security, and administrative tasks. A smaller property, on the other hand, may only require the services of an on-site resident manager, or even just the occasional use of a handyman.

When determining a property's staffing needs, the manager should begin by listing all of the essential tasks associated with keeping the property functioning. How often those tasks need to be performed? How much time per week or month does each task require? This analysis is similar to creating property's operating budget, except that time rather than money is budgeted.

Once all of the tasks are listed, the manager can group the tasks together into categories. These categories can be the basis for job descriptions, or even for setting up whole departments if the property is a large one. Based on the total number of weekly or monthly hours assigned to each category, the manager can decide how many full-time and/or part-time staff are needed, as well as which tasks could be more efficiently outsourced to contractors. While estimating the number of staff needed, the manager must remember to account for sick leave and vacation days.

There are two competing interests at play when determining staffing: 1) limiting labor costs by employing as few (and as inexpensive) employees as possible, versus 2) the need to keep the property in optimal condition. Optimal condition isn't perfect condition, but rather the condition that yields the greatest operating income while still maintaining the property's value. Optimal condition cannot be achieved by understaffing. A poorly maintained property, or a property whose management is unresponsive to complaints, will have unnecessary vacancies and will lose out on potential income. Deferred maintenance can also cause the property to lose value.

Staffing Options

A property manager has several options when it comes to hiring staff. He can hire staff to work on-site only at one property, itinerant staff to work at multiple properties, or independent contractors to perform temporary or intermittent tasks. All three types of workers could also be used to work together on certain tasks or issues. For instance, a problem with a building's cooling system might require cooperation between the building's on-site manager, the management firm's handyman, and a contractor with expertise in cooling systems.

On-Site Staff. On-site staffers, as the name implies, work on the premises of a single property. Many properties are too small to support an on-site staffer, but larger properties of all types will need on-site staff. Managers of large apartment buildings need to be available to respond to tenant problems at any time. Similarly, managers of office complexes or shopping malls need to provide cleaning and security services around the clock. Some large properties require full-time leasing agents, as well as support staff such as accountants, human resources specialists, or receptionists.

The most common task performed by on-site staff is maintenance; this is usually limited to simple tasks, such as basic upkeep and minor repairs that a handyman could complete. Only the very largest properties have enough work to keep skilled specialists, such as plumbers or electricians, on staff. For smaller properties, these needs are usually fulfilled by contractors.

On-site workers are usually paid out of the property's operating funds. They may be employees of either the property owner or the property management firm. Even when on-site workers are employed by the property owner, the property manager may take on the role of employer, taking responsibility for all hiring and firing, training, supervision, and payroll administration.

Multi-Site Staff. Many property management firms manage several properties that are within a reasonable distance of each other. If this is the case, staff can easily work at more than one property, traveling between sites as needed. Multi-site (or itinerant) staffers often work in maintenance, particularly if they have a specialization that wouldn't justify full-time employment at one property. A computer support person might also work at multiple sites, keeping computer systems functioning in the offices of several different properties.

Multi-site staff are usually employed by the property management company; however, if a client owns multiple properties near each other, multi-site staff might be employed directly by the property owner. If employees of the management firm work at properties owned by different clients, the firm will charge labor costs to each property owner on an hourly basis.

Contractors. Having full-time employees is expensive and time-consuming in terms of recordkeeping and payroll processing. A management firm may instead choose to delegate many important duties to contractors. Contractors generally must be paid a significantly higher rate per hour of work, but they do not require benefits or as much administration. Contractors also can be deployed only when needed, instead of being kept permanently on payroll whether needed or not. Either the property management firm or the property owner can be the one who hires and pays contractors.

Contractors are most commonly used for jobs that require special skills or licensing and that are only performed periodically. This kind of work includes elevator maintenance, electrical work, and pest control. Contractors are also used for work that's needed only on a seasonal basis, such as lawn care or snow removal, or that needs to be performed only occasionally, like window washing. A manager may also use contractors to handle temporary office staffing shortages, in the same way a typical business office hires "temps."

A property manager may also opt to use contractors for regular tasks such as janitorial or security services. This simplifies the property manager's job: someone else is responsible for hiring, training, and handling payroll and tax reporting. Using contractors for these types of jobs may also reduce the property manager's liability should something go wrong. If a contractor (as opposed to an employee) has primary responsibility for security or maintenance services and a customer is harmed, the property owner may get at least partial reimbursement for the amount of damages from the contractor.

A property manager should engage in due diligence before hiring any contractor. If the manager is hiring for a position that requires a license, the manager should make sure that the contractor is currently licensed. In addition, the manager should verify that the contractor is bonded and carries appropriate insurance. It is also important to contact the contractor's references and obtain a criminal background check on anyone who will work on-site regularly. (Bonding and insurance are discussed in Chapter 15.)

Before soliciting bids from contractors, a property manager should write up exact specifications for the job, describing how it should be done, what materials should be used, and when it must be completed. Contractors will base their bids on these criteria. In some cases, a contractor may only be able to provide an estimate instead of a firm price; perhaps it's not clear exactly how long the project will take or what parts or supplies will be needed. In the estimate, the contractor should list the hourly rates for labor and travel, as well as the costs of anticipated parts or materials.

The property manager usually chooses the contractor who can provide the necessary level of service at the least expensive price. It's always important for the manager and contractor to use a written contract that contains a termination provision in case the work is unsatisfactory or is interrupted before completion.

Types of Staff and Functions

While small properties often require one staff person to wear many different hats, larger properties may have multiple staff members divided into different departments. These departments (or categories) include managerial staff, administrative staff, service staff, maintenance staff, and security staff. In this chapter, we'll limit our discussion to these basic categories; we'll go into greater detail about the staffing requirements for particular types of properties in Chapters 10–13.

Management Staff. Larger residential properties generally need an around-the-clock management presence on the premises. Some states require apartment buildings with a certain number of units to have resident managers. For instance, California law requires a resident manager in buildings with 16 or more units. In states without such a requirement, the owner has more discretion, but she is likely to find that a building with more than 15 or 20 units generates enough tenant requests and leasing activity that a resident manager is desirable. An on-site manager is also usually needed for larger commercial properties during their hours of operation.

While any resident manager or on-site manager will perform at least some clerical tasks and interact with tenants, the exact duties of a resident or on-site manager vary depending on the manager's skills. One with a background in leasing might have only the most basic maintenance skills, and would need to rely more heavily on contractors. On the other hand, a resident or on-site manager trained in repair work might need to rely on someone else for lease negotiations and marketing.

The most important limitation on what a resident manager or on-site manager can and cannot do may be legal. As we've discussed, state law may require property managers to have a real estate license or property manager's license. In states that require licensure, an unlicensed resident or on-site manager will typically be limited to simpler tasks like showing rental units or spaces and collecting rents, and must leave negotiating and finalizing leases to a licensed property manager or the property owner.

Very large properties may have not just an on-site manager, but also one or more full-time leasing agents. In a large residential building, the leasing agent sometimes works out of a rental center rather than the management office. Leasing agents are often independent contractors and are paid by commission. Leasing agents may be very active when a new building first opens, and then transfer leasing tasks to the property management office when the building fills up.

Administrative Staff. For smaller and medium-sized properties, the on-site or resident manager usually handles administrative and clerical tasks, such as keeping tabs on rent receipts or maintenance purchase orders. However, the on-site or resident manager of a large property may require one or more administrative support staff members for these types of tasks. For instance, the manager might delegate accounting or marketing tasks to specialized assistants. Offices in very large properties may need an office manager, a receptionist, and human resources or computer support staff.

The property manager should arrange bonding for any staff members who handle money. Bonding companies typically require a credit report and police background check for each person who is bonded. The staff member must give written authorization for the company to perform these checks.

Service Staff. Service staff (including doormen, information desk staff, porters, and concierges) provide assistance directly to tenants or visitors. Service staff are generally found only in very large or very high-end residential properties, or in large commercial properties like malls or hotels.

Maintenance Staff. Large residential and commercial properties usually have enough work to keep an on-site maintenance staff busy. This is especially likely when tenant requests for maintenance and repairs are coupled with the continual need to maintain the common areas. On-site maintenance staff include a janitorial or cleaning crew, and, if the property has extensive grounds, gardeners or groundskeepers as well. A skilled handyman may also work full-time on-site.

Security Staff. Large properties need full-time staff to ensure the safety of tenants and their guests. This includes security guards and watchmen to patrol the property. It may also include front desk attendants and staff to monitor security cameras. Restaurants, bars, and entertainment venues may also require bouncers or other crowd control staff. We will discuss security concerns in greater detail in Chapter 15, in the context of risk management.

Hiring and Training Staff

The quality of hiring decisions can make the difference between an effective, smoothly functioning staff or a staff that is a constant source of managerial headaches. But even when a well-qualified staff has been selected, they can't simply be turned loose; the property manager needs to train and supervise employees.

Hiring. The first task in the hiring process is acquiring a pool of applicants. The usual starting point is placing help-wanted ads on employment websites or in the local newspaper. Such postings should include a job description, but managers are still likely to receive a flood of applications from persons unqualified for the position. Rather than wade through applications, a manager may prefer to rely on personal referrals from colleagues or professional associations. For properties with a large staff, the property manager can fill positions by promoting from within.

Employment agencies. A property manager may also hire workers through an employment agency. The manager gives a job description as well as experience and training requirements to an outside firm that will, in exchange for a fee, provide a list of qualified candidates. This is a time-saver for busy managers, and it will often pay for itself. Also, using an employment agency may help decrease the property manager's risk of liability for an employee's misconduct. Skilled recruitment firms are less likely to miss red flags in an applicant's background or employment record. If they do miss something, some of the liability for failure to properly screen employees may transfer to the employment agency.

For a permanent hire, employment agencies usually charge a one-time fee, often a percentage of the employee's annual salary. Alternatively, many employment agencies will "lease" an employee on a long-term basis. The property manager pays the agency a monthly fee, and the agency will, out of those payments, pay the employee's salary and benefits. Some employers may find that having an outside agency handle the paperwork, pay the salary and employment taxes, and deal with employee benefits makes the arrangement worthwhile.

Training. Once a new staff member is brought aboard, the manager's next task is to train her. All employees should be familiar with the duties they're expected to perform as well as the resources available to help perform them. The property manager may need to train not just direct hires, but also staffers supplied by a contractor or employment agency.

Every manager should have an **employee manual** that explains the company's rules. All new staff members should receive this manual. The employee manual is important not only because it gives guidance to new hires, but also because it offers the employer legal protection. If the employee manual establishes antidiscrimination policies and payment procedures in writing, in advance, it can strengthen an employer's defense in the event of a lawsuit over sexual harassment or unpaid benefits. We discuss this aspect of the employee manual further in Chapter 15.

An employee manual should include:

- basic rules of employment, such as work hours, pay periods, holidays and vacations, and sick leave;
- policies and procedures for discipline, grievances, and firing;
- discrimination and sexual harassment policies, ethical requirements and conflict of interest rules, and other expectations regarding workplace conduct; and
- information about the company, such as its mission statement and organizational chart.

The manager may give new staffers one-on-one training. It's important to make sure that staff members who deal with tenants or visitors bring a positive, customer-service mindset to their interactions. It can be helpful to role-play with new employees and prepare them for typical exchanges. New employees should also receive comprehensive training on dealing with emergencies.

Thorough training helps managers ensure that new hires can perform their jobs properly and safely. Of course, the manager will need to provide ongoing supervision as well. Regular performance reviews should be scheduled at least once a year. Comprehensive reviews early in an employee's tenure may help a manager decide if additional training is warranted, if the employee might be better utilized in a different capacity within the company, or if the job description itself needs adjustment (to include more or different duties and responsibilities). The reviews can also support a manager's decision to terminate an employee, should a claim of illegal termination be filed.

Compensation. Skilled employees are a manager's greatest asset, and it's important to compensate them adequately. This keeps their morale high and reduces unnecessary turnover. A well-paid employee may actually save the manager money in the long run, by avoiding frequent job openings, the inconvenience of a hiring process, and the delay that occurs as new hires get up to speed.

The way a staff member is compensated helps determine whether he is an employee or an independent contractor. This distinction matters because the government treats these two types of workers differently.

As we discussed in Chapter 3, an **independent contractor** is hired (and paid) to perform a particular task. She uses her judgment as to how exactly to perform that task, usually with a minimum of supervision. Many independent contractors are outside experts brought in to resolve a problem with a property, such as a plumber hired to fix a leaking pipe. However, an independent contractor may also work full-time on-site.

An **employee**, by contrast, performs a variety of ongoing tasks for an employer, and receives a greater level of supervision. The employer generally expects the employee to work set hours and follow specific instructions, and pays her a salary or hourly wages.

> **Example:** A leasing agent who uses his own resources to find tenants, and who is compensated by commissions rather than a fixed salary, is probably an independent contractor. However, an administrative assistant who works in the same office as the leasing agent and assists him with leasing tasks is paid a fixed rate for each hour she works and answers to the building's manager. She is an employee.

The IRS publishes detailed rules for distinguishing employees from independent contractors. The distinction matters to the employer because he must contribute toward unemployment insurance and worker's compensation on the employee's behalf. He must also withhold money from an employee's salary to pay certain taxes: federal and state income taxes, and Social Security and Medicare withholding. (Note that state laws vary considerably regarding whether brokerage firms must pay unemployment insurance and workers' comp for their affiliated agents. To find out more about these and other employment laws, it's best to consult an attorney.)

Employees are entitled to legal protections that don't apply to independent contractors. For instance, the federal **Fair Labor Standards Act** (FLSA) requires employers to pay employees a minimum wage. It also sets the maximum number of hours that hourly employees can work per day or week without triggering overtime pay.

Employment Laws

A manager must comply with a number of other important state and federal employment laws. Among the most important laws are:

- the Family and Medical Leave Act, which requires employers to give unpaid time off to employees in certain circumstances;
- the Fair Labor Standards Act, which, as mentioned above, governs minimum wage and overtime pay for employees;
- Title VII of the Civil Rights Act of 1964, which prohibits employment discrimination if it is based on certain protected characteristics (perhaps most significantly, the law prohibits sexual harassment); and
- the Americans with Disabilities Act, which prohibits disability-based discrimination in hiring, and also requires making facilities (such as managerial offices) that are open to the public accessible to the disabled.

We will discuss these and other statutes in Chapter 14. For now, we'll simply note that these laws exist and any manager who hires workers will have to be familiar with them. If a legal problem arises, it's advisable to get advice from an employment attorney.

A manager who hires employees or contracts out for help may also need to be aware of applicable union rules. Janitors, electricians, plumbers, and various other skilled workers often belong to unions. If a manager has hired union employees, union rules might limit his future ability to hire nonunion workers or workers from competing unions.

> ▶ *Progressive Discipline*
>
> It is better for managers to engage in progressive discipline, where a series of disciplinary steps are taken—each one more serious than the last—than to ignore problematic behavior for a long time and then react suddenly and negatively. Employees should get the chance to correct their behavior and learn from their mistakes.
>
> Step one in the progressive disciplinary process is typically a verbal warning, which calls attention to the violation of company policies. (This should be noted in the employee's personnel file.) A second step would be a written warning, a copy of which is placed in the personnel file. The third step could be a period of probation. Only after the probationary period has passed and the problem has still not been corrected should the employee be terminated. A third party, such as the manager of another department, should attend disciplinary meetings so there is a more objective witness present.

Firing. Employee termination probably gives rise to more lawsuits than any other single action by an employer, so we'll give the topic extra attention here. In most states, employment is "at will," meaning that either employer or employee can terminate the employment relationship at any time. Even in those states, though, firing cannot violate antidiscrimination or anti-retaliation (whistleblower) laws, nor can it violate the terms of collective bargaining agreements.

To avoid leaving the door open to lawsuits for unlawful termination, an employer should keep careful records of each step in the termination process. The event or behavior prompting termination should be thoroughly documented. The documentation should focus objectively on how work fell short of expectations, rather than speculating on underlying causes. Management should also make sure that terminations are handled consistently from person to person; variations in how different employees are treated for similar violations could give rise to claims of discrimination.

Terminating a resident manager raises a unique consideration. The resident manager's workplace is also his home, so he may need additional time to find a new place to live after termination. A period of a week or more may be appropriate before requiring a terminated resident manager to vacate. At any rate, an employment agreement with a resident manager should always specify that possession of a unit is tied to employment, and rights to occupy the unit cease upon termination of employment.

Maintenance

Maintaining the property is one of the most important tasks for a property manager. It's not an area to skimp on or take shortcuts. In fact, everything else a property manager does will matter very little if maintenance is neglected. Poor maintenance eventually reduces the property's value. It also makes the property less desirable to current and potential tenants, increasing the vacancy rate and forcing decreases in rent. Proper maintenance, on the other hand, can reduce operating costs by lowering utility bills or insurance premiums, and it can also reduce an owner's potential liability to tenants or visitors because of unsafe conditions.

Types of Maintenance

Managers usually break down maintenance activities into three categories: custodial maintenance, preventive maintenance, and corrective maintenance. The boundaries between these categories aren't always clear, though, and many experts include a fourth category: construction.

Custodial Maintenance. Other terms for custodial maintenance include routine maintenance, janitorial maintenance, or housekeeping. Custodial maintenance includes tasks performed weekly, daily, or even hourly, such as vacuuming, dusting, garbage removal, floor waxing, and restroom cleaning. Custodial maintenance also includes chores that are performed less frequently but still fairly regularly, like lawn mowing and pool cleaning, as well as seasonal tasks like cleaning out gutters. Lastly, this kind of maintenance includes rarely performed cleaning jobs like power-washing building exteriors and walkways.

Custodial maintenance is important to tenants; they may not notice obsolete equipment or systems, but they certainly will notice overflowing garbage cans, stained carpets, or dirty bathrooms in a building's common areas.

Preventive Maintenance. Preventive maintenance refers to a program of regular upkeep that helps keep equipment, furnishings, and fixtures in good shape. Most preventive maintenance activities (such as oiling moving parts in machinery and changing filters or belts) take place on a scheduled basis. Preventive maintenance needs vary considerably from one building to the next, depending not just on the size of the building and the types of systems it has, but also on the age of the components.

Staff should leave complex or specialized preventive maintenance tasks to expert contractors. In fact, the law generally requires this when dealing with safety items such as elevators or the fire control system.

Corrective Maintenance. Even the diligent performance of preventive maintenance can't completely prevent equipment and other building components from occasionally failing. Corrective maintenance involves fixing such things as broken washing machines, leaky roofs, or cracked windows.

Like custodial maintenance, corrective maintenance also affects a tenant's perception of the property. Prompt, effective responses to requests for repairs make tenants happy. Also, a prompt response may also prevent a small problem from turning into a large one.

Delaying a repair until it's more convenient or more cash is available is called **deferred maintenance**. Deferred maintenance is a form of depreciation. (Depreciation is a property's loss of value from any cause.) Management can cure this form of depreciation, at least initially. However, if at some point repairs become impossible, or their cost of would exceed the amount the repairs would add to the property's value, then the property has suffered **incurable depreciation**.

In older buildings (but also in some unlucky new buildings), maintenance problems may crop up at a faster rate than provided for in the budget. In such cases, some deferred maintenance may be unavoidable. The manager will need to prioritize repairs, attending to problems that affect health and safety first, and perhaps breaking less urgent problems down into smaller, more affordable segments.

Construction. Some experts treat construction as a fourth category of maintenance. Although the word calls to mind tearing down buildings and rebuilding them from the ground up, the term here refers to remodeling and refurbishment. Much of this could actually be called "cosmetic maintenance." Most buildings usually undergo a number of updates, in terms of fixtures and overall appearance, over the course of their lives.

Construction commonly occurs during the transition period between two tenants. In a commercial building, construction often goes beyond merely repainting or laying new carpet; a landlord may need to move walls or install new equipment to meet an incoming tenant's specifications. Even for residential properties, the gap between tenants is often a good time to repaint or replace carpets or wallpaper. This type of maintenance can also include replacing outdated or energy-inefficient kitchen appliances or windows. The property's exterior trim or landscaping could even be upgraded, to increase the property's curb appeal and justify higher rents.

Developing a Maintenance Program

The property manager needs to take many things into consideration when designing a maintenance program. She'll need to complete a fair amount of research to see what will need maintenance when, figure out the best recordkeeping system for the property, and determine what schedules and reports need to be created.

Preliminary Research. When developing a maintenance program, a property manager will need to do some preliminary research. He'll need to list:

- all aspects of the property that need maintenance,
- the type of maintenance required,
- how often maintenance needs to occur, and
- how much time it will take.

To obtain this information, the manager begins by consulting the on-site maintenance staff. These staff people know, for example, how long various tasks take and the type of maintenance required. Research also often includes getting opinions from outside contractors. The manager should review the recommended maintenance schedules listed in the operating manuals and warranties of all of the property's equipment. Finally, the manager may need to do some investigating to find out where to order replacement parts—suppliers tend to change over time.

When developing a maintenance program, a manager needs to know something about federal, state, and municipal regulations that apply to the property. For example, with an industrial tenant, the manager may need to understand the basic requirements for handling toxic or hazardous substances. The same may be true with a residential building if asbestos or lead-based paints are present. Since any modifications to the property must comply with accessibility provisions of the Americans with Disabilities Act, managers need at least some familiarity with that statute's requirements (see Chapter 14). Generally, the manager should consult a lawyer or other expert when it comes to legal compliance.

Recordkeeping. Most managers use software to organize a maintenance program. Specialized software helps schedule repairs and track progress, and also provides reminders of easy-to-forget preventive maintenance tasks.

Not all software has the same capabilities. At a minimum, the program should:

- schedule and retain work orders,
- track tenant repair requests,
- pay vendors,
- monitor and pay contractors, and
- integrate maintenance costs into the property's financial software.

Ideally, the manager can use the software to itemize equipment and other assets (like the appliances in all units, or all the vacuum cleaners used by staff), as well as supplies and materials. If the maintenance software can link to the property's financial software, a manager can learn how much money is left in the budget. This information helps her decide whether she can perform a particular repair or replacement immediately or should defer it.

An effectively designed maintenance program will pay off over time through increased efficiency. For instance, maintenance software can generate lists that help group repairs and inspections in a logical manner. Maintenance software can also provide repair histories, revealing troublesome equipment that might make better sense to replace than to keep on repairing.

> **Example:** Each year, the manager of the Merced Industrial Complex reviews software-generated repair histories for the various building components. He notices that the complex's Acme-brand air handler units in the HVAC system suffer significant breakdowns about every four years. The manager consults with HVAC experts and learns that this failure rate exceeds industry averages by 25%. New equipment will pay for itself in approximately four years. The manager adds the cost of new units to the capital expenditures budget for the following year.

Schedules and Reports. The manager generates two documents that are instrumental to carrying out the maintenance program: an inspection schedule and a maintenance schedule.

Inspection schedules. If any component of a property has even a remote chance of failing, maintenance staff should inspect it regularly. Often the janitorial staff checks elements of the building (such as carpeting and plumbing fixtures) as part of their daily or weekly cleaning routine. Other building components, such as the roof, may get inspected only a few times a year. An infrequent inspection doesn't make it any less crucial, of course. Discovering and patching a small roof leak after a quarterly inspection, for example, could prevent major water damage from a torrential rainstorm later on.

An **inspection report** (see Figure 9.1) lists all of the elements that are scheduled to be inspected on a particular date. The manager or maintenance employee works her way through the list, noting each item's condition and indicating any needed repairs (along

Figure 9.1 Inspection report

Property Inspection Report				
Property: _____				
Inspection date: _____ Inspected by: _____				
Feature	**Condition**	**Work Needed**	**Cost (est.)**	**Next Insp.**
Walkways & parking lots				
Landscaping				
Foundation				
Exterior walls				
Windows				
Roof				
Gutters				
Lobby & hallways				
Interior walls				
Elevators				
Stairways				
HVAC equipment				
Electrical system				
Plumbing system				
Safety equipment				
Garbage & recycling areas				
Pest control				

with estimated repair costs). The form also includes the date of the next inspection. It's a good idea to document any problems by taking digital photos and adding them to the maintenance records.

As mentioned, some items get inspected more often than others. In general, elements of the building's interior need to be checked far more frequently than exterior items. Separate interior and exterior inspection forms are commonly used for that reason. Some managers use inspection forms that include subcategories for complicated systems. Instead of listing the heating and cooling system as one item, for example, a form might have separate entries for each subcomponent, such as the oil filter, oil reservoir, air filter, and blower.

Managers may also use one form for the public areas of a building's interior and more detailed lists for each tenant unit or space within the building. Inspections of tenant interiors rarely take place during periods of occupancy, but inspection reports do get prepared when the tenancy ends. Units or spaces occupied by long-term tenants should be inspected at least occasionally, perhaps annually.

Maintenance schedules. The other important maintenance document that we'll talk about is the maintenance schedule. This schedule lists preventive maintenance or

Figure 9.2 Maintenance schedule

Maintenance Schedule		
Task	**Frequency**	**When (✓)**
Skim swimming pool and add chemicals	Daily, in season	
Check common areas for burned-out lights	Weekly	
Polish lobby fixtures	Weekly	
Mow and water lawns	Weekly, in season	
Test fire safety equipment	Monthly	
Test elevators	Monthly	
Check furnace filters, clean or replace as needed	Monthly	
Wash windows in common areas	Quarterly	Jan April July Oct
Inspect for roof leakage	Three times a year	Jan May Sept
Clean gutters	Twice a year	March Nov
External window washing	Annually	May
Inspect and touch up exterior paint	Annually	June
Patch and restripe parking lot	Annually	July
Recharge fire extinguishers	Annually	November

cleaning tasks, and states how often they must be performed. The form also includes space for noting when the tasks are completed. Figure 9.2 shows a sample maintenance schedule.

A manager who uses multiple inspection schedules is likely to use multiple maintenance schedules as well. A custodial schedule, for instance, would list the areas of the building that should be cleaned every day (such as the lobby and restrooms). Another schedule will list areas that need less frequent cleaning (such as supply closets, utility areas, and equipment rooms).

Preventive maintenance schedules list each piece of equipment on the property that needs regular service. The list states how often different parts of the equipment need cleaning or replacement. For instance, furnace air filters might need quarterly replacement, while the oil filters and nozzles require annual replacement. Establishing a preventive maintenance schedule for systems that are older and more troublesome may take some trial and error. This is also true if the manufacturers' original documents can't be found and recommended service schedules aren't known.

Based on her preliminary research, the manager knows roughly how long each maintenance task takes. This helps her schedule these tasks efficiently, not giving personnel too much or too little to do. Of course, any schedule needs to include a certain amount of leeway for dealing with the emergencies that will inevitably crop up.

Managers should also take into account the needs of the tenants when scheduling maintenance. Maintenance activities should not unduly disturb or inconvenience tenants. If a maintenance task calls for workers to enter a tenant's unit, it's best to schedule the work during times when the tenant is away. The same goes for exterior projects that are particularly noisy (such as leaf blowing) or unpleasant-smelling (such as roof repairs).

On the other hand, it's good for tenants to witness some maintenance work. It helps tenants realize that management is actively working to improve the property. Having groundskeepers or custodial workers busy in public areas during business hours will re-inforce these perceptions.

Components of Managed Property

Let's take a moment to briefly discuss the various elements of a property that require maintenance. This is merely an overview. Each type of rental property requires different types of maintenance, so we'll examine particular areas in greater detail in the chapters that discuss the different types of property.

Grounds. The amount and type of grounds maintenance required depends both on the local climate and the time of year. In the spring and summer, a groundskeeper will need to keep the lawns mowed and flower beds weeded. Some landscaping work is usually needed each spring, to plant new flowers or to reseed lawns; in the fall, leaves must be raked; winter may require the removal of dead plant material and other clean up. Of course, litter should always be picked up as soon as it appears, year-round.

To avoid injuries to residents and others, staff should inspect the grounds after inclement weather to look for fallen or broken branches or any damaged outdoor improvements.

Driveways and Walkways. In many parts of the country, driveways and walkways need particular attention during the winter. Remove snow or ice as soon as possible, not just for people's convenience but also to lessen the possibility of slip-and-fall injuries. In all seasons, maintenance staff should watch for, and repair, cracked or uneven pavement. Some property managers pressure wash walkways and concrete driveways occasionally to brighten their appearance and reveal hidden cracks and chips that need repair. (However, care must be taken when pressure washing not to cause chips and other damage.)

Parking Areas. Parking areas, just like driveways, should be kept clear of snow and ice, and patched when cracks or potholes appear. In addition, parking areas will periodically need resurfacing due to the cumulative effects of traffic and harsh weather.

Building Exteriors. Exterior building walls accumulate dirt; periodic pressure-washing refreshes the property's appearance. Staff should clean signs and light fixtures regularly, and replace burned-out bulbs promptly. Don't let damage to a building's exterior surface go unrepaired. Peeling or cracking paint must be touched up between complete repaint-ings. Building staff may be able to repair minor cracks and chips in brickwork, concrete walls, and foundations, but a professional mason should repair more significant damage.

Windows. Custodial staff or contractors should wash a building's windows (both interior and exterior) periodically. In a commercial property, windows in public areas, such as those next to entrances or facing the lobby, should be washed often, perhaps even daily. Office or apartment windows typically don't require the same level of attention; a manager may hire a contractor to wash them all at once, perhaps once a year (although many apartment managers don't do it that often). If windows open and have moving parts, they'll require regular preventive maintenance to keep them functioning.

Roofs and Gutters. While roofs don't need custodial maintenance, a manager should have them inspected a few times a year (and after any unusually strong winds or heavy snow or rain) for any signs of damage or leakage. This is particularly important for buildings with flat roofs, since rain tends to puddle up. Most roofs need to be replaced several times over the building's life. Gutters should be cleaned out at least once a year, and also need occasional replacement, usually on the same timeline as the roof.

Interior Areas. A building's public areas—chiefly lobbies, corridors, restrooms, and elevators—require regular cleaning. Floors should be waxed, carpets vacuumed, and metallic surfaces polished. In addition, interior walls must be cleaned as needed, and repainted occasionally. To make maintenance easier, property owners should select washable types of paint or wallpaper, and choose carpet that is easy to vacuum and resists heavy foot traffic.

HVAC. A building's heating, ventilation, and air conditioning (HVAC) system removes stale air and introduces fresh air. It also helps ensure that temperature and humidity remain at reasonably constant and pleasant levels. A faulty heating or cooling system can quickly cause the building to become intolerable for tenants. This makes preventive maintenance of the HVAC system a high priority. Maintenance staff may perform simple tasks like changing filters or cleaning ducts. However, managers typically contract out most HVAC repair and maintenance (except in very large properties that employ a full-time staffer in this role).

Amenities. While amenities like swimming pools and fitness centers can be strong selling points to potential tenants, they also require a significant amount of maintenance. A fitness center typically requires more cleaning than other common areas. Pools also require daily attention, including cleaning the water and maintaining chemical levels. Local health codes may mandate regular water sample testing, and establish other sanitation guidelines. Of course, the area surrounding the pool must be kept clean and free of clutter, to help prevent slip-and-fall injuries. Fencing and warning signs must also be maintained.

Elevators. Unsafe elevators pose a hazard to life and limb, making their maintenance particularly important. State law and sometimes municipal ordinances regulate elevator maintenance and recordkeeping. For instance, laws may require that only properly licensed personnel can perform elevator maintenance work, and that service records be updated whenever any maintenance is performed.

A manager can help minimize wear and tear on elevators by making sure that tenants and visitors use them properly. For instance, the manager should make sure that tenants and delivery people do not use passenger elevators to transport freight (if there's a separate freight elevator). In any case, building rules should require that anyone who transports freight must use proper padding to protect the elevator's interior.

Fire Safety. As with elevators, fire safety systems and procedures matter a great deal: lives are at stake, and state and municipal regulations apply. Managers or service contractors should frequently inspect equipment associated with fire safety, such as smoke detectors, alarm systems, and sprinkler systems, and make sure they're working properly. Fire exits, fire doors, and fire escapes must be clearly marked, free of obstacles, and in working order.

Many jurisdictions require smoke detectors, and may also require sprinkler systems in larger buildings, especially high-rise structures. Certificates of inspection for these systems usually must be posted on-site. Fire extinguishers must be kept charged, and tags on the extinguishers must include a record of when they were charged. Regulations generally require the presence of lighted exit signs and emergency lighting, and in some cases maps that show evacuation routes. (We discuss fire safety requirements from the risk perspective in Chapter 15.)

Many jurisdictions require fire department personnel to periodically inspect apartment houses and commercial properties for fire hazards and fire code violations. Managers should regard the fire department as an ally, not an adversary, and consider requesting inspections and asking the inspector for advice about maintenance and safety issues.

Pest Control. Pest control activities vary considerably from city to city and even from building to building. Most managers need to contract with licensed exterminators for regular visits. Cockroaches plague much of the country, and managers may also have to combat termites, rats, ants, bedbugs, or even birds or other wildlife.

Buildings that house restaurants or other food services are particularly susceptible to pests. Local health regulations may require these businesses to spray and take other measures. A building manager can also help with pest control by keeping garbage confined to designated areas and ensuring its regular disposal. Custodial staff should regularly clean garbage rooms and dumpsters and seal wall cracks and other openings to stop vermin from entering buildings.

Despite a manager's best efforts, periodic extermination often becomes necessary. Unfortunately, piecemeal spraying of the individual tenant units or spaces (such as when a problem is reported or a space vacated) doesn't usually work. Spot spraying only serves to drive the pests into neighboring units or spaces. Spraying or fumigating the entire building at once is more effective, although difficult to coordinate.

Arranging for Repairs

Arranging repairs means lots of paperwork, regardless of whether contractors or staffers perform the actual repair. Management needs to retain the paper trail generated by the repair process as part of the property's records. Documents to keep include:

- repair requests,
- work orders and the work log,
- purchase orders, and
- inventory control lists for supplies.

Figure 9.3 Maintenance work order

Work Order

Work order number: _____   Date: _____

Property: _____   Assigned to: _____

Description of work to be done, including location on property: _____

_____

_____

_____

Task completed? Explain status. _____

_____

_____

Time required: _____   Labor charges: _____

Materials used: _____   Cost of materials: _____

_____   Total cost: _____

Repair Requests. Repair requests from tenants are common. The tenant might fill out a form and drop it off with the manager. (Ideally, the tenant should sign the form; that way, it serves as written permission for the landlord to enter the premises to do any necessary work.) Tenants can also report problems to management by phone; if so, a staffer can complete the request form.

Many property managers maintain websites that have an online form for requesting repairs and reporting other issues. These online systems often have the ability to send email confirmations to the tenant, stating the time and date the repair will occur. Confirmation emails should also note whether the repair will cost the tenant anything and, if so, how much. Lastly, the system can generate a request for feedback from the tenant regarding whether the issue was resolved after the repair.

A manager should emphasize to tenants that they can't request services directly from outside repair people and expect to get reimbursed. The manager should also make it clear that tenants cannot ask on-site staff for repairs; all requests must go through management.

Managers should discourage tenants from trying to fix problems themselves. Most tenants are happy to delegate the responsibility of fixing things to the manager (this is one of the main advantages of renting). Nonetheless, sometimes over-enthusiastic do-it-yourselfers attempt to perform minor work, which can turn a small problem into a huge one.

Work Orders. A work order should accompany every maintenance project. A **work order** is a short document that describes what will be done, when it will be done, and who will do it. (See Figure 9.3 for a sample work order.) The manager usually fills out the first part of the form, and the person who completed the task fills out the rest of the form, describing the materials used, the time taken, the cost of materials and the charge for labor, if any. Usually the manager retains a copy and so does the worker—at least if it's a contractor and not a staff member.

Work Logs. With most properties, work orders get recorded in a work log. The log (see Figure 9.4 for an example) gives the work order number, if any, and briefly describes the project. After the project is completed, the log entry is updated with the names of those who performed the work, how long it took, and how much it cost. For on-site staffers, managers might ask each staff member to maintain his own work log so that the manager can monitor worker productivity.

Figure 9.4 Maintenance work log

Maintenance Work Log

Property: _____

Owner: _____

Work Order No.: _____

Description of job: _____
(See work order for more information)

Rental unit or location on property: _____

Tenant name, if applicable: _____

Source of or reason for order:
☐ Routine inspection
☐ Tenant's request or complaint
☐ Owner's instructions
☐ Required by law or gov't agency
☐ Other: _____

Request or instructions received:
☐ In person
☐ By phone
☐ By letter
☐ By email
☐ Through website

Date of request: _____   Legal deadline, if any: _____

Work order date: _____   Completion date: _____

Work assigned to: _____

Time spent on job: _____

Cost: _____

Work inspected and approved by: _____

Notes: _____

_____

_____

_____

Ordering Supplies. Another important aspect of maintenance is ordering and keeping track of supplies. A building needs a proper stock of cleaning supplies, hardware, and replacement parts. To keep on top of the constant flow of items into and out of the building's supply closets, a manager should have both a record of purchases and a system for keeping track of inventory.

Purchases are usually tracked with documents called purchase orders. A **purchase order** includes information such as the name of the vendor, the date of the order, the quantity and price of items ordered, and the delivery date and terms of acceptance. Purchase orders are particularly helpful to a manager of a larger property who has multiple staff members buying supplies.

An inventory control system may be as simple as a checkout list in the supply room, or it may involve the use of specialized software. Whatever system is used, when someone removes an item from inventory they should note it so that the manager knows how much of a particular item remains. Inventory control systems make it clear when it's time to reorder and also help reduce the theft of supplies.

 ## Hiring a Contractor

A manager facing a large repair project may choose to use a general contractor to oversee the project. The general contractor will hire subcontractors to perform specific tasks. Alternatively, a manager with some knowledge about the construction process may take on the lead role himself, and save money by directly hiring different contractors to perform their specialized tasks.

Regardless of whether a manager is hiring a general contractor or a subcontractor, he may use one of two types of construction contracts: competitive bids or negotiated contracts. In the **competitive bidding process**, a manager will entertain bids from various contractors, and choose the most attractive bid.

By contrast, in the **negotiated contract process**, a manager (usually one who is experienced and well-connected with the local construction community) will contact reputable contractors, one for each field, and ask them to collaborate on one joint proposal, which includes an estimate of the project's total cost. The manager and owner can then accept or reject the bid as a whole.

A payment schedule should be agreed to before the work begins. It is customary for the owner or manager to pay a large amount up front and another significant portion when the project is partially done, withholding the final portion (such as 10%) until after the job is done. This final payment protects the property owner, just in case additional work is necessary. While most contractors are paid a flat fee, a manager may agree to pay a contractor on a **cost-plus basis**. Under this system, a contractor will be paid the actual cost of the project plus an agreed-upon fee. This type of deal may encourage greater efficiency on the contractor's part.

Tenant-Arranged Repairs

The residential landlord-tenant laws in most states allow tenants to arrange repairs and deduct the costs from rent if the unit's habitability is at stake and the landlord refuses to make repairs. (Of course, a competent manager should never let a property's condition deteriorate to that point in the first place.) The tenant must follow a specific procedure to take advantage of this "self-help" remedy. This includes giving written notice to the landlord and waiting a certain amount of time for the landlord to respond before ordering the work. If the tenant meets these requirements and completes the repairs, it can be expensive for the landlord. The tenant might use a contractor who's pricier than the manager's usual provider, or the manager might have to pay to undo work that doesn't meet the owner's specifications.

Under the Fair Housing Act, a disabled residential tenant doesn't have to get a landlord's permission to modify her unit if she needs the modification for full use and enjoyment of the property. Typical modifications include adding grab bars in the bathroom or more accessible door handles. The law doesn't require the landlord to pay for these modifications. Also, the landlord can require the tenant to restore the unit to its original condition at the lease's end (also at the tenant's expense).

It's important to keep on hand only the inventory that's actually needed. Buying in bulk can save money, but maintaining too much inventory locks up funds that the manager or owner could use elsewhere. It's also a good idea to standardize purchases among all units. The fewer colors of paint and brands of appliances used, the less space and money must be devoted toward keeping paint and parts in stock.

Maintenance and Alterations Between Tenancies

The most serious maintenance and remodeling work within a unit or space occurs after the tenant vacates. Office and retail spaces usually undergo extensive work between tenancies as they are reconfigured or rebuilt to meet a new tenant's specifications. This process is typically repeated every time a new tenant moves into the space. (We will discuss the leasing of vacant commercial space in greater detail in Chapters 11–13.)

In a residential unit, maintenance between tenancies may be as simple as taking a day or two to thoroughly clean the apartment. However, more serious work may be necessary to correct deferred maintenance, or to update the unit so the rent can be increased. This may include repainting, recarpeting, and replacing appliances or fixtures.

Residential maintenance staff sometimes use a **unit preparation checklist**, also known as a unit make-ready report (see Chapter 10 for an example). Such a checklist makes it harder to accidentally overlook items. Action items listed in the report include checking the plumbing system and cleaning all bathroom fixtures; inspecting and cleaning all kitchen appliances and cabinets; inspecting and cleaning windows and screens; looking over all painted surfaces for peeling, stains, nail holes, and cracks; checking and cleaning blinds or drapes; and checking and cleaning carpets and floors.

The apartment manager and the tenant should inspect the unit together, both at move-in and move-out. After each inspection, they should sign a document called a **walk-through checklist** or move-in/move-out inspection form. (Again, there is an example in Chapter 10.) The form creates a written record of any damage that occurred during the tenancy (beyond normal wear and tear). If the manager needs to withhold part or all of the security deposit to pay for repairs, the form provides justification.

Environmental Issues

Escalating energy costs have increased the importance of properly maintaining energy-thirsty equipment. For instance, regular replacement of filters will increase furnace efficiency, saving many dollars in energy costs. Pursuing across-the-board energy efficiency may require extensive retrofitting, especially in older buildings. This can involve replacing appliances or windows with more efficient Energy Star® rated versions, installing timed thermostats or motion-sensing lights, and installing low-flow toilets.

Before making these types of improvements, the manager should perform a cost-benefit analysis. Will the amount of money saved on energy costs exceed the cost of replacing the equipment? If not, the improvement would not be worthwhile. In general, retrofitting more than pays for itself (especially if there are tax benefits associated with the improvement). However, it's important to consider not just the initial cost of the improvement, but also its cost over time. For example, if a new furnace saves energy, the analysis takes those savings into account. But the manager must also look at the furnaces's cost over time. Does the new furnace last as long? Are parts more expensive? This kind of analysis, looking at the long-term costs of equipment, is called **life-cycle costing**.

Managers should also remember that some of the most cost-effective energy-saving strategies are the simplest and cheapest, such as requesting that tenants report leaking faucets, or asking custodial staff to turn off lights when they've finished cleaning. Installing compact fluorescent lights in place of incandescent bulbs is another easy, money-saving step.

Another environmentally related maintenance issue is air quality inside the building. A poorly designed or operated HVAC system can hurt air circulation. Bacteria, compounds from cleaning solutions, and gas from building elements can be permanently trapped in the building's atmosphere. The pollution can cause "sick building syndrome" for the building occupants. Sufferers experience headaches, eye, nose, and throat irritation, dry or itchy skin, nausea, dizziness, or fatigue. Regular maintenance of the HVAC system (especially duct cleaning) and use of less caustic cleaning supplies may help prevent or at least reduce these problems.

Employee Safety

There's one more important consideration when planning and carrying out maintenance tasks: employee safety. The Occupational Safety and Health Administration (OSHA) sets job safety standards, and OSHA inspectors visit job sites and issue citations for violations of safety rules. (We'll discuss this again in Chapter 14.)

Environmental Hazards

There are various materials that might be present in a building or on the grounds that create environmental hazards. Not only can these materials reduce the property's value, they can also cause health problems for tenants and their guests. Federal and state regulations mandate how to handle or dispose of many of these materials. In some cases, the property's owner may be responsible for an expensive cleanup project.

Hazards a property manager might encounter include:

Asbestos. Asbestos is a fibrous material that can cause lung cancer if it crumbles and is inhaled. It is sometimes found in insulation or roofing materials in older buildings. Trained professionals can remove or encapsulate it.

Radon. Radon is an odorless and colorless gas that is carcinogenic. It may collect in basements in certain parts of the country, although this risk can be mitigated by sealing cracks and providing better ventilation.

PCBs. Polychlorinated biphenyls are chemicals found in electrical transformers that release toxic dioxin gas if they leak or are burned. Materials containing PCBs must be removed by authorized hazardous waste haulers.

Lead-based paint. The use of paint containing lead additives was ended in 1978, but buildings built before this may contain lead-based paint, either exposed or under newer layers of paint. Paint chips are a poisoning hazard for young children. The paint should be stripped or removed only by professionals. Federal law requires residential property owners to disclose the presence of any known lead-based paint to potential tenants.

Urea formaldehyde. Formaldehyde gas can be found in adhesives used in certain wood products such as paneling and cabinets, and used to be found in foam insulation. It is carcinogenic and thus hazardous when materials containing it are initially installed, although the gas does dissipate over time.

Mold. While mold does not pose a health hazard to most people, it can be a source of misery to persons with respiratory health problems or allergies. Mold grows in enclosed spaces where there is water leakage; it can be remediated by cleaning and repair of mold-damaged surfaces.

Underground storage tanks. Some properties may have underground tanks for storing heating oil. These tanks gradually rust, and may leak oil into the soil. Unused tanks should be removed or filled with concrete. Prospective buyers of properties with underground storage tanks may want to have a soil inspection to make sure nothing has leaked into the soil. Soil contamination can require a long and expensive cleanup process.

Compliance with job safety regulations is especially important when staffers deal with dangerous machinery or chemicals. For example, a manager must make sure that workers using power tools wear the proper safety equipment, such as safety glasses and gloves. Similarly, workers using harsh cleansers or other toxins or flammables must wear protective gear and dispose of the material properly.

Chapter Summary

1. The number of staff varies considerably depending on the size of the property and what tasks need to be performed. Staffing options include permanent on-site staff, itinerant staff who work at multiple sites, and contractors hired for specific tasks.

2. Staff members at a property may include managerial staff, administrative staff, service staff, maintenance staff, and security staff.

3. A manager should prepare an employee manual and give it to new staff members, outlining basic rules of employment and policies for discipline and grievances. Staff should also receive hands-on training.

4. Employees are compensated differently from independent contractors. Contractors, who are hired to perform a particular task, are usually paid a fixed amount or a commission, and taxes are not withheld. Employees operate under closer supervision, are paid a salary or wages, and have taxes withheld from their earnings.

5. Maintenance is broken down into three basic categories: custodial, preventive, and corrective. Custodial maintenance is routine cleaning and housekeeping. Preventive maintenance is oriented toward keeping equipment and systems functioning, while corrective maintenance is fixing unexpected problems. Refurbishment construction is sometimes considered a fourth category of maintenance.

6. A maintenance program involves a maintenance schedule and an inspection schedule. A maintenance schedule establishes when and where preventive maintenance tasks must be performed; the inspection schedule tells when to inspect equipment for potential problems.

7. Components and systems in a property that require upkeep include the grounds, driveways and walkways, parking lots, building exteriors, windows, interior surfaces, the HVAC system, pools, elevators, and fire safety systems.

8. Records must be kept as part of the process of arranging and ordering repairs, and include repair requests, work orders, work logs, purchase orders, and inventory controls.

9. A property manager should seek to save money through energy-efficiency strategies, which may include retrofitting the property with more efficient appliances and systems. Managers should be aware of potential health hazards, such as poor indoor air quality or the presence of asbestos or lead-based paint.

Key Terms

On-site staff – An on-site staff member works for a property manager on a single property.

Multi-site staff – Some property management firms may employ itinerant staffers, who perform maintenance or other tasks at multiple properties.

Contractor – A person hired to perform specific tasks rather than being kept on the manager's payroll. Contractors are more expensive than employees on an hourly basis but don't require benefits or a long-term commitment.

Management staff – Workers at a property who negotiate leases, perform recordkeeping tasks, and interact with tenants.

Employee manual – A handbook given to new hires that explains company policies on work hours and pay periods, discipline and grievance policies, and policies concerning discrimination and sexual harassment.

Employee – A person who works under close supervision, is compensated by salary or wages, may receive benefits, and has taxes withheld from paychecks. Contrast with an independent contractor.

Custodial maintenance – Tasks performed frequently to keep a building clean and orderly, such as vacuuming and restroom cleaning.

Preventive maintenance – A scheduled program of upkeep tasks intended to keep equipment and fixtures properly functioning and to prevent excessive wear and tear.

Corrective maintenance – Fixing broken machinery or fixtures as problems arise.

Deferred maintenance – Corrective maintenance that needs to be performed but is postponed, causing a reduction in the property's value.

Construction – Remodeling or refurbishment of a property; may also be known as cosmetic maintenance.

Inspection schedule – A plan for how often equipment or areas of a building need to be inspected for problems.

Maintenance schedule – A set plan for the cleaning and upkeep of various parts of a building.

HVAC – An acronym for heating, ventilation, and air conditioning, referring to all equipment associated with air circulation and climate control.

Work order – A document describing what needs to be done in a maintenance project, when it needs to be done, and who should do it, partly completed by the manager and partly by the worker.

Repair request – A form allowing tenants to report problems that need repair or other maintenance work.

Work log – A comprehensive list maintained by a manager of all maintenance work performed on a property.

Purchase order – A document used to keep track of purchases of supplies or other items; includes information such as the vendor, date of purchase, price, and quantity.

Inventory control system – A written or computerized method of keeping track of consumption of supplies and the remaining inventory.

Unit preparation checklist – A checklist used in vacancy periods between tenancies, to make sure that all steps in the cleaning and refurbishment process are completed. Also called a unit make-ready report.

Chapter Quiz

1. A handyman skilled in HVAC systems is employed by a property management firm that manages a number of commercial buildings. He receives a regular salary, and travels from building to building to work on projects as needed. This is an example of:

   a) an independent contractor
   b) itinerant staff
   c) just-in-time staff
   d) on-site staff

2. A property manager may choose to use a contractor for:

   a) jobs that are infrequently performed but require special skills, like elevator repair
   b) long-term positions, when the manager doesn't want to handle the associated payroll and tax duties himself
   c) seasonal tasks like lawn care or snow removal
   d) All of the above

3. A leasing agent working full-time at a large apartment complex would be considered part of the building's:

   a) administrative staff
   b) maintenance staff
   c) management staff
   d) service staff

4. All of the following will be discussed in a management firm's employee manual, except:

   a) discrimination and sexual harassment policies
   b) procedures for discipline and grievances
   c) procedures for evicting tenants who haven't paid rent
   d) work hours, pay periods, and sick leave

5. All of the following are true concerning an independent contractor, except:

   a) he uses his judgment to perform the task, rather than being heavily supervised
   b) he works as many hours as needed to complete the task
   c) the employer must withhold income taxes and Social Security from his pay
   d) the employer will not be responsible for paying benefits to the contractor

6. Which federal law establishes the maximum number of hours that an hourly employee may work in a day or a week, before overtime pay requirements apply?

   a) Americans with Disabilities Act
   b) Fair Labor Standards Act
   c) Family and Medical Leave Act
   d) Occupational Safety and Health Act

7. An example of custodial maintenance is:

   a) fixing a broken oil pump in a furnace
   b) lubricating moving parts in the elevator
   c) repainting a vacant unit between tenancies
   d) vacuuming the lobby carpet

8. A maintenance staffer changes the air filters in a building's HVAC system, according to an established schedule. This is an example of:

   a) corrective maintenance
   b) cosmetic maintenance
   c) custodial maintenance
   d) preventive maintenance

9. When an apartment is vacant between tenancies, the property manager arranges to replace a refrigerator and a picture window with more energy-efficient versions. This would be considered:

   a) construction
   b) corrective maintenance
   c) custodial maintenance
   d) deferred maintenance

10. The first step in creating a maintenance program is for the manager to:
    a) decide what level of maintenance each component needs
    b) determine how long each task will take to do
    c) find how frequently each task will need to be done
    d) inventory all equipment and items on the property that will need to be maintained

11. A manager compiles a list of all equipment and systems in a building that should be examined by a maintenance employee on a particular date. This is an example of a/an:
    a) inspection schedule
    b) maintenance schedule
    c) repair request
    d) work order

12. A document lets a maintenance worker know that the furnace's air filters need to be replaced in June, but the oil filter doesn't need to be replaced until November. This would be a/an:
    a) inspection schedule
    b) maintenance schedule
    c) unit make-ready report
    d) work log

13. State or local regulations place strict controls over all of the following components of a property, except for:
    a) elevators
    b) fire sprinklers
    c) smoke detectors
    d) roofs

14. Rather than compensating a contractor through a flat fee, a manager offers to compensate the contractor by paying the actual costs of the project, plus an additional 15% as profit. This is known as:
    a) cost-plus basis
    b) life-cycle costing
    c) net payment
    d) flexible payment

15. Before a new tenant moves in, the building manager and the tenant should:
    a) complete the move-in/move-out inspection form
    b) inspect the unit together
    c) put together a list of remodeling projects that will occur once the tenant moves in
    d) Both A and B

Answer Key

1. b) Persons who are permanently employed by a property manager or managerial firm, but who work at multiple buildings rather than at one site, are known as itinerant or multi-site staff.

2. d) Contractors are often hired for specific repair or construction projects, and they may also be used for seasonal upkeep tasks. They also may be used on a long-term basis when it's not convenient for a manager to hire an employee.

3. c) Although leasing agents may work out of a model unit rather than the managerial office, they are still considered part of management staff.

4. c) While a manager will certainly have a set procedure for handling unpaid rents, this is not a topic for the employee manual, which covers rules in the relationship between employer and employee.

5. c) An employer does not withhold anything from the compensation paid to an independent contractor. By contrast, federal and state income taxes and Social Security are withheld from an employee's wages.

6. b) The Fair Labor Standards Act (FLSA) sets minimum wage and overtime rules.

7. d) Vacuuming carpets is an example of custodial maintenance, which consists of day-to-day cleaning and upkeep activities.

8. d) Preventive maintenance is a program of scheduled tasks performed to keep equipment functioning properly. Changing filters is a typical example, along with cleaning and lubricating moving parts.

9. a) Construction is often considered a maintenance category unto itself. Sometimes known as cosmetic maintenance, it includes remodeling and refurbishment, and may mean replacing appliances or other fixtures.

10. d) Before a manager can make decisions about what maintenance is required, how often it must be done, or how long it will take, the manager should take stock of all aspects of the property that will need maintenance.

11. a) An inspection schedule lists all the components of a building that need to be inspected by a maintenance person.

12. b) The maintenance schedule establishes when preventive maintenance needs to be performed, often at a level of detail involving various parts of a complicated system.

13. d) Specialists in elevator repair and pest control may be subject to licensing requirements, and states and localities have extensive fire safety regulations. Working on a roof isn't regulated in the same way.

14. a) Cost-plus basis is a method of compensating contractors that may be used when a manager already has a trusted relationship with the contractor and wants to encourage efficiency on the contractor's part.

15. d) If the manager and new tenant agree in person on the condition of the property at the beginning of a tenancy, and put that agreement into writing, that diminishes the likelihood of disputes later over who caused damage to the unit.

Chapter 10

Managing Residential Property

Introduction

In the previous chapters, we've examined various elements of a property manager's duties, including developing a management plan, marketing, leasing, staffing and maintenance, and working with both clients and tenants. In this chapter, we'll take a closer look at these elements in the specific context of residential property.

We'll start by describing the different categories of managed residential property and then discuss the steps involved in residential management planning. Next, we'll look at various strategies used to market residential property. Then, we'll turn to leasing residential units, operating residential properties, handling tenants, and handling security deposits. We'll end with a discussion of some management issues specific to certain types of residential property.

Residential Property Management

Residential property management differs from commercial property management in many ways. First, residential property is continuously in use. Residential property managers are on-call around the clock, especially in regards to maintenance and repair issues. Also, residential lease terms tend to be significantly shorter than commercial lease terms. Higher tenant turnover means residential managers spend a greater proportion of their time marketing, showing spaces, and finalizing leases. Residential tenants can be quite personally invested in their rental units; consequently, it's important for a residential manager to possess good people skills. And finally, residential managers must be familiar with an array of federal, state, and local laws regarding landlord-tenant relations, many of which are discussed here and in Chapter 14.

Managed Residential Property

Various types of housing are often under professional management, including single-family homes, duplexes, triplexes, and apartment buildings. Many common interest developments, such as condominiums, cooperatives, and planned unit developments, also rely on some degree of professional management. Property managers may be employed in manufactured home parks, subsidized housing, and housing for the elderly.

Of course, apartment complexes are probably what comes to mind first when thinking of residential property management. In this chapter, our discussion will focus primarily on these multi-family rental properties. Then, in the last section of the chapter, we'll look at special management considerations for other types of housing.

Types of Multi-Family Rental Properties. Even within the category of multi-family rental properties, a range of sizes and building configurations exists. Anyone who's ever searched for an apartment knows that units with similar descriptions can vary widely in terms of age, amenities, floor plans, and location. Still, apartments can generally be categorized according to size and configuration as one of the following:

- **Traditional buildings.** These properties are one to three stories high, with no more than a dozen one- or two-bedroom units. The buildings are often older and rarely feature elevators (for this reason, they're sometimes referred to as "walkups"). They're generally preferred by couples and singles, as opposed to families.
- **Mid-rise buildings.** Usually located in urban areas near a city's downtown core, these are four- to nine-story properties that typically contain studios and one-bedroom units rented by working singles.
- **High-rise buildings.** These properties, which are ten stories or more and can contain hundreds of units, are located in urban areas where land is very expensive and vertical development is a necessity. Some high-rises, categorized as luxury buildings, feature units with large living spaces, views, and amenities such as pools, fitness centers, front desk attendants, and parking garages.
- **Garden apartments.** This type of property, designed to appeal to families, consists of multiple low-rise buildings on a larger parcel of land, in a suburban setting where land is less expensive. Units typically contain two or three bedrooms and the buildings often feature attractive landscaping and amenities such as pools or play areas.
- **Converted loft buildings.** Light industrial and warehouse space located in urban areas is sometimes converted into living spaces with open, undivided interiors. These units tend to appeal to singles, young adults, and older couples that are downsizing.

Residential Management Planning

As with any type of property, the successful management of residential property requires good planning. Two critical elements of management planning are creating the management plan and developing an operating budget.

Management Plan

The management plan represents the manager's strategies for handling the property and serves as a roadmap for ongoing management activities. To develop the plan, the property manager performs a preliminary study that includes five types of analysis: regional analysis, neighborhood analysis, property analysis, market analysis, and analysis of alternatives. (Management plans are discussed in detail in Chapter 4.)

The **regional analysis** considers the economic and demographic conditions that affect the supply of and demand for residential property in the surrounding region. Certain types of data are especially key to the residential market, such as the population's average age and family size. These figures help determine which type and size of housing units are most desirable. Similarly, employment trends are important: as salaries and employment rates rise, so does demand for more expensive housing. It's also a good idea to research the region's major industries and employers, and look into the quality of local schools.

The manager can use a variety of sources of data to research these elements, including the U.S. Census Bureau, state and local government agencies, local business and civic groups, and local chapters of REALTORS® and other professional organizations.

In the **neighborhood analysis**, the property manager identifies the neighborhood's physical or intangible boundaries. She then gathers data about the neighborhood's characteristics, population, and location. A residential neighborhood analysis will consider everything from vacancy and rental rates to transportation issues and zoning; however, it should focus particularly on the demographics of local residents, as they form the pool of potential tenants.

Factors that affect the desirability of a particular neighborhood include crime rates, access to public services, and access to public transportation and major thoroughfares. Desirability is also affected by proximity to schools, shopping centers, cultural centers, recreational facilities, and business zones and/or major employers. The manager also considers neighborhood employment and income data, and current occupancy and rental rate trends. The manager may rely on sources of data similar to those used for the regional analysis, but she'll want to inspect the neighborhood in person as well.

In the residential **property analysis**, the manager gathers and evaluates information about the property's physical attributes, attractiveness and condition, current management, and financial status. While the owner can provide much of the necessary data, the manager must personally inspect the property. Because **curb appeal** (the building's exterior appearance and condition) is particularly important for residential property, the manager needs to investigate not only the building's size and configuration, but also its age, condition, and appearance.

Next, the manager uses data gathered in the regional, neighborhood, and property analyses to perform a **market analysis**. In this analysis, the manager determines appropriate rental rates for the subject property by locating competitive units and evaluating their current rental rates.

The manager begins by choosing comparable housing units. She'll consider the number and type of apartments available locally; the average age and character of the buildings; the features (size, layout, amenities) of a typical unit; current rental rates for average units; and occupancy levels. Some of this information may be gathered by studying advertisements for competing properties. However, the manager should visit at least some of the competition in person to get a better sense of their condition and appearance.

Units used as comparables must be truly comparable. For example, the manager must evaluate furnished units against furnished units, and unfurnished units against unfurnished units. The manager should pay close attention to certain factors that some prospective tenants consider "dealbreakers." That includes the cost of utilities and who pays them; proximity to major arterials or public transportation; the availability of laundry facilities, parking and other amenities; and policies regarding pets.

Using a comparison grid worksheet (such as the one shown in Figure 10.1) allows the manager to compare the different properties side-by-side and estimate dollar values for each feature or amenity. The manager then adjusts the rent of each comparable unit to account for each difference between the comparable property and the subject property. The resulting amount reflects what the comparable would rent for if it had the same features and amenities as the subject. The manager uses the comparables' adjusted rents to evaluate the subject property's current rent schedule and decide whether to raise or lower the rent amounts or leave them alone. For brand-new buildings (which don't yet have rental schedules), the manager uses the data from the comparables to set rents.

The manager may need to adjust the rent amounts of individual units to reflect particular advantages or disadvantages. For example, a unit may be more attractive than other units in the building because it has a view or a balcony; conversely, another unit may be less attractive because it's positioned closest to the freeway.

> **Example:** Brian's market analysis of the Sunshine Studios building shows that the appropriate average rental rate for the studio units is $600 per month. However, only the ground-floor units feature private patios, and while most of the building's units have updated kitchens, ten of the units still have their original kitchens. Brian decides to raise the price of the ground-floor units to $675 per month, and lower the price of the units with older kitchens to $550 per month.

The final analysis in the preliminary study is the **analysis of alternatives**. If the manager believes that any operational or physical changes to the property may be appropriate, he will perform a cost-benefit analysis of the changes and present the client with a written proposal summarizing his findings.

 Rent Control

Rent control ordinances set maximum limits on the amount of rent that a landlord may charge. New York and San Francisco are two cities that have some form of rent control ordinances. Rent controls are intended to make property available at reasonable rates when there is a housing shortage.

Many economists believe that rent controls are not effective in accomplishing their primary goal of providing affordable housing. They argue that rents become high because demand for housing exceeds supply. In order for rents to come down, demand and supply must be brought into balance, either by reducing demand or by increasing supply. Rent controls usually have little positive effect on either of these goals. Artificially low rents may in fact increase demand. In addition, the resulting low yields to property owners may discourage the construction of new housing.

Figure 10.1 Comparison worksheet for market analysis – residential property

Market Analysis Comparison Grid for Residential Property

Subject property: _Casablanca Apartments, 1674 Weldon Place N._   Date: _June 19_

Type of unit: _1-bedroom on second floor in garden apartment complex_

	Subject	Comparable 1	Comparable 2	Comparable 3
Property Name		Vanguard	Stillmont	Annabel Lee
Rental rate (monthly)		$1,610	$1,590	$1,585
Concessions (–)		none	none	none
Effective rent		$1,610	$1,590	$1,585
Vacancy rate		7.5%	9%	7%

Elements	Description	Difference	$ adj.	Difference	$ adj.	Difference	$ adj.
Location	near shops	near lake	–10	same	—	near freewy	+5
Prestige	good	superior	–5	same	—	same	—
Access to transportation	very good	inferior	+5	inferior	+5	same	—
Nearby tenant services	very good	inferior	+5	same	—	same	—
Crime and safety issues	good	same	—	same	—	same	—
Buildings & Site							
Number of bldgs/units	10/40	9/54	+5	9/36	—	10/35	—
Age of building(s)	14 years old	15 yrs	—	10 yrs	–5	17 yrs	—
Grounds	adequate	superior	–10	superior	–5	same	—
Building exterior(s)	good	same	—	same	—	inferior	+5
Entry and/or lobby	N/A						
Other common areas	good	same	—	same	—	same	—
Systems & Operations							
Energy efficiency (HVAC)	adequate	same	—	superior	–10	same	—
Elevators	N/A						
Staffing	good	superior	–5	same	—	same	—
Security	good	same	—	same	—	same	—
Parking							
Lot, covered, or garage	covered	lot	+10	garage	–5	same	—
Visitor spaces available	adequate	inferior	+5	inferior	+5	superior	–5
Tenant parking cost	$75/mo.	$65	–10	$90	+15	$60	–15

Adjustments should be stated in dollars per month. For example, +10 means the comparable's rental rate is increased by $10.00 per month, and –22 means the rate is decreased by $22.00 per month.

Elements	Subject Description	Comparable 1 Difference	$ adj.	Comparable 2 Difference	$ adj.	Comparable 3 Difference	$ adj.
Amenities							
Pets allowed	yes	yes	—	yes	—	yes	—
Internet/cable TV	yes	yes	—	yes	—	yes	—
Clubhouse or party room	no	yes	–5	yes	–5	no	—
Rec or exercise facilities	small ex room	superior	–5	superior	–5	none	+10
Laundry facilities	en suite	same	—	same	—	shared	+20
Other	nonsmoking	same	—	smoking	+10	same	—
Rental Unit							
Location in complex	away from street	same	—	on street	+15	same	—
Square footage (est.)	1,100 sq.ft.	1,115	–22	same	—	1,115	–22
Layout	excellent	inferior	+5	inferior	+5	inferior	+5
Overall quality/condition	good	same	—	superior	–10	same	—
Number of bathrooms	1½	same	—	same	—	same	—
Storage	very good	same	—	inferior	+5	same	—
Carpets & flooring	good	inferior	+5	same	—	inferior	+5
Window treatments	good	inferior	+5	same	—	same	—
Stove & refrigerator	adequate	superior	–7	superior	–7	same	—
Dishwasher	adequate	superior	–3	superior	–3	same	—
Other appliances	good	same	—	same	—	same	—
Air conditioning	good	same	—	same	—	inferior	+3
Balcony, deck, or patio	yes	none	+15	same	—	superior	–5
Fireplace	none	none	—	none	—	none	—
Other	cathedral ceiling	inferior	+5	inferior	+5	inferior	+5
Utilities Paid by Owner	none	none	—	none	—	none	—
Adjustment Totals		65 + –82 = –17		65 + –55 = +10		58 + –47 = +11	
Adjusted Rent		$1,593		$1,600		$1,596	
Adjusted rent per sq.ft.		$1.428		$1.454		$1.431	
Total no. of adjustments		20		17		12	
Comments:							

Operating Budget

The second important element of management planning concerns finances. As we discussed in detail in Chapter 5, a property manager must create an annual **operating budget** that reflects the property's anticipated monthly income and expenses over the upcoming year. Unless the building is brand-new, these figures are usually based on numbers from the previous year.

Income. The primary source of income for a residential property is rent. Since tenant turnover is a significant issue for most residential properties, the budget will include a **bad debt and vacancy factor**: a percentage deduction that accounts for losses in income due to vacancies and difficulties collecting rent. The bad debt and vacancy factor is expressed as a percentage of the property's potential gross rental income and is based on the amount of rent that was actually collected in recent years.

Additional sources of income include parking and storage fees, revenue from laundry and vending machines, and even "unscheduled" income such as late fees or forfeited security deposits.

Expenses. Typical residential property expenses include wages for the property manager and any other staff, supplies and administrative costs, maintenance and repairs, any owner-paid utilities, and property taxes and insurance. Note that the budget usually doesn't include mortgage payments; debt service isn't considered part of the property's operational expenses.

Preparing the Budget. The manager must carefully consider all factors that could affect occupancy over the coming year. She weighs items such as changes in economic conditions, housing trends, or construction of competitive units nearby.

Most residential property managers use a **net operating income (NOI) budget** format. This format lists the property's potential gross income, effective gross income, and expenses, and then provides a projected net operating income figure. (See Figure 5.2 for an example.) However, other formats may be used, depending on the owner's needs. For example, a **cash flow budget**, which includes mortgage payments as expenses, might meet the owner's needs better. (Budgeting is discussed in greater detail in Chapter 5.)

Marketing Residential Property

Property managers can employ any of a variety of marketing techniques, but a few methods tend to be particularly effective for residential properties. When planning a marketing campaign for a specific rental property, a property manager should consider the target audience and choose methods that are not only effective but reasonable in terms of time, energy, and expense. The techniques that work best for one type of housing may not be right for another type.

The most frequently used methods of marketing multi-family properties include newspaper advertisements, For Rent magazines, and Internet websites. Rental centers and leasing agents may also be used to market units in larger properties.

Print Ads

For decades, the preferred method of marketing residential units was printed ads in local newspapers. Managers used short **classified ads** to communicate basic information about a rental unit, such as the rent amount, location, and number of bedrooms and bathrooms. Larger and more expensive **display ads**, on the other hand, were used when the manager wanted to provide photographs or more details about a property and its amenities. While some managers continue to use newspaper advertising, many have turned to Internet advertising.

In some areas, an ad in a **For Rent magazine** is the most cost-effective option for advertising apartment units, especially those in high-end apartment buildings. For Rent magazines are publications that are usually printed monthly and distributed for free at newsstands or shopping centers.

Internet Advertising

For most residential managers, online advertising offers an inexpensive way to reach a large pool of potential tenants. Even the most basic website can contain a fairly large amount of information about a property. Internet advertising removes geographical limitations: anyone, anywhere, can view online ads. This facilitates housing searches by out-of-towners who haven't had a chance to visit the area in person.

The simplest type of Internet ad is a short listing on a classified ad website, such as craigslist or sites associated with newspapers; these ads usually contain a brief description of the unit and perhaps a few photos. Prospective renters can search these listings online, narrowing their searches by neighborhood, price, number of bedrooms, and other factors. These ads can be very effective for marketing any type of residential unit.

Alternatively, the manager of a larger apartment complex may prefer to use a dedicated website that has been set up solely for the purpose of advertising units in that building. Brokerage firms that handle property management often maintain these types of sites as well. A listing on one of these websites is usually fairly detailed, with descriptions of the unit's amenities and finishings. It may also include photos, floorplan illustrations, and even a short video of the unit's interior.

Of course, managers aren't limited to just one type of ad. Often, managers will use a brief online ad or print media classified ad to direct prospective tenants to a more detailed online listing.

Example: Henry places a short online classified ad that reads:

> *Lovely 1-bdrm units available in desirable Shoreline Sands complex. $850/month, all utilities included. Visit www.shorelinesands.com for more information.*

The www.shorelinesands.com website contains large color photos of the apartment complex, including aerial shots and images of residents using the pool and tennis courts. Each available unit has its own page that lists the unit's features and amenities, and shows a floorplan illustration and a 360-degree video of the unit's living room.

Model Units and Rental Centers

In a larger apartment complex or development, the manager may opt to maintain a **model unit** (or show unit) for prospective renters to visit. This marketing tactic is similar to staging a home for sale: it allows prospects to tour an attractively furnished, decorated space and spend a few minutes imagining themselves living in it. Ideally, the model unit is professionally furnished and decorated; naturally, it should be kept in clean, show-ready condition.

The manager of a large property may also opt to market units using a **rental center**: an office or room used only for meeting prospective tenants and distributing information and marketing materials. Depending on its size and location, a rental center may even draw in passersby who are interested in the displays.

> **Example:** Blackpoint Tower's rental center is a spacious office on the ground floor of the complex. Aerial photographs, floorplan drawings, and a model of the tower are all on display; a table holds a stack of brochures that list the development's features and amenities. On one wall, a TV monitor shows a video that features the interiors of a few sample units and describes the neighborhood and local attractions. In the corner, a sitting area allows prospective tenants to meet with management representatives to discuss the property, arrange to tour a model unit, and possibly complete a rental application.

Leasing Agents

Another marketing strategy used for larger properties is the employment of **leasing agents**. Leasing agents are trained in sales techniques and may be able to present a property more effectively and close a deal (obtain a signed lease agreement) faster than the property management's regular staff. Leasing agents are often well suited to rental center atmospheres.

Additional Considerations

Keep in mind that regardless of the specific marketing methods and strategies used, all advertising must comply with any applicable federal, state, and local fair housing and antidiscrimination regulations. For example, all display ads and printed materials must contain the equal housing logo. If photos of people are used, the models must be diverse enough to give the impression that the housing is open to everyone. Fair housing and other antidiscrimination laws are discussed in detail in Chapters 6 and 14.

Finally, it's important to understand that even the most sophisticated marketing campaign can be derailed if a building lacks **curb appeal**. A well-written ad can entice a prospective tenant into visiting a property. However, if she arrives and the building appears tired and run-down, she may not bother entering to see the available unit. In addition, many potential renters locate available units simply by walking or driving around the desired neighborhood. Even if a property displays a "Vacancy" sign, prospective tenants may decide it's not worth inquiring about the unit if the building's condition and landscaping are unattractive.

A good manager keeps building interiors properly maintained and exterior paint and masonry in reasonably good condition. Landscaping need not be elaborate, but the grounds should be kept clean, the grass mowed, and so on.

Leasing Residential Property

If the manager's marketing efforts are successful, the next step is leasing. The leasing process involves accepting applications, screening and selecting tenants, and signing leases.

Application Process

A residential property manager uses a lease application form to obtain information from a lease applicant. The information helps determine whether the applicant can afford the unit and is otherwise a good match. Most managers use a standardized application form, which allows the manager to collect all of the relevant information in an organized manner. It also helps prevent any claims of discrimination, since every applicant is asked the same questions in the same format.

Most lease application forms ask for the following information:

- the applicant's name and social security number;
- the name(s) of anyone else (including minor children) who will be occupying the apartment;
- the applicant's current address and phone number, the length of time at that residence, the reason for leaving, and the name/contact information of the current landlord (if any);
- the same information as above, for the applicant's previous residence;
- the applicant's current employer, job title, salary, length of time at that position, and the immediate supervisor's name/contact information;
- the same information as above, for the applicant's previous employer;
- bank names and account numbers for any checking or savings accounts, credit cards, and outstanding loans;
- permission to verify the information provided in the application, including authorization to run a credit check and criminal background check; and
- the applicant's signature.

The application may also ask for references and emergency contact information. The manager will want to see the applicant's identification (such as a driver's license) and make a photocopy of it.

The application should clearly state the amount of any fee or deposit charged at the time of the application, and indicate whether the money is refundable. A few property managers require the applicant to make a deposit to hold the vacancy open while the application and credit/background checks are completed. If the manager denies the application, she returns the deposit to the applicant. If the application is approved and the tenant signs a lease, the deposit is applied to the tenant's security deposit. The manager may also charge a fee for running credit or background checks. It's important to note that state law may limit the amount of any application fee charged. It may also be illegal to charge an application fee when no vacancies currently exist.

Screening and Selecting Tenants

The next step in leasing is to process the applications received and determine which (if any) applicants would make suitable tenants. Of course, a primary consideration is whether the prospective tenant is likely to pay rent in a consistent and timely fashion. To find this out, the manager looks into the applicant's credit history, income, and debt levels. We addressed this topic in Chapter 7, so here we'll just emphasize a few points. Keep in mind that many managers use a screening service to handle some or all of the steps we're going to describe.

The manager usually begins the screening process by obtaining the applicant's **credit report** from one or more of the three major credit reporting agencies (Equifax, Experian, and TransUnion). A credit report presents information about an individual's loans, credit purchases, and debt repayment over the previous seven years, forming a snapshot of the person's debt level and credit history.

For each account or loan appearing on the credit report, a payment record shows whether the payments were made on time. If an applicant is chronically late making payments, he may have the same trouble paying rent on time. The credit report also reveals any outstanding court judgments or bankruptcy filings. Finally, the report contains a credit score, issued by the reporting agency, which quantifies the applicant's overall credit history. Managers often require that lease applicants have a certain minimum credit score.

If the manager is satisfied with the applicant's debt level and repayment history, she'll turn to income verification and analysis. First, the manager contacts the applicant's employer to verify that the tenant accurately reported items such as salary and length of time at the position. The manager must then decide whether the applicant's income is sufficient to ensure regular and timely rent payments.

Remember that when making these inquiries, the manager must comply with the requirements of the federal Fair Credit Reporting Act and similar state laws, such as California's Consumer Credit Reporting Agencies Act. For example, the manager must notify the lease applicant that her credit (and/or background information) is being checked. (This is why the lease application should contain a statement authorizing the manager to check the applicant's credit.)

Similarly, if a manager decides to deny an application based on a credit report, the applicant must be notified in writing of her right to obtain additional information from the credit agency that provided the credit report. The applicant should also be notified of the right to dispute any inaccuracies in the report. (See Chapter 14 for more information on credit reporting regulations.)

Of course, aside from financial considerations, the manager must decide if the applicant looks like a good tenant in other respects. Will she take care of the property? Will she get along with the neighbors? And finally, does she have the potential to become a long-term tenant? The manager may contact the applicant's current and previous landlords to find out whether she was a good tenant and to verify the lengths of these tenancies. Longer tenancies indicate a more reliable prospect.

Again, it's important to comply with fair housing laws. The same level of inquiry should be applied to all lease applicants; if a certain kind of check is run on one applicant, that check must be run on all applicants. (See Chapter 14 for further discussion of fair housing laws.)

Residential Lease Agreements

Once the manager has screened and selected a prospective tenant, the next step is signing the lease agreement. A variety of pre-printed residential lease agreement forms are available. Managers of smaller properties may opt to buy one of these forms, filling in the terms by hand each time an agreement is prepared. For a larger multi-unit building, it may make more sense to use a computer-generated agreement created specifically for that property; this agreement can be filled out online and then printed for signing. Note that in some states, residential leases must be in "plain language." This means that the agreements must be written in terms that can be understood by the average person.

Even when a standard form is used, and the agreement contains simple, straightforward language, it's always a good idea to review the lease terms with the tenant to make sure he understands them.

We just noted that some states require plain language in residential leases. States impose many other requirements on residential leases in their residential landlord-tenant acts. Because these acts have such a big impact on the content of residential leases, we'll discuss them briefly before turning to particular lease provisions.

Residential Landlord-Tenant Acts. Every state has a residential landlord-tenant act. Many of these laws are based on the **Uniform Residential Landlord and Tenant Act** (URLTA), a model landlord-tenant act created to help achieve consistency in this area of the law. Many states and municipalities have adopted the URLTA in whole or in part.

Typically, state statutes don't impose much regulation on commercial leases; legislatures assume that commercial tenants have more knowledge and sophistication than residential tenants, and are better able to protect themselves. In contrast, residential landlord-tenant acts are usually lengthy statutes that spell out the rights and duties of the parties in great detail. These laws address the amount of and handling of security deposits, notice requirements for landlord entry, responsibility for maintenance of the premises, notice requirements for termination of the lease, grounds for eviction and, in some cases, the procedures for the eviction itself. Landlord-tenant laws also address the remedies available if a party breaches a lease or violates a provision of the statute.

Another important topic addressed by residential landlord-tenant acts is habitability. As discussed in Chapter 8, every residential lease contains an implied promise by the landlord to keep the premises fit for habitation. This is the **implied warranty of habitability**. However, residential landlord-tenant acts generally make this landlord duty explicit. Typically, the landlord must keep the building weather-tight, arrange for garbage removal, and make heat, water, and light available.

Most state laws require immediate action by the landlord to remedy anything that makes the premises uninhabitable. For instance, after receiving notice from a tenant that there is no water, heat, or electricity, the landlord must remedy the problem within 24 hours. Longer time limits apply for less serious conditions. The URLTA, for example, gives a landlord 14 days to remedy a routine maintenance issue. If the landlord doesn't fix a problem within the proper period, the tenant can move out and recover her security deposit.

Of course the tenant also has some responsibilities in this regard. In most states, for instance, the tenant cannot create an unsanitary condition in the unit.

Lease Provisions. Most residential leases contain provisions addressing most, if not all, of the following:

- parties and occupants,
- lease term,
- rent,
- description of the premises,
- security deposit,
- utilities,
- assignment and subleasing,
- rules,
- maintenance,
- possession,
- entry and inspection, and
- pets.

Parties and occupants. Every competent adult who will occupy the unit should sign the lease. The lease should make all these parties jointly and severally liable for the rent payments. This protects the owner; in the event that one person moves out unexpectedly, the remaining tenants will be required to cover that person's share of the rent.

If a tenant (such as a student) has little credit history and/or income, a co-signer may be required. A **co-signer** is another party (such as a parent) who agrees to accept liability for any default by the tenant. A co-signer must sign the lease agreement but is listed separately from the actual tenants.

 Overcrowding

Overcrowded conditions in rental units can be a serious problem, especially in densely populated areas with expensive housing. At best, overcrowding puts unnecessary stress on the housing's physical structures; at worst, it can have serious public health implications. In an effort to prevent overcrowding, many states have adopted the Uniform Housing Code's occupancy requirements. For example, section 503(b) of the Uniform Housing Code requires every residential rental unit to have at least one room that is at least 120 square feet, while other rooms used for living purposes must be at least 70 square feet. In addition, if a room is used for sleeping, the minimum floor area must be increased by 50 square feet for each occupant in excess of two. (There are different rules for apartments that qualify as "efficiency units.")

The lease should also list any other persons who will occupy the apartment (such as minor children), even though they aren't parties to the lease. Include each person's full name, age, and relationship to the signing parties. The number of occupants cannot exceed the limits set by state law or local housing codes.

Lease term. The lease agreement should contain a statement of the lease term, including the beginning and ending dates. Most residential lease agreements provide for term tenancies. In a **term tenancy**, the lease agreement is for a particular length of time and contains a specific termination date. Although there's no standard term for residential leases, one-year terms are common. At the end of the lease term, the tenancy terminates automatically.

If the lease agreement doesn't include a termination date, the tenancy is a periodic tenancy. A **periodic tenancy** renews itself automatically at the end of each period unless one party gives notice that she is terminating the tenancy. Often, this period is one month, giving rise to the term "month-to-month tenancy." Some periodic tenancies are specifically created by lease agreement; in other cases, a periodic tenancy arises when a term tenancy ends.

> **Example:** Mario rents a house from the Doziers. The lease agreement defines the lease term as "…for one year, starting October 1, and month-to-month thereafter." Under the terms of the agreement, the lease term ends on September 30 of the following year. However, Mario remains in the apartment and continues to pay rent to the Doziers. He now holds a month-to-month tenancy.

Whether a term tenancy or periodic tenancy is the best arrangement depends on the current market and the owner's preference. A term tenancy offers stability; a periodic tenancy offers more flexibility. Although owners and managers tend to prefer a term tenancy, the flexibility of a periodic tenancy may make sense in a market with rapidly rising rents.

If units in a larger building are leased using term tenancies, it's a good idea to try to stagger the lease termination dates throughout the year. Otherwise, the advertising, showing, and leasing tasks required during a short period of time every year could overwhelm the manager. Staggering lease terms may not be an option, however; for example, in a college town, many tenants are students who want lease terms that correspond to the school year. In fact, in those areas, it's not uncommon for leases to run only nine months: September through May. During the summer, the units are unoccupied or leased at a discount to students who remain in the area.

If an option for renewal is given to the tenant, language in the lease should specify when and how the option may be exercised.

Rent. Residential leases nearly always spell out the rent due date. Landlords usually require payment at the beginning of the rental period (typically, the first of the month). If a lease does not specify when the rent is to be paid, however, it is not due until the end of the rental period.

Often the landlord requires the tenant to pay the first month's rent (and sometimes the last month's rent as well) in advance, when the lease is signed. If the lease term happens to begin in the middle of the month, the first month's rent payment should be prorated, with successive payments due on the first of the month. (This ensures that all units have the same rent due date.)

If late payments will incur late fees, this must be stated along with the amount of the fee and the conditions under which it will be charged.

> **Example:** The Silvers sign a one-year apartment lease that begins July 1. The rent is $750 a month and is due on the first of the month. There is a three-day grace period for rent payments; any payments received after the third of the month are subject to an additional $50 late fee.

The lease should also state the acceptable methods of payment. Some managers accept payments by mail; others require payments made directly to a lockbox in the rental building. In some cases, tenants can pay rent via electronic funds transfer from the tenant's bank account to the manager's trust account.

Description of the premises. The lease must identify the rented premises, using the property's address. It should also describe the condition of the premises; sometimes this description takes the form of a **walk-through checklist** (which may also be called a move-in/move-out inspection form or MIMO; see Figure 10.2 for an example). It's always a good idea for the manager and tenant to walk through the rented unit at the beginning of the lease term, noting any existing damage or other issues. The tenant is expected to leave the unit in the same condition in which she received it, and having a written record of the unit's original condition will help avoid disputes.

Security deposit. Most residential property managers require a security deposit from the tenant when the tenant signs the lease. The deposit gives the manager some protection should the tenant damage the property or fail to pay the rent. We discuss handling security deposits in more detail later in this chapter.

Utilities. Residential leases vary greatly in assigning responsibility for utilities such as electricity, gas, water, garbage, and sewer services. In some cases, the tenant pays for all of her utilities; in others, the tenant is only responsible for certain bills, such as electricity. Alternatively, the owner may pay all of the utilities and in turn charge a higher rent.

In some older apartment buildings, the units don't have individual utility meters. In this situation, the tenants may split the building's total utility costs evenly, or the utilities may be entirely covered by the owner.

Assignment and subleasing. As discussed in greater detail in Chapter 7, assignment and subleasing are situations in which the tenant transfers part or all of the remaining lease to another party. In an assignment, the original tenant remains secondarily liable for the rent; in a sublease, she remains primarily liable.

Most residential leases specifically prohibit the tenant from assigning the lease to another party or subleasing the premises without prior written consent. This protects the manager and owner from finding themselves suddenly saddled with a tenant who isn't creditworthy or is otherwise unsuitable.

Sometimes a prospective tenant anticipates needing to move out before the end of the lease term. For example, he may be searching for a home to buy, or may believe an out-of-town job transfer is on the horizon. Such a tenant can seek language in the assignment

Figure 10.2 Walk-through checklist

CALIFORNIA
ASSOCIATION
OF REALTORS ®

MOVE IN / MOVE OUT INSPECTION
(C.A.R. Form MIMO, Revised 11/07)

Property Address _____ Unit No. _____
Inspection: Move In _____ (Date) Move Out _____ (Date)
Tenant(s) _____

When completing this form, check the Premises carefully and be specific in all items noted. Check the appropriate box:
N - NEW   S - SATISFACTORY/CLEAN   O - OTHER   D - DEPOSIT DEDUCTION

	MOVE IN N S O Comments	MOVE OUT S O D Comments
Front Yard/Exterior		
Landscaping	☐ ☐ ☐ _____	☐ ☐ ☐ _____
Fences/Gates	☐ ☐ ☐ _____	☐ ☐ ☐ _____
Sprinklers/Timers	☐ ☐ ☐ _____	☐ ☐ ☐ _____
Walks/Driveway	☐ ☐ ☐ _____	☐ ☐ ☐ _____
Porches/Stairs	☐ ☐ ☐ _____	☐ ☐ ☐ _____
Mailbox	☐ ☐ ☐ _____	☐ ☐ ☐ _____
Light Fixtures	☐ ☐ ☐ _____	☐ ☐ ☐ _____
Building Exterior	☐ ☐ ☐ _____	☐ ☐ ☐ _____
Entry		
Security/Screen Doors	☐ ☐ ☐ _____	☐ ☐ ☐ _____
Doors/Knobs/Locks	☐ ☐ ☐ _____	☐ ☐ ☐ _____
Flooring/Baseboards	☐ ☐ ☐ _____	☐ ☐ ☐ _____
Walls/ Ceilings	☐ ☐ ☐ _____	☐ ☐ ☐ _____
Light Fixtures/Fans	☐ ☐ ☐ _____	☐ ☐ ☐ _____
Switches/Outlets	☐ ☐ ☐ _____	☐ ☐ ☐ _____
Living Room		
Doors/Knobs/Locks	☐ ☐ ☐ _____	☐ ☐ ☐ _____
Flooring/Baseboards	☐ ☐ ☐ _____	☐ ☐ ☐ _____
Walls/Ceilings	☐ ☐ ☐ _____	☐ ☐ ☐ _____
Window Coverings	☐ ☐ ☐ _____	☐ ☐ ☐ _____
Windows/Locks/Screens	☐ ☐ ☐ _____	☐ ☐ ☐ _____
Light Fixtures/Fans	☐ ☐ ☐ _____	☐ ☐ ☐ _____
Switches/Outlets	☐ ☐ ☐ _____	☐ ☐ ☐ _____
Fireplace/Equipment	☐ ☐ ☐ _____	☐ ☐ ☐ _____
Dining Room		
Flooring/Baseboards	☐ ☐ ☐ _____	☐ ☐ ☐ _____
Walls/Ceilings	☐ ☐ ☐ _____	☐ ☐ ☐ _____
Window Coverings	☐ ☐ ☐ _____	☐ ☐ ☐ _____
Windows/Locks/Screens	☐ ☐ ☐ _____	☐ ☐ ☐ _____
Light Fixtures/Fans	☐ ☐ ☐ _____	☐ ☐ ☐ _____
Switches/Outlets	☐ ☐ ☐ _____	☐ ☐ ☐ _____

Tenant's Initials   (_____)(_____)   Tenant's Initials   (_____)(_____)
Landlord's Initials (_____)(_____)   Landlord's Initials (_____)(_____)

MIMO REVISED 11/07 (PAGE 1 OF 5) Print Date

Reviewed by _____ Date _____

EQUAL HOUSING
OPPORTUNITY

MOVE IN / MOVE OUT INSPECTION (MIMO PAGE 1 OF 5)

Reprinted with permission, CALIFORNIA ASSOCIATION OF REALTORS®. Endorsement not implied.

Property Address: _____   Date: _____

MOVE IN
N S O Comments

MOVE OUT
S O D Comments

Other Room _____
Doors/Knobs/Locks
Flooring/Baseboards
Walls/Ceilings
Window Coverings
Windows/Locks/Screens
Light Fixtures/Fans
Switches/Outlets

Bedroom # _____
Doors/Knobs/Locks
Flooring/Baseboards
Walls/Ceilings
Window Coverings
Windows/Locks/Screens
Light Fixtures/Fans
Switches/Outlets
Closets/Doors/Tracks

Bedroom # _____
Doors/Knobs/Locks
Flooring/Baseboards
Walls/Ceilings
Window Coverings
Windows/Locks/Screens
Light Fixtures/Fans
Switches/Outlets
Closets/Doors/Tracks

Bedroom # _____
Doors/Knobs/Locks
Flooring/Baseboards
Walls/Ceilings
Window Coverings
Windows/Locks/Screens
Light Fixtures/Fans
Switches/Outlets
Closets/Doors/Tracks

Bedroom # _____
Doors/Knobs/Locks
Flooring/Baseboards
Walls/Ceilings
Window Coverings
Windows/Locks/Screens
Light Fixtures/Fans
Switches/Outlets
Closets/Doors/Tracks

Tenant's Initials (_____)(_____)
Landlord's Initials (_____)(_____)

Tenant's Initials (_____)(_____)
Landlord's Initials (_____)(_____)

Reviewed by _____ Date _____

MOVE IN / MOVE OUT INSPECTION (MIMO PAGE 2 OF 5)

Property Address: _____ Date: _____

	MOVE IN				**MOVE OUT**			
	N	**S**	**O**	**Comments**	**S**	**O**	**D**	**Comments**
Bath #_____								
Doors/Knobs/Locks	☐	☐	☐	_____	☐	☐	☐	_____
Flooring/Baseboards	☐	☐	☐	_____	☐	☐	☐	_____
Walls/Ceilings	☐	☐	☐	_____	☐	☐	☐	_____
Window Coverings	☐	☐	☐	_____	☐	☐	☐	_____
Windows/Locks/Screens	☐	☐	☐	_____	☐	☐	☐	_____
Light Fixtures	☐	☐	☐	_____	☐	☐	☐	_____
Switches/Outlets	☐	☐	☐	_____	☐	☐	☐	_____
Toilet	☐	☐	☐	_____	☐	☐	☐	_____
Tub/Shower	☐	☐	☐	_____	☐	☐	☐	_____
Shower Door/Rail/Curtain	☐	☐	☐	_____	☐	☐	☐	_____
Sink/Faucets	☐	☐	☐	_____	☐	☐	☐	_____
Plumbing/Drains	☐	☐	☐	_____	☐	☐	☐	_____
Exhaust Fan	☐	☐	☐	_____	☐	☐	☐	_____
Towel Rack(s)	☐	☐	☐	_____	☐	☐	☐	_____
Toilet Paper Holder	☐	☐	☐	_____	☐	☐	☐	_____
Cabinets/Counters	☐	☐	☐	_____	☐	☐	☐	_____
				_____				_____
Bath #_____								
Doors/Knobs/Locks	☐	☐	☐	_____	☐	☐	☐	_____
Flooring/Baseboards	☐	☐	☐	_____	☐	☐	☐	_____
Walls/Ceilings	☐	☐	☐	_____	☐	☐	☐	_____
Window Coverings	☐	☐	☐	_____	☐	☐	☐	_____
Windows/Locks/Screens	☐	☐	☐	_____	☐	☐	☐	_____
Light Fixtures	☐	☐	☐	_____	☐	☐	☐	_____
Switches/Outlets	☐	☐	☐	_____	☐	☐	☐	_____
Toilet	☐	☐	☐	_____	☐	☐	☐	_____
Tub/Shower	☐	☐	☐	_____	☐	☐	☐	_____
Shower Door/Rail/Curtain	☐	☐	☐	_____	☐	☐	☐	_____
Sink/Faucets	☐	☐	☐	_____	☐	☐	☐	_____
Plumbing/Drains	☐	☐	☐	_____	☐	☐	☐	_____
Exhaust Fan	☐	☐	☐	_____	☐	☐	☐	_____
Towel Rack(s)	☐	☐	☐	_____	☐	☐	☐	_____
Toilet Paper Holder	☐	☐	☐	_____	☐	☐	☐	_____
Cabinets/Counters	☐	☐	☐	_____	☐	☐	☐	_____
				_____				_____
Bath #_____								
Doors/Knobs/Locks	☐	☐	☐	_____	☐	☐	☐	_____
Flooring/Baseboards	☐	☐	☐	_____	☐	☐	☐	_____
Walls/Ceilings	☐	☐	☐	_____	☐	☐	☐	_____
Window Coverings	☐	☐	☐	_____	☐	☐	☐	_____
Windows/Locks/Screens	☐	☐	☐	_____	☐	☐	☐	_____
Light Fixtures	☐	☐	☐	_____	☐	☐	☐	_____
Switches/Outlets	☐	☐	☐	_____	☐	☐	☐	_____
Toilet	☐	☐	☐	_____	☐	☐	☐	_____
Tub/Shower	☐	☐	☐	_____	☐	☐	☐	_____
Shower Door/Rail/Curtain	☐	☐	☐	_____	☐	☐	☐	_____
Sink/Faucets	☐	☐	☐	_____	☐	☐	☐	_____
Plumbing/Drains	☐	☐	☐	_____	☐	☐	☐	_____
Exhaust Fan	☐	☐	☐	_____	☐	☐	☐	_____
Towel Rack(s)	☐	☐	☐	_____	☐	☐	☐	_____
Toilet Paper Holder	☐	☐	☐	_____	☐	☐	☐	_____
Cabinets/Counters	☐	☐	☐	_____	☐	☐	☐	_____

Tenant's Initials (_____)(_____)   Tenant's Initials (_____)(_____)

Landlord's Initials (_____)(_____)   Landlord's Initials (_____)(_____)

MIMO REVISED 11/07 (PAGE 3 OF 5)

Reviewed by _____ Date _____

EQUAL HOUSING OPPORTUNITY

MOVE IN / MOVE OUT INSPECTION (MIMO PAGE 3 OF 5)

Property Address: _____ Date: _____

| | **MOVE IN** | | | **MOVE OUT** | | | |
| | N | S | O | Comments | S | O | D | Comments |

Kitchen

	N	S	O	Comments	S	O	D	Comments
Flooring/Baseboards	☐	☐	☐	_____	☐	☐	☐	_____
Walls/Ceilings	☐	☐	☐	_____	☐	☐	☐	_____
Window Coverings	☐	☐	☐	_____	☐	☐	☐	_____
Windows/Locks/Screens	☐	☐	☐	_____	☐	☐	☐	_____
Light Fixtures	☐	☐	☐	_____	☐	☐	☐	_____
Switches/Outlets	☐	☐	☐	_____	☐	☐	☐	_____
Range/Fan/Hood	☐	☐	☐	_____	☐	☐	☐	_____
Oven(s)/Microwave	☐	☐	☐	_____	☐	☐	☐	_____
Refrigerator	☐	☐	☐	_____	☐	☐	☐	_____
Dishwasher	☐	☐	☐	_____	☐	☐	☐	_____
Sink/Disposal	☐	☐	☐	_____	☐	☐	☐	_____
Faucet(s)/Plumbing	☐	☐	☐	_____	☐	☐	☐	_____
Cabinets	☐	☐	☐	_____	☐	☐	☐	_____
Counters	☐	☐	☐	_____	☐	☐	☐	_____

_____
_____

Hall/Stairs

	N	S	O	Comments	S	O	D	Comments
Flooring/Baseboards	☐	☐	☐	_____	☐	☐	☐	_____
Walls/Ceilings	☐	☐	☐	_____	☐	☐	☐	_____
Light Fixtures	☐	☐	☐	_____	☐	☐	☐	_____
Switches/Outlets	☐	☐	☐	_____	☐	☐	☐	_____
Closets/Cabinets	☐	☐	☐	_____	☐	☐	☐	_____
Railings/Banisters	☐	☐	☐	_____	☐	☐	☐	_____

_____
_____

Laundry _____

	N	S	O	Comments	S	O	D	Comments
Faucets/Valves	☐	☐	☐	_____	☐	☐	☐	_____
Plumbing/Drains	☐	☐	☐	_____	☐	☐	☐	_____
Cabinets/Counters	☐	☐	☐	_____	☐	☐	☐	_____

_____
_____

Systems

	N	S	O	Comments	S	O	D	Comments
Furnace/Thermostat	☐	☐	☐	_____	☐	☐	☐	_____
Air Conditioning	☐	☐	☐	_____	☐	☐	☐	_____
Water Heater	☐	☐	☐	_____	☐	☐	☐	_____
Water Softener	☐	☐	☐	_____	☐	☐	☐	_____

Other _____

_____
_____
_____
_____
_____
_____
_____
_____
_____

Tenant's Initials (_____)(_____)   Tenant's Initials (_____)(_____)

Landlord's Initials (_____)(_____)   Landlord's Initials (_____)(_____)

MIMO REVISED 11/07 (PAGE 4 OF 5)

Reviewed by _____ Date _____

MOVE IN / MOVE OUT INSPECTION (MIMO PAGE 4 OF 5)

Property Address: _____   Date: _____

	MOVE IN				**MOVE OUT**			
	N	S	O	Comments	S	O	D	Comments

Garage/Parking

Garage Door	☐	☐	☐	_____	☐	☐	☐	_____
Other Door(s)	☐	☐	☐	_____	☐	☐	☐	_____
Driveway/Floor	☐	☐	☐	_____	☐	☐	☐	_____
Cabinets/Counters	☐	☐	☐	_____	☐	☐	☐	_____
Light Fixtures	☐	☐	☐	_____	☐	☐	☐	_____
Switches/Outlets	☐	☐	☐	_____	☐	☐	☐	_____
Electrical/Exposed Wiring	☐	☐	☐	_____	☐	☐	☐	_____
Window(s)	☐	☐	☐	_____	☐	☐	☐	_____
Other Storage/Shelving	☐	☐	☐	_____	☐	☐	☐	_____

_____

Back/Side/Yard

Patio/Deck/Balcony	☐	☐	☐	_____	☐	☐	☐	_____
Patio Cover(s)	☐	☐	☐	_____	☐	☐	☐	_____
Landscaping	☐	☐	☐	_____	☐	☐	☐	_____
Sprinklers/Timers	☐	☐	☐	_____	☐	☐	☐	_____
Pool/Heater/Equipment	☐	☐	☐	_____	☐	☐	☐	_____
Spa/Cover/Equipment	☐	☐	☐	_____	☐	☐	☐	_____
Fences/Gates	☐	☐	☐	_____	☐	☐	☐	_____

_____

Safety/Security

Smoke/CO Detector(s)	☐	☐	☐	_____	☐	☐	☐	_____
Security System	☐	☐	☐	_____	☐	☐	☐	_____
Security Window Bars	☐	☐	☐	_____	☐	☐	☐	_____

_____

Personal Property

_____

Keys/Remotes/Devices

Keys _____

Remotes/Devices _____

☐ **Attached Supplement(s)** _____

THIS SECTION TO BE COMPLETED AT MOVE IN: Receipt of a copy of this form is acknowledged by:

Tenant _____ Date _____

Tenant _____ Date _____

New Phone Service Established? ☐ Yes ☐ No   New Phone Number _____

Landlord (Owner or Agent) _____ Date _____

Landlord _____

     (Print Name)

THIS SECTION TO BE COMPLETED AT MOVE OUT: Receipt of a copy of this form is acknowledged by:

Tenant _____ Date _____

Tenant _____ Date _____

Tenant Forwarding Address _____

_____

Landlord (Owner or Agent) _____ Date _____

Landlord _____

     (Print Name)

Published and Distributed by:
REAL ESTATE BUSINESS SERVICES, INC.
a subsidiary of the California Association of REALTORS®
525 South Virgil Avenue, Los Angeles, California 90020

MIMO REVISED 11/07 (PAGE 5 OF 5)

Reviewed by _____ Date _____   EQUAL HOUSING OPPORTUNITY

MOVE IN / MOVE OUT INSPECTION (MIMO PAGE 5 OF 5)

clause that says the landlord will not unreasonably withhold approval of an assignment. The tenant might also request language stating that the landlord won't impose a fee or penalty for an assignment.

Rules. A significant portion of the lease agreement will likely be devoted to explaining the rules that apply to the tenant's activities and use of the premises. Some of these rules and regulations are imposed by federal, state, or local law; others are management policies. Violation of the rules constitutes a breach of the lease and may be cause for eviction.

As we explained in Chapter 7, the tenant can't use the property for illegal activities; for instance, she can't run a drug lab out of her home. In addition, the lease almost always limits the use of the premises to residential purposes only. So even if local zoning regulations allowed the premises to be used as an auto repair shop or beauty salon, for example, the tenant still could not do so.

Maintenance. The lease should set forth any maintenance tasks the tenant is expected to handle. In a single-family home, this might include mowing the lawn and other yardwork. If the tenant's duties exceed what would be considered normal, the manager should carefully go over the requirements with the tenant at the lease signing or even earlier.

Possession. The date on which the lease term begins is usually also the date on which the tenant takes possession. If, for some reason, the premises aren't ready for the tenant on the promised date, the owner will probably need to compensate the tenant for any resulting costs incurred by the tenant (such as a hotel bill or storage facility costs).

Entry and inspection. The tenant's right of possession must be balanced against the landlord's right to entry. A lease typically provides for inspection of the leased premises by the manager during the lease term, under specified conditions. As a general rule, a residential tenant may not unreasonably refuse the manager's legitimate requests to enter the unit to inspect it, perform repairs, provide other agreed-upon services, or show the unit to prospective buyers or tenants.

The state's residential landlord-tenant act typically spells out how much notice a residential landlord must give before entering the premises. For example, for a routine repair the landlord might have to give a tenant at least 48 hours' notice before entering. On the other hand, no notice to the tenant is necessary if the landlord must enter the premises to address an emergency, such as a broken water pipe.

Pets. Most managers would probably prefer to prohibit pets in their rental units, due to the potential for noise, damage, and hassle. However, the reality is that a significant percentage of prospective tenants own pets, and excluding them can dramatically reduce the number of potential renters.

Fair housing laws require managers to allow service animals. Although most people think of service animals as dogs, some jurisdictions have expanded the definition of "service animal" to include cats, birds, and other animals.

Whether or not tenants are permitted to keep pets, the lease should have a clause spelling out what is and isn't allowed. Some apartment buildings don't even allow visiting animals on the premises; if this is the case, it should be clearly stated in the lease.

Pet Policies

Buildings that allow pets need a pet policy. The policy should specify which species (and possibly breeds) of animals are permitted, and place a maximum on the number of animals each tenant can keep. Size and weight restrictions may be imposed as well. Animals should be vaccinated and licensed as required by law, and the owners may be required to carry renter's insurance that covers pet damage and liability for pet-caused injuries. Tenants should be required to clean up after their animals and to keep them confined or restrained when appropriate (for example, dogs must be leashed in common areas). Finally, the landlord should ask for an additional damage deposit for each pet to cover any repairs or extra cleaning that may be needed after the tenant moves out.

Although it's not legally necessary, for larger properties it may be a good idea to establish a leash-free pet exercise area. Providing a separate, enclosed area for tenants to let their animals run around unfettered can help minimize cleanup and leash enforcement issues in other common areas of the property.

Lease Renewals

The time and effort required to market, show, and rent out a unit can be avoided if the existing tenant renews her lease for another term. The manager can take steps to encourage tenants to renew. A few months before the current lease expires, the manager might send the tenant a renewal notice explaining any changes in rent or lease terms, and include a copy of a new lease. To offset the impact of any rent increase, the manager might offer to upgrade the unit in some manner. For example, he might install new carpeting or repaint the bathrooms.

Residential Operations

Now we'll turn to a few aspects of day-to-day operations. In this section, we'll discuss how to staff a residential building. We'll also make some comments about the maintenance, including the preparing of units for new tenants.

Staffing

The size and organization of staff needed to complete a property's operational tasks will depend, naturally, on the size and type of property being managed. While management of a small apartment building can often be handled by a single off-site manager, in a larger property, a full-time resident manager and additional maintenance staff may be necessary.

Resident Managers. Property owners often opt to hire resident managers who live on-site and handle certain management tasks in exchange for reduced or free rent. If the resident manager has basic maintenance skills, she can save the owner a significant amount of money by handling jobs that would otherwise require a service call by a plumber, electrician, or handyman. A manager who lives on-site is also often better able to enforce parking, pet, noise, and other policies. This system benefits tenants as well; they appreciate having a resident manager who can respond to complaints and maintenance requests quickly and around the clock.

In some situations, state law may require that a resident manager be present. For example, in California a residential building with 16 or more units must have a resident manager.

Because resident managers may need to interact with tenants on a fairly personal level—for example, by entering residences or responding to maintenance requests at odd hours—persons hired in this position should have good interpersonal skills.

Maintenance Staff. Every residential property has maintenance needs: common areas must be kept clean, landscaping tended, and light bulbs changed. With a smaller property, maintenance can often be handled by a single person. However, in a larger residential property, some or all of the maintenance tasks require janitorial and maintenance personnel. Whether on-site or outsourced staff is more appropriate depends on the tasks and costs involved.

Generally, it's less expensive and easier to control projects undertaken by employed staff. Certain exceptions exist, however. For example, while routine lawnmowing is easily handled by an on-staff maintenance person, it may be a good idea to have major seasonal cleanup, significant plantings, or other landscaping projects performed by a professional.

Other Staff. Aside from a resident manager and maintenance crew, a variety of other management staff may be required. Larger apartment buildings often employ front desk attendants and security staff; upscale properties may have doormen and concierges.

Maintenance

Residential properties often offer a variety of amenities and facilities. Many larger complexes have exercise rooms and equipment, as well as swimming pools with hot tubs and saunas. Some properties also have outdoor recreational areas, such as patios, picnic areas, playgrounds, tennis courts, and gardens. Generally, tenants can use these facilities for no additional charge.

Other amenities are offered to tenants for a fee, such as parking spaces, storage units, and laundry rooms. Vending machines and indoor or outdoor spaces that can be reserved for events can also be used to generate income.

Obviously, the more amenities a property has, the greater the maintenance needs. The landlord takes that into account when deciding whether to offer an amenity or determining a fee, if any, for its use.

The maintenance tasks required for a residential property vary widely depending on the property's size, type, and location. The maintenance requirements for a high-rise apartment building with a large lobby and several elevators differ dramatically from those of a small one-story garden apartment building. Climate also plays a role. In some areas of the country, snow and ice removal from driveways and walkways is a major concern in winter; in other areas, the summer months mean daily pool maintenance.

Regardless of these differences, all residential properties have some common maintenance concerns. The grounds must be kept tidy, and common areas kept clean and well-lighted. Individual units must have functioning heating systems, and appliances and plumbing must be kept in working order. For further discussion of specific maintenance tasks, see Chapter 9.

Preparing Units for New Tenants. One significant maintenance task is preparing a unit for a new tenant. The size of the unit, the length of time the previous tenant resided there, and the condition in which she left the unit all affect how much of an undertaking this project is.

Before a tenant moves out, the parties must complete the move-out portion of the move-in/move-out checklist. (See Figure 10.2 for an example of this checklist.) The manager can use the comment section to note issues that must be addressed before the new tenant moves in. If necessary, the manager can create a separate list of action items for the unit. (See Figure 10.3.) For instance, all plumbing, heating systems, appliances, light fixtures, and smoke alarms must be in working condition before the new tenant moves in. The walls are typically repainted between tenants and, if the previous tenancy lasted more than a few years, it may be time to replace the carpet and window coverings. Even if the unit is in good condition, cosmetic upgrades, such as replacing kitchen or bathroom fixtures, may be a good idea.

Working with Residential Tenants

Of course, one of a residential property manager's main functions is to act as a liaison between the owner and tenants. Here we'll discuss some ways a residential manager can communicate with her tenants. We'll also discuss issues concerning rent collection, tenant complaints, and lease agreement violations.

Communicating with Tenants

Residential property managers use a variety of methods to communicate with individual tenants, make general announcements, and receive complaints and suggestions. Monthly newsletters are a simple and inexpensive way to update tenants about the property or remind them of rules or coming changes. Email newsletters cost less than a print version, but a print version may get more attention. The manager should not email a tenant unless the tenant has consented to receiving this form of communication. Website postings are an easy way to impart general information to tenants, although the manager can't count on tenants visiting the site.

As far as tenant complaints and suggestions go, tenants should always be able to reach a property manager by phone. In addition, an increasingly common method for this sort of communication is email. Of course, some managers opt to use the tried-and-true suggestion

Figure 10.3 Unit preparation checklist

Rental Unit Preparation Checklist and Report

Property: _The Sarasota_   **Initial inspection date:** _September 6_

Bldg & Unit: _C-309_   **Inspected by:** _L. Baumann_

Date vacated: _August 31_   **Occupancy date:** _October 1_

Reinspected and approved by: _____

Tasks	Done ✓	Work Needed	Done ✓	Approved ✓
Doors				
Keys and locks work smoothly				
Doors unwarped, close properly; lubricate hinges if needed				
Thresholds and stripping: in good condition, properly affixed				
Windows				
Windows slide or open easily; lubricate if needed				
Panes: undamaged; wash insides, note whether outsides need washing				
Screens: no tears, proper fit				
Blinds: check operation, untangle cords				
Clean blinds, tracks, and sills				
Remove any drapes left behind				
Walls & Ceilings				
Paint: check for peeling or discoloration; repainting needed?				
Plaster: no cracks or holes, no damage to taped seams				
Baseboards and moldings: clean and firmly affixed				
Dust to remove cobwebs				
Floors				
Flooring: no cracks, burns, or other damage; replacement or refinishing needed?				
Clean and polish all flooring as appropriate for type				
Carpeting: not damaged or worn; replacement needed?				
Vacuum carpeting; shampoo if needed, and/or treat any stains				

Tasks	Done ✓	Work Needed	Done ✓	Approved ✓
Kitchen & Appliances				
All appliances: check operation and condition and note if replacement necessary; if not, wash exterior and interior				
Stove: check burners for smoking, replace burner pans, clean oven				
Microwave: use radiation detector to check for leakage				
Refrigerator: deodorize interior, check operation of icemaker				
Dishwasher: run full cycle to check operation				
Washer/dryer: run cycle; check dryer hose, lint screen for damage				
Sink: run disposal; check water pressure, faucet drips, and drain				
Shelves and cupboards empty, clean; cupboard doors shut well				
Countertops: no scorching or other damage; wash surfaces, clean edge stripping				
Bathroom(s)				
Disinfect all surfaces and fixtures				
Check condition of tiles, grout				
Toilet: check flushing and filling; examine base for leakage; tighten seat bolts, flushing handle				
Basin and tub: check for dripping faucets, rust stains; clear drains; discard shower curtain if left				
Towel racks, grab bars, toilet paper holder, soap dish: firmly affixed, clean				
Clean mirrors, medicine cabinet				
Electrical & HVAC				
Lighting fixtures: check operation, replace all bulbs				
Switches, outlets: clean and tighten face plates				
Heaters: check functioning; thermostats, vents, registers				
Air conditioning: check functioning; clean or replace filter				
Replace smoke detector batteries				

box placed in the building lobby. The manager may also periodically distribute surveys to tenants.

Rent Issues

Residential managers rarely send out regular rent bills, as the rent amount is usually the same each month. Rent payments must be made in the form and manner stated in the lease agreement. Whatever form the rent payments take—cash, personal checks, or electronic funds transfer—the manager handles them in accordance with state laws governing trust funds. As always, it's important to keep good records and provide regular reports to the owner.

From time to time, a tenant may want to deduct money from rent as compensation for a broken appliance. A tenant may also want reimbursement for purchasing supplies or performing a repair or maintenance task normally handled by management. However, deductions complicate recordkeeping, so generally, it's best to insist that such matters be handled separately from rent payments. (We'll discuss the repair and deduct issue in greater detail in the next section.) As we stated in Chapter 9, managers should discourage tenants from handling repairs because of problems with recordkeeping, cost, and quality.

Collecting rent also means handling occasional rent delinquencies. This job entails sending out late notices as well as collecting late fees. Remember that any steps a manager takes to collect overdue rent payments must comply with applicable state and federal laws regulating collection efforts. For example, the federal Fair Debt Collection Practices Act, among other things, restricts the hours during which collection calls can be made. It also allows the debtor to specify times and places that she cannot be contacted at all. Although this law only applies to third party "debt collectors" (such as a collection agency hired by a manager), some states have similar laws that regulate collection efforts by an original creditor (including a landlord and his agent, the property manager).

Breach of the Lease Agreement

What happens if the landlord or the tenant breaches the lease agreement? If a residential landlord breaches a lease provision, the tenant has a number of options. State residential landlord-tenant law often governs the specifics of these remedies, imposing notice requirements and other limitations.

- **Repair and deduct.** If a tenant gives a landlord notice of a problem and the landlord fails to repair it, the tenant may have the repair work performed professionally and deduct the cost of the repair from the next month's rent. The tenant usually must wait for the landlord's repair deadline to expire (the deadline depends on the nature of the repair), and also provide the landlord with the contractor's estimate before having the repairs made. There is often a dollar limit on the amount that the tenant can spend and deduct in this way. (In many states the limit is one month's rent per repair, and a certain number of repairs per year.)
- **Self repair.** The self repair remedy is similar to the repair and deduct remedy, but the tenant undertakes the work herself rather than hiring a contractor. The tenant

must provide a written estimate beforehand and allow the landlord to inspect the work after completion. The tenant can be held liable for any work that does not meet code requirements.

- **Depositing rent into an escrow account.** If a landlord refuses to make a repair, the tenant may opt to pay rent into an escrow account until the landlord takes care of the repair. The tenant must give the landlord proper notice when using the escrow remedy. Once the landlord has made the necessary repairs, she can apply to the court for release of the escrowed rent funds. Escrow procedures are complicated, however, so a tenant considering the escrow remedy should contact a landlord-tenant attorney before proceeding.
- **Vacating the premises.** If the landlord fails to address a critical issue, the tenant can terminate the lease agreement and move out after giving written notice to the landlord. State law determines the amount of notice required. The landlord must refund any prepaid rent as well as any security deposit (or provide a written accounting for any deposit amount withheld).
- **Filing a lawsuit or entering arbitration.** The tenant can sue the landlord and seek a court order requiring the landlord to fulfill the terms of the lease. However, some leases state that a party with a dispute must first submit the issue to **arbitration** (a binding hearing conducted by a private individual, often a retired judge). Alternatively, a tenant may voluntarily choose arbitration, since it's faster and cheaper than going to court. Note that many leases provide that the prevailing party will be reimbursed for her attorney fees, regardless of whether arbitration or a court is used.

On the other hand, if the tenant fails to fulfill her obligations under the lease, the landlord's chief remedy is to evict the tenant. To protect residential tenants, state laws impose a number of requirements on a landlord who wants to evict someone. The manager can't simply lock the tenant out, for example. Instead, she must follow detailed legal procedures spelled out in the state's eviction statute. (We'll discuss the eviction process in detail in the next section.)

Fair Housing Considerations

Every residential property manager must be familiar with the requirements of the federal Fair Housing Act and other federal and state fair housing laws. We discuss these rules in Chapter 14, but we'll briefly outline some of their requirements here.

Disabled Tenants. Under the federal Fair Housing Act, a residential landlord must allow a disabled tenant to make reasonable modifications to the property at the tenant's expense, so long as the modifications are necessary for the tenant's full use and enjoyment of the premises. (The tenant can be required to restore the premises to their original condition at the end of the tenancy.) Landlords must also make reasonable exceptions to their rules to accommodate disabled tenants. For example, even if landlords forbid pets, they can't refuse to rent to someone with a guide dog.

Familial Status. Discrimination on the basis of familial status refers to discrimination against a person because he has a child (under 18 years old) living with him. Parents, legal guardians, pregnant women, and those in the process of obtaining custody of a child are protected against housing discrimination on the basis of their familial status.

While the Fair Housing Act makes it unlawful to discriminate in renting because the applicant is pregnant or lives with a child, the manager can make a rental decision based on whether the family's size would mean the number of occupants in the unit would exceed the limit set by local law.

"Adults only" apartment or condominium complexes are forbidden, as are complexes divided into "adult" and "family" areas. However, the law includes an exemption for properties that qualify as housing for older persons. See Chapter 14 for details.

The reality is that families with children—like many categories of renters—can present certain challenges (mainly noise issues and safety concerns). While it can be a good idea to institute policies addressing these issues (for example, "quiet hours" between 9:00 PM and 8:00 AM), the manager must draft these policies fairly and enforce them uniformly.

Tenant Complaints and Tenant Unions

Of course, keeping tenants happy is central to the property manager's job. A big part of what makes tenants happy is a manager who keeps the property clean and in good repair, and who responds promptly and professionally to requests and complaints. Generally, one on-site manager can do a good job of handling tenants for about 50 units. If the manager tries to handle more, the quality of service suffers. This means tenant dissatisfaction, which sooner or later leads to loss of rent revenue.

Poor responses to tenant requests can also lead to the formation of tenant unions. These organizations sometimes form in response to a particular incident, but can also grow out of a more generalized discontent with conditions in a building. Once a union forms, its demands can be difficult to deal with. It's best to create an environment where tenants feel no need to band together against management. Good communication with residents and prompt responses to maintenance and repair requests go a long way toward preventing discontent.

Unfortunately, at one point or another even the best-run property has a tenant who seems impossible to satisfy. In most cases, the manager can do little besides carefully document the difficulties with the tenant as they arise. This helps provide a defense in case the tenant later claims the refusal to renew her lease is illegal discrimination.

Handling Residential Security Deposits

Most state residential landlord-tenant acts place significant restrictions on how a landlord handles security deposits. For instance, a written, signed rental agreement is generally required before the manager can collect a security deposit from the tenant. The rental agreement often serves as the written receipt for the deposit. It acknowledges that the landlord has collected the specified dollar amount as security for the tenant's performance under the terms of the agreement.

Some states limit the size of a security deposit to the amount of one month's rent. Security deposit refunds may also be subject to a deadline, as discussed below.

Certain states require security deposits be held in trust accounts, while other states simply require the landlord to provide the tenant with the name and address of the bank where the deposit will be held. If received by a property manager, deposits should be delivered to the owner or placed in a trust account in accordance with state law. Many states require the landlord to pay interest to the tenant; some even specify a minimum interest rate.

When the Tenancy Ends

Within two to three weeks after the tenant moves out (depending on state law), the landlord must do one of two things. He must either refund the entire deposit or provide a written itemized statement of repair expenses and unpaid rent amounts that were deducted from the deposit, plus any remaining refund.

The landlord can use the deposit to cover only the damage that exceeds normal wear and tear. For example, using deposit funds to replace old carpet or repaint faded walls is not allowed. However, paying to repair broken windows or fix holes in the wall is a legitimate use of the tenant's security deposit, as long as the damage was caused by the tenant.

The property manager should keep a copy of all repair bills and be prepared to provide copies to the tenant upon request. (Some states require managers to give copies of repair bills to the tenant along with the initial notice of deduction.)

A landlord who fails to return the tenant's security deposit (or to provide written documentation of the amounts deducted) within the mandatory time limit may end up paying the tenant more than just the amount of the original deposit. Many states add penalties to the past-due amounts. Some state laws provide for treble damages; that is, if the landlord failed to refund the tenant's $1,000 deposit, he could end up owing the tenant $3,000.

Sale of the Property. Residential landlord-tenant acts spell out what happens to deposits when ownership of a property changes hands. When a rental property is sold (including

---

 ### *"Useful Life" Rule*

While a landlord can't deduct normal wear and tear from a security deposit, he can deduct a percentage of the replacement cost if the tenant has created damage over and above the normal wear and tear of an item. The landlord calculates the amount of the deduction according to the "useful life" rule.

Let's see how this rule works. Suppose tenant Jerry burns a large hole in the living room window's custom drapes. The drapes are three years old, and are already showing signs of age. Their expected useful life is only eight years. The drapes cannot be repaired, and it will cost $1,200 to replace them. The landlord can deduct $750 from the tenant's security deposit, which represents the five remaining years of useful life of the drapes (5/8 × $1,200 = $750).

by foreclosure), the original owner must either transfer the tenant's security deposit to the new owner through the escrow process, or return the deposit to the tenant. In the latter case, the new owner will then collect a new security deposit from the tenant.

If the deposit is transferred to a new owner, the seller must give the tenant written notice of the transfer, along with the new owner's name, address, and telephone number. If a new property manager will be handling the tenant's funds, the manager's name, address, and phone number should also be included in the notice. When the tenancy ends, the tenant should recover her deposit from the new owner. If the original owner failed to transfer the deposit or return it, the tenant can generally sue the original owner for the funds.

Some states allow the seller to keep the security deposit funds instead of transferring them at closing, in order to cover property damage and/or unpaid rent. The seller then either refunds the remaining balance to the tenant or transfers the balance to the new owner. In either case, of course, the seller must give written notice explaining the amounts deducted. In addition, if transferring the remainder of a deposit to the new owner, the notice explaining the deductions must include the name, address, and telephone number of the new owner.

> **Example:** John buys a 12-unit apartment building from Sharon. Before the sale closes, John orders an inspection of the building. The inspector finds serious tenant-caused damage to one of the units, and John asks Sharon to have the repairs made before closing. Sharon has the work done and deducts $845 from the tenant's $1,500 security deposit. She transfers the $655 balance to John and provides the tenant with an itemized description of charges for the repairs, together with John's name, address, and telephone number.

Managing Specific Types of Residential Property

Throughout this chapter, we've focused primarily on management of multi-unit rental properties—apartment buildings and complexes. We'll end the chapter with a look at some issues that arise in management of other types of residential property.

Single-Family Homes

A significant portion of the rental market consists of single-family homes. Property managers often handle rental homes for owners who either live out of town or who are first-time investors and feel uncomfortable or uninterested in managing property.

A manager often spends considerably more time managing single-family homes than he does managing an equivalent number of apartments. That's primarily because the homes are spread out geographically. Transit time adds up whenever the manager needs to show a property or respond to a tenant's request for repairs. Maintaining the grounds and buildings of various individual properties is also far more time-consuming than maintaining these elements in a single apartment complex.

On the other hand, single-family home renters tend to be less transient than apartment renters. The longer tenancies mean less time spent on marketing and leasing tasks. In addition, single-family homes often have significantly higher rent than comparably sized apartment units; higher rents usually translate into higher management fees.

What Counts as a Single-Family Home?

Residential property managers often categorize duplexes, triplexes, and town-homes (multi-story homes built closely together, sometimes sharing common walls) as "single-family homes." This categorization makes sense because the management considerations for these types of dwellings tend to be closer to those of single-family homes than those of larger apartment buildings.

Common Interest Developments

Common interest developments (CIDs) are residential developments in which each resident owns her own unit (or has a proprietary lease to it) and also holds a shared interest in the common areas. Examples include condominiums, cooperatives, and planned unit developments. Common interest developments provide alternatives to ownership of a traditional single-family home. They have become popular because of their efficient use of increasingly valuable land.

Common interest developments usually have a **community association** (sometimes called an owners association or homeowners association) that often employs a part-time or full-time property manager. The manager may be known as a **community association manager**.

In this section, we'll discuss the different types of CIDs and different tasks associated with community association management. Remember, though, that CIDs are resident-owned property, not income-generating property. Some units may be rented out, but the property manager's duties will still differ significantly from those involved in managing income-producing property.

Types of CIDs. There are three main types of CIDs: condominiums, cooperatives, and planned unit developments.

Condominiums. Someone who buys a unit in a condominium owns the unit itself in severalty, but shares ownership of the common elements with other unit owners as tenants in common. **Common elements** (also called common areas) are aspects of the condominium property that all of the unit owners have the right to use, such as the driveway, lobby, courtyard, or elevator. The land itself, the roof, and any recreational facilities such as a swimming pool are also considered common elements.

Some features may be designated as **limited common elements**, which are reserved for the owners of certain units. For example, an assigned parking space would be a limited common element. A feature such as a balcony, which is designed for use with a particular unit but is outside of the unit itself, would also be a limited common element.

Each unit owner obtains separate financing to buy his unit, receives an individual property tax bill, and may acquire a title insurance policy for the unit. A lien can attach to a single unit, so that the unit can be foreclosed on separately without affecting the other units in the condominium.

The condominium is managed by the **owners association**, which collects regular and special assessments from each owner for the maintenance, repair, and insurance of the common elements. (The regular assessments, often collected on a monthly basis, are sometimes called condo fees or dues.) Every unit owner is a member in the association. Management decisions are made by an elected board of directors.

A unit owner may occupy her unit herself, or rent to a tenant. Either way, only owners—not renters—can be members of the association and participate in elections.

Cooperatives. The residents of a cooperative building don't own their units (a nonprofit corporation does). Instead, the residents own shares in the corporation and have long-term proprietary leases on their units. The corporation that owns the cooperative may employ a property manager to handle the property.

To establish a cooperative, the corporation obtains a mortgage loan to buy or construct the building, and other funds are raised by selling shares in the corporation to prospective tenants. The rent that each tenant pays to the corporation is a pro rata share of the mortgage, taxes, operating expenses, and other debts for the whole property. The cooperative corporation is managed by an elected board of directors. If one tenant defaults on her share of the mortgage payments, the other tenants must make up the difference or risk having the mortgage on the entire project foreclosed. This is also true for tax assessments and other liens.

In some cooperatives, a tenant cannot transfer stock or assign his proprietary lease to a new tenant without the consent of the governing board or a majority of the members. This approval process is used to screen out undesirable tenants; however, discrimination in violation of fair housing laws is not allowed.

Most cooperatives were created in large eastern cities during the first half of the twentieth century, before the condominium form of ownership had been developed. Nowadays, when a multi-family building is constructed as (or converted to) a common interest development, it's much more likely to be a condominium than a cooperative.

Planned unit developments. In a planned unit development (PUD), a buyer purchases a single-family home and the parcel of land on which it is located, along with a shared interest in the development's common areas. These parcels may be relatively small, in order to maximize the space available for common areas; in fact, housing density may be twice that of a typical subdivision.

A PUD's common areas might include a park or other open areas, a swimming pool or other recreational facilities, and even a retail shopping area. As in condominium developments, owners in a PUD belong to a homeowners association and are typically subject to numerous restrictions in the form of CC&Rs (covenants, conditions, and restrictions).

Managing a CID. The needs of a smaller community interest development may be simple enough that professional management isn't necessary. However, CIDs with more than a few units generally require professional management. The association consists of individual unit owners—not financial or real estate professionals—who may have neither the knowledge nor the inclination to handle long-term budgeting, large-scale repairs, and other issues.

The community association may hire a property manager as a part- or full-time employee; alternatively, a property manager may be retained as a consultant. Some states have special licensing requirements for community association managers; elsewhere, a real estate license (or no license at all) is needed. The Community Associations Institute offers a Professional Community Association Manager designation that can be earned by completing certain education and experience requirements.

The manager's role varies greatly depending on the type, size, and needs of a particular CID. However, her primary tasks usually mirror those of a multi-unit property manager: overseeing the property's operations and maintenance, collecting monthly assessments and paying bills, accounting, enforcing rules, and handling complaints from residents. Often, the manager helps market units that are up for sale (or helps lease units on behalf of their owners). A community association manager can also assist with long-range budgeting.

> **Example:** Most condominium associations maintain a reserve fund to help cover costs of major repairs or improvements, such as roof replacement or central heating repairs. The association funds the reserve account with monthly assessments. When the assessment amount is adjusted, typically on an annual basis, the manager can help determine an amount that will ensure adequate reserves.

Management fees. A community association may compensate its manager in a number of ways. One common compensation structure is a base monthly salary plus fees for providing additional after-hours services, such as attending board meetings or handling emergency maintenance issues. On the other hand, it usually makes sense to pay part-time managers an hourly rate.

Manufactured Home Parks

Over the last few decades, manufactured homes (sometimes called mobile homes) have evolved from house-trailers in trailer parks to modern manufactured homes: large factory-built structures that can be transported to a full-sized lot and permanently installed. Once placed, a manufactured home can be virtually indistinguishable from a conventional home. Nevertheless, residential zoning often prohibits placing manufactured homes in neighborhoods of traditionally constructed houses, so many manufactured homes are still located in manufactured home parks. Some of these parks are designated "senior communities" or "retirement communities" and marketed accordingly; this doesn't violate fair housing laws as long as the park meets the accepted definition for housing for the elderly.

Typically, manufactured home park residents own their home, but rent the site on which the home is placed. (In some areas, it's more common for a tenant to rent both the mobile home and the site.) The park usually employs an on-site property manager to handle leasing, rent collection, maintenance, and other general property management tasks. Other duties depend on the mix of residents; for example, if the park has a large number of families, the manager may be responsible for planning community activities or maintaining a clubhouse or playground.

Leasing a space in a manufactured home park obviously differs from leasing other residential property. When a tenant moves, finding a new space to lease and physically moving the home can be difficult and costly. For this reason, many states have special manufactured/mobile home landlord-tenant laws that govern lease agreements and other aspects of the landlord-tenant relationship; a manufactured home park manager should be very familiar with any such law that applies in her state. Eviction procedures, notice requirements, and other rules often differ from the requirements that apply to other residential tenants.

In addition, state law may impose restrictions on a landlord who wants to close a manufactured home park or convert it to another use. For example, the landlord may be required to give tenants up to a year's notice of plans to close the park.

Subsidized Housing

The term **subsidized housing** refers to residential rental property for lower-income tenants whose rent is subsidized by the government. Subsidized housing may be either public housing or government-assisted housing.

Public Housing. Public housing is owned and managed directly by a government body, such as a city or county housing authority. Some public housing consists of single-family homes, but the majority is multi-unit buildings. A prospective tenant applies directly to the local housing authority; rental units are offered to eligible applicants as they become available. The tenant signs a lease agreement with the housing authority and may need to put down a security deposit.

Government-Assisted Housing. This type of housing is privately owned and managed, but a portion of the tenant's rent is paid by a government agency. A variety of federal, state, and local housing assistance programs exist, but the largest federal program is the housing choice voucher program. In this program, an eligible renter receives a voucher from the local housing authority and then locates a suitable rental unit whose owner will accept the voucher. The tenant must pay the difference between the actual rent charged and the amount subsidized by the government program.

Management of subsidized housing can present some unique challenges. The manager must understand the requirements of the housing program in which the property is participating, be familiar with an array of specialized housing regulations, and be comfortable dealing with housing authorities and other government agencies. The manager is often responsible for screening lease applicants to ensure that their income levels meet the requirements for eligibility, as well as recertifying current tenants on a regular basis. Typically, the manager must submit a number of forms and reports to the appropriate housing authority or agency throughout the year.

At the same time, the manager must still perform the usual tasks associated with managing residential property—usually within a smaller budget that reflects the reduced amount of rental income. Additional financial pressure stems from the fact that subsidized housing is often more densely populated, and this can translate into higher maintenance and security costs. Subsidized housing also tends to have higher turnover rates and collection costs. However, investment in this kind of property can pay off for some owners.

Housing for the Elderly

As the U.S.'s population ages and baby boomers retire, senior housing communities are rapidly growing in popularity. As mentioned earlier in this chapter, a residential housing complex can be designated as seniors housing without violating fair housing laws, as long as the housing meets certain requirements. (See Chapter 14.)

A variety of types of housing for the elderly exists. Some developments, known as independent living communities, offer individual residences and a variety of recreational amenities; they are geared toward active retirees looking for security and social interactions. Other properties, known as assisted living facilities, are intended for those who need nursing, personal care, food preparation, and other support services. Some developments include both kinds of housing.

Management of housing for the elderly often requires providing a range of services different from (or in addition to) the services provided in other types of residential management. For example, food preparation and transportation services may be offered, as well as recreational activities, housekeeping, and medical services. Management may spend a significant amount of time handling medical emergencies and communicating with tenants' families. In addition, state and federal governments closely regulate housing for the elderly; the property manager must be familiar with the regulations and ready for periodic inspections or audits.

Chapter Summary

1. The largest category of residential property under professional management is multi-family apartment buildings, which includes smaller traditional buildings, mid-rise buildings, high-rises, garden apartments, and converted lofts.

2. Residential management planning requires creating a management plan and developing an operating budget. Most residential managers use a net operating income budget format.

3. Residential properties are marketed using print ads (in newspapers and For Rent magazines), Internet ads (on classified sites and dedicated websites), model units and rental centers, and leasing agents. All advertising must comply with fair housing laws. Maintaining the property's curb appeal (exterior appearance) is also important to the leasing effort.

4. Residential managers use standardized lease application forms to gather information about applicants' rental history, credit history, income, and employment. This information, along with credit and background checks, is used to screen applicants and select tenants.

5. Residential lease agreements generally contain provisions addressing the parties, lease term, payment of rent, security deposit, utilities, maintenance responsibilities, entry and inspection of the property, and management rules.

6. The number of staff persons needed to operate a residential property depends on the size and type of property. Some buildings may need only a single off-site manager; others require resident managers, maintenance staff, front desk attendants, and security personnel.

7. Maintenance staff may have to clean the public areas of an apartment building, such as lobbies, on a daily basis. Other tasks such as snow removal are seasonal.

8. The manager acts as a liaison between the owner and tenants. The manager communicates with tenants, collects rent, enforces lease agreements, and handles tenant complaints.

9. When a residential tenancy ends, the security deposit must be returned to the tenant along with a written itemization of any amounts withheld. If the rented property is sold or foreclosed, the deposit is either returned to the tenant or transferred to the new owner.

10. Other types of property commonly under professional management include single-family homes, common interest developments (condominiums, cooperatives, and planned unit developments), manufactured home parks, subsidized housing, and housing for the elderly.

Key Terms

Bad debt and vacancy factor – In an operating budget, a percentage deduction that accounts for losses in income due to vacancies and difficulties collecting rent.

Net operating income budget – A budget format that lists potential gross income, effective gross income, and expenses, before providing a projected net operating income.

Model unit – A furnished and decorated rental unit kept in show-ready condition for prospective renters to tour.

Rental center – A space dedicated to marketing activities such as distributing information and materials and meeting with prospective renters.

Leasing agent – A trained salesperson hired specifically to help with marketing and leasing activities.

Curb appeal – A building's exterior appearance.

Credit report – A report from one of the three major credit reporting agencies that summarizes an individual's loans, credit purchases, and debt repayment history.

Co-signor – Another party, such as a tenant's parent, who agrees to accept liability for any default by the tenant.

Term tenancy – A tenancy for a particular length of time, with a definite end date.

Periodic tenancy – A tenancy that automatically renews itself at the end of each period unless one party gives notice of termination.

Security deposit – A deposit from the tenant that gives the landlord some protection in the event that the tenant damages the property or fails to pay rent; security deposits are trust funds that must be handled in accordance with state law.

Resident manager – A property manager who resides on-site, often in exchange for reduced or free rent; may be required by state law for buildings of a certain size.

Uniform Residential Landlord and Tenant Act – A model landlord-tenant law created in an effort to provide some consistency in state and local residential landlord-tenant acts; many states have adopted it.

Implied warranty of habitability – A provision implied in every residential lease that the landlord will keep the leased premises fit for habitation. State residential landlord-tenant acts have generally codified the warranty into a set of requirements.

Common interest developments – Residential developments in which each resident owns her own unit (or has a proprietary lease to it) and also holds a shared interest in the common areas.

Community association – An association of owners in a common interest development that manages the development, often with the assistance of a professional property manager; also known as an owners association or homeowners association.

Condominium – A common interest development in which a unit owner owns her unit in severalty but shares ownership of the common areas with the other unit owners.

Cooperative – A common interest development in which ownership is held by a corporation; residents own shares in the corporation and hold proprietary long-term leases to their units.

Planned unit development – A common interest development consisting of individually-owned single-family homes and parcels, and shared common areas (such as parks and recreational facilities).

Public housing – Residential property owned and managed by a government body or agency.

Government-assisted housing – Privately owned and managed residential property where a government agency pays a portion of the tenants' rent.

Chapter Quiz

1. When warehouse space is converted into residential property, the units are known as:
   a) high-rises
   b) garden apartments
   c) lofts
   d) low-rise buildings

2. A cluster of low-rise apartment buildings in a suburban area, with a swimming pool and a recreation room, would be referred to as:
   a) garden apartments
   b) high-rise buildings
   c) mid-rise buildings
   d) lofts

3. In developing a management plan, a property manager researches the rental rates of similar units located nearby. This is known as a/an:
   a) property analysis
   b) market analysis
   c) analysis of alternatives
   d) neighborhood analysis

4. In the analysis of alternatives, the manager:
   a) researches regional and local employment trends
   b) considers the features and amenities of comparable rental units
   c) performs a cost-benefit analysis of proposed operational or physical changes to the property
   d) gathers information about the property's physical attributes and condition

5. A marketing method that is particularly useful for residential properties is a/an:
   a) For Rent magazine
   b) online classified ad
   c) rental center
   d) All of the above

6. If a lease applicant has minimal credit history but otherwise appears acceptable, the manager is likely to require a:
   a) co-signer
   b) sublease clause
   c) security deposit equal to six months' rent
   d) All of the above

7. The Fair Housing Act prohibition against discrimination on the basis of familial status would protect a/an _____ from housing discrimination.
   a) Unwed couple
   b) Pregnant woman
   c) Married couple who has their 19-year-old college student son living with them
   d) Tenant who uses a wheelchair and requires a first-floor apartment

8. When a property manager receives a security deposit, she must:
   a) keep the funds, in cash, in a locked safe in her office
   b) deliver the funds to the owner or deposit them into a trust account
   c) immediately deposit them into the building's operating account
   d) Any of the above

9. If a tenant transfers all of her remaining obligations under a lease to a new party, this is known as:
   a) assignment
   b) surrender
   c) abandonment
   d) eviction

10. Jim's lease states a beginning and an end date. He has what type of tenancy?
   a) Term
   b) Periodic
   c) Month-to-month
   d) Periodic term

11. Managers try to stagger lease terms in order to:
    a) satisfy state law
    b) spread out leasing tasks
    c) decrease maintenance requirements
    d) None of the above; managers avoid staggering lease terms

12. A prohibition against tenants running businesses out of their apartments would be found in the _____ provision.
    a) assignment
    b) entry and inspection
    c) renewal option
    d) use

13. Residential amenities might include:
    a) carpeted hallways
    b) renewal options
    c) free storage lockers
    d) Both B and C

14. A common interest development in which residents own shares in a corporation and hold long-term leases in their units is a:
    a) condominium
    b) cooperative
    c) planned unit development
    d) manufactured home park

15. A low-rise apartment complex that is owned and operated by a county housing authority would be classified as:
    a) government-assisted housing
    b) an assisted living facility
    c) an independent living community
    d) public housing

Answer Key

1. c)   Light industrial and warehouse space is sometimes converted into living spaces known as lofts.

2. a)   Garden apartments are low-rise suburban apartment complexes.

3. b)   In a market analysis, the manager locates comparable rental units and uses their rental rates to set a rent schedule for the subject property.

4. c)   The manager uses the analysis of alternatives to propose any changes to the property that he believes are appropriate.

5. d)   Print ads, online ads, and rental centers are all used in marketing residential properties.

6. a)   A co-signer is a third party (such as a parent) who will not reside in the unit, but signs the lease and agrees to accept liability for any default by the tenant.

7. b)   Familial status under the Fair Housing Act includes any adult with a child under age 18 living with him or her—and it includes a woman who is pregnant.

8. b)   Security deposits are trust funds and must be handled in accordance with state law, which usually requires delivery to the owner or deposit into a trust account.

9. a)   Lease agreements usually prohibit the tenant from assigning the lease without prior written consent.

10. a)   Term tenancies have a fixed beginning and end date. Periodic tenancies are ongoing; typically they run month-to-month.

11. b)   Staggering lease terms means that tasks such as showing apartments and screening candidates are spread throughout the year. The manager isn't overwhelmed by a mass of expiring leases.

12. d)   Most residential leases contain a use provision that limits the tenant to residential use of the premises.

13. c)   Amenities are nonessential services or enhancements to the property offered by a landlord. An option to renew might favor a tenant but it isn't considered an amenity.

14. b)   In a cooperative, the building is owned by the corporation.

15. d)   Public housing is a term used to describe residential housing that is owned and operated by a government body or agency.

Chapter 11

Managing Office Property

Outline

Introduction

In the last chapter, we examined residential property management. Now we're going to turn our attention to managing the various types of commercial property. Commercial property is any property that isn't residential; the category includes office buildings, stand-alone stores, shopping centers, factories, and warehouses. Because the management needs of these different kinds of commercial properties vary so greatly, we will discuss office property in this chapter, and retail property and industrial property in Chapters 12 and 13, respectively.

We'll begin by discussing office properties in general, and then we'll examine management planning and marketing. Next, we'll take a look at the process of tenant selection and lease negotiation. Finally, we'll end the chapter with a discussion of general operations, including security, maintenance needs, tenant relations, and reports to owners.

Types of Office Properties

Let's begin with an orientation about office buildings: where they're located, who owns them, and how they're classified.

Location of Office Space

When many people think of office property, they think of high-rise buildings that dominate a city's skyline, clustered together in the downtown core. For much of the twentieth century, most office space was indeed found in a city's **central business district** (CBD). However, the advent of the automobile and the freeway system changed that dramatically.

Today, metropolitan areas have multiple business centers, with clusters of medium-rise and even high-rise buildings located around regional transportation and shopping nodes (sometimes called edge cities). Much of the nation's recently constructed office space is found in these areas, or in office parks spread along suburban arterials. **Office parks** typically consist of several one- or two-story buildings clustered together on landscaped grounds. Tenants often include call centers or companies that need to combine both office and warehouse or light industrial space (office park zoning often allows light industrial use).

In cities, mixed-use buildings are increasingly common. These medium-rise or high-rise buildings typically have retail space on the ground floor facing the street, and office space on the floors above.

Methods of Ownership

Historically, small private investors (individuals or small business entities) owned most commercial investment property. That is still true today for many small- or medium-sized office buildings, particularly in suburban areas. However, the cost to construct and maintain high-rise structures has, for the most part, kept small investors from owning these types of buildings. Large investment syndicates now own most big multi-story office buildings, especially the towers found in central business districts.

Another ownership trend is the increasing popularity of office condominiums. Instead of renting space from commercial landlords, small businesses buy space within multi-story projects. This arrangement lets small businesses build equity and enjoy the benefits of ownership without the expenses associated with owning a freestanding building. On the other hand, these owners typically have to pay maintenance (or owners association) fees, which adds to the cost of condominium ownership. One drawback of office condominium ownership is that a business facing changing economic conditions may find it difficult or impossible to expand or decrease its space, something that is easier to do when leasing.

Classification of Office Buildings

The Building Owners and Managers Association (**BOMA**), a trade association for property managers, created widely-used classifications for different grades of office space. These classifications help managers market their properties better, and help potential tenants find properties that are appropriate for their needs.

BOMA classifies office space as Class A, Class B, or Class C, based on various factors including building finishes, amenities, location, and market perception. (Amenities are services in the building available to tenants, and may include coffee shops or snack bars, copying and express mail services, and physical fitness or child care centers.) The criteria used to classify property are fairly subjective; the classification of a property as a Class A property or a Class B property is affected by the other office space in that market. This means that the lines drawn between classes may differ from area to area—a building might be Class A in one city, but Class B in another.

 BOMA Definitions

Here are BOMA's building classification standards for metropolitan areas.

- **Class A.** Class A buildings are the most desirable and, accordingly, the most expensive buildings in the market. BOMA defines them as the "most prestigious buildings competing for premium office users with rents above average for the area." Class A buildings have high-quality finishes and state-of-the-art systems in addition to optimal locations. Most are relatively new structures, although the class may include expertly renovated older structures.

- **Class B.** Class B buildings compete "for a wide range of users with rents in the average range for the area." Building finishes are fair to good, but these properties can't compete in the upper end of the market, either because of their age, their lack of amenities, or their location.

- **Class C.** Class C buildings compete "for tenants requiring functional space at rents below average for the area." These are usually older buildings that started life as Class A or B buildings. While adequately maintained, they are starting to show some obsolescence in their amenities and systems. Tenants who need a cost-effective space and who aren't as concerned about public perception are likeliest to be interested in Class C space.

The purpose of the classification system is to standardize discussions about the properties that are available in a certain market. However, because the classifications are so subjective, BOMA discourages publishing the classification rating for an individual property. Instead, they recommend that building managers include a handout in the marketing package that lists the accepted definition of the A, B, and C classes in that particular market, along with typical rental rates per square foot for each class in that market. This allows a manager to place her property in a larger context, and she can then discuss the advantages of her property over similar properties in the market.

Management Planning for Office Property

Developing an effective management plan is the first step in managing an office property. In Chapter 4, we discussed the components of the management plan—the regional analysis, neighborhood analysis, property analysis, market analysis, and analysis of alternatives. Here, we'll look at these five types of analysis in the context of office property.

Regional Analysis

As you recall, the regional analysis looks at the bigger picture: the metropolitan area where the property is located. (Sometimes nearby metro areas are considered, too, especially if the metro area where the property is located is relatively small.) The regional analysis should consider the current status of office space in the metro area: is there an oversupply or undersupply of office space? However, the analysis should consider the future as well: does current construction activity mean there will be too much office space available in a few years?

Employment levels affect the demand for office space, so the regional analysis must take into account future employment growth. The analysis should list which sectors of the regional economy are growing, what businesses might enter the metro area in the coming years, and what type of office space these new businesses might need. For instance, growth in law firms or investment firms would require more traditionally configured space with private offices and meeting rooms, while growth in online commerce might lead to more demand for open space for call centers. Census data and local business journals can help provide some of this information. (See Chapter 4 for a general discussion of data sources for management planning.)

The property manager should also consider how technological advances might shape future demand for office property. For instance, as more workers gain the ability to telecommute, the demand for traditional office space may decrease.

Neighborhood Analysis

Compared to the regional analysis, the focus of the neighborhood analysis is much narrower; it looks at the area immediately surrounding the property. The relative prestige of a building's location and its access to utilities, transportation, and any off-site parking are crucial. The manager should also note in the analysis whether services are nearby, such as copy shops, daycare centers, and restaurants.

Office tenants often want to locate near businesses of similar quality, so the neighborhood analysis should honestly evaluate the quality and nature of other businesses in the neighborhood. This information will be helpful later when the manager is creating a marketing plan that realistically targets potential tenants.

> **Example:** While surveying the neighborhood, the manager determines that the nearby office buildings are almost uniformly Class C. Tenants are small, lackluster companies. The manager should avoid marketing the property by claiming that the property is prestigious, since prospective tenants would be disappointed by the neighborhood when they came to view the property.

As mentioned, the neighborhood analysis includes a look at transportation. How well the neighborhood is served by nearby arterials, highways, and mass transit is an important consideration for office tenants. Hundreds or even thousands of workers descend on a large office building each day for work, so convenient methods of transportation are vital. The manager should note any transportation problems, such as chronic traffic congestion in the neighborhood.

Other neighborhood characteristics to note include health and safety issues, such as adequate street lighting, police presence, and regular garbage collection.

Property Analysis

After examining the economic health of the region and the desirability of the neighborhood, the manager performs a property analysis. The manager inspects the site and the building, and determines how well the property is currently managed. The property manager can then use this information to plan for the future. Should the building be upgraded or repaired? Are expenses too high, or perhaps not high enough (which could be why repairs are urgent)? Is the rent collection process efficient?

Site. The property manager will be interested in any on-site parking, walkways leading to the building, exterior lighting, and landscaping. Is the amount of on-site parking sufficient for the needs of the tenants and their clients? (The amount of parking needed will typically depend on the type of tenants.) Is the property's access to transportation routes adequate—for example, can the site handle deliveries made by trucks? Are entryways adequate for the entry and exodus of employees at the beginning and end of the work day? Do the exterior elements, such as landscaping, lighting, and fencing, increase tenant safety and add to the attractiveness of the building?

Building. The building portion of the property analysis should examine the building's square footage, age, general physical condition, elevator and HVAC systems, telecommunications infrastructure, and other components. Some office tenants have very specific electrical requirements: they need more outlets than usual, industrial-grade wiring, and heavy duty air conditioning for computer equipment. This is unlikely to be a problem for a newer building, but may be a challenge for some older buildings. (While older buildings can be retrofitted to suit these needs, it may not be economical to do so.)

Management. An important part of the property analysis is the evaluation of current management. Are tenants satisfied with staff and services? Is the owner satisfied? Are rents collected efficiently and on time? Is the owner happy with the format and frequency of operating reports? Is the vacancy rate in line with the market vacancy rate? Are expenses reasonable, considering the type and age of the building?

If the answer to any of these questions is no, the manager will want to include her ideas for improvement in the management plan.

To determine whether the property's expenses are in line with average expenses for similar properties, the manager could simply ask colleagues who manage other buildings. Local chapters of trade associations may also have some helpful data. However, for the majority of managers, the most useful sources of information are the national surveys from IREM and BOMA.

IREM publishes an annual volume called "Income/Expense Analysis: Office Buildings." This publication offers a sample of over 3,000 properties in over 100 metropolitan areas around the nation, sorted according to criteria such as building type, age, size, and range of rental rates. The report contains information about typical percentage amounts spent on management fees, amenities, and other items. The manager can look at data at the national, regional, or metropolitan level.

BOMA also offers huge quantities of information concerning expenses. Their annual "Experience Exchange Report" contains averages of operating income and expenses at local, regional, and national levels.

Market Analysis

Once the office property and the surrounding neighborhood have been analyzed, the next step is to complete the market analysis. As we explained in Chapter 4, the first step of the market analysis is to determine the property's market. This is done by choosing a relevant submarket of similar office properties within the geographical area. Only then can the manager pick comparable properties to help her establish appropriate rental rates for the subject property.

At least three comparables should be chosen. Information about those comparables is then collected; the rental rates of the comparable properties are particularly important. Finding rental rates for comparable office properties can be difficult, however. While the leasing agents for many office buildings publish an asking rental rate, the actual rental rate is usually negotiated over a period of weeks or months. Discovering the agreed-upon rate can be challenging. As mentioned earlier, IREM's "Income/Expense Analysis: Office Buildings" is a good resource for the general range of rental rates in a given area. However, information about a particular property requires more targeted research. Colleagues sometimes share useful information; many local business journals and associations maintain online databases of existing leases.

The information gathered about the chosen comparables is typically laid out in a grid similar to the one in Figure 11.1. It should provide space for each comparable's rental rate (stating the base rent, any concessions, and the pass-through expenses, along with rent factors like the R/U ratio—see Chapter 7), and it should list all of the features that are likely to have an impact on how much rent potential tenants would be willing to pay.

The property manager then compares the condition and features of each comparable to those of the subject property. For each difference, the manager makes an adjustment to the comparable's rental rate. If the comparable has a feature that the subject lacks or

Figure 11.1 Comparison worksheet for market analysis – office property

Market Analysis Comparison Grid for Commercial Property

Subject property: *Fairmont Building, 1384 Fourth Avenue*   Date: *June 19*

Type of property: *Space in Class B office bldg; 3-year lease*

	Subject	Comparable 1	Comparable 2	Comparable 3
Property Name		Cairn Bldg	Harmon Bldg	Bazelon Tower
Base rent (sq. ft./year)		$30.80	$32.00	$34.20
Concessions (–)		$3.85	$3.90	$4.10
Pass-through expenses (+)		$5.90	$6.15	$6.80
Tenant improvements (+)		not included	not included	not included
Total (effective rent)		$32.85	$34.25	$36.90
Vacancy rate		4%	7%	6%

Elements	Description	Difference	$ adj.	Difference	$ adj.	Difference	$ adj.
Location	CBD, west end	same	—	same	—	east end	—
Prestige	good	same	—	same	—	superior	–1.50
Transportation access	excellent	same	—	same	—	inferior	+1.20
Business services	very good	same	—	same	—	same	—
Employee services	good	same	—	same	—	superior	–0.20
Crime and safety issues	good	same	—	same	—	superior	–0.40
Other	across from park	no	+0.20	no	+0.20	no	+0.20
Building & Site							
Age of building	38 years old	42 yrs	+0.20	40 yrs	+0.10	35 yrs	–0.30
Overall curb appeal	very good	inferior	+1.00	inferior	+1.00	same	—
Grounds	very good	same	—	inferior	+0.30	same	—
Building exterior	very good	inferior	+0.20	same	—	same	—
Entry and/or lobby	small, dim	superior	–0.50	superior	–0.50	superior	–0.50
Other common areas	good	same	—	same	—	same	—
Other	—						
Special Factors (list)							
Extra storage available	heated bsmt	none	+0.50	none	+0.50	inferior	+0.30
Roof garden/patio	good	same	—	none	+0.20	none	+0.20

Adjustments should be stated in dollars per square foot per year. For example, +0.20 means the comparable's rental rate is increased by twenty cents per square foot, and –1.50 means the rate is decreased by $1.50 per square foot.

Elements	Subject	Comparable 1		Comparable 2		Comparable 3	
	Description	Difference	$ adj.	Difference	$ adj.	Difference	$ adj.
Systems & Operations							
Energy efficiency (HVAC)	good	same	—	same	—	superior	–1.00
Elevators	freq. repairs	superior	–1.00	same	—	superior	–1.00
Telecommunications	good	inferior	+0.50	same	—	superior	–0.50
Staffing	adequate	superior	–0.30	same	—	inferior	+0.30
Security	good	same	—	inferior	+0.30	same	—
Other	—						
Parking							
Lot, covered, or garage	garage	same	—	same	—	same	—
Parking ratio or index	N/A						
Visitor spaces available	adequate	same	—	inferior	+0.50	superior	–0.50
Tenant parking cost	included	same	—	same	—	same	—
Rental Space							
Location within building	middle floor	similar	—	similar	—	similar	—
Layout issues; floor plate	standard	same	—	same	—	same	—
Quality	very good	same	—	inferior	+0.60	same	—
Condition	very good	inferior	+1.00	same	—	inferior	+1.00
Storage	good	same	—	inferior	+0.70	inferior	+0.70
Special features	—						
Other	—						
Adjustment Totals		+3.60, –1.80		+4.40, –0.50		+3.90, –5.90	
Net Adjustments		+1.80		+3.90		–2.00	
Adj. rent per rentable sq.ft.		$34.65		$38.15		$34.90	
R/U ratio (×)		1.10		1.10		1.12	
Adj. rent per usable sq.ft.		$38.12		$41.97		$39.09	
Total no. of adjustments		10		11		16	
Comments:							

is in better condition than the subject, the comparable's rental rate is adjusted downward (decreased) by an appropriate amount. If the comparable lacks a feature that the subject has or is in worse condition, the comparable's rental rate is adjusted upward. For example, in Figure 11.1, the subject office building has better access to transportation than one of the comparables. Based on experience, the manager estimates that the difference is worth $1.20 per square foot per year; so the manager adds $1.20 to the comparable's annual rent per square foot. The final result of all the adjustments indicates what the comparable would lease for if it were essentially identical to the subject property.

After going through this process for all of the comparables, the manager uses his judgment to evaluate whether any of them is a more reliable indicator of the subject property's current rental value than the others. At this point, the manager has enough information to set the rental rates for the managed property.

> **Example:** A manager is performing a market analysis of a 20-story Class B office building located five blocks from the center of the CBD. She finds three comparable properties, all Class B buildings of similar size, within the surrounding several blocks. Comparable 1, after accounting for the R/U ratio and other expenses, has an adjusted effective rent of $35 per square foot, while Comparable 2 rents for $40 per square foot, and Comparable 3 rents for $42 per square foot.
>
> The manager finds that the overall condition and quality of finishes of Comparable 1 make it a better match for her client's building than either 2 or 3, so she gives Comparable 1's adjusted rent more weight than the others. Based on this market analysis, the manager decides that $37 per square foot is the appropriate rental rate for the managed property.

In some markets, the rent is typically expressed as cost per square foot per month; in others, it's cost per square foot per year. (It doesn't matter which is used, as one can be turned into the other simply by multiplying or dividing by 12.)

Rental rates for larger buildings. With a large office building, the rental rates may vary depending on the location of the office space within the building. In a high-rise building, for example, the upper floors, which have more prestige (and better views), usually command higher rents. Rents would also vary if the rental space on one side of the building offered views of a lake or mountain, and the other side faced the street or another building.

High-rise office buildings frequently have retail space on the ground floor occupied by small vendors, such as coffee shops or newsstands. This retail space will often have a different rental rate than the office space on the floors above.

Analysis of Alternatives

Sometimes a competitive rental rate isn't enough to cover the property's expenses, or it may not provide the owner with the desired return on his investment. In this case, the property manager has three alternatives: 1) reduce operating expenses, 2) generate additional revenue, or 3) convince the owner to lower expectations on his desired yield. (These options can be combined, of course).

The data sources we mentioned earlier may be used to determine if the property's expenses are in line with industry standards. If they're not, the manager may be able to find ways to reduce expenses without compromising the quality of the services provided to the tenants or the upkeep of the building. Generating additional revenue often requires upfront expenditures, but the expense may pay off in the long-term. For instance, a substantial upgrade of the building's interior finishes or its mechanical systems could translate into a significantly higher rent per square foot. Convincing the owner to reduce his expectations may be difficult, but if the property manager has done her homework and is armed with plenty of objective market data, such an attempt may be successful.

Marketing Office Space

Coming up with an effective management plan and determining a competitive rental rate will be a wasted effort if potential tenants never hear about the property. Thus, as with other types of property, marketing is a vital part of managing office property. As you know, marketing is not a matter of simply putting up a few For Rent signs and waiting; it should be a thoughtfully planned effort. Even if there is currently no vacant space in the property, marketing efforts should be ongoing. Although office tenants don't move as frequently as residential tenants, a manager should be prepared to fill a vacancy quickly.

As we discussed in Chapter 6, there are a number of advertising media that can be used to attract prospective tenants, including:

- signs,
- brochures,
- the Internet,
- newspapers and magazines,
- direct mail,
- public relations,
- retail centers,
- referrals, and
- cold calling.

Each medium could be used for general advertising purposes or to appeal to particular tenants or types of tenants. It's often effective to market an office property to particular types of tenants by emphasizing certain characteristics. For example:

- information on the building's up-to-date infrastructure for high-end computing could be sent to high-tech companies;
- lower fees for common area maintenance, lower utility costs, and an open floor plan might appeal to companies running large call centers;
- the building's prestigious address might be attractive to high end financial businesses; or
- a building's location near a rapidly growing suburb might appeal to professionals such as accountants, attorneys, and doctors.

Types of Advertising

Let's take a closer look at how some types of advertising media are particularly suited to marketing office property.

Internet. It's increasingly common for individual office buildings to have their own websites. These websites, which are updated frequently, describe the building and its amenities, and list any space that is available. Ideally, these websites will include interactive features, such as clickable maps, suggested floor plans, and virtual tours of amenities and common areas. A building website could also include photos of nearby amenities—restaurants, parks, and so forth.

Business is increasingly international, and the Web is an economical and relatively easy way to reach potential office tenants worldwide.

Print and Broadcast. While classified ads and free real estate magazines are often used to market residential rental property, they aren't likely to work well for office property, except perhaps modest-sized office buildings suited to small businesses.

However, well-selected print media can be used to target niche markets. For instance, a display ad in the regional bar association's monthly magazine could pay off when marketing office space to lawyers; similarly, a medical office building might advertise in a medical association periodical. More generally, larger buildings might advertise in local business journals or magazines targeted at local business leaders. Very large properties might even place display ads in business publications with a national reach.

Radio and television ads are rarely used to market office space; broadcast media reach too many people, almost none of whom want to lease office space.

Public Relations. The manager of an office building may hire a public relations firm to raise a project's profile, or may undertake a simple PR campaign himself. For instance, the manager might write press releases for local news publications, touting a building's opening or reopening after a remodel. Another topic likely to generate interest would be a move-in by a prestigious new tenant.

The manager may also use empty space in the building to host (and possibly subsidize) events of interest to the office community. Events could include conferences or continuing education classes, such as training for insurance agents, accountants, or lawyers.

Rental Center. Many large office buildings have a model office space. The model provides workspace for leasing agents and a comfortable setting for negotiations, and it also helps potential tenants envision how their space might be used. The opportunity to see finished, built-out space is particularly important when the space is currently unfinished. If a building is new to the market, the manager might consider using the model office to host an open house.

Cold Calling. Cold calling potential tenants, either by phone or in person (sometimes called **canvassing**), can be the most persuasive marketing method of all, as long as contacts are selected carefully. Cold calling will reach some prospects who are actively considering a move but may also plant a seed in the minds of those who aren't. A look at business journals, newspaper financial sections, or company annual reports can help an office building manager locate companies that are experiencing rapid growth and so may need additional space.

Cold calling should always be done systematically; start with nearby businesses and then progress outward in larger circles. For large buildings, cold calling can be delegated to full-time leasing agents. Of course, those making cold calls must comply with Do Not Call laws.

Cold calling is often regarded as time-consuming and frustrating: dozens of calls are typically made before one interested party is found. However, compared to the costs associated with most other forms of advertising, cold calling can be an economical way to find prospects.

Leasing Office Space

If your marketing efforts have been successful, you now have several prospective tenants to choose from. In this section, we're going to discuss selecting office tenants and negotiating lease terms, and we'll also make a few points about retaining good tenants.

The Tenant Selection Process

Chapter 7 described the general process for qualifying and selecting commercial tenants, and that discussion certainly applies to office tenants. Here we're going to discuss a few issues that are of special importance in the office property context. First we'll look at evaluating a potential tenant's space and service requirements in order to make sure that the property is a good fit. Then we'll consider how the concept of tenant mix affects the selection of office tenants.

Space Requirements. While a prospect's financial status is arguably the most important element to examine in the tenant selection process, the manager should also give careful thought to the prospect's space requirements. If the available space is too large or too small or can't be configured correctly, the tenant is best served by looking elsewhere. Thus, a manager often analyzes a prospect's space needs even before showing her any office space.

> ### ▶ Questions to Ask Potential Tenants
>
> - How long have you been in your current space?
> - What is your current rent?
> - Why are you looking to move?
> - Where are you looking to move, and what kind of space are you interested in?
> - What other spaces are you looking at?
> - When would you like to move?
> - How much space do you need?
> - How many employees will you have in the space?
> - How much parking will you need?
> - Are there any unusual services or functions that you'll need?
> - Do you expect your space requirements to change in the near future?

The manager and prospect will meet to discuss how many employees will work in the new space, what kind of tasks they will perform, and how much growth is expected.

The configuration of the space is a particular concern. Columns, elevator shafts, stairwells, and various other elements may prevent building out the space in a way that suits the prospect's needs. Or perhaps there is not enough space along outer walls for private offices with windows (a feature that may be necessary if the prospective tenant has several executives who all expect private offices with windows). Likewise, the building layout might prevent the creation of special-use spaces that a tenant requires, like a large conference room, computer room, or library.

The need for future expansion must also be considered. A prospective tenant who foresees rapid growth should rent a larger space than is initially needed. If a tenant has enough employees at the beginning of the tenancy to fill the entire space, it will be quite challenging to add more employees later. Reconfiguring the space to allow for additional employees can be more expensive than planning for growth at the outset.

Service Requirements. After considering space requirements, a property manager should determine whether the services available in the building will meet the prospective tenant's needs. For example, what level of security does the prospect need? Do their business hours differ from the other tenants in the building? What about lobby and elevator usage?

A manager who doesn't anticipate these issues, and doesn't account for them in the lease terms (by requiring the tenant to pay for increased costs), may end up with an unprofitable lease. However, spending money to meet a potential tenant's needs shouldn't be dismissed out of hand. Making the required improvements might make the building more profitable in the long run.

> **Example:** A high tech company wants to lease space in Wharf Building 1. Outfitting this older building with a new telecommunications infrastructure and a more advanced security system to meet the prospect's needs will improve the building as a whole and help it attract future tenants at higher rental rates.

Tenant Mix. Tenant mix—the hallmark of shopping center tenant selection—is also important when selecting tenants for office properties. Choosing tenants who complement each other can prevent tenant squabbles over overcrowded parking lots, obnoxious customers, or excessive noise. And of course, tenant mix affects each tenant's bottom line: too many similar businesses in the building may create too much competition, while having related businesses in the same building can translate into more customers for all the tenants.

The identity of the building's principal tenant often determines the tenant mix. For instance, if a national bank is a building's principal tenant, smaller firms from the financial services industry will be attracted to the building. Likewise, a prominent law firm may attract accounting firms, escrow companies, messenger services, and other related businesses.

Lease Provisions

Once the manager has determined that a prospect is right for the building in terms of space needs, service requirements, and tenant mix, the next step is to negotiate the terms of the lease. (This step is also necessary to some degree with tenants who are renewing leases.) In Chapter 7, we discussed the various issues that arise in most commercial lease negotiations, so here we'll focus on a few issues that are of particular importance in office leasing.

Rent. While residential tenants rarely get the chance to negotiate their rent payments, rent negotiations play a prominent role in the leasing of office property. The prospective tenant's ability to negotiate a lower rental rate will depend in large part on the current market for office space. If the vacancy rate for office space is high, property managers may be willing to be reduce the rental rate. On the other hand, if office space is tight, managers can negotiate from a position of strength and hold out for a higher rent.

Square footage. Office rent is generally a flat rate based on the square footage of the leased space, plus an additional amount for the common areas. Thus, it's important for the lease to accurately specify the square footage of both the tenant's usable space and the building's common areas. (Many office property managers use BOMA's standard methods to measure their building's rentable and usable square footage.)

As explained in Chapter 7, the amount of rent paid for common areas is determined in part by the ratio of rentable space to the usable space (the R/U ratio). R/U ratios can be converted into a percentage, sometimes referred to as a **loss factor**. Typical loss factors for office buildings run between 10% and 18%.

Pass-through charges. Some expenses are passed through to the tenant; others are the property owner's responsibility. The lease should clearly state which types of expenses the tenant will be expected to pay. Generally, if the landlord classifies something as a building expense (such as parking lot maintenance), the office tenant will pay a prorated portion of it. However, the landlord generally pays for major building improvements (called capital improvements), such as a new roof or heating system. Tenants often prefer the lease to state that the distinction between expenses and capital improvements should be based on generally accepted accounting principles, to prevent the landlord from labeling items as expenses that are actually capital improvements. (For more on pass-through charges and leases, see Chapter 7.)

Escalation clauses. Office leases are usually fairly long-term, so inflation can quickly make a rent that seems reasonable the first year, for example, seem significantly below market the fourth year. An escalation clause avoids this problem. As you may recall from Chapter 7, escalation clauses—which are commonly included in commercial leases—call for periodic increases in the rent amount. The increase may be based on the rate of inflation (by using an index or another accepted measure of inflation), or it can be based on actual increases in the property's operating expenses.

Build-Out. One crucial—and complicated—point that must be negotiated is the build-out of unfinished office space. Lease provisions that address build-out are often so complicated that an addendum or an entirely separate agreement is used to lay out the details. While it's beyond the scope of this book to thoroughly discuss this subject, we'll touch on shell space, building standards, payment terms, and tenant specifications.

Shell space. When a building is new, the interior space is usually left unfinished, so it can be **built out** to the tenants' specifications. Since each tenant has unique needs, it makes sense to leave unleased space unfinished until a tenant is found, rather than to configure the space first only to have to change it later.

Unfinished commercial space is known as **shell space**. Shell space is made up of exterior walls, a roof, a concrete floor, and utility connections. When the space is leased, the interior walls, carpeting or floor tile, ceiling tiles, paint or wallpaper, and interior plumbing and electrical are added. The tenant chooses the configuration, and the owner generally oversees the construction. Sometimes the tenant is responsible for the build-out, but this is uncommon. When the management takes care of all the work, it is sometimes referred to as providing the tenant with space in **turnkey condition**.

Even if a building isn't new, vacant space is often reduced to shell space before marketing efforts begin, in order to show prospects a blank slate. If the space is left in the previous tenant's configuration, it's more difficult for prospects to picture themselves moving into the space. And, of course, the new tenant is likely to want to tear everything down to the bare floor and start again anyway. (Occasionally a smaller office tenant on a shoestring budget may use some or all of the existing layout, in order to save money.)

Build-out costs. Build-out costs include the construction work itself, along with architectural, engineering, and design fees. "Open layouts" are the most economical to build; space that is partitioned into many private offices is considerably more expensive. The build-out of specialized space—such as a medical office, with its many small rooms, multiple sinks, and shielding for X-ray equipment—can easily run double the cost of an ordinary office build-out.

Unless the market for office space is tight, property owners usually pay for at least some of the build-out costs. The owner will specify—or the parties will negotiate—a **tenant improvement allowance** (such as $25 per square foot). If the build-out costs more than this, the tenant will cover the excess.

The amount of the tenant improvement allowance often depends on the rental rate that's negotiated. A high rent often means a generous improvement allowance. The inverse is also true—if the tenant has negotiated a relatively low rent, the landlord is less likely to throw in a large improvement allowance.

Building standards. Typically, the tenant can't choose any kind of build-out. Property owners often specify a uniform type of finish work for the entire building (these standards can be added as an addendum to the management agreement). A consistent level of workmanship and a similar aesthetic look and feel throughout the building increase its overall value, in the same way that a reasonable amount of conformity in a residential neighborhood adds value to the homes there.

Some very large office buildings have their own in-house staff of construction workers and space planners to assist with build-outs; this makes it easier for management to preserve building standards. It's more convenient for the tenant as well. Absent in-house staff, managers will use contractors they trust and have worked with before. Only a tenant with considerable clout can insist on using its own contractors. However, exceptions are sometimes made for tenants with special aesthetic or other construction needs, provided the tenant can guaranty high-quality contractors who are especially suited to the work.

Tenant specifications for work. The parties will usually lay out the tenant's specifications for improvements in an addendum to the lease or a separate **work letter** that is prepared later. It's a good idea for the tenant to hire an interior designer or an office space planner to help with the specifications. These professionals can easily pay for themselves by producing superior plans. While office layout may not be quite as important as the layout for retail or industrial space, efficiency certainly matters; and since office leases tend to be long-term, small improvements can add up to a big savings. Larger office buildings often have space planners on staff, and this service can be offered to tenants for free or at a reduced rate. There are also various software programs that can help with space planning.

Utilities. The lease should state explicitly which utility services the landlord will provide and when. In many cases, the landlord provides heating and air conditioning during business hours but not after hours. The tenant may have to pay extra to keep the office space at normal temperatures during off hours.

Sometimes the lease requires the landlord to pay for the tenant's electricity and other utilities costs up to a certain dollar amount, with the tenant paying for any overage.

Tenant Services. If there are facilities within the building that are shared among the tenants, the terms of their use should be dictated clearly in the lease. The terms might include restrictions on the use of shared conference rooms or exercise facilities, the cost of concierge services, or the rates for reserved spaces in the building's parking garage.

In office buildings, janitorial services are often provided by the property management. The lease should spell out in detail what will be cleaned and when. Office tenants with significant customer traffic, such as lawyers and financial planners, may require more frequent janitorial service.

Lease Term. As with other kinds of commercial property, office leases generally run for multi-year periods, such as five or ten years. The parties often make a significant investment of time and money to build-out unfinished space, and it takes time to recoup this investment. Long lease terms offer the advantage of low turnover, but this also means managers must select tenants wisely, since they will be around for years to come.

Retaining Tenants

Office building vacancies can take time to fill even in healthy markets, and the build-out process is expensive, so it's important for managers to try to retain existing tenants. To strengthen relationships with current tenants, managers can organize events such as luncheons, contests, or charity drives. Events like these not only improve management-tenant relationships, but also help build relationships between the tenants. Sending monthly or quarterly newsletters to the tenants is also a good idea.

Arguably, the most important part of tenant retention is the lease renewal discussion. The manager should contact the tenant at least six months before the lease is set to expire, asking about the tenant's plans and space needs. The recommended approach is to try to renew the lease at current market rates, offering other tenant concessions if necessary; renewing at market rates helps maintain the value of the building. Tenant concessions can be purely financial (such as a few months of free rent) or can consist of improvements to the tenant space, such as increased rights to use common areas or additional parking spaces. The manager should offer concessions that cost less—or certainly no more—than the expenses associated with finding a new tenant.

Operations and Reporting

The operational requirements of an office building vary widely depending on the size of the building. For small buildings, onsite management may not be necessary or feasible. When this is the case, tenants should be given contact information for the offsite management office. Tenants must be able to reach management staff during normal business hours, and an emergency number should be provided for situations that need immediate attention, regardless of the hour.

Larger buildings or office complexes can usually support an onsite office. The office should be centrally located and have a similar quality of finishes as a typical leased space. In some cases, the only personnel at the office will be the building manager and perhaps an administrative assistant; however, in large buildings, the management staff may include assistant managers, tenant relations coordinators, a tenant improvement construction coordinator, and a supervisor for the maintenance and security department.

Security

Security personnel help keep tenants and their possessions safe from crime, as well as offering assistance during emergencies. These personnel should be trained to respond to fires, earthquakes, power failures, water line breaks, bomb threats, and accidents and injuries. Large office buildings usually have one or more security guards on duty at all times. During business hours, security services often consist of simple gatekeeping (controlling access to the building). This task is typically handled by staff seated at an information desk in the lobby.

During off-hours, security staff may monitor security cameras and make random sweeps of the building, checking for intruders or other problems. The largest buildings will have around-the-clock guards in the lobby. In buildings with 24-hour security, people can usually pass freely through the building during business hours, but during evening or weekend hours they will need to display identification cards or sign in and out, or do both. Elevator service may be limited and require a key card.

Low-rise buildings in office parks typically don't have around-the-clock security, although large office parks may provide a security detail to patrol parking lots. Managers of buildings with limited security needs often use the services of a security firm, rather than hiring their own staff. Of course, janitors or other maintenance staff working after-hours can be on the lookout for security issues.

There's more to security issues than staffing. Property managers shouldn't overlook the physical aspects of building security. Alarm systems are customary in all sizes of office buildings. There are many different types of systems to consider—often used in conjunction with each other—including infrared, motion detection, or magnetic contacts on doors and windows. Video camera surveillance is also used in larger buildings, although to be effective, there must be personnel to monitor the camera feeds.

Larger, more sophisticated buildings install electronic access systems on both outer doors and office doors; doors are opened with entry codes or by swiping employee identification cards. Electronic methods are popular because they make key control easier; traditionally, a locksmith was needed to change lock cylinders throughout the building whenever a tenant moved out. Electronic systems simply require reprogramming whenever building occupancy changes.

Maintenance

In addition to providing security staff, building management often provides maintenance and janitorial staff. The property manager may hire staff, or may use the services of a janitorial/maintenance company.

The type of services offered depends on the building's size and of course what kind of janitorial services the tenants need.

> **Example:** Office building A houses several accounting firms, two law firms, and three firms that offer financial services. Customers visit these businesses all day long, and the restrooms must be cleaned several times a day.
>
> Office building B houses a large call center, a data processing firm, and a hard drive recovery center. These businesses rarely—if ever—have customers who visit the premises, and they only want to pay for cleaning the common areas once a day.

Smaller buildings, such as those in office parks, tend to have little in the way of public areas. These buildings may require individual tenants to provide their own janitorial services. Smaller buildings also have fewer and easier-to-maintain mechanical systems, meaning they can be serviced by outside companies.

Janitorial staff may report directly to the building manager. However, in larger buildings there might be more of a hierarchy: a supervisor for each shift, along with one maintenance superintendent to oversee all janitorial activities. A large building is also likely to have a chief engineer onsite to oversee the physical systems (HVAC, plumbing, lighting, etc.).

Working with Office Tenants

Of course, the security and maintenance of the office building is only part of the property manager's job. As you learned in Chapter 8, the manager needs to build relationships with her tenants by welcoming them at the beginning of their occupancy, communicating with them on a regular basis, and—probably most importantly—providing timely responses to requests and complaints.

The proper collection of rent is also a part of tenant relations. We've already discussed rent collection in previous chapters, so here we'll just take a moment to discuss a couple of points related to rent collection when tenants have headquarters (and accounts payable departments) in another state or country.

Every commercial lease should include a clause in which the tenant names an employee or other representative who is officially responsible for receiving rent bills and paying them. This is doubly important if the tenant isn't headquartered locally. A clause like this can help squelch protests about miscommunication, improperly routed rent bills, or the imposition of late fees. Note that the clause should also require the tenant to notify the manager if the name or address of the contact person changes.

Reports to the Owner

The complexities of rent provisions and other financial terms in the typical office lease usually mean that reports to the owner are fairly complex. Fortunately, the manager may choose from a number of property management software packages specifically tailored for office properties.

Chapter 5 describes the most common items normally included in owner reports. We'll conclude this chapter by briefly addressing some reporting matters of particular concern to the office property manager.

Rent Roll. As you know, managers provide property owners with rent rolls that list monthly rent collections. Office property rent rolls can be complicated, though. Office rents normally include pass-through and CAM charges. While the lease will characterize these charges as rent, they should nonetheless be listed separately in the rent roll to allow year-over-year comparisons. In addition, there should also be separate entries for any amounts paid under rent escalation provisions. This helps the manager and the owner evaluate how well the escalation is working. Does the escalation clause result in the tenant paying too low or too high a rent? The answer will matter greatly at renewal time when there's a chance to renegotiate the clause.

Delinquency Reports. The manager's reports usually differentiate between delinquencies of rent and delinquencies of pass-throughs and other charges. This is true even though the charges are generally treated as past due rent under the lease (as well as in any collection actions). Sometimes, a tenant pays the basic rent but disputes the payment of a pass-through charge and withholds payment of that amount. In this case, the separate accounting helps the property manager and the owner understand the tenant's claim and determine whether the holdback amount is proper. If more than one tenant disputes an amount due under the same lease provision, this suggests that the lease provision is ambiguous and should be revised in the future.

Chapter Summary

1. Office buildings are found in downtown business districts, office parks, and around shopping areas and transportation nodes. Large investment syndicates own most high-rise office buildings.

2. Office properties are traditionally classified as Class A, Class B, or Class C space, depending on their age, amenities, and prestige. The different classes have correspondingly different rental rates.

3. Office property values and rents are heavily determined by location; desirability is influenced by proximity to other office properties of similar prestige containing similar types of tenants.

4. The management plan for an office property is similar in organization to the plans created for other kinds of property: it includes a regional analysis, neighborhood analysis, property analysis, market analysis, and analysis of alternatives.

5. Techniques a manager may use to market office space include print media, public relations, rental centers, and cold calls.

6. When evaluating prospective tenants, a manager keeps several factors in mind: the tenant's space requirements, service requirements, and the building's tenant mix.

7. Office space is often leased as unfinished shell space, to be built out by the tenant; the work will be performed according to building standards and tenant specifications, and management usually gives the tenant an improvement allowance.

8. Staffing and maintenance needs depend on building size and the types of tenants. Smaller office buildings often contract out security and janitorial services. Larger buildings usually maintain at least two shifts of janitorial staff and have round-the-clock security.

9. Reports to office property owners often involve more detail than for other property types. Both reports should reflect pass-through charges and escalation payments, listed separately in order to allow comparison from one period to the next and to assist in identifying any problematic lease provisions.

Key Terms

Central business district – The downtown core of a city where high-rise office buildings are heavily concentrated.

Office park – An office property that consists of several one- to two-story buildings clustered together on landscaped grounds.

BOMA – A trade association for property managers, which has formulated classifications for office space based on various factors such as building finishes, amenities, location, and market perception.

Class A space – The most desirable and prestigious office buildings in a particular market, with rents above average for the area.

Class B space – Office buildings that compete for a wide range of users in the average rental range for the area.

Class C space – Office buildings that offer functional space for tenants at below-average rents, but that may have obsolete systems or amenities.

Tenant mix – The blend of tenants in a property; office property managers should strive for an appropriate mix, avoiding new tenants who are incompatible with current tenants or who may have a negative impact on the building's reputation.

Regional analysis – Analysis at the metropolitan level that considers factors such as future employment growth.

Neighborhood analysis – Analysis of a property's location, including its prestige and accessibility to transportation.

Property analysis – Analysis that focuses on the building, its site, and management; part of the goal is to classify the building as Class A, B, or C property.

R/U ratio – A ratio of the tenant's usable space to the usable space in the entire building; the ratio is used to calculate how much the tenant will pay for shared common space.

Market analysis – A method of analysis that compares the subject property to competing properties in the same market.

Built-out – An office space that has been finished to a tenant's specifications.

Shell space – Space that has not been built out, but is awaiting a tenant's improvements.

Building standard – The minimum construction standards for any build-out or improvement made in tenant spaces; the standard may also state the amount of work that management will provide for tenants at no additional charge when building out unfinished space, though this is subject to negotiation during the leasing process.

Space requirements – The amount of square footage needed by a potential tenant to accommodate its employees and planned operations.

Turnkey condition – A space that is fully improved and ready for occupancy.

Chapter Quiz

1. Compared to managing residential buildings, all of the following are true of managing office buildings, except:

   a) less turnover

   b) longer lease terms

   c) management only with tenant and owner needs in mind

   d) remodeling in between tenants

2. A high-rise office building in a central business district is well-maintained, but is several decades old and doesn't have the same amenities as nearby prestigious buildings. This would most likely be considered:

   a) Class A space

   b) Class B space

   c) Class C space

   d) flex space

3. Which of the following describes Class C office space?

   a) Functional space at below average rent

   b) Average quality and average rents

   c) Superior finishes in heart of downtown business core

   d) Home office space

4. While developing a management plan, the manager notes where the building is located in relation to the central business district's focal point and evaluates access to key transportation corridors. This is a part of the:

   a) building analysis

   b) market analysis

   c) neighborhood analysis

   d) regional analysis

5. When measuring the space that will be rented to a tenant, the manager takes into account not only the number of square feet inside the tenant's premises, but also a portion of the shared space in the building. This is the:

   a) gross area

   b) net area

   c) rentable area

   d) usable area

6. A manager calculates the ratio of a tenant's usable space to the usable space in the building. This is known as the:

   a) absorption ratio

   b) add-on ratio

   c) break-even ratio

   d) R/U ratio

7. While preparing a management plan, the manager looks for properties that will compete with the subject property for tenants. The analysis compares rental rates, features, and amenities between the comparable property and the managed property. This is known as a:

   a) property analysis

   b) building analysis

   c) market analysis

   d) site analysis

8. Which of the following marketing methods is the manager of an office property least likely to use to attract potential tenants?

   a) Classified ads in newspapers

   b) Direct mail

   c) Referrals

   d) Rental center

9. The first tenant to lease a space in a newly constructed office building finds that the space is unfinished, with nothing but the exterior walls, a concrete floor, and utility connections. This is known as:

   a) built-out space
   b) shell space
   c) standard space
   d) turnkey condition

10. When negotiating a lease, the tenant and owner agreed that the owner will pay $50,000 toward the costs of building out the space to the tenant's specifications. Any additional construction expenses will be the tenant's responsibility. Fifty thousand dollars is the:

    a) break-even amount
    b) build-out bonus
    c) security deposit
    d) tenant improvement allowance

11. Minicorp signs a lease for office space in a large multi-tenant building. Minicorp's lease is likely to be a:

    a) tenancy at will
    b) gross lease
    c) month-to-month lease
    d) multi-year lease

12. A building manager considers the role of technological change and how it will affect the types of jobs created in the future in his metropolitan area. This would be part of his:

    a) regional analysis
    b) neighborhood analysis
    c) property analysis
    d) market analysis

13. When interviewing a potential tenant who is interested in leasing space in her office building, a manager asks about the nature of the tenant's business, how many employees will work there, and whether they'll be mostly executive or clerical workers. The manager is evaluating the tenant's:

    a) business reputation
    b) financial condition
    c) service requirements
    d) space requirements

14. During the workday, building management typically provides janitorial services covering all of the following areas, except:

    a) grounds
    b) interior leased spaces
    c) lobby
    d) public restrooms

15. Which of the following is not a factor that's considered when deciding which classification an office building should receive?

    a) Prestige
    b) Building finishes
    c) Amenities
    d) Rental rates

Answer Key

1. c) Property managers must consider not only the tenants, but also the tenants' clients and other members of the public who pass through the building. Office leases are long-term leases, often with extensive remodeling of the space in between lease terms.

2. b) Class B space includes buildings that compete for a variety of users in the average price range for a market; it often includes buildings that are well-kept but don't compete at the upper end of the market because of obsolescence.

3. a) Class C is the lowest BOMA classification and includes office space that, while functional, is not in good enough shape or location to command even the average rents of Class B space.

4. c) Neighborhood analysis focuses on issues such as the relative prestige of a building's location, its access to transportation and parking, and proximity to useful services.

5. c) Rentable area includes not only space exclusively controlled by a tenant, but also a share of common spaces available to tenants.

6. d) The R/U ratio, used to determine how much a tenant will pay in addition to the rent for the square footage within his unit, is a ratio of the tenant's usable area to the total usable area of the entire building.

7. c) A market analysis compares the subject property to competing properties in the same market.

8. a) Classified advertising in generally distributed newspapers is unlikely to attract prospective tenants for office property.

9. b) Shell space is unfinished space that is waiting for the tenant's improvements before it is ready for occupancy.

10. d) The amount a building owner will contribute toward the cost of the improvements requested by a new tenant is known as a tenant improvement allowance. Anything beyond that amount is the tenant's responsibility.

11. d) Office property leases are usually for multi-year periods, rather than month-to-month or year-to-year.

12. a) Regional analysis is forward-looking, and considers the entire metropolitan area or an even larger area.

13. d) When determining whether the available space will meet the tenant's requirements for size and configuration possibilities, a manager needs to know about the tenant's type of business, number of employees, and possible expansion plans.

14. b) The grounds, lobby, and public restrooms usually require constant upkeep during the day given their volume of use. Leased spaces are typically cleaned only after hours, though, so as not to interfere with work.

15. d) Rental rates don't determine how an office property is classified. In fact, how a building is classified (Class A, B, or C) is a key determinant of rental rates.

Chapter 12

Managing Retail Property

Outline

Introduction

The retail property manager faces a wide range of challenges. For instance, marketing efforts must be directed at not just tenants, but also retail customers. Rent payment calculations tend to be more complicated for retail properties. The manager must also continuously monitor a retail property to make sure it remains competitive and appealing; this can be especially difficult amid changing demographics and a constantly shifting retail landscape.

In this chapter, we'll examine the types of properties and tenants that a retail property manager might work with. We'll then turn to the special considerations involved in management planning for retail property. Next we'll consider the complexities of marketing and leasing retail space. Finally, we'll discuss operations, particularly marketing to retail consumers, and also touch on reports to the owner.

Types of Retail Property and Tenants

Let's begin by looking at the various types of retail properties and their tenants. While it's important to be familiar with all types of retail properties, this chapter will focus on shopping centers, since most professional property managers work with this type of property rather than with individual stores.

Types of Shopping Centers

While shopping centers are the most typical retail arrangement, their size, scope, and layout vary. Shopping centers have traditionally been categorized according to the size of their market area; in other words, the retail customer base will determine the size of the shopping center and, in turn, the category into which it falls.

While the rules aren't written in stone, the industry recognizes five main shopping center categories: strip or convenience, neighborhood, community, regional, and super-regional. (We'll also mention some additional classifications at the end of this section.)

Strip Mall. The strip mall (sometimes called a convenience shopping center) is usually located on a major thoroughfare, either on the boundary of an urban area or further out into the suburbs. A strip mall contains anywhere between 5,000 and 30,000 square feet of **gross leasable area**, or **GLA**. (The GLA includes all of the tenant spaces but not the shopping center's common areas.) A strip mall is usually configured in a simple L-shape or as a row of buildings set back from the street, with parking spaces in front. This type of center serves the smallest market area. An **anchor tenant** (a larger, more prominent tenant) may or may not be included; if so, the anchor tenant is likely to be a small drugstore or a chain convenience store.

Neighborhood Shopping Center. Next largest in size is the neighborhood shopping center. The neighborhood center usually consists of 30,000 to 150,000 square feet of GLA. It supports a market area of at least 1,000 families within a radius of one to two miles. Anchor tenants are most often supermarkets, but may also be large drugstores or home improvement stores. The configuration is similar to the strip mall, but is larger and may include one or more outparcels, often occupied by chain restaurants. (An **outparcel** is a retail space that is separate from the main shopping area but still within the boundaries of the parking lot.)

Community Shopping Center. The community shopping center is similar to a neighborhood center, but on a much larger scale. Community shopping centers typically contain 150,000 to 400,000 square feet of GLA, and require a customer base of at least 5,000 families within a five-mile radius. Anchor tenants are usually supermarkets, smaller department stores, and home improvement centers. The configuration can range from that of a large strip to an L or U shape, and is generally an open-air complex surrounded by parking areas.

Regional Shopping Center. The regional shopping center attracts customers from surrounding areas who are in search of products—or a selection of products—that can't be found closer to home. Regional centers typically contain 300,000 to a million square feet of GLA. They serve an average market area of 50,000 to 150,000 families within a 10- to 50-mile radius. Anchor tenants can include up to four major department stores (traditional, discount, or specialty), as well as large multi-screen movie theatres. At this size, a variety of configurations are used: single-story enclosed, single-story open-air, and multi-story malls with up to six floors. The single-story enclosed version is the most common.

Superregional Shopping Center. As the name suggests, the superregional shopping center is a larger version of a regional center. It typically has more than four major department stores for anchors, and usually contains over one million square feet of GLA. Superregional malls differ from regional malls only in terms of size, number of anchor tenants, and market area.

Specialized Shopping Centers. Before we move on, let's discuss a few types of specialty shopping centers that are worth singling out: the outlet, power, and lifestyle shopping centers. They are usually regional shopping centers.

Outlet and discount shopping centers. Outlet and discount centers differ in one important way from most of the centers we've just discussed: they typically do not have anchor tenants. Outlet centers consist of name-brand stores selling overruns and factory seconds at discount prices. The brand names and reduced prices attract customers from up to 50 miles away. These centers range in size from 50,000 to 500,000 square feet of GLA. Discount retailers, who sell non-branded merchandise, may also occupy space inside these outlet centers to be near their bargain-minded shoppers.

Developers usually locate outlet and discount centers far from urban centers and suburbs; the reduced rents in small towns allow them to keep prices low.

Power shopping centers. A model that's relatively new is the power center, a shopping center featuring a collection of market-dominant chain stores (known as "category killers") clustered together in one center. Because each store is the dominant player in its own product line, these stores have little in common with each other. Thus, they don't benefit significantly from the customer traffic generated by their co-tenants; people come simply to shop at a particular store. The combined GLA in these centers can range from 300,000 to over a million square feet. Power centers are typically built for access by private vehicle rather than pedestrian foot traffic.

Lifestyle shopping centers. Lifestyle shopping centers are relatively new to the retail marketplace; they first appeared in the U.S. in the 1980s and became very popular

 Shopping Centers: Here to Stay?

It's sometimes said that the regional mall has been going out of style for 30 years. This bit of industry humor, referring to a repeated prediction that fails to materialize, testifies to the regional mall's staying power through good and bad economic times. Before the 2008 recession, the general consensus was that trendier lifestyle centers, power centers, and mixed-use projects would soon surpass the decades-old format of the regional enclosed mall. As it turned out, the tried-and-true model weathered the recession reasonably well, better than any other type of shopping center. From the first quarter of 2008 through the first quarter of 2011, the vacancy rate for regional malls posted the smallest amount of vacancy increase:

Shopping center type	Vacancy increase (2008-2011)
Regional malls	2.1%
Neighborhood centers	2.4%
Lifestyle centers	2.6%

Some experts attribute this resiliency to the fact that the classic regional mall is typically positioned in a solid trade area, with good demographics and a reliable tenant mix. Whatever the reasons, it appears the regional mall is here to stay.

in the 1990s. These open-air centers cater to affluent consumers, combining a boutique-like shopping experience with the easy access and parking of a neighborhood shopping center. These centers routinely incorporate dining and entertainment into the tenant mix, often including a multiplex cinema and several restaurants. These centers typically have around 50,000 square feet of GLA. Lifestyle centers may or may not have anchor stores.

Types of Retail Tenants

Let's turn our discussion now to the different types of retail tenants. Keep in mind that retail tenants include those who sell services as well as goods. Thus, the retail category encompasses not only stores but also businesses such as banks, portrait studios, watch and jewelry repair shops, and even optometrists.

Anchor Tenants. In nearly all shopping center configurations, anchor tenants are the most important type of tenant. Anchor tenants occupy the largest and most prominent spaces in a center, and they generate traffic for the center's smaller retail tenants. Accordingly, banks will ordinarily not finance the development of a new shopping center until the developer has signed lease agreements with the anchor tenants.

Depending on its size, a shopping center may have anywhere from one to ten anchor tenants. These tenants are usually large department stores, but may also be big box retailers or other major national chain stores. Because of an anchor tenant's importance to the shopping center in terms of securing financing and attracting customers, it enjoys a privileged position when it comes to lease negotiations.

Small Shops/Specialty Stores. Small shops and specialty stores generally carry a better-than-average selection of a certain type of item, such as handbags, cookware, or athletic shoes, and have a knowledgeable sales staff to go along with their products. While specialty stores are not the main customer draw for a shopping center, many customers will travel to a center to patronize a particular specialty store.

Grocery Stores and Restaurants. Many shopping centers have a grocery store as well as one or more restaurants. These businesses often occupy outparcels, as they tend to open earlier and/or close later than the regular retail stores in the center.

Services. Most retail centers include some service retailers. We gave several examples of service retailers above. Other services include dry cleaners, beauty salons, and fitness centers. Appropriately chosen service retailers broaden the appeal of a shopping center.

Management Planning for Retail Property

We covered the management plan generally in Chapter 4; here, we'll discuss aspects of the regional, neighborhood, property, market, and alternatives analyses that are unique to retail properties.

Regional Analysis

Regional factors to analyze include transportation issues, the health of local industries, tourism, recreational opportunities, and—somewhat uniquely for retail properties—climate. Climate has a big impact on the success of malls that are pedestrian friendly or otherwise open to the weather. The popularity of specific recreational activities in the region (which also tend to be climate-dependent) can help determine everything from the physical look of a mall to the kinds of clothing stores that are likely to do well.

Consumer Profile. The manager must also research demographic information to understand local buying power and purchasing preferences. The manager collects data on age, employment, education and income level, family configuration, and buying habits; this information is known as a **consumer profile**. Here are some of the most commonly used sources of data (all published by the U.S. Department of Commerce):

- U.S. Census (conducted every ten years with annual updates published in the Statistical Abstract of the United States);
- American Housing Survey (regional information on housing quality, neighborhood quality, and personal income);
- Consumer Expenditures Survey (spending patterns of American consumers, broken down by merchandise category); and
- current business reports (monthly compilations of retail trade sales and inventories).

Nongovernment resources are also available. For example, the *Sales & Marketing Management's Annual Survey of Buying Power* offers detailed listings on consumer spending habits in every major metropolitan area in the U.S. Local trade and business journals occasionally publish similar information for their areas.

Armed with information from these sources, the manager can begin to build a profile of the region's consumers.

Neighborhood Analysis

One of the key issues for a retail neighborhood analysis is local transportation. How will people get to the shopping center? Could access be improved? (If so, the analysis of alternatives should address this.)

The manager should also evaluate the economic condition of the neighborhood. Obviously, upscale shopping centers will do better if they are reasonably close to their customers. Locating shopping centers in relatively run-down neighborhoods generally makes it harder to attract customers, and may result in vandalism and graffiti.

Property Analysis

As we explained in Chapter 4, a property analysis assesses the property's physical attributes and general condition, as well as the property's marketing and leasing operations, management quality, and financial condition. Physical components prone to wear, especially the roof and HVAC systems, need close examination. In addition, the manager must evaluate the adequacy of parking, landscaping, and interior visual elements (such as potted plants or water features) that are intended to appeal to customers.

Tenant Mix. One thing that makes the property analysis for retail property unique is the time and energy spent on studying the **tenant mix**—evaluating how compatible each store is with neighboring stores and with the shopping center as a whole.

The selection of an individual retail tenant can have an enormous financial impact on other tenants as well as the property itself. The customers brought in by one tenant can mean success or failure for other retailers in the shopping center.

> **Example:** Customer Bob visits the new Rolling Rock Mall to buy a food processor at Ludlow's department store. He's daydreaming about the delicious meals he will prepare when he passes a cutlery shop a few doors down from Ludlow's. As he glances at the display window, he remembers that he needs a new chef's knife to replace his current dull, worn knife. He goes in and finds just the knife he wants.
>
> On his way out of the cutlery shop, Bob sees a specialty cheese shop. He realizes that he can finally buy a wedge of the hard cheese he loves, now that he has a knife with the heft to cut it. This illustrates the magic of a good tenant mix: in a single customer visit, the cutlery shop benefits from the traffic to one store, and provides traffic to another.

A shopping center manager must constantly monitor the tenant mix; shoppers' tastes can shift and what works well for several years may gradually become less effective. Each time a space in the shopping center becomes vacant or a lease is up for renewal, the manager should consider what type of tenant will best meet the goals of the center.

Generally, tenant mix should reflect the demand for various categories of merchandise in the relevant market. The government publications mentioned earlier will tell the manager how consumers spend their dollars in various merchandise sectors. These merchandise sectors include categories such as shoes, office supplies, and home furnishings. Analyzing these figures reveals the market segments with the largest sales potential. The manager then targets retailers in these segments for inclusion in the tenant mix, in proportion to demand.

A comprehensive discussion on formulating the optimal tenant mix is beyond the scope of this chapter, but keep in mind that creating a successful tenant mix is more a matter of experience than instruction.

Determining Tenant Mix in a New Development. Typically, much of the tenant mix in a new retail development is determined well in advance. The developer conducts her own market analysis and then approaches potential anchor tenants and signs them before construction begins. Based on the initial market analysis, the developer may also have a good idea about what types of retailers would make the most sense for the remaining space. This information is a good starting point for a property manager charged with taking on the management of the new shopping center.

Market Analysis

The market analysis for retail properties typically addresses two issues: the property's ability to attract customers and the property's ability to attract tenants.

Attracting Customers. A key factor in a retail property's appeal to tenants is its ability to attract customers. The market analysis should define what kind of customers the shopping center wants to attract; rather than trying to appeal to everyone, most shopping centers target a certain range of customers. The property manager must determine where these customers currently shop, what they shop for, and how much they spend. Only then can the manager analyze how attractive the subject property will be to these shoppers.

Attracting Tenants. The second part of the market analysis is a study of competing properties. Competing retail properties include shopping centers and sometimes stand-alone stores as well.

Whether a similar shopping center or store is considered competition depends in part on its proximity to the subject property. For instance, a strip mall manager looks at strip centers in nearby commercial neighborhoods. On the other hand, a regional mall manager looks much farther afield, at other regional malls; the appeal of a nearby strip mall is more or less irrelevant.

Whether a given shopping center is considered competition also depends on the types of merchandise sold there. Proximity and types of merchandize often intersect: a shopper may drive 40 miles to comparison shop for a specialty item (such as designer apparel), but not for household supplies or groceries.

Analysis of Alternatives

As you know, the analysis of alternatives describes property elements that could or should be changed to increase the property's competitiveness. With a shopping center, the number of alternatives to analyze is nearly endless. Many alternatives involve the shopping center's appearance. Cosmetic upgrades don't have to cost a great deal. For instance, fresh, attractive landscaping can be a quick, cost-effective enhancement. Upgrades can also be made to the interior common areas: new seating, new trash receptacles, and additional plantings. A more significant alternative would be storefront facelifts, including new paint, signage, lighting, and awnings.

Parking is always an important element for retail properties. However, if more than enough parking already exists, replacing some of the excess parking with additional store space would bring in more rent and customer traffic.

Fundamental to the analysis of alternatives is the question of highest and best use. Is there a more profitable use of the property? Generally, for retail property, the answer is no. However, if the shopping center is struggling or in a neighborhood that is undergoing significant change, the answer may be different.

> **Example:** A neighborhood in the city is undergoing a renewal; housing prices are rising and several boutiques and upscale restaurants have moved into this commercial zone. An older, slightly run-down strip mall in the area is starting to look a little out of place. In addition, rising property taxes are cutting into the owner's meager profits.
>
> The company managing the property performs an analysis of alternatives, and recommends tearing down the strip mall and replacing it with a three-story mixed-use building that has underground parking, ground-floor retail, and upper-story residential condo units.

Marketing Retail Space to Tenants

We'll now turn to the critical task of marketing retail space to prospective tenants. Naturally, in the case of a new shopping center, the overriding goal of the marketing effort is to "lease up" the property. The leasing program remains important afterwards, too, because tenant turnover continues to create new vacancies. Chapter 7 discusses leasing in general, so here we will discuss the responsibilities of the leasing team in a shopping center context.

Leasing Team

With community, regional, and superregional shopping centers, a team of people generally handles the leasing effort (at least during lease up). The size and membership of the team varies depending on the size of the retail property and the number of spaces to be leased. The leasing team for a large new shopping center with a lot of vacant space may include the following:

- **Shopping center manager.** The manager usually develops the marketing plan and the leasing program, so she often leads the leasing team, selects its members, and directs its activities.
- **Leasing agent.** The leasing agent is a salesperson trained in renting commercial space who is hired to focus on prospecting for tenants, selling the space, and closing the deal. He may be an employee of the property management firm or of the property owner, or he may work for a brokerage firm that specializes in retail leasing. Leasing agents are paid on commission, and are most useful during a large lease-up. If only a few vacancies need to be filled, the shopping center manager usually handles leasing agent duties.
- **Marketing director.** The marketing director's principal activity is to market the shopping center and its tenants to consumers; she generally has only an advisory role in leasing activities. But that advisory role is important. As the marketing director, she knows the local retail market—what retailers are moving into the area, as well as existing retailers who may want to move or expand.
- **Property owner.** Although the owner has the ultimate authority to approve and reject tenants, she often doesn't actively serve on the leasing team. Regardless, the manager and leasing agent should keep the owner informed about current market conditions and trends. This allows the owner to make informed decisions about prospective tenants.

In addition to these members of the leasing team, lawyers, accountants, and other professionals will provide services as needed.

Finding and Marketing to Potential Tenants

The leasing team starts its work by reviewing the management and marketing plans. After team members have educated themselves, they can begin selling the property to prospective tenants.

Leasing Package. One of the first steps in the marketing effort is to create a leasing package, especially if the property is newly built. The materials in the package depend on the team's marketing strategy as well as the particulars of the property itself. However, the leasing package for all but the smallest shopping center generally includes the following:

- **Layout drawing.** This is a diagram that shows all existing tenants and their locations in the shopping center. A separate tenant list may be used if it's not feasible to note all tenant locations on the drawing.
- **Brochure.** The brochure usually includes illustrations (either photos or drawings) plus a brief description of the architecture and common areas, anchor tenants and their anticipated customer draw, and any amenities that would interest retailers.
- **Regional map.** The map shows public transit lines, expressways and exits, and major thoroughfares. Geographic information system (GIS) information may be added, along with brief references to demographic information, such as average household income per neighborhood.
- **Demographic and lifestyle profile.** A complete statement of demographic information for the relevant market is a must. The information should be broken down into various radius distances to show the primary, secondary, and tertiary zones of the customer base. This crucial information allows a prospective tenant to estimate potential sales.
- **Traffic counts.** Local governments often conduct vehicle traffic surveys on busy arterials and interchanges, as well as near popular shopping areas. These counts are considered effective indicators of potential retail sales.
- **General sales numbers from current tenants.** A brief overview of the sales figures for various categories of merchants should be given (for example, "$11 million in annual gross sales for six women's career clothing stores"). Sales figures for an individual store should never be disclosed.
- **Marketing and promotions.** The package should include a description of the shopping center's marketing program, along with a calendar of planned marketing campaigns and promotional events, news coverage of past events, and the like. Prospective tenants want to see that the center actively promotes and markets itself, particularly if regular contributions to a marketing fund are required. (The marketing fund is explained later in this chapter.)

Finding Prospects. The shopping center manager and/or the leasing agent(s) should compile a list of sources for potential tenants, and then begin prospecting. Display advertising in local business journals, direct mail campaigns, billboards, and on-site signage all help generate interest among retailers. Additionally, team members should have personal contacts that will help identify potential tenants.

Generally, the most cost-effective way to share leasing information is via the shopping center's own website. Interactive maps and virtual tours can enhance the information in the leasing package, and prospects may request more information with the click of a button.

Many commercial property websites list available retail space. These websites resemble online classified ads, but allow someone looking for commercial space to use more sophisticated search parameters. Interested retailers can narrow a property search by entering the desired location, square footage, building type, and rental rate. Most commercial property management and brokerage offices also maintain these kinds of sites for their clients.

Leasing Retail Space

Once the manager begins marketing to potential tenants, she must also begin to think about selecting tenants and negotiating the lease. Here we'll briefly discuss how to evaluate and choose tenants, and then move on to an examination of some commonly negotiated lease provisions. We'll also discuss lease provisions in the anchor tenant context. Finally, we'll say a few words about using lease summaries.

Evaluating and Selecting Tenants

As we've discussed, one of the most important characteristics of retail property is the synergistic relationship between the tenants in a shopping center: the draw of one store helps other stores in the center. Thus, the retail property manager wants to achieve the right tenant mix.

A manager who prepared a thorough analysis of local retail sales in his management plan should already know which categories of retailers would create the ideal tenant mix. The manager now needs only to evaluate individual prospective tenants. He scrutinizes each potential tenant with the same care that an employer evaluates a job applicant.

- Does the prospect have a healthy sales history?
- Does the prospect carry an adequate inventory and replenish it with current, seasonally appropriate merchandise?
- Would the prospect's current sales volume increase the shopping center's profitability?
- Would relocating to the shopping center be likely to change the prospect's sales volume?
- Is the space under consideration the best choice for this prospect in terms of customer traffic to and from neighboring tenants?

The manager and/or leasing agent should also determine whether the projected **rent-to-sales ratio** is acceptable. To calculate the rent-to-sales ratio, divide the minimum rent by projected sales. A store with a ratio above 15% is generally not producing enough profit and poses an unacceptably high risk of default on the lease.

Example: Retail space has just opened up in the popular Red Springs Shopping Center. It normally generates a minimum rent of $25 per square foot. Two prospective tenants are under consideration. Store A projects its monthly sales at $180 per square foot, while Store B projects monthly sales of $140 per square foot.

Store A: $25 ÷ $180 = .138 = 13.8%
Store B: $25 ÷ $140 = .178 = 17.8%

Everything else being equal, Store A is the more attractive tenant because it presents the least risk of default. Even if Store B were the only applicant interested in the space, the manager would probably avoid committing to a long-term lease; Store B's rent-to-sales ratio is too high for comfort.

Lease Provisions

Retail tenants and the spaces they rent vary widely, so the particulars of retail leases also vary. However, most retail leases have a similar structure and include some of the same provisions. Here, we'll discuss provisions that govern percentage rent and pass-through charges, the two most hotly negotiated items. We'll also look at various provisions concerning tenant operations, such as store hours, use of the premises, and so on.

Percentage Rent. Retail rent typically consists of two parts, a **minimum rent** amount (also called base rent) and **percentage rent**. Minimum rent is straightforward: it's the set amount of rent due each month. All commercial tenants pay minimum rent. A retail lease may provide for periodic increases in the minimum rent to account for rising costs, using an escalation clause (see our discussion of rent in Chapter 7). However, minimum rent increases aren't as common in retail leases as they are in other commercial leases. On the other hand, percentage rent clauses (a concept unique to retail property) are found in most retail leases.

In a **percentage lease**, the rent amount is based on the tenant's monthly or annual gross sales. Thus, the more sales, the higher the rent paid. This benefits both tenant and landlord: the tenant has to pay higher rent only as sales increase, and the landlord receives more rent as overall prices increase (creating higher sales figures). Percentage rent provisions also encourage the shopping center to focus on marketing the property as a whole: the more customers come to the shopping center, the greater the benefit for both the tenants and the property owner.

Breakpoints. Typically, percentage lease provisions specify one or more breakpoints. **Breakpoints** are gross sales amounts above which the percentage rent kicks in. Breakpoints may be determined either "naturally" or "artificially."

Natural breakpoints are calculated using the minimum rent amount. For example, suppose the percentage to be applied is 5% of all sales over and above the natural breakpoint, with minimum rent set at $5,500. The natural breakpoint is determined by dividing the minimum rent by the percentage:

$$\text{Base rent} \div \text{Percentage rate} = \text{Breakpoint}$$
$$\$5,500 \div 5\% = \$110,000$$

This is considered "natural" because the tenant is essentially paying 5% on all sales. Note that the rent provision guarantees the first 5% as minimum rent no matter what sales actually are. Only if sales exceed the breakpoint will the tenant owe anything more than minimum rent. (The additional amount is sometimes called overage rent.)

The parties can negotiate a higher or lower amount than the natural breakpoint. If so, that figure is considered an artificial breakpoint. A property manager with strong bargaining power, or who has given generous concessions in other areas, may seek an artificial breakpoint that's below the natural breakpoint. With a lower breakpoint, the percentage rent kicks in sooner than it would with the natural breakpoint. In the above example, for instance, the breakpoint could be lowered to $95,000. This could add as much as $750 worth of additional rent ($110,000 – $95,000 = $15,000; $15,000 × .05 = $750). Since the minimum rent is fixed, a lower artificial breakpoint results in higher total rent payments.

On other hand, if the tenant is in a stronger bargaining position, he may negotiate a breakpoint that is higher than the natural one, so that lower total rent may be paid.

Determining gross sales. To compute the amount of percentage rent due, the property manager usually uses the tenant's gross sales figures. However, the lease may allow deduction of certain items from gross sales, such as sales tax and customer refunds. It's in the best interest of both parties to clearly define gross sales in the lease. This reduces the chance of later arguments about the amount of percentage rent due.

Tenants (except, possibly, large anchor tenants) must report their gross sales to the landlord every month. These reports, called tenant sales reports, are typically due within 20 days after the last day of the month being reported. The manager uses the report to determine the amount of percentage rent due for the next month. However, since the manager based the calculation on the previous month, the amount of percentage rent paid is provisional. The tenant's actual sales for the month may be higher or lower. At the end of the year, the tenant usually provides a year-end gross income statement prepared by an independent certified public accountant. The landlord then compares this annual statement to the monthly statements. If the tenant overpaid, it receives a refund; if the tenant underpaid, it must pay the landlord the additional amount.

Retailers are sometimes tempted to underreport their sales in order to pay less percentage rent. Because of this, most leases give the manager the right to audit the tenant's financial records. Penalties for delinquent or inaccurate reporting are typically included in the lease's sales report provision.

Variable scale. The percentage rent provision may include a maximum dollar limit. Alternatively, or in addition, the provision may use a tier arrangement, with the percentage rent rate falling as each successively higher sales amount is reached. These limits keep the total rent amount from becoming too large.

> **Example:** AB Foods, a large grocery chain, has just finalized lease negotiations for a store in the new Pine Street Shopping Center. Because of AB's national prominence and its ability to draw customers, the landlord agreed to a decreasing percentage rate on all gross sales above $200 million per year. Here's how AB's percentage rent would be calculated if its gross sales total $320 million for the year:
>
> **Percentage Rent Lease Terms**
>
> | | |
> |---|---|
> | Minimum rent | $12 million (6% to breakpoint) |
> | Sales breakpoint ($12 million ÷ 6%) | $200 million |
> | Percentage rent above breakpoints | 1st tier: 3% of next $50 million |
> | | 2nd tier: 1.5% of next $250 million |
>
> **Rent calculation for the year ($320 million in gross sales)**
>
> | | |
> |---|---|
> | Minimum rent | $12,000,000 |
> | Percentage rent, 1st tier ($50 million × .03) | $1,500,000 |
> | Percentage rent, 2nd tier ($70 million × .015) | $1,050,000 |
> | **Total Rent** | **$14,550,000** |

Recapture Clause. Sometimes the landlord wants an escape hatch (called a recapture clause) in case the new tenant doesn't reach the optimal sales level and is unable to pay the desired percentage rent. The **recapture clause** requires the tenant to achieve a minimum sales figure. If the tenant fails to meet this goal, the landlord may terminate the lease, retake (recapture) the premises, and seek a more promising tenant.

Straight Percentage

One of the less common percentage rent arrangements is the straight percentage lease. As the term implies, rental payments under a straight percentage lease are based solely on the tenant's gross income for the period; the manager applies a fixed percentage rate to the income and charges no minimum rent. This type of lease is generally reserved for seasonal retail occupancies and other leases of a more temporary nature.

Late Charges. As with other kinds of leases, a retail lease usually imposes a penalty if a rent payment is late. Additionally, most percentage leases require the tenant to submit monthly sales reports to the manager by a certain date. The lease should impose a penalty if the tenant fails to meet this deadline. However, the lease usually requires the manager to give the tenant written notice and a certain number of days' grace period before assessing these penalties.

Pass-Through Charges. Most commercial leases include provisions for pass-through charges. As we discussed in Chapter 7, these charges distribute the property owner's operating expenses (such as taxes, insurance, and common area maintenance charges) among the tenants, based on the amount of space each tenant occupies. There are a couple of ways to calculate the exact percentage for the pro rata share.

The **leasable area formula**, which is preferred by tenants, assigns a pro rata percentage to a tenant by dividing the GLA of the entire property (including vacancies) into the tenant's GLA.

The **leased space formula**, preferred by landlords, assigns a pro rata percentage to a tenant by dividing the total currently leased GLA into the tenant's GLA. This formula results in a larger percentage for the tenant than the leasable area formula when the center is less than 100% occupied. The leased space formula shifts the burden of expenses associated with empty space from the landlord to the tenants.

Example: Ace 5 Shopping Center has just begun its second year in operation, but has secured tenants for only half of the center's total GLA. Total GLA for the center is 800,000 square feet, and total pass-through expenses are roughly $325,000 per year for the entire property. Tenant A occupies 15,000 square feet. Here are the two calculations for Tenant A's pro rata share:

Leasable area formula:
Tenant's GLA ÷ Total GLA = Tenant's pro rata share
15,000 ÷ 800,000 = 1.875%
Pass-through charges of $325,000 × 1.875% = $6,093.75

Leased space formula:
Tenant's GLA ÷ Currently leased GLA = Tenant's pro rata share
15,000 ÷ 400,000 = 3.75%
Pass-through charges of $325,000 × 3.75% = $12,187.50

The fact that the premises are only half occupied doubles the tenant's share of expenses under the leased space formula.

CAM charges. As you've learned from previous chapters, CAM charges are common area maintenance expenses. For a shopping center, common areas include parking lots, loading docks, interior service areas, and mall pedestrian areas.

Calculating CAM expenses under a retail lease can be quite complex. For instance, at an indoor shopping mall the outparcel tenants—and many anchor tenants—typically pay CAM charges only for parking and exterior areas (since they don't rely as heavily on the interior areas). This leaves the smaller inside tenants to pay all of the interior CAM expenses. In order to bill these expenses separately, the landlord must maintain an account for interior CAM charges and also one for exterior CAM charges. That way, he can calculate the tenants' pro rata shares for each.

A tenant who pays both interior and exterior CAM charges will usually pay one rate for interior CAM charges and another (somewhat smaller) percentage for exterior CAM charges. (Exterior CAM charges are usually smaller because more tenants are sharing the cost).

Because the tenant's CAM charges are based on the landlord's actual expenses in maintaining the common areas, the tenant has the right to inspect the landlord's invoicing and bookkeeping for accuracy. The lease should contain a provision that addresses the tenant's right to audit, with reasonable limits on time, place, and billing periods.

Tenant Operations Provisions. Now that we've discussed the provisions for percentage rent and pass-through charges, we'll address lease provisions that govern tenant operations (use, store hours, and so on).

Tenant use. The goods and services sold by each tenant must vary enough that the stores aren't competing with each other for the bulk of their business (unless the center's strategy is to deliberately attract comparison shopping). The lease provision that the landlord uses to prevent excessive competition is called the **use clause**. This provision limits a tenant's use of the leased premises to what is specifically listed in the clause.

> **Example:** Here's a typical use clause for an office supply store:
>
> *Premises will be used as an office supply store for the sale of products limited to paper goods, forms, filing supplies, ink and toner, mailing and shipping supplies, desk accessories, and office furniture. Tenant is prohibited from selling computers, computer equipment, and electronics, or from offering repair services. Tenant may not sell snacks or coffee supplies in bulk, but may offer individually wrapped candy and snacks for immediate consumption; sales area for candy and snacks is limited to 15 square feet.*

Imagine that a computer retailer, for example, wants to rent space in our hypothetical shopping center. The retailer worries about competition from the office supply business. Thanks to the use restriction in the office supply store's lease, the property manager can assure the prospective tenant that the office supply store can't sell or service computers and computer equipment.

A retailer with clout sometimes seeks a lease provision that bars the landlord from entering into subsequent leases with retailers who sell competing merchandise or services.

This is called an **exclusivity clause**. For example, an exclusivity clause might prevent the landlord from leasing to anyone else who sells a certain designer clothing line.

Landlords sometimes negotiate a provision that prohibits the tenant from opening a branch store within a certain radius. This clause, sometimes referred to as a **noncompete clause**, prevents the tenant from siphoning off customers to a different location. (Note that the term noncompete may also be used to describe an exclusivity clause.)

Store hours. Nearly all retail leases require the tenant to remain open during normal shopping hours. The overall success of the shopping center (and of each individual tenant) depends on a customer base that expects all stores to be open when they come to shop. If the mall is open until 9:00 pm, but a customer finds several stores dark when he visits at 7:30 pm, that customer may take his business elsewhere. Further, a store that isn't open during normal business hours won't realize as much in gross sales. This means the landlord may collect less percentage rent.

Usually included in the requirement to remain open during normal retail hours is the obligation to maintain adequate inventory and sales staff.

Most shopping center leases also prohibit the tenant from remaining open longer than the shopping center's regular hours; longer hours require extra security, additional utilities, and possibly higher insurance rates. However, landlords generally allow an outparcel tenant, such as a restaurant or supermarket, to open earlier and stay open later than the mall's normal hours. In fact, longer hours are often necessary to make the restaurant or supermarket profitable.

Insurance. Given a shopping center's numerous employees and many customers, injuries are bound to occur. Some degree of property damage is also inevitable. Both the landlord and the tenants need to obtain adequate insurance. As with other types of commercial properties, the policies on retail properties typically name both the landlord and the tenant as co-insureds. The property manager usually treats shopping center policies as a CAM expense and bills tenants on a pro rata basis.

Signage and advertising. Retail tenants usually design and install their own signs, but managers should retain control over the size, color, materials, and placement of the signs. The lease usually requires the tenant to submit the specifications to the manager for prior approval.

A retail lease also typically requires the tenant to spend a certain minimum amount on advertising (a flat rate or a percentage of gross sales, for example). Alternatively, the advertising clause may require the tenant to advertise a minimum number of times per month in designated publications and advertising circulars. The tenants may also have to contribute to a marketing fund. The property manager administers the marketing fund, using it to pay for advertising that benefits the entire shopping center. (We'll discuss marketing funds later in the chapter.)

Security deposits. The retail property manager collects security deposits from tenants for the same reason that a residential manager collects deposits from renters: to protect the property owner should the tenant default on the lease. Sometimes, the tenant can negotiate an early refund of part or all of the deposit after meeting predetermined sales goals for a specified number of months.

Most anchor tenants and large national chain stores can cover the cost of a lease default, so they're usually not required to pay a security deposit.

Leasing to Anchor Tenants

As we've mentioned, anchor tenants have more clout than the typical tenant. This certainly helps the anchor during lease negotiations. Here we'll look at a few common lease provisions and discuss how the terms of an anchor lease tend to differ from those found in an ordinary retail lease.

Lease Term. Anchor tenants invest significant money and planning into their locations, and the success of a shopping center depends on their presence. Therefore, both parties want longer lease terms than is common for ordinary retailers. The terms might run as long as 20 to 30 years.

In some yet-to-be-built malls, anchor tenants lease the ground from the landlord and build their own stores. (This is mainly true of outparcel tenants.) Since these tenants are going to pay for constructing the building, and will own it, they often require even longer lease terms.

Rent. Anchor tenants often pay a relatively low base rent, at least for the first few years of the lease term. The initial minimum rent amount is often just enough to cover the landlord's costs for that portion of the property. However, as long as the anchor tenant's business is successful, the landlord will make up for that low base rent by collecting percentage rent during that early period.

Because anchor tenant leases tend to run for such long periods of time, they often contain escalation clauses as well as percentage rent clauses. Escalation clauses attempt to account for factors such as inflation and demographic shifts that are inevitable over the long haul. A tenant's sales don't always reflect these changes and percentage rent alone may fail to keep up with the times.

CAM Charges. We mentioned earlier that anchor tenants often negotiate their way out of paying their pro rata share of CAM charges. However, these tenants usually agree to pay CAM charges on their share of the parking area, the logic being that while they can operate quite successfully without the benefit of the interior common areas, they do require parking.

This doesn't mean anchor tenants don't care about interior common areas. In fact, the opposite is true; an anchor tenant often imposes requirements for common area use and upkeep, since poorly maintained or overly crowded common areas can hurt the anchor's business. The provisions regarding the common areas may be in the body of the lease or attached as a separate document called a CAM agreement.

Continuous Operation. During economic downturns, anchor tenants sometimes decide it makes financial sense to "go dark." In other words, they continue to pay the base rent but cease retail operations on the premises. Most anchors are part of large chains and can afford this strategy. An anchor tenant might do this even in good times if it's opened another store in a nearby, more attractive shopping center.

Tenant Operations

Many retail tenants, particularly those with more bargaining power, seek some wiggle room in the tenant operations provisions. Here are a few examples.

- **Go-dark allowance.** Retail leases generally require the tenant to stay open for business every day. However, small or midsize tenants may seek a certain number of days per year during which they are allowed to close, for example, to conduct inventory or to observe holidays.
- **Go-dark contingency.** Some retail tenants want a modification to the continuous operation provision, giving them the right to close if other tenants do. Such a modification may give the tenant the right to remain closed during the lease-up phase in a new center, or if certain anchor tenants are closed for any reason.
- **Additional use options.** Some tenants seek the option to add or convert to another use. For example, a camera store may want the right to sell certain other kinds of consumer electronics, or a sporting goods store may want to convert to a store that specializes in outdoor clothing only. Such allowances must be negotiated cautiously; the manager has to keep noncompete clauses with other tenants in mind.

Obviously, a dark anchor will cast a shadow over the entire mall. A continuous operation provision limits the right of the anchor to go dark, or at least gives the landlord the right to terminate the lease if the tenant ceases or suspends retail activities.

Lease Summary

As with all commercial properties, retail leases are usually quite lengthy and complex. While the manager should always have access to the complete lease document if questions arise, she usually needs access to only the key lease terms. The **lease summary** serves this need, as it includes only the essential terms for each tenant.

The summary is typically about one page for each tenant, allowing the manager to see at a glance the:

- minimum rent and sales breakpoint,
- amount and date of any scheduled adjustment to minimum and/or percentage rents,
- amount of CAM charges,
- square feet of gross leasable area, and
- lease termination date.

Operations and Reports to the Owner

Now that we've examined the steps involved in marketing and leasing to retail tenants, let's take a closer look at operations, specifically security and maintenance. After discussing operations, we'll look at ways to market shopping centers to consumers. We'll conclude the chapter with a short look at making reports to the owner of retail property.

Operations

An important part of retail property management is making sure the premises appeal not only to tenants but also to customers. A shopping center that appears to be unsafe or in poor repair will drive away customers. Therefore, security and maintenance are vital to a retail property's success.

Security. The size of the property, its location, and its operating hours largely determine what kinds of security measures are necessary. The manager also needs a good handle on the area's crime statistics. In a safe neighborhood, for example, on-site security personnel may not be necessary for a small neighborhood shopping center or a strip mall. In such cases, contracting with an independent service for regular security patrols might be sufficient. On the other hand, a small property with a history of trouble may require an on-site guard, at least during evening hours. Obviously, a large regional or superregional mall warrants a full-time security presence regardless of its location.

Customers may ask on-site security staff to help with flat tires or dead car batteries. The manager and owner should develop a policy for handling these requests. Helping customers with these types of problems means purchasing and maintaining the necessary equipment.

Another unique security consideration with retail property is detaining suspected shoplifters and handling unruly or destructive shoppers. Security procedures should spell out what the staff can and cannot do about these problems. Leaving matters to a guard's discretion will lead to problems sooner or later. Clear procedures and solid training can limit liability in the event of a lawsuit.

Maintenance. Retail tenants often handle routine maintenance for their own space. That leaves the shopping center manager to develop and implement a maintenance program for the common areas. Chapter 9 addresses maintenance in detail, so here we'll limit the discussion to a few matters specific to retail property.

Shopping center maintenance varies according to property size, customer traffic, and season. For instance, restrooms in a busy mall may need hourly cleaning, while restrooms in a smaller shopping center may need to be cleaned two or three times a day. During winter months, snow removal from parking lots and walkways may comprise a large portion of the custodial maintenance budget. In harsh winter weather, customers track water, snow, sand, and chemicals into the common areas, so the staff must monitor and clean interior floors more often. This not only helps maintain the mall's appearance, it also limits liability for slip and fall injuries.

If the shopping center has a food court, the property manager is responsible for the disposal of food waste and keeping surfaces clean. In addition, the manager should handle any pest control issues. Food preparation and cleanup is normally regulated by local health codes, and the manager must ensure compliance.

Marketing Shopping Centers to Consumers

Now let's turn our attention to how a shopping center markets itself to consumers. While individual retail stores do their own advertising, it's imperative for a shopping center to have its own marketing strategy. The shopping center's marketing director generally handles all aspects of the center's promotion and advertising.

Dependable funding and a detailed plan are crucial elements of a successful consumer marketing campaign.

Funding the Marketing. Generally, either the property owner, a merchants association, or a marketing fund provides the money for a shopping center's marketing efforts.

Owner-financed funding. With the owner-financed approach, the shopping center owner pays the cost of any marketing that benefits all of the retailers. The tenants do not get involved, nor do they pay any dues or fees. Naturally, most owners would rather not carry this financial burden alone. For that reason, landlords tend to negotiate leases that require contributions from tenants, as described below.

Merchants association funding. The first cooperative efforts in shopping center marketing involved merchants associations. Though not as common as they once were, merchants associations still exist. Under the association approach, all the stores in a shopping center have a provision in their lease requiring them to join the association and pay monthly dues. The owner also contributes a certain amount. A board of directors elected by the association's members runs the organization and meets regularly to plan promotional and advertising activities. Many retailers and board members don't have the time or expertise to develop an effective marketing plan, so they rely on the expertise of the shopping center's marketing director.

Merchants associations were the most common organizational approach in the U.S. until the early 1980s, when the marketing fund displaced them as the favored model.

Marketing fund. The property owner has complete control of the marketing efforts paid for by a marketing fund. The leases require each tenant to contribute to the fund every month. (The property owner also usually contributes.) The lease often provides for automatic annual increases in the contribution amount.

An advisory board represents the retailers and makes suggestions to the owner regarding allocation of the funds. The board consists of representatives of the anchor tenants and perhaps two or three other retailers in the center. These representatives serve in a strictly advisory capacity; while they have some influence over the landlord's marketing decisions, they exercise no actual control.

Each tenant's contribution is based on the amount of square footage it leases. However, anchor tenants often pay less per square foot to the marketing fund than other, smaller retailers. This is because anchors spend large amounts on their own marketing, which brings many customers to the shopping center.

Elements of the Marketing Campaign. A detailed marketing plan is essential to the success of any shopping center's consumer marketing efforts. Sophisticated tenants often insist on a lease provision that describes the landlord's marketing responsibilities, particularly when the tenant is contributing to a marketing fund.

The marketing director typically prepares an annual marketing plan with input from the landlord, the manager, and representatives of the retailers. (This collaborative style of marketing campaign is sometimes referred to as a "coordinated" marketing plan.) The manager and marketing director should make a point of meeting with each tenant to explain the marketing plan and how it will benefit that tenant and the shopping center as a whole.

Media selection. The marketing plan should employ all reasonable means of gaining exposure to customers, including newspapers, mailings, billboards, television, radio, and the Internet. (Internet marketing utilizes property websites, social media, email, and local online coupon promotions.) The media director wants to remind potential customers on a regular basis to shop at the center.

Events. Aside from regular advertising campaigns, the property manager and marketing director should also plan at least one or two event-type promotions each year. These kinds of promotions generate energy and community involvement. Possible events include fundraisers for local charities, seasonal sales and clearances, health and fitness promotions (with information booths and equipment displays), and special interest events such as hobby and craft fairs or comic book trade shows. If well-conceived, these events attract the attention of local news media and can thus yield free advertising in the form of news features and mentions in event calendars.

Grand openings. The marketing plan for a new shopping center naturally involves considerable advance planning. For a larger shopping center, the marketing director begins planning grand opening events and promotions up to a year in advance. The property manager and the marketing director should keep all tenants and prospective tenants apprised of developments during this planning stage.

Advertising for a grand opening should include a mix of Internet and traditional media (including newspaper, direct mail, and radio spots). Press releases make up an important part of the media blitz. Grand opening banners should be placed on the exterior of the more prominent buildings. The marketing director or the manager chooses or approves the size, font, and color schemes of the banners.

The marketing director should work with all of the retailers to ensure that the tenants' individual grand openings complement those of the entire shopping center. Grand opening events can be spread out over several weeks to maximize the effect.

Reports to the Owner

We're going to conclude the chapter with a discussion of reports to the owner. We've repeatedly noted the importance of keeping the owner apprised of shopping center matters. Some of this communication takes the form of discussions, either via phone calls or in face-to-face meetings. Of course, retail managers must also make the standard written reports described in Chapter 5.

One report that's unique to retail is the **sales analysis report**. We'll focus on that here. As the name implies, the sales analysis report tracks tenant sales figures, which determine the amount of percentage rent collected.

The format of the report depends on the size of the shopping center and the number of tenants in the various retail categories. At a minimum, the analysis includes sales figures for each retailer broken down by month and year. It also includes the number of square feet and dollars of sales per square foot for each retailer. It should note the annual breakpoint and percentage rent owed, if any.

Ideally, the analysis also compares each tenant's current sales performance to both its past performance and to industry averages. (Various trade publications provide industry sales averages.) If the property is a large center with many tenants in various retail categories (such as apparel, food, or gifts), the report should include a sales breakdown by retail category. That way, the owner and manager can compare the center's sales in each category to local and regional averages.

All of these various income statistics allow the owner to determine her return on investment and judge how well the property is doing compared to competing shopping centers. The data may also indicate the need for changes to the tenant mix or adjustments to the marketing efforts.

Chapter Summary

1. Shopping center properties vary greatly from one another in size, tenant mix, number of anchor tenants, and customer base. Along with strip malls, types of shopping centers include neighborhood, community, regional, superregional, outlet and discount, power, and lifestyle.

2. Management planning for retail property differs in several important ways from other commercial properties. First, the market analysis must account for the subject property's ability to compete not only for tenants, but for retail customers. Second, the property analysis must include an assessment of each individual retail space for compatibility with surrounding retail tenants and with the shopping center as a whole (the tenant mix).

3. The leasing strategy for a new retail property depends on its size, age, budget, and the anchor tenants that have committed. In most cases a leasing team is beneficial. For smaller properties, some of these roles may be handled by a single person. A leasing package is useful in marketing to potential tenants, and generally includes property diagrams, maps, demographic data, traffic counts, and information on planned shopping center marketing.

4. The typical retail lease includes provisions for minimum rent. In addition to minimum rent, retail tenants usually pay percentage rent based on their gross sales. Generally all tenants pay percentage rent each month based on the retailer's sales reports. Some retailers negotiate maximum or variable scale percentages.

5. Most retail leases require the tenant to pay a percentage of the shopping center's operating expenses, known as pass-through charges. These include taxes, insurance, and CAM expenses. Because the charges are supposed to be a percentage of the owner's actual expenses, tenants have the right to audit the landlord's records on those expenses.

6. A retail lease normally imposes requirements on a tenant's operations. These may include restrictions on sales of certain kinds of merchandise, noncompete clauses, prescribed store hours, and provisions that prevent a store from "going dark."

7. Anchor tenants typically receive important leasing concessions because they bring in customers for the center's other retailers. These concessions may include low minimum rent, discounted CAM charges, and the anchor's right to control some of the landlord's common area management practices.

8. Maintenance for shopping centers varies with property size and customer volume. Winter in many areas places heavy demands on staff due to snow and ice. Security for a shopping center involves on-site staff and outside help.

9. Retail leases usually require the tenant to contribute to a marketing fund to pay for the center's consumer marketing efforts. Ideally, a marketing director handles marketing for the shopping center.

10. The shopping center property manager's reports to the owner require a retail-specific approach, including collecting and analyzing tenant sales reports. The owner wants to know how well the individual stores are doing compared to similar stores, and how well the shopping center as a whole is doing compared to the competition.

Key Terms

Gross Leasable Area (GLA) – The GLA is a measure of square footage that includes all of the tenant spaces but not the common areas.

Anchor tenant – A large retail tenant that occupies a prominent space in a shopping center and is expected to draw the majority of customers to the property. Because of their importance to the center's success, anchor tenants usually receive significant leasing concessions.

Outparcel – A retail space that's not attached to the main shopping center, but occupies a separate space within the boundaries of the shopping center, usually surrounded by its parking lot.

Consumer profile – A collection of demographic and lifestyle information on consumers in a retail property's market area, including age, employment, education and income levels, family configuration, and buying habits.

Tenant mix –The proportion of different types of retail tenants and their physical arrangement on the property. Because customer traffic in a shopping center is so interdependent, the tenant mix has a sizeable impact on sales performance.

Leasing team – A team of leasing professionals that optimizes leasing efforts for a retail property. Depending on the property's size and percentage of vacant space, the team can include a combination of leasing agents, brokerage agents, marketing director, property manager, and owner.

Minimum rent/base rent – The baseline rent in a retail lease. Regardless of the retailer's sales for the period, it must pay the stated minimum rent.

Percentage lease – A common retail lease arrangement in which the tenant must pay a stated percentage of gross sales in addition to minimum rent.

Breakpoint – The dollar amount of gross sales that must be achieved before the effective percentage rate exceeds minimum rent, triggering percentage rent due for the period.

Recapture clause – A lease clause that sets a certain level of gross sales for a new retail tenant to achieve within a certain time; if the tenant fails to meet this sales goal, the landlord may terminate the lease and rent to a new tenant.

Leasable area formula – One of two methods of calculating a tenant's prorated percentage for pass-through charges. The leasable area formula divides total GLA of the entire property (whether vacant or occupied) into the total GLA occupied by the subject tenant.

Leased space formula – The alternative method of calculating a tenant's prorated percentage for pass-through charges. The leased space formula divides total leased GLA into the GLA occupied by the subject tenant. When there are vacancies, this formula results in a higher percentage, and thus higher pass-through charges, for each existing tenant.

Common area maintenance (CAM) charges –The costs, charged to tenants, of maintaining the common areas, such as parking lots, mall walkways and escalators, and landscaping. Most retail tenants pay a prorated share of CAM costs based on the square footage of their premises.

Exclusivity clause – A use clause in a lease that prevents the landlord from entering into new leases with retailers who sell competing merchandise or services.

Noncompete clause – A provision in a lease that prevents a tenant from opening a similar store or branch within a specified radius.

Lease summary – A summary of the lease terms (such as minimum rent, CAM charges, and lease termination date) for each tenant.

Sales analysis – An important periodic financial report prepared for the owner of a retail property that compares each tenant's sales, and the shopping center's as a whole, to industry averages.

Chapter Quiz

1. The distinctive element of a market analysis for a retail property, as opposed to other kinds of property, is:
   a) looking at what tenants pay for similar space elsewhere
   b) assessing the market to determine the property's ability to compete for the customers of the property's tenants
   c) conducting a local census
   d) looking at demographics

2. Anchor tenants enjoy significant bargaining power during lease negotiations because:
   a) their customer draw benefits the entire shopping center and attracts other retailers
   b) they often occupy outparcels
   c) developer financing usually cannot be obtained unless all or most anchor tenants are signed
   d) Both a) and c)

3. The consumer profile is:
   a) a statistical measure of consumer inflation
   b) a collection of statistical demographic information on consumers in the region
   c) part of the property analysis for a retail property
   d) an ongoing survey conducted in the common areas of the mall

4. Evaluation of a retail property's tenant mix is important:
   a) during initial lease-up of a new property
   b) prior to lease renewal negotiations on an existing property
   c) on an ongoing basis
   d) All of the above

5. The distinctive element of a property analysis for a retail property. as opposed to other kinds of property is:
   a) investigating the property's physical characteristics to determine the extent of functional obsolescence
   b) assessing the property's marketing and leasing activities
   c) investigating the use of each space to assess its customer draw and compatibility with neighboring tenants
   d) None of the above

6. The kind of rent that is based on a retail tenant's gross sales is called:
   a) minimum rent
   b) percentage rent
   c) CAM rent
   d) artificial breakpoint rent

7. Tenant A wants to pay as little as possible in CAM charges. Which of the following should he negotiate for?
   a) Leasable area formula to be used in calculating proration percentage for pass-through charges
   b) Leased space formula to be used in calculating proration percentage for pass-through charges
   c) Maximum percentage rent provision
   d) Limited marketing fund

8. Why should a property manager maintain two separate CAM budgets?
   a) Different tenants want different CAM charges
   b) Tenants have a right to audit all expenses, so the manager will want a presentable set of books
   c) Some tenants pay exterior CAM charges only, so the charges will be different than those paid by tenants responsible for both interior and exterior CAM charges
   d) Both a) and b)

9. Which of the following marketing approaches gives individual retailers the most control?

   a) Owner-financed
   b) Merchants association
   c) Marketing fund
   d) Marketing plan

10. Which of the following marketing promotions is most likely to attract free local media attention?

    a) End-of-summer mall-wide clearance event
    b) Mall-wide sale with discounts on one particular type of merchandise
    c) Health and fitness event with a variety of health information booths and exercise equipment displays
    d) Local online coupon promotion

11. A retail lease includes a penalty for a tenant's delinquency in submitting periodic gross sales reports because the manager:

    a) needs the figures to calculate the percentage rent due
    b) needs current figures to prepare sales analysis reports for planning and the owner's review
    c) wants to preserve the right to audit the retailer's books
    d) Both a) and b)

12. Which of the following is most likely to save the retail property manager time in the day-to-day monitoring of tenant operations?

    a) Lease summary
    b) Penalty provisions for delinquent rent and reporting
    c) CAM agreement with an anchor tenant
    d) None of the above

13. Which of the following is NOT a reason for a retail property owner's interest in the sales analysis report?

    a) Comparing sales performance of the property with the local competition
    b) Identifying low-performing retailers for planning and future leasing decisions
    c) Monitoring income from percentage rent, which is variable
    d) Selecting a leasing team

14. Which of the following types of retail properties do not necessarily have anchor tenants?

    a) Outlet and discount shopping centers
    b) Superregional shopping centers
    c) Neighborhood shopping centers
    d) Regional shopping centers

15. Which kind of shopping center generally benefits the least from customer traffic generated by the tenant mix?

    a) Lifestyle
    b) Power
    c) Community
    d) Strip mall

Answer Key

1. b) The market analysis for any kind of property concerns itself with competition in the market area. The unique element for a retail property is competition for retail customers.

2. d) Anchor tenants are the main customer draw, and other potential tenants are often persuaded to lease space in a center based on who the anchor tenants are. In new retail developments, the developer's financing is typically contingent on committed anchor tenants.

3. b) The consumer profile is a collection of demographic and lifestyle statistics applicable to consumers in a retail property's market area. It is prepared as part of the market analysis.

4. d) A retail property manager should continually evaluate the tenant mix, whether the property is new or well-established. For an older property with no upcoming lease expirations, there may or may not be vacant space to fill but, in either case, the manager should always be aware of what types of retailers would enhance the existing tenant mix.

5. c) While all of the choices are involved in a property analysis, only a retail property manager must inquire into a tenant's customer draw and merchandising compatibility with neighboring tenants.

6. b) Percentage rent is a typical arrangement in retail leases. It calls for the payment of rent in addition to the minimum amount, based on a percentage of the retail tenant's gross sales for the period.

7. a) CAM charges are part of the pass-through charges. The prorated percentage to be applied to individual tenants is calculated using either the leasable area formula or the leased space formula. Because the leasable area formula results in a lower percentage when vacancies exist, tenants prefer this method.

8. c) A property manager should keep two separate CAM budgets because some tenants, such as anchor stores and outparcel tenants, do not pay interior CAM charges.

9. b) The merchants association requires contributions from retailers, who elect members to the association's board of directors. The board meets regularly to make routine decisions regarding marketing and promotional activities. The landlord plays a much bigger role in the other approaches to marketing a shopping center.

10. c) Special events that foster community involvement or offer lifestyle improvement information are most likely to get the attention of the local press, which may run a story on the upcoming event or include it in a calendar of local events.

11. d) A penalty for delinquent retailer sales reports helps to ensure timely submittal of the reports, which are needed to calculate percentage rent as well as to prepare accurate sales analysis reports. The right to audit a retailer's books is another issue and should be addressed in a separate lease provision.

12. a) A well-prepared lease summary condenses all of the most-needed lease information into a short document for each retail tenant. This saves the manager time in day-to-day operations by avoiding the need to study the lease document itself, which can be lengthy.

13. d) The periodic sales analysis is of interest to the property owner for monitoring the property's sales performance against the competition, for monitoring sales performance of individual tenants, and for monitoring income from percentage rent.

14. a) Brand names at reduced prices are the main customer draw in outlet and discount shopping centers, so anchor tenants are generally not necessary.

15. b) The power shopping center features several market-dominant chain stores clustered in one property. Because these stores dominate sales of their respective product lines, they generally don't benefit that much from customer cross-traffic.

Chapter 13
Managing Industrial Property

Outline

Introduction

What exactly is industrial property? The simplest definition is that **industrial property** is property used for the production, storage, and distribution of products.

Production involves transforming raw materials into products (refining and manufacturing) or assembling components into products (fabrication). Storage means the warehousing of products or raw materials; warehouses comprise a major category of industrial property. Finally, distribution refers to the packaging and transporting of products.

Industrial property management is considered by many experts to be less complex than other types of commercial management. Several factors help explain this view. For starters, the typical industrial lease term tends to be much longer than other types of commercial leases, meaning that there's less tenant turnover to deal with. Further, few industrial tenants require much in the way of build-out of office or other space, something management deals with quite often with other kinds of commercial property. Finally, many industrial tenants handle repairs and other maintenance on their own, without involving management.

On the other hand, managers with industrial tenants face some unique challenges. The manufacturing processes used by industrial tenants shift as new techniques develop and new competition enters the market. These changes may run afoul of zoning laws or lease use provisions. Additionally, industrial tenants are considerably more likely to create environmental problems than other types of commercial tenants.

In this chapter, we will look at the basics of what an industrial property manager needs to know. First, we'll take a look at the various types of industrial property. Then we'll discuss how managers develop management plans for industrial property, how industrial property is marketed, and how leases are negotiated. We'll finish the chapter with an explanation of operations and reporting functions.

Types of Industrial Property

There are three basic ways to classify industrial property: by the use of the building, by whether the building is single- or multi-tenant, and by whether the property is free-standing or part of an industrial park.

Use of the Building

Probably the chief criterion for classifying industrial buildings is use. Buildings may be considered general purpose, special purpose, or single purpose.

General Purpose Buildings. Industrial tenants use general purpose buildings for a wide range of activities: warehousing, research, assembly, and even light manufacturing. In other words, general purpose buildings are used when a heavy-duty structure and specialized or high-volume utilities are unnecessary.

In most regions, the general purpose building is the most common type of industrial property. The majority of "shell buildings" fall into this category. Shell buildings are single-story, high-ceilinged structures that have little or no interior finishing. They are

Trends in Warehouse Space

Big box retailing has created demand for big box storage facilities. Yesteryear's large warehouses featured floor areas of perhaps 120,000 square feet and ceiling heights of around 20 feet. No more. Square footage now often reaches 400,000 or 500,000 square feet, with ceilings towering upwards of 36 feet (roughly three stories). Some 800,000 square foot giants even exist.

For obvious reasons, these behemoth storage facilities tend to be built a good distance from cities, where land is cheap. This drive for cheap land has meant moving well inland from traditional warehouse locations, which have historically clustered around ocean and river ports.

In the last few years, the trend of locating farther away from ports has ebbed somewhat. Increasingly, businesses sell to customers across the world, which means that they must be able to move their goods to ports. The time and fuel required to reach a distant port have prompted some of these companies to decide it's worth spending money on the higher rent of more centralized locations.

usually built in industrial parks. Shell buildings are often built "on spec"; that is, without prospective tenants lined up.

Special Purpose Buildings. Special purpose buildings, also known as special use buildings, are suitable for only a single category of use. This includes buildings that can handle heavy manufacturing—buildings with reinforced floors and walls that support heavy machinery, high-volume water and electrical service, and perhaps specialized fire control systems.

We mentioned that warehouses may be general purpose buildings. However, some warehouses fall into the special purpose category.

> **Example:** Star Property Management oversees three warehouses run by a company that provides paper record storage to businesses and government. These buildings were designed to allow careful control of temperature and humidity. In addition, they have extra fireproofing and boast special fire control equipment. These are special purpose buildings.

Special purpose warehouses also include those used to store flammable or toxic chemicals, refrigerated foodstuffs, and other materials that require a special environment.

Single Purpose Buildings. The single purpose building, also known as the single use building, is our last category of use-based classification. This category could in fact be viewed as a subcategory of the special purpose classification. At any rate, single purpose buildings have extremely limited uses, and are in some cases usable by only one particular tenant. Many buildings operated by utility companies fall into this category: pumping stations, heating plants, and water treatment facilities. Agricultural buildings are often single use; grain silos are an example. Manufacturing examples include steel rolling mills and airplane hangars.

Often the user owns these buildings. However, because of the capital required to build a specialized industrial facility, investors may construct these buildings on behalf of the tenant. Or the industrial user may build the facility and then arrange a **sale-leaseback**, selling the property to investors to acquire funds for industrial operations. The user then leases the building from the new owners via a long-term lease that was arranged as part of the sale. (Other types of commercial tenants may also employ this arrangement.)

Sometimes businesses, especially industrial businesses that require a special purpose building, sign a long-term lease on raw land. (This is called a **ground lease**.) The tenant then constructs his own specialized facilities on the land. This arrangement appeals to the landowner, who may not want to tie up capital constructing a complex facility.

Ground lease terms typically run at least a few decades, often more. With the extra-long term, the tenant knows that he won't be forced off the property before he's had the chance to recoup the cost of building the facilities. And since advances in technology may render these facilities obsolete by the end of the long lease term, vacating the property when the lease expires may not cause problems for the tenant. If the tenant does vacate at that point, the landlord may be able to convert the building into a less specialized use. For example, many old factories have been turned into mixed-use office and retail centers.

Single-Tenant vs. Multi-Tenant Buildings

Along with the use categories, buildings may be classified as either single-tenant or multi-tenant. While a tenant might prefer to be the single occupant of the building, this may not be the most profitable arrangement for the landlord.

This is particularly true with old rambling structures and oddly-shaped buildings. For example, the former mills found along waterways often have nooks and crannies that are of little interest to major tenants who typically need large, open areas. Yet a small startup may fit perfectly into one of those smaller spaces. In addition, some of these old plants have frontage along sidewalks or canals—a perfect spot for a restaurant or small shop. The property owner could get a higher rent and the neighborhood would benefit from the services provided by these small businesses.

Developers occasionally construct new multi-tenant industrial buildings. These buildings tend to be relatively small, not much more than 100,000 square feet. They usually contain just a few tenants who are engaged in compatible uses (such as light fabrication).

Separate Parcel vs. Industrial Park

The last industrial property classification that we'll discuss is a distinction between industrial buildings located on separate parcels of land versus those that are part of an industrial park. The idea of a building on its own separate parcel is fairly straightforward, so here we'll concentrate on explaining industrial parks (or business parks, as they're also called).

Almost all industrial parks are organized as subdivisions. The owner or developer subdivides the land before construction, much like with a residential subdivision. One owner may own and manage the entire park, and lease out individual buildings or parts of buildings to tenants.

Alternatively, the condominium form of subdivision may be used for industrial parks. The owners of the various buildings are members of an owners association, with the power to vote on issues affecting the park. The owners pay association dues to cover the expenses of park operations. The association must maintain the park's common areas—generally, this includes the grounds as well as any roadways, utility lines, and any other elements that belong to the park as a whole. Responsibility for building exteriors may also fall into this category. Usually, the owners association hires a property management company to manage the park.

Industrial parks were developed in part to present a more attractive image for industry. In fact, many manufacturing businesses consider the park where their plant is located to be clean enough, and the grounds attractive enough, to locate their offices there. Before industrial parks came into vogue, manufacturers commonly rented urban office space some distance away from their plants. However, a single site offers obvious advantages to the manufacturer. Thus, many industrial parks include some office space, and perhaps even some retail (depending on whether local zoning laws permit anything other than industrial uses in the subdivision).

Management Planning for Industrial Property

As with any other type of property, the manager of industrial property must develop a management plan. The plan includes a regional, neighborhood, property, and market analysis, as well as an analysis of alternatives. Chapter 4 outlined the basics of management planning; the principles covered there apply to almost any kind of commercial property, including industrial.

One of the main goals of the management analysis is to identify the property's strong points to aid in the marketing effort. However, the analysis also identifies any weaknesses related to the property. For those flaws that are curable, the analysis will suggest steps that would remedy the problems.

Sources of Data

The industrial property manager's research for her analysis begins with sources that we've mentioned in other chapters. These include business newspapers and journals, which provide a picture of local and regional economic conditions and trends. The local chamber of commerce can provide data about the number and size of relevant businesses in the area, and trade associations can provide information about a specific industry. The transportation picture is crucial to most industries; a manager can obtain traffic counts, information about planned road building/expansion projects, and other useful data from the city, county, and state transportation offices.

General commercial management magazines always feature some news and analysis concerning industrial property. Demographics are especially important for labor intensive industries; a picture of the labor force can be derived from U.S. Census data and the local

Labor Intensive Industries

Labor intensive industries are industries that employ a relatively high number of workers for a given amount of space. An electronics plant, which requires many assembly workers, is labor intensive. The degree of intensity is often expressed as the number of employees per acre. A very labor intensive industry might employ 80 or 90 workers per acre, for example.

An example of an industry that isn't labor intensive is chemical refining. Refining plants typically rely on processing machinery and related equipment and employ a relatively small staff to monitor the process—perhaps ten per acre. Such industries may be referred to as "labor extensive," though the term isn't used much.

employment office. The Society of Industrial and Office Realtors® publishes a "Comparative Statistics of Industrial and Office Real Estate Markets," which contains data on industrial property vacancy rates, rent amounts, sale prices, and some limited information on expenses.

Managers of special purpose and single purpose buildings should possess a good understanding of the particular industry the building is suited for. Industry journals and other industry-specific publications are helpful sources of information.

Regional Analysis

The management planning process begins with a look at regional issues. The regional analysis examines area demographics, economic conditions, transportation, utilities, tax rates, and potential business incentives.

Demographics. Like other businesses, most industrial firms need to know about the area's employment and turnover rates, education (including skills training), income, average age, and major occupations. Degree of unionization is important to some businesses. Again, census data is the chief source for this information, as well as employment offices.

Not all industries are equally concerned with demographics. Labor-oriented industries place intense emphasis on this data, while resource-oriented industries—which must locate where the resources are—show less interest. Nonetheless, resource-oriented industries must hire workers, too, and so they will pay some attention to information about the local labor force.

Economic Conditions. The economic analysis includes a consideration of prices, the health of industry in the area, and the outlook for business in general. The economic analysis also discusses data concerning current and predicted employment rates and wages.

Transportation. The creation of industrial parks in outlying areas—where land is relatively cheap—became possible after the development of the freeway system. The freeway system is a "two-way street," allowing businesses to get their goods on the road and also

Figure 13.1 Industrial electrical rates by region (cents per kilowatt hour)

New England	12.13
Middle Atlantic	7.48
East North Central	6.53
West North Central	6.23
South Atlantic	6.54
East South Central	6.07
West South Central	5.34
Mountain	6.16
Pacific	7.69

Source: U.S. Energy Information Administration, 9/2012

allowing workers to commute from distant areas. Easy access has diminished the importance of locating a business along railways or near ports and airports.

Threatening this trend somewhat are rising fuel costs, traffic congestion, and deteriorating highways (as governments have less money for road maintenance). The transportation analysis should include an evaluation of the quality of the region's road, airport, port, and railroad infrastructure, and give an estimate of what the future holds for local transportation.

Utilities. Many manufacturers, particularly those making food, paper, or chemicals, or those refining ores or petroleum, use a great deal of water. Fabrication plants use water for cutting, washing, and cooling. Many of these same industries also consume substantial amounts of electricity. The regional analysis should assess the ability of local utility companies to service the needs of potential tenants, as well as review the utility rates.

Industries that don't need to locate near cheap utilities (or natural resources or transportation points) are sometimes called **footloose industries**. In theory, a footloose industry can locate almost anywhere. However, while the term "footloose" is easy enough to define, few industries fully qualify. Electronics firms, research facilities, and call centers (at least smaller ones) are among those that are relatively footloose.

Footloose industries tend to pick their spots based on quality of life. Quality of life refers to a combination of factors such as climate, housing costs, recreational opportunities, schools, and crime rates. Of course, footloose industries are at least somewhat influenced by general business costs (like rent, labor, utilities, and taxes), and these costs will also affect where those industries choose to locate.

Tax Rates. Tax rates affect all businesses but, unlike many retail or office tenants, tax rates often directly impact an industrial tenant's choice of locations. In fact, a region may offer low tax rates to industries in order to attract these important employers to the area. We'll return to this point shortly.

The property manager's regional analysis looks at state and local tax rates and, to a lesser extent, federal tax rates. Federal taxes typically don't vary from one location to

Classifying Industries by Location Needs

When analyzing regional issues to determine the suitability of a property for different types of tenants, keep in mind these categories of industries:

Resource (or supply) oriented. Industries that need to locate near the source of raw materials, components, or supplies so as to minimize costs of transportation. Examples: lumber mills, fruit and vegetable canners, oil refineries.

Energy (or utility) oriented. Industries that choose a location near inexpensive electricity or plentiful water. (Water is important in many types of manufacturing.) Examples: aluminum plants, chemical manufacturers, glassmakers.

Labor oriented. Industries that tend to choose a location based on the availability of cheap and plentiful labor (unskilled or semiskilled). Examples: auto manufacturing, computer assembly plants, garment makers.

Transportation oriented. Industries that require volume shipping will generally choose locations near a railway, highway, airport, or port. Examples: wholesalers and distributors, freight forwarders.

Market oriented. Industries that need to locate near consumers of their products (whether these consumers are individuals or businesses). Most makers of heavy or bulky products fall into this category, since they want to locate near their customers to reduce transportation costs. The soft drink industry is a good example; the product is heavy and somewhat bulky (considering its cost-to-size ratio), so bottling plants tend to be built near large cities where much of the product is consumed.

---

another, so we will limit our discussion here to state and local taxes. A detailed analysis of taxation generally requires the assistance of accountants or other tax experts.

Governments need tax money to operate; this means, for example, that a locality which boasts low property taxes might have high income taxes, or vice versa. And if all the various taxes in a locality are low, potential tenants might wonder if this translates into poor public services (for instance, weak schools or badly maintained roads). While a particular industrial tenant may not utilize schools or certain other government services directly, its employees will, so the quality of government services usually remains important.

There are three categories of taxation to examine: business taxes, property taxes, and personal income taxes.

Business taxes. Definitions vary, but we use the term business taxes to refer to: 1) corporate income and business gross receipts taxes, 2) employment taxes, and 3) sales tax.

Most states levy income taxes on corporations, with rates ranging from 2% to 9%. About ten states levy a **gross receipts tax**. It's called a gross receipts tax because there are no deductions for operating expenses such as rent and payroll. The gross receipts tax either takes the place of, or supplements, a corporate income tax.

Employment taxes (sometimes referred to as payroll taxes) also vary by state, though significantly less so than corporate income or gross receipts taxes. State employment taxes include an unemployment compensation tax and workers' compensation tax.

Finally, many states require businesses to collect a sales tax on goods sold at retail and, in some places, on the sale of services too. A state sales tax normally has only an indirect effect on industrial businesses, since most of them don't sell at the retail level.

Property taxes. Real property owners pay an annual property tax based on the value of their property. Although these taxes are levied on the owner, not the tenant, most industrial property owners pass these taxes on to their tenants. In addition to taxing real property, some states also tax certain business personal property, such as inventory or equipment. The rate of the property tax varies from state to state, ranging from a fraction of a percent to as much as four percent or more. Counties and local governments may impose property taxes too, meaning that the total tax rate can vary within the state. That difference can make one county or city more attractive to an industrial tenant than a neighboring county or city.

Personal income taxes. Many states charge a personal income tax. Like corporate income tax, these rates vary considerably. Accordingly, when the owners of any industrial business are otherwise free to choose between two or more states when deciding on a location, the amount of state income tax the owners will have to pay personally will also factor into the decision.

Government Incentives for Business. Our discussion of taxes provides the groundwork for a very important part of the manager's regional analysis. In the last few decades, many state and local governments have courted businesses—particularly industrial ones—by offering tax relief and other incentives. The goal is to encourage businesses to locate or remain in the jurisdiction. Governments want businesses to locate in their area because this increases revenue (through property and business taxes), and also because it increases job opportunities for residents. Skilled manufacturing and high tech industry jobs, which generally pay well, are especially prized. We'll look briefly at some of the more common types of incentives, but keep in mind that the analysis of government incentives can be technical and often requires expert advice.

Tax incentives. Many state and local governments offer tax relief to new or expanding industrial employers. For instance, if there is a tax on personal property (such as inventory or industrial equipment), that tax may be waived or reduced for a certain period to encourage growth.

Real property taxes may be similarly reduced.

> **Example:** A state's law authorizes counties to offer reduced property taxes (up to 50%) to new or expanding industrial employers. The abatement period may last up to ten years. The state hopes to attract new industry and encourage the owners, managers, and tenants of outmoded or rundown buildings to make improvements. This will add vitality to the region as well as increase local property values. The abatements can also help existing businesses remain competitive and reduce the temptation to move elsewhere.

Financing incentives. In addition to tax relief, governments sometimes provide financing assistance for larger industrial development projects, chiefly in manufacturing. This is especially true in areas considered economically depressed. The assistance usually takes the form of tax-exempt industrial revenue bonds (IRBs). Investors essentially lend money for a project when they buy the bonds. Since the interest these investors earn on IRBs is tax exempt, the borrower (the owner and/or the industrial tenant) can pay a lower rate of interest than typically required with other types of financing.

Occasionally, local governments facing stubborn development problems will actually buy the land themselves and then sell it to investors at attractive prices. The federal Small Business Administration also gets involved in providing incentives, offering lending at attractive rates.

Regulatory and other incentives. Governments also offer incentives for industrial development by relaxing regulations, either temporarily or permanently. Regulatory incentives may include the easing of zoning requirements. These types of incentives might also include some form of compromise on environmental restrictions, at least temporarily.

California and other states offer paid job training programs, which helps attract industries who need skilled workers. In some cases, the government pays private industry councils to provide the job training.

Federal incentives. The federal government offers various tax incentives to encourage industrial development, particularly to industries favored by public policy, such as wind farms and other alternative energy producers.

Another form of federal incentive are **foreign trade zones** (FTZs). Almost every state has at least one FTZ, and many states, especially coastal ones, have numerous ones. FTZs are considered to be outside of U.S. Customs Territory for the purpose of paying customs duty. Customs doesn't levy tariffs on foreign goods entering FTZs until the goods leave the zone. Merchandise that is shipped to foreign countries from FTZs is also exempt from duty payments. Finally, state and local governments may exempt certain merchandise held in FTZs from inventory taxes. Thus, goods may be stored inside an FTZ indefinitely, awaiting peak market prices without incurring tax expenses. FTZs can make it easier to keep manufacturing plants (and jobs) in the U.S. by allowing companies to avoid paying duties and local taxes until they are ready to sell or use the goods.

Neighborhood Analysis

The neighborhood analysis for an industrial property is similar to that performed for any other type of commercial property. However, some parts of the neighborhood analysis, including the sections that review zoning, access to transportation, and municipal services, are especially important for industrial properties. We'll focus on those topics here.

Zoning. Most cities and counties have at least two or three classes of industrial zones, such as:

- light industrial (clean assembly, research and development);
- medium industrial (warehouses, woodworking, construction yards); and
- heavy industrial (refining, cement plants, plastics and other manufacturing).

Areas zoned for heavy industry usually allow the presence of lighter industries within the zone. So, for example, a heavy industrial zone might allow warehouses.

The manager should keep in mind that zoning boards occasionally grant exceptions (called variances) to zoning restrictions. The board will grant a proposed variance if the request is reasonable and won't harm neighboring property owners. It's a good idea to have a land use attorney prepare the variance application. (See Chapter 14 for a further discussion of variances and zoning generally.)

Local Access to Transportation. As we mentioned earlier, the regional analysis includes an analysis of the overall transportation picture: the area's freeways, rail lines, airport, and water port, if any. However, an industrial tenant also needs to know about local access to transportation. Is there a spur servicing the main rail line? Is there easy access to the freeway? The neighborhood analysis must answer these and similar questions.

Freeway access especially can pose a problem. Trucks are challenged by sharply winding roads, poor quality road surfaces, and low overpasses. While these types of road access problems can be fixed, it is usually very expensive to do so. Owners and tenants of industrial properties in the area may want to band together to help remedy these infrastructure weaknesses, through lobbying efforts and perhaps by direct investment.

Municipal Services. The term municipal services refers mainly to waste disposal, firefighting, and police protection. Many industries work with hazardous and flammable materials; a well-equipped, modern firefighting department is a big plus.

Industrial tenants also need to know whether the municipality (or private companies) can handle the particular kind of waste they produce, both as to type and volume. Tenants also want to know how much the disposal will cost.

Property Analysis

The third part of the management analysis is the property analysis. This analysis looks at the site and the building, as well as the property's finances and operations. Here we'll focus on some physical aspects of a rental property that industrial tenants find particularly important.

Building. The analysis of the building is the main part of the property analysis, and this section is often quite detailed, especially for special purpose or single purpose buildings.

Square feet. One of the most important features of an industrial building is its size. The property manager's analysis of square footage includes a figure for the rentable square footage and also one for the usable square footage.

Both of these terms are defined in Chapter 7. To review, the rentable square footage is the total amount of square footage enclosed by the exterior walls of the tenant's space, as well as a share of any common areas. It typically includes the space taken up by stairwells, elevator shafts, and HVAC equipment rooms. It also includes a proportional share of any common building areas, such as a percentage of a shared lobby or lunchroom. Usually the measurement excludes loading docks, parking (outside, covered, or below-ground), and patio or awning-covered areas.

The usable square footage, as the name implies, is the amount of space that a tenant can actually occupy with its people and equipment. Generally, the usable square footage is less than the rentable square footage, especially with multi-story, multi-tenant buildings. Many industrial buildings are single-story and single-tenant, however, and these two figures tend be very similar for these types of structures.

Ceiling height and other structural requirements. Most manufacturers prefer single-story, high-ceilinged buildings that can accommodate tall machinery and other equipment. Warehouses with high ceilings can accommodate high storage stacks, which lowers operating costs.

Naturally, heavy equipment or tons of stored goods requires a sturdy floor. An engineer can determine a floor's maximum load, a figure that some tenants may want to know.

Plumbing and wiring capacity. As previously mentioned, many kinds of industries require heavy-duty utility service, such as three-phase electrical service. While the regional analysis evaluates the ability of utility companies to provide the necessary service, the property analysis addresses the capacity of plumbing and wiring on the premises.

Fire safety systems. Industrial properties generally pose a higher risk of fire than other types of property because of the materials and machinery used on the premises. Fire safety begins with an automatic fire detection system. An automatic sprinkler system is also mandatory in all but the smallest commercial buildings. The fire safety analysis looks at these systems and also includes an evaluation of how fireproof the building itself is.

Sophisticated fire prevention features may include smoke and heat vents in the roof, which open automatically when needed. These large vents also provide firefighters with targeted access for their fire hoses, which means reduced water damage. The presence of exterior doors for fire access serves a similar purpose.

Shipping and receiving facilities. Loading docks, preferably covered, are a necessity for many industries. In addition, or as an alternative to docks, some buildings have "drive-in" doors, which allow trucks to enter the building to load or unload. Drive-ins, like loading docks, are features that can often be added to buildings if tenant demand warrants it.

Parking. The parking analysis looks at how many parking spaces the property has and compares this figure to what is actually needed. The manager must also analyze the security of the parking lot, and the quality of access to and from the lot. Parking issues are critical for labor intensive industries. On the other hand, some properties require little in the way of a parking analysis. This would be true of a warehouse property tenant that employs relatively few workers.

Market Analysis

As you know, a market analysis is a way for the manager to examine comparable properties to help her set rental rates and learn about any features that competing properties offer but the subject property lacks. Finding comparable properties for most light industrial and warehouse space is fairly easy; these buildings tend to be generic and are common in almost every area.

However, as we mentioned at the beginning of the chapter, industrial properties include special purpose and single purpose buildings. These properties are by nature unusual, so finding comparable properties may require looking outside the county or even the state. In looking at distant properties, the manager must be careful. While a distant building may look comparable at the property analysis level, regional and neighborhood factors—such as utility rates and access to transportation—may differ markedly, making a rent rate comparison more complicated. Generally, however, a special use or single use building will have its own rental history that will help guide the evaluation.

Analysis of Alternatives

In the analysis of alternatives section, the manager discusses whether adding new features is possible and cost-effective. The analysis can also include an evaluation of the option of setting a lower rent rather than adding any features.

The manager will consider modest improvements first, including cosmetic upgrades, such as improved landscaping, more modern signage, and freshly painted exteriors. More significant—and more expensive—changes to consider might include increasing or decreasing the amount of parking. Even if the amount of parking needs no adjustment, the manager might consider refurbishing the paved areas (resurfacing, restriping, and adding curbs). Other possible changes include replacing old, energy-inefficient windows and upgrading wiring. Older properties especially may benefit from an improvement in freight facilities, such as the addition of truck wells to loading docks.

The most serious alternatives to consider are a complete overhaul of the building or a change of use. Industrial requirements for space often evolve more quickly than with other types of commercial business. Especially with older properties, the manager may have to consider fairly drastic changes. For example, an old factory space may need such a thorough revamping to become competitive that it may be more economical to convert it to warehouse use or even office space (if zoning allows).

Marketing Industrial Property

Most of our discussion about marketing in Chapter 6 also applies to industrial property. However, marketing industrial property does involve some special considerations.

Using Leasing Agents

Usually a leasing agent—not the property manager—handles the marketing and leasing of an industrial property. These agents are sometimes called **industrial brokers** if they specialize in industrial property. (Most leasing agents handle all kinds of commercial property, including office and retail space).

There are various reasons why managers of industrial property rely on leasing agents. Most importantly, many industrial properties are extremely specialized. Finding tenants for unique properties usually requires a broad geographical search, often national or even international. There simply aren't that many potential tenants for specialized properties in any one region. Leasing agents at a regional or national brokerage firm can embark on a large-scale search more easily than most property managers can, and they can network with other leasing agents.

Nonetheless, it is up to the owner to decide whether to use the property manager or a leasing agent for marketing and leasing activities. Certainly some industrial property managers handle these tasks, especially with smaller properties.

Property Listing

An industrial property listing is typically quite basic; the listing information includes the location, a photo or two (a street view and, for larger properties, an aerial shot), and a handful of basic facts about the property.

> **Example:** Light industrial space in Urbana, Illinois
> - Building area: 42,284 sq. ft. (including office)
> - Construction: Tilt slab concrete
> - Sprinkler: Yes
> - Ceiling height: 21 foot, clear span
> - Power: 12000 amp – 480 volt three phase
> - Zoning: General Industrial (GI)
> - Parking: 60
> - Loading: 4 truck-height loading docks, 1 overhead door
> - Rent: $4.75 per sq. ft. triple-net lease

The listing in this example is somewhat more detailed than many listings. Often listings for general purpose buildings limit themselves to basics, giving the square footage, ceiling height, and number and type of loading facilities (again, along with photos). Only potential tenants who are serious enough to request further information will receive more complete details about the property's features. Of course, the leasing agent or manager also provides additional information during showings.

Prequalifying Tenants and Showing the Property

Before showing property, the manager or leasing agent should prequalify prospective tenants. There's no point showing the property to a prospect who can't afford it, or who fails to meet the property owner's standards in some other way.

The prequalifying process is mainly a financial analysis of the prospect's business to determine ability to pay rent. We discuss this type of financial analysis in Chapter 5. However, certain factors make financial screening of industrial tenants especially crucial. Removing a defaulting tenant from of any type of commercial property is hard, but that difficulty is magnified considerably when the tenant—who has a long term lease—has installed expensive machinery and modified the premises.

Prequalifying also includes a basic evaluation of the prospect's business operations to make sure that they're appropriate for the premises. In addition, learning about the potential tenant's business operations serves another role—it helps the manager or leasing agent tailor the showing of the property. Armed with some knowledge of the prospect's business, someone showing the property can easily point out features that are suited to the potential tenant's needs.

Even if a leasing agent conducts the showing, the property manager will usually attend the showing. It's especially beneficial for the manager to attend when a group of employees from the interested company comes to the showing. The group may wish to split up and focus on different aspects of the building. If so, it's helpful to have more than one person who can show the property and answer questions.

Leasing Industrial Property

As with marketing, leasing may be handled by a commercial broker rather than by the property manager. Regardless of who handles the negotiations, however, the principles remain the same. (For a general discussion of lease negotiation and lease provisions, refer back to Chapter 7.)

Negotiation

A leasing team often handles the lease negotiation for larger industrial properties. The team members may include a leasing agent, the property manager, and the owner herself. The team will also usually employ a lawyer and/or an accountant to analyze the impact of the lease provisions.

Environmental experts may also play at least a background role during lease negotiations, especially if the property was previously used for heavy industry. As mentioned, these types of properties sometimes have environmental problems.

Lease Provisions

As with other kinds of commercial leases, industrial leases tend to be long and complicated. Here we'll take a look at some of the more important lease provisions, focusing on aspects of special concern for industrial properties. We'll discuss provisions covering the lease term, rent and pass-throughs, use restrictions, insurance, and environmental matters.

Term. Lease terms for ordinary industrial property often last at least ten years and frequently longer. This helps the parties recover the cost of their investments in the property. As noted earlier, many industrial tenants, especially manufacturers, make costly modifications to the building and install expensive equipment. The industrial property owner may also invest significantly. For example, the owner might have to upgrade electrical service for a new tenant or improve access to the property.

With ordinary warehouse space and other more generic industrial properties, where the investment in modification and equipment is more modest, lease terms may be shorter.

The owner of a single use building knows that finding a replacement tenant would not be easy, and that converting the building to other uses would be difficult or impossible. Similarly, the single use tenant knows how hard it would be to find substitute facilities. For this reason, owners and tenants of single use properties tend to agree to extremely long lease terms, usually many decades. In fact, a 100-year lease term is not unheard of.

Rent and Pass-Throughs. Industrial leases are usually fully net. In other words, the landlord passes the property's taxes, insurance, and maintenance costs on to the tenant. Utilities are usually metered and paid directly by the tenant. This is important, as industrial tenants typically have extremely expensive utility bills.

An industrial lease is occasionally an **industrial gross lease**. This lease is a true gross lease only in the first year (see Chapter 7 for a full discussion of gross leases). In that first year, called the **base year,** the tenant pays a flat rent that includes some or all of the landlord's operating expenses. In subsequent years, however, the tenant pays any increases in the landlord's operating expenses over the amount established in the base year. If there are increases (and inevitably there are), the industrial gross lease begins to resemble a net lease, as it covers the landlord's operating expenses.

Square footage. As with other kinds of commercial leases, the rent in an industrial lease is usually based on the space's rentable square footage. Often the lease states both the rent per square foot and the amount of rentable square feet. Alternatively, the landlord may simply state the rent as a flat amount. This avoids squabbles about how the square footage should be calculated.

If square footage is used, the lease may specify the industrial floor measurement standard published by BOMA, or detail some other method for measuring the space. However, even with an agreed-upon method, it's possible to come up with a different number each time the space is measured. This is especially true with complicated spaces.

This sample lease clause shows one way of handling space measurement:

> Tenant may have the Premises measured by a qualified engineer or architect acceptable to Landlord. If the rentable square feet of the Premises as calculated by the engineer or architect is less than 216,537 square feet, then the rent shall be adjusted accordingly. If Tenant does not have the Premises measured within 90 days after Commencement Date, then the Premises shall be deemed to contain 216,537 square feet.

Escalation clause. Most industrial leases contain a rent escalation clause. Longer-term leases make these clauses especially necessary; otherwise, the landlord may be stuck for many years with a below-market rental rate. As mentioned in Chapter 7, the rent increase is either a pre-set amount each year or a floating amount equal to the increase in inflation. Escalation clauses that track inflation often use the Consumer Price Index (CPI) for the area.

However, rather than a floating amount, it's more common to use a fixed amount of annual increase because of the certainty it provides to both parties. The annual increases are usually determined by a fixed percentage—for example, 3%—but they don't have to be. Fixed rent increases can be laid out in a lease attachment, making it easy for both parties to tell at a glance what's expected in the future (see Figure 13.2).

Use restrictions. A use clause limits what a tenant can do with the premises. Many shopping center leases, for example, employ a use clause to prevent one business from competing with another. In the industrial setting, however, competition rarely matters that much to the parties. Instead, use clauses are imposed by the landlord in order to protect the property.

For example, with a light industrial or warehouse property, the use clause might limit the tenant to "light assembly" or "warehouse use." This prevents the tenant from adding

Figure 13.2 Sample rent escalation schedule for a ten-year industrial lease

	Per Sq. Ft.	Annual Rent	Monthly Rent
Year 1	$5.20	$ 969,992.40	$80,832.70
Year 2	$5.36	$ 999,092.17	$83,257.68
Year 3	$5.52	$1,029,064.94	$85,755.41
Year 4	$5.63	$1,049,646.24	$87,470.52
Year 5	$5.74	$1,070,639.16	$89,219.93
Year 6	$5.85	$1,092,051.94	$91,004.33
Year 7	$5.97	$1,113,892.98	$92,824.41
Year 8	$6.09	$1,136,170.84	$94,680.90
Year 9	$6.21	$1,158,894.26	$96,574.52
Year 10	$6.21	$1,158,894.26	$96,574.52

Lease Exhibit D

or switching over to heavier manufacturing processes, with the wear and tear and other problems that those kinds of uses bring.

The use clause may also prohibit the tenant from using environmentally toxic chemicals, or limit their use to a certain stated maximum. Generally, however, the lease addresses environmental issues separately (as we'll discuss shortly).

Inspections. A use clause won't mean much if the manager fails to periodically inspect the property to ensure that the tenant is complying with the use restrictions. Inspections can also help ensure a tenant's compliance with environmental, zoning, and other laws. If the inspection uncovers a use that violates both the law and the lease provision, the easiest approach may be to place a call to government inspectors and let them handle the matter.

Insurance. Industrial uses often pose fire hazards. In addition, the machines used for manufacturing and loading operations create a higher risk of serious accident than is found in retail and office settings. Manufacturers may also use hazardous chemicals. For these and other reasons, the insurance provision in industrial leases may be even more important than it is with other types of commercial leases.

The lease should state what types of coverage the tenant will obtain and in what amounts. Relevant policies include pollution liability, property and casualty, workers' compensation, boiler and machinery, business interruption, commercial automotive, and commercial general liability.

As with any commercial lease, the insurance provision should require the tenant to provide proof of insurance on an annual basis. Some leases state a minimum rating grade for the insurance company. This prevents the tenant from procuring cheap insurance from a shaky company (which is a special concern during recessionary times). Most landlords designate A.M. Best as the rating agency, but Moody's and Standard and Poor's also issue insurance company ratings.

Environmental Matters. The provision on environmental issues often has several parts. One part is a clause that prohibits or limits the tenant's use of environmentally hazardous materials. Of course, with some industries, the tenant can't avoid using environmentally hazardous materials. In these cases, the use provision may impose volume limits or handling requirements.

The section on liability for environmental damage may also include a clause—called an indemnification or hold harmless agreement—in which the tenant promises to pay the owner's legal costs and any resulting fines or damages in the event of a lawsuit or regulatory action.

Yet a property owner should never rely completely on indemnification language; these agreements are only as good as the tenant's financial ability to back them up. Environmental cleanup costs can be staggering and can easily bankrupt a tenant. As we'll discuss in Chapter 14, many environmental cleanup laws are strict liability laws. In other words, the owner could find himself responsible for cleanup costs even if he wasn't responsible for the contamination. Thus, the lease should provide for a monitoring process to help prevent environmental damage from occurring.

Example:

> *Testing.* At tenant's expense, landlord may have testing wells drilled on the property and have the ground water tested to detect the presence of hazardous substances. Landlord will supply tenant with test results.

Operations and Reporting

Managing and reporting tasks for industrial property are much the same as for other kinds of commercial property. However, there are a few industrial property-related issues that are worth mentioning regarding maintenance, security, and reporting to the owner.

Maintenance

Responsibility for maintenance varies somewhat by the type of property. With a multi-tenant building, the manager has to take responsibility for the common areas, including the roof and the building exterior. The expenses of maintaining these elements are billed back to the tenants on a pro rata basis as common area maintenance charges.

In a single-tenant industrial building that isn't part of an industrial park, the tenant might very well be responsible for maintaining everything or almost everything. This is especially likely with a single purpose building, because the maintenance there is often quite specialized and integral to the tenant's operations. Thus, the lease will usually assign maintenance responsibilities to the tenant, with the property manager playing a monitoring role.

In an industrial park, regardless of whether the buildings are single-tenant or multi-tenant, the management generally has responsibility for maintaining the building exterior and grounds. Again, all these expenses are charged back to the tenants.

Security

Industrial property poses some unique security challenges. The equipment and products inside industrial properties, especially warehouses, can attract thieves. Many industrial buildings are single-story and have skylights and vents that may present access opportunities. If the manager is responsible for burglar alarms, she should consult with a security expert periodically. The technology in this area changes rapidly.

Industrial tenants who do a lot of shipping and receiving may tend to leave loading dock doors open. If there are multiple tenants in the building, and the landlord has ignored chronic laxness on the part of a particular tenant, liability for any resulting loss is a possibility. Whether the building is single- or multi-tenant, the lease should require that occupants keep their entrances secure. Most industrial properties hire security guards to patrol the premises. The manager should instruct the guards to report instances of unsecured freight doors and similar problems.

Reports to the Owner

As with other types of property, the manager of industrial property prepares various standard operating and financial reports for the owner. In some cases, a particular problem with the property may justify additional reports.

Probably the most common reason for special reporting with industrial property is the discovery of environmental damage on the property. After identifying an environmental problem, federal and state environmental agencies typically impose monitoring and cleanup requirements. They may also require ongoing reporting. The property manager should make his own reports to the owner concerning steps taken to deal with the environmental problem. As we noted earlier, the property owner may be liable for contamination on her property regardless of who caused it.

Chapter Summary

1. Industrial property is property used for the production, storage, and distribution of products. Production involves transforming raw materials into products or assembling components into products. Storage refers to the warehousing of products or raw materials. Distribution refers to the packaging and transporting of products.

2. Industrial property may be classified by use (general purpose, special purpose, or single purpose), by occupancy (single-tenant or multi-tenant), and by whether the property is a freestanding parcel or part of a subdivision (an industrial park).

3. The management analysis for industrial property is similar to the analysis employed for other types of property. However, the aspects that are emphasized often differ. For instance, an industrial property analysis usually places more emphasis on labor demographics, transportation, and government incentives than is typical with other types of property.

4. A leasing agent usually handles the marketing and leasing of industrial property. Compared to property managers, leasing agents typically have better resources for carrying out the kind of large-scale search for tenant prospects that's often necessary when leasing industrial properties.

5. Lease provisions that are of particular importance in an industrial lease include the lease term (terms tend to be long), rent and pass-through charges (industrial leases are net leases, though sometimes not in the first year), use restrictions (designed to avoid damage to the property), maintenance (industrial tenants often have more responsibility for maintenance than other kinds of tenants), and environmental matters (many industries work with environmentally hazardous materials).

6. The basic concerns in operating industrial property don't differ greatly from other kinds of commercial property. Maintenance is something of an exception, however: many industrial tenants handle all or most of their own maintenance. Security also poses special challenges because of the valuable products and equipment kept on many industrial premises. Lastly, the manager must diligently monitor industrial processes for environmental hazards. Operating reports to the owner should address any environmental problems.

Key Terms

Industrial property – Property used for the production, storage, and distribution of products.

Special purpose buildings – Buildings suitable for only a limited number of uses, such as heavy manufacturing.

Single purpose buildings – Buildings usable for only one purpose, such as a specialized type of industrial production.

Sale-leaseback – An arrangement in which a business sells the property it owns (and uses) to an investor and becomes the new owner's tenant. The tenant uses the proceeds from the sale to fund operations.

Ground lease – An arrangement where a business (often industrial) leases raw land from the owner on a long-term basis and then builds his own specialized facilities on the land.

Industrial park – A preplanned development that contains industrial buildings and sometimes office buildings as well.

Demographics – Characteristics of a human population, such as average family size, median age, and household income.

Zoning – Ordinances that divide a community into areas set aside for specific types of land use, such as agricultural, residential, commercial, or industrial.

Labor intensive industry – An industry that employs a relatively large number of workers for a given amount of space.

Footloose industry – An industry that doesn't need to locate near particular resources, energy sources, transportation centers, or markets. Tax rates or quality of life issues may end up determining where footloose businesses locate.

Resource oriented – An industry that needs to locate near the source of raw materials, components, or other supplies to reduce the cost of transportation.

Energy oriented – An industry that chooses a location near inexpensive electricity or plentiful water. (Many types of manufacturing require large amounts of water.)

Transportation oriented – An industry that engages in volume shipping, requiring a location near railways, highways, airports, or ports.

Market oriented – An industry that needs to locate near consumers of its products, because the business sells heavy or bulky products and locating near the purchasers reduces transportation costs.

Government business incentives – Tax relief and other incentives offered by state or local governments to court industry and other businesses, such as financing assistance and regulatory easing.

Foreign trade zones (FTZs) – Geographical areas where the government provides tax relief to importing and exporting industries.

Industrial broker – A leasing agent who specializes in industrial properties.

Industrial gross lease – A lease in which the tenant pays a flat rent for the first year (the base year); in subsequent years, the tenant pays the landlord's operating expenses to the degree they have increased since the base year.

Use restriction – A lease clause limiting the tenant's use of the property; for example, for a warehouse building, a use restriction limits the tenant to "warehouse uses."

Chapter Quiz

1. Is a warehouse considered retail or industrial property?

   a) Retail

   b) Industrial

   c) Either retail or industrial depending on what is stored

   d) Neither; it's a category by itself

2. Which of the following is a general use building?

   a) Light industrial building

   b) Refrigerated warehouse

   c) Grain loading facility

   d) Steel mill

3. A sale-leaseback involves an industry or other business:

   a) leasing space to itself

   b) subleasing space

   c) selling a property and moving elsewhere

   d) leasing a building from the buyers to whom the business recently sold the property

4. Building owners in the Morgan Industry & Office Park belong to an owners association and have a partial ownership interest in the park's private roadways and certain other shared elements. The park is a:

   a) cooperative

   b) condominium

   c) voluntary association of separate parcels

   d) None of the above

5. Which of the following is most likely a labor intensive industry?

   a) Ore refining

   b) Electronics assembly

   c) Chemical manufacture

   d) Oil refining

6. Clyde Forge casts aluminum engine blocks and other parts, using a great deal of power and water. Most likely the primary classification of this industry would be:

   a) resource oriented

   b) transportation oriented

   c) utility oriented

   d) market oriented

7. XYZ, Inc. is a footloose industry. This means that the company's:

   a) workers generally walk to work

   b) location needs are weak

   c) location needs are strong

   d) location changes fairly often

8. A locality has low rates across the board for its various types of taxes. What is a possible disadvantage with this?

   a) It's possible that government won't have enough funds to provide needed services

   b) Rates have nowhere to go but up

   c) Competition from businesses moving to the area is likely to develop

   d) None; little or no taxation is always best for business

9. Which of the following is NOT a typical incentive offered by government to encourage industry to locate in a given area?

   a) Lowered property tax rates

   b) Job training programs

   c) Financing assistance

   d) Wage subsidy to help cover the cost of higher-salary employees

10. A metal fabrication plant is likely to be located in which zone?

    a) Light industrial

    b) Medium industrial

    c) Heavy industrial

    d) Commercial

11. Rentable square footage is:

    a) the area available for the tenant's actual use

    b) the gross area that the tenant rents

    c) the total amount of space a landlord has to lease in a building, excluding common areas

    d) another term for usable square footage

12. Klein Chemicals wants to rent space for a new manufacturing facility. What length lease term are they likely to seek?

    a) Short term

    b) Medium term

    c) Long term

    d) Any length, depending on which term offers the lowest annual rent

13. In an industrial gross lease, who pays the operating expenses?

    a) Landlord throughout the lease term

    b) Tenant throughout the lease term

    c) Landlord during the first year; the tenant handles any increases thereafter

    d) Tenant during the first year; the landlord handles any increases thereafter

14. What clause is generally necessary to make a use restriction fully effective?

    a) Inspection

    b) Escalation

    c) Insurance

    d) Maintenance

15. An industrial broker handles marketing and leasing at Cascade Industrial Park. Nonetheless, the property manager is likely to:

    a) contribute information to the marketing campaign

    b) attend showings of the property

    c) join the lease negotiation team

    d) All of the above

Answer Key

1. b) Warehouse property falls under the industrial category.

2. a) General use includes light industrial properties; while most warehouses are also general use, the features necessary for refrigerated storage make the building too specialized to be considered general use.

3. d) In a sale-leaseback, a business that owns the property that it uses for its business sells the property in order to raise capital. As part of the sale, the business signs a lease with the buyers that allows the business to rent the property so that it doesn't have to move its operations.

4. b) This form of organization describes a condominium. Many industrial parks are organized as condominiums.

5. b) Electronics assembly usually involves a fair amount of hand labor, making it a labor intensive industry. The other industries mentioned typically employ a few machine operators and engineers and other support staff, but much of the building space is taken up with processing machinery, and the storage of raw and finished product, rather than being occupied by a large number of workers.

6. c) Manufacturers that consume large amounts of power and water are considered utility oriented and often locate where these utilities are relatively cheap.

7. b) A footloose industry can locate almost anywhere because its business doesn't have strong location needs such as transportation access or cheap utilities.

8. a) Governments use tax revenues to provide services such as fire, police, schools, and roads, a benefit for both businesses and employees. However, if tax revenue is too low, the quality of these services tends to deteriorate.

9. d) Governments don't generally offer salary subsidies and, if they did, it would more likely be targeted at lower-level unemployed or underemployed workers in need of training, rather than high salary individuals.

10. c) Metal fabrication would probably be restricted to a heavy industrial zone. Cleaner, lighter manufacturing might fall under medium industrial, while clean assembly could qualify as light industrial.

11. b) Rentable square footage may be referred to as gross square footage—it's the square footage on which rent is calculated, a number that is usually significantly higher than the actual usable space.

12. c) The company will have to install lots of processing machinery and will probably seek a long term lease, perhaps 20 years or more. Long lease terms are typical for heavy industry.

13. c) With an industrial gross lease, the tenant pays a flat rent for the first year. This rent is called gross, rather than net, because it includes some or all of the landlord's operating expenses. However, after the first year (the base year), any increases in the landlord's operating expenses are passed on to the tenant.

14. a) Generally speaking, a use provision in an industrial lease prohibits a tenant from changing to a heavier category of use. The intent is to protect the property from environmental or other damage. The manager should include a right to inspect in the lease, so that he can make sure the tenant's operations stay within the bounds imposed by the use clause.

15. d) Even with a property where the manager doesn't handle marketing and leasing, the manager nonetheless usually contributes information to the marketing plan (based on her experience and her management analysis) and also participates in other aspects of the leasing process.

Chapter 14

Complying with Federal, State, and Local Laws

Introduction

An array of federal, state, and local laws regulate many different aspects of a property manager's work. Property managers should make compliance with these laws a top priority. In previous chapters, we've mentioned legal requirements that apply in various contexts and circumstances. This chapter provides an overview of the laws that establish those requirements. We'll cover federal statutes that apply to leasing and managing property in any of the 50 states, and we'll also describe the types of state and local laws that may apply in a particular locale. These laws include:

- antitrust laws, which are aimed at limiting anticompetitive business practices;
- disclosure laws, which require landlords to notify tenants about potential hazards or problems;
- tenant screening laws, which impose certain duties on landlords during the application process;
- antidiscrimination laws, which prevent landlords from discriminating against members of protected classes;
- employment laws, which protect the owner's or manager's employees in a variety of ways; and
- land use and environmental laws, which may affect how a manager can use a property.

Federal, State, and Local Laws

To understand the laws that pertain to property managers, it's helpful to have a general understanding of the different types of laws that exist in the United States. Federal laws apply to everyone in the country; state laws apply to everyone in a particular state; and local laws apply only to those in a particular city, county, or other local jurisdiction. The laws that affect property management are most often state laws, but there are quite a few exceptions to this general rule, such as federal environmental and civil rights laws, and local zoning ordinances and subdivision regulations.

Laws can also be classified as statutory laws or administrative regulations. **Statutory laws** are enacted by a legislative body (such as the U.S. Congress, a state legislature, or a city council) to govern a particular issue. **Administrative regulations** are adopted by federal, state, or local administrative agencies, such as the federal Department of Housing and Urban Development, the state real estate licensing agency, or the county building department.

Generally, if the same issue is addressed by more than one law or regulation, the one that imposes the most restrictive requirements must be followed. Similarly, when one law provides a more generous remedy to an injured party than another law, that party can usually bring her claim under the more helpful law.

Antitrust Laws

A property manager may recognize the more obvious dangers of violating landlord-tenant laws or fair housing laws, but she may overlook the very real risk of running afoul of antitrust laws. **Antitrust laws** were designed to prevent business agreements and practices that unreasonably restrain trade. Antitrust laws encourage competition between businesses. When businesses join forces to control prices or limit supply, customers typically end up paying higher prices and the economy suffers. A competitive marketplace, on the other hand, leads to better products and better prices for the consumer.

The main federal antitrust law is the **Sherman Act**, which prohibits any conspiracy or other agreement that restrains trade. Under the Sherman Act, a **conspiracy** occurs when two or more business entities participate in a common scheme, the effect of which is the unreasonable restraint of trade.

If a property manager violates antitrust laws, she risks both civil and criminal liability. An individual found guilty of violating the Sherman Act can be fined up to one million dollars and/or sentenced to serve up to ten years' imprisonment. If a corporation is found guilty of violating the Sherman Act, it can be fined up to one hundred million dollars.

While some states also have their own antitrust statutes, we're going to focus here on federal antitrust law.

Prohibited Activities

Property managers must be careful to avoid engaging in three types of activities that are prohibited by antitrust law: price fixing, tie-in arrangements, and market allocation.

Price Fixing. The law defines price fixing as the cooperative setting of prices or price ranges by competing firms. The typical real estate example of price fixing is a group of real estate agents getting together to set commission rates.

As we discussed in Chapter 4, property managers often determine rental rates for the properties they manage by discovering what the competition is charging for similar properties. While researching local market rates is lawful, managers should be careful when asking competitors about rental rates; it's a good idea to check with your brokerage or with a real estate attorney to make sure you don't violate antitrust laws. At a minimum, antitrust law prohibits you from agreeing with the owner or manager of a competing property to charge a minimum rental rate for a particular kind of rental property.

> **Example:** Property manager Fred calls his colleague Louise over at Apartment House X across the lake. "What are you charging for one-bedrooms with views?" Fred asks her. "$1,250," she replies. "And I don't see any point in you undercutting me."
>
> Fred promises to charge no less than Louise for one bedrooms with lake views. This is illegal price fixing.

Note that just as competing real estate agents cannot cooperate in setting commission rates, property management firms cannot agree to charge a standard management fee.

Tie-In Arrangements. A **tie-in arrangement** (also known as a **tying arrangement**) occurs when a buyer is required to purchase one product or service in order to purchase another product or service.

> **Example:** Hamid is the chairman of the board for a large condominium complex. He contacts Lewis, a licensed real estate agent, about managing the complex. Lewis agrees, but only on the condition that the residents agree to list their units with Lewis when they decide to sell. Requiring Hamid to do this as a condition of managing the property is an illegal tie-in arrangement; Lewis is violating antitrust laws.

This scenario is an example of a **list-back agreement**. List-back agreements violate antitrust law if the listing requirement is a condition of the management agreement. Note, however, that two parties may mutually agree to a list-back agreement without violating antitrust laws. So if the condominium residents truly wanted to enter into a list-back agreement with Lewis, the agreement wouldn't be illegal.

Market Allocation. Another business practice prohibited by antitrust law is **market allocation**. It's illegal for competitors to agree not to sell: 1) in specified areas, or 2) certain products or services in certain specified areas, or 3) to certain customers in specified areas. This means that competing property managers or management firms cannot allocate business between them; to do so would limit competition.

Is all market allocation illegal? No, only market allocation between competitors violates antitrust laws. It's perfectly acceptable for an individual management firm to decide it will service a specific market area. It is also acceptable for a firm to allocate territory to its employees. However, territory allocations are only permissible within the firm, not between two competing firms.

> **Example:** ABC Management assigns Mario to handle properties on the east side of town, and assigns Ingrid to handle properties on the west side of town. This practice does not violate antitrust law.
>
> However, if ABC Management and XYZ Realty agree that ABC Management will handle all properties on the west side of town, and XYZ Realty will handle all properties on the east side of town, this would be a violation of antitrust law.

The same is true with regard to allocating customers. Competing management firms may not agree to allocate business among themselves based on the type of customer (retail versus residential, for example). But an individual firm may allocate different types of customers to different employees.

Disclosure Laws

A variety of state and federal laws require property managers to make disclosures about a property and its condition to prospective tenants.

Disclosure of Latent Defects

Under principles of general agency law, a property manager owes prospective tenants a duty of good faith and fair dealing. This requires a manager to disclose all material facts about the property. A **material fact** is often defined as any fact that could reasonably be expected to influence the tenant's decision whether or not to rent. For example, a **latent defect**—a hidden defect that is not discoverable by ordinary inspection—is a material fact. If the manager fails to disclose a known latent defect to a prospective tenant, the manager may be liable for any injury suffered by the tenant as a result of the defect.

> **Example:** Bryant is the leasing agent for a retail space in downtown Floraville. When he shows the space to Sally, who plans to open a fabric store, he doesn't mention the fact that the roof has leaked during previous winters. Three months after Sally opens her store, a particularly bad storm comes through Floraville, the roof leaks, and part of Sally's inventory is ruined. Bryant will be liable for her losses.

In many states, a seller in a real estate sales transaction must provide the buyer with a written disclosure statement listing any known defects in the property. While lease transactions don't normally involve the same sort of formal disclosure statement, it's always a good idea to make any required latent defect disclosures in writing, as soon as possible—perhaps even when showing a property to a prospective tenant. In any event, these disclosures should be made before a lease is signed.

Megan's Law

Since 1996, a federal law has required every state to have a registration program for sex offenders convicted of crimes against children. The federal law is commonly called **Megan's Law** (the law was passed after Megan Kanka was murdered by a sex offender); many of the state laws modeled after it are also called Megan's Law. Upon release from incarceration, sex offenders must register with a law enforcement agency, and they must also notify the agency whenever they move.

Each state makes information concerning registered offenders, including their addresses, available to the public, although specific rules vary from state to state. In some cases, when a registered offender moves into a residential neighborhood, authorities are required to notify the community. Some states require all residential leases to contain a clause disclosing the existence of the state's registered sex offender database. State statute usually dictates the language that must appear in the lease.

If a prospective or current tenant asks a property manager whether there are any registered sex offenders in the area, the manager should refer the tenant to the law enforcement agency that makes that information available. However, if a manager knows that a registered sex offender is, in fact, living in the vicinity of a rental unit, state law may require the manager to disclose this to prospective tenants. It's important for a manager to know her state's specific rules concerning this type of disclosure.

Note that some state laws prohibit a manager from denying someone housing based on that person's registered sex offender status.

Lead-Based Paint Disclosures

Lease transactions that involve housing built before 1978 are subject to a federal law concerning lead-based paint. About three-quarters of the homes built before 1978 contain some lead-based paint. The paint is usually not dangerous if properly maintained, but if it deteriorates and is ingested or inhaled, it may cause brain damage and organ damage in young children.

This law requires a residential landlord to do all of the following:

- disclose the location of any lead-based paint that he is aware of in the home (in both the dwelling unit and the common areas, if any);
- provide a copy of any report concerning lead-based paint in the home, if it has been inspected; and
- give tenants a copy of a pamphlet on lead-based paint prepared by the U.S. Environmental Protection Agency (EPA).

Specific warnings must be attached to the lease, along with signed statements from the parties acknowledging the delivery and receipt of the various items listed above. The signed acknowledgements must be kept for at least three years as proof of compliance.

Landlords who fail to fulfill their obligations under this law may be ordered to pay the tenant treble damages (three times the amount of any actual damages suffered by the tenant). Civil and criminal penalties may also be imposed.

 Lead-Based Paint and Renovation

While undisturbed lead-based paint isn't particularly dangerous, activities like sanding or demolition can create hazardous paint dust and chips. For this reason, the EPA now regulates contractors performing renovation, repair, and painting projects that will disturb lead-based paint in homes, child care facilities, and schools built before 1978. These contractors must take an eight-hour training course to become EPA-certified renovators. The training covers lead-safe work practices, which are designed to ensure that work areas are contained, dust is minimized, and cleanup is thorough. In addition, contractors must provide an EPA-printed pamphlet on lead hazards to building owners and occupants, and the families of children under age six that attend child care facilities.

The law exempts renovation work that will not affect more than six square feet of interior painted surfaces or more than twenty square feet of exterior painted surfaces (as long as no window replacement or demolition is involved).

Bedbug Disclosure Laws

In recent years, bedbugs have become a serious problem in New York City: in 2009, the city received over 11,000 calls about bedbugs, compared to 537 calls in 2004. In response, the state legislature passed a "Bedbug Disclosure Law" in 2010. Landlords across New York state are now required to let prospective tenants know, in writing, if a bedbug infestation has occurred in an individual unit or building within the past year and, if so, whether eradication steps were taken. The disclosure rule does not apply to current tenants, only prospective tenants. Landlords have complained about the requirement, arguing that the required disclosure form does not distinguish between serious building infestations and isolated incidences in which a few bugs were spotted and eliminated. Regardless, New York City's vacancy rates remain low.

Certain types of transactions are exempt from the lead-based paint disclosure law. These include transactions involving "zero-bedroom units" (such as efficiency or studio apartments, dormitories, and room rentals); leases for less than 100 days; housing for the elderly or disabled (unless young children live there); rental housing that has been checked by a certified inspector and found to be free of lead-based paint; and foreclosure sales.

Other Disclosure Laws

Depending on state law, a property manager may be required to provide tenants with a variety of other disclosures. For example, is the property in a flood zone or does it have a history of flooding? If so, the manager may have to disclose this in writing. In some states, the same is true if the property has a history of mold or ongoing pest control problems. In other states, indoor air quality must be tested, along with groundwater and soil, with the results provided to tenants. It's important for property managers to remain aware of the disclosure requirements particular to their states.

Laws Affecting Tenant Screening

Federal and state laws affect how a property manager screens rental applications. These laws include the federal Fair Credit Reporting Act, the USA PATRIOT Act and Executive Order 13224, and state laws governing inquiries into citizenship status.

Fair Credit Reporting Act

As part of the process of screening a prospective tenant, a property manager usually obtains a copy of the applicant's credit report from a private credit reporting bureau. A credit report contains the applicant's identifying information, loan and payment history, employment information, and matters of public record, such as civil judgments, tax liens, and bankruptcies.

The three major credit reporting bureaus in the U.S. are Equifax, Experian, and TransUnion. The **Fair Credit Reporting Act** (FCRA) is a federal law that regulates how credit reporting bureaus collect and use the consumer credit information compiled in their credit reports. The FCRA is intended to improve the accuracy of the information collected, and to protect the privacy of the individuals whose information is compiled by the credit bureaus.

The FCRA applies to any transaction in which a consumer credit report on a prospective tenant is obtained, including residential and commercial lease transactions. The manager must inform the prospective tenant that he will check her credit history, along with other aspects of her background—such as employment, residence, and criminal history. These disclosures must be made in writing. For this reason, a rental application form will usually contain a clause for the applicant to sign, indicating her consent to the credit and background checks. (Some managers use a separate consent form.)

Under the FCRA, if a rental application is rejected based on the information contained in the applicant's credit report, the manager must inform the applicant of this fact in writing. The letter must also notify the applicant of her rights under the FCRA. Among other things, the individual is entitled to:

- obtain additional information from the credit reporting bureau that provided the report;
- dispute any inaccurate or incomplete information in the report;
- have inaccurate, incomplete, or unverifiable information in the report corrected or deleted;
- have access to her file limited to those with a valid need (such as prospective landlords); and
- have negative information in her file deleted after a certain number of years.

The Fair Credit Reporting Act is enforced by the Federal Trade Commission. A property manager who fails to comply with the law, either negligently or willfully, faces the risk of criminal and civil penalties.

USA PATRIOT Act and Executive Order 13224

When screening prospective tenants, property managers must also comply with the federal USA PATRIOT Act and Executive Order 13224, which went into effect following the terrorist attacks of September 11, 2001. (Following the convention used by most authorities, we'll simply refer to the act and order as the "Patriot Act.") The Patriot Act is intended to hinder the efforts of terrorist organizations, in part by making it harder to launder money used to fund the organizations. To that end, the Patriot Act prohibits U.S. individuals and businesses from entering into any type of business transaction (including lease transactions) with any person, group, or entity listed on the **Specially Designated Nationals and Blocked Persons List** (SDN list). The SDN list, which is published by the Office of Foreign Assets Control, contains thousands of names and is updated regularly.

Criminal Background Checks

It's always a good idea for a property manager to run criminal background checks on prospective employees, particularly when hiring for positions involving significant interaction with tenants (for example, workers who enter units to perform repairs or maintenance, or those having access to applicants' credit reports). Background information can be obtained from private companies (including some credit reporting bureaus) in the form of consumer reports.

The FCRA regulates the information collected and provided in these reports in the same way that it regulates credit reports. For example, the job applicant must consent to the background check in writing, and the property manager must certify that he will not misuse any information obtained. If the manager rejects a job applicant based on the results of the background check, the manager must inform the applicant and notify her of her rights under the FCRA. And the manager must be careful to dispose of the information properly (such as shredding paper documents and deleting electronically stored files).

Both residential and commercial property managers must be careful to avoid entering into lease agreements or management agreements with anyone on the SDN list. Managers should always check the names of prospective tenants and clients against the SDN list, which can be found on the Treasury Department's website. It's also a good idea to periodically run the names of current tenants and clients against the list. A property manager who frequently needs to screen tenant applicants, prospective clients, or other parties may opt to use a software program dedicated to checking names against the SDN list. Managers should check all names, and never limit their searches to persons of a certain race, religion, or background.

If a manager finds a potential match on the SDN list, she should try to use any and all identifying information available to confirm whether that person or entity really is the person or entity on the list. Then the Office of Foreign Assets Control should be contacted to verify the match. If the Office confirms the match, any funds held on behalf of the person or entity (such as a security deposit) must be frozen.

The government imposes stiff penalties for violating the Patriot Act. Civil fines range between $11,000 and $275,000 per violation; criminal violations can result in fines as high as $1 million per violation and up to 12 years in jail.

Citizenship Status Inquiries. Given the amount of proactive tenant screening expected of a manager under the Patriot Act, it may be surprising to learn that managers are not expected to verify a prospective tenant's (or client's) citizenship status. In fact, in some states and cities, a manager is prohibited from asking about citizenship status at all. It's important for a property manager to familiarize himself with the rules that apply in his particular area.

Antidiscrimination Laws

Another group of laws important to property managers is antidiscrimination laws, which include federal civil rights laws; federal, state, and local fair housing laws; and the Americans with Disabilities Act. Keep in mind that antidiscrimination laws apply not only to a manager's activities before a lease agreement is signed, but to the ongoing landlord-tenant relationship as well.

Civil Rights Laws

The **Civil Rights Act of 1866** is a federal antidiscrimination law that states that "all citizens of the United States shall have the same right, in every state and territory as is enjoyed by white citizens thereof to inherit, purchase, lease, sell, hold, and convey real and personal property." The law prohibits any discrimination, based on race or color, in real estate transactions, including the leasing of residential and commercial property.

> **Example:** Barrett is the property manager of the Hilltop apartment complex. He's had a recent run of difficult tenants, including several families of a particular race whose apartments regularly emitted very strong food odors that bothered the other tenants. Hoping to avoid similar issues in the future, Barrett decides to require a much larger security deposit from prospective tenants of that race, thinking it will discourage them from renting at Hilltop. This policy is illegal under the Civil Rights Act of 1866.

Someone who has been discriminated against in violation of the Civil Rights Act of 1866 can sue in federal court. The court can issue an injunction ordering the defendant to stop discriminating or to take affirmative steps to correct the violation. This might involve an order requiring the defendant to sell or lease the property to the plaintiff. The court can order the defendant to pay the plaintiff actual damages to compensate for financial losses, humiliation, and suffering caused by the discrimination. In addition, the defendant might be ordered to pay punitive damages (an additional sum to punish the defendant for wrongdoing).

Another federal antidiscrimination law, the federal **Civil Rights Act of 1964**, prohibits discrimination based on race, color, religion, or national origin in many programs and activities for which the federal government offers financial assistance. However, this narrow scope means that its impact on rental properties has been quite limited.

A civil rights act enacted a few years after the 1964 act, the **Civil Rights Act of 1968**, plays a much greater role with rental properties. We'll discuss that next, in our analysis of fair housing laws.

Fair Housing Laws

The **Fair Housing Act** helps provide fair housing opportunities throughout the United States. This federal law, contained in Title VIII of the Civil Rights Act of 1968, makes it illegal to discriminate on the basis of **race, color, religion, sex, national origin, disability,** or **familial status** in the sale or lease of residential property or in the sale or lease of vacant land for the construction of rental buildings. The law also prohibits discrimination in advertising, lending, real estate brokerage, and other services in connection with residential real estate transactions.

Although there are several categories of exemptions to the Fair Housing Act, these exemptions do not apply to a property manager involved in a transaction. While the number of groups covered by the act is broader than the Civil Rights Act of 1866 (which only covers race and color), the Fair Housing Act is also narrower in scope; it applies only to residential transactions, not those involving commercial or industrial properties.

Prohibited Acts. The Fair Housing Act prohibits any of the following acts if they are done on the basis of race, color, religion, sex, national origin, disability, or familial status:

- refusing to show or rent a residential property;
- refusing to negotiate for the rental of residential property, or otherwise making it unavailable;
- changing the terms or conditions of a lease for different potential tenants;
- using advertising that indicates a preference or intent to discriminate;
- representing that property is not available for inspection or rent when it is in fact available;
- coercing, intimidating, threatening, or interfering with anyone on account of his enjoyment, attempt to enjoy, or encouragement or assistance to others in enjoying the rights granted by the Fair Housing Act.

Also prohibited are the discriminatory practices known as blockbusting and steering:

- **Blockbusting** (also known as panic selling or panic peddling) occurs when someone tries to induce homeowners to sell or—more relevant to the property management context—rent their properties by predicting that members of a certain race (or other protected class) are moving into the neighborhood, and that this will lead to undesirable consequences such as lower property values or an increase in crime. If this increases turnover in the area, the blockbuster profits by collecting commissions on the induced sales or rentals.
- **Steering** refers to channeling prospective buyers or tenants toward or away from specific neighborhoods based on their race (or religion, national origin, etc.) in order to maintain or change the character of those neighborhoods.

    Example: ABC Management "encourages" its rental agents to show Asian clients only rental units located in predominantly Asian neighborhoods, with the idea that they would be more "comfortable" there. This is illegal steering.

It's important to note that although the Fair Housing Act's prohibitions come into play most frequently during the leasing process, the law prohibits discriminatory behavior throughout the entire tenancy as well. Managers must be careful to comply with the law when handling all aspects of the landlord-tenant relationship. Services must be provided to all tenants equally, and policies and rules must apply to all tenants uniformly.

Disability and Familial Status. Originally, the act did not include disability or familial status as protected classes; these were added to the law in 1988. (Those who fall into one of the groups covered by the Fair Housing Act—or other civil rights laws—are known as members of a **protected class**.)

Disability. Under the Fair Housing Act, it's illegal to discriminate against someone because she has a physical disability or mental impairment that substantially limits one or more major life activities. This class includes people suffering from chronic alcoholism, mental illness, or AIDS. But the act does not protect those who threaten the health or safety of others, or who currently use controlled substances.

A residential landlord must allow a disabled tenant to make reasonable modifications to the property at the tenant's expense, so long as the modifications are necessary for the tenant's full use and enjoyment of the premises. (However, the landlord can require the tenant to restore the premises to their original condition at the end of the tenancy.) Land-lords must also make reasonable exceptions to their rules to accommodate disabled tenants. For example, even if landlords don't allow pets, they can't refuse to rent to someone with a guide dog.

Special wheelchair accessibility rules apply to newer residential construction with four or more units. For instance, units may be required to have wider doorways and wheelchair ramps.

Familial status. Discrimination on the basis of familial status refers to discrimina-tion against a person because he has a child (under 18 years old) living with him. Parents, legal guardians, pregnant women, and those in the process of obtaining custody of a child are all protected against discrimination on the basis of their familial status. (However, the Fair Housing Act doesn't override local laws limiting the number of occupants permitted in a dwelling.)

"Adults only" apartment or condominium complexes are generally forbidden, as are complexes divided into "adult" and "family" areas.

> **Example:** Bob, the manager at Shoreline Apartments, tells all prospective renters with small children that they may only rent units on the first floor of the complex. He explains that this policy is merely a safety precaution, as the second-floor units have balconies from which children could fall and injure themselves. He points out that the first-floor units rent for about $100 less per month than comparable units upstairs. Bob's policy is discriminatory, as it treats families with children differently from other prospective tenants.

The Fair Housing Act's bar on discrimination based on familial status has an impor-tant exemption for properties that qualify as "housing for older persons." Children can be excluded from properties that fit into one of the following categories:

1. properties developed under a government program to assist the elderly;
2. properties intended for and solely occupied by persons 62 years old or older;
3. properties that adhere to a policy that designates intent to house persons who are 55 or older, if at least 80% of the units are occupied by at least one person who is 55 or older.

HUD and Enforcement. The Fair Housing Act is enforced by the federal Department of Housing and Urban Development (HUD), through its Office of Fair Housing and Equal Opportunity. HUD also issues regulations to promote the purpose of the Fair Housing Act.

Figure 14.1 Fair housing poster

U.S. Department of Housing and Urban Development

EQUAL HOUSING
OPPORTUNITY

We Do Business in Accordance With the Federal Fair Housing Law

(The Fair Housing Amendments Act of 1988)

It is Illegal to Discriminate Against Any Person Because of Race, Color, Religion, Sex, Handicap, Familial Status, or National Origin

■ In the sale or rental of housing or residential lots

■ In advertising the sale or rental of housing

■ In the financing of housing

■ In the provision of real estate brokerage services

■ In the appraisal of housing

■ Blockbusting is also illegal

Anyone who feels he or she has been discriminated against may file a complaint of housing discrimination:
1-800-669-9777 (Toll Free)
1-800-927-9275 (TDD)

U.S. Department of Housing and Urban Development
Assistant Secretary for Fair Housing and Equal Opportunity
Washington, D.C. 20410

Previous editions are obsolete

form HUD-928.1A(8-93)

One such regulation requires brokers and other persons involved in real estate transactions to display a fair housing poster (see Figure 14.1) at their place of business.

As part of its enforcement process, HUD sometimes uses **testers**—individuals who play the role of a person wanting to buy or rent housing. A tester evaluates compliance with fair housing laws and is allowed to file a complaint if discrimination is found. Testers do not identify themselves as testers; instead, they act like typical potential renters and purchasers.

If a person feels that his rights under the Fair Housing Act have been violated, he may file a complaint with HUD (within one year of the alleged discrimination). Alternatively, he may file a lawsuit in federal or state court. If someone is found to have violated the Fair Housing Act, the HUD administrative law judge or the court may issue an injunction ordering the violator to stop the discriminatory conduct or to take affirmative steps to correct a violation.

In addition to injunctive remedies, the violator may also be ordered to pay actual damages and attorney's fees to the complainant. Actual damages can include compensation for humiliation suffered as a result of discrimination, as well as for financial losses. A federal court can also order the violator to pay punitive damages to the complainant. If the case is brought by the Attorney General, instead of punitive damages the court can order a civil penalty ranging from a maximum of $55,000 for a first offense up to a maximum of $110,000 for a third or subsequent offense. A HUD administrative law judge can also impose a civil penalty; the maximum penalty in this case ranges from $16,000 for a first offense up to $65,000 for a third or subsequent offense.

State and Local Fair Housing Laws. Most states have laws designed to promote fair housing, and many counties and cities may have their own antidiscrimination ordinances as well. Some of these laws and ordinances impose requirements similar to those found in the federal Fair Housing Act. Others, though, are noticeably stricter; for example, they have more limited exemptions or include additional protected classes, such as age, sexual orientation, marital status, or source of income.

> **Example:** Sally manages a number of single-family houses in a residential neighborhood in New Jersey. She has a long-standing policy of renting only to married couples, as she believes they take better care of the homes and yards. She also finds married couples to be quieter and far more likely to renew their leases year after year.
>
> Sally's policy of renting only to married couples discriminates on the basis of marital status. The policy is perfectly legal under the federal Fair Housing Act, since this law doesn't include marital status as a protected class. However, New Jersey's state fair housing law does name marital status as a protected class, so her policy violates that law.

Americans with Disabilities Act

While the Fair Housing Act and other fair housing laws apply only to residential property, the Americans with Disabilities Act (ADA) is a federal antidiscrimination law that applies to many types of commercial property. The ADA helps ensure that disabled persons have equal access to public facilities. The ADA requires any business or other facility open to the public to be accessible to the disabled. (Private clubs and religious organizations are exempt from the ADA.)

The ADA prohibits discrimination on the basis of disability in any commercial facility or place of public accommodation. The act defines a **disability** as any physical or mental impairment that substantially limits one or more of the individual's major life activities. The definition of **public accommodation** encompasses establishments open to the public, such as hotels, restaurants, retail stores, banks, and schools. It also includes professional offices, such as property management and real estate brokerage offices. This means that property management firms and real estate brokerages are required to comply with the ADA.

Commercial facility is defined even more broadly than public accommodation; it includes any private entity with facilities open to the public, as long as the operation of the facilities affects commerce. This can include not just offices, but even factories and warehouses. Property managers working with commercial property owners must be prepared to advise their clients of the ADA's requirements, and help to ensure their buildings comply.

> **Example:** Bruno is the property manager of two non-residential buildings. The tenant in the first building is a light manufacturing firm that fabricates eyeglass frames. The second building is leased to a small accounting firm that receives clients on a regular basis. The first building is considered a commercial facility; the second building is not just a commercial facility but also a place of public accommodation. Both buildings must comply with ADA accessibility requirements.

Requirements of the ADA. To ensure the accessibility of public accommodations, the ADA requires all of the following, as long as they are **readily achievable** (readily achievable means easily accomplishable and able to be carried out without much difficulty or expense):

- Reasonable modifications must be made to policies, practices, and procedures in order to make goods or services accessible to individuals with disabilities.
- Architectural barriers, structural communication barriers, and transportation barriers must be removed so that goods and services are accessible to the disabled.
- Auxiliary aids and services must be provided so that no disabled person is excluded, denied services, segregated, or otherwise treated differently from other individuals.
- Any new commercial construction must be accessible to the disabled, unless structurally impractical.

For example, the owner of a two-story commercial building with no elevator may have to install automatic entry doors and a buzzer at street level. This way, customers of a second-floor business can ask for assistance. A commercial building owner might also be required to install wheelchair ramps, add grab bars to restroom stalls, and take a variety of other steps to make the building's facilities accessible.

Enforcement. An individual who has suffered discrimination (or who reasonably believes that she will be discriminated against) in violation of the ADA may sue the offender. If the complaint concerns a rental housing violation, the plaintiff could sue both the property owner and the manager. Instead of suing, an individual may also file a complaint with the U.S. Attorney General, who will investigate the alleged violation.

Penalties for ADA violations include an injunction to stop the violation, monetary damages for the victim(s), and civil penalties payable to the government.

Property Manager's Role. If a tenant runs a business that qualifies as a commercial facility or place of public accommodation, both the landlord and the tenant are responsible for complying with ADA requirements. This means that if a tenant violates the ADA, both the tenant and the landlord can be held liable.

> **Example:** Let's return to our example of Bruno, the property manager. At the beginning of the lease term for the second building, the tenant (the accounting firm) and Bruno agree that since the firm will be receiving clients in offices on the second floor, the building's elevator must be updated with buttons with raised letters and braille markings. The tenant, however, never gets around to making these changes and Bruno fails to follow-up. Several months later, a visually impaired client lodges an ADA complaint against both the accounting firm and Bruno, based on the elevator's lack of properly marked buttons.

The lease should specify which party (the landlord or the tenant) is responsible for checking the premises for compliance and for making necessary modifications. Some leases designate the tenant as responsible for ADA compliance within its own rental unit, and make the landlord responsible for the common areas. Even if the tenant is responsible for its own space, the manager should conduct her own inspections as well—both when the lease begins and periodically throughout the lease term.

Most new construction meets ADA requirements. Even if not, bringing a newer property into compliance with the ADA may involve only a few relatively simple changes. But for older buildings, the necessary renovations and upgrades can be substantial and quite expensive.

It's critical that a property manager learn about the ADA requirements. A good starting point is the ADA Compliance Guidebook, published by the Building Owners and Managers Association. BOMA also publishes and sells several other publications on ADA compliance. HUD provides detailed guidance as well.

Federal Employment Laws

Now let's take a look at some of the federal laws that govern employment. Perhaps the most fundamental federal employment law is the Fair Labor Standards Act, which regulates such matters as minimum wage and overtime requirements. But there are other laws that provide additional employee rights and protections. For example, requirements under the Occupational Safety and Health Act help guarantee workplace safety.

Note that most of these laws apply only to firms with a minimum number of employees. For instance, the Family and Medical Leave Act applies only to firms with more than 50 employees. Bear in mind, though, that more stringent state laws on discrimination or family leave may apply and trump a federal law. Employment law is complicated and an attorney's advice should be sought if there are questions.

Fair Labor Standards Act

The Fair Labor Standards Act (FLSA) is administered by the Wage and Hour Division of the U.S. Department of Labor. The act sets forth rules for minimum wage, overtime, and

Case Law: Minimum Wage

In 1937, Elsie Parrish, a chambermaid at a hotel in Wenatchee, Washington, brought suit to recover the difference between the wages paid to her by the hotel and the minimum wage under Washington state law. The hotel argued that the minimum wage law was unconstitutional because it violated the due process clause of the Fourteenth Amendment and the "freedom of contract."

The U.S. Supreme Court disagreed with the hotel's claim. Freedom of contract is a qualified right, not an absolute one. The state legislature is well within its police power to legislate for the health and safety of its citizens. Furthermore, the "exploitation of a class of workers who are in an unequal position with respect to bargaining power and are thus relatively defenseless against the denial of a living wage is not only detrimental to their health and well-being, but casts a direct burden for their support upon the community." *West Coast Hotel Co. v. Parish,* 300 U.S. 379 (1937).

recordkeeping for all full- and part-time employees covered by the act. The law applies in both private and government sectors.

Basic Wage Requirements. As of 2012, the federal minimum wage for employees is $7.25 per hour. Individual states may set higher minimum wage requirements, but the basic wage for any employee in any state can never fall below $7.25 per hour. (About a third of the states have higher minimums than the federal amount.)

It's illegal for an employer to dock an employee's wages to recover the cost of uniforms, equipment, or similar items, or to make up for damaged or missing (or even stolen) items or funds, if that deduction would reduce the total wages due an employee to below the minimum wage.

> **Example:** In Sam's state, the minimum wage is $7.25 an hour. Sam's employer, a gas station, has a policy that cash register shortages will be deducted from its employees' paychecks. Sam makes $7.50 an hour and worked 20 hours last week (for a total paycheck of $150). After a particularly busy shift, Sam's cash register is short $10. Despite the gas station's policy of deducting cash register shortages from an employee's paycheck, Sam's employer cannot deduct the full $10. A deduction of $10 would bring Sam's average hourly wage below the minimum required by federal law. ($150 − $10 = $140; $140 ÷ 20 hours worked = $7.00 per hour.)

Wages must be paid on the regularly scheduled payday for the pay period worked. For example, an employee who worked 20 hours and is normally paid on Friday, must be paid for the entire 20 hours on Friday; his employer cannot pay the employee for 10 hours on Friday and the remainder on the following Monday.

Overtime. Under the FLSA, if an employee works more than 40 hours in a week, he must be paid at a rate of one and one-half times his regular rate of pay for those additional hours. Deductions for shortages and other items cannot be used to reduce the amount of overtime pay due under the FLSA.

Exempt Employees. The FLSA excludes some employees from coverage. Some workers are exempt only from the overtime pay provisions, while others are exempt from both the minimum wage provisions and the overtime provisions. Examples of exempt employees include commissioned salespeople; executive, administrative, and professional employees; computer professionals; certain farmworkers; and some seasonal and recreational employees.

Keep in mind that the burden of proving that an employee is exempt rests on the employer. Never simply assume that an employee is exempt; it's best to get legal advice.

What the FLSA Doesn't Cover. The Fair Labor Standards Act doesn't cover all aspects of an employee's job. For instance, there's no federal requirement that limits workers to an eight-hour day. The FLSA also does not require any of the following:

- vacation, holiday, severance, or sick pay;
- meal or rest periods;
- time off for holidays;
- premium pay for holiday or weekend work;
- pay raises; or
- a termination notice, reason for termination, or immediate payment of final wages.

Recordkeeping Requirements. The FLSA requires employers to keep basic records regarding each covered employee's name and address, wage and occupation, age (if under 19), total hours worked each work day and work week, total regular hours and overtime hours worked per week, deductions from earnings, total wages paid each pay period, hour and day when the work week begins, and date of payment and pay period covered.

This information doesn't have to be kept on a specific form, and employers are not required to use a time clock.

Occupational Safety and Health Act

Another federal employment law is the Occupational Safety and Health Act. The U.S. Congress enacted OSHA in 1970 in an effort to help prevent work-related injuries, illnesses, and deaths. The **Occupational Safety and Health Administration** (also called OSHA) enforces the act. The agency works with states to ensure safe and healthy work environments through research, inspection, training, and education in occupational health and safety.

All employers covered by the act must post a federal or state OSHA poster that provides employees with information on their health and safety rights in the workplace.

Recordkeeping and Reporting Requirements. Employers with 11 or more employees must keep records of work-related injuries and illnesses. However, employers in low-hazard industries (such as retail, professional services, and real estate) are generally exempt from these requirements; they are not required to keep records unless asked in writing by OSHA to do so.

All businesses covered by the law must report any work-related fatality, as well as any illness that results in the hospitalization of three or more employees.

Americans with Disabilities Act

Congress passed the Americans with Disabilities Act (ADA) to help ensure that disabled persons have equal access to public facilities. As we've already discussed, the ADA prohibits discrimination on the basis of disability in any place of public accommodation (a business or other facility open to the public).

The ADA also makes it illegal to discriminate in employment against an otherwise qualified individual because she has a disability. The ADA's prohibitions against employment discrimination are enforced by the U.S. Equal Employment Opportunity Commission (EEOC) in conjunction with state and local agencies.

Employers may not discriminate in the recruitment, hiring, firing, training, assignment of jobs, promotions, pay, benefits, layoffs, granting of leave, or any other employment activity. These rules apply to employers with 15 or more employees.

The ADA protects those who are currently disabled or were disabled in the past. And even if the employer only believes the individual to be disabled (when in fact, the employee is not), the law protects that person from discrimination.

Reasonable Accommodations. In some cases, the ADA requires employers to help disabled workers by making changes to the workplace. These changes are called **reasonable accommodations**. The act defines a reasonable accommodation as any change or adjustment to a job or work environment that allows a qualified applicant or employee with a disability to participate in the job application process, to perform the essential functions of a job, or to enjoy benefits and privileges of employment equal to those enjoyed by employees without disabilities.

For example, reasonable accommodations might include:

- providing or modifying equipment or devices;
- adjusting or modifying applications, examinations, training materials, or policies;
- providing readers and interpreters; and
- making the workplace readily accessible to and usable by people with disabilities.

The employer doesn't have to make an accommodation if he can show that it would pose an **undue hardship**. Undue hardship exists if the accommodation cannot be achieved except with significant difficulty or expense.

Who is Covered. To be protected under the ADA, disabled individuals must meet a two-prong test. First, the individual must be qualified to perform the essential functions of the job. (The applicant can be required to have specific education, training, experience, or licenses, among other things.) Secondly, the individual must be able to perform the essential functions of the job with reasonable accommodation.

An employer cannot refuse to hire an otherwise qualified individual just because he can't do a particular task that is not an essential function of the job.

Example: Molly is disabled and uses a wheelchair. She applies for a desk job at a real estate firm. She is well-qualified, and she needs no accommodation to perform the essential functions of the job. It would be illegal for the firm to refuse to hire Molly because she wouldn't be able to climb the stairs to the extra storage room, because doing so is not an essential function of the job she has applied for.

Family and Medical Leave Act

Most businesses offer employees at least some paid leave in the form of holidays, vacation time, or sick days. The amount of paid leave usually depends on the employee's position with the company and length of service. In some situations, a company may permit unpaid leave as well. In determining its leave policies, companies should take into account federal and state laws related to family and medical leave.

The federal **Family and Medical Leave Act** (FMLA) entitles eligible employees to take up to 12 weeks of unpaid, job-protected leave in a 12-month period for specified family and medical reasons. FMLA applies to state, local, and federal employers, including government agencies and schools. It also applies to private-sector employers who employed 50 or more employees in 20 or more work weeks in the current or preceding calendar year. Eligibility for FMLA benefits requires the employee to have worked for a covered employer for a total of 12 months, and for at least 1,250 hours over the previous 12 months.

An employee returning from leave under FMLA must be restored to her original position within the company, or one that is equivalent (with equivalent pay, benefits, and other terms of employment). In addition, employers must maintain group health coverage for employees who take leave under FMLA (if such health coverage was provided before the employee's leave). However, employers may require employees to pay health insurance premiums while on unpaid leave.

Title VII of the Civil Rights Act of 1964

Earlier in the chapter we mentioned the Civil Rights Act of 1964, noting that it plays a limited role in housing discrimination. However, the act plays a more significant role in combatting employment discrimination. Title VII of the act prohibits discrimination in employment based on race, color, religion, sex, or national origin.

Harassment based on sex includes harassment due to pregnancy, childbirth, or related medical conditions. It also includes sexual harassment. Sexual harassment can occur in a variety of circumstances. Here are some harassment rules to keep in mind:

- The victim as well as the harasser may be either male or female.
- The victim and the harasser don't have to be of the opposite sex.
- The harasser can be the victim's supervisor, co-worker, tenant, or visitor.
- The victim can be anyone affected by the offensive conduct.
- Unlawful sexual harassment doesn't necessarily involve firing or other economic injury to the victim.
- The harasser's conduct must be unwelcome.

Someone victimized by sexual harassment or any other form of employment discrimination based on Title VII can file a complaint with the EEOC.

Land Use Laws

Depending on the types of property a manager handles, she may need some knowledge of land use controls. Land use controls include zoning ordinances; health, safety, and building codes; subdivision/condominium laws; and environmental laws. These laws limit the ways in which private property owners (and tenants) may use property.

Zoning

Local governments enact zoning regulations to maintain a community's quality of life by limiting the sprawl and clutter of unplanned development. To that end, zoning regulations seek to control population density, provide aesthetic guidelines, and help preserve open space and access to air and daylight. One way that zoning ordinances accomplish this is by dividing a community into areas (zones) that are set aside for specific types of uses. There are zones for residential, commercial, agricultural, and industrial uses. Each of these basic zoning categories may have subcategories. For instance, an industrial district could be divided into a light industrial zone and a heavy industrial zone, while a residential district could be divided into single-family zones and multi-family zones.

Keeping different types of uses in separate zones helps ensure that only compatible uses are located in the same area. Areas zoned for incompatible uses may be separated by **buffer zones** (parks, playgrounds, or undeveloped open space). Some places have **overlay zoning**, which permits a mixture of different uses in a specific area. For example, a planned unit development might include single-family and multifamily homes, retail businesses, and open space, with no clear delineation as to where in the development these differing uses are placed.

Zoning laws typically regulate more than just a property's general use. For instance, in addition to permitting a certain type of business in a particular area, zoning ordinances may dictate the business's signage and outdoor displays. The law might also require a certain number of parking spaces for a business, and impose rules on handling and storing hazardous materials.

Zoning ordinances also regulate the height, size, and shape of buildings, as well as their use. The laws usually include setback and sideyard requirements, which prescribe the minimum distance between a building and the property lines. (Setback and sideyard rules often don't apply in high-density downtown areas.)

Zoning Exceptions. Zoning ordinances do allow exceptions. A zoning exception or a rezone request can come from an individual property owner, a developer, or a city or county government. The local zoning authority, called a zoning hearings board or board of adjustment, hears the requests.

Variances. In some cases, if the applicable zoning law is strictly enforced, the property owner's injury would far outweigh the benefit of enforcing the zoning requirement. Under these circumstances, the zoning authority may grant a **variance**. A variance allows a property owner to build or maintain a structure or use that would otherwise be prohibited by the zoning ordinance. For example, a variance might authorize construction of a house even though the topography of the lot makes it virtually impossible to comply with normal setback requirements.

A variance usually will not be granted unless the property owner faces severe practical difficulties or undue hardship (not created by the property owner herself) as a result of the zoning. The owner usually has to prove that the zoning prevents a reasonable use of the land, not merely the most profitable use.

> **Example:** Mabel wants to run a bed and breakfast out of her home, but she lives in a single-family residential zone that does not permit home-based businesses. Mabel couldn't get a variance by claiming that a bed and breakfast would be much more profitable than a single-family home.

Most variances authorize only minor deviations from the zoning law. A variance should not change the essential character of the neighborhood or conflict with the community's general plan.

Nonconforming use. In some cases, if the zoning in a neighborhood changes, an existing use that does not conform to the new zoning doesn't need to change right away. The existing use is known as a nonconforming use (or a grandfathered use), and is typically allowed to remain. However, nonconforming uses aren't perpetual. They can't be enlarged, resumed if they're shut down, or rebuilt if they're destroyed.

> **Example:** Earl owns a building that he leases to a small corner grocery store in a neighborhood that has just been zoned strictly residential. His tenant may continue to operate the store without the city's permission. If the store burns down, though, the nonconforming use ends; Earl can't replace the destroyed building with a new store.

Sometimes a zoning authority places time limits on nonconforming uses. For example, a small industrial operation in a neighborhood recently zoned residential may be given ten years to move.

Property Manager's Role. While a manager won't be called on to interpret zoning law (this is a task reserved for a land use attorney), it's a good idea to have at least a basic understanding of the applicable zoning ordinances. Commercial property managers should be aware of the legal limitations that apply to their tenants' businesses. And even residential property managers may find themselves referring to zoning laws if, for example, a tenant decides he wants to run a hair salon out of his apartment or begins parking his boat on his lawn.

Health, Safety, and Building Codes

Every state has health, safety, and building codes that affect the use of real property. These codes set standards for garbage removal and pest control, require the use of smoke and carbon monoxide detectors, and require grounded outlets near sinks and other water sources. Some state laws address every conceivable health or safety issue. Others set minimum standards and leave it up to state or local agencies to provide the details.

Many county and city governments have their own health, safety, and building codes. If local codes conflict with state codes, the stricter law generally applies.

Example: Pete manages a property in Smalltown. State law requires rental buildings to have a smoke detector in every bedroom. Smalltown's local code requires rentals to have a smoke detector in every bedroom, plus one detector in the kitchen and one detector in each communal living space (such as living rooms and family rooms). Pete must comply with Smalltown's stricter requirements when installing smoke detectors in his rental property.

Local building, safety, and health codes can be quite comprehensive. The municipal code of Seattle, for example, imposes the following conditions on the availability of heating in the units of apartment buildings:

> *Maintain heat in all occupied habitable rooms, baths and toilet rooms at an inside temperature, as measured at a point 3 feet above the floor and 2 feet from exterior walls, of at least 68 degrees Fahrenheit between the hours of 7:00 a.m. and 10:30 p.m. and 58 degrees Fahrenheit between the hours of 10:30 p.m. and 7:00 a.m. from September 1st until June 30th, when the owner is contractually obligated to provide heat.*

Even if a structure was built before a new, stricter standard was enacted, the property owner may have to update the building to meet the newer tougher standard.

Building Codes and Construction. A city or county typically requires a permit before anyone constructs a new building, or remodels or significantly repairs an existing one. The owner of a single-family rental, for example, needs a permit to build a deck and might even need one to build a fence. The permit requirement allows officials to examine the building plans to make sure the construction will satisfy building codes and zoning ordinances. In some cases, an official will inspect the property during construction. Once the completed construction has been inspected and found satisfactory, the building department issues a **certificate of occupancy** (sometimes called an occupancy permit).

City or county inspectors periodically inspect most multi-family residential properties and commercial properties. Penalties for code violations include fines (sometimes assessed on a daily basis) and orders to bring the building into compliance. In extreme cases, buildings may be closed down, and property owners could even face jail time.

Of course, the property manager is also responsible for making sure that a building remains compliant with health, safety, and building codes. Laws change frequently, so the manager must stay alert to new requirements. Both property owners and managers may find it useful to visit state government websites; these websites often list landlord-tenant related laws. City clerk's offices may have relevant information as well. If not, a property manager should consult a lawyer or search the local municipal code (usually available online), looking for information on:

- fire codes,
- health and safety codes,
- building codes, and
- mechanical (heating and electrical) requirements.

Common Interest Development Laws

As we discussed in Chapter 10, some property managers specialize in community association management. This kind of management entails working with the associations that manage condominiums, cooperatives, and planned unit developments. A community association manager's role might include budget planning, overseeing common area repairs and maintenance, collecting association assessments, and handling resident complaints and concerns.

Every state has laws governing at least some aspects of the creation and operation of community associations; naturally, community association managers must be familiar with the various legal requirements imposed by these statutes. These laws often dictate how records must be kept, how association funds are used, and how assessments are imposed and collected. Of course, if a manager is responsible for collecting and handling association assessments, he must be careful to comply with state law regarding the handling of trust funds.

In some states, a person managing a community association may need a real estate license or a community association manager's license. The licensing requirement may depend on the number of units contained in the association, or on the size of the association's budget.

Conversion. Sometimes the owner of an apartment complex will find it profitable to change the complex into a condominium. This process, called conversion, may be regulated to protect renters who will be displaced. For instance, when an apartment building is converted to a condominium project, the owner may be required to give tenants six months' advance written notice of the conversion.

Environmental Laws

Property managers need some familiarity with the local, state, and federal environmental laws. For example, federal and state environmental laws place restrictions and requirements on development activity; local ordinances often regulate waste disposal, recycling, and energy use. These laws may affect the ways owners and tenants can use their land.

Environmental Impact Assessments

The **National Environmental Policy Act** (NEPA) requires federal agencies to prepare an environmental impact statement for any private land use or development that requires the approval of a federal agency. An **environmental impact statement** (EIS) summarizes a proposed project's background information and its probable environmental effects (both positive and negative). The EIS also evaluates alternatives to the proposed project that might reduce any harmful environmental impacts. The federal agency involved in the project uses the EIS as guidance in finalizing plans or determining approval of the project.

Many states have enacted their own versions of NEPA. These laws, known as "little NEPAs," function as state equivalents of the federal law. They require environmental impact reports for public or private projects when state or local approval is involved and the project is likely to have a significant impact on the environment. The state laws are often more restrictive than the federal version.

Building additions, larger-scale remodeling or rehabilitation, and condominium conversions are all examples of projects that may require environmental impact assessments.

A Bad Reflection

The owners and property managers of an office complex in Ontario, Canada, were recently sued by two environmental groups for causing the deaths of an estimated 800 migratory birds during 2008 and 2009. According to the environmental groups, the birds were killed when they collided with the mirrored windows of the complex's three high-rise buildings. The groups sued under Ontario's Environmental Protection Act, which prohibits the discharge of contaminants (in this case, reflected light) that cause or are likely to cause harm to animals. If the environmental groups win, the windows will need to be retrofitted, and the owners and managers may be liable for thousands of dollars in fines.

Although this is a Canadian lawsuit brought under Canadian law, it's not hard to see how an analogous case might be brought in the United States under the Endangered Species Act.

While a property manager won't ever be directly involved in preparing an environmental impact assessment, managers should understand what these assessments entail.

Endangered Species Act

The federal Endangered Species Act (ESA) forbids any action that might harm a plant or animal species that is listed as endangered. This means it is illegal to do anything that kills, injures, or harasses a listed plant or animal. In addition, the law prohibits actions that reduce or degrade the habitat of a listed species. A violation of the ESA is referred to as a "taking" and may result in stiff fines and prison time.

> **Example:** George manages a large apartment complex located near a breeding site of the endangered Pacific pocket mouse. He is overseeing the addition of ten new parking spaces for the property. On his way to the construction site, he accidentally runs over a nest of endangered mice. Obviously, George has committed a taking by killing the mice. Less obvious is the fact that the construction and paving may also qualify as a taking, since it is so close to the breeding site and harms the mouse's habitat.

CERCLA

The federal statute that authorizes toxic waste cleanups by federal authorities and establishes rules for making polluters pay for remediation is the Comprehensive Environmental Response, Compensation, and Liability Act (CERCLA). In order to avoid burdening taxpayers with cleanup costs, CERCLA casts a broad net when looking for parties to pay the cleanup bill. CERCLA is known as a "strict liability" law; it imposes liability on both property owners and operators at the time the pollution occurred, and potentially on any subsequent owners and operators of the contaminated property. This means that not only will the actual polluting parties be liable, but any parties who own or operate the property later may also be liable. Significantly, "operators" has been interpreted to include property managers.

> **Example:** ABC Realty managed a strip mall owned by DevCorp several years ago. One of the strip mall tenants was a dry cleaning business. The mall was then sold to BigBiz, with management taken over by 123 Realty. Recently, it was discovered that the soil underneath the mall is contaminated by chemical solvents spilled by the former dry cleaning business. Liability for the cleanup costs may fall on the owners and operators at the time the pollution occurred (DevCorp, ABC Realty, and the tenant dry cleaning business), as well as the subsequent owners and operators (BigBiz and 123 Realty).

Defenses and Exceptions. The law does provide several important exceptions to strict liability that may apply to parties that own or acquire property that has been contaminated through no fault of their own. Under certain circumstances, if a party can prove that she qualifies as an innocent landowner, a contiguous property owner, or a bona fide prospective purchaser, she cannot be forced to pay for remediation. An **innocent landowner** is someone who acquires contaminated property without knowing about the contamination. A **contiguous property owner** is someone whose property has been contaminated by an adjacent property owned by someone else. And a **bona fide prospective purchaser** is someone who purchases a property knowing (or having reason to know) that the property is contaminated.

Also, although CERCLA applies to both residential and commercial property, the government generally won't take enforcement action against a residential owner, unless the owner:

- causes a release (or a threat of a release) of hazardous substances;
- fails to cooperate with an EPA or state cleanup effort; or
- develops or improves the property in any manner that is inconsistent with residential use.

CERCLA isn't the only toxic waste cleanup law. Many states have their own analogous cleanup statutes—for example, California's Hazardous Substances Act and Washington's Model Toxics Control Act—which assign liability in the same manner as CERCLA.

Obviously, these laws may impose serious financial burdens on owners, buyers, and managers of polluted properties. Managers, especially those handling industrial properties, should be on the lookout for any signs of pollution caused by tenants.

Local Environmental Laws

In addition to the federal and state environmental laws discussed above, many cities and municipalities have local ordinances regulating a variety of aspects of waste disposal and recycling. For example, residential properties are generally required to have weekly garbage service. Recycling (and sometimes composting) is mandated in some municipalities. Hazardous waste and yard waste is usually handled separately from other household waste.

Some local ordinances impose energy conservation measures as well; for example, the use of compact fluorescent bulbs, insulated water heaters, and exterior door weatherstripping may be required. It's important for both residential and commercial property managers to stay on top of the applicable requirements.

Chapter Summary

1. The different types of laws that apply to property management include federal and state statutes, administrative regulations, and local ordinances and regulations.

2. Antitrust laws are designed to encourage competition between businesses. The main federal antitrust law is the Sherman Act, which prohibits any agreement that has the effect of unreasonably restraining trade. The law prohibits property managers from engaging in price fixing, tie-in arrangements, and market allocation.

3. A property manager must disclose all material facts about a property, particularly latent defects, to prospective and current tenants. A latent defect is a hidden defect; it isn't discoverable through ordinary inspection.

4. Under the Fair Credit Reporting Act, a manager must inform a prospective tenant before checking her credit and other background history. If a rental application is rejected based on information contained in a credit report, the manager must inform the applicant of this fact in writing and notify the applicant of her legal rights. The Patriot Act prohibits a manager from entering into any type of business transaction (including lease transactions) with any person, group, or entity listed on the Specially Designated Nationals and Blocked Persons List (SDN list).

5. The Civil Rights Act of 1866 is a federal antidiscrimination law that prohibits any discrimination based on race or color in real estate transactions, including the leasing of residential and commercial property. The federal Fair Housing Act makes it illegal to discriminate on the basis of race, color, religion, sex, national origin, disability, or familial status in the sale or lease of residential property. The Fair Housing Act is enforced by HUD. Property managers must also comply with state and local fair housing laws.

6. Under the federal Americans with Disabilities Act (ADA), any business or other facility open to the public must be accessible to the disabled.

7. Employment laws, both state and federal, affect how a property manager must treat employees and job applicants. Federal employment laws that the manager should be familiar with include the Fair Labor Standards Act, Americans with Disabilities Act, Occupational Safety and Health Act, Family and Medical Leave Act (FMLA), and Title VII of the Civil Rights Act of 1964.

8. Property managers may need to be familiar with a variety of land use laws, including zoning ordinances, health, safety, and building codes, and common interest development laws.

9. Environmental protection laws that can affect a property manager's work include the National Environmental Policy Act, the Endangered Species Act, CERCLA, and local ordinances regulating waste disposal, recycling, and energy conservation.

Key Terms

Statutory laws – Laws enacted by a legislative body, such as Congress, a state legislature, or a city council.

Administrative regulations – Rules adopted by officials in charge of a federal, state, or local administrative agency.

Antitrust laws – Laws intended to encourage competition between businesses.

Sherman Act – A federal antitrust law that prohibits any agreement that has the effect of unreasonably restraining trade.

Conspiracy – When two or more business entities participate in a common scheme, the effect of which is the unreasonable restraint of trade.

Price fixing – The cooperative setting of prices or price ranges by competing firms.

Tie-in arrangement – An arrangement in which a buyer must purchase one product or service in order to purchase another product or service.

Market allocation – Competing businesses agreeing not to sell: 1) certain products or services in certain specified areas; 2) in specified areas; or 3) to certain customers in specified areas; illegal under the Sherman Act.

Material defect – Any fact about a property that could reasonably be expected to influence the tenant's decision whether to rent.

Latent defect – A hidden defect, one that is not discoverable by ordinary inspection.

Megan's Law – A federal law requiring every state to have a registration program for sex offenders convicted of crimes against children.

Lead-based paint disclosures – Landlords renting housing built before 1978 must disclose the presence of lead-based paint, which is a health hazard to children.

Fair Credit Reporting Act (FCRA) – A federal consumer protection law intended to improve the accuracy of information collected by credit agencies, and protect the privacy of borrowers.

Specially Designated Nationals and Blocked Persons List – A list of persons, groups, and entities with whom U.S. individuals and businesses are prohibited from entering into any transaction (including leases).

Civil Rights Act of 1866 – A federal law prohibiting any discrimination, based on race or color, in real estate transactions, including the leasing of residential and commercial property.

Federal Fair Housing Act – A federal law prohibiting discrimination on the basis of race, color, religion, sex, national origin, disability, or familial status in the sale or lease of residential property or in the sale or lease of vacant land for the construction of rental buildings.

Protected class – A group of people who are protected by a civil rights law and share a certain feature or characteristic, such as the disabled or people with children.

Blockbusting – When someone tries to induce homeowners to sell or rent their properties by predicting that members of another race (or other protected class) will be moving into the neighborhood, lowering property values.

Steering – Channeling prospective buyers or tenants toward or away from specific neighborhoods based on their race (or religion, national origin, etc.) in order to maintain or change the character of those neighborhoods.

Familial status – A protected class under the Fair Housing Act, defined as having a child (under 18 years old) living with you (or being in the process of obtaining custody of a child).

Americans with Disabilities Act (ADA) – A federal law that requires any business or other facility open to the public to be accessible to the disabled. It also makes it illegal to discriminate against the disabled in employment.

Disability – Under the ADA and the Fair Housing Act, any physical or mental impairment that substantially limits one or more of the individual's major life activities.

Public accommodation – Under the ADA, a business open to the public, such as a hotel, restaurant, or theater.

Commercial facility – Under the ADA, any private entity with facilities open to the public, as long as the operation of the facilities affects commerce.

Readily achievable – Under the ADA, an accommodation that is readily achievable is one that's easily accomplishable and able to be carried out without much difficulty or expense.

Fair Labor Standards Act (FLSA) – A federal law setting a minimum wage and a maximum numbers of hours that can be worked without triggering overtime requirements.

Occupational Safety and Health Act (OSHA) – A federal law creating various workplace safety requirements.

Reasonable accommodation – Under the ADA, any change or adjustment to a job or work environment that allows a qualified applicant or employee with a disability to participate in the job application process, to perform the essential functions of a job, or to enjoy benefits and privileges of employment equal to those enjoyed by employees without disabilities.

Undue hardship – Under the ADA, an employer must make a reasonable accommodation unless it poses an undue hardship, meaning the accommodation cannot be achieved without significant difficulty or expense.

Family and Medical Leave Act (FMLA) – A federal law requiring employees to give unpaid time off to employees under certain circumstances.

Title VII of the Civil Rights Act of 1964 – A federal law prohibiting discrimination in employment.

Zoning ordinances – Laws dividing a community into areas (zones) set aside for specific types of uses, such as residential, commercial, agricultural, or industrial; these laws help ensure that only compatible uses are located in the same area.

Buffer zones – Areas separating two different zoning uses, such as a park, playground, or open space between a single-family zone and a commercial zone.

Overlay zoning – Zoning which permits a mixture of different zoning uses in a specific area.

Variance – Authorization by the local zoning authority to build or maintain a structure or use that is prohibited by the zoning ordinance; requires a showing that current zoning rules prevent a reasonable use of the land.

Building codes – Local ordinances setting standards for construction methods and materials; intended to protect the public from unsafe or unworkmanlike construction.

Certificate of occupancy – A certificate issued by a local building authority after a new building has been inspected and found satisfactory.

Environmental impact assessments – Reports prepared by a federal or state agency that summarize a proposed project's probable environmental effects and list alternatives to the proposed project.

Endangered Species Act (ESA) – A federal law prohibiting any action that kills, injures, or harasses an endangered plant or animal, or adversely affects the habitat of an endangered plant or animal.

CERCLA – The Comprehensive Environmental Response, Compensation, and Liability Act, a federal law that authorizes and funds the cleanup of severely polluted sites; extends liability for remediation costs to owners who took possession after pollution occurred.

Chapter Quiz

1. Laws passed by a state legislative body are known as:

   a) administrative regulations
   b) statutes
   c) ordinances
   d) federal laws

2. If two competing property management firms discuss their management fee rates, this is:

   a) permissible under the Sherman Act
   b) price fixing
   c) market allocation
   d) a tie-in arrangement

3. If a property management firm assigns smaller retail properties to one manager and larger properties to another, this is:

   a) permissible under the Sherman Act
   b) price fixing
   c) market allocation
   d) a tie-in arrangement

4. A defect that isn't detectable upon ordinary inspection is a:

   a) material fact
   b) latent defect
   c) Both A and B
   d) None of the above

5. Sarah, a prospective tenant, asks a property manager about registered sex offenders in the area. The manager should:

   a) refuse to answer
   b) assure Sarah that he would never rent to a registered sex offender, under any circumstances
   c) refer Sarah to the local law enforcement agency that maintains this information
   d) All of the above

6. Which of the following properties would be subject to the lead-based paint disclosure law?

   a) An apartment building with all studio units, built in 1949
   b) A single-family residence built in 1979
   c) A duplex built in 1977
   d) All of the above

7. The federal law regulating the information collected by Equifax, Experian, and Transunion is called the:

   a) Patriot Act
   b) Fair Debt Collections Practices Act
   c) Civil Rights Act of 1964
   d) Fair Credit Reporting Act

8. When screening a prospective tenant, a manager should:

   a) verify the person's citizenship status
   b) check the person's name against the SDN list
   c) obtain permission before running a background check
   d) Both b) and c)

9. The antidiscrimination law that prohibits discrimination based on race or color in all real estate transactions is the:

   a) Civil Rights Act of 1866
   b) Civil Rights Act of 1964
   c) federal Fair Housing Act
   d) Americans with Disabilities Act

10. Which of the following is not a protected class under the federal Fair Housing Act?

   a) Familial status
   b) National origin
   c) Marital status
   d) Sex

11. Refusing to rent to families with young children would be permissible:
    a) under no circumstances
    b) as long as there is sufficient alternative housing nearby
    c) if the building was developed under a government program to assist the elderly
    d) if none of the current residents have young children

12. Which of the following would be subject to the requirements of the ADA?
    a) Dentist's office
    b) Church youth group's office
    c) Private men's club
    d) Triplex

13. The Fair Labor Standards Act regulates:
    a) the amount of leave a worker can take for medical reasons
    b) minimum wage and overtime hours
    c) workplace safety
    d) weights and measures used in industry

14. Which of the following would the ADA prohibit?
    a) Lack of protective blade guards on a saw used in a meat-packing plant
    b) Lack of bathrooms in a meat-packing plant that could accommodate a wheelchair
    c) Failure to hire a meat-cutter because he needed to work seated due to a disability
    d) Both b) and c)

15. Which of the following parties might be held liable under CERCLA for a chemical spill at an industrial plant that seeps into the ground and contaminates the soil?
    a) The current tenant
    b) The current property owner
    c) Any future owners of the property
    d) All of the above

Answer Key

1. b) Laws passed by a state legislative body are known as statutes.

2. b) This would probably be viewed as price fixing, which is illegal under antitrust law.

3. a) An individual firm is allowed to allocate its clients or territory among its own employees.

4. c) This is the definition of a latent defect, which is a material fact that must always be disclosed to prospective tenants.

5. c) The best course of action would be to refer Sarah to the law enforcement agency that makes sex offender database information available.

6. c) Residences built after 1978 are exempt from the disclosure law, as are zero-bedroom (studio) unit properties.

7. d) The Fair Credit Reporting Act regulates how credit reporting agencies collect and use consumer credit information.

8. d) Managers aren't expected to (and may be prohibited from) verifying a prospective tenant's citizenship status.

9. a) The Civil Rights Act of 1866 prohibits discrimination based on race or color in real estate transactions.

10. c) Marital status is not a protected class under the federal Fair Housing Act. However, some state and local antidiscrimination laws do include it as a protected class.

11. c) An exemption to the Fair Housing Act's prohibition on familial discrimination exists for properties that qualify as "housing for older persons."

12. a) The ADA applies to commercial facilities and places of public accommodation. It doesn't apply to religious organizations, private residences, or private clubs.

13. b) The FLSA sets a minimum wage and overtime rules. Blade guards and other safety matters would fall under OSHA. Medical leave is addressed by the Family and Medical Leave Act (FMLA).

14. d) The ADA requires accommodation of the disabled in public places, such as a business. It also prohibits employment discrimination against the disabled. It would be a reasonable accommodation to allow a disabled meat-cutter to work seated.

15. d) CERCLA imposes liability on the actual polluting parties as well as current and subsequent property owners.

Chapter 15

Risk Management

Outline

Introduction

Risk management refers to actions taken to reduce the size and frequency of legal claims against clients (property owners), and/or against the manager herself, by tenants, employees, and others. Managing risk also includes steps taken to reduce the risk of damage to the property.

We'll begin with the risk of employees injuring people or damaging property, and how to reduce that risk through careful hiring, training, and supervision. Then we'll look at reducing risk to the property by performing safety-oriented inspections and maintenance. After that, we'll turn to emergency preparedness and ways to address the risk posed by hazards such as fires or earthquakes. Following that, we'll examine security issues—ways to reduce the risk posed by crime. Our last topic concerns handling risk through insurance. Despite the manager's best efforts, injuries and damage to the property will occasionally occur, and insurance can lessen the financial impact of these events.

Reducing Risk from Employees and Contractors

Most property managers need to hire help at some point. Some employ a large staff; others contract with one or two people as needed for particular tasks, such as elevator repair or legal advice. But employing workers poses risk. The worker may act negligently or even maliciously (intentionally) and end up harming persons or property. If the manager carelessly hired, trained, or supervised that employee, the manager faces liability.

Let's begin by discussing the dangers of manager negligence in hiring and retaining employees and contractors.

Negligent Hiring

If a manager hires someone that she knows (or should know) could be a danger to others, and that person goes on to injure someone, the injured person may sue the manager for negligent hiring. To prove negligent hiring, the injured party must show that:

- the manager knew (or should have known) that the employee was a danger to employees, tenants, or others;
- the danger was known (or should have been known) at the time the employee was hired;
- the employee injured a coworker, tenant, or third party; and
- the reason the employee was dangerous was related to the injury caused.

> **Example:** Sunset Management hires Dan to work as a janitor in an office complex. Several months later, Dan is accused of assaulting one of the tenants, using his keys to access the tenant's office after hours. A background check reveals that Dan has a history of assault and has even served a lengthy prison term. The manager should've performed a background check during the hiring process, and thus could easily end up liable for the tenant's medical care and lost wages, and perhaps pain and suffering too. (We'll discuss the role insurance might play in this kind of situation at the end of the chapter.)

The best way to avoid negligent hiring is to thoroughly screen each job applicant during the hiring process. A criminal background check is a good start. However, employers should also check an applicant's references, credentials, and prior work history. If the employee passes a background check and then hurts someone or damages property, the manager can defend against a suit for negligent hiring by pointing out that she used a reasonable hiring procedure. Many companies offer employment screening online for a fee. If the manager is already using a service to screen tenants, he can check to see if the company provides employment screening services as well.

Negligent Retention

Sometimes an employer learns an employee is dangerous after hiring him. What if the manager fails to terminate that employee and the employee goes on to harm someone? In this case, the employer faces liability for negligent retention.

The initial applicant screening will help provide some protection against a claim of negligent retention. Also, at the first plausible suggestion that an employee has done something illegal, the manager should update her background check on the individual.

Contractors

Liability for negligent hiring and negligent retention also applies to independent contractors. (For a discussion of the distinction between employees and independent contractors, see Chapter 9.) The manager should screen all contractors carefully and require (in writing) each contractor to run background checks on its own employees.

Also, the manager should make sure that all contractors she hires are properly insured (and bonded, if necessary). Failing to take that step may leave the manager exposed.

> **Example:** A property manager hires an independent contractor to update the plumbing in several apartment units. Unfortunately, the contractor accidentally floods some of the units. If the contractor isn't insured, the management company could be left with the bill.

How can a manager tell if a contractor has adequate insurance? One way is to request a certificate of insurance. A **certificate of insurance** is a document issued by an insurance company stating the type of coverage the policyholder has, its effective dates, and the amount of coverage.

Training

Careful hiring is just the first step in decreasing employee risk. The manager must also properly train his employees. This is a critical element of risk management; aside from improving job performance, proper training helps reduce the odds of employees accidentally damaging property or injuring others.

Training consists of one-on-one guidance or mentoring, group training sessions, and outside education. Training should emphasize the prevention of sexual harassment and discrimination, two particularly troublesome areas we'll discuss shortly. And employee training should always include a thorough review of the employee handbook, one of the manager's most important training and risk mitigation tools.

Employee Handbook. Employees need a handbook they can study and refer to—both during training and afterwards. A thorough, up-to-date employee handbook suggests that the manager takes his training and supervision responsibilities seriously. (Of course, the manager must back this up with quality training and supervision.) An employee handbook that contains clear rules of conduct may reduce the manager's liability if an employee's behavior causes a problem. On the other hand, a poorly written handbook can cause misunderstandings, confusion, and even legal disputes.

The employee handbook should include clear, objective descriptions of unacceptable behavior towards other staff as well as tenants. Concrete examples of unacceptable behavior can be particularly helpful.

> **Example:** Pam is putting together an employee handbook for use at the large apartment complex she manages. She could write "no fraternizing with tenants," but a more useful (and less ambiguous) rule that would reduce the risk of unacceptable behavior might state:
>
> *Employees should not fraternize with tenants. Unacceptable behavior includes, but is not limited to:*
> - *attending tenant parties where alcohol is served,*
> - *allowing tenants to enter employee-only areas for any reason, or*
> - *doing work or odd-jobs for tenants for payment outside of your usual duties.*
>
> *If there are any questions about what behavior is acceptable, please see the manager.*

The handbook should also describe the procedures for receiving and responding to claims of sexual harassment and discrimination. Again, aside from reducing incidents, the presence of solid procedures (provided they're followed, of course) may help eliminate or reduce liability if someone brings a claim.

Sexual Harassment. We discussed sexual harassment generally in Chapter 14. To review, the law defines sexual harassment as any sort of unwelcome sexual advance or other sexual conduct that makes the workplace intimidating or hostile.

It can be difficult to recognize when behavior crosses the line into illegal harassment. For instance, a single act may be considered sexual harassment if it's physical (such as unwanted touching), while less invasive conduct (such as a romantic invitation) may be considered sexual harassment only if it is part of a pattern of behavior. Both during training and in the handbook, the manager should provide clear, relevant examples of harassing behavior and other types of inappropriate conduct.

Housing Discrimination. Employees who interact with tenants can run afoul of state and federal antidiscrimination laws in a variety of ways. Unlawful rental housing discrimination can be subtle, and many types of people are protected. For an overview of antidiscrimination laws, see Chapter 14.

To reduce risk in this area, managers should make sure that the employee training program carefully goes over all state and federal fair housing laws. A section of the employee handbook should be devoted to recognizing and avoiding discriminatory behavior. Training should focus on how avoid discrimination while selecting and evicting tenants and handling tenant complaints and maintenance requests.

Training is an ongoing process. This is particularly true with regard to compliance with fair housing laws. Over time, these laws—or at least the interpretation of them—tend to change. Periodically, the manager should go over current legal requirements with her

Labor Laws

Many state and federal laws regulate employment practices, and managers must be familiar with the specific legal requirements that apply to them. Among other things, these laws regulate:

- the minimum wage, the number of hours that can be worked, and overtime requirements;
- meals and breaks;
- recordkeeping requirements (new employees, taxes, and wage reporting);
- workplace safety;
- accommodations that must be made for disabled workers;
- unemployment taxes; and
- workers' compensation.

Some of these laws apply only when the employer has a certain minimum number of employees; others always apply. A manager should check the state's website for more information on the labor laws that apply to his business.

employees. This aspect of training doesn't necessarily have to involve significant resources. Sometimes a simple email to the workforce reminding them about an issue or providing an update on an antidiscrimination statute or other law will be sufficient.

Supervision

The last tool that we'll discuss for reducing risky behavior by employees is supervision. We mentioned that solid screening and training can be a legal defense if an employee hurts someone or damages property. However, a court or agency won't give screening and training much weight if the manager's ongoing supervision was inadequate. Regular staff meetings, employee reviews, and the mere presence of an attentive manager can all help reduce the odds of employee negligence. Regular contact with the employee may also reduce the chance of intentional misconduct, although of course this kind of wrongdoing is less easy to control.

Disciplinary Procedures. Proper supervision includes following the disciplinary procedures described in the employee handbook. Consistent use of disciplinary procedures sends a message to the workforce that management won't tolerate risky behavior or wrongdoing. In particular, managers should respond to harassment complaints quickly—the longer the behavior continues, the greater the potential damages and the more employee morale suffers. The parties involved should be treated fairly and with dignity, but the complaint must be taken seriously.

Depending on the gravity of the employee's misconduct, the manager may:

- offer the employee additional training,
- put the employee on probation, or
- terminate the employee.

Whatever the course of action, the manager should document both the problem and the management's response.

Reducing Risk from the Property

Now let's focus on steps the manager should take to decrease the risk of injury from safety hazards on the property. Left unchecked, safety issues usually result in claims against the property owner. The manager reduces this kind of risk with employee training (which we've just discussed), and with preventive and corrective maintenance, addressed in Chapter 9. The manager must also conduct safety inspections and then follow up on any problems with repairs or other actions. (Note that risk management related to safety hazards on the property also results in reducing the risk of damage to the property itself.)

Inspections

The manager should personally inspect the property for safety issues and other problems as soon as she takes over management responsibilities. These inspections should continue on a regular basis thereafter, at least once a year. More frequent inspections make sense for many properties.

It's a good idea to hire professionals to inspect specialized equipment. In fact, some equipment, such as elevators, should always be inspected by professionals. The manager may also want to order professional inspections of complicated, trouble-prone building elements, such as the roof.

Anyone who inspects the property should use a checklist to note safety problems such as torn carpeting, loose stairs and railings, and cracks in walkways. It's also important to note any cleanup issues that affect safety, such as ice or snow in entryways or paint rags in a hallway (which pose a fire hazard). Whoever performs the inspection should record the date of the inspection, as well as the nature of any repairs or other service required.

Repairs

As we've mentioned in Chapter 8 and elsewhere, the manager should address problems revealed by an inspection in a timely manner. Safety issues, however, such as a loose tile in a lobby floor or burnt-out bulbs in a stairwell, require immediate attention. A quick response reduces the risk of someone getting hurt and then accusing the manager or owner of negligence.

Some repair tasks require specialists. If the manager tries to complete a complicated repair himself or uses an inexperienced staff member to do so, this could damage the property or result in injuries to tenants. Equipment and building elements that require repair by licensed professionals include boilers, elevators, pipes, and wiring.

If a safety problem can't be fixed right away, the manager should warn tenants, staff, and guests of the hazard.

> **Example:** There's a broken concrete step at a building's entrance that presents a tripping hazard. The manager has arranged for someone to repair the step, but it will take a few days before the work can be completed. In the meantime, the manager should put up yellow caution tape, traffic cones, or other barricades to warn people to avoid the broken step.

As we discussed in Chapter 9, the manager should keep a maintenance work log. Whoever makes the log entries should describe the problem, the date the problem was fixed, and who performed the repair. It's also a good idea to note the methods used to warn people of danger before and during the repair. Software programs that include work logs usually allow photographs of the worksite to be attached to the file; this helps prove what precautions were taken.

Keeping track of tenant repair requests and the repairs made in response to them helps protect the landlord from a claim that he failed to respond in a timely manner to a safety problem. Note that these records can also help disprove accusations of illegal discrimination. If a disgruntled tenant, for example, claims that the manager responds more quickly to repair requests from white tenants than to requests from minority tenants, the manager has the records to refute this allegation.

Emergency Preparedness

Having well-planned procedures in place before an emergency occurs can help limit financial losses from property damage and injuries. Emergencies include potentially catastrophic events such as fire, earthquakes, and flooding. However, emergencies also include individual problems, such as a tenant or staff member getting hurt on the premises (or suffering some other medical problem) and requiring an emergency response.

We'll discuss three aspects of emergency preparedness: an emergency plan and procedures manual, emergency preparedness training, and emergency-oriented maintenance and inspections.

Emergency Plan

An emergency plan addresses the actions that staff and tenants should take during various kinds of emergencies. This plan is embodied in the emergency procedures manual. The manager communicates the emergency plan to the staff using this manual and also via training. The manager should also communicate relevant aspects of the plan to tenants through meetings and emergency drills, information in the tenant handbook, and website material.

Note that some jurisdictions require the owner to have an emergency plan tailored to the property; managers should check local ordinances to make sure that their plans comply with the law.

Emergency Procedures Manual

A solid, thoughtfully prepared emergency procedures manual helps tenants and staff safely react to an emergency. As with an employee handbook, the manual can also help the manager defend against negligence claims if an emergency results in harm to persons or property. The manual indicates that the manager was prepared for emergencies and took reasonable precautions to protect tenants, employees, and property.

The manual should be kept in a central, accessible location, with copies placed in other locations as necessary. (For instance, one copy should be kept in the facilities room, where utility shutoffs are located). Some manuals, at least for large institutions, address a great number of topics and may be hundreds of pages long. Most property managers create manuals with a more modest range of topics and length. Here, we're going to focus on some of the most important topics: utilities shutoffs, evacuation, use of fire equipment, communications, and security.

Utility Shutoffs. In some emergencies, such as a fire or flood, the manager may have to turn off the water, gas, and electricity to some or all of the premises. The manager and staff should know the location of shutoff valves and switches and how to use them. (Utility companies can provide detailed instructions.) With larger properties, the manager should create a map that shows the location of the shutoffs, along with directions on operating them. The map should be included in the emergency procedures manual, and large-scale copies of the map should be posted in utility areas and the property office. The map should also indicate the location of any tools needed to operate these shutoffs. (The tools should be labeled, easy to find, and as near as reasonably possible to the shutoffs.)

The manager of a single-family home or other residential building too small to have an on-site staff member should show tenants the location of utilities shutoffs and how to use them. The manager should also leave a copy of the emergency procedures manual (or relevant excerpts) with the tenants.

Evacuation Plan. During the emergency planning phase, the manager determines the evacuation routes for getting tenants and staff out of the building. Often, the manager consults with experts (such as fire department personnel) for assistance in developing these routes. The procedures manual includes diagrams of the evacuation routes; instructions on achieving a safe orderly departure from the building accompany these diagrams. Managers should post evacuation diagrams and instructions in hallways and elsewhere; local law may require this.

It's a good idea to hold annual evacuation drills (often called fire drills). This allows the manager to check that equipment and alarms work properly. He can also see how well the evacuation plan works.

Elderly or disabled tenants may need extra help during an emergency. Emergency plans should take this into account.

> **Example:** The tenant in Unit 1B is deaf. Her apartment has a flashing fire alarm. She supplements this with a vibrating warning system tied into the building's fire alarm; the vibrations alert her of the danger if she's sleeping. (These systems typically employ a vibrating pad on the tenant's bed or pillow.) In addition, the manager notes in the emergency procedures manual that, if safe to do so, the office manager or the first company employee on the scene should personally ensure that the tenant evacuates the building.

Security. The emergency procedures manual should address security issues both during and after a disaster. Fire or flooding, for example, may leave some or all of a building exposed to intruders. Of course, securing damaged areas of a building takes second place to securing the safety of tenants and staff. However, after the immediate threat to personal safety has passed, the manager or someone else designated in the emergency procedures manual should act quickly to secure the premises.

> **Example:** The Delta Office Plaza emergency procedures manual designates Lloyd, the assistant manager, as the one in charge of security during a disaster response. A fire in one of the ground floor offices destroys several windows and damages the building's side entrance door. After the tenants evacuate and the fire is put out, Lloyd consults with the fire department. He then has the staff handyman place plywood over the broken windows. The handyman also screws plywood over the door opening. Lloyd, after consultation with the manager, decides to hire a security guard during the nighttime hours until the doors and windows are fully repaired.

Communications. The emergency procedures manual should address communications during a disaster. With larger properties, the manual usually lays out a phone tree. Each staff member has the duty to call two or three other staff people who in turn notify others. This way, no one person is completely tied up making calls. Also, a phone tree gets the job done faster.

The procedures manual should contain the phone numbers and other contact information for key management personnel and the owner. It should also include contact information for the various utilities, police, fire, and other emergency services. Naturally, the manager must update this contact information periodically.

 File Backup

Floods, fires, and other natural disasters can destroy on-site records, so it's important to keep electronic or paper copies of important documents in a safe, off-site location. Take special care with:

- insurance policies;
- surveys, building plans, and blueprints;
- financial documents, such as mortgages and other loan agreements;
- tenant leases and disclosures signed by tenants, such as lead paint disclosures;
- documents showing compliance with federal or state housing programs;
- ledgers, and invoices or receipts;
- tax returns and supporting documents; and
- employee records, and documents showing compliance with labor laws.

Keep in mind that state law may require managers to keep some information—such as an employee's social security number—private.

Training

Unfortunately, after creating a fine emergency procedures manual, managers sometimes place the binder on a shelf and forget it. Don't let this happen. Give key staff members copies of the manual and make sure that they receive training in its contents. This can be done as part of a new employee's training, or provided as separate training.

> **Example:** Fire erupts in a unit of the Medville Apartments. An untrained staff member might have run down the hall, knocking on doors and telling people to get out. But thanks to her training, the staff member in charge knew that the first step was to call 911. She and other staff members then supervised an orderly evacuation. Because the staff member was trained properly, firefighters were able to put out the fire before it spread to surrounding units, and everyone escaped safely.

First Aid. The emergency procedures manual should list the names and cell phone numbers of any staff members trained in first aid. In addition, the manual should include a map showing the location of all first aid kits. The most basic preparedness for medical emergencies requires having one or more well-stocked first aid kits in convenient locations. In fact, the federal Occupational Safety and Health Administration (OSHA) requires first aid kits in workplaces. This would include a property management office. Local or state safety codes, especially for residential properties, may also require first aid kits (at least in larger buildings).

OSHA's requirements for some workplaces extend beyond requiring first aid kits. Unless a hospital or clinic is close by, or emergency medical technicians can respond within a few minutes (far from guaranteed in many locations), at least one staff member must be trained in first aid. This generally includes learning how to administer cardiopulmonary

 Automated External Defibrillators (AEDs)

When a person suffers a heart attack it takes a only few minutes for serious brain and tissue damage to occur. CPR training is invaluable, but some managers take the additional step of acquiring an automated external defibrillator (AED). An AED is a portable electrical device that automatically analyzes someone's heart and determines if there's a problem. If appropriate, the device gives the user the option to defibrillate (send a shock to) the victim's heart, hopefully restoring a normal rhythm.

If an AED is kept on site, train all staff to use it. The AED supplier may offer training; alternatively, the Red Cross can provide the training. However, these devices are very simple and safe to use. A readout on the device explains each step that has to be taken.

AEDs are somewhat expensive (about $1,000 – $3,000). Yet managers of larger buildings or buildings that cater to the elderly may feel they need them. The good news is that some states offer a tax credit to offset the purchase of an AED.

resuscitation (CPR). Training for all staff members is ideal. Contact the local Red Cross for class information and on-site training options.

Maintenance and Inspections

We discussed the importance of regularly inspecting the property in Chapter 9 and elsewhere. Emergency preparedness also calls for periodic inspections that focus on safety and emergency equipment.

Fire Safety Equipment. Smoke detectors and carbon monoxide detectors should be inspected regularly. Tenants should know how to test the smoke and carbon monoxide detectors inside their unit or space. Manager should remind tenants to change the batteries and clean the detectors at least once (if not twice) a year. Note that even if the detectors are hard-wired into the building's electrical system, they contain back-up batteries in case of a power failure. These batteries should also be changed annually. As with any safety-related issue, the manager should respond immediately to a tenant complaint of a malfunctioning smoke or carbon monoxide detector.

It's essential to ensure that the building's fire alarm system works properly. The manager can run a system check during the annual fire drill. Address any problems with the system immediately.

Many state or local governments impose detailed fire equipment requirements for certain types of properties. For example, depending on the size or type of building, local ordinances may require a certain number of fire extinguishers per floor, or the presence of a sprinkler system. Industrial properties in particular have to comply with extensive fire safety requirements.

In many cases, state law requires owners to provide each tenant with information about the building's fire and safety equipment. Chiefly, this means informing tenants about the number and location of smoke detectors and fire extinguishers. The law may also require the landlord to inform tenants about various other fire safety matters, such as the location of alarm boxes and exit routes.

Workplaces, such as the property office, must have portable fire extinguishers. Employers have to train their employees in the proper use of these fire extinguishers. The manager should arrange to have all fire extinguishers serviced according to the manufacturer's directions. (This includes extinguishers in the common areas and, at least with residential units, those in the private spaces, too.)

Lights and Emergency Lighting. Proper lighting is crucial during nighttime emergencies or when the smoke from a fire reduces visibility. Staff should inspect hallway and stair lighting frequently, and replace any burned out bulbs.

State and local governments may require emergency lighting in residential apartment buildings, and even in some commercial buildings. Stairways and hallways may need floor lighting to illuminate escape routes. Larger buildings may also require back-up generators to power emergency lights in high-traffic areas.

Earthquake Retrofitting. In earthquake-prone areas, managers of older buildings should have the building evaluated for the risk of damage or collapse in a serious quake.

Soft-Story Construction in California

A soft-story building is one that has wood frame apartment(s) built above parking spaces that are separated by posts. Soft-story buildings are very common in California, yet they are particularly vulnerable in earthquakes.

In the 1994 Northridge earthquake, 34,000 soft-story living units were damaged or destroyed, and 16 deaths were attributed to the collapse of soft-story construction. A 1999 survey conducted in nine counties in California's Bay Area region found that 15,000 soft-story buildings still existed, but only about 1% of property owners had completed the recommended seismic retrofitting.

Since then, many local communities have passed soft-story ordinances requiring property owners to submit engineering reports that identify the buildings' weaknesses. However, most ordinances do not require landlords to do any retrofitting.

If structural problems exist, consider retrofitting to strengthen the building. Earthquake retrofitting includes various modifications, chief among them adding bracing to walls and bolting framing to the concrete foundation. While often quite expensive, retrofitting may be less costly than the damage caused by an earthquake. Some insurers offer a discount for retrofitting.

New construction or major improvements to existing buildings generally have to meet building code standards for seismic activity. In some areas, an entire building may need to be brought up to code if the manager plans to make significant changes to any portion of the building.

Security Issues

All property managers—regardless of the type the property they manage—have to address security. If crime and related personal safety issues go ignored and tenants feel unsafe, lease renewals will suffer. And if the property gains a reputation for criminal activity, new tenants will be hard to find. The failure to address security issues can also cause other problems, including lawsuits, property damage and loss, and government fines.

The manager must take tenant security-related complaints very seriously. These complaints can range from simple calls about a burnt-out light bulb to reports of criminal activity such as vandalism. Along with promptly responding to complaints, the manager should take preventive measures. In this section, we'll cover complying with state and local laws, the use of security personnel and equipment, and the handling of particular types of crime.

Door and Lock Requirements

Most state and local governments require residential units to have deadbolts on exterior doors. Locks may have to be of a certain type or quality to help prevent a criminal from cutting through them. Generally the law requires lockable windows too. Some states also require locks for sliding glass doors, or a bar that sits in the slider track and prevents someone opening the door from outside. Buildings with casement windows may have similar requirements.

In most cases, front doors must be made of steel or solid wood. The law often requires chains or peepholes so that a tenant can observe who is outside before opening the door.

Some states require landlords (mainly residential) to rekey or change the locks between tenants. This must be done, at the landlord's expense, within a certain number of days of a new tenant moving in. Failure to change the locks exposes the landlord to the possibility of penalties and also liability for any resulting theft or injuries. Also note that residential landlords in some states must change the locks if a victim of domestic violence requests it.

Even when the law doesn't require the landlord to change locks between tenants, it's still a good idea to do so (for both residential and commercial properties). This practice reduces the risk that someone with an old key can access the premises for criminal purposes. (To make it more difficult for a stranger to use a lost key, never put a unit number or other identifying information on the key itself.)

Security Personnel and Equipment

Property managers, especially those working with commercial or large residential properties, try to prevent criminal activity by employing security personnel, using surveillance cameras and alarms, and installing exterior lighting.

Security Personnel. Security guards can note suspicious activity, control access to the building, and possibly intervene when crimes occur (or at least call 911). Retail properties, such as malls, and certain other commercial properties may hire their own security personnel; alternatively, the property manager may contract out for security services.

Security personnel—whether employees or independent contractors—should be given very specific guidelines as to how to perform their jobs (for instance, when to stop someone who appears to be shoplifting). Management should also give personnel detailed rules about the amount of force, if any, they can use when intervening in suspicious activity. Are guards allowed to detain persons until police arrive and, if so, how? Or are they only permitted to question people?

Contract security personnel should be insured, and the manager and property owner named as insured parties on the policies. A manager who hires a security guard directly should talk with her insurance broker. Is there sufficient coverage if someone sues over a guard's actions? (We discuss insurance in more detail at the end of this chapter.)

Surveillance Cameras. Small video cameras hooked up to hard drives or other storage media are a relatively inexpensive way to provide broad surveillance for large properties. A guard at a desk can monitor many cameras simultaneously, and sometimes just the knowledge that the area is under surveillance deters would-be criminals.

Cameras can be installed at entrances to the building and also overlooking parking lots. Interior areas worth video monitoring include lobbies, hallways, and garages.

Generally, the law permits cameras except in areas where people have a reasonable expectation of privacy, such as bathrooms and dressing rooms. A manager worried about the placement of surveillance cameras should consult a security expert.

Alarms. Commercial buildings often have alarm systems to protect the property during non-business hours. Whether management or the tenant provides the alarm system tends to vary according to the type of property. With commercial single-tenant buildings, for example, the tenant usually provides the alarm. With commercial multi-tenant buildings, the tenants typically provide alarms for their own interiors and the landlord provides alarms for entrances and other common areas.

Some residential rental properties install alarm systems in the tenant units. However, the landlord might be held liable if a residential tenant relies on an owner-provided alarm that fails to work at a critical time. To help avoid this problem, the manager should:

1. Test the alarm before a tenancy begins; if it doesn't work, fix it before the tenant moves in.
2. Show the tenant how to use the alarm, even if she doesn't think she will use it.
3. Have the tenant sign a form that states she's been shown how to use the alarm, that she understands it's her responsibility to set the alarm, and that she will inform management immediately if the alarm malfunctions.

Fix any malfunctioning alarms as soon as possible. An unreasonable delay may mean liability if someone suffers an injury or property damage before the repair. Yet a manager should avoid promising to fix an alarm (or make any other safety-related repair) "immediately" or by a specific date or time. Doing so might create liability if the repair doesn't take place as quickly as promised and an injury or property loss occurs as a result.

Lighting and Landscaping. There are some fairly simple preventive measures that the manager can take to make the property less inviting to criminals. For example, the manager should inspect the building and grounds with an eye toward eliminating dimly lit areas and overgrown landscaping. Managers should closely examine particularly vulnerable areas, such as an out-of-the-way laundry room or an isolated section of the parking garage. Add lighting if needed, and keep shrubbery trimmed, especially along walkways and near parking lots.

Sometimes managers can take advantage of safety inspection services provided by insurance companies or local law enforcement agencies. A safety inspection can help the manager assess the hazards presented by a property and then formulate a plan for reducing those hazards. Going this route poses a risk, however; the management must take the safety recommendations seriously. Receiving a warning from an inspector about a safety hazard and then failing to act on her recommendations may bring liability for negligence if someone gets hurt. (Ignoring the recommendation may also affect insurance coverage or rates.)

Crimes of Particular Concern

Several types of crimes are of particular concern to property managers and owners, including vandalism and graffiti, drug manufacture and sales, and computer crime and identity theft.

Graffiti and Vandalism. The manager should clean up and repair any graffiti and vandalism promptly. If graffiti or vandalism is a regular occurrence, security patrols are probably necessary. It may be tempting to ignore minor incidents, since it takes time and money to fix the damage and the problem is likely to reoccur. However, the presence of graffiti and damaged or broken building elements suggest to criminals that the property is poorly guarded, inviting more dangerous types of crime. The unsightliness of graffiti and other damage discourages tenant applications and renewals, and drives down the property's value. The failure to remedy these problems suggests to prospective tenants that the manager might not respond to their own repair requests adequately. Also, damage from vandalism (such as a broken window) could lead to injuries.

Keep in mind that the landlord's insurance policies may require him to keep the property repaired. In addition, the owner's mortgage financing agreement typically requires prompt removal of graffiti and repair of vandalism.

Drug Activity. Drug activity must not be tolerated on the property. If the offender is a tenant, the manager should enforce the lease provision that prohibits illegal behavior and evict the tenant. If the lawbreakers are guests or people loitering in the area, the manager can take measures to discourage the illegal activity, such as calling the police, adding lighting, and installing security cameras.

The insurance policy and financing documents we just mentioned probably also require the landlord to deal promptly with drug activity. In addition, the owner who repeatedly fails to address drug activity could find her property declared a public nuisance by the authorities, resulting in fines and even criminal charges. (A **public nuisance** is any activity that threatens the public's safety, morals, or general welfare.) In extreme cases, law enforcement can cause a forfeiture of the property.

Meth labs. The illegal manufacture and use of methamphetamine is fairly widespread in some areas. "Meth labs" are extremely dangerous. The manufacturing process poses a risk of explosion or fire, and uses chemicals and produces waste that are hazardous to health.

The after-effects of methamphetamine production can linger for years. Residential space used as a meth lab cannot be occupied until it's been thoroughly cleaned by professionals trained in removing hazardous materials. In some states, landlords must disclose to prospective tenants that the property was used for methamphetamine production. Even if not specifically required, the duty to disclose latent defects may make this disclosure a necessity.

The cost to clean an apartment that was used as a meth lab can run many thousands of dollars. It's expensive, but the law requires the cleanup. And if a tenant gets sick because the landlord failed to properly clean up after a meth lab, the result could be a million-dollar lawsuit.

The manager should train staff to look for signs of meth production and to report suspicious behavior immediately. The Drug Enforcement Administration website provides information on how to recognize the signs of methamphetamine production.

Computer Crime and Identity Theft. Most property managers use computers to store tenant bank account numbers, social security numbers, and other sensitive information. Thus, it's important to protect computer systems so that this information doesn't end up in the wrong hands.

By stealing someone's stored account numbers and similar information, a thief can assume the victim's identity and make fraudulent purchases and commit other crimes in the victim's name. To reduce the risk of identity theft, the manager should use the latest computer security software. She should set up a computer firewall and install antivirus programs, running frequent scans to check for problems. Whenever possible, the manager should use software to encrypt private information.

But computers aren't the only source of identity theft: paper records are also vulnerable. Simple precautions, such as not putting social security numbers on leases or other documents, are a good start. Files should be kept under lock and key or protected by password. Only personnel with a legitimate need should have access to the personal information of tenants and employees. In addition, the manager should shred sensitive paper files after they're no longer needed.

Insurance

No matter how carefully a property manager works to reduce risk, accidents happen; that's where insurance comes in. Insurance reduces the financial impact of personal injuries and property damage.

Let's take a look at how insurance works. The insured party (also called a policyholder) enters into a contract with the insurance company. This contract between the insured and the insurance company is called the policy. In exchange for a fee paid by the insured (the premium), the insurance company agrees to compensate the policyholder up to the amount of the policy for any kind of loss covered by the policy (less any deductible, as we'll discuss shortly).

A person can purchase insurance only if he has an **insurable interest**: an ownership interest or some other right in the property being insured.

> **Example:** The owner of an apartment building purchases insurance (hazard insurance) that will cover loss of the building or damage to it in the event of a fire. This insurance won't, however, cover the contents of a tenant's apartment, because the owner has no financial stake in the tenant's property. The tenant would need to purchase her own insurance (renter's insurance) to cover the belongings in her unit.

This insurable interest requirement means that in most property management situations, the policyholder must be the property owner, not the manager. However, the property manager may be responsible for finding the best insurance policy (generally, the most complete coverage at the lowest rate) on the owner's behalf.

Different types of properties face different types of risk, requiring different kinds of policies and amounts of coverage. Obviously, a small residential rental property has different insurance needs than a factory or warehouse.

Insurance is complicated, so it's important to consult an insurance agent or broker for professional advice. Nonetheless, the manager should understand the fundamentals. In this section, we'll cover the basics of coverage limits and deductibles, policy types, and making claims.

Coverage and Deductibles

The first step in determining what type of insurance coverage to buy is assessing the risk involved. A retail complex in a flood zone, for example, will need flood coverage; properties in other areas might need earthquake coverage.

Frankly, it's too expensive to insure against every possible loss. The manager will have to weigh the cost of the policy against the potential size and likelihood of various types of losses. The manager can make suggestions about policy types and coverage amounts, but ultimately the owner should select a policy based on the advice of an insurance broker.

Coverage Limits. Insurance policies commonly contain two coverage limits: one limit on the amount the insurance company will pay per incident, and another limit on the total amount the insurance company will pay per year.

> **Example:** Sam has an insurance policy that will pay up to $5,000 per incident to cover losses due to vandalism, up to a total of $15,000 per year. Over the course of a year, Sam submits four vandalism-related claims for $3,500, $5,000, $4,000, and $4,500.
>
> The insurance company pays each of the first three claims in full, as they are within both coverage limits. However, the total of those three claims is $12,500. Even though the fourth claim is below the individual limit of $5,000, Sam's yearly limit is $15,000. For the fourth claim, the company will pay $2,500 and Sam will be responsible for the remaining $2,000.

To save money on premiums, the buyer of an insurance policy might want to insure less than the full value of the property. Less coverage means smaller premiums. However, insurers generally require that property be insured to at least 80% of its value. Some insurers require 100%.

The property manager should make sure that the owner pays the premiums every year, and recommend increases to the coverage amount when necessary.

> **Example:** The owner of a building purchases a $160,000 hazard insurance policy when the building's value is $200,000. Fifteen years later, when the building is worth $400,000, a fire burns the structure to the ground. If the insurance coverage has remained at $160,000, the insurance company will only pay $160,000, leaving the property owner with a loss of about $240,000.

Replacement Value vs. Actual Cash Value. Insurance that covers the physical premises (such as hazard insurance policies or machinery and equipment policies) reimburses the owner either for the property's replacement value or for its actual cash value. Actual cash value is the market value of the property before the damage or loss; it's also called depreci-ated value. This distinction can make a big difference in how much the insured recovers.

> **Example:** A small retail building was purchased ten years ago and its depreciated value is $575,000. To build a replacement building would cost about $800,000. The building is completely ruined by flooding and subsequent mold. If the owner's insurance company pays only the actual cash value ($575,000), the owner will have to come up with the re-maining $225,000 to rebuild a similar building. However, if the insurer pays the building's replacement value, the owner will receive $800,000 to rebuild the structure.

Of course, a policy that pays replacement value will have higher premiums than one that pays actual cash value. It could be worth the extra cost, especially if the building is fairly old.

Deductibles. Our insurance examples thus far have omitted discussion of deductibles for simplicity's sake. But as anyone who's ever made an insurance claim knows, the insured generally has to pay a deductible. With a homeowners policy, for example, the insured might be responsible for the first $500 of any claim. The insurer pays the claim amount over the $500 deductible up to the policy's limits. If the insured suffers another incident, she must again pay the deductible before receiving any coverage.

Commercial insurance policies differ somewhat from typical consumer insurance poli-cies. For instance, because the coverage amounts are so large, so are the deductibles. The deductible for an office building hazard policy, for example, might be as much as $10,000 or considerably more.

Commercial deductibles are often aggregate rather than per incident. The insured may make various small claims throughout the year; once the claims add up to the deductible amount, the insurance company pays any overage (again, up to the policy's limits).

Occasionally the deductible on a commercial policy is stated as a percentage of the claim amount. The deductible might be 10%, for instance. With percentage deductibles, it's common to have a minimum and maximum dollar amount.

> **Example:** Acme Safe Manufacturing has a hazard policy deductible of 10%, with a minimum deductible amount of $1,500 and a maximum of $25,000. If Acme files a claim for a $2,000 loss, they must pay $1,500 of that loss themselves (even though this amount, $1,500, greatly exceeds 10% of the claim). What if Acme suffers a $500,000 loss? The maximum amount limit cuts the company's deductible to $25,000. Twenty-five thousand is considerably less than the $50,000 the company would have to pay with a straight 10% deductible.

Types of Insurance

There are many different types of insurance policies. We'll discuss the most common types here; however, an insurance broker should advise the property owner as to the ap-propriate coverage for her particular property.

Hazard Insurance. Hazard insurance is also known as homeowner's insurance or prop-erty insurance. Most lenders require hazard insurance as a condition for making a mortgage loan. Basic coverage hazard insurance usually protects against problems (referred to as perils) such as fires, lightning, windstorms, and vandalism. Broad coverage hazard insurance may also protect against problems like falling objects, water damage from faucets and plumbing, and damage or collapse due to the weight of ice or snow. It's important to read the policy carefully to understand exactly what perils are covered and under what circumstances.

Alternatively, many owners prefer to pay somewhat more for the extra coverage provided by **special form insurance**. Rather than protect against certain named risks (such as those listed above), the policy instead protects against all risks except those named in the policy. This all-risk policy puts the burden on the insurer to prove that a particular claim falls within a narrow set of excluded events.

Earthquake and Flood Insurance. General hazard insurance policies don't cover earthquake or flood damage. The loss from such events is usually so large that most insurance companies require owners who want flood or earthquake coverage to purchase additional endorsements or policies. An **endorsement** is a written attachment to an insurance policy contract, in which the insurance company agrees to additional coverage in exchange for an additional fee.

Earthquake insurance can be quite expensive. The manager must attempt to determine whether the risk justifies the cost. Note that earthquake insurance usually covers quake-caused physical damage to foundations and other structures. The policy might not cover damage to personal property items inside the building. However, quake-related damage from broken water pipes or a resulting fire may already be covered by the property's hazard insurance policy. The manager should check with the insurance broker to clarify exactly what is covered.

Flood insurance, like earthquake insurance, can cost quite a bit. However, the expense may be worth it, particularly for a property located in a flood zone. (In fact, lenders generally require flood coverage for properties in those areas.) The federal National Flood Insurance

▶ Types of Homeowner (HO) Policies

HO-1 – Basic Form Homeowner Policy. Covers a number of named perils, such as fire, lightning, windstorm, vandalism, theft, and personal liability.

HO-2 – Broad Form Homeowner Policy. Covers more named perils than an HO-1 policy, including water damage from broken plumbing, and damage from falling objects.

HO-3 – Special Form Homeowner Policy. An all-risk policy that covers all perils unless they are specifically excluded. (Major exclusions include floods, earthquakes, mold, and damage caused by war, riot, and nuclear disaster)

HO-4 – Renter's Insurance. Protects a renter, as opposed to an owner. Generally covers the same perils named in an HO-2 or HO-3 policy, as well as damage to property or injuries to persons visiting the unit.

Program (NFIP) offers coverage in some parts of the country. To determine if a property falls within an area covered by the NFIP, enter the property's address at the NFIP website.

Business Interruption Insurance. Hazard insurance will compensate the owner for the cost of a building damaged or destroyed by fire or other disaster. But the owner usually also suffers a loss of income from the disaster. Hazard insurance won't cover that. Property repairs could take months; replacing a completely destroyed property could take years. In the meantime, tenants generally don't have to pay rent if the building can't be used.

To counteract this risk, owners can purchase business interruption coverage. (It's also known as loss of rents coverage.) The price is based on the rental value of the units or space.

> **Example:** A small office building has eight tenants and generates approximately $32,000 per month in rental income. Fire guts the building. The hazard insurance policy covers the cost of rebuilding the structure, which will take about ten months. While the hazard insurance won't compensate the owner for the $320,000 in lost rental income for those ten months, the business interruption insurance covers the bulk of it.

Machinery and Equipment Insurance. Standard hazard insurance policies traditionally excluded coverage for losses due to steam boiler explosions or breakdowns. As a result, some insurers began offering boiler and machinery insurance (also known as equipment breakdown coverage). This kind of policy covers damage to a boiler or to other heavy production machinery and equipment. The owner of a refrigerated warehouse, for example, might purchase this insurance to cover breakdown of the refrigeration units. The policy could also cover the HVAC systems, and electrical, computer, or communication systems. Sometimes coverage also includes bodily injury related to a covered accident or breakdown.

Workers' Compensation Insurance. Workers' compensation insurance (also called industrial insurance) protects both employees and employers from the financial impact of work-related injuries. The employer pays premiums into a state fund. In turn, that fund pays for an injured worker's medical and rehabilitative care. Injured workers may also be eligible for partial wage replacement. Workers covered by workers' compensation generally can't sue employers over work-related injuries.

Workers' compensation is mandatory for any company that has even one employee. Failure to pay workers' compensation premiums can result in interest and penalties. Under some state laws, the employer may deduct a portion of the premium from the employee's pay.

Note that in some states, businesses must pay workers' compensation for independent contractors as well as for employees.

Basic Liability Insurance. The landlord can obtain liability insurance to help protect herself from claims by tenants, guests, and visitors for property damage or bodily injury caused by the landlord's negligence. Liability insurance also covers the costs of defending a lawsuit, such as hiring an attorney. In most cases, the property manager and the owner will each need their own policy.

The payment of claims with liability insurance is different than with other types of insurance. The party who suffered the loss or injury receives the proceeds, not the policyholder.

Example: Sunrise Properties owns a 20,000-square-foot office complex, and carries a $5,000,000 liability insurance policy. A visitor slips on ice outside the complex and sues Sunrise for $100,000. The insurance company eventually settles the claim for $20,000. The insurance company pays the $20,000 to the injured party, not to Sunrise Properties.

The amount of liability coverage needed varies with the type of property. The amount of coverage isn't based on the property's value. Instead, the insured needs to buy a policy that will cover the potential claims for damage or bodily injury.

Example: Juan manages a 12-unit older apartment building in a rundown part of town. Because of the building's age, some of the property's elements are worn or do not meet current health and safety code requirements (such as minimum railing heights). This increases the odds of a tenant getting injured. Juan encourages the owner to buy a larger–than-average liability policy. The property is worth about $875,000, but the owner purchases a liability policy that will pay up to $5,000,000 in claims.

Property managers should consult an insurance broker for a recommendation on the amount of liability coverage for the manager's property or business.

Commercial General Liability Insurance. Unfortunately, personal injury and property damage claims aren't the only types of lawsuits brought by tenants, guests, and visitors. Even the most careful property owner or manager can find herself being sued for slander or libel, invasion of privacy, retaliatory or unlawful eviction, or discriminatory rental practices. To address these risks, the property owner usually needs commercial general liability insurance. (Many basic liability policies don't cover these kinds of claims.) Like the all-risk hazard insurance policy, this policy covers every risk except those specifically excluded.

Automobile Insurance. Vehicles used for business purposes should have commercial automobile liability insurance coverage. Multiple business vehicles can be insured under the same commercial auto policy. The policy should name all the employees who drive company vehicles. Also, if an employee will use her own vehicle for company business, she should add the management business and the owner to her personal policy as additional insured parties. Alternatively, the manager and owner may be able to add a "non-owned auto liability endorsement" to their own policies.

Renter's Insurance. As we noted earlier, the property owner's hazard insurance policy doesn't cover damage or loss to a tenant's personal property. Thus, the manager should notify residential tenants in writing that they should purchase insurance to cover their personal property. (Actually, most commercial leases require this coverage; some residential leases do, too.)

Residential tenants can purchase an HO-4 policy. This policy covers furniture, clothing, electronics, and so on. An HO-4 policy also usually provides some liability protection if the tenant's negligence injures someone. Retail, office, and industrial tenants should obtain policies that cover their equipment and other personal property.

Errors and Omissions Insurance. Errors and omissions (E&O) insurance is a type of liability insurance that helps protect a service provider (the property manager) against a

Other Types of Insurance

Depending on the type of property they own, landlords may also want to consider some of the following additional types of insurance.

Demolition insurance – Covers the cost of removing the remains of structures on the property that were destroyed by fire or other causes.

Inland marine insurance – Covers outdoor fixtures, such as signs and lighting, as well as movable equipment, such as lawn mowers.

Ordinance insurance – Covers the costs that occur when a building must be brought up to code.

Sewer backup insurance – Covers damage to the premises caused by clogged sewers.

Blanket insurance – Covers multiple properties owned by the same landlord at different locations under a single policy.

claim of negligence made by the client (the property owner). This type of insurance is also known as professional liability insurance. As a general rule, the property manager's E&O coverage should equal approximately 10% of the total amount of funds (such as rent and security deposits) that she handles each year. That's usually enough to cover accounting mistakes and other financial oversights.

Some states require property managers to carry errors and omissions insurance. Even if there's no legal requirement, the employment contract between the owner and manager often requires the manager to carry the policy.

Bonding. A fidelity bond (or surety bond) covers losses due to an employee or contractor committing embezzlement, fraud, or similar criminal acts. Bonds are very much like insurance.

The property owner often requires the manager, and any management employees who handle the owner's funds, to obtain a bond. The manager may also buy bonding on her employees to protect herself from losses due to employee dishonesty.

> **Example:** Sam manages ABC Apartments. One of Sam's assistants embezzles $85,000 by writing checks to himself from ABC's account. Fortunately, Sam's property management company is bonded. ABC's owner will be reimbursed by the bond company.

The manager should consult the bonding company for the appropriate amount of the bond.

Insurance Claims

It's usually the property manager's job to file an insurance claim if the managed property suffers damage. The claim may be small (for example, to cover the cost of a new plate glass window) or it may be enormous (such as when fire destroys a large property).

To handle these claims professionally, the property manager must understand the owner's insurance policies' limits and coverage, as well as how the claims process works.

If it looks like a claim must be filed, notify the insurance company immediately. The insurer may require mitigation steps, such as putting a tarp over a roof that's been damaged by a falling tree. It's always a good idea to photograph both the original problem and also any steps taken to prevent additional damage.

Recordkeeping. A property manager should keep files for each insurance policy and for each claim that she files—both for the properties she manages and for her own property management business as well. The files should include:

- copies of policies and contact information for the insurance agent and the insurance company's claims departments (the phone number to make an emergency claim—such as damage from a catastrophic fire—may be different from the number used for more routine claims);
- copies of any claims;
- receipts for any claim-related items or services purchased;
- copies of all correspondence between the property manager and the claims adjuster or insurance agent, and a log of claim-related phone calls, with the time, date, and subject of each conversation.

The manager should keep this information handy at all times, with backup copies maintained online or at an off-site location.

Chapter Summary

1. An effective risk management strategy can reduce the number of lawsuits against the property manager and owner, and help reduce the severity of injuries and property damage.

2. Property managers who employ staff must avoid negligent hiring, properly train and supervise employees, and provide employees with a detailed employee handbook outlining the policies and procedures.

3. To lessen the chance of injuries and lawsuits, and to reduce insurance claims, property managers must obey all health and building codes, perform inspections to identify maintenance and safety issues, and deal with problems in a timely manner.

4. A property manager needs to prepare for emergencies (such as fires, floods, earthquakes, and accidents), train staff in the use of a first aid kit, and create an emergency procedures manual with detailed information regarding utility shut-off valves, evacuation routes, and other emergency procedures.

5. Crime prevention begins with compliance with state and local laws regarding locks and keys. Other security measures, such as hiring a guard, using surveillance cameras, and installing alarms, may be appropriate depending on the type of property. The manager should immediately address even small problems related to security, such as broken light bulbs and vandalism. He should be especially vigilant about drug-related activity. Failure to comply with drug laws may result in fines, criminal prosecution, and seizure of the rental property.

6. An insurance company will reimburse the policyholder up to the amount of the policy for losses due to property damage or personal injury. Common types of insurance include hazard insurance, business interruption coverage, liability insurance, and commercial auto insurance. The property manager should carry E&O insurance and the manager and his employees should be bonded.

Key Terms

Risk management – The actions taken by a landlord to minimize the risk (and extent) of financial losses from natural disasters, accidents, and wrongdoing.

Negligent hiring – A situation where an employer may be liable to someone injured by an employee if the employer knew or should have known that the employee posed a risk to others.

Employee – Anyone who performs a service for another, when the employer has the right to control both what will be done and how it will be done.

Independent contractor – Someone who is hired to perform a particular job and to use her own judgment as to how the work will be done.

Certificate of insurance – A document issued by an insurance company that states the type and amount of coverage held by the insured party.

Retrofitting – Updating an existing building by adding bracing and other improvements that make the structure less susceptible to an earthquake.

Public nuisance – Any activity that threatens the public's safety, morals, or general welfare.

Insurable interest – An ownership interest or some other right in the property being insured.

Hazard insurance – Insurance that protects against the cost of damage to the property from hazards such as fires, storms, and vandalism; also known as property insurance.

Special form insurance – A type of hazard insurance that protects against all types of risks except those specifically excluded from coverage.

Endorsement – A written attachment to an insurance policy contract, in which the insurance company agrees to additional coverage in exchange for an additional fee.

Business interruption coverage – Insurance that protects against lost income after a fire or other disaster destroys a business; also known as a loss of rents policy.

Workers' compensation – Insurance that protects both employees and employers from the financial impact of work-related injuries; also known as industrial insurance.

Liability insurance – Insurance that protects the landlord against claims by tenants, guests, and visitors for property damage or bodily injury caused by the landlord's negligence.

Fidelity bond – A bond (similar to insurance) that covers losses caused by employees who commit criminal acts such as fraud or embezzlement.

Chapter Quiz

1. Marie manages a small office building. Marie hires Paul to answer the phones without checking his references or doing a background check. After Paul assaults one of his coworkers, it's discovered that he has a criminal record for similar assaults. Marie may be liable for:
   a) criminal negligence
   b) aiding and abetting a criminal
   c) negligent hiring
   d) criminal hiring

2. To protect employees against financial loss due to work-related injuries, the business owner is required to provide:
   a) workers' adjustment insurance
   b) workers' compensation insurance
   c) business interruption coverage
   d) liability coverage

3. To reduce the risk of injury or death on the property, the manager should:
   a) perform regular safety and maintenance inspections
   b) ensure that staff are trained in basic first aid and CPR
   c) create an emergency procedures manual
   d) All of the above

4. Information regarding unacceptable behavior toward tenants would be found in a/an:
   a) emergency procedures manual
   b) employee handbook
   c) certificate of insurance
   d) Either a) or b)

5. If a manager fails to deal with ongoing tenant drug activity, the government might declare the property a:
   a) public nuisance
   b) private nuisance
   c) local nuisance
   d) criminal mischief hazard area

6. A manager receives a complaint that an apartment's burglar alarm isn't working. The manager should do all of the following, except:
   a) record the problem in the tenant repair request log
   b) promise to solve the problem immediately
   c) fix the alarm before addressing an earlier complaint of a squeaky door
   d) hire a professional to address the problem if the manager can't fix it

7. The manager of an older building in California has hired contractors to add bracing to the building's walls and to bolt the framing to the foundation. This is an example of:
   a) retroactive compliance
   b) risk transference
   c) retrofitting
   d) constructive repairs

8. The emergency procedures manual addresses:
   a) location of utility shutoffs
   b) evacuation routes
   c) disciplinary procedures
   d) Both a) and b)

9. A property manager requires any contractors she hires to carry $1,000,000 of liability insurance. To ensure the contractor is adequately insured, the manager should request a/an:
   a) certificate of insurance
   b) good faith estimate
   c) notarized copy of the contractor's policy
   d) authorized endorsement

10. Who is most likely to have an insurable interest in Jim's property?

    a) Sally, who takes out a liability policy
    b) Jim, who takes out a hazard insurance policy for his property
    c) Marcus, the property manager for Jim's property
    d) Bill, Jim's insurance broker

11. A hazard insurance policy that covers damage from fires and windstorms, but also protects against falling objects and water damage, is probably a/an:

    a) basic coverage policy
    b) broad form policy
    c) HO-3 policy
    d) short form policy

12. Juan's property insurance doesn't cover earthquakes. He'd like to add this coverage to the policy. The additional coverage is provided by means of a/an:

    a) new policy
    b) provisional clause
    c) extra-hazard clause
    d) endorsement

13. Carol's 15-year-old home has a market value of approximately $350,000. When a fire destroys the property, Carol's insurance only pays her $225,000. The deductible is $3,000. The policy's coverage is based on the property's:

    a) salvage value
    b) replacement value
    c) depreciated (cash) value
    d) discounted value

14. Commercial general liability insurance is a type of:

    a) basic coverage policy
    b) broad coverage policy
    c) business interruption coverage
    d) all-risk policy

15. To protect against dishonest employees, a property owner may require that the property manager obtain a/an:

    a) all-risk policy
    b) fidelity bond
    c) employee risk policy
    d) None of the above

Answer Key

1. c)   Under the theory of negligent hiring, a manager may be liable if she knew or should have known that the employee posed a danger of committing that kind of crime.

2. b)   Workers' compensation insurance protects both employees and employers from the financial loss associated with work-related injuries. Workers' compensation insurance is mandatory for employers with one or more employees.

3. d)   All of these precautionary measures are a good way to reduce the risk of injury or death (as well as property damage).

4. b)   An employee handbook should contain (among other things) information regarding company policies on unacceptable behavior toward tenants.

5. a)   Failure to deal with criminal activity on a property may lead to the landlord being sued for creating a public nuisance (an activity that threatens the public's safety, morals, or general welfare).

6. b)   A manager should never promise to fix a safety-related issue by a specific date or time, as it would open the manager up to liability if something should happen before the alarm is fixed. Instead, the manager should inform the tenant that the repair will be made as soon as possible.

7. c)   Retrofitting refers to updating existing buildings with newer materials and modern techniques that make the structure less susceptible to an earthquake.

8. d)   The emergency procedures manual doesn't address discipline; that topic is covered in the employee handbook.

9. a)   A certificate of insurance is a document issued by an insurance company that can be used to verify the type and amount of coverage held by the insured.

10. b)   Only a person with a stake in the property being insured can take out a hazard insurance policy.

11. b)   A broad form hazard insurance policy protects against the hazards covered in a basic coverage policy, such as fires and windstorms, but also covers additional risks, such as falling objects and water damage.

12. d)   An endorsement is an attachment to the insurance policy contract, in which the insurer agrees to additional coverage in exchange for an additional fee.

13. c)   An insurance policy may be based upon a property's depreciated value, which is the value of the building before it was destroyed, rather than the cost to replace the building with a new one.

14. d)   Commercial general liability insurance is a type of all-risk policy that will cover all types of liability claims, except for those specifically excluded from coverage.

15. b)   A fidelity bond is a special type of insurance that covers losses caused by dishonest employees who engage in criminal acts such as fraud or embezzlement.

Glossary

Abandonment—Failure to occupy and use property, which may result in a loss of rights.

Absorption rate—The length of time it would take for all existing vacant space in a market to be leased, at current rates of leasing activity.

Acceptance or denial letter—A letter sent by a property manager to applicants notifying them if an application was accepted or denied; the FCRA requires that denials based on credit factors be explained to the applicant.

Accommodation, public—Under the Americans with Disabilities Act, a business open to the public, such as a hotel, restaurant, or theater.

Accommodation, reasonable—Under the ADA, any change or adjustment to a job or work environment that allows a qualified applicant or employee with a disability to participate in the job application process, to perform the essential function of a job, or to enjoy benefits and privileges of employment equal to those enjoyed by employees without disabilities.

Account, operating—A checking account used for ordinary receipts and expenditures, into which the manager deposits the property's rents and other income, and out of which he pays the operating expenses.

Account, pooled trust—A trust account in which multiple clients' trust funds are placed.

Account, reserve fund—An account, often interest-bearing, that is used to accumulate reserves to pay for capital expenditures (such as a roof replacement or new appliances).

Accounting, accrual-basis—Accounting system where income is recorded when due and expenses when incurred.

Accounting, cash-basis—An accounting system where income is recorded when received and expenses are recorded when paid.

Accounting, modified cash-basis—An accounting system where annual or semi-annual expenses are debited monthly as they accrue, but income is recorded only when received.

Accounting software—Software designed to handle accounting and generate financial reports for the owner.

Accredited Residential Manager (ARM)—See: Manager, Accredited Residential.

Accrual-basis accounting—See: Accounting, accrual-basis.

ADA—See: Americans with Disabilities Act.

Add-on factor—See: Factor, add-on.

Additional named insured—An extension of coverage, under an owner's insurance policy, to include a property manager.

Adjusted basis—See: Basis, adjusted.

Administrative regulations—Rules adopted by a federal, state, or local administrative agency.

After-tax cash flow—The overall cash flow minus the income taxes paid on the property's income; the best reflection of an owner's spendable cash flow.

Agency law—A body of law governing fiduciary relationships, such as that between property manager and owner.

Agent—A person authorized to represent another (the principal) in dealings with third parties.

Agent, general—An agent authorized to handle all of the principal's affairs in one area or in specified areas.

Agent, leasing—A trained salesperson hired specifically to help with marketing and leasing activities.

Agent, special—An agent with limited authority to do a specific thing or conduct a specific transaction.

Amendment—A written modification to a contract that occurs after both parties have signed the document.

Americans with Disabilities Act (ADA)—A federal law requiring facilities that are open to the public to ensure accessibility to disabled persons, even if that accessibility requires making architectural modifications. The ADA also requires employers to make reasonable accommodations for disabled employees.

Analysis, break-even—Calculation of a rental rate based on the lowest possible rent that covers operating expenses, debt service, and the owner's desired yield.

Analysis, cost-benefit—A technique used to analyze the costs and benefits, over a given period of time, of a physical or operational change to a property.

Analysis, market—An evaluation of how the subject property compares to competing properties in the pertinent market.

Analysis, neighborhood—Analysis of a property's immediate location, including its prestige and accessibility to transportation.

Analysis, property—Analysis that focuses on the building and its site, as well as its operations and financial footing.

Analysis, regional—A preliminary study that focuses on the general economic and demographic conditions that affect the supply of and demand for property in the area where the subject property is located.

Analysis, sales—An important periodic financial report prepared for the owner of a retail property that compares each tenant's sales, and the shopping center's as a whole, to industry averages.

Analysis of alternatives—The process of evaluating possible operational or physical changes that are intended to increase a property's income, preserve the property's value, or comply with legal or insurance requirements.

Anchor tenant—A large tenant that occupies a prominent space in a shopping center or office building that is expected to draw the majority of customers to the property.

Antitrust laws—Laws that prohibit any agreement that has the effect of restraining trade, including conspiracies.

Appraisal—An estimate or opinion of the value of a piece of property as of a particular date. Also called valuation.

Appreciation—An increase in value; the opposite of depreciation.

Articles of incorporation—A document filed with state officials that establishes a corporation, lists the name and address of each incorporator, explains the share structure, and includes a general statement of purpose.

Artificial person—A legal entity such as a corporation, which the law treats as an individual with legal rights and responsibilities; as distinguished from a natural person, a human being. Sometimes called a legal person.

Asset—Anything of value that a person owns.

Asset manager—See: Manager, asset.

Assign—To transfer rights (especially contract rights) or interests to another.

Assignee—One to whom rights or interests have been assigned.

Assignment—1. A transfer of contract rights from one person to another. 2. In the case of a lease, when the original tenant transfers her entire leasehold estate to another. Compare: Sublease.

Assignor—One who has assigned his rights or interest to another.

Assumption—When a buyer takes on personal liability for paying off the seller's existing mortgage or deed of trust.

Auditing—Verification and examination of records, particularly the financial accounts of a business or other organization.

Automated external defibrillator (AED)—A portable electrical device that can be used to restore a heart to its normal rhythm after a heart attack.

Automatic renewal clause—A lease provision that ensures automatic renewal of the lease unless the tenant or the landlord gives the other party notice of an intent to terminate.

Bad debt and vacancy factor—See: Factor, bad debt and vacancy.

Balance sheet—See: Financial Statement.

Base rent—See: Rent, base.

Basic coverage insurance—See: Insurance, basic coverage.

Basis—A figure used in calculating a gain on the sale of real estate for federal income tax purposes. Also called cost basis.

Basis, adjusted—The owner's initial basis in the property, plus capital expenditures for improvements, and minus any allowable depreciation or cost recovery deductions.

Basis, cost-plus—A way of paying a contractor that, rather than using a flat fee, pays the contractor for the actual cost of the project plus an agreed-upon percentage of profit.

Basis, initial—The amount of the owner's original investment in the property; what it cost to acquire the property, which may include closing costs and certain other expenses, as well as the purchase price.

Blind ad—An ad that violates state licensing law by failing to state the licensee's firm's name as licensed.

Blockbusting—Attempting to induce owners to list or sell their homes by predicting that members of another race or ethnic group, or people suffering from some disability, will be moving into the neighborhood; this violates antidiscrimination laws. Also called panic selling.

Board of directors—The body responsible for governing a corporation on behalf of the shareholders.

BOMA—See: Building Owners and Managers Association International.

Branding—The process of developing an image for a company, product, or person in the public marketplace.

Breach—Violation of an obligation, duty, or law; especially an unexcused failure to perform a contractual obligation.

Break-even analysis—See: Analysis, break-even.

Breakpoint—The dollar amount of gross sales that must be achieved before the effective percentage rate exceeds minimum rent, triggering percentage rent due for the period.

Budget, capital—A budget showing how reserve funds will be used to replace equipment or make improvements over time.

Budget, net operating income—A budget format that lists potential gross income, effective gross income, and expenses, before providing a projected net operating income.

Budget, operating—A budget that estimates a property's income and expenses for the coming year on a month-by-month basis.

Budgeting, incremental—A budget compiled based on a property's historical performance numbers, updated to reflect current prices.

Budgeting, zero-based—A budget based not on a property's historic performance, but on figures for comparable properties in the same market.

Buffer zone—An undeveloped area of land that separates two areas zoned for incompatible uses.

Build out—Creating a desired rental space from a larger, unfinished space.

Build-to-suit—A leasing mode in which the landlord builds and finishes a tenant's space according to the tenant's specifications, and then leases the building to the tenant.

Building codes—Regulations that set minimum standards for construction methods and materials.

Building Owners and Managers Association International (BOMA)—A professional organization for property managers.

Building standard—The level of work that management will provide for tenants at no additional charge when building out unfinished space.

Built-out—Commercial space that has been finished to a tenant's specifications.

Business cycle—The pattern of repeated waves of growth and decline that characterizes the movement of the economy.

Business interruption insurance—See: Insurance, business interruption.

Buyer's market—A situation where prices fall, as sellers compete with each other to find buyers for a widely available product.

C corporation—See: Corporation, C.

CAM charges—See: Common area maintenance charges.

CAN-SPAM Act—A federal law that prohibits unsolicited emails.

Capital—Money (or other forms of wealth) available for use in the production of more money.

Capital assets—Assets held by a taxpayer other than: 1) property held for sale to customers in the ordinary course of the taxpayer's business; and 2) depreciable property or real property used in the taxpayer's trade or business. Thus, real property is a capital asset if it is held for personal use or for profit.

Capital budget—See: Budget, capital.

Capital expenditure—Money spent on improvements and alterations that add to the value of the property and/or prolong its life.

Capital gain—Profit realized from the sale of a capital asset. If the asset was held for more than one year, it is a long-term capital gain; if the asset was held for one year or less, it is a short-term capital gain.

Capital improvement—Any improvement that is designed to become a permanent part of the real property or that will have the effect of significantly prolonging the property's life.

Capital loss—A loss resulting from the sale of a capital asset; it may be long-term or short-term, depending on whether the asset was held for more than one year or for one year or less.

Cash-basis accounting—See: Accounting, cash-basis.

Cash flow—The residual income after deducting from gross income all operating expenses and debt service. Also called spendable income.

Cash reserves—Funds set aside for planned and unplanned upgrades and significant repairs.

CC&Rs—A declaration of covenants, conditions, and restrictions; usually recorded by a developer to place restrictions on all lots within a new subdivision.

Census Bureau—The federal government entity that collects and makes available demographic and economic data.

Central business district (CBD)—The downtown core of a city where high-rise office buildings are heavily concentrated.

CERCLA—See: Comprehensive Environmental Response, Compensation, and Liability Act.

Certificate of insurance—A document issued by an insurance company that states the type of coverage held by the insured party, as well as the amount of coverage.

Certificate of occupancy—A permit issued by local authorities allowing occupancy, once new construction has been completed in compliance with local building codes.

Certified Property Manager (CPM)—See: Manager, Certified Property.

Civil rights—Fundamental rights guaranteed to individuals by the law. The term is primarily used in reference to constitutional and statutory protections against discrimination or government interference.

Civil Rights Act of 1866—A federal law guaranteeing all citizens the right to purchase, lease, sell, convey, and inherit property, regardless of race or ancestry.

Civil Rights Act of 1964—A federal law prohibiting discrimination on the basis of race, color, national origin, religion, sex, handicap, or familial status in education, employment, access to public accommodations, and in many programs for which the government provides financial assistance.

Civil Rights Act of 1968—A federal civil rights law that includes the federal Fair Housing Act, which strengthened the protections against discrimination in housing.

Class A space—The most desirable and prestigious office buildings in a particular market, with rents above average for the area.

Class B space—Office buildings that compete for a wide range of users in the average rental range for the area.

Class C space—Office buildings that offer functional space for tenants at below-average rents, but that may have obsolete systems or amenities.

Closely held corporation—See: Corporation, closely held.

Co-signor—Another party, such as a tenant's parent, who agrees to accept liability for any default by the tenant.

Cold calling—A marketing technique involving phone or in-person contact with potential customers with whom there has been no previous contact.

Commercial facility—Under the ADA, any private entity with facilities open to the public, as long as the operation of the facilities affects commerce.

Commingling—Illegally mixing trust funds held on behalf of a client with personal funds.

Commission—1. The compensation paid to a brokerage for services in connection with a real estate transaction (usually a percentage of the sales price or rent amount). 2. A group of people organized for a particular purpose or function; usually a governmental body, such as the Real Estate Commission.

Common area maintenance (CAM) charges—The costs, charged to tenants, of maintaining the common areas, such as parking lots and landscaping; most commercial tenants pay a prorated share of CAM costs based on the square footage of their premises.

Common areas—1. The land and improvements in a condominium, planned unit development, or other housing development that are owned and used collectively by all of the residents, such as parking lots, hallways, and recreational facilities available for common use. Also called common elements. 2. In a building with leased units or spaces, the areas that are available for use by all of the tenants.

Common elements, limited—In a condominium, areas outside of the units (such as balconies or assigned parking spaces) that are designated for the use of particular unit owners, rather than all of the residents.

Common interest developments—Multi-resident developments in which each resident owns his own unit and also holds a shared interest in the common areas.

Community association—An association of owners in a common interest development that manages the development, often with the assistance of a professional property manager; also known as an owners association or homeowners association.

Comparable—A recently sold and similarly situated property that is used as a point of comparison by an appraiser using the sales comparison approach.

Comprehensive Environmental Response, Compensation, and Liability Act (CERCLA)—A federal law authorizing federal cleanups of pollution; in some cases, it extends liability for remediation costs to owners who took possession after pollution occurred.

Concession—Any incentive that a building owner gives to a prospective tenant during the lease negotiation process.

Condominium—A type of common interest development, where each co-owner has a separate interest in an individual unit, combined with an undivided interest in the common areas of the property.

Conspiracy—An agreement or plan between two or more persons to perform an unlawful act.

Construction—See: Maintenance, cosmetic.

Constructive eviction—See: Eviction, constructive.

Consumer Price Index (CPI)—An index that tracks changes in the cost of goods and services for a typical consumer. Formerly called the cost of living index.

Consumer profile—A collection of demographic and lifestyle information on consumers in a retail property's market area, including age, employment, education and income levels, family configuration, and buying habits.

Continuous operation provision—A clause in most retail leases requiring the tenant to stay open during all of the shopping center's hours of operation.

Contract—An agreement between two or more persons to do or not do a certain thing, for consideration.

Contract rent—See: Rent, contract.

Contractor—One who contracts to perform labor or supply materials for a construction project, or to do other work for a specified price.

Contractor, independent—See: Independent Contractor.

Conversion ratio—A measure of how many prospects it takes to get a signed lease, expressed as a percentage.

Cooperative—A building owned by a corporation or association, where the residents are shareholders in the corporation; each shareholder receives a proprietary lease on an individual unit and the right to use the common areas.

Corporate officers—Those appointed by a corporation's board of directors to run the business on a day-to-day basis.

Corporation—An association organized according to certain laws, in which individuals may purchase ownership shares; treated by the law as an artificial person, separate from the individual shareholders.

Corporation, C—A type of corporation that is subject to double taxation.

Corporation, closely held—A type of corporation with comparatively few shareholders.

Corporation, S—A type of corporation that can pass its income on to shareholders without first paying corporate income taxes.

Corrective maintenance—See: Maintenance, corrective.

Cosmetic maintenance—See: Maintenance, cosmetic.

Cost-benefit analysis—See: Analysis, cost-benefit.

Cost per prospect—The amount of money spent on each type of advertising divided by the number of prospects the advertising generates.

Cost-plus basis—See: Basis, cost-plus.

Cost recovery deduction—A depreciation deduction from income taxes.

Covenant of quiet enjoyment—A covenant implied in any lease, that assures the tenant of freedom from any unreasonable intrusion by the landlord or anybody else.

CPI—See: Consumer Price Index.

CPM—See: Manager, Certified Property.

Credit report—A report from one of the three major credit reporting agencies that summarizes an individuals' loans, credit purchases, and debt repayment history.

Curb appeal—The overall exterior appearance of a property.

Custodial maintenance—See: Maintenance, custodial.

Damages—In a civil lawsuit, an amount of money the defendant is ordered to pay the plaintiff.

Damages, compensatory—Damages awarded to a plaintiff as compensation for injuries (personal injuries, property damage, or financial losses) caused by the defendant's act or failure to act.

Damages, liquidated—A sum that the parties to a contract agree in advance (at the time the contract is made) will serve as full compensation in the event of a breach.

Debt investment—See: Investment, debt.

Debt service—The amount of money required to make the periodic payments of principal and interest on an amortized debt, such as a mortgage.

Deduction—An amount a taxpayer is allowed to subtract from his income before the tax on the income is calculated (as distinguished from a tax credit, which is deducted from the tax owed).

Default—Failure to fulfill an obligation, duty, or promise, as when a borrower fails to make payments, or a tenant fails to pay rent.

Defect, latent—Defects that are not visible or apparent (as opposed to patent defects).

Defect, material—Any fact about a property that could reasonably have a negative influence on the tenant's decision whether to rent.

Defect, patent—A problem that is readily observable in an ordinary inspection of the property. Compare: Latent Defect.

Deferred maintenance—See: Maintenance, deferred.

Demand—Desire to own coupled with ability to afford; this is one of the four elements of value, along with scarcity, utility, and transferability.

Demographics—Characteristics of a human population, such as average family size, median age, and household income.

Department of Housing and Urban Development (HUD)—The federal department charged with enforcing the Fair Housing Act.

Deposit insurance—See: Insurance, deposit

Depreciation—1. A loss in value (caused by deferred maintenance, functional obsolescence, or external obsolescence). 2. For the purposes of income tax deductions, apportioning the cost of an asset over a period of time.

Depreciation, curable—Deferred maintenance and functional obsolescence that would ordinarily be corrected by a prudent owner, because the correction cost could be recovered in the sales price.

Depreciation deductions—Under the federal income tax code, deductions from a taxpayer's income to permit the cost of an asset to be recovered; allowed only for depreciable property that is held for the production of income or used in a trade or business. Also called cost recovery deductions.

Depreciation, incurable—Deferred maintenance, functional obsolescence, or external obsolescence that is either impossible to correct, or not economically feasible to correct, because the cost could not be recovered in the sales price.

Disability—According to the Americans with Disabilities Act and Fair Housing Act, a physical or mental impairment that substantially limits a person in one or more major life activities.

Discrimination—Treating people unequally because of their race, religion, sex, national origin, age, or some other characteristic.

Diversification—Investing in a mix of different investment types, such as stocks, bonds, and real estate.

Dividends—Income from a corporation that is periodically distributed to its shareholders.

Do Not Call Law—A federal law that prohibits calling individuals who have registered with the Do Not Call registry.

Double taxation—When income from a corporation is taxed at the corporate level, and then taxed again at the individual shareholder level.

Earthquake insurance—See: Insurance, earthquake.

Economic rent—See: Rent, economic.

Effective gross income (EGI)—See: Income, effective gross.

EGI—See: Income, effective gross.

EIS—See: Environmental impact statement.

Employee—Someone who works under the direction and control of another. Compare: Independent contractor.

Employee manual—A handbook given to new hires that explains company policies on work hours and pay periods, discipline and grievance policies, and policies concerning discrimination and sexual harassment.

Endangered Species Act—A federal law prohibiting any action that kills, injures, or harasses an endangered plant or animal, or adversely affects the habitat of an endangered plant or animal.

Endorsement—A written attachment to an insurance policy contract, in which the insurance company provides additional coverage in exchange for an additional fee.

Environmental impact assessments—Reports prepared by a federal or state agency that summarize a proposed project's probable environmental effects and list alternatives to the proposed project.

Environmental impact statement—A written report analyzing a construction project's impact on the environment; required for projects that are likely to have a significant impact on the environment.

Equal Credit Opportunity Act—A federal law prohibiting providers of credit from discriminating based on race, color, religion, national origin, sex, marital status, age, or because the applicant receives public assistance.

Equity—The difference between a property's market value, and the liens against the property.

Errors and omissions insurance—See: Insurance, errors and omissions.

Escalation clause—A clause in a lease or mortgage that provides for payment or interest adjustments (usually increases) if specified events occur, such as a change in the property taxes or in the prime interest rate.

Estate for years—See: Tenancy, term.

Eviction—The legal process for removing a tenant from a rental property before the end of the lease term.

Eviction, actual—Physically forcing someone off of real property (or preventing them from re-entering), or using the legal process to make them leave. Compare: Eviction, constructive.

Eviction, constructive—When a landlord's act (or failure to act) interferes with the tenant's quiet enjoyment of the property, or makes the property unfit for its intended use, to such an extent that the tenant is forced to move out.

Eviction, for cause—State or local laws often prohibit a landlord from evicting a tenant without one of the reasons specifically listed in the law.

Eviction, self-help—When a landlord uses physical force, a lock-out, or a utility shut-off to evict a tenant, instead of the legal process. This is generally illegal.

Expenses, fixed—A property management expense that remains the same, regardless of rental income.

Expenses, maintenance—Cleaning, supplies, utilities, tenant services, and administrative costs for income-producing property.

Expenses, operating—For income-producing property, the fixed expenses, maintenance expenses, and reserves for replacement; does not include debt service.

Expenses, variable—Expenses incurred in connection with property that do not occur on a set schedule, such as the cost of repairing a roof damaged in a storm.

Expiration—The end of a tenancy when an agreed-upon date is reached; the method by which most leases end.

Facilities manager—See: Manager, facilities.

Factor, add-on—An additional flat fee charged to commercial tenants to account for rental of common areas, used in place of an R/U ratio.

Factor, bad debt and vacancy—A percentage deducted from a property's potential gross income to determine the effective gross income, estimating the income that will probably be lost because of vacancies and tenants who don't pay.

Fair Credit Reporting Act (FCRA)—A federal consumer protection law intended to improve the accuracy of information collected by credit agencies, and protect the privacy of borrowers.

Fair Debt Collection Practices Act—A federal law that provides debtors with certain protections from debt collection actions.

Fair Housing Act—A federal law prohibiting discrimination in the sale or lease of residential property on the basis of race, color, religion, sex, national origin, handicap, or familial status.

Fair Labor Standards Act (FLSA)—A federal law setting a minimum wage and a maximum numbers of hours that can be worked without triggering overtime requirements.

Familial status—A protected class, under the Fair Housing Act, which includes those living with a child (under 18 years old) or expecting a child through pregnancy or adoption.

Family and Medical Leave Act (FMLA)—A federal law requiring employers to give unpaid time off to employees under certain circumstances.

FCRA—See: Fair Credit Reporting Act.

Fidelity bond—A special form of insurance that covers losses caused by dishonest employees who engage in criminal acts such as fraud or embezzlement.

Fiduciary—A person who holds a special position of trust and confidence in relation to someone else.

Fiduciary duties—Duties that an agent owes to a principal as part of an agency relationship.

Fiduciary relationship—A relationship of trust and confidence, where one party owes the other (or both parties owe each other) loyalty and a higher standard of good faith than is owed to third parties. For example, an agent is a fiduciary in relation to the principal; husband and wife are fiduciaries in relation to one another.

Financial statement—A summary of facts showing the financial condition of an individual or a business, including a detailed list of assets and liabilities. Also called a balance sheet.

Fixed expenses—See: Expenses, fixed.

Fixed lease—See: Lease, fixed.

FLSA—See: Fair Labor Standards Act.

FMLA—See: Family and Medical Leave Act.

Footloose industry—An industry whose location is not controlled by labor or resource concerns.

For cause eviction laws—See: Eviction, for cause.

For Rent magazine—A magazine-style publication offered for free, consisting of advertisements for residential rentals.

Fully net lease—See: Lease, fully net.

Functional obsolescence—A loss of value due to design defects or outdated elements.

General agent—See: Agent, general.

General partnership—See: Partnership, general.

General real estate taxes—Taxes levied every year on a property owner, based on the property's value.

Generational marketing—See: Marketing, generational.

GLA—See: Gross leasable area.

Government-assisted housing—See: Housing, government-assisted.

Government business incentives—Incentives offered by state or local governments to court industry and other businesses, such as tax relief, financing assistance, and regulatory easing.

Green certification—A certification available to building managers with training in environmentally friendly technology and practices.

Gross area—A measure of space that includes the entire floor area enclosed within the outer walls.

Gross income—See: Income, gross.

Gross leasable area (GLA)—The amount of square footage within a commercial building's exterior walls; the space available to be rented.

Gross lease—See: Lease, gross.

Ground lease—See: Lease, ground.

Habitability—See: Implied warranty of habitability.

Hazard insurance—See: Insurance, hazard.

Highest and best use—The use which, at the time of appraisal, is most likely to produce the greatest net return from the property over a given period of time.

Housing, government-assisted—Residential property that is privately owned and managed, but where a portion of the tenants' rent is paid by a government agency.

Housing, public—Residential property owned and managed by a government body or agency.

Housing, subsidized—Government-funded housing for low-income tenants; can be either public housing or government-assisted housing.

HUD—See: Department of Housing and Urban Development.

HVAC—An acronym for heating, ventilation, and air conditioning, referring to all equipment associated with air circulation and climate control.

Illiquidity—Difficulty in quickly or efficiently converting an asset into cash.

Impact fees—An upfront fee charged to developers to help offset the cost of additional public services required by a new development.

Implied warranty of habitability—A warranty implied by law in every residential lease, that the property is fit for habitation.

Incidental or interim owner—See: Owner, incidental or interim.

Income approach to value—One of the three main methods of appraisal, in which an estimate of the subject property's value is based on the net income it produces; also called the capitalization method or investor's method of appraisal.

Income, effective gross—A measure of a rental property's capacity to generate income; calculated by subtracting a bad debt/vacancy factor from the economic rent (potential gross income).

Income, gross—A property's total income before making any deductions (for bad debts, vacancies, operating expenses, etc.).

Income, net operating (NOI)—The amount of money left over from gross income after paying the property's operating expenses: Gross Income – Operating Expenses = Net Operating Income.

Income, passive—Income a taxpayer earns from an enterprise (such as a limited partnership) that he does not materially participate in; the IRS classes rental income as passive income.

Income, potential gross—A property's economic rent; the income it could earn if it were available for lease in the current market.

Income-producing property—See: Property, income-producing.

Incremental budgeting—See: Budgeting, incremental.

Incurable depreciation—A decline in property value that cannot be remedied with repairs to the property. Also refers to a decline in value where the cost of repairs would exceed the value those repairs would add to the property.

Independent contractor—A person who is hired to perform a particular job and to use her own judgment as to how the work will be done. Compare: Employee.

Industrial gross lease—See: Lease, industrial gross.

Industrial park—A preplanned development that contains industrial buildings and sometimes office buildings as well.

Industrial property—See: Property, industrial.

Initial basis—See: Basis, initial.

Inspection schedule—A plan for how often equipment or areas of a building need to be inspected for potential problems.

Institute of Real Estate Management (IREM)—A professional organization for residential and commercial real estate managers.

Institutional owner—See: Owner, institutional.

Institutional property—See: Property, institutional.

Insurable interest—An ownership interest or some other right in the property being insured.

Insurance, basic coverage—Hazard insurance that protects against a limited number of perils, such as fire and windstorm.

Insurance, business interruption—Insurance that protects against lost income after a fire or other disaster destroys a business; in the rental property arena, also known as a "loss of rents" policy.

Insurance, deposit—Insurance provided by the Federal Deposit Insurance Corporation (FDIC) protecting depositors against the risk of failure by their financial institutions.

Insurance, earthquake—Additional insurance, usually purchased as an endorsement to a hazard insurance policy, that covers damage from an earthquake.

Insurance, errors and omissions—Insurance coverage that will pay for harm caused by an agent's (or firm's) unintentional mistake or negligence.

Insurance, hazard—Insurance against damage to real property caused by fire, flood, theft, or other mishap. Also called casualty insurance.

Insurance, liability—Insurance that protects the policy holder against claims by tenants, guests, and visitors, for damage to property or bodily injury caused by the landlord's negligence.

Insurance, renter's—Insurance that protects a tenant's personal property within the rental unit or space.

Insurance, special form—A type of homeowner hazard insurance that protects against all types of risks except those specifically excluded from coverage.

Insurance policy—The contract between an insurer (or insurance company) and an insured (or policyholder).

Inventory control system—A written or computerized method of keeping track of consumption of supplies and remaining inventory available.

Investment—An allocation of funds (investment capital) that is expected to generate a profit for the investor.

Investment, debt—An investment where an investor lends money to an individual or business entity.

Investment, ownership—An investment where the investor acquires an asset or an ownership interest in an asset.

Investment capital—See: Capital.

Investor-owner—An individual or entity that owns property for the production of rental income.

IREM—See: Institute of Real Estate Management.

Joint and several liability—See: Liability, joint and several.

Joint venture—Two or more individuals or companies that join together to carry out one project or a related series of projects, but not as an ongoing business. Compare: Partnership.

Just cause exception—A prohibition against termination of a periodic tenancy by a landlord unless the tenant has committed a significant breach of the lease agreement, such as failure to pay rent or illegal use of the property.

Labor intensive industry—An industry that employs a relatively large number of workers for a given amount of space.

Latent defect—See: Defect, latent.

Lead-based paint disclosures—Disclosures to prospective tenants that federal law requires of landlords who rent housing built before 1978, regarding the presence of lead-based paint, a health hazard to children.

Leading indicators—Widely accepted criteria used by economic forecasters to measure the economy's overall health.

Leasable area formula—One of two ways to calculate a tenant's prorated percentage for pass-through charges; it involves dividing the total gross leasable area (GLA) of the entire property (whether vacant or occupied) into the total GLA occupied by the subject tenant. Compare: Leased space formula.

Lease—A conveyance of a leasehold estate from the fee owner to a tenant; a contract in which one party pays the other rent in exchange for the possession of real estate. Also called a rental agreement.

Lease, fixed—A lease in which the rent is set at a fixed amount, and the landlord pays most or all of the operating expenses (such as utilities, taxes, insurance, and maintenance costs). Also called a flat lease, gross lease, or straight lease.

Lease, fully net—A lease where all operational costs are passed through to the tenant; also called a triple net lease or net-net-net lease.

Lease, gross—A lease where the landlord absorbs operational costs such as maintenance, taxes, and insurance, rather than directly charging the tenant her share of these amounts.

Lease, ground—A very long-term lease where a tenant leases undeveloped land and then builds improvements suited to its intended use.

Lease, industrial gross—A lease in which the tenant pays a flat rent for the first year (the base year); in subsequent years, the tenant pays the landlord's operating expenses to the degree they have increased since the base year.

Lease, net—A lease where the landlord passes through to the tenant a pro rata share of operational costs, such as maintenance, taxes, and insurance, so that the rent itself is pure net income.

Lease, percentage—A lease where the landlord charges a fixed amount of minimum or base rent plus an agreed-upon percentage of the tenant's gross sales.

Lease, sandwich—A lease where a new tenant takes possession and is liable for rent to the original tenant.

Lease, triple-net—A lease where the tenant is responsible for taxes, insurance, utilities, and a share of common area maintenance costs.

Lease term—In a lease contract, the amount of time a property will be leased.

Lease-up—The period when a new rental property enters the market and is seeking its first tenants.

Leased space formula—One of two ways to calculate a tenant's prorated percentage for pass-through charges; it involves dividing total leased gross leasable area into the GLA occupied by the subject tenant. Compare: Leasable area formula.

Leasing agent—See: Agent, leasing.

Leasing team—A team that engages in leasing efforts for a property; the team may include leasing agents, brokerage agents, marketing director, property manager, and owner.

Letter of intent—A preliminary nonbinding agreement used in contract lease negotiations to state basic lease terms, such as the start date and rent amount, while detailed negotiations are worked out.

Letter of transmittal—A cover letter found in a management plan, from the property manager to the client.

Leverage—Using borrowed money to invest in an appreciable asset.

Liability insurance—See: Insurance, liability.

Liability, joint and several—A form of liability in which two or more persons are responsible for a debt both individually and as a group.

Liability, limited—When a business investor is not personally liable for the debts of the business, as in the case of a limited partner or a corporate shareholder.

Liability, unlimited—When a business owner is personally liable for the business's debts.

Liability, vicarious—A legal doctrine stating that a principal can be held liable for harm to third parties resulting from an agent's actions.

Liable—Legally responsible.

Lifestyle shopping center—An open-air shopping center occupied by upscale specialty stores.

Limited common elements—Parts of a property that are outside of a unit but reserved for a particular unit, such as a balcony.

Limited liability—See: Liability, limited.

Limited liability company (LLC)—A form of business entity that offers both limited liability for its owners and certain tax benefits.

Limited partnership—See Partnership, limited.

Liquidated damages—See: Damages, liquidated.

Liquidity—The ability to convert an asset to cash quickly.

LLC—See: Limited liability company.

Maintenance, corrective—Ongoing repairs that are made to a building and its equipment to restore it to good operating condition.

Maintenance, cosmetic—Remodeling or refurbishment of a property.

Maintenance, custodial—Tasks performed frequently to keep a building clean and orderly, such as vacuuming and restroom cleaning.

Maintenance, deferred—Corrective maintenance that needs to be performed but is postponed, causing a reduction in the property's value.

Maintenance, preventive—A scheduled program of upkeep tasks intended to keep equipment and fixtures properly functioning and to prevent excessive wear and tear.

Maintenance schedule—A plan for where and when cleaning and upkeep of various parts of a building should happen.

Management agreement—The contract that establishes and defines the working and agency relationship between a property owner and her property manager.

Management plan—A property manager's strategy for the physical and financial management of a property.

Management proposal—An analysis of a property, usually proposing changes; if the owner approves the proposal, it becomes the basis for a management plan.

Management staff—Workers at a property who negotiate leases, perform recordkeeping tasks, and interact with tenants.

Manager, Accredited Residential (ARM)—A professional designation offered through the Institute for Real Estate Management for those specializing in residential management.

Manager, asset—A person who handles long-term planning for a property or portfolio of properties.

Manager, Certified Property (CPM)—A property manager who has satisfied the requirements set by the Institute of Real Estate Management of the National Association of Realtors®.

Manager, facilities—A property manager employed by an institutional owner.

Manager, resident—A property manager who resides on-site, often in exchange for reduced or free rent; may be required by state law for buildings of a certain size.

Manager, site—A manager who works on-site, such as a resident manager in a residential building or a building manager in an office building. Responsible for day-to-day tasks required to manage a single property, including leasing, rent collection, physical maintenance, and handling tenant complaints.

Manufactured home park—A community for manufactured or mobile homes, typically where a resident owns the manufactured home itself but rents the site where it is installed.

Market—Any venue in which buyers and sellers exchange a product.

Market allocation—An illegal act under the Sherman Act, where competing businesses agree not to sell: 1) certain products or services in certain specified areas; 2) in specified areas; or 3) to certain customers in specified areas.

Market analysis—See: Analysis, market.

Market rent—See: Rent, market.

Market value—The price that an informed buyer would pay for a property on the open market under normal conditions.

Marketing—The process by which a business promotes and sells a product or service to customers.

Marketing, generational—A way of segmenting a market, not just by age but also by social, economic, and psychological factors.

Marketing, targeted—Dividing a large group of potential customers into smaller groups, then focusing marketing efforts on one or two key segments of those groups.

Marketing, viral—A type of marketing that occurs when customers market a product or service for a seller, usually by word of mouth or on the Internet.

Material breach—A breach of a lease or other contract serious enough to justify termination of the contract.

Material defect—See: Defect, material.

Material fact—Information that has a substantial negative impact on the value of the property, on a party's ability to perform, or on the purpose of the transaction.

Megan's Law—A law that requires state authorities to make information about sex offenders available to the public.

Metropolitan statistical area (MSA)—An area, along with adjacent territory, with at least one urbanized population area of 50,000 or more and a high degree of social and economic conformity.

Minimum rent—See: Rent, base.

Model unit—A furnished and decorated rental unit kept in show-ready condition for prospective renters to tour.

Modified cash-basis accounting—See: Accounting, modified cash-basis.

Monetary policy—The Federal Reserve Board's effort to control the supply and cost of money in the United States.

Monthly statement—A financial report given to the owner that shows actual income and expenses for a given month, usually compared to the budgeted income and expenses.

MSA—See: Metropolitan statistical area.

Multi-site staff—Itinerant staffers employed by certain property management firms, who perform maintenance or other tasks at multiple properties.

Narrative report of operations—A letter to a property management client more thoroughly explaining information summarized in numeric form in a financial report.

National Apartment Association (NAA)—A professional organization whose members include managers of apartment properties.

National Association of Residential Property Managers (NARPM)—A professional organization for managers of single-family residences and other small residential properties.

National Environmental Policy Act (NEPA)—A federal law requiring the preparation of an environmental impact statement before any governmental action that would have a significant effect on the environment.

Negligence—Conduct that falls below the standard of care that a reasonable person would exercise under the circumstances; carelessness.

Negligent hiring—A legal doctrine that makes an employer liable to persons who are injured by an employee, if the business owner knew or should have known that the employee posed a risk to others.

Neighborhood—A geographic area in which the residents share common characteristics or the properties share a similar land use.

Neighborhood analysis—See: Analysis, neighborhood.

NEPA—See: National Environmental Policy Act.

Net lease—See: Lease, net.

Net operating income (NOI)—See: Income, net operating.

Net operating income budget—See: Budget, net operating income.

NOI—See: Income, net operating.

Noncompete clause—A provision prohibiting the landlord from leasing space to competing businesses; this provision is sometimes found in shopping center leases.

Notice of belief of abandonment—A notice given by a landlord who believes a tenant has abandoned the premises; if the tenant does not respond, the landlord may remove and dispose of the tenant's personal property.

Notice to quit or cure—A notice given by a landlord to a tenant who has become delinquent on rent or is otherwise violating lease terms, stating that legal action will be taken if the violation is not rectified.

Occupational Safety and Health Act (OSHA)—A federal law that establishes workplace safety standards.

Office of Financial Assets Control (OFAC)—The federal agency that maintains the Specially Designated Nationals watch list.

On-site staff—Staff members who work for a property manager on a single property.

Operating account—See: Account, operating.

Operating budget—See: Budget, operating.

Operating expenses—See: Expenses, operating.

Operating expense ratio—The percentage of effective gross income spent on the property's operating expenses, which can be compared to industry averages to determine management efficiency.

Option to renew—A provision in a lease contract that gives the tenant the option to renew his lease at the end of the lease term for another similar rental period.

Ordinance—A law passed by a local legislative body, such as a city council. Compare: Statute.

Ordinary repairs—Routine repairs (corrective maintenance) that keep the property in ordinarily efficient operating condition.

OSHA—See: Occupational Safety and Health Act.

Outparcel—A retail space that is not attached to the main shopping center, but occupies a separate space, or pad, within the boundaries of the shopping center, usually surrounded by its parking lot.

Overbuilding—A phase in the real estate cycle where more properties enter the market than demand can bear.

Overlay zoning—Zoning which permits a mixture of different zoning uses in a specific area.

Owner, incidental or interim—A property owner who didn't anticipate owning property, such as an individual who inherited property or a lender who obtained property through foreclosure.

Owner, institutional—A corporate, educational, or government entity that owns the property it uses.

Ownership—Title to property, dominion over property; the rights of possession and control.

Ownership investment—See: Investment, ownership.

Partnership—An association of two or more persons to carry on a business for profit. The law regards a partnership as a group of individuals, not as an entity separate from its owners. Compare: Corporation, Joint venture.

Partnership, general—An association of two or more individuals who co-own and operate a business.

Partnership, limited—An association of business co-owners, where general partners are liable but limited partners do not have managerial control and have limited liability.

Pass-through—An operational cost that a landlord charges to a tenant under a net lease, such as taxes, insurance, or common area maintenance costs.

Passive income—See: Income, passive.

Payback period—The period of time it takes to offset the cost of an improvement.

Percentage lease—See: Lease, percentage.

Periodic tenancy—See: Tenancy, periodic.

Personal guaranty—When a landlord leasing to a small business tenant requires the owners to personally sign the lease, making the owners personally liable for a breach of the lease.

Physical deterioration—Loss in value (depreciation) resulting from wear or tear or deferred maintenance.

Planned unit development (PUD)—A development (usually residential) with small, clustered lots designed to leave more open space than traditional subdivisions have.

Pooled trust account—See: Account, pooled trust.

Portfolio—The mix of investments owned by an individual or company.

Potential gross income—See: Income, potential gross.

Power center—A large shopping center, consisting of a number of big box stores, usually not connected to each other.

Preliminary study—The process of research and analysis used by a property manager to determine a property's current status and future prospects.

Preventive maintenance—See: Maintenance, preventive.

Price fixing—The cooperative setting of prices by competing firms; price fixing is an automatic violation of antitrust laws.

Principal—One who grants another person (an agent) authority to represent him in dealings with third parties.

Product—Anything that can be marketed or sold to the public.

Property analysis—See: Analysis, property.

Property, income-producing—Property that generates rental income, rather than property held merely for appreciation.

Property, industrial—Property used for the production, storage, and distribution of products.

Property, institutional—Property owned by institutional owners, which requires management but does not generate income.

Property management—The administration, operation, and maintenance of real estate.

Property management company—A firm that provides property management services to property owners.

Property manager—A person hired by a property owner to administer, market, and maintain property, especially rental property.

Property, residential—Properties where tenants live, including single-family homes, apartment complexes, and duplexes.

Property, special purpose—A property that does not fit neatly into the residential, commercial, or industrial categories, such as a hospital, school, or church. See also: Special purpose industrial buildings.

Prospect cards—Forms that are used in person or online to gather information about individual prospects, such as name, address, the type of property they are looking for, and how the prospect heard about the property.

Prosperity—The phase in a business cycle where growth is sustained and stable.

Protected classes—Groups of persons sharing a certain characteristic, who are protected under a civil rights law such as the federal Fair Housing Act.

Public accommodation—See: Accommodation, public.

Public housing—See: Housing, public.

Public nuisance—Any activity that threatens the public's safety, morals, or general welfare.

Public relations—The process of creating and keeping a positive image in the community, including among clients and customers.

PUD—See: Planned unit development.

Purchase order—A document used to keep track of purchases of supplies, including information such as the vendor, date of purchase, price, and quantity.

Qualification package—The collection of documents submitted by a commercial tenancy applicant; these include financial statements, business plans, tax returns, and budgets.

Qualified prospect—A person who has the need for a product or service and the ability to purchase that product or service.

Quiet enjoyment—Use and possession of real property without interference from the previous owner, the lessor, or anyone else claiming title. See also: Covenant of quiet enjoyment.

Reach—The size of an audience targeted by an advertisement.

Readily achievable—Under the ADA, an accommodation that can be carried out without much difficulty or expense.

Real estate cycles—Cycles of growth and contraction that occur specifically within the real estate sector; these often closely track broader business cycles.

Real estate investment trust (REIT)—A real estate investment business that has at least 100 investors that qualifies for tax advantages if organized and managed in compliance with IRS rules.

Reasonable accommodation—See: Accommodation, reasonable.

Recapture clause—1. A provision in a percentage lease that allows the landlord to terminate the lease and regain the premises if a certain minimum volume of business is not maintained. 2. A provision in a ground lease that allows the tenant to purchase the property after a specified period of time.

Recession—The phase in a business cycle when the economy is contracting, characterized by increased unemployment and falling prices.

Recovery—The phase in a business cycle where growth starts to resume after a recession has bottomed out.

Regional analysis—See: Analysis, regional.

Regional shopping center—A large mall of 300,000 square feet or more, drawing customers from throughout a metropolitan area.

REIT—See: Real estate investment trust.

Remodeling—Renovations to already existing rental space.

Rent—Compensation paid by a tenant to the landlord in exchange for the possession and use of the property.

Rent, base—The fixed rental amount that a tenant is responsible for, before accounting for pass-through charges or a percentage of gross sales under a percentage lease. Also called minimum rent.

Rent bill—The monthly rent invoice for commercial tenants. The bill takes into account any percentage rent and the tenant's share of operating expenses, such as taxes, insurance, utilities, and maintenance charges.

Rent control—An ordinance in certain cities limiting how much rent a landlord may charge for certain properties.

Rent, contract—The rent that is actually being paid on property that is currently leased.

Rent, economic—The rent that a property would be earning if it were available for lease in the current market.

Rent, market—The amount an owner could rent a property for, if it were currently available in the rental market.

Rent roll—A report on rent collections; a list of the total amount of rent earned, both collected and uncollected.

Rentable area—A measure of office space that includes not only usable area but also a portion of common areas; the foundation of the BOMA method of measurement.

Rental center—A space dedicated to marketing activities such as distributing information and materials and meeting with prospective renters.

Rental downtime—The period of time that leased space lies vacant (and generates no income) while a landlord looks for a tenant and prepares the space.

Rental ledger—A list of the property's tenants, noting for each tenant the rent rate, security deposit, lease expiration date, payments made, late charges incurred, and balances owed.

Rental schedule—A list of the rental rates assigned to the different types of units or spaces in a managed property.

Renter's insurance—See: Insurance, renter's.

Repair request—A form allowing tenants to ask for repairs or other maintenance work.

Reservation fee—A fee charged by a landlord to hold a space for several days for a prospective tenant while performing background checks.

Reserve account report—A list of deposits into and withdrawals from a property's reserve fund account.

Reserve fund account—See: Account, reserve fund.

Resident manager—See: Manager, resident.

Residential property—See: Property, residential.

Resource oriented industry—An industry that must locate near a source of raw materials or supplies.

Retaliation—Raising rent or any other retaliatory action by a landlord against a tenant who has submitted a complaint or maintenance request.

Retrofitting—Updating a building using newer materials and modern techniques to make the structure less susceptible to earthquake damage.

Return—A profit from an investment. Also referred to as return on investment (ROI).

Right of first refusal—A right that gives the holder the first opportunity to purchase or lease a particular parcel of real property, should the owner decide to sell or lease it.

Risk management—The set of actions taken by a landlord to minimize the risk of financial losses from natural disasters, accidents, and wrongdoing.

R/U ratio—The ratio of rentable area to usable area; the ratio is used to calculate how much the tenant will pay for shared common space. Can be expressed as a percentage, often referred to as a loss factor.

S corporation—See: Corporation, S.

Sale-leaseback—A form of real estate financing in which the owner of industrial or commercial property sells the property and leases it back from the buyer; in addition to tax advantages, the seller/lessee obtains more cash through the sale than would normally be possible by mortgaging the property, since lenders will not often lend 100% of the value.

Sales analysis—See: Analysis, sales.

Sandwich lease—See: Lease, sandwich.

Screening services—Companies that, for a fee, will provide background information about a tenant applicant, including employment history, past addresses and landlords, credit history (credit report), and some limited legal history.

Securities—Investments where the investor does not have a managerial interest, only the right to receive payments (such as with shares of stock).

Security deposit—Money a tenant gives a landlord at the beginning of the tenancy to protect the landlord in case the tenant defaults; the landlord may retain all or part of the deposit to cover unpaid rent or repair costs at the end of the tenancy.

Self-help eviction—See: Eviction, self-help.

Seller's market—An environment where prices go up as buyers compete with each other for a scarce product.

Sexual harassment—Any sort of sexual conduct that makes a workplace hostile or intimidating.

Shell space—Office space that has not been built out, but is awaiting a tenant's improvements.

Sherman Act—A federal antitrust law prohibiting any agreement that has the effect of a restraint on trade, such as price fixing and tie-in arrangements.

Single purpose building—A building usable for only one purpose.

Site manager—See: Manager, site.

Sole proprietorship—A business owned by one individual.

Space requirements—The amount of square footage needed by a potential commercial tenant to accommodate its employees and planned operations.

Special agent—See: Agent, special.

Special assessment—A tax levied to pay for a particular improvement or project that benefits certain properties, rather than all properties in the jurisdiction.

Special form insurance—See: Insurance, special form.

Special purpose industrial buildings—Buildings suitable for only a limited number of uses, such as heavy manufacturing.

Special purpose property—See: Property, special purpose.

Specially Designated Nationals and Blocked Persons List—A list of persons, groups, and entities with whom U.S. individuals and businesses cannot do business (including leasing).

Statement of disbursements—A list of all of a property's expenses incurred during a specific operating period.

Statement of operations—A periodic report showing the overall condition of the property and the total money received and disbursed for a given period.

Statute—A law enacted by a state legislature or the U.S. Congress. Compare: Ordinance.

Steering—Channeling prospective buyers or tenants to or away from particular neighborhoods based on their race, religion, national origin, or ancestry.

Subagent—A person that an agent has delegated authority to, so that the subagent can assist in carrying out the principal's orders; the agent of an agent.

Sublease—See: Lease, sandwich.

Submarket—In a market analysis, a smaller segment (such as luxury high-rise rental units) of the larger relevant market (such as residential apartment buildings).

Subsidized housing—See: Housing, subsidized.

Substitution, principle of—A principle of appraisal holding that the maximum value of a property is set by how much it would cost to obtain another property that is equally desirable, assuming that there would not be a long delay or significant incidental expenses involved in obtaining the substitute.

Summary of operations—A brief description of a property's income and expenses in a financial report.

Supply—The quantity of a particular product available in a market.

Surrender—When the tenant and the landlord mutually agree to terminate a lease before its expiration date.

Syndicate—An association formed to operate an investment business. A syndicate is not a recognized legal entity; it can be organized as a corporation, partnership, or trust.

Targeted marketing—See: Marketing, targeted.

Tax deductions—Expenses that may be deducted from income prior to determining the amount of tax owed, when calculating income taxes.

Tenancy, periodic—A leasehold estate that continues for successive periods of equal length (such as from week to week or month to month), until terminated by proper notice from either party. Also called a month-to-month (or week-to-week, etc.) tenancy. Compare: Term tenancy.

Tenancy, term—A leasehold estate set to last for a definite period (one week, three years, etc.), after which it terminates automatically. Also called a tenancy for years. Compare: Periodic tenancy.

Tenant—Someone in lawful possession of real property; especially, someone who has leased property from the owner.

Tenant handbook—A document or manual containing rules, policies, and contact information, given to tenants at move-in.

Tenant improvement allowance—A certain amount of money given to a commercial tenant by the property owner to build out or remodel the premises at the start of a tenancy.

Tenant mix—The mix of tenant types found in a property; landlords try to avoid adding new tenants that are incompatible with current tenants or that may have a negative impact on the property's reputation.

Term tenancy—See: Tenancy, term.

Termination agreement—A document that formalizes the termination of a property management agreement and spells out the status of all major management duties and expenditures.

Tester—An individual who plays the role of someone seeking to buy or rent property, as part of HUD's enforcement of the Fair Housing Act.

Tie-in arrangement—An agreement to sell one product, only on the condition that the buyer also purchases a different product.

Title VII—The portion of the federal Civil Rights Act of 1964 that prohibits employment discrimination.

Traffic report—A summary used by a property manager to list basic information about the number and type of prospects who call or visit and how they heard about the property.

Triple-net lease—See: Lease, triple-net.

Trust—A legal arrangement in which title to property (or funds) is vested in one or more trustees, who manage the property on behalf of the trust's beneficiaries, in accordance with instructions set forth in the document establishing the trust.

Trust funds—Money or things of value received by an agent, not belonging to the agent but being held for the benefit of others.

Turnkey condition—Describes a space that is fully improved and ready for occupancy.

Undue hardship—Under the ADA, a disability accommodation is not required if it would pose an undue hardship; that is, the accommodation cannot be achieved without significant difficulty or expense.

Uniform Residential Landlord and Tenant Act (URLTA)—A model landlord-tenant law created in an effort to provide consistency in how the landlord-tenant relationship is regulated in different jurisdictions; adopted in some form in 21 states.

Unit preparation checklist/Unit make-ready report—A checklist used in vacancy periods between tenancies, to make sure that all steps in the cleaning and refurbishment process are completed.

Unlawful detainer—A legal action to regain possession of real property; especially, a suit filed by a landlord to evict a defaulting tenant.

Unlimited liability—See: Liability, unlimited.

URLTA—See: Uniform Residential Landlord and Tenant Act.

Usable area—A measure of office space based on the number of square feet that can actually be occupied by a tenant.

Use clause—A provision in a lease that limits the tenant's use of the property to a particular purpose or purposes, and prohibits illegal or hazardous uses.

Vacancy and collection loss factor—See: Factor, bad debt and vacancy.

Variable expenses—See: Expenses, variable.

Variance—Permission (from the local zoning authority) to use property or build a structure in a way that violates the terms of the zoning ordinance.

Vicarious liability—See: Liability, vicarious.

Viral marketing—See: Marketing, viral.

Walkthrough—An inspection by a landlord and tenant at the beginning of a rental term, before move-in, conducted to note any damage to the rental property and to protect the tenant's security deposit from being used to repair pre-existing damage.

Walkup—An older apartment building where there is no elevator to upper-story units.

Work log—A comprehensive list maintained by a manager of all maintenance work performed on a property.

Work order—A document describing what needs to be done in a maintenance project, when it needs to be done, and who should do it, partly completed by the manager and partly by the worker.

Workers' compensation—State-mandated insurance coverage for injured workers (also known as industrial insurance). Real estate brokerages must pay workers' compensation premiums on all their agents in most states.

Yield—The return of profit to an investor on an investment, stated as a percentage of the amount invested.

Zero-based budgeting—See: Budgeting, zero-based.

Zoning—Government regulation of the uses of property within specified areas.

Index